Business and Finance: Global Perspectives

Business and Finance: Global Perspectives

Edited by
Kayla Dawson

Willford Press
www.willfordpress.com

Published by Willford Press,
118-35 Queens Blvd., Suite 400,
Forest Hills, NY 11375, USA

ISBN: 978-1-68285-678-9

Cataloging-in-Publication Data

Business and finance : global perspectives / edited by Kayla Dawson.
p. cm.
Includes bibliographical references and index.
ISBN 978-1-68285-678-9
1. Business. 2. Finance. 3. Management. I. Dawson, Kayla.
HF1008 .B87 2019
650--dc23

For information on all Willford Press publications
visit our website at www.willfordpress.com

Willford Press

Printed in China.

Contents

Preface

The main aim of this book is to educate learners and enhance their research focus by presenting diverse topics covering this vast field. This is an advanced book which compiles significant studies by distinguished experts in the area of analysis. This book addresses successive solutions to the challenges arising in the area of application, along with it; the book provides scope for future developments.

Business is the practice of earning money by engaging in activities like buying, selling and producing goods or services. Business ownership is classified into partnership, cooperative, franchises, corporation, etc. Companies can also be distinguished into public and private companies. The activities crucial to a business are accounting, manufacturing, safety, research and development, and sales. Finance is a significant aspect of any business. It deals with the management of assets, liabilities and overall money management. Some common financial theories include financial economics, financial mathematics, behavioral finance and experimental finance. This book discusses the fundamentals as well as modern approaches of business and finance. It consists of contributions made by international experts on these subjects. For all readers who are interested in business and finance, the case studies included in this book will serve as an excellent guide to develop a comprehensive understanding.

It was a great honour to edit this book, though there were challenges, as it involved a lot of communication and networking between me and the editorial team. However, the end result was this all-inclusive book covering diverse themes in the field.

Finally, it is important to acknowledge the efforts of the contributors for their excellent chapters, through which a wide variety of issues have been addressed. I would also like to thank my colleagues for their valuable feedback during the making of this book.

Editor

Incorporating Ethics into Strategic Management with Regards to Generation Y's View of Ethics

Celikdemir DZ* and Paker IT

Department of International Logistics Management, Faculty of Economics andAdministrative Sciences,Yasar University, Turkey

Abstract

Generation Y, also called the Net Generation or Millennial refers a collaborator of the population larger than the Baby Boom generation. With approximately 80 million people born from mid-1980 to 2000, this group is the most recent generation to enter the workforce. Workplaces are being redefined and organizations are being pressed to adapt as this new wave of workers inspire into business environments. It is widely accepted that distinct generational experiences shape ethical ideologies and ethical ideologies in turn affect the way people function in the workplace. Age-based differences in perspective and complaints about other generations are certainly not a new phenomenon. Businesses committed to high ethics standards know how important it is to create a shared sense of values and a cohesive culture rooted in integrity, where organizational values and personal values align. Shaped by significant events, societal trends, and the cultures of their organizations, each generation develops its own unique perspective of what constitutes right and wrong behavior on the job. Correspondingly, Gen Y's unique collaboration experiences are likely to shape their ethical ideologies and consequent workplace judgments and actions. In this study, we examine Gen Y's ethical ideology and its reflections on strategic management essentials. This group of people is an important part of the workforce since they are the near future managers of the business life. The purpose of the research is to better understand the impacts of Generation Y's ethical ideology and how this ideology reflects to their practice in business. In order to analyze their ethics view, qualitative approach is held. Interviews with individuals whom are to be considered as employees from Gen Y are conducted to identify ethical attitudes and behaviors. Especially, the changing ethics view on corporate business life and the effects on strategic management are focused in this research. The research will try to explore how ethical ideology has changed conditionally with the changing generation behaviors. The interviews are held with 8 employees. The interviews are transcribed into data which are analyzed by the researches to identify the findings. Qualitative approach is advantageous since it helps to gain detailed feedback about feelings, attitudes and behavior. The research will contribute to the literature by considering the impact of varying ethics view for Generation Y and how it reflects to the business life environment in today's global world.

Keywords: Ethics; Generation Y; Strategic management

Introduction

Generation Y, with approximately 80 million people born from mid-1980's to 2000, is the most recent generation to enter the workforce. Much has already been written about the changing work styles, wants and needs of this generation, and the need for radical responsive changes in the workforce, including the way managers lead this new generation of workers [1]. There is a clear need for research that focuses specifically on Generation Y (Gen Y). Such understanding is essential for managing current workplace ethical conduct and for understanding the impacts on ethical climates of organizations in the near future. In this article, we examine how Gen Y ethical ideologies relate to ways they work with others, lead others, and judge ethically questionable behaviors. With respect to leading others, we focus on the servant leadership construct because of its special emphasis on personal integrity and ethical conduct [2,3].

To understand the ethical ideologies of Gen Y, we first must consider their distinct cohort experiences. Academic literature has argued that ethical judgments, decisions, and behaviors tie back to the unique experiences that shape generational cohorts [4]. Generational theory points to common experiences in political, social, and historic contexts as being major influencers of ethical values, especially during the time when an individual is coming of age. Ramsey et al. note that the literature "provides evidence of persistence in ideologies created by unique historical events," and that "a cohort process rather than an aging process tends to explain the differences in ethical judgments".

Businesses committed to high ethics standards know how important it is to create a shared sense of values and a cohesive culture rooted in integrity, where organizational values and personal values align. Strong ethics cultures rely, in part, on a clear, shared understanding of "right" and "wrong," so employees understand their responsibilities and clearly know what it means to "do the right thing." Age-based differences in perspective and complaints about other generations are certainly not a new phenomenon. Every generation has a moment (or several) when they throw up their hands and ask, "What's wrong with them? Why don't they just get it? Why are they so slow to learn?" The differences become even more important when it comes to workplace conduct, e.g., everything from appropriate use of the company credit card to gathering information on competitors to sexual harassment.

Generational differences in perspective and in work style can make the difficult task of culture-building even more challenging. When

***Corresponding author:** Deniz Zaptcioglu Celikdemir, Department of Chair and Professor of International Logistics Management, Faculty of Economics and Administrative Sciences, Yasar University, University Street , No. 37-39, Wooded Road, Bornova, Izmir 35100, Turkey
E-mail: deniz.celikdemir@yasar.edu.tr

communication goes awry and cues are misread, it is easy for shared values to manifest themselves in different and even contradictory ways. Shaped by significant events, societal trends, and the cultures of their organizations, each generation develops its own unique perspective of what constitutes right and wrong behavior on the job. Businesses are not powerless against the forces of generational change and the challenges faced by less-experienced workers. Companies committed to integrity can and do make concerted efforts to meet the ethics challenges they face – by putting in place robust ethics and compliance programs and building strong ethics cultures. But as it turns out, ethics and compliance programs and ethics cultures influence the generations differently.

While this generation does appear to hold some core ethical values, they also hold a relational view of ethics which influences how these values play out. We posit that this interesting mix of experiences and characteristics of Gen Y'ers affects (a) their ethical ideology [4], which in turn influences, (b) their workplace leadership style, (c) their approaches to workplace team situations, and (d) their responses to individual and collaborative workplace ethical violations.

Literature Review

The features of gen Y

Generation Y are a group of people born during the '80s and the early '90s. The name is based on Generation X, which is the peer group that came before them. Generation Y people may be known as echo boomers because they are the children of baby boomers, or someone who was born during the period of increased birth rates that occurred between 1946 and 1964. The Generation Y cohort is also referred to as Millennials, the Internet generation and/or the Net generation. Generation Y legal professionals are in their 20s and are just entering the workforce. With numbers estimated as high as 80 million, Generation Y is the fastest growing segment of today's workforce.

Here are the some main characteristics of this group of people:

- One of the most specific features of Generation Y is that they grew up with technology and rely on it to perform their jobs better. Armed with iPhones, laptops, cellphones and other gadgets, Generation Y is plugged-in 24 hours a day, 7 days a week. This generation prefers to communicate through e-mail and text messaging rather than face-to-face contact and prefers webinars and online technology to traditional lecture-based presentations. Learning for them is more than just traditional brick and mortar college campuses. They also have access to presentations via webinars and online classes.

The fast-track has lost much of its appeal for Generation Y who is willing to trade high pay for fewer billable hours, flexible schedules and a better work/life balance. While older generations may view this attitude as narcissistic or lacking commitment, discipline and drive, Generation Y legal professionals have a different vision of workplace expectations and prioritize family over work.

Nurtured and pampered by parents who did not want to make the mistakes of the previous generation, Generation Y is confident, ambitious and achievement-oriented. They have high expectations of their employers, seek out new challenges and are not afraid to question authority. Generation Y wants meaningful work and a solid learning curve.

As children, Generation Y participated in team sports, play groups and other group activities. They value teamwork and seek the input and affirmation of others. Part of a no-person-left-behind generation, Generation Y is loyal, committed and wants to be included and involved.

Generation Y craves attention in the forms of feedback and guidance. They appreciate being kept in the loop and seek frequent praise and reassurance. Generation Y may benefit greatly from mentors who can help guide and develop their young careers.

As adults, Gen Y's are confident in themselves and their future, motivated, goal oriented, optimistic, assertive, and they believe they are "right". As a result, they feel pressured to succeed and think others should be flexible with them when they want to negotiate scheduling conflicts. They prefer to work in groups, and are group oriented rather than being individualistic [5]. An egalitarian leadership style (democratic approach) is best suited to this generation because they do not particularly conform well to hierarchies. Gen Y also has been classified as exceedingly narcissistic. In fact studies done by Twenge and Foster have shown that the average college student in 2006 was 30 % more narcissistic than the average student in 1982 [6]. This implies a focus on self at others' expense, or at least a failure to consider the impact of one's workplace behaviors on others—a critical component of higher-level ethical perspectives and of effective interpersonal work behaviors (e.g., teamwork).

Taking into account the personal characteristics of this generation, it can be said that they show very distinct differences when it comes to business life. Gen Y's appear to observe fewer boundaries than previous generations and are more flexible about when and how to apply them. In being more open and transparent, they become more likely to discuss work activity with a wider range of people both in public and in private. Their flexibility might make Gen Y's more likely to engage in or tolerate behavior that many consider unacceptable. Additionally, they are the most at-risk group of the four generations, as they are more likely to observe misconduct and experience retaliation after reporting it. However, there is some encouraging news about the youngest generation. Gen Y's entering the workforce have shined the light more readily on misconduct than the youngest entrants in previous years. In fact, Gen Y's were more likely than their older cohorts to utilize the resources of ethics and compliance offices. Finally, Gen Y's are more likely to respond to the elements of ethics and compliance programs that include social interaction and provision of support (e.g., helplines, mechanisms for seeking advice, training) (2013 Ethics Resource Center).

This age group is moving into the labor force during a time of major demographic change and sixty-year-olds are working beside 20-year-olds. Freshly minted college graduates are overseeing employees old enough to be their parents. And new job entrants are changing careers faster than college students change their majors, creating frustration for employers struggling to retain and recruit talented high-performers. Unlike the generations that have gone before them, Gen Y has been pampered, nurtured and programmed with a slew of activities since they were toddlers, meaning they are both high-performance and high-maintenance. They also believe in their own worth. "Generation Y is much less likely to respond to the traditional command-and-control type of management still popular in much of today's workforce," says Jordan Kaplan, an associate managerial science professor at Long Island University-Brooklyn in New York. "They've grown up questioning their parents, and now they're questioning their employers. They don't know how to shut up, which is great, but that's aggravating to the 50-year-old manager who says, 'Do it and do it now.'

Strategic management

Strategy as a word traces back to Greek. As a term it is related with words "army" and "lead". In Greek, it means "a general" and its definition is "to destroy enemies through effective use of resources" [7]. However, its use in business appeared after World War II within the changes taking place throughout the world which was leading to a competitive environment. The changes in firms and in technology ended up with an increment in the competition which caused an unstable environment [8]. Many scholars have studied strategy as a concept in field of business [9-12]. According to the studies of scholars, business strategy should be used as a tool which would enable organization to realize its main goals through effective use of resources in accordance with the outcomes of organization's environmental and situational analysis. Therefore, strategic management is defined as the implementation of business strategy which has been developed [7].

Strategic management analyzes the internal and external environment of an organization to enhance the use of resources to attain its organizational goals. It also helps organization to deal with change [7]. Throughout the strategic management literature, it is mentioned that organization is an open system which survives within an independently given environment [13]. It is crucial for managers to sustain accordance between organizational needs and environmental constraints [14]. Thus, it can be stated that strategic management forms a framework for organization. While forming the framework, the most familiar method is SWOT analyses which points out the strengths and weaknesses of an organization through internal analysis and also determines the opportunities and threats waiting by external analysis [15]. This would help managers to figure out their business strategies and long term plans. Also, it would enable them to adapt to changes taking place in their environment which may help to gain competitive advantage. Through the environmental scanning, managers are able to formulate and implement strategies. For the last step, they should evaluate and control whether these strategies enable them to attain their goals which are set in their plans [16].

After environmental scanning is completed by using SWOT analysis, the organization should formulate their strategies. In this phase, the organization should define its mission and vision statements clearly. Also, it should determine its objectives, strategy and policy guidelines. Mission describes the purpose of the organization, it reflects its present situation whereas vision defines what the organization aims to become, it reflects its expected future state [16]. Following, this they should implement strategies and policies in action to realize their objectives. By measuring the performance of the organization, the evaluation and control stage would be completed. The aim of strategic management is to increase the performance of the organization. It helps organizations to enhance their effectiveness and efficiency. Therefore, the last step which is evaluation and control would let managers to see if the whole processes succeed or not.

Ethical strategic management

Ethics has become a hot topic in business world due to the scandals such as Enron, WorldCom which have occurred in recent 20 years. Ethical issues have become crucial for businessmen and managers in order to save their organizations and to provide them with a good reputation [17]. Providing ethical behavior is one of the aims of managers. However, there are many organizational and situational factors which affect ethical behavior in an organization [18]. Even, the managers should use ethical way of thinking while making decisions. Ethical decision making has also gained importance in business world. To prevent unethical behavior and ethical lapses, managers should be able to use ethical decision making models. The situational and organizational factors which lead to ethical or unethical behavior are also impactful in ethical decision making [18].

As being the strategic decision makers, managers are always questioned whether their responsibilities are limited with shareholders or they have broader responsibilities. Strategic managers should consider all stakeholders while making decisions about the welfare of the organization. For organizations to exist and improve themselves, they should take stakeholders and ethical issues into consideration [17]. Thus, throughout the literature, it is mentioned that ethics and social responsibility can enhance firm's performance. Hosmer stated that ethics can be regarded as a good investment [19]. In his view, it helps organization to have good relationship with its internal and external stakeholders since it enables to build trust among these. One of the organizational aims is to increase sales, productivity and enhance the performance. Therefore, implementing ethics and social responsibility in strategies or long term plans can help organizations to enhance their performances.

Since employees are influenced by the characteristics of their own organization [18], implementation of ethics in organizational infrastructure and strategic management is crucial. Corporate ethical values are one of the dimensions of ethical behavior in business and they also lead to ethical behavior in an organization. Other factors which increase ethical behavior are the code of ethics, ethical leadership and support of whistle blowing. Code of ethics whether being principle or policy based statements influences the corporate culture and determines the procedures and guidelines for ethical behavior. There are various positions or departments such as ethics committees or chief ethics officers in organizations to provide ethical behavior and to prevent unethical acts. Also ethics trainings programs are included in most of the organization to enhance ethical behavior [17,20]. Besides these organizational factors, individual factors such as personality and moral development are also effective in creating ethical behavior [17,18,21]. Also, managers should make ethical decisions when they encounter with ethical dilemmas or conflicts. They may use ethical decision making based on models or ethical approaches. It is expected for managers to be ethical by using justice approach which would lead to equality and fairness in the organization among employees in terms of salary, promotion and treatment [17]. If an organization is an ethical one by providing the requirements, then the employees would be more motivated and be willing to work more efficiently and effectively. This would also enable firm to increase its performance and efficiency.

Managers consider ethics as a business issue such as costs, profits and growth. In the planning stage, they should consider all stakeholders of the organization and ethics. Ethics should be incorporated in their corporate strategy. Ethics in planning process would enhance the trust of stakeholders which would result with commitment and higher performance. This would even help the organization to gain competitive advantage. According to him, ethics should be implemented overall management of the firm [19].

Incorporating ethics and social responsibility in corporate strategies and strategic management would enable the organizations to be good citizens [19]. Even though being a good citizen may increase the costs of the organization, it may increase its performance as well. It may increase the costs since implementing ethics training programs or recruiting experts such as ethics chief officer will be recorded as expenses for the organization. However, all these steps regarding to incorporating ethics in the organization would bring a good reputation for the company. A good reputation increases the motivation and strengthens trust of employees which would lead to higher job satisfaction and performance. It would also attract high quality of employees. Scholars found out that people have higher tendency to work in ethical organizations. At the same time, it will take attention of the customers and society which will enable the promotion of the organization. Studies indicated that most American firms which has superior reputation based on their ethical acts, have the superior financial performance [17].

The organization' values should be congruent with the employee's values to maintain ethical behavior in that organization. Employee's aims and targets should be in accordance with the organization. If the strategy development models do not consider ethics and ambition, then it would be high likely for that organization to experience unethical behavior [22]. For example, as a strategic managements model, personal and organizational balanced scorecards can be taken into account as Rampersad did. Rampersad developed and used these models to point out the importance of ethics in strategic management model in his study [23]. He linked the critical factors to performance measures in his own model. Personal ambition and personal behavior should be balanced to lead to ethical behavior. He used Kaplan and Norton's Organizational Balanced Scorecard for his study [24,25]. Personal ambition, goals and organizational ambition, goals should be in accordance with each other. Concordance between values, mission and vision of the organization and the employee should be provided to have ethical behavior.

All the factors encouraging ethical behavior are part of strategic management. Even though most organizations mentioned that they are ethical in their mission statements and implement code of ethics, practices and managerial ethics in strategies and infrastructure of the organization, it is still questionable whether they perform ethical acts in real life. This should go beyond the statements or strategies by being realized in real life through the decisions and the moves of the organizations.

Methodology

Research goal

As a research method, interview is used. An interview is held with each respondent. Each interview is recorded and then converted into transcripts. Each interview is held in either respondent's office or home. The confidentiality of the respondents is provided and they are being informed about the confidentiality of their identities to make them feel comfortable which will enable the researchers to get impartial results. Questions regarding their perception of ethics and business life are asked to each of the respondents. Their answers which are transcribed are analyzed by the researchers.

Sample and data collection

Sample of the study consists of 8 people who are all members of Generation Y and who are working. There are 4 male and 4 female who attended to the study. The entire sample has bachelor's degree.

Interview Questions:

The questions which are given below are asked to each respondent.

1. If an action could harm an innocent one, but helps you to gain positive reputation in your career, what would you do?
2. While working on a project, a team work is needed, if one of your group members does not attend to the meetings, what would you do?
3. Did you ever use a false excuse to delay turning in a report?
4. What does ethical behavior mean to you?
5. Do you think an organization should implement ethics in its long term plans or strategies?
6. Would you prefer to work in a company which has incorporated ethics in its strategic management?
7. Do you think ethics would enhance company's performance?
8. Would you take an action even though it is legal but not ethical?

Analyses and results

The female and male respondents were equally distributed and all of them have a college degree and working in a corporate company.

- Of all the respondents 5 of them said that, even if an action could harm an innocent but helps to gain positive reputation in their career, they would act professional and do the action.
- All of the respondents agree on that, if one of their group members does not attend to the meetings in a group project, they would report him/her to the managers and they would try to take him/her out of the project.
- Of all the respondents 6 of them said that, they have never delayed turning a report before, but even if they did they would have tell the truth.
- Interviewee's most common perceptions of ethics include precepts, being honest, able to make an empathy, and never to harm another for your own sake
- All of the interviewees agree on that a company should implement ethics in its long term plans because this is one of the factors that increase performance.
- All of the interviewees said that they would prefer to work in companies which have incorporated ethics in strategic management.
- Of all the respondents 7 of them said that ethics would enhance company's performance while 1 one of them said that ethics and performance are two different issues.
- Of all the respondents 6 of them said that to take an action which is legal but unethical will harm the company in its long term, while 2 of them said that in accordance with law unethical behaviors can take place for company's benefit.

As a result of our research, it can be said that Gen Y has a high tolerance on implementation of ethics in strategic management. Even though at some point they may think that for the sake of the company sometimes ethical essentials may be flexible, they resist this flexibility when their personal gain is in question. Because of this, generation feel comfortable with themselves, they prefer to tell the truth in every situation, even if they pass a deadline. Communication is an important aspect in Gen Y's life. The effects can be seen too. Their perception of ethics or an ethical behavior depends on getting use of empathy. They think very professionally on business that, even though when a friend of them doesn't work for the project, they don't feel sorry to escalate him/her from the group. And finally this group of people believes that ethics is something above the laws and that's why they do not prefer to take an action which is legal but unethical.

Conclusion

As also mentioned in the literature, especially, in business life individuals whom are part of Gen Y give more importance to ethics than other members of any generation. Ethics is crucial for them and they conform to ethical codes, guidelines or principles. Whenever they encounter with an ethical conflict, they seem to make a decision based on ethicality of that act. It can be assumed that they are followers of deontology as an ethical approach. They do not hesitate to get use of whistle-blowing whenever they find out misconduct or unethical behavior. People who do not comply with ethical principles could easily be left out by this generation even if they are friends or someone from their in-group.

The research of the study also indicated results which are in accordance with the literature. Based on the literature, it is expected for Gen Y to perform ethical behavior and take ethical principles into consideration in business life through their actions. The study deployed a qualitative research method which in depth interviews was held with the participants of Gen Y. All of the participants were holding a bachelor's degree and were employed. Depending on the answers given by participants, the findings indicated that whenever they encounter with misconduct or an unethical act, they try to solve the issues following ethical guidelines or principles. They may easily end up their business or professional relationship with a friend when they realize that their friend is behaving unethically. The answers of participants show that ethics is a priority for them in their business life. They claim that they prefer being ethical over gaining success, good reputation or gaining more profits. Majority of the participants mentioned that it is more important for them to be ethical in business life and they may give up good reputation or chances or promotion in order to perform ethical behavior. They also stated that they prefer to work in organizations which incorporated ethics into their infrastructure and strategic management. High percentage of the participants included that the organization must reflect its ethical behavior with its act rather than just stating in its mission statement or principles. According to participants, long term business plans and strategies of the organizations should also be shaped in accordance with ethical principles. They highlighted the importance of implementing ethics into strategic management of an organization. They believe that incorporating ethics into strategic management would enable the organization to increase its performance. Thus, it can be stated that the results were as expected.

Since Gen Y are now in the business life and expected to be the future managers and leaders in business world, it is important for them to have an ethical point of view especially in terms of professional life. Ethics has gained critical importance due to ethical lapses and scandals which have occurred lately. Therefore, ethical managers and leaders are demanded in business world. Many training programs have been developed in order to enhance ethics in organizations. Managers are forced to attend to these ethics training programs to prevent unethical behavior in organizations. The organizations should incorporate ethics in its strategic management by adapting its infrastructure accordingly and implementing codes of ethics, supporting whistle-blowing and ethical leadership. Besides implementing ethics in their mission statements, business plans and strategies, they should demonstrate it with their acts and actions. Since Gen Y gives priority to ethics and ethical behavior, it would be high likely for them to incorporate ethics into strategic management which would indeed increase the organization's performance as well. As Gen Y being the future managers, it would be much easier for organizations to implement ethics into strategic management within employment of Gen Y in their organizations.

The study contributes to literature since it highlights on Gen Y and their ethical view on incorporating ethics into strategic management. Most of the studies regarding ethical strategic management does not consider category of generation, therefore, the study fills a gap in the literature by taking generation differences into consideration in ethical strategic management. Also, most of the empirical researches on this subject are studied in Western countries. Since this study takes place in non-western country, it brings a different perspective. The study could also be considered for managerial implications. The business men may consider recruiting members of Gen Y since their priority is ethics in professional life, it would enable them to enhance ethics and incorporate ethics into strategic management.

References

1. Tolbize A (2008) Generational differences in the workplace. Research and Training Center on Community Living. University of Minnesota, Minneapolis.
2. Page D, Wong TP (2000) A conceptual framework for measuring servant leadership. In S Abjibolosoo (Ed), The human factor in shaping the course of history and development. University Press of America, Lanham.
3. Ehrhart MG (2004) Leadership and procedural justice climate as antecedents of unit-level organizational citizenship behavior. Personnel Psychology 57: 61-94.
4. Strutton D, Pelton LE, Ferrell OC (1997) Ethical behavior in retail settings: Is there a generation gap? Journal of Business Ethics 16: 87-105.
5. Howe N, Strauss W (2000) Millenials rising: The next great generation. Random House, New York.
6. Twenge JM, Foster JD (2008) Mapping the scale of the narcissism epidemic: Increases in narcissism 2002–2007 within ethnic groups. Journal of Research in Personality 42: 1619-1622.
7. Bracker J (1980) The Historical Development of the Strategic Management Concept. The Academy of Management Review 5: 219-224.
8. Ansoff HI (1965) Corporate Strategy. Mc Graw-Hill, New York.
9. Neumann JV, Morgenstern O (1947) Theory of games and economic behavior. Princeton University Press.
10. Drucker P (1954) The Practice of Management. Academy of Management, Harper & Brothers, New York 17: 16-23.
11. Schendel D, Hofer C (1979) Introduction. D Schendel and C Hofer (eds), Strategic Management: A New View of Business Policy and Planning (Little Brown, Boston, MA) pp: 1-12.
12. Mintzberg H (1979) The Structuring of Organizations. Prentice- Hall, US pp: 322-353.
13. Thompson JD (1967) Organizations in Action: Social Science Bases of Administrative Theory. Transaction Publishers, New Jersy.
14. Lawrence PR, Dyer D (1983) Renewing Americon industry. Human Resource Management 22: 475-478.
15. Faulkner DO, Campbell A (2003) The Oxford Handbook of Strategy: A Strategy Overview and Competitive Strategy. Oxford, UK.
16. Wheelen TL, Hunger DJ (2012) Strategic Management and Business Policy: Toward Global Sustainability. Pearson Learning Solutions, Iowa State University, USA.
17. Daft RL (2010) Management. South-Western Cengage Learning, USA.
18. Hunt SD, Vitell S (1986) A General Theory of Marketing Ethics. Journal of Macromarketing 6: 5-16.
19. Hosmer LT (1994) Strategic planning as if ethics mattered. Strategic Management Journal 15: 17-34.

20. Miller DS, Catt SE, Carlson JR (1996) Fundamentals of Management: a framework for excellence. West Publishing Company, Minneapolis.

21. Ferrell OC, Fraedrich J, Ferrell L (2010) Business Ethics: Ethical Decision Making & Cases. South-Western Cengage Learning, USA.

22. Rampersad HK (2003) The links between individual learning, collective learning and ethics. Training and Management Development Methods 17: 1.

23. Rampersad HK (2003) Total Performance Scorecard: Redefining management to achieve performance with integrity. Butterworth-Heinemann Business Books, Elsevier Science, Massachusetts.

24. Kaplan RS, Norton DP (1996) The Balanced Scorecard: translating strategy into action. Harvard Business School Press, Boston.

25. Kaplan RS, Norton DP (2000) The Strategy focused Organization: how balanced scorecard companies thrive in the new business environment. Harvard Business School Press, Boston.

2

Determinants of Financial Self Sufficiency of Andhra Pradesh Microfinance Institutions

Beg K*

Department of Commerce, Aligarh Muslim University, Aligarh, India

Abstract

Microfinance aims to reduce poverty and generate profit by providing financial services to poor and unprivileged section of society. The southern state of Andhra Pradesh in India which is known as Mecca of Microfinance accounts for about 30% of the credit extended by MFIs. Andhra Pradesh Microfinance Crisis 2010 lead to the shutdown of many emerging and small MFIs and loss of loan portfolio rose to the extent of Rs 7,200 crore. Financial sustainability became very challenging issue for Microfinance institutions. This study uses cross sectional high quality panel data from MIX (Microfinance Information Exchange) market of 10 microfinance institutions of Andhra Pradesh, for the period 2005 to 2013 to examine the patterns of financial viability. This study employed pooled OLS model, fixed effect model and Random effect model of panel data in order to check consistency of results.

Keywords: Financial sustainability; Microfinance institutions; Mi-crofinance crisis

Introduction and Issues

Microfinance institutions (MFIs) have proved to be very important in growth and development of a country. MFIs enhance financial deepening in an economy thereby contributing to an economy's development by providing financial services to the extremely poor section of society. Nowadays, MFIs face challenge of sustainability and outreach. There has been increased pressure on MFIs to decrease dependence on donations, grants and subsidized funding. As providing Microfinance services is a costly business due to high transaction and information cost. At presents, large number of Microfinance programs is still depending on donors, grants and donations which mean that MFIs are not financially sustainable. In 1990s, the issue of sustainability of MFIs gave rise to important debate between financial system approach and poverty lending approach (Robinson, 2001) [1].

According to the report of Deutsche bank (2007) only 1-2% of MFIs in the world are financially sustainable [2]. 8% of all MFIs are close to being profitable. 70% of all MFIs are heavily dependent on subsidy. Microfinance in India has grown at tremendous pace in recent years, achieving significant outreach amongst the poor household across the country. According to the status of Microfinance report 2011-12 there are about 1,000 MFIs in country working in various legal forms, Puhazhendhi [3]. The southern state of Andhra Pradesh accounts for about 30% of the credit extended by MFIs. According to the article published in, "Business Standard" the number of Self-help groups is declining over the years an indication of weakening SHG movement in India. NABARD has also raised alarm over rising Non Performing Assets (NPAs) or Bad loans in SHG bank linkage model. Andhra Pradesh Microfinance crisis lead to the following repercussions that Non Performing Assets (NPAs) of Andhra's MFIs is an all time high of over 96% in the year 2011. Smaller emerging MFIs shut down their business operations and loss of MFI portfolio to the extent of Rs. 7,200 crore.

Research objectives

The study is focused on achievement of following objectives.

1. To determine the factors affecting financial sustainability of microfinance institutions in Andhra Pradesh.

2. To analyze the effect of increasing interest rates on Financial Performance of Andhra Pradesh MFIs.

Literature Review

Schafer and Fukasawa in this paper titled "Factors determining operational self sufficiency among Microfinance institutions" investigate about the factors affecting operational self sufficiency of MFIs [4]. The empirical investigation is based on the data of 1,000 MFIs retrieved from MIX market for the year 2006 and 2008 scattered in different part of the world. Their empirical findings by multiple regression analysis revealed that number of borrowers, write off ratio were found to be important determinants of operational self sufficiency. Moreover, there was no significant difference in 2006 before the worldwide financial crisis and in 2008.

Zerai and Rani examined technical efficiency of Ethiopian micro finance institution (MFIs) by utilizing data of 19 micro finance institutions taken from mix market with the help of stochastic frontier analysis [5]. The findings of the study revealed that average efficiency score of 71.72% of Ethiopian MFIs. Assets, operational sustainability, depth of outreach have significant impact on efficiency. The empirical findings confirm tradeoff between efficiency and outreach of Ethiopian MFIs.

Cull, Demirgüc-Kunt and Morduch examines by using dataset of 245 microfinance Institution effect of prudential supervision on MFI profitably outreach to small scale borrowers and women [6]. Their finding suggest that profit oriented micro finance institution respond to supervision by maintaining profit rates and but at the cost outreach to women and poor client that are costly to reach. Their empirical finding shows that supervision has a negative effect on outreach, because supervision is positively related with average loan balance while it is negatively related with the percentage of women borrowers.

***Corresponding author:** Kashif Beg, Department of Commerce, Aligarh Muslim University, Aligarh, Uttar Pradesh, India
E-mail: Kashifbeg90@gmail.com

Gutiérrez-Nieto, Serrano-Cinca and Molinero in their paper discussed about dual performance of MFIs i.e social and performance [7]. Out of data set of 450 institutions for the year 2003 from mix microfinance information exchange only 89 MFIs were selected for which complete information was available. Data elopement analysis (DEA) was used to calculate the social and financial efficiency of MFIs. Operating cost and assets gross loan portfolio used as inputs. Gross loan portfolio and financial revenue are used as outputs for measuring financial efficiency. No. of active borrowers and indicator of benefit to the poorest are used as output variable to calculate social efficiency. The result of financial efficiency and social efficiency was correlated with various financial ratios to withdraw the result and interpretation. The findings of this paper suggest that except one, no MFIs are socially efficient but financially efficient MFIs exist. There is low positive relationship between social and financial efficiency of MFIs.

Tehulu used unbalanced panel data from 2004 to 2009 of 23 microfinance institutions in east Africa to identify the factors affecting financial sustainability. The study used binary probit and ordinary probit regression models to identify the factors. The empirical result regression revealed that management efficiency and portfolio at risk is negative and significantly related with financial sustainability. Management inefficiency, portfolio at risk, loan intensity and size are important factors of financial sustainability [8].

Gonzalez examined the technical efficiency of micro finance institution by using DEA and also identify differences in efficiency with the help of Tobit regression average loan size, proportion of assets used as performing portfolio, scale of operation, ratio of payroll to expenses, age, structure of the board and for profit status of MFIs are the indicators used to determine differences in efficiency [9]. The empirical evidence shows tradeoff between sustainability and outreach in Mexican MFIs. Moreover, this study provides an idea how to use tools to analyze the relative technical efficiency of MFIs.

Rai in his research work "A comparative analysis of the financial performance of micro finance institution of India and Bangladesh" analyzed the financial performance of Indian MFIs and compared it with MFIs of Bangladesh from different point of view by using various performance indicators and Ratios [10]. Mann Whitney U test is used to compare financial performance of India and Bangladesh MFIs. Kruskal Wallis one way ANOVA is used to analyze age wise performance of Indian MFIs after categorizing MFIs into young, mature and old. This study covers the period of 2007-08. There is no significant difference between the means of Bangladesh and Indian MFIs on operational self sufficiency, yield on gross loan portfolio and return on assets. NBFC MFIs are financially more viable and outreach is high.

Masood and Ahmad measured the technical efficiency of micro finance institution by applying stochastic frontier approach of unbalanced panel data of 40 micro finance institutions withdrawn from mix market for the period 2005-08 [11]. The objective of the study is to benchmark the best practice MFIs by assigning ranks and to determine the factors responsible for variation in efficiency level. The findings of the study revealed that efficiency level of micro finance institution is very low and it is increasing during the study period and there is no evidence of trade off. MFIs in southern part of India are more efficient than other MFIs. Moreover unregulated MFIs are more efficient than regulated MFIs.

Gutierrez et al. employed data envelopment analysis (DEA) approach to efficiency to prove that ratio analysis does not capture DEA efficiency. This study highlights an important aspect that, "how DEA model be specified i.e. which input and output variables should be chosen [12]. A methodological approach based on multivariate analyses is applied in order to choose appropriate model specifications and to produce ranking of MFIs in terms of efficiency. The finding of the study is based on data obtained data of 30 MFIs from micro rate web page from the year 2003. The selection of inputs and outputs indicators is based on Yaron's (1994) outreach and sustainability framework. The study reveals that level of MFIs depend on the particular model. This model is also relevant for efficiency assessment.

Hassan and Sanchez investigates about the technical and scale efficiency of MFIs by using Data elopement analysis. The data of 215 MFIs was taken from mix (A CGAP data base of MFIs around the globe). These MFIs are scattered in region of Latin America, Middle East and North Africa and South Asia. The efficiency of MFIs is analysed following both production approach and intermediation approach. The inputs indicators for the intermediation approach are operating expenses, total financial expenses and labour. The indicators used as output in intermediation approach are gross loan portfolio, total funds and financial revenues. On the other hand, operating expenses and labour are used as input in production approach and Numbers of active borrower is as only input. The empirical findings of the study depicts that technical efficiency is higher for formal MFIs. South Asian MFIs have higher efficiencies in comparison to latin America and middle east and north African MFIs. The efficiencies are of pure technical nature i.e. MFIs are wasting their resources and not producing enough outputs [13].

Data and Methodology

The empirical findings of the study are based on the financial data of Microfinance institutions withdrawn from MIX market (Microfinance Information Exchange database). Mix market provides information about historical and social performance information data of more than 2100 microfinance institutions worldwide serving about 94 million clients. The study is based on the unbalanced panel data consists of 10 Microfinance institutions representing over the period 2005 to 2013 with total 76 observations. As of 31st March 2013 around 200 Indian Microfinance institutions reported data to the MIX. Out of 18 Andhra's Microfinance institutions 10 have been selected for this study. The criteria for selecting the MFIs were based on the time period of 9 years (2005-2013). However data provide by these institutions was incomplete. We have selected those institutions which report at least 5 years data from the period 2005 to 2013 to MIX database. On the basis of this criterion 10 MFIs have been selected. Therefore on the basis of sample size and time period our data is unbalanced panel data with 76 observations.

After fulfilling the above criteria, the unbalanced panel data of 10 microfinance institutions for 9 years period 2005 to 2013 is used for analysis and interpretation. These microfinance institutions are representative of around of around 55% of total number microfinance institutions in Andhra Pradesh given their size and age. It has been attempted to include all categories of size (large, medium and small) and age (old, medium and young) MFIs.

Sampling technique

The purposive sampling technique on the basis of following points given below is adopted. Only those MFIs which follow the followings assumptions are selected for the present study.

1. Only those MFIs which report data to the MIX market

(Microfinance information exchange) of Andhra Pradesh are taken into consideration for this study.

2. Out of the 18 Andhra MFIs which report data to the MIX 10 MFIs have been selected. Only those MFIs which are operating during the period 2005-2013 are selected.
3. Only those MFIs which report at least five years data during the period 2005-2013 is selected for the present study.
4. MFIs do not provide full information regarding the variables. Some observations are missing in the data.
5. After fulfilling the above criteria, the unbalanced panel data of ten firms for nine years during the period (2005 to 2013) are taken into consideration.

The use of panel data enhances tracking variables changes in measured variables and relationship overtime [14]. It allows us to control for unobserved characteristics of individuals cases or MFIs and facilitates causal inferences in situations where inferring causality would be very difficult in case if we had only single year cross sectional data. According to Gujarati, by studying repeated cross sectional data of same cases or firms, Panel data is considered better to study dynamic changes [15]. Furthermore, panel or longitudinal data help us to study the importance of lags in the behavior. We used the pooled OLS model, fixed effect model and random effect model of panel data. However, we try to check the consistency of results by using all the three models independently. Finally Gretl version 1.9.12 software is used to generate regression results and panel diagnostics command in Gretl to determine most appropriate model. On the basis of result of F test, Hausman test and Breusch pagan test most appropriate model is determined and finally our result and interpretation is based on most appropriate model.

Dependent and independent variables

This section states about definitions of independent variables and their expected hypothesis sign related to factors affecting financial sufficiency model. Hypotheses of the study, In line with the main objective of the study, the researcher have developed the following hypotheses based on the theories and empirical studies discussed in literature related to financial self sufficiency.

Dependent variable

Financial self sufficiency (FSS): The key dependent variable in our analysis of profitability is the financial self sufficiency (FSS) ratio, a measure of an institution's ability to generate sufficient revenue to cover its costs. Values below one indicate that it is not doing so. The financial self sufficiency ratio is the best measures of financial performance because the data readjusted as described below and because it offers a more complete summary of inputs and outputs than standard financial ratios such as return on assets or equity.

FSS=Operating Income (Loans+Investments) Operating Costs+Loan Loss Provisions+Financing Costs+Adjusted Cost of Capital

Independent variables and expected hypothesis

Real gross portfolio yield: Portfolio yield is a percentage that shows the institutions ability to generate revenue to covers its Financial and operational expenses. It represents the average gross returns as a proportion of portfolio outstanding. It shows the amount received from interest payments during the period by Microfinance institutions. In case the MFIs following cash accounting system the portfolio yield will not include (interest and fee) income generated by delinquent loan. It indicates the efficiency of micro finance institution in generating cash revenue from their outstanding loan portfolio. In simple words Portfolio Yield shows how much on average the MFIs receives in interest payment on its loan. It is a good indicator of delinquency as if Portfolio at risk is low (as reported by MFI) if the yield is lesser than expected than there is delinquency [16].

The study of indicates the coefficient for gross loan portfolio yield is positive and significant with all three measures of financial performance (financial self sufficiency, operational self sufficiency and return on assets indicating that individual based lenders earns more profit than their average interest are higher [17]. However the result is quite different for village banks or solidarity lenders. For Group lenders and solidarity lenders there is not significant relationship between interest rates and profitability even after controlling for cost? Rahman and Mazlan empirical findings revealed significant and positive relationship between yield on gross loan portfolio and financial self sufficiency [18]. The study of De Crombrugghe et al. founds the gross portfolio yields affects the financial self sufficiency [19]. The finding of the study show financial self sufficiency is positive through interest and fees revenues. The study of Woller and Schreiner shows that real portfolio yield is statistically significant determinant of financial self sufficiency [20]. Adongo and stork found that all the financial institutions during the selected period were financially unsustainable [21]. The study suggests that they were not charging enough interest rates that can cover all financial costs and non-financial costs and risk of their operation. The study of Cull et al. shows that interest rates are related with improved financial performance for individual lenders only [17]. Nyamsogoro empirical findings revealed positive relationship between yield on gross loan portfolio and financial self sufficiency [22]. Hence, based on the earlier empirical evidences, the following hypothesis is framed.

H_1: There exists a positive relationship between yield on gross loan portfolio and financial self sufficiency.

Capital cost to total assets ratio: The capital cost to total assets ratio is used as standard inverse proxy of leverage, especially in banking research because regulatory attentions are paid to capital assets ratio [23]. In context of financial performance agency costs hypothesis states that increasing leverage or decreasing capital assets ratio is associated with reduction in agency cost of outside equity and improvement in financial performance. Kar concludes that reduction in capital cost ratio may raise efficiency [24]. Gebremichael predicted positive relation between capital assets ratio and financial self sufficiency [25]. Accordingly the following hypothesis is predicted.

H_2: There exists a negative relationship between capital cost to assets and financial self sufficiency.

Gross loan portfolio to total assets ratio: Gross loan portfolio to total assets ratio is an indicator of financing structure. It is the ratio of adjusted gross loan portfolio to adjusted total assets. It is an indication of their focus of lending as otherwise these funds could have been utilized for some income generating purpose. Tehulu also predicted that loan intensity affects positively to financial sustainability and his findings show that the coefficient of gross loan portfolio to total assets ratio is positive and significant at 5% level [8]. Cull et al. empirical findings revealed positive relationship between gross loan portfolio to total assets ratio and financial sufficiency [26]. Kar also expected uncertain relationship between gross loan portfolio and financial self sufficiency [24]. However, based on the prior empirical evidence, we predict positive relationship between financial performance and gross loan portfolio to total assets ratio. Accordingly, the following hypothesis is suggested

H_3: There exists positive relationship between gross loan portfolio to total assets ratio and financial self sufficiency.

Average loan balance per borrower: Average loan size is taken as proxy for depth of outreach. It measures the efficiency of microfinance institutions in selling loans. It is calculated by dividing average gross loan portfolio by number of active borrowers. The size of loan can affect FSS and even portfolio at risk. However, larger loans may be more risky than smaller loans, but their cost per rupee is assumed to be small, if there is some fixed cost per loan. The size of the loan is often taken as indicator of coverage i.e. ability of MFIs to reach poor, as poor people are expected to avail for smaller loan than larger amount of loan. It is interesting to determine how important the effect of the size of the loan and to determine how MFIs perform for given loan size. The findings of the study of Gonzalez shows that larger loans are associated with higher cost efficiency and thereby profitability [9]. However the findings of Cull et al. are against the findings of above two studies [26]. The study revealed that the Micro banks or MFIs which provide smaller loans are not less profitable than those which provide bigger loan. The findings of the study revealed that the average loan sizes are not strongly associated with financial performance indicators. Institutions which provide larger loans are not less profitable than which provide bigger loan amount. Woller and Schreiner found that the depth of outreach is inversely related with financial self sufficiency [20]. Nyamsogoro study also indicates that average loan size is positively and significantly related with financial self sufficiency [22]. Adongo and Stork found that profitability is related with bigger or wealthier loan size per borrower [21]. Therefore, based on the review of prior empirical and theoretical evidences the following hypothesis is suggested.

H_4: There exists a positive relationship between average loan balance per borrower and financial self sufficiency.

Portfolio at risk (30 days): Portfolio at risk indicates that how much an MFI is efficient in making collections of loans. Higher PAR indicates inefficiency of MFIs i.e. indicates lower repayment rates. Lower the PAR the more inefficient the microfinance institutions will be and thereby financially sustainable. Portfolio at risk captures the accounting convention that loans exceeding 30 days overdue pose an unacceptably high risk of non-repayment [24]. He predicted an inverse relationship between PAR (30) and profit efficiency and his findings show negative insignificant relationship between PAR (30) and firm performance. The study of Cull et al. conclude that higher interest rates are associated with higher rates of non-repayment but for individual based lenders only [26]. Moreover, according to one specification individual based lenders charging higher interest rates higher profit than those charging interest intermediate rates. Tehulu also found that credit risk measured by PAR (30) days found to have a negative and significant impact on financial sustainability of MFIs [8]. The empirical findings of Nyamsogoro disclosed that, there is a statistically significant and negative relationship between portfolio at risk and financial sustainability [22]. Thus, in the line with prior studies the following hypothesis is proposed.

H_5: There exists a negative relationship between portfolio at risk and financial self sufficiency.

Personnel productivity ratio: Personnel productivity measures the amount of quality services delivered by microfinance institutions staff to their customers. The finding of the Cull et al. shows that there is negative relationship between charging higher interest rates and having a large customer base. Accordingly, the following hypothesis is suggested [26].

H_6: There exists an uncertain relationship between labour cost to assets and financial self sufficiency.

Size: The size of an MFI is defined as natural logarithm of total assets of the MFIs. Hermes et al. [27]; Mersland and Strom [28]; Bogan, Johnson, and Mhlanga [29]; Hartarska [30] shows that the MFI size do not effects its financial sustainability. While study of Mersland and Strom, Bogan et al., Hartarska used total value of its assets as MFIs size indicator [28-30]. The study of Hartarska shows that the MFIs size did not affect its financial sustainability [30]. While the study of Mersland and Strom, and Bogan et al. revealed that the size of an MFI is associated with its financial sustainability [28,29]. The empirical finding of Cull et al. shows that size of MFI is statistically significant and positively linked to its financial performance [26]. The study of Nyamsogoro found that the size of MFI significantly affects its financial sustainability [22]. Similar findings were also disclosed by the study of Cull et al [26]; Robinson [1]; Bogan et al. [29]; Mersland and Strom [28]. Therefore in the line with prior empirical findings, the following hypothesis is suggested.

H_7: There exists a positive relationship between size of MFIs and financial self sufficiency.

Age of MFIs: The study of Cull et al. revealed that the age of MFIs is significantly and positively related with all three measures of sustainability i.e. (FSS, OSS and ROA) [26]. The study of Gonzalez depicts that the age of Indian MFIs never comes up significant with financial self sufficiency and operational self sufficiency [9]. The findings of Robinson imply that age is significant variable to effect financial self sufficiency [1]. The findings by Nadiya show that relationship between age of MFIs and operational self sufficiency is not significant for determining changes in operational self sufficiency [31]. The study of Bogan et al. shows that the age of MFIs is related to financial sustainability [29]. Nyamsogoro found that age of microfinance institution is not significantly related with financial self sufficiency [22]. Hence, in the line with prior studies the following hypothesis is proposed.

H_8: There exists a positive relationship between age of MFIs and financial self sufficiency (Table 1).

Operational model for financial self sufficiency (FSS)

$$\text{MODEL } (FSS)_{i,t}=\alpha_i+\beta_1(YOGP)_{i,t}+\beta_2\ (CCTA)_{i,t}+\beta_3\ (GLPTA)_{i,t}+\beta_4\ (L\_ALBPB)_{i,t}+\beta 5(P30)_{i,t}+\beta_6\ (PEA)_{i,t}+\beta 7(L\_ASS)_{i,t}+\beta 8\ (AGE)_{i,t}+\varepsilon_{i,t}$$

Where (FSS)=dependent variable {(Financial Self Sufficiency (FSS) in percentage for firm "i" during time period "t")}

$\boldsymbol{\alpha_i}$=Constant

$\beta_1\ (YOGP)_{i,t}$=coefficient of Independent variable, yield on gross loan portfolio for firm "i" during time period "t"

$\beta_2\ (CCTA)_{i,t}$=coefficient of Independent variable, Capital/Assets ratio for firm "i" during time period "t"

$\beta_3\ (GLPTA)_{i,t}$=coefficient of Independent variable, Gross loan portfolio to total assets ratio for firm "i" during time period "t"

$\beta_4\ (L\_ALBPB)_{i,t}$=coefficient of Independent variable, Average loan balance per borrower for firm "i" during time period "t"

$\beta_5\ (P30)_{i,t}$=coefficient of Independent variable, Portfolio at risk (30) days for firm "i" during time period "t"

β_6 $(PEA)_{i,t}$=coefficient of Independent variable, Labour cost to total Assets ratio for firm "i" during time period "t"

β_7 $(L\_ASS)_{i,t}$=coefficient of Independent variable, Size (log of Total Assets) for firm "i" during time period "t"

β_8 $(AGE)_{i,t}$=coefficient of Independent variable, AGE of MFIs for firm "i" during time period "t"

$\varepsilon_{i,t}$=Error term

Descriptive Statistics

The Table 2 shows the results of descriptive statistics of dependent and independent variables employed in the study. The average loan size is generally used as a measure of depth of outreach. Smaller amount of loan indicates better outreach to poor. The descriptive statistics for mean value of average loan size per borrower is 4.98 in its natural logarithm value. In real term the value for the mean is (149.94$) indicating that MFIs provide (150$) per borrower. The maximum value of loan balance per borrower is (235$) is an indication of serving non poor clients. However the minimum value of (77$) is an indication of better outreach to poor. If FSS value is one or greater than one, it indicates that MFIs are financially self-sustainable. On the other hand less than one indicates that MFIs are not financially self-sustainable. As per the result of descriptive statistics for FSS, the mean value is 0.657 (65.7%) indicates that MFIs in the sample are not financially self-sufficient. The capital cost to assets ratio has an average value of (0.070). It means that around 7% of equity financing is done against total assets by microfinance institutions. Furthermore, the minimum value is 0.0008 and maximum value is 0.365. It indicates that proportion of equity financing is quite low against the total assets.

The result of pair wise correlation is reported in Table 3. The results of correlation analysis show that all the variables except age and (l_ass) are below the threshold limit of (0.7). The result revealed that the variable age is highly correlated with size at (0.73). We further computed variance inflation factor (VIF) for each coefficient to detect the culprit variable causing multicollinearity. The results of VIF values are reported in Appendix Gujarati (2003) and Hair et al. (2006) suggest that variance inflation factor above 10 causes multicollinearity [14,15]. Following the Hair et al. criteria of VIF [14] it is evidence from the result of VIF values of independent variables in all the models ranges from 1 to 3 i.e. within the threshold for nonexistence of multicollinearity. It implies that regression coefficient will be fairly estimating the model.

Results of Financial Self Sufficiency Model by Pooled OLS model, Fixed Effect Model and Random Effect Regression Models

In this section the result of factors affecting financial self sufficiency model is shown by pooled OLS model, random effect model and fixed effect model. In order to check consistency, we employed all the three models of panel data. Finally, our result and interpretation is based on most appropriate model which is chosen on the basis of result of F test to make choice between pooled OLS and fixed effect model, Breusch pagan test to make choice between pooled OLS and random effect model. Finally, Hausman test to make choice between random and fixed effect model.

S/N	Variable Standard Name	Description	Variable description as used in regression	Expected effect on the FSS
1	Real Gross Portfolio Yield	(Yield on gross portfolio (nominal) - Inflation rate)/ (1+Inflation rate)	YOGP	Positive
2	Capital to Assets ratio	Adjusted total equity/Adjusted total assets	CCTA	Negative
3	Gross loan portfolio to total assets ratio	Gross loan portfolio/total assets	GLPTA	Positive
4	Average loan balance per borrower	Adj. GLP/Adj. Number of Active Borrowers	l_ALBPB	Positive
5	Portfolio at risk	The fraction of loan portfolio that is overdue past 30 days or more; that is PAR 30=Portfolio at risk/ Gross loan portfolio	P30	Negative
6	Labour cost to assets	Personnel expenses/total assets	PEA	Positive or negative
7	SIZE OF MFI	The size of MFIs measured by value of its Assets	l_ASS	Positive
8	MFI AGE	Years since its establishment to when evaluation is considered. It also measure length of it outreach.	AGE	Positive

Table 1: Definitions of independent variable and their expected hypothesis sign related to Financial self sufficiency model.

Descriptive statistics of dependent and independent variables					
Variable	**Mean**	**Standard**	**Minimum**	**Maximum**	**No. of observations**
FSS	0.657846	0.313578	0.0360245	1.78001	76
YOGP	0.109191	0.197436	0.1304	0.9954	76
CCTA	0.0705189	0.0574553	0.0008	0.3655	76
GLPTA	1.11314	0.997195	0.6528	8.916	76
p30	0.192328	0.320923	0	0.9954	76
PEA	0.0471257	0.0163077	0.0165	0.0917	76
l_Ass	17.3295	1.99854	13.9942	20.6751	76
AGE	15.5263	5.37767	4	27	76
l_ALBPB	4.9821	0.241976	4.34381	5.45959	76
ALBPB	149.947	35.3323	77	235	76

Note: FSS=financial self sufficiency ratio, YOGP=yield on gross loan portfolio to total assets ratio, CCTA=Capital cost to total assets ratio, GLPTA=gross loan portfolio to total assets ratio, P30=Portfolio at risk (30) days, PEA=Labour cost to total assets ratio, l_ASS=Log of total assets (size), AGE=age of MFIs since its establishment, l_ALBPB=log of average loan balance per borrower, ALBPB=Average loan balance per borrower

Table 2: Descriptive statistics.

Summary of panel data

In this section the coefficients of econometric regressions (pooled, fixed and random) have been summarized to facilitate an overall overview. The Table 4 shows panel data regression for the year 2005-2013 with financial self sufficiency as dependent variable. The table reports summary of pooled OLS, fixed effect and random effect model of financial self sufficiency (FSS) on (GLPTA), yield on gross loan portfolio (YOGP), capital cost to assets (CCTA), gross loan portfolio to total assets (GLPTA), average loan balance per borrower (ALBPB), portfolio at risk (30) days (p30), labour cost to assets (PEA), size of MFI, Assets (ASS), age of MFIs in years (AGE).

Table 4 shows the results from pooled, fixed, and random models. The dependent variable is the financial self sufficiency. According to the result of panel diagnostic command (Result reported in Appendix A and B) fixed effect model is more appropriate and consistent than Pooled OLs and Random effect model. *,**,*** significant at 10%, 5% and 1% level respectively. Figures that are in bold are p values. Figures in parenthesis are t values based on Robust (HAC) standard errors. Figures in brackets are coefficients (Table 4).

This study employed pooled OLS model, fixed effect model and Random effect model of panel data in order to check consistency of results. Though, our results and interpretation is based on most appropriate model which is determined on basis of result of F test, Breusch-pagan test and Hausman test. The result reported in Appendix (B) of panel diagnostic command for FSS model shows that the F statistic value is 3.03 with P value is (0.004) a low p value counts against the null hypothesis that the pooled OLS model is adequate, in favour of the fixed effects alternative. Secondly Breusch-Pagan test is applied on FSS model in order to decide between pooled regression and random effects model. The LM statistic value is 2.18 with P value 0.139. As the P value is much greater than the 5% level of significance. Therefore, our Null hypothesis articulated as pooled regression is more consistent and appropriate than the random effects model remains accepted. Finally the choice between fixed effects and random effects tested through Hausman's specification test. The null hypothesis is framed as random effect is more appropriate and consistent to fixed effects model. The result of Hausman test in Appendix B for FSS model indicates that the low p value of 0.03 is much less than the 5% level of significance. A low p value counts against the random effects model is consistent, in favour of the fixed effect model. Hence, fixed effect is more consistent than the random effects model. The results indicate that fixed effect model is more appropriate than pooled OLS and Random effect model. Therefore results and interpretation for financial self sufficiency (FSS) model is based on the fixed effects model which is discussed in detail in next section.

The explanatory power (R^2) for FSS model is 0.38 in case of pooled OLS model. This reflects that 38% change in FSS model can be explained jointly by the given firm or MFIs specific factors; while the remaining 62% is attributed to the factors outside the model. In case of fixed effect for FSS model explanatory power (R^2) is 0.58 which reflects that 58% changes can be explained by the firm specific determinants, while 42% is attributed to the factors outside the model. Moreover, the value of (R^2) for FSS random effect model is 0.38 reflecting that 38% change in FSS model is due to Firm specific variable and remaining 62% is attributed to the factors outside the model.

Findings and Discussion of Financial Self Sustainability (FSS) Model

Yield on gross loan portfolio

The yield on gross loan portfolio measure of average interest rate on loan to customers is strongly significant and positively associated at 1% significance level in Pooled model. It indicates that increasing interest rates improves financial sustainability of Andhra Microfinance institutions. The econometric result of regression analysis revealed that for one unit increase in a yield on gross loan portfolio financial self-sustainability ratio is expected to increase by 0.66 units, holdings all other variables constant. This suggest that yield on gross loan portfolio is significant variable influencing financial sustainability of microfinance institutions. It also indicates that MFIs tend to be more profitable when interest rates are higher. Finally, it can be concluded that increasing interest rates is clearly associated with improved level of financial self sufficiency. The findings of this study are consistent with that of Nyamsogoro, De Crombrugghe et al. concluded that yield on gross loan portfolio positively affect the financial sustainability of microfinance institutions [19,22]. The findings of the Cull et al. revealed that yield on gross loan portfolio is significant and positively associated across all the measures of financial self-sustainability i.e. Return on Assets, Financial sustainability, Operational self-sustainability for individual based lenders only [26]. The findings of this study are consistent with our findings. Therefore based on regression results, the alternative hypothesis articulated as yield on gross loan portfolio is positively associated with financial self sufficiency is accepted.

Capital cost to assets

The study finds an insignificant negative relationship of capital cost to assets with financial self sufficiency. Therefore on the basis of our

	AGE	CCTA	FSS	GLPTA	L_ALBPBG	L_ASS	P30	PEA	YOGP
AGE	1								
CCTA	-0.3077	1							
FSS	-0.32014	0.035301	1						
GLPTA	0.22275	-0.1773	-0.37808	1					
L_ALBPB	0.053976	0.110357	0.070101	-0.08627	1				
L_ASS	0.732431	-0.33276	-0.05729	-0.07058	0.086663	1			
P30	0.284837	-0.21015	-0.34307	0.457572	0.16452	0.040008	1		
PEA	0.240223	0.212528	0.061753	-0.23289	-0.44092	0.254694	-0.23841	1	
YOGP	0.025384	-0.00825	0.24652	-0.11474	-0.02301	-0.06441	0.322258	0.223271	1

Source: *Gretl output.*

Note: FSS=financial self sufficiency ratio, ALBPBG=Average loan balance per borrower to GNI per capita, YOGP=yield on gross loan portfolio to total assets ratio, CCTA=Capital cost to total assets ratio, GLPTA=gross loan portfolio to total assets ratio, P30=Portfolio at risk (30) days, Pea=Labour cost to total assets ratio, I_ASS=Log of total assets (size), AGE=age of MFIs since its establishment, ALBPB=Average loan balance per borrower

Table 3: Multicollinearity results.

Variables	Pooled OLS regression model	Fixed effect regression model	Random effects regression
Const	(-0.172192)	(-0.499381)	(-0.172192)
	[-0.0643]	[-0.5390]	[-0.2207]
	0.94891	0.59194	0.82599
YOGP	-0.541798	-0.451348	-0.541798
	[3.2606]	[2.3153]	[3.1016]
	0.00175***	0.02415**	0.00282***
CCTA	(-0.71581)	(-0.476002)	(-0.71581)
	[-0.7853]	[-0.5966]	[-1.0325]
	0.43502	0.55311	0.30557
GLPTA	(-0.00126836)	-0.0310568	(-0.00126836)
	[-0.4954]	[0.7628]	[-0.0345]
	0.62196	0.4487	0.97259
l_ALBPB	-0.212125	-0.130244	-0.212125
	[1.2702]	[0.6904]	[1.3699]
	0.2084	0.49269	0.17529
p30	(-0.370474)	(-0.336808)	(-0.370474)
	[-2.0084]	[-2.0049]	[-2.9955]
	0.04864**	0.04965**	0.00384***
PEA	(-0.736011)	(-1.08831)	(-0.736011)
	[-0.0853]	[-0.3375]	[-0.2716]
	0.93225	0.73694	0.78674
l_ASS	-0.0603387	0.145989	-0.0603387
	[0.8008]	[2.8237]	[2.0243]
	0.00125***	0.00650***	0.04693**
AGE	(-0.438934)	(-0.731365)	(-0.438934)
	[5.8795]	[-2.7452]	[-2.9228]
	0.00001***	0.00804***	0.00473***
R^2	0.385346	0.58225	0.388844
Adjusted R^2	0.311955	0.459806	0.31587
F-statistic	5.250555	4.755233	5.328531
P – value (F)	0.000041	3.86E-06	0.000035
Durban-Watson	1.427617	1.437774	1.655338

Robust (HAC) standard error,
Included 10 cross-sectional units,
Time-series length: minimum 5, maximum. *,**,*** significant at 10%, 5% and 1% level respectively.

Table 4: Model: Dependent variable: Financial self sufficiency.

result capital cost to assets is insignificant variable influencing financial self sufficiency of Andhra Microfinance institutions. The result of cull et al. indicated that coefficients on the capital cost variables show differences in the way of different type of lenders (Individual, Group and solidarity) generate profits [26]. The findings revealed that, there is no significant difference between capital cost and financial sustainability measure for group lenders. Therefore based on the regression results we reject the alternative hypothesis articulated as there is negative relationship between capital cost to assets and financial self sufficiency.

Gross loan portfolio to total assets

Gross loan portfolio is insignificant predictor in determining financial self sufficiency. The findings shows that Gross loan portfolio to total assets ratio is insignificant variable influencing financial self sufficiency of Andhra Microfinance institutions. However, the findings of cull et al. revealed loan to assets ratio is significant and positively associated with measures of financial sustainability [26]. Therefore based on the regression result the alternative hypothesis is rejected which was formulated as there is positive relationship between gross loan portfolio to total assets and financial self sufficiency.

Log of average loan balance per borrower

The average loan size defined as the average gross loan divided by the number of borrowers. The coefficient is positively associated but insignificant in fixed effect regression model. The result of regression analysis shows that average loan size is not a significant predictor. Therefore, our findings suggest that average loan balance per borrower is not an important factor influencing financial self sufficiency. Our findings are consistent with the findings of cull et al. which indicates that average loan size is not strongly significant with financial sustainability of Microfinance institutions [26]. The study of Nadiya et al. is also against the findings of this study, which shows that operational self sufficiency is significantly and negatively associated to average loan size per borrower [31]. Our findings is also against the findings Gregoire and Tuya, Adongo and stork, Gonzalez, Nyamsogoro which revealed that financial sustainability is significantly and positively linked to average loan size [9,21,22,32]. Therefore, based on the regression result from the study, the alternative hypothesis articulated as there is positive relationship between average balance per borrower and financial self sufficiency is rejected.

Portfolio at risk (30) days

The portfolio at risk measures indicates how much a Microfinance institutions is efficient in making collections of loans. The higher the portfolio at risk indicates lower repayment rates, an indication of inefficient MFI. In simple words, a high portfolio at risk ratio would limit the income derived from Microfinance operations and therefore amount of lendable funds reduces. This would result in rationing of credit and ultimately the continuous supply of quality loan services would be affected and have a negative impact on financial sustainability of MFIs. The result of regression analysis revealed that the coefficient is significant at 5% level and negatively associated with financial self sufficiency. It indicates that Less efficient the MFIs are (higher par) ultimately less will be its financial sustainability. The result of regression analysis confirms the alternative hypothesis that significant reduction in portfolio at risk (30) days should have a positive impact on financial sustainability of MFIs i.e. portfolio at risk is expected to be negatively associated with financial sufficiency. Our findings are consistent with prior empirical findings of Nyamsogoro, Ayayi and sene shows that, there is negative relationship of portfolio at risk with financial sustainability [22,33].

Labour cost to assets (pea)

Labour cost to assets is insignificant negative predictor in determining financial self sufficiency of Andhra Microfinance institutions. Our findings are contrary to findings of Cull et al, shows that labour cost are associated with improved profitability for individual based lenders [26]. For group based lenders the coefficient on their labour cost variable is negative and significant. The findings of this study show that coefficient is negatively associated but insignificant in Random effect model i.e. most appropriate model as per the result of panel diagnostic. Therefore based on the regression result from the study, we fail to reject the null hypothesis which was formulated as there is no significant relationship between labour cost to assets ratio and financial sustainability.

Size (total assets)

Total Assets is the proxy measure for the size of MFIs. The econometric result of regression analysis revealed that Total Assets is strongly significant at 1% level and positively associated with financial self sufficiency. It indicates that, MFI size does improve its financial sustainability. It means that a change in the size (total Assets) causes a change in financial sustainability positively. The econometric result revealed that for one unit increase in Size of MFIs, financial self sufficiency ratio is expected to increase by (0.03) units, holdings all other variable constant. The findings of this study are consistent with that of Cull et al. [17,26]. He found that MFIs size is positively and significantly linked to financial self sufficiency. Our findings are also consistent with Bogan et al, Hartarska and Nadolnyak, Coleman and Osie and Robinson [1,29,34,35]. However or findings is contrary to the findings of Hartarska [30]. Thus, the findings support the alternative hypothesis articulated as size of MFIs affects financial sustainability positively.

AGE (log value)

The age of MFI refers to the period; MFI has been in operational since it came into existence. The variable age is expected to be positively related to financial self sufficiency. However, the fixed effect regression model shows that age of MFIs is highly significant at 1% level and negatively associated with financial self sufficiency. It indicates that MFIs age does not improve its financial sustainability. It also means that mature MFIs are not financially sustainable. This result is quite strange because with increasing age MFIs must become efficient. Our findings contradict with the study of cull et al. which shows that MFIs age is significantly and positively related with financial self sufficiency [26]. Our findings also contradict with findings of Nadiya et al and Nyamsogoro which shows that age is not significant factor influencing financial self sufficiency [22,31]. Based on the result of fixed effect regression, the alternative hypothesis articulated as, age of MFIs expected to be positively associated with financial self sufficiency is rejected.

Conclusion

Our findings revealed that the important determinant of financial self-sustainability are yield on gross loan portfolio, portfolio at risk (30) days, size and age. The p values of independent variables are highly significant at 1% level in both model FSS model only portfolio at risk is significant at 5% level in FSS model. However labour cost to assets ratio, average loan balance per borrower, gross loan portfolio to total assets ratio and capital cost to assets ratio are insignificant predictor of financial self sufficiency. The findings of yield on gross loan portfolio are consistent with the study of Nyamsogoro and De Crombrugghe et al. found that yield on gross loan portfolio significantly and positively affects the financial performance [19,22]. The finding of portfolio at risk is consistent with the findings of Nyamsogoro and Ayayi and Sene concluded that there is negative association between portfolio at risk and financial sustainability [22,33]. The findings of yield on gross loan portfolio that increasing interest rates are associated with improved financial performance is consistent with De Crombrugghe et al, Cull et al. and Nyamsogoro [19,22,26]. To be financially sustainable Andhra's MFIs must charge optimum enough interest rates in order to cover not only for operating cost but also for the possible losses as a result of loan default. But, it must be done cautiously considering the impact of increasing loan interest rate on loan repayment and depth of outreach to poor clients (Appendix A).

References

1. Robinson M (2001) The microfinance revolution: Sustainable banking for the poor. The World Bank, Washington, DC.
2. Deutsche Bank Research (2007) Microfinance: An emerging investment opportunity. Frankfurt am Main: Deutsche Bank.
3. Puhazhendhi V (2013) Microfinance India: State of the sector report 2012. SAGE Publications India.
4. Schäfer K, Fukasawa Y (2011) Factors Determining the Operational Self-Sufficiency among Microfinance Institutions. Advances in Business Research 2: 171-178.
5. Zerai B, Rani L (2012) Technical Efficiency and Its Determinants of Micro Finance Institutions in Ethiopia: A Stochastic Frontier Approach. African Journal of Accounting, Economics, Finance and Banking Research 8: 1.
6. Cull R, Demirgüç-Kunt A, Morduch J (2011) Does regulatory supervision curtail microfinance profitability and outreach? World Development 39: 949-965.
7. Gutiérrez-Nieto B, Serrano-Cinca C, Molinero CM (2009) Social efficiency in microfinance institutions. Journal of the Operational Research Society 104-119.
8. Tehulu TA (2013) Determinants of financial sustainability of microfinance institutions in East Africa. European Journal of Business and Management 5: 152-158.
9. Gonzalez A (2007) Resilience of microfinance institutions to national macroeconomic events: An econometric analysis of MFI asset quality. MIX Discussion Paper, 4317.
10. Rai AK (2012) A comparative analysis of the financial performance of microfinance institutions of India and Bangladesh (Unpublished Doctoral dissertation, Jaypee institute of information technology).
11. Masood T, Ahmad M (2010) Technical efficiency of microfinance institutions in India-a stochastic frontier approach. MRPA, 25454.
12. Gutierrez-Nieto B, Serrano-Cinca C, Molinero CM (2007) Microfinance institutions and efficiency. Omega 35: 131-142.
13. Hassan KM, Sanchez B (2009) Efficiency analysis of microfinance institutions in developing countries. Networks Financial Institute Working Paper.
14. Hair JF, Black WC, Babin BJ, Anderson RE, Tatham RL (2006) Multivariate data analysis. Upper Saddle River, Pearson Prentice Hall, NJ.
15. Gujarati DN (2003) Basic Econometrics. (4thedn) McGraw Hill.
16. Sa-Dhan (2006) Microfinance Manager Series (No.16).
17. Cull R, Demirgüç-Kunt A, Morduch J (2006) Financial performance and outreach: a global analysis of leading microbanks. World Bank Policy Research Working Paper, 3827.
18. Rahman MA, Mazlan AR (2014) Determinants of Financial Sustainability of Microfinance Institutions in Bangladesh. International Journal of Economics and Finance 6: p107.
19. De Crombrugghe A, Tenikue M, Sureda J (2008) Performance analysis for a sample of microfinance institutions in India. Annals of Public and Cooperative Economics 79: 269-299
20. Woller G, Schreiner M (2002) Poverty lending, financial self-sufficiency, and the six aspects of outreach. Disc. Paper, Ohio.
21. Adongo J, Stork C (2005) Factors influencing the financial sustainability of selected microfinance institutions in Namibia. Namibian Economic Policy Research Unit.
22. Nyamsogoro GD (2010) Financial sustainability of rural microfinance institutions (MFIs) in Tanzania. Doctoral dissertation, University of Greenwich.
23. Berger AN, Bonaccorsi di patti E (2006) Capital structure and firm performance: a new approach to testing agency theory and an application to the banking industry. Journal of Banking and Finance (30), 1065-1102
24. Kar AK (2010) Sustainability and Mission Drift in Microfinance: Empirical Studies on Mutual Exclusion of Double Bottom Lines. Helsinki: Hanken School of Economics.
25. Gebremichael BZ (2013) Efficiency, outreach and sustainability of Ethiopian microfinance institutions. Doctoral Dissertation, Andhra University, India.
26. Cull R, Demirgüç-Kunt A, Morduch J (2007) Financial performance and outreach: a global analysis of leading microbanks. The Economic Journal 117: F107-F133.

27. Hermes N, Lensink R, Meesters A (2011) Outreach and efficiency of microfinance institutions. World Development 39: 938-948.

28. Mersland R, Strøm RØ (2009) Performance and governance in microfinance institutions. Journal of Banking & Finance 33: 662-669.

29. Bogan V, Johnson W, Mhlanga N (2007) Does Capital Structure Affect the Financial Sustainability of Microfinance Institutions? Cornell University 454: 1-28.

30. Hartarska V (2005) Governance and performance of microfinance institutions in Central and Eastern Europe and the newly independent states. World development 33: 1627-1643

31. Nadiya M (2011) An inside View of the Factors Affecting the operational self-sufficiency of Indian Microfinance institutions: A mixed method enquiry. Oikos Foundation for Economy and Ecology.

32. Gregoire JR, Tuya OR (2006) Cost efficiency of microfinance institutions in Peru: A stochastic frontier approach. Latin American Business Review 7: 41-70.

33. Ayayi AG, Sene M (2010) What drives microfinance institution's financial sustainability. The Journal of Developing Areas 44: 303-324.

34. Hartarska V, Nadolnyak D (2007) Do regulated microfinance institutions achieve better sustainability and outreach? Cross-country evidence. Applied Economics 39: 1207-1222.

35. Coleman AK, Osei KA (2008) Outreach and profitability of microfinance institutions: the role of governance. Journal of Economic Studies 35: 236-248.

3

Factors Influencing General Problems Encountered by the First Generation Entrepreneurs in Madurai, Tamilnadu

Selvaraj N[1]*, Suganya M[1] and Balajikumar P[2]

[1]*Commerce Department, Saraswathi Narayanan College, Madurai, Tamilnadu, India*
[2]*Management Department, Saraswathi Narayanan College, Madurai, Tamilnadu, India*

Abstract

Entrepreneur is one of the important inputs in the economic development of a country or of regions within the country. Entrepreneurial competence makes all the difference in the rates of economic growth. As the only source to unemployment, they definitely opt for a career in entrepreneurship. There is no need to possess previous experiences in business or no need to run the family business. A study on the first generation entrepreneurs in the small scale industry in Madurai city is a maiden attempt made by the research. The main objectives of the present study are the problems encountered by the first generation entrepreneurs in small scale industry. Factor analysis was done with 12 variables (OPINION) Orthogonal Varimax Rotation for the opinion of the respondents towards the much influencing factors to start enterprises by the first generation entrepreneurs, have an impact on their behavioral attitudes in the study area. In the glow of the research conducted, to enhance the entrepreneurship culture in the minds of the youngsters as well as in the interest of the nation. Proper entrepreneurship education should be given at school. Best young entrepreneurship idea oriented students are to be identified at high school/higher secondary school level and they should be under keen observation by the entrepreneurship incubators.

Keywords: Entrepreneur; Orthogonal varimax; Small scale industry; Training and finance

Introduction

Entrepreneur is one of the important inputs in the economic development of a country or of regions within the country. Entrepreneurial competence makes all the difference in the rates of economic growth. The small-scale industrial sector and business are left completely by private entrepreneurs. Several factors go into the making of an entrepreneur. Individuals, who initiate, establish, maintain and expand new enterprises, constitute the entrepreneurial class. The socio-political and economic conditions, the availability of industrial technology and know-how, state of art and culture of business and trading, existence of markets for products and services and the incentives and facilities available for starting an industry or business, all have a bearing on the growth of entrepreneurship [1]. Conducive environment is created through the policies and interest of the government in economic and industrial development.

First generation entrepreneurs

There are millions of unemployed youth in the country and by this time, this number would have increased substantially. Instead of being a part of that group which keeps knocking from pillar to post, checking with employment exchanges, relatives, friends, and neighbors and still not able to get a job to their liking and then settle for a second or third rate job, they can also choose to be like Mr. Patel of 'Nirma' who was a chemist's assistance once and now owns a Rs. 2500 crore company. The original Mr. Bata who was a cobbler once has stores in more than 30 countries all over the world now.

As the only source to unemployment, they definitely opt for a career in entrepreneurship. There is no need to possess previous experiences in business or no need to run the family business. For the first time in a family if any person comes forward with a vision to set up a business/industry or with entrepreneurship ideas, he/she is called first generation (in his/her family) entrepreneur and the word is common to both sex.

Significance of the Study

A study on the first generation entrepreneurs in the small scale industry in Madurai city is a maiden attempt made by the research. The first generation entrepreneurs do not know even the basics of entrepreneurship and under this situation how they can come up as successful entrepreneur is the problem identified by the researcher [2]. Besides these problems many first generation entrepreneurs are coming up to business and getting success every day. This study aims to scan the problems faced by them and to reveal the remedial measures that will guide the rest of the world especially to the unemployed educated youth to know success route.

Statement of the Problem

It is evident that the first generation entrepreneurs in and around Madurai city are engaged in various activities like industrial engineering, trade, agricultural engineering, tourism development, catering technology and hotel management, food production, ready-made garments manufacturing, soft-drinks production, bakery, flour mills, electrical and electronic goods manufacturing, polythene bags and PVC pipe manufacturing, steel and wooden furniture manufacturing and travel business [3]. Entrepreneurs engaged in these types of activities are based on their knowledge and skills acquired through formal education. Entrepreneurs of first generation are not doing well though they have entered into small-scale industrial ventures. They face a lot of operational problems while managing their establishments. The problems are, lack of raw-material, finance, marketing, government, funding agencies, competition and support from the family. Because of the multi-various problems the entrepreneurs feel frustrated, and they

***Corresponding author:** Dr. Selvaraj N, Assistant Professor of Commerce, Saraswathi Narayanan College, Madurai, Tamilnadu, India
E-mail: selvaraj_narayanan@yahoo.com

could not concentrate in sustaining the growth of their business.

Objectives of the Study

The main objectives of the present study are the following:

1. To unearth the problems encountered by the first generation entrepreneurs in small scale industry in Madurai city.

2. To offer the summary of findings, suggestions and conclusion on the study of first generation entrepreneurs.

Period of study

The present study is based on the primary. The primary data have been collected from the respondents directly for the period of study is impounded to one year. (i.e., 2014-2015).

Collection of data

The present study covers both primary data. The required primary data were collected through structured questionnaire.

Framework of analysis

In this paper, an attempt has been made to identify the factors which influenced the first generation entrepreneurs to identify their skills. For this, 12 statements relating to the other general problems encountered by the first generation entrepreneurs have been selected to identify the significant dimensions of the factors, with the help of factor analytical technique.

In the present study, the principal factor analysis method with orthogonal varimax rotation is used to identify the factors influencing the overall skills and ability of the entrepreneurs in the study area.

Factor analysis was done with 12 variables (OPINION) Orthogonal Varimax Rotation for the opinion of the respondents (sample first generation entrepreneurs) towards the other general problems encountered by the first generation entrepreneurs, have an impact on their behavioral attitudes in the study area.

The rotated factor matrix for the variables relating to other problems encountered by the first generation entrepreneurs and entrepreneurship attitude of the respondents in the study is given as follows.

From Table 1, it is observed that the first factor is designed as "GOVERNMENT NORMS/TRAINING/FINANCE" on the basis of the loaded variables. In the first factor three variables in this category are significant with high factor loading. It indicates that among the various performance scales, 'EDP–Activities improvement', 'Total Govt. support', and 'Contribution of Financial Institutions timely Assistance' are important attributes in this category. Thus, "GOVT. NORMS/TRAINING/FINANCE" is required as an important factor to influence the first generation entrepreneurs in their walk of business life, in Madurai city.

The second factor is narrated as "FINANCE SUPPORT" on the basis of the loaded variables. Five variables in this category are important with high factor loading. It indicates that among the various performance scales, 'Financial assistances against educational certificates,' 'Poor service by Banks', 'Special consideration to FGEs', 'All time support from Govt.' and 'Active Trade Associations', are important attributes in this category. Thus, it indicates entrepreneurs to get funds or financial assistance to run their enterprises, but he finds problem in availing such services affecting, them in the study area [4-6].

The third factor is identified as "PRACTICAL EXPOSURE", on the basis of the loaded variables. Two variables in this category are important with high factor loading. It indicates that among the various performance scales, 'Poor subsidy support from Govt.' and 'Learning out of experience' affects attributes in this category. Thus, the "PRACTICAL EXPOSURE" which influences the first generation entrepreneurs, is identified by the researcher in the study area.

It is concluded from the above factor analysis that the following factors are identified to influence the first generation entrepreneurs with reference to the advantages in the study area:

1. Govt. Norms/training/finance
2. Finance support
3. Practical exposure

Factors influencing much, to start enterprises by the first generation entrepreneurs

In the present study, the principal factor analysis method with orthogonal varimax rotation is used to identify the factors influencing

Sl. No.	Opinion Variables	Rotated Factor Loadings			h²
		F1	F2	F3	
1.	EDP – Activities improvement	.99207	-.02744	.02723	.98571
2.	Total Govt. support	.99207	-.02744	.02723	.98571
3.	Contribution of Financial Institutions timely Assistance	.99207	-.02744	.02723	.98571
4.	Financial assistances against educational certificates	.00973	.96797	-.00902	..93715
5.	Poor service by Banks	.00973	.96797	-.00902	..93715
6.	Special consideration to FGEs	.08338	.73155	-.33245	..65264
7.	All time support from Govt.	-.25032	.59771	.19697	.45872
8.	Active Trade Associations	.11802	.58119	-.52699	..62943
9.	Cumbersome procedures	.20330	-.10319	.86861	..80645
10.	Need of Education and experience to Entrepreneurship	-.11910	.26136	.74281	..63396
11.	Poor subsidy support from Govt.	.20709	-.36237	.58440	.51572
12.	Learning out of experience affects	.42245	.05619	-.54262	.50231
	Eigen values	3.65491	3.30817	2.08757	
	Percentage of variation	30.5	27.6	17.2	
	Cumulative percentage	30.5	58.0	75.3	

Table 1: Rotated Factor Matrixes for the Other General Problems Encountered by the Respondents.

Sl. No.	Opinion Variables	Rotated Factor Loadings				h²
		F1	F2	F3	F4	
1.	Unemployment	.99178	-.01282	-.00542	.05087	.91568
2.	Enterprising Nature	.99178	-.01282	-.00542	.05087	.98640
3.	Diversification of employment	.99178	-.01282	-.00542	.05087	.75219
4.	Ambition/Goal in life	.45151	.06967	-.42463	-.34284	.98640
5.	Economic factors	.00201	.94236	.10529	-.12862	67773
6.	Success stories of entrepreneurs	-.00732	.90802	.03765	-.10480	.98640
7.	Courageous to face/take risk	.08455	.70630	-.10939	-.39969	.82139
8.	Threats available in previous employment	-.28082	.64811	-.02885	.50245	.50657
9.	To use idle funds ideally	.07646	.63044	-.57402	.00626	.73284
10.	To attain social status	-.08351	.15192	.88744	-.06151	.76188
11.	To make use his own Knowledge For social development	.19834	-.11560	.70902	.45416	.83696
12.	Property inherited/acquired	.15834	-.25724	.10392	.79592	.73553
	Eigen values	3.47792	3.25319	1.92052	1.04814	
	Percentage of variation	29.0	27.4	16.0	8.7	
	Cumulative percentage	29.0	56.1	72.1	80.8	

Table 2: Rotated Factor Matrixes for the Much Influencing Factors to Be A First Generation Entrepreneur.

the overall skills and ability of the entrepreneurs in the study area.

Factor analysis was done with 12 variables (OPINION) Orthogonal Varimax Rotation for the opinion of the respondents (sample first generation entrepreneurs) towards the much influencing factors to start enterprises by the first generation entrepreneurs, have an impact on their behavioral attitudes in the study area.

The rotated factor matrix for the variables relating to the influencing factors to turn as entrepreneurs by the respondents in the study is given as follows.

From Table 2, it is observed that the first factor is designed as "INTERNAL FACTORS" on the basis of the loaded variables. In the first factor four variables in this category are significant with high factor loading. It indicates that among the various performance scales, 'Unemployment', 'Enterprising Nature', 'Diversification of employment' and 'Ambition/Goal in life', are important attributes in this category. Thus, "PERSONAL CHARACTER" is identified as an important factor to influence the respondent to take a new 'avatar' as an entrepreneur and become as first of its kind in his family, in Madurai city [7].

The second factor is narrated as "EXTERNAL FACTORS" on the basis of the loaded variables. Five variables in this category are important with high factor loading. It indicates that among the various performance scales, 'Economic factors', 'Success stories of entrepreneurs', 'Courageous to face/take risk', 'Threats available in previous employment', and 'To use idle funds ideally', are important attributes in this category. Thus, it is indicating respondents to get ready for a paradigm shift from individual to entrepreneur to overcome the problems which are influenced by various above factors, affecting the first generation entrepreneurs in the study area.

The third factor is identified as "SOCIAL FACTORS", on the basis of the loaded variables. Two variables in this category are important with high factor loading. It indicates that among the various performance scales, 'To attain social statuses' and 'To make use his own Knowledge for social development' are important attributes in this category. Thus the "SOCIAL FACTORS" also influences the first generation entrepreneurs and it is identified by the researcher in the study area [8].

The fourth factor is identified as 'FAMILY FACTOR", on the basis of the loaded variables. Only one variable in this category is playing significant role with high factor loading. It indicates that among the various performance scales, 'Property inherited/acquired' is the important attribute in this category. Thus, the 'FAMILY FACTOR' that influences the first generation entrepreneurs to get into business, is also identified by the researcher in the study area.

It is concluded from the above factor analysis that the following factors are identified to influence the first generation entrepreneurs with reference to the locational advantages in the study area:

1. Internal factors
2. External factors
3. Social factors
4. Family factors

Suggestions

In the glow of the research conducted, the following suggestions are furnished to enhance the entrepreneurship culture in the minds of the youngsters as well as in the interest of the nation.

Proper entrepreneurship education should be given at school level and the same concept is to be included under common based syllabus in a compulsory way.

Best young entrepreneurship idea oriented students are to be identified at high school/higher secondary school level and they should be under keen observation by the entrepreneurship incubators.

More support from the Governments of State and as well as Central is to be extended and the District Industries Centre should be modernized under the direct control of the District Collector to identify the right project, right entrepreneurs at right time in order to avoid political interference, delayed/poor services.

Subsidies, tax concession, relaxation of norms, may be introduced to new/first generation entrepreneurs.

Financial assistances may be approved against the educational certificates to the first generation/new entrepreneurs to motivate them by and large.

Conclusion

Among the external influencing factors, assistance from financial institutions and assistances from government are expected more but emerged to some extent as the most significant factors. Almost all the entrepreneurs are of the opinion that they would not have perhaps been able to implement the project without financial assistance, infrastructural facilities and the like. These factors are not the prime motivators but play the role of contributing factors in the implementation of the entrepreneurial idea. Availability of technology either from indigenous sources or from foreign collaborators also attracted a few entrepreneurs to take up manufacturing activities.

References

1. Arthur HC (1959) "Business Enterprise in its social setting" Harvard University Press, Cambridge.
2. Kanka SS (2000) "Entrepreneurial Development" S Chand and Co, New Delhi.
3. Khan MY, Jain PK (2007) "Financial Management" Tata McGraw-Hill publishing company limited, New Delhi.
4. Kothari CR (2009) "Research Methodology" New Age International publishers, New Delhi.
5. Krishnaswami OR, Ranganatham M (2009) "Methodology of Research in Social Sciences" Himalaya publishing house, Mumbai.
6. Pannerselvam R (2009) "Research Methodology" PHI-Learning, New Delhi 2009.
7. Brimmer AF (1995) "The setting of entrepreneurship in India" Quarterly Journal of Economics.
8. Joseph V (2005) "Rural entrepreneurs in India" Kissan world.

4

Financial Ratios (Accounting Ratios) and Survival of Microfinance Institutions in Ghana

Sarkodie EE[1]*, Addai I[1] and Asiedu DK[2]

[1]*Department of Accounting Studies Education, College of Technology Education, Kumasi, Ghana*

[2]*University of Education, Winneba, College of Technology Education, Kumasi, Ghana*

Abstract

Accounting Ratio is a way of expressing the relationship between one accounting result and another, which is intended to provide a useful comparison. Accounting ratios assist in measuring the efficiency and profitability of a company based on its financial reports. Accounting ratios are important for financial decision making irrespective of the size of the institution. The Bank of Ghana has the constitutional mandate to oversee the activities of all financial institutions in Ghana including the Microfinance institutions. This core mandate of Bank of Ghana is basically guided by the use of accounting ratios. The ratios per their style have the power to determine the risk exposure of financial institutions. Over the past five years the Ghanaian economy has witnessed the collapse of certain microfinance institutions that the public assumed to be highly visible in the financial market. The study therefore provided a logistic regression model with 117 observations to determine whether accounting ratios have the power to predict the fortunes of microfinance institutions in Ghana. An increase in the current ratio reduces the log-odds of a firm's survival by -1.461987. An increase in the acid test ratio improves the log-odds of survival by 6.847345. An increase in the debt equity ratio increases the chances of survival of a firm by 1.055941. Current ratio and acid test ratio were statistically significant at 10 percent whilst debt equity ratio was statistically significant at 5 percent. The study implies that microfinance institutions should be mindful of the current ratio, acid test ratio and the debt to equity ratio.

Keywords: Financial ratios; Stock; Business; Microfinance; Enterprise

Introduction

A financial ratio or accounting ratio is a relative magnitude of two selected numerical values taken from an enterprise's financial statements (wiki). Accounting Ratio is a way of expressing the relationship between one accounting result and another, which is intended to provide a useful comparison. Accounting ratios assist in measuring the efficiency and profitability of a company based on its financial reports. Accounting ratios form the basis of fundamental analysis. An accounting ratio compares two aspects of a financial statement, such as the relationship (or ratio) of current assets to current liabilities. The ratios can be used to evaluate the financial condition of a company, including the company's strengths and weaknesses (Investopedia) [1].

Financial ratios quantify many aspects of a business and are an integral part of the financial statement analysis. Financial ratios are categorized according to the financial aspect of the business which the ratio measures. Liquidity ratios measure the availability of cash to pay debt. Activity ratios measure how quickly a firm converts non-cash assets to cash assets. Debt ratios measure the firm's ability to repay long-term debt. Profitability ratios measure the firm's use of its assets and control of its expenses to generate an acceptable rate of return. Market ratios measure investor response to owning a company's stock and also the cost of issuing stock. These are concerned with the return on investment for shareholders, and with the relationship between return and the value of an investment in company's shares. Financial ratios allow for comparisons;

1. Between companies
2. Between industries
3. Between different time periods for one company
4. Between a single company and its industry average

Ratios generally are not useful unless they are benchmarked against something else, like past performance or another company. Thus, the ratios of firms in different industries, which face different risks, capital requirements, and competition, are usually hard to compare.

The objective of this study was to find out whether accounting ratios have the capacity to tell the fortunes of microfinance institutions. The research questions that were asked included:

1. Does Current Ratio predict survival?
2. Does Quick Ratio predict survival?
3. Does Debt to Equity Ratio predict survival?

This study will contribute to microfinance management and policy making in the financial market at large.

Literature Review

Naser [1] conducted a study to find out if Financial Ratios Reliably Measure the Performance of Banks in Bahrain. The study covered the calculation of important financial ratios of major financial institutions in Bahrain as well as comparing their performance in the context of the global financial crisis. It also compared ratios of conventional banks with Islamic financial institutions in Bahrain. These ratios defined profitability, financial performance, size and type of banks. The result of the analysis of ratios for measuring financial performance showed

***Corresponding author:** Sarkodie EE, University of Education, Winneba, College of Technology Education, Department of Accounting Studies Education, Kumasi, Ghana, E-mail: effahsarkodie@yahoo.com

that there is corporate excellence in asset management and value equity shares. The study also recommended that the analysis could be used as a basis for preventative actions for future bankruptcy and market risk.

Lenders often rely on ratio analysis because it allows them to see how one's business is doing and how compare it compares to other businesses which they have loaned money to. The potential loan creditor also requires information about security that the Ratio Analysis can be provided [2].

Ratio analysis is a useful tool for business owners as well. It measures the health of the business whether it is a bank or a multinational corporation. It helps to measure the performance of the business, to diagnose potential problems and to see how well it is doing over time.

Finch [3] stated that financial ratios are one of the most common tools of managerial decision making. A ratio is to compare one number to another-mathematically, a simple division problem. Financial ratios involve the comparison of various figures from the financial statements in order to gain information about a company's performance. It is the interpretation, rather than the calculation, that makes financial ratios a useful tool for business managers. The future decisions can be evaluated in terms of measuring the behavior of the firm value, given a decision to be analyzed. However, examining historical financial statements analysis has the limitations in reaching the optimal financial decisions. Ratios may serve as indicators, clues, or red flags regarding not worthy relationships between variables used to measure the firm's performance in terms of profitability, asset utilization, liquidity, leverage, or market valuation [4].

Singh [5] in his study identified commonly used ratios in the lodging industry and discovered their importance for lodging financial executives. In his point of view, financial ratios have always been a valuable tool for lodging industry managers. Ratios allow the user to summarize and analyze related data to provide meaningful information for making decisions [6,7].

Problem Statement

Accounting ratios are important for financial decision making irrespective of the size of the institution. The Bank of Ghana has the constitutional mandate to oversee the activities of all financial institutions in Ghana including the Microfinance institutions. This core mandate of Bank of Ghana is basically guided by the use of accounting ratios. The ratios per their style have the power to determine the risk exposure of financial institutions [1]. Bank of Ghana is indeed noted for strict adherence to these accounting ratios. However, over the past five years the Ghanaian economy has witnessed the collapse of many microfinance institutions that the public assumed to be highly visible in the financial market. Some of these collapsed institutions include Noble Dream Microfinance, Above All Financial Services and KAD Microfinance. This study therefore tried to calculate some of these accounting ratios of microfinance institutions in Ghana including those that have collapsed and those that are still in operation. The study thereafter provided a logistic regression model to determine whether accounting ratios have the power to predict the fortunes of microfinance institutions in Ghana.

Methodology

Model specification

This study adopted Logistic regression modeling technique. The choice of this methodology is based on the fact that the regress and of the model is binary. The logistic regression is specified as

$$\ln[P_i/(1-P_i)] = \lambda_0 + \lambda_1 cr + \lambda_2 atr + \lambda_3 der + +\mu$$

Where: cr= Current ratio , atr= Acid Test Ratio, der=Debt Equity Ratio, μ= Error term, $\lambda_0..\lambda_3$= The parameters to be estimated. $[P_i/(1-P_i)]$ = The Odds of survival of Microfinance institutions.

Definition of variables

Current Ratio is a relationship of current assets to current liabilities. Current Assets are the assets that are either in the firm of cash or cash equivalents or can be converted into cash or cash equivalents in a short time (say, within a year's time) and Current Liabilities are repayable in a short time. It is calculated as follows:

$$\text{Current Ratio} = \frac{\textit{current assets}}{\textit{current liabilities}}$$

The objective of calculating Current Ratio is to assess the ability of the enterprise to meet its short-term liabilities promptly. It shows the number of times the current assets can be converted into cash to meet current liabilities. As a normal rule current assets should be twice the current liabilities. Low ratio indicates inadequacy of the enterprise to meet its current liabilities and inadequate working Capital. High Ratio is an indication of inefficient utilization of funds. An enterprise should have a reasonable current ratio. Although there is no hard and fast rule yet a current ratio of 2:1 is preferable.

Acid Test Ratio: is a relationship of liquid assets with current liabilities and is computed to assess the short- term liquidity of the enterprise in its correct form.

This is calculated as follows:

$$\text{Acid Test Ratio} = \frac{\textit{current assets}}{\textit{current liabilities}}$$

Quick assets= Current assets - (stock + Prepaid Expenses) Liquid assets are the assets, which are either in the form of cash or cash equivalent or can be converted into cash within a very short period. Liquid assets include cash, bills receivable, marketable securities and debtors (excluding bad and Doubtful debts), etc. Stock is excluded from liquid assets as it may take some time before it is converted into cash. Similarly prepaid expenses do not provide cash at all and are thus excluded from liquid assets. A quick ratio of 1:1 is usually considered favorable, since for every rupee of current liabilities, there is a rupee of current assets. A high Acid Test ratio compared to current ratio may indicate under stocking while a low liquidity ratio while a low Acid Test ratio indicated overstocking.

Debt-Equity Ratio- It is computed to ascertain the soundness of the long-term financial position of the firm. This ratio expresses the relationship between debt (external equities) and the equity (internal equities) Debt means long term loans, i.e., debentures, long-term loans from financial institution. Equity means shareholders' funds, i.e., preference share capital, equity share capital, reserves less losses and fictitious assets like preliminary expenses. The ratio is ascertained as follows:

$$\text{Debt} - \text{equity Ratio} = \frac{\text{Debt}\left(\text{long} - \text{term loans}\right)}{\text{Equity}\left(\text{shareholders' Funds}\right)}$$

Higher Ratio indicates risky financial position while lower ratio indicates safe financial position. Acceptable Debt-Equity Ratio is 2:1 which means debt can be twice the equity. This ratio is significant to

Survive	Coef.	Std. Err.	z	P>|z|	[95% Conf. Interval]	
cr	-1.461987*	.7994525	-1.83	0.067	-3.028885	.1049107
acr	6.847345*	3.87012	1.77	0.077	-.7379499	14.43264
der	1.055941**	.3075388	3.43	0.001	.4531757	1.658706
_cons	-.9088469	.6503588	-1.40	0.162	-2.183527	.365833

*Significant at 10 percent, ** significant at 5 percent.

Number of observation = 117, Log likelihood chi square=35.18 Prob > chi^2 = 0.0000

cr= current ratio, atr= acid test ratio, der= debt-equity ratio, _cons=constant term

Table 1: Logistic Regression Results.

access the soundness of long –term financial position. It also indicates the extent to which firm depends upon outsiders for its existence. It portrays the proportion of total funds acquired by a firm by way of loans.

Data, population and sample

The study relied purely on cross sectional and secondary data collected from one hundred and seventeen microfinance institutions (117) in Ghana. The secondary source is from the annual audited accounts of these microfinance institutions. The population in this study includes all microfinance institutions in Ghana.

Results and Discussion

The table below is a logistic regression results which indicates that one hundred and seventeen microfinance institutions were used and there was no missing value. The log likelihood ratio of 35.18 with a chi square of 0.0000 is an indication that the model as whole fits better than a model with no predictors.

Number of observation = 117, Log likelihood chi square=35.18 Prob > chi^2 = 0.0000

cr= current ratio, atr= acid test ratio, der= debt-equity ratio, _cons=constant term

An increase in the current ratio reduces the log-odds of a firm's survival by -1.461987. That is as the firms' current assets increases too much relative to their current liabilities they stand the risk of collapsing. In other words, microfinance institutions may not be able to meet their liabilities if they create huge loans, which are usually a greater percentage of their current assets. Besides the current ratio proved statistically significant at 10 percent error level. This indeed, emphasizes that the variable is scientifically a true determinant of the log-odds of survival.

An increase in the acid test ratio improves the log-odds of survival by 6.847345. That is if microfinance institutions put much of their resources into very liquid assets then there is a higher possibility of its survival. This stems from the fact that microfinance institutions can easily lay hands on these liquid assets to settle their current liabilities. Therefore, to avoid risk of collapsing microfinance institutions must put resources into liquid assets. It is moreover, observed that, the acid test ratio is statistically significant at 10 percent error level.

An increase in the debt-equity ratio also enhances the log-odds of a firm's survival. From the Table 1 an increase in the debt equity ratio increases the chances of survival of a firm by 1.055941. This means that if the microfinance institution is able to access long term loans from other financial institutions, then it will enhance the firms chances of survival. Moreover, the debt-equity ratio is statistically significant at 5 percent error level.

Implications of the Study

The study implies that microfinance institutions should be mindful of the current ratio, acid test ratio and the debt to equity ratio.

Summary and Recommendations

Microfinance institutions may have at the heart to make profit by way of giving out several loans. However, increasing loans does not necessarily increase profit since the business can collapse through the loans giving. It is advised per the findings of this study that short term loans to customers would be of great advantage to the microfinance institutions. Also, microfinance institutions ability to invite long term loans from other financial institutions could be of great help to the microfinance institutions. This is because increasing long term loan accessibility can improve their chances of survival. In this regard an alliance of microfinance institutions would help form syndicate which can aid the assessment of long term loans from banks. Frequent monitoring of the microfinance institutions ratios would help to prevent collapsing.

References

1. Najjar NJ (2013) Can Financial Ratios Reliably Measure the Performance of Banks in Bahrain? Int J Eco Financ 5: 3.
2. Lambert RA, Larcker DF (1987) An analysis of the use of accounting and market measures of performance in executive compensation contracts, J Accont Res 2: 85-125.
3. Finch H (2005) Financial Ratios. Reference for business.
4. Murthy SRY (2004) Financial Ratios of Major Commercial Banks.
5. Ward S (2003) Is Your Business Sick? Give Your Business a Health Checkup with These Three Ratios.
6. Lang M, Maffett M, Owens E (2010) Earnings comovement and accounting comparability: The effects of mandatory IFRS adoption', Working paper, UNC-Chapel Hill.
7. Lynch RM, Willamson RW (1983) Accounting for Management. New York: McGraw-Hill.

5

A Study on Budgetary Control with Special Reference to Coimbatore District Co-Operative Milk Producer's Union Limited, Coimbatore

Amala V Venkatasami*
GIM, Coimbatore, India

Abstract

The Study entitled "A Study on budgetary control" (with special reference to Coimbatore district co-operative milk producers union limited, Coimbatore).

Coimbatore district co-operative milk producers union restricted may be a co-operative sector endeavour, engaged within the process of milk and amp; producing the milk product, it recently launched 3 new variants of union milk. District co-operative milk producers union restricted is found within the central a part of Coimbatore. The company workplace of the union relies at Madras, covering four districts of Annur, Tirupur, Sulthapet, Shanmugapuram.

The budget management is enjoying a significant role within the organization. The role of fund management is that the essence of a business. The knowledge is that the blood and fund management may be a heart; within the body the centre plays the role of supply pure blood to all or any the weather of the body together with the brain. The fund management plays precisely the same role within the organization. The system ensures that associate degree applicable information is collected from the varied sources. Processed and sent more to all or any the destitute destinations.

The system is predicted to meet data desires of a private, a gaggle of individual, a gaggle of economic functionaries, the managers and therefore the high management that the fund management is incredibly necessary in fashionable organization.

Thus I have been chosen the budgetary control as the specific area of the study. Therefore a study has been taken up on "A study on budgetary control" (With special reference to Coimbatore district co-operative milk producers union limited, Coimbatore).

Introduction

Budget and budgetary control

A budget is a plan expressed in quantitatively, usually monetary term, covering a specific period of time, usually one year. In other words a budget is a systematic plan for the utilization of manpower and material resources.

Budgetary management is that the method of firm of budgets about varied activities and comparing the budgeted figures with the particular performance for inward at deviations, if any. Consequently, there can't be monetary fund management while not budgets. Monetary fund management may be a system that uses budgets as suggests that of coming up with and dominant.

The on tops of definitions reveal the subsequent necessities of monetary fund control:

1. Institution of objectives for every operate and section of the organization.
2. Ascertainment of the causes for such deviations of actual from the budgeted performance.
3. Taking appropriate corrective action from completely different on the market alternatives to realize the specified objectives.

Advantages of monetary fund management

The advantages of monetary fund management could also be summarized as follows:

1. It facilitates reduction of value.
2. Budgetary management guides the management in coming up with and formulation of policies.
3. Budgetary management facilitates effective co-ordination of activities of the varied departments and functions by setting their limits and goals.
4. It ensures maximization of profits through value management and optimum utilization of resources.
5. It helps to the management economical and economic production management.
6. It facilitates corrective actions, whenever there's inefficiencies and weaknesses comparison
7. Actual performance with budget.
8. It guides management in analysis and development.
9. It ensures economy in operating.
10. It helps to adopt the principles of ordinary cost accounting.

Scenario of Dairy Industry in India

Dairy is place where handling of milk products is done. Technology refers to the afflictions of scientific knowledge for practical purpose.

***Corresponding author:** Amala Venkatasami, M.B.A, GIM, Coimbatore, India, E-mail: venkat.asha1988@gmail.com

Dairy technology has been defined as that branch of dairy science, which deals with the processing of manufacturing of milk products on industry scale.

The Indian dairy industry has made rapid progress since independence. A large number of modern milk plants and product factors has been established these organized dairies have been successful engaged in routine commercial production of paste section milk and various dairy products. With modern knowledge of the protection of milk during transportation, it becomes possible to locate dairies where land was less expensive and corps could be growth more economically.

In Indian, the market milk technology may be considered to have commenced in 1950, with the functioning of milk colony, and milk product technology in 1956, with the establishment of Amul dairy Anand.

Dairy industry in India

More than 2500 million people economically active in agriculture in the world probably 75% regional of them are wholly or partly dependent on livestock forming. India which has 66% of economically active population engaged in agriculture. It drives 31% of GDP from agriculture. The share of livestock is estimated at 21% of total agriculture sector.

National Dairy Development Board (NDDB)

The nation dairy board was creating to promote, finance and activities that seek strength farmer cooperatives and support national policies that are favourable to the growth of such fundamental to NDDB'S effort are cooperative principle and cooperative strategies.

The national dairy development board is an institution of nation importance setup by an act of parliament of India. The main office is located in Anand, Gujarat with regional offices throughout the country. NDDBS subsidiaries include mother dairy, Delhi it was founded by Dr .Varghese kurien and Dr. Amrita Patel is the current chairman of the national dairy development board Anand.

NDDB has now integrated 96000 dairy cooperative in what it calls the Anand pattern linking the village society to the state federations in a three-tire structure.

NDDB launched its perspective plan for 4 thrust areas:

1. Quality assurance,
2. Productively,
3. Institution building,
4. National information.
5. Dairy co-operative account for the major share of processed liquid milk marketed in the country. Milk is processed and marketed by 170 milk producers' cooperative unions, which federate into 15 state co-operative milk marketing federations.
6. The diary development board's program and activities seek to strengthen the functioning of diary co-operatives, as producer-owned and controlled organizations. NDDB supports the development of diary co-operatives by providing them financial assistance and technical expertise, insuring a better future for Indian farmers.

Over the years, brands created by co-operatives have become synonymous with quality and value. Brands like Amul (GCMMF), Vijaya (AP), Verka (Punjab), Saras (Rajasthan), Nandini (Karnataka), Milma (Kerala), Gokul (Kolhapur), Aavin(Tamilnadu), are those that have earned customers confidence.

Some of the major diary co-operatives federations include

1. Andra Pradesh Diary Development Co-operative Federation Ltd., (APDDCF)
2. Bihar State Co-operative Milk Producers Federation Ltd., (COMPFED)
3. Gujarat Co-operative Milk Marketing Federation Ltd., (GCMMF)
4. Hariyana diary Development Co-operative Federation
5. Himachal Pradesh state Milk Producers Federation Ltd., (HPSCMPF)
6. Karnataka co-operative Milk Producers Federation Ltd., (KMF)
7. Kerala state co-operative Milk Producers Federation Ltd., (KCMMF)
8. Madhya Pradesh state co-operative Dairy Federation Ltd., (MPCDF)
9. Maharashtra Rajya Shakari Maryadit Dugdh Mahasangh Orissa State Co-operative Milk Producers Federation Ltd., (OMFED)
10. Prdeshik Co-operative Dairy Federation Ltd., (UP PCDF)
11. Punjab State Co-operative Dairy Federation Ltd., (MILK FED)
12. Rajasthan co-operative Dairy Federation Ltd., (RCDF)
13. Tamilnadu co-operative Dairy Federation Ltd., (TCMPF)
14. West Bengal co-operative Milk Producers Federation Ltd., (WBCMP

Milk production from 1996 to 2020

1996: 52 million

2013: 100 million

2014: 108 million

(Projected) 2020: 150 million

India is one of the leading World's major Milk Producers Unions in the year of 1997-1998 of 71% where others are comparatively less and Australia has a least Score of 9%. But expected to increase in the upcoming years towards 2020.

The Coimbatore District Co-Operative Milk Producer's Union Ltd

The dairy development department was established in 1958 at Tamilnadu. The administrative and statutory control over all the milk co-operative in the state were transferred to the dairy development was made as the functional limited was registered in the state on 1st Feb 1981.

The commercial activities of the development such as milk procurement, processing, chilling, packing and sale of milk to the consumers etc... hither to dealt with by the Tamilnadu dairy development corporation ltd, were transferred to the newly registered

Tamilnadu. Co-operative milk producers federation limited, popularly known as "Aavin".

In the wake of liberalization policy, private dairies have also entered into field of dairying. As per the directions of the humble chief minister of Tamilnadu high priority has been given for performance of milk co-operative by adopted a systematic approach and strategy in milk co-operative societies, union and federation in the state of Tamilnadu.

The cattle population in India is approximately 15% of total cattle population in the world India stood no.1 position in milk production Tamilnadu is one of the leading states in milk production. The milk production in Tamilnadu per is 45.88 lakhs litres. This union was started on 15/09/1987.

Registered societies =655

Functioning societies =527

Total members =112597

Female members =29607

Daily avg. milk procurement/day= 300000 litres

Daily avg. milk sales/day= 250000 litres

Objectives of the Dairy Development Department

1. Assure a remuneration price for the producers by the members of the milk producers cooperative societies through a stable steadily and well organized market support.
2. Distribution of quality milk and milk products to the consumer at reasonable price.
3. Keeping these objectives in mind, a number of activities are undertaken by the dairy development department.
4. Provision of tree veterinary health cover to all animals owned by the members of milk cooperatives.
5. Implementation of artificial insemination of farmers with the modern animal husbandry methods and practice.
6. All activities which are essential for the up gradation of the mulch animals and improving productivity.

Functions of District Co Operatives

There are 17 district cooperatives milk producers union functioning in the state of Tamilnadu covering 30 districts. There are 15 districts in district cooperative milk producers union with an installed processing of 19.42llpd. There are 36 chilling capacities of 13.55ll pd.

1. Establishment of chilling centres.
2. Formation of new milk router to collect milk produced by the members of the societies.
3. Collection of milk from society process and part in modern dairy plants by maintaining quality standards.
4. Supply of quality milk to Chennai metro under hygienic conditions.
5. Fixation of procurement and selling price of milk.
6. Increase of liquid milk sales by introducing innovative sales promotional activities.
7. Supply of input to the members of the societies.
8. Render veterinary health service and emergency service to the cattle of members of primaries to impart training on first aid and an artificial insemination to the staff of member's societies.

Product available

1. Butter
2. Milk and cream
3. Ripening
4. Aging
5. Churning
6. Draining and washing
7. Salting and working
8. Packing and storage
9. Curd
10. Flavored milk and others

Review of Literature

Badu and Daniel study was a budget may be a practical statement ready before a present amount of your time of the policy to be pursued throughout that amount for the aim of getting given objectives. Budgeting associate degree monetary fund management systems play a number one role in each company or establishment by serving to in establishing an economical internal control system for making property competitive advantage. The Tennessee board of Regents (2006) defines budgeting because the method whereby the plans of industries area unit understood into associate degree itemized, licensed and systematic arrange of operation, expressed in financial terms for a given amount. Budgeting, at each management level and operation level appearance at the long run and lays down what needs to be achieved. "A budget may be a quantitative expression of an inspiration of action ready prior to of the amount to that it relates. it's an inspiration expressed in terms cash ready and approved before the budget amount that show financial gain, expenditure and capital to be used [1]. The approach the research worker won't to conduct this analysis. The chapter contains analysis framework, population and sample, sample technique, information assortment instrument, information assortment activities furthermore as methodology of information analysis.

Inadequate monetary resources will undermine the effective implementation of organic process comes in MMDAs. Budgets area unit necessary as they providentially manage scarce monetary resources and at identical time function a way of expenditure authorization, management and analysis base. Monetary management is so necessary side of public administration of each nation and it's one in all the weather that builds government effective. It involves monetary prediction, monetary designing and budgeting, monetary reportage and auditing. Currently sensible monetary management is getting used by donors as a precedent for debt relief like HIPC and different monetary help to developing countries. The preparation method for the annual budget involves an excellent deal of energy, time, and expense. Hence, it's necessary that a rustic should be able to follow accurately all the ways of making ready associate degree annual budget. In budgeting, the main focus isn't solely to arrange the budget, however additional significantly to own a follow-up operation for budgeting and to act in keeping with legendary information. Information collected were altered, evaluated and measured against the analysis to confirm their completeness, consistency, accuracy and connexion. Microsoft package was utilized in the process of primary and secondary information gathered through the administration of the info assortment instruments. This is often to change information gathered to be conferred into tables, graphs and charts for qualitative explanations and analysis on budgeting and monetary fund controls.

The planning, programming and budgeting process is the central feature of defence management for providing resources to the defence force to ensure the defence and protection of the state in alignment with national security and defence policy. Thus, defence budgets should be the result of good short, medium, and long-term plans that are based on open and clear defence and national security policy. Descriptive and qualitative analyses demonstrate that there was no strict accountability, which allow creating sense of institutional budget perception. There is no reasonable cost estimation practice. Lack of adequate and experienced budget workers is other issue that contributes to worsen the problems. It should also prepare annual plan and budget based on the strategy. One of the responsibilities of budget users is controlling costs and constantly improving the ways of doing things. A budget has been approved by the legislature and monies appropriated, the goal is to ensure the efficient and effective use of resources to implement sectorial priorities. This requires careful monitoring and evaluation of operational performance both within the armed forces and by civil servants. As indicated in the introductory part of the paper, statistical package for social science (SPSS) application has been applied to analyze the data. The descriptive analyses were also supported by the open-ended responses given during the collection of data, interview responses, reports, and literature reviews.

Budgetary control as a proven management tool helps organization management enhances improved performance of any economy in a different ways. Its primary function is to serve as a guide in financial planning operation; it also establishes limits for departmental excesses. It helps administrative officials to make careful analysis of all existing operations, thereby justifying, expanding, eliminating or restricting present practice. The inability to recognize the problem concerned and fixing a boundary of investigation creates an obstacle for the successful implementation of budgeting and control. Budgeting is a familiar and very important type of short range plan; a plan that is expressed in a numerical terms how the resources of a company can be distributed to attain a desired profit. Since working out a budget force a company to determine how much money will be coming in, what cost will be incurred, it serves a dual purpose to become a controlling as well as a planning operation. The use of the budget as a yardstick in the daily activities of the operation, performance measurement and its evaluation, analysis of key elements of the questionnaire, lessons learned to arrest any shortfalls and the way forward in meeting budget target are ascertained. In all, a total of 44 out of 61 responded to the questionnaire.

"The processes by which managers assure that resources are obtained and used effectively and efficiently in the accomplishment of the organization's objectives". The many methods for managing the strategic management and budgeting processes; the right methods for any particular firm according to the author depend on factors such as its industry, size, number of divisions, product lines or business units, management preferences, history and culture. Regardless of how these processes are managed, they share a single goal: improving the ability of both strategic management and budgeting to contribute to business performance. A strategic review committee often consists of executives representing diverse areas who meet to address challenges to the firm's strategic direction. Such committees supplement the annual strategic planning processes. By including executives from throughout the firm, including those responsible for a firm's strategic management and budgeting processes, ramifications arising from changes in one area of the firm for others are more quickly identified. The sources of literature, techniques employed in data collection, research purpose, data analysis as well as critiques to the method use. In a research process, it is important that information provided satisfies the purpose and should be reliable as well. Therefore this will depend on the method of data collection employed. The reason to this is due to the fact that if data collected does not suit the purpose, then it would be difficult to analyze and the research would be considered as inappropriate.

Avatar PRASAD 2010 Budget and monetary fund management, each at management and operational level appearance at the long run and lays down what should be achieved. Management checks whether or not or not the plans area unit accomplished, and puts into result corrective measures wherever deviation or deficiency is going on. This study examines however budget and monetary fund management will impact on the performance of the IT sectors of Manasi data technologies Pvt. Ltd. This reviewed the performance of the IT trade in previous and gift times. It's discovered that the performance of this trade depends on the planning, development, implementation and management of computer-based data systems, significantly package applications and constituent. A budget fixes a target in terms of rupees or quantities against that the particular performance is measured. A budget is closely associated with each the management operate yet because the accounting operates of a company. Budget provides as a valuable aid to management through designing, coordination and management. It's a tool that measures the social control performance of a company. It promotes sensible morale and generates harmony within the organization. Applications that don't add production will value firms a lot of greenbacks. Imagine what number potential customers would go away an internet web site if the links didn't work properly. Sound quality assurance programs utilizing high-quality testing tools area unit needed to make sure client satisfaction. A scientific approach to facilitate effective management performance is profit designing and management or budgeting. Budgeting is so associate degree integral a part of management in an exceedingly means, a monetary fund system has been delineate as a historical combination of a "goal setting machine for increasing associate degree enterprises profits and a goal achieving machine for facilitating structure coordination and designing whereas achieving the budgeted targets".

The slow house of structure performance in Nigeria has been attributed partly to inadequacy within the method and implementation of budget and monetary fund management. This paper aims at filling the gap as a method of teaching managers associate degree operators of companies World Health Organization area unit capable of reversing the present low structure performance to an improved one. This study examines however budget and monetary fund management will impact on the performance of some chosen producing firms listed in the Nigerian exchange through a fault finding sampling technique. Monetary fund management as a pertinent management tool propels organization and enhances improved performance of the economy in an exceedingly kind of ways in which. It holds a primary operate of serving as a guide to monetary designing operators; it additionally establishes a boundary for division excesses. Budgets were initial introduced within the Twenties as tools for cost management and cash flows in large industrial organizations. Drury states that it absolutely was throughout the1960s that firms began to use budgets to work out what individuals required to try to do within the Nineteen Seventies, performance improvement was supported meeting monetary targets instead of effectiveness, companies then long-faced issues within the 1980s and 1990s after they weren't willing to expend money on innovations so as to remain with the rigid budgets. Firms were solely involved with meeting sales targets, that they thought-about as necessities, to the harm of consumer's satisfaction and how they were being treated. Consistent with conductor, management involves the creating of selections based mostly on relevant data that results in plans and actions that improve the employment of the productive assets and services offered to organizations management. Effective and economical management is alleged to be based on standards with that actual performance is compared. If there aren't any standards, then there is no effective live of attainment.

Prentice Hall Budgets, by definition, got to be ready in advance; and for this reason, they're usually brought up in terms of their being a part of a feed forward system. Feedback could be a term of times detected each in accounting and normal use. Feed forward, on the opposite hand tends to be less of times detected, however this word incorporates the foremost necessary facet of budgeting: observing things before, brooding about the impact and implications of things before trying to require management of things before. Monetary fund management relates to the institution of budgets relating the responsibilities of budget holders the wants of a policy. Monetary fund management additionally relates to the continual comparison of actual with budgeted results: it will this to undertake to make sure that the objectives of that policy area unit achieved; or to supply a basis for the amendment of these objectives. Jones and Pendlebury provide US some insight into the start of the budgeting cycle after they gift a "Timetable for preparation of elaborated revenue budget and capital programmed" for a neighbourhood Authority. They show that the method starts in Gregorian calendar month within the year preceding the budget amount with the draft budget manual being sent to Finance Officers, World Health Organization can discuss this draft with their division workers (with a read to adoption or amendment). The interrelatedness aspects of this instance have most likely not fazed US therefore far: the character of interrelationships is that they usually go unnoticed! So as to hit the purchases in units, we've got had to work out the gap and shutting stock amounts, and that we got the sales units. Thus, if we've got calculated the stock budgets incorrectly, the acquisition amounts are wrong, and also the purchases budgets are dishonest.

It was reported that "nothing was given out of the treasure without a written order. History has in that joseph budgeted and stored gains. Budgets were first introduced in the 1920s as a tool to manage and cash flows in large industrial organization.1990s when they were not willing to spend money on innovations in order to stay with the rigid budgets. Glautier [1] state that" the emergence of scientific management philosophy with the advent of industrial capitalism for the industrial revolution of the eighteenth century, which presented a challenge for industrial management. Omolehisw defined, a budget as a plan of dominant individuals in an organization expressed in monetary terms and subjects to the constraints imposed by the participants and the environments, indicating how the available resources may be utilized, to achieve whatever the dominant individuals agreed to be organization priorities. The impressive thing about this definition is that, it recognizes. The constraints imposed on budget by other participants who are to ensure that the objectives and targets. Thaka unfortunately, many organizations make poor investments decisions from investing tool little in positive net present value projects and much in negative net present value projects resulting in investment [2].

Whereas fund management may be a probably vital tool once the economic surroundings are unstable and unpredictable, the analysis of its development demonstrates that its use has dramatically dilated over the time since firms are ready to run forecasts. So as to assist them develop fund management, firms have enforced ways that have reduced risks and therefore improved their ability to create correct forecasts. Such ways have taken several forms and varied from one firm to a different [3-5]. They materialized as various types of agreement, together with cartels, through ways to result market leadership, or via policies of nationalization. In those firms wherever the surroundings was stable and risk limitation wasn't vital, fund management may well be used for numerous internal functions. During this respect, the analysis of the management of firms helps US to spot the needs that fund management is used. It's found that fund management permits for bigger enlargement opportunities and provides the suggests to strengthen the management of management at intervals major firms [6]. Our observations highlight a contradictory side of fund control: whereas it's relevant at intervals associate unstable surroundings, it performs best in associate surroundings that is much managed [7,8].

Research and Methodology

Research methodology

The research methodology is characterized into three different groups

1. First groups we include those methods which are concerned with the collection of data
2. Second group consists of these statistical techniques used for establish relationship
3. Third group consists of those methods which are used to evaluate the accuracy of the results

Research design

The research design adopted for the Research work is "Analytical Research "design in which what, when, why and how the topic is used in this study [9].

Statement of the problem

1. The purpose of the study is to estimate of receipts and payments of revenue and capital items in future. Hence the study has been entitled as "A study on budgetary control (with special reference to Coimbatore district co-operative milk producers union limited, Coimbatore) [10-12].
2. To analyze how budgetary control helps the milk union to select best course of action.
3. To provide a detailed plan of action for a business over a period of time.
4. To revise the budget in the light of changed circumstances.

Objectives of the Study

1. To analyze how budgetary control helps the milk union to select best course factors.
2. To revise the budgets in the light of changed circumstances.
3. To give suggestion towards correlation preparation method.

4. To suggest measures to reduce the costs and improve the financial position.
5. A budgetary control department fulfil the needs of organizations.

Statistical tools used

The following techniques can be used in connection with analysis and interpretation of financial statements.

1. Ratio analysis
2. Correlation
3. Operating expenditure estimate

Limitations of the study

1. The study is only limited to the available information in the department.
2. The success utility of budgeting depends in the co-operation and participation of all members of management.
3. The establishment of a budgeting process takes time. Also sometimes too much are expenses.
4. Efforts may therefore not be made to exceed the performance beyond the budgeted targets.
5. Effective implementation of budgetary control depends upon willingness, co-operation and understanding among people reasonable for execution. Lack of co-operation leads to inefficient performance.
6. Frequent changes may be called for in budgets due to first changing industrial climate.

Data analysis and Interpretation

Ratio analysis

Data has been analysed from the various ratios and the results had been showed below (Table 1).

Correlations

Relationship between stock turnover ratio and net profit ratio analysis: Null hypothesis: There is no relationship between Stock turnover ratio and Net profit ratio.

Alternative hypothesis: There is relationship between Stock turnover ratio and Net profit ratio (Table 2).

Correlation formula: $\mathbf{r} = \dfrac{\Sigma \mathbf{xy}}{\sqrt{\sum \mathbf{x}^2 * \sum \mathbf{y}^2}}$

$\mathbf{r} = 0.54$

$\mathbf{r} = 103.59 / \sqrt{664.34 * 23.72}$

$\mathbf{r} = 0.825$

$\bar{x} = \Sigma x/n\ (209.49/5) = 41.89$

$\bar{y} = \Sigma y/n\ (6.678/5) = 1.34$

Relationship between operating ratio and capital turnover ratio

Null hypothesis: There is no relationship between operating ratio and capital turnover ratio.

Alternative hypothesis: There is relationship between operating ratio and capital turnover ratio (Table 3).

Correlation formula: $\mathbf{r} = \dfrac{\Sigma \mathbf{xy}}{\sqrt{\sum \mathbf{x}^2 * \sum \mathbf{y}^2}}$

$r = 3.61 / \sqrt{3.434 * 5.121}$

$\mathbf{r} = 0.861$

$\bar{x} = \Sigma x/n\ (449.25/5) = 89.85$

$\bar{y} = \Sigma y/n\ (13.73/5) = 2.75$

Relationship between working capital turnover ratio and operating profit ratio:

Null hypothesis: There is no relationship between working capital turnover ratio and operating profit ratio.

Alternative hypothesis: There is relationship between working capital turnover ratio and operating profit ratio (Table 4).

Correlation formula: $\mathbf{r} = \dfrac{\Sigma \mathbf{xy}}{\sqrt{\sum \mathbf{x}^2 * \sum \mathbf{y}^2}}$

$\mathbf{r} = 255.21 / \sqrt{9983.89 * 22.25}$

$\mathbf{r} = 0.54$

$\bar{x} = \Sigma x/n\ (208.03/5) = 41.61],$

$\bar{y} = \Sigma y/n\ (10.635/5) = 2.1]$

Estimated expenditure

2009-10, 2010-11, 2011-12, 2012-13 and 2013-14 financial year expenditure of Coimbatore district co-operative milk producer's union ltd, Coimbatore, was estimated (Table 5).

Findings and Suggestion

1. In the year 2013-2014 the gross profit ratio was increased and the net profit in the year 2012-13 was decreased.
2. In the year 2013-14 the operating ratio was increased but decreased in the next year and the operating profit ratio in the year 2009-10 was decreased.
3. Fixed asset turnover ratio is increasing and working capital turnover ratio is decreased
4. Total asset turnover ratio and stock turnover ratio is increasing.
5. Current and liquid ratio shows increasing trend.
6. Fixed assets ratio and proprietary ratio is increasing.
7. The opening of milk products (Figure 1) 2011-12 it increased and purchase (Figure 2) of the milk from milk unions 13-14 was increased compared to the previous year.
8. Trade charges (Figure 3) paid and due 2013-14 it increased, and tax paid 12-13 was increased compared to the previous year.
9. Tax paid (Figures 4 and 5), Interest paid (Figure 6), Provisions (Figure 7) (bonus, Gratuity) decreased compared to the previous year.
10. There is no relationship between Stock turnover ratio and Net profit ratio.

Particular	2009-10	2010-11	2011-12	2012-13	2013-14
G.P Ratio	9.567	11.147	10.088	8.956	10.986
N.P Ratio	0.137	0.159	0.654	0.057	5.671
Operating Ratio	90.433	88.853	89.912	91.039	89.014
Operating Profit Ratio	0.547	1.138	1.681	0.986	6.283
Capital Turnover Ratio	2.325	4.745	2.497	2.097	2.064
Fixed Asset Turnover Ratio	10.901	11.977	12.600	13.671	12.774
Working Capital Ratio	16.107	14.690	-127.328	43.738	6.165
Total Asset Turnover Ratio	1.493	14.546	1.456	1.383	1.383
Stock Turnover Ratio	61.169	37.221	39.986	45.227	25.888
Current Ratio	1.259	1.244	0.973	1.089	1.878
Liquid Ratio	1.230	1.227	0.954	1.064	1.619
Absolute Liquid Ratio	0.397	0.579	0.267	0.383	0.477
Fixed Asset Ratio	0.213	0.396	0.198	0.153	0.162
Proprietory Ratio	1.023	0.952	0.965	0.459	0.729

Table 1: Analysed data from the various ratios.

Particular	Rs	Rs	Rs	Rs	Rs	Total
X	61.169	37.221	$\bar{x}$ 39.986	45.227	25.888	209.49
Y	0.137	0.159	0.654	0.057	5.671	6.678
$X=x-\bar{x}$	19.28	-4.669	-1.904	3.337	-16.002	
$\chi=y-\bar{y}$	-1.203	-1.181	-0.686	-1.283	4.331	
X^2	371.72	21.79	3.63	11.14	256.06	664.34
λ^2	1.45	1.39	0.47	1.65	18.76	23.72
$X\lambda$	23.19	5.51	1.31	4.28	69.30	103.59

Inference: Calculate value is (0.825).There is no relationship between Stock turnover ratio and Net profit ratio. Hence Null hypothesis is accepted. Correlation of co-efficient in the above table lays between -1 to +1.

Table 2: Relationship between stock turnover ratio and net profit ratio.

Particular	Rs	Rs	Rs	Rs	Rs	Total
X	90.433	88.853	89.912	91.039	89.014	449.25
Y	2.325	4.745	2.497	2.097	2.064	13.73
$X=x-\bar{x}$	0.583	-0.997	0.062	1.189	-0.836	
$\lambda=y-\bar{y}$	-0.425	1.995	-0.253	-0.653	-0.686	
X^2	0.34	0.99	0.004	1.41	0.69	3.434
λ^2	0.181	3.98	0.06	0.43	0.47	5.121
χ^λ	0.25	1.99	0.02	0.78	0.57	3.61

Inference: Calculate value is (0.861).There is no relationship between operating ratio and capital turnover ratio. Hence Null hypothesis is accepted. Correlation of co-efficient in the above table lays between -1 to +1.

Table 3: Relationship between operating ratio and capital turnover ratio.

Particular	Rs	Rs	Rs	Rs	Rs	Total
X	16.107	14.690	-127.328	43.738	6.165	208.03
Y	0.547	1.138	1.681	0.986	6.283	10.635
$X=x-\bar{x}$	-25.503	-26.92	85.718	2.128	-35.45	
$\lambda=y-\bar{y}$	-1.583	-0.992	-0.449	-1.144	4.153	
χ^2	650.40	724.69	7347.58	4.528	1256.70	9983.89
λ^2	2.506	0.984	0.202	1.309	17.247	22.25
χ^λ	40.37	26.70	38.49	2.43	147.22	255.21

Inference: Calculate value is (0.54).There is no relationship between working capital turnover ratio and operating profit ratio. Hence Null hypothesis is accepted. Correlation of co-efficient in the above table lays between -1 to +1.

Table 4: Table refers to relationship between working capital turnover ratio and operating profit ratio.

S.NO	Particular	2009-10	10-11	11-12	12-13	13-14
1	Opening products of the milk	28127929	29172936	48363067	30793481	47565412
2	Purchase	1099339346	1326740095	1369801002	1596786477	1736798698
3	Trade charges paid and due	187670500	209735504	248478475	261637560	325478580
4	Tax paid	6283155	10096781	12491021	18776311	14416230
5	Esta.charges paid and due	94119640	126431457	149609521	146892079	141639902
6	Interest paid	147050	121895	41489	0	0
7	Provisions(bonus, sub,due to co-op union, gratuity)	3425968	3323703	3274643	3172699	3042470
8	Reserve created	49707385	68843991	46361957	68127322	12201097

Table 5: 2009-10, 2010-11, 2011-12, 2012-13 and 2013-14 financial year estimated expenditure.

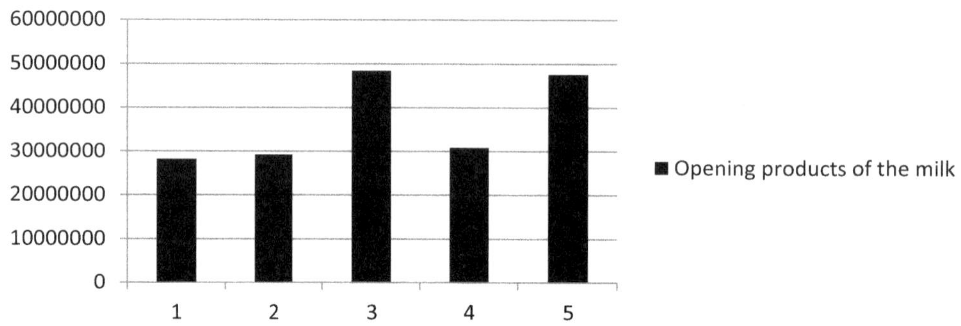

Interpretation: Opening products of the milk from the year 2009-14. Opening products of the milk in the year 2011-12 increased and in 2012-13 decreased.

Figure 1: *Showing classification of opening products of the milk analysis.*

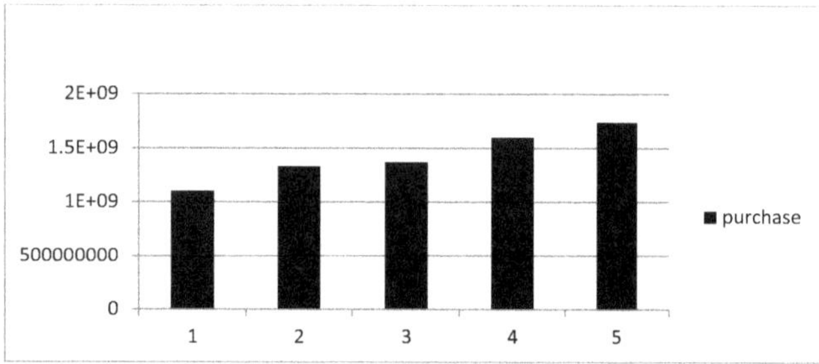

Interpretation: Purchase of milk from milk union from the year 2009-2014. Purchase of milk from milk unions in the year 2013-14 increased and in 2009-10 decreased.

Figure 2: Chart showing classification of purchase of the milk from milk unions.

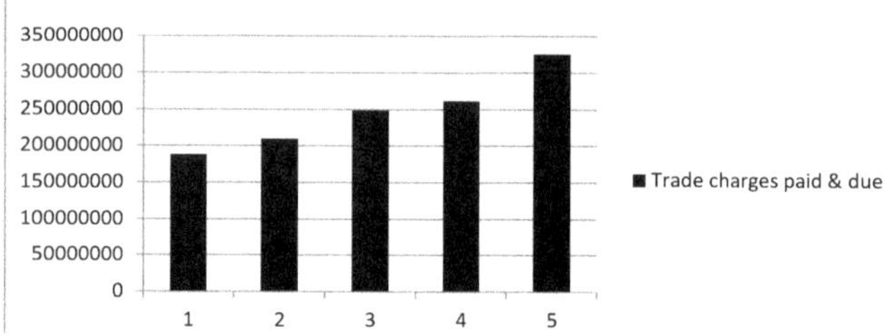

Interpretation: The above table shows that trade charges paid and due in 2009-14. Trade charges paid and due in the year 2013-14 increased and in 2009-10 decreased.

Figure 3: Chart showing classification of trade charges paid and due.

11. There is no relationship between operating ratio and capital turnover ratio (Figure 8).

Suggestions

As the result of study budgetary control of Coimbatore district co-operative milk producers union limited the given the following suggestions.

1. It is Essential to maintain the good management control
2. It is Mandatory that the organisation has to always maintain the good working capital
3. Maintain the good corporate governance
4. Fluctuations are common in every organization but sustainability is very important so to maintain the stability.
5. The processes of indent taking and billing through on line transaction processing systems is very important.
6. Use the new technologies to maximize the quality of output.

Conclusion

It is interesting to note that budgetary control Coimbatore district co-operative milk producers union limited is doing well and growing phenomenally. Based on the finding and experience the researcher had, while conducting the study on "budgetary control department" as a researcher I came to the following conclusion.

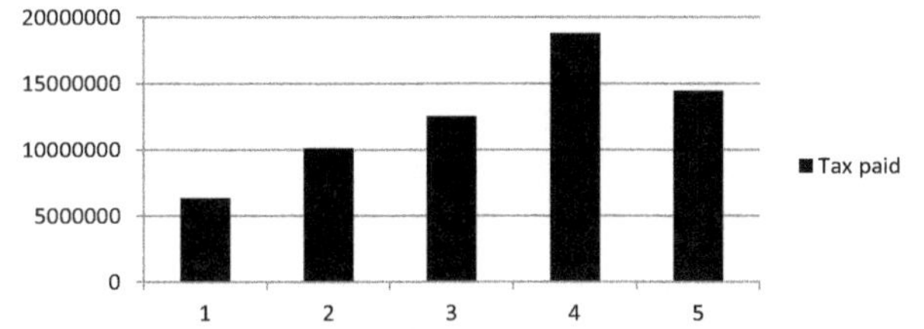

Interpretation: The above table shows that tax paid from the year 2009-13. Tax paid in the year 2011-12 increased and in 2012-13 decreased.

Figure 4: Chart showing classification of tax paid.

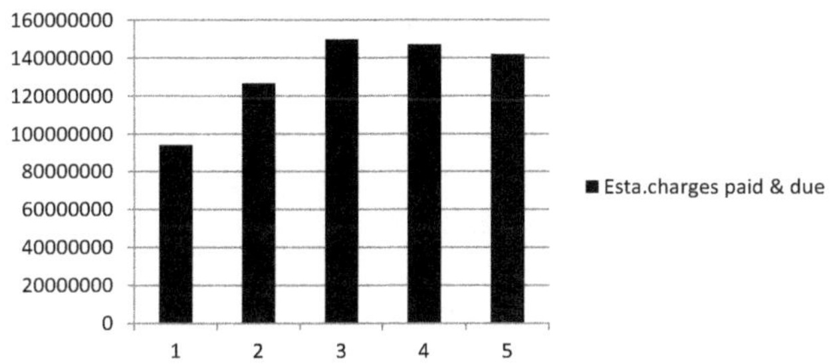

Interpretation: The above table shows that establishment charges paid and due from the year 2009-2013. Establishment charges paid and due in the year 2010-11 increased and in 2011-12 decreased.

Figure 5: Chart showing classification of establishment charges paid and due.

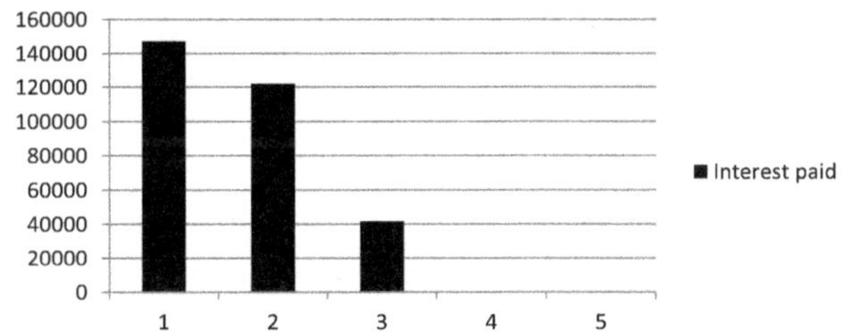

Interpretation: The above table shows that interest paid and due from the year 2008-13.Interest paid in the year 2008-09 increased and in 2010-11, 11-12, 12-13 decreased.

Figure 6: Chart showing classification of Interest paid.

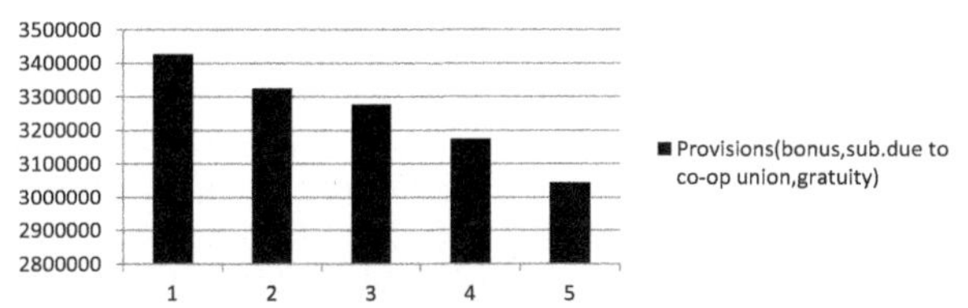

Interpretation: The above table shows that provisions (bonus, sub. due to co-op union) in 2008-13. Provisions (bonus, sub. due to co-op union) in the year 2008-09 increased and in 2010, 2011, 2012, 2013 decreased.

Figure 7: Chart showing classification of provision (bonus, Sub. due to co-operative union, gratuity).

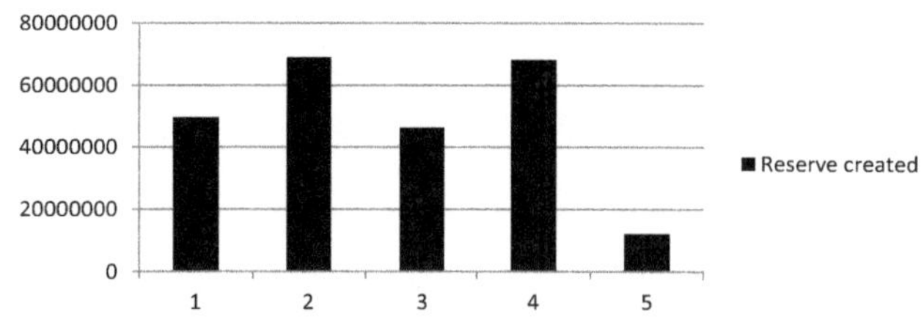

Interpretation: The above table shows that reserve created (depreciation reserve, Audit objection, interest overdue) and due in 2008-13. Reserve created (depreciation reserve, Audit objection, interest overdue) in the year 2009-10 increased and in 2010-11, 2012-13 decreased.

Figure 8: Chart showing classification of reserve created.

1. Budgetary control department works as a back bone of top management. It is one of the important plan for every management for their Business
2. With the support of good budgetary control the management of marketing, finance, production and personnel become more efficient. So it is essential to regulate proper Budgetary control for all organisation.

References

1. Lockyer K (1983) Fundamental of Budget preposition ethics: A Development.
2. "Glautier" (1997) Accounting Theory and Practice (6thedn.) Pitman Publishing, London.
3. Pandey IM, Vikas publication house pvt ltd, Financial Management (9thedn.) New Delhi pp. 754-758.
4. Otley S (1987) Budget Use and Management Performance. Journal of Accounting Research publication 16.
5. Dowdy S, Wearden S (1983) Statistics for research. Wiley, Himalayan publishing p: 2008
6. Kothari CR (2004) Research Methodology. New age international publishers, New Delhi.
7. Maheshwari SN, Maheshwari SK (2012) Accounting for Management. Vikas Publication House Pvt Limited.
8. Jawahar L. Cost Accounting. Tata McGraw-Hill Publishing Company Limited, pp. 775-784.
9. Batty J (1963) Management Accounting including Financial Management and Control. Macdonald and Evans.
10. Batty J (1979) Accounting for Managers. Heinemann Publishers.
11. Buyers, Holmes G (1984) Principle of Cost Accounting. Cassell Ltd.
12. Chartered Institute of Management Accountants (2000) Management Accounting Official Terminologies. CIMA.

Is CSR a Luxury that SMEs in Africa Cannot Afford?

James AP*

BSc (Hons) MA (PCET) DBA, 41 Burgess Road, Stratford, London, UK

Abstract

Corporate Social Responsibility (CSR) is a subject that divides academic opinion. The current literature on the subject provides a dichotomy of views from the perspective of supporters who argue that businesses do well by doing good. Critics, from mainly the free enterprise movement, argue that CSR is 'just a fad' and that by diverting valuable resources into activities that have no direct bearing on a company's bottom-line is unscrupulous and unprincipled. There is also the argument that CSR engagement place undue burden on SMEs in Africa that can ill afford them while protecting foreign companies.

The cost associated with the phenomenon is one of the key reasons for the current position which is also not helped by the lack of scientific measurement of the impact of CSR engagement on a company's performance. However, there is evidence from CSR literature which supports the view that there are long-run benefits for companies adopting CSR strategies including enhanced reputation, enhanced staff loyalty and cost savings.

This paper argues that there is a strong business case for CSR engagement by SMEs in developing countries in spite of the associated costs and concludes that CSR engagement enhances SMEs in developing countries' social, environmental and financial performance.

Keywords: Small and Medium Scale Enterprise (SME); Corporate social responsibility; Stakeholders; Organisational responsibility; Philanthropic responsibilities; Shareholder value; Corporate citizenship; Transnational corporations

Introduction

Corporate social responsibility (CSR) is difficult to pin down in terms of a clear definition, because there are different facets to its meaning and application. According to Fisman, Heal and Nair (n. d.) there is a lack of well-defined analytical framework which generates difficulties in the study of corporate social responsibility (CSR) since the term seems to have different connotations to different audiences. Raynard and Forstater [1] quote from various literature and provide the following definitions:

CSR is "the continuing commitment by business to behave ethically and contribute to economic development while improving the quality of life of the workforce and their families as well as of the local community and society at large." (World Business Council for Sustainable Development)

"Being socially responsible means not only fulfilling legal expectations, but also going beyond compliance and investing more into human capital, the environment and relations with stakeholders." (The European Commission)

CSR means "operating a business in a manner that meets or exceeds the ethical, legal, commercial and public expectations that society has of business."

Visser [2], defines CSR as "the way in which business consistently creates shared value in society through economic development, good governance, stakeholder responsiveness and environmental improvement" (p. 7). The simplest and probably the best definition that seems to capture the various aspects of CSR is the one that defines the concept as 'businesses doing well by doing good". From the literature on the subject, I find this simple definition to encapsulate the spirit as well as the essence of CSR as it implies that as businesses carry out their activities in the interest of the wider stakeholders, the primary goal of investors is also facilitated.

CSR involves the transformation of businesses from mere profit motivated machinery into corporate citizens who are actively promoting moral principles and responsible practices which engender sustainable operations and transparent entities in their dealings with both internal and external stakeholders [3]. Many corporations including Enron, WorldCom, Tyco, Adlephia have been affected by 'doubts and distrust' by the investing public as a direct results of poor and unethical business practices leading to their demise (p. 1).

The shift from profit maximisation to ethical and responsible practices is captured clearly in Carroll's pyramid of CSR, [4]. As illustrated in Figure 1 below, Carroll argues that business concerns may be arranged in a hierarchical order with the most important concerns at the bottom of the pyramid. It therefore follows that there is a linear development of organisational responsibility which suggests that firms will prioritise their objectives ranging from economic responsibilities to philanthropic responsibilities.

The pyramid (Figure 1) is a clear illustration of the transformation of business motivation from 'the business of business is business,' argued by the neo-classical economists, to corporations as members of the global community, with responsibility and accountability to states and civil society. The change in emphasis means shifting from treating pollution etc. as 'externalities' to including all costs to environment, community etc. in market transactions. The concept of corporate citizenship has gathered momentum due to its mutual benefit to both society and businesses. According to Lenssen et al. [5], innovative companies are moving from building 'shareholder value' to 'shared

***Corresponding author:** James AP, BSc (Hons) MA (PCET) DBA, 41 Burgess Road, Stratford, London, E15 2AD, UK
E-mail: attapanin@hotmail.com

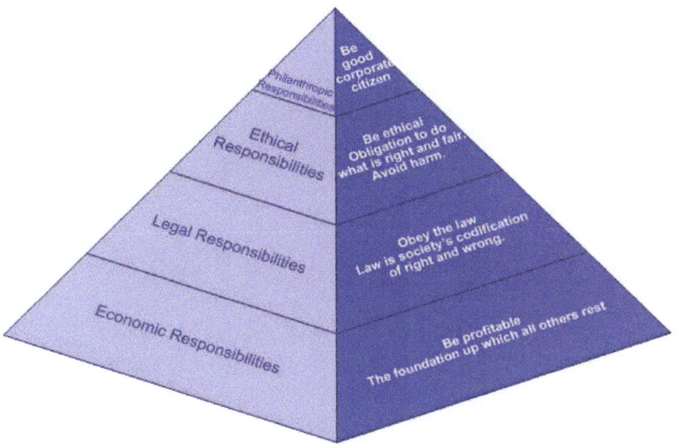

Carroll's CSR Pyramid

Figure 1: Carroll's CSR Pyramid and its applications to small and medium sized businesses.

value' for all stakeholders; from 'quarterly capitalism' to 'long-term capitalism'. They are also providing resources, open access systems and capital to entrepreneurs and communities to support technology and knowledge transfers. Companies that integrate future development concerns into their business model will be ideally placed to secure long-term licenses to operate, develop loyal new consumer bases, and innovate in new market segments.

In this regard, the days of profit maximization regardless of its social and environmental implications appear to be gone for good and any company that decides to risk societal backlash in the name of profit maximization does so at its own peril.

Historical Development

CSR is not just a recent phenomenon to the business environment. Although Raynard and Forstater [1] are of the view that there has been a radical change in the relationship between the private sector and both state and civil society in the form of CSR engagement and expectations over the past two decades, it is the position of the CSR literature that the principle and idea behind the CSR concept has been around for decades, if not centuries [2,6]. The CSR debate over the relationship between business and society dates back to the late nineteenth century "when the power of corporations was in ascendancy and periods in which society attempted to regulate the growth of corporate power" [6]. During this era, the emergence of large corporations and the 'robber barons' led to the development of the anti-trust movement and society began to look suspiciously at the activities of these large and powerful corporations and their owners. The corporations responded by engaging in philanthropic activities in order to prove that government regulations were unnecessary [6,7] posits that the Great Depression in the 1930s produced a second wave of regulation which led to Roosevelt's New Deal in the US and nationalisation and regulation by the post-war Labour government in the UK. The tension between business and society continued into the 1960s and 1970s as concerns were raised regarding the growing social and environmental impact of transnational corporations (TNCs), leading to a third period of efforts to regulate corporate activities.

Global restructuring and the rise of neoliberalism in the 1980s led to a shift away from state intervention in both developed and developing countries [8]. National policies at the time towards TNCs shifted away from regulations and gave rise to 'intense competition to attract foreign direct investment' which led to the exploitation of state resources as governments became fearful of the TNCs who were prepared to relocate their production facilities to countries with more favourable regimes. Bendell [9] argues that by the 1980s, it was becoming clear that the various multilateral initiatives and agreements that had been introduced in the previous decade were doing little or nothing to address corporate power.

Recent work on CSR began with the work of Keith Davies, a Professor at the University of Arizona who argued that some socially responsible business decisions can be justified by a long, complicated process of reasoning as having a good chance of bringing long-run economic gain to the firm, thus paying it back for its socially responsible outlook. He sets forth his now-famous Iron Law of Responsibility, which held that the social responsibilities of businesspeople needed to be commensurate with their social power (Corporate Social responsibility and related terms, n. d.). There is no doubt that the process of globalisation has also added more impetus to the growing debate on the equitable sharing of the benefits of international investment, trade, growth and development [1]. In regards to this, and in the view of the proponents of CSR, civil societies have become increasingly aware of the social and environmental impact of TNCs activities and are thus demanding that these corporations make a fair contribution to the communities whose lives are impacted on by their activities. In making the business case for CSR engagement, the Boston College Centre for Community Relations (2000) argued that some of the factors that have had significant effect on the increased CSR engagement by business include globalisation and the associated growth in competition, increased size and influence of companies, retrenchment and repositioning of government and its roles, increasing competition for talents and expertise, growth of global civil society activism and increased importance of intangible assets. It therefore appears that CSR engagement is not only expedient for the growth of modern corporations but it now needs to have a strategic focus for both multi-national corporations (MNCs) whose cross border interactions rely on governments and civil societies with considerable understanding of corporate citizenship and high expectations and small and medium enterprises (SMEs) whose activities have significant impact on the development of national economies as well as local communities and the environment. The views of Raynard and Forstater is that companies, especially SMEs in developing countries now recognise that 'improving their own impacts and addressing wider social and environmental problems will be crucial in securing their long-term success' (p. 1). In fact, Willard went on to underscore that 'good environmental and social programmes make good business sense' (p.2) and creates a win/win/win approach for corporations, society and the planet.

The Benefits to SMEs in Developing Economies for CSR Engagement

In answering the question as to whether the SMEs in developing countries should engage in CSR activities, it is essential to discuss what is in it for them. What do they stand to gain by taking on additional commitments that some may argue do not directly add value to their core business? Before going into the details of the importance of CSR to SMEs it is necessary to emphasise the significance of SMEs in developing economies, especially those of the sub-Saharan African region. The point is made that it is the activities of SMEs that will drag citizens of these nations out of poverty [1]. For this to materialise, access to international markets will be crucial. This is where CSR engagement becomes imperative as it provides a link to TNCs who are increasingly making it a condition for doing business with those SMEs in developing economies.

It must be noted that as more and more TNCs rely on supplies from SMEs in developing nations, their reputation and the brand image is intrinsically linked together. The activities of the SMEs that are deemed unethical tarnish the reputation of the parent companies in the developed economies where there is the expectation of adherence to higher social responsibilities. Many companies have suffered the consequences of the actions of their supplier chain businesses in developing countries. These include recent cases of Primark and the collapse of the Rana Plaza factory in Bangladesh where over 11000 people lost their lives. Nike has been shamed by its sweatshop outsourcing factories which has tarnished the image of the company and is still struggling to restore its reputation [10].

To avoid these embarrassments, TNCs make CSR engagement a condition for doing business with SMEs in developing countries. Raynard and Forstater, asserted that increasingly, TNCs are including social and environmental criteria alongside the more traditional considerations of quality and price. In recent years, there has been a flurry of activities relating to codes of conducts for sub-contractors concerning environmental and labour standards ensuring that these companies in countries with limited CSR expectations live up to international standards to meet society's call for higher moral and ethical practices.

Another benefit of the TNCs and SMEs interface with regards to CSR engagement is the rising acknowledgement that "forming trading links and development partnerships, which help SMEs gain access to markets, finance, training, physical infrastructure and business support services can be one of the key ways that they can have a positive impact on poverty" (p.41). At the recent annual general meeting of the African Development Bank (AfDB) held in Arusha, Tanzania, the AfDB's President Donald Kaberuka, announced the official launch of the African Guarantee Fund (AGF), a market-friendly guarantee scheme which aims at easing access to finance for African small SMEs. This was funded and supported by the governments of Denmark and Spain to "provide financial guarantees to financial institutions to stimulate financing to SMEs and unlock their potential to deliver inclusive growth in the region" [11]. These partnerships support the activities of respective SMEs and enhance their performance especially by increasing their bottom-line in the process.

Table 1 below also summarises how the Japanese government supports SMEs in sub-Saharan Africa through the One Village, One Product (OVOP) programme which is expected to alleviate constraints on the development of SMEs [12]. The first column lists the market failures and constraints which confront SMEs, and the second column indicates whether OVOP addresses these constraints. The other columns identify examples of OVOP support and complementary actions by local governments. The last column suggests additional/alternative sources of donor assistance.

There are also long-run benefits for companies adopting CSR strategies. Some of these benefits include:

- Cost- savings – Waste and energy consumption adds significantly to SMEs operational costs. By adopting policies to control these, SMEs are likely to cut down significantly on such avoidable expenses, thereby impacting positively on efficiency and profitability. A university in Ghana was recently able to cut down on its electricity bill by almost a third as a result of installing solar panels in place of the traditional energy supply.

- **Enhanced staff loyalty:** Companies with advanced human resource development programmes (e.g. high investment in training, family-friendly policies, incentives and reward schemes) enjoy higher levels of loyalty and lower levels of absenteeism, and will also find it easier to recruit, develop and retain staff. I recently conducted a simple experiment in my classroom by asking 125 A' level students who are about to enter university whether the reputation of an organisation will be one of their considerations when looking for a job in the future. I was astonished to find that 85 out of the 125 indicated that they will refuse to work for a company with poor CSR reputation, even in this difficult and competitive job market. Although this is not a precise science, yet it goes a long way to indicate employment trends with future generations.

- TNCs are able to use their strong influence on governments to establish/encourage decisions and policies that support ethical standards and human resource policies that ultimately improve business performance. The actions of TNCs are influencing governments in developing countries to adopt more positive environmental and ethically friendly policies likely to favour organisations that align their strategic policies with favourable socially responsible practices.

- Finally, and most crucially, developing countries are more likely to be affected by environmental disasters, all things being equal, than developed nations. Western developed nations have the capacity,

Constraint in SMEs	Japanese assistance for OVOP	Examples of OVOP related involvement	Examples of complimentary actions by host Government	Examples of other donor assistance
Low skills	Directly by providing ex-pat skills and training courses in japan	Packaging, Labelling, Accounting Marketing etc.	Training	Limited,GTZ
Lack of technology standard and knowledge	Directly by providing advice and training courses	Quality Control, Kaizen, S5, TQM JIT etc	No	Limited, standards support by the EC UNIDO on standards
Lack of external links such as in value chains	Directly by linking SMEs to Japanese markets	Trade fair in Japan website	Trade fair	e.g. IDRC
Lack of access to credit	Indirectly via government policy	No	Yes, sometimes. cooperatives secretariats	World bank, DFID etc
Weak BDS market	No. OVOP provides BDS itself and does not promote the BDS market	No	No	Donor committee on small enterprise, DFID etc
Infrastructure	No, only small equipments are provided	Cooling tanks for milk plants	No	World Bank, EC
Regulatory framework and governance framework more widely	No, only limited guidance for OVOP framework will be provided	No	Limited	World Bank UNDP UNID DRD etc.

Table 1: Japanese government supports SMEs in sub-Saharan Africa.

technology and resources to recover from environmental catastrophes better than developing countries. Recent 'cries for help to the Western world after earthquakes, famine, diseases and other environmental problems by developing nations are testimonies of how almost helpless developing countries are when it comes to emergency assistance. It is therefore in the interest of these nations to take the responsibility to support any initiative that minimises the chances of such environmental tragedies.

In summary, the conclusions can be drawn to the fact that all parties concerned stand to benefit from a stable environment that is less likely to play havoc with people's daily lives and for that reason, any attempt to protect the environment and adoption of ethical policies is in the interest of citizens of developing nations. SMEs in these parts of the world can make significant contribution to sustainable development by adopting policies that facilitate tackling capacity constraints and building the drivers of responsible business [13]. Baker [14] states it quite emphatically that, there are areas where companies have to do the right thing. The business case for action on climate change is not that you will necessarily get competitive advantage for so doing (although you might if you are clever) but because your business model is fundamentally screwed if we don't have a planet, and every business, every law-maker and every individual citizen has a part to play in that (p. 5).

The case against CSR in developing economies

In spite of the overwhelming evidence supporting the need for SMEs in developing nations to have a more strategic focus in CSR engagement, critics argue that CSR is 'just a fad' and that by diverting valuable resources into activities that have no direct bearing on a company's bottom-line is unscrupulous and unprincipled. Belsky [15] draws from the conclusion of a recent study and assert that "firms that are focused on pursuing a socially responsible agenda are more likely than other businesses to behave in socially irresponsible ways".

The argument from the free enterprise movement can be summed up in a quote by Milton Friedman in a New York Times article thus, any business executives who pursued a goal other than making money were, he said, "unwitting puppets of the intellectual forces that have been undermining the basis of a free society these past decades." They were guilty of "analytical looseness and lack of rigor." They had even turned themselves into "unelected government officials" who were illegally taxing employers and customers [16].

The free enterprise movement argue that by creating jobs and contributing to the coffers of governments, businesses contribute their fair share to communities and they do not need to accept the pressure of 'do gooders' who expect board of directors to use the legitimate returns on investment to appease society. According to the neoliberal economists, the responsibility of providing for communities lies firmly at the doors of governments. It is also the role of governments to ensure businesses operate within the law and as far as each party is doing their jobs well, there is no need for businesses to take on the role of governments.

Milton Friedman, a neo liberalist economist wrote in the New York Times on September 13, 1970 and said that:

There is one and only one social responsibility of business-to use its resources and engage in activities designed to increase its profits so long as it stays within the rules of the game, which is to say, engages in open and free competition without deception or fraud.

His views were supported by the neoliberal journalist Janet Albrechtsen who, writing in an opinion piece for the Australian newspaper recently wrote:

The fundamental flaw with corporate social responsibility, and why it is a backward step, is the underlying premise that capitalism and companies have something to be embarrassed about, that they must justify their existence by going in search of some higher moral purpose. This shame-faced capitalism is an unfortunate development. The idea pushed by advocates that the pursuit of private profit is inconsistent with public good does not stack up. How quickly we forget that Adam Smith knew a thing or two about human nature ... Smith pointed out that "it is not from the benevolence of the butcher, the brewer or the baker that we expect our dinner, but from their regard to their own self-interest" [17].

According to Baker [14], some of the main arguments raised against CSR include the following:

- Businesses are owned by their shareholders - money spent on CSR by managers is theft of the rightful property of the owners
- The leading companies who report on their social responsibility are basket cases - the most effective business leaders don't waste time with this stuff
- Our company is too busy surviving hard times to do this. We can't afford to take our eye off the ball - we have to focus on core business
- It's the responsibility of the politicians to deal with all this stuff. It's not our role to get involved
- I have no time for this. I've got to get out and sell more to make our profit line.
- Corporations don't really care-they're just out to screw the poor and the environment to make their obscene profits

Karnani, wondered whether companies can do well by doing good and asserts that the idea that companies have a responsibility to act in the public interest and profit from it is fundamentally flawed [18]. He goes further to posit that the whole idea of businesses trumpeting the case for CSR is not only an illusion but potentially a dangerous one. He argues that, in cases where private profits and public interests are aligned, the idea of corporate social responsibility is irrelevant: Companies that simply do everything they can to boost profits will end up increasing social welfare. In circumstances in which profits and social welfare are in direct opposition, an appeal to corporate social responsibility will almost always be ineffective, because executives are unlikely to act voluntarily in the public interest and against shareholder interests (p. 1).

Others argue that CSR has ulterior motives. One study showed that over 80% of corporate CSR decision-makers were very confident in the ability of good CSR practice to deliver branding and employee benefits (Arguments against CSR, n. d.). To take the example of simple corporate philanthropy, when corporations make donations to charity they are giving away their shareholders' money, which they can only do if they see potential profit in it. This may be because they want to improve their image by associating themselves with a cause, to exploit a cheap vehicle for advertising, or to counter the claims of pressure groups, but there is always an underlying financial motive, so the company benefits more than the charity. In other words, CSR is a cheap PR exercise designed to promote the image of an organisation for marketing and other financial purposes. By appealing to customers' consciences and desires, CSR helps companies to build brand loyalty and develop a personal connection with their customers.

In Africa and the developing world the arguments against CSR engagement is often a cynical one. Critics argue that CSR engagement place undue burden on companies that can ill afford them while protecting foreign companies. Even well-meaning governments have expressed the concern that CSR standards are a mechanism for retaining jobs, trade and investment in developed countries at the expense of developing economies, which tend to compete through lower labour costs and less stringent environmental regulations (Raynard and Forstater, [1]. The CSR standards often include the payments of relatively high wages, higher quality standards, and other conditions that may not be particularly relevant in the context of the developing nations. For example, what is often perceived in the Western world as inhumane conditions may actually be the lifeline for a family in those parts of the world and that without those jobs, a family may starve or a child may not go to school. Coming from a Ghanaian background, I remember back in the days when a group of us will work for several hours every Saturday in a foreign owned company, under what one may say 'sweat-shirt' conditions to be able to pay our school fees in the secondary school. Without that labour and 'meagre' wages neither of us could have completed secondary school. It is the conviction of the author that, the argument needs to be balanced and looked at in a holistic context. Although this is not an excuse for businesses to exploit their employees or 'force' them to work under difficult conditions, there ought to be support for the SMEs in developing economies by their upstream supply chain TNCs by way of fair prices for their produce to encourage them to maintain higher standards without jeopardising jobs.

The other costs associated with CSR engagement are the monitoring and auditing costs which are related to the administration and auditing of systems associated with licensing. Raynard and Forstater [1] cite the example of one firm in China which was audited by teams from 40 customers in a single month. Expecting a small company in any part of Africa to bear such costs would be prohibitive and unrealistic leaving such firms to abandon any consideration for engaging in CSR practices, regardless of the long term benefits.

Conclusion

Clearly there is a strong business case for CSR engagement by SMEs in developing countries in spite of the associated costs. The evidence of this could be found in the masses of research linking social, environmental and financial performance which have concluded that doing good can also be good for business. In Africa and the developing world, there is a greater need for the case for businesses and governmental institutions to take responsibility and work towards environmental and humanitarian protections as the consequences of failure could have a more devastating effect on the citizens of developing nations than it would for developed countries for reasons highlighted above. Visser [2] quoted Josiah Charles Stamp as saying that "it is easy to dodge our responsibilities, but we cannot dodge the consequences of dodging our responsibilities" (p. 3). This is very true in the case of CSR engagement by businesses, especially, those in developing countries.

Although there are costs associated with engaging with CSR, a strategic approach backed with higher standards will enable SMEs in developing economies gain access to contracts with TNCs which is likely to secure jobs and enhance a business' bottom-line. A World Bank sponsored conference concluded that SMEs were motivated to be socially responsible by moral values and financial incentives, but face key challenges in implementing CSR. These include a lack of time and resources, a low margin of error, informal status, ad-hoc management styles, family ownership of businesses, and competition with others [19]. These factors are complex and may be country-specific which may require a strategic and coordinated effort. The international community probably led by United Nations Industrial Development Organisation (UNIDO) may need to support in this process to facilitate a comprehensive understanding of the economic, humanitarian and environmental values in CSR engagement by SMEs in developing countries.

References

1. Raynard P, Forstater M (2002) Corporate social responsibility: Implications for small and medium enterprises in developing countries.
2. Visser W (2013) The age of responsibility: CSR 2.0 and the new DNA of business. John Wiley and Sons Ltd. United Kingdom.
3. Colley J, Doyle J, Logan G, Stettinius W (2005) What is corporate governance? McGraw-Hill Companies, Inc. USA.
4. Dudovskiy J (2012) Carroll's CSR pyramid and its applications to small and medium sized businesses.
5. Lenssen JH, Wassenhove LV, McWilliams A, Siegel D (2012) Corporate social responsibility: a theory of the firm perspective. The Academy of Management Review 26: 117-127.
6. Jenkins R (2005) Globalization, corporate social responsibility and poverty. International Affairs 81: 525-540.
7. Richter J (2001) Holding corporations accountable: Corporate conduct, international codes, and citizen action, London: Zed Books.
8. Broomhill R (2007) Corporate social responsibility: Key issues and debates. Dunstan Paper No. 1/2007.
9. Bendell J (2004) Barricades and boardrooms: A contemporary history of the corporate accountability movement. UNRISD Technology, Business and Society Programme Paper. Number 13.
10. Nisen M (2013) How Nike solved its sweatshop problem. Business Insider.
11. Kakuyu E (2012) African guarantee fund for small and medium-sized enterprises, African Development Bank Group.
12. Kurokawa K, Tembo F, Velde DWT (2008) Donor support to private sector development in sub-Saharan Africa: Understanding the Japanese OVOP programme.
13. Trust M KU, Yambayamba K (2005) How can corporate social responsibility deliver in Africa? Insights from Kenya and Zambia.International Institute for Environment and Development, Vol 3.
14. Baker M (2008) Arguments against corporate social responsibility – redoubled.
15. Belsky G (2013) The downside of corporate social responsibility.
16. Denning S (2013) The origin of 'the world's dumbest idea': Milton Friedman, Forbes.
17. Albrechtsen J (2006) This business of moral coercion is just a hoax. The Australian 29 March 2006. Arguments against CSR (n. d.).Corporate Watch.
18. Karnani A (2010) The case against corporate social responsibility.
19. Hermes S, Jarvis M, Atacik MC, Schwittay A, El-Sharkawy A (2004) Can small be responsible? The possibilities and challenges of corporate social responsibility among small and medium enterprises.

Finance Bank Zambia Plc Retail Customers' Perceptions of Service Quality

Machayi J and Ahmed EM*

Faculty of Business, Multimedia University, Malaysia

Abstract

The study examined the nature of factors that influence customer's perception of service quality provided by Finance Bank Zambia Plc. is a private sector indigenous bank in the country. This is an analytical study based mainly on the primary data collected through a scientifically developed questionnaire and secondary information sources. Based on the outcomes originating from the literature review, this research has used a modified SERVQUAL scale. The questionnaire to customers was administered on a sample size of 357, chosen on a convenient basis across the branch network. These statistical methods used are as follows: frequencies - to describe the respondent's characteristics; means - to identify level of perception (questionnaire statements); Independent-Samples T-Test - to identify the significance of differences in the means of retail customers and branch staff perceptions of service quality; factor analysis: to identify the differences between customers and bank branch staff in terms of the degree of importance they attached to various dimensions of service quality and Cronbach's coefficient alpha test: to examine scale reliability and internal consistency. All factors namely tangibility, responsiveness, empathy, assurance, image, convenience reliability, access and ATM effectiveness qualified to be designated as important because their mean index scores were above 2 and 50% or more of respondents affirmed them to be either 4-very important or 3-important.

Keywords: Retail customers; Perceptions; Service quality; Finance bank; Private sector

Introduction

The banking sector is the backbone of any financial system of the economy. Commercial banks play an important role in the development of Zambian economy through mobilization of resources and their better allocation. Service quality has continued to gain importance due to its unique characteristics involving intangibility, inseparability, variability and perishability. Researchers have come up with different dimensions of service quality. Service quality has become a principal competitive weapon in the banking industry. Services are intangible and also not easily duplicated. Quality on the other hand, is differentiable and stems from the expectations of customers. Hence, it is necessary to identify and prioritize the customers' expectations for service quality and incorporate the expectations into a service process for improving quality. The key variables in meeting customer expectations begin with identifying the specific characteristics of service quality as perceived by the customer who defines the nature and importance of service quality.

Among the service industry stakeholders, the banking sector is perhaps the largest one that caters to the needs of people belonging to all sections of society. Moreover, perceived service quality tends to play a significant role in the interaction between customers and the service providers.

In addition, Finance Bank is large enough to capture and represent almost all the critical dimensions of total service quality that management may have to encounter in order to manage a service organization effectively.

Amid intense competition and the dynamic business environment, surviving in the market has become a key challenge for many service organisations. Service quality has become one of the key tools for surviving and gaining competitive advantage in banking industry, since its offering comprised mainly of intangible elements. Thus service quality has taken considerable interest in marketing literature. The banks perception of service quality may be quite different from what retail customers perceive as service quality. It is therefore, important for the bank to understand customer's perception of service quality in the light of great competition, numerous customer complaints and movement of customers from one bank to another.

Service quality has drawn the attention of researchers and managers because it is known to reduce costs and increase customer satisfaction, which are usually associated with customer loyalty which leads to increased economic returns for the company. Also, service quality was found to have a relationship with repeat purchase intention by Perez and Chen and consumption behavior by Dabholkar [1-3]. Therefore, service quality is a measure of the performance of an organization, which makes it important for both academics and practitioners to consider according to Karatepe [4]. According to Cook research indicates that companies with excellent customer service have reported a 72% increase in profit per employee compared to similar organizations that have poor customer service; it is also five times costlier to attract new customers than to retain existing customers [5].

Rust stated that service quality survey results can be used by managers to make important marketing decisions and to project the impact of different courses of action [6]. According to Bridges and Freytag firms might have to invest in finding new customers and/or retaining current customers, depending on the market situation [7]. According to Athanassopoulos offensive marketing involves attracting new customers, while defensive marketing involves keeping existing customers [8].

Having a defensive marketing strategy is better because it is cheaper to retain existing customers for many reasons, such as lower expenses for advertising to attract new customers with whom it takes time to establish loyalty. As discussed earlier, providing high levels of service quality is one way to keep customers both satisfied and loyal.

***Corresponding author:** Elsadig Musa Ahmed, PhD, Professor, Faculty of Business, Multimedia University, Melaka, Melaka 75450, Malaysia
E-mail: elsadigmusa@yahoo.com

According to Lages and Fernandes service quality became prominent since the 1970s because in many industrialized economies the service sector accounts for more than half of the GDP [9]; this represents the service sector without considering the manufacturing sector, which has also started to provide services according to Gupta [10]. According to Zeithaml employment in the service sector has been larger than in the manufacturing sector in the United States since 1929 [11], with 55% of the labor force working in the service sector; this increased to 82% in 2006, and services represent 80% of the GDP. This is an indication of the magnitude of the service industry and thus the need for high levels of service quality.

Due to the changing and competitive environment, financial services organisations have become increasingly marketing oriented. This has led to banks development of strategic plans, which respond to customers' needs, attitudes and behaviour. It has increasingly become cheaper to retain existing customers through provision of excellent service and development of long-term relationships.

There is lack of ample evidence of research on service quality in the banking industry in Zambia. Most research studies accessed are comparative studies of customer's perception of service quality of banks in other countries. Therefore, this study is required in that it will assess customer's perception of service quality in order to understand their expectations.

It is therefore, important not to misconstrue perception for judgement of service levels but rather an expectation. Bank staff was included to have a feel of the expectation of those involved in delivery service to possibly weigh in on how they may be used in service quality improvement strategies.

The major limitation of this study may arise from the fact that it is only based on Finance Bank. The study may not give a thorough understanding of the antecedents and dimensions of service quality that influence customer's perception of service quality. The overall issue of customer's perception of service quality is still unresolved. There is need to widen the understanding of service quality in the banking industry especially factors that drive customers' perception. This can only be achieved if a more encompassing study with large sample size and scope is conducted. It will be significant for banks to understand customers' perception of service quality in the banking industry and the drivers of such perceptions will be a sound basis for continuous improvement in the quality of service offered to customers, customer satisfaction and customer retention.

Service quality has become an important factor among the customers in retail banking. For the success and survival in the Zambian banking sector, provision of high service quality is necessary in meeting several requirements such as customer satisfaction and its consequent loyalty, attracting new customers and to increase the market share and profitability. Service quality is consistently viewed in the literature as a unique construct from customer satisfaction. The consumer considers that the service quality stems from a comparison of what he feels about the service and what is the performance of that service offering. In short, in order to evaluate the service quality the discrepancy between the consumers' perceptions should be calculated.

All the nine service quality offering variables will influence the overall service quality. Earlier to this Gronroos also proposed a conceptual model for service quality and also identified the possible determinants of service quality [12].

The marketing of financial services has also developed rapidly over the years. Management and marketing skills are considered crucial in the now very competitive world of financial services. Without a good reputation for understanding customer problems and requirements a bank will lose existing customers and fail to at least its market share of new business.

Research background

Due to the changing and competitive environment, financial services organisations have become increasingly marketing oriented. This has led to banks development of strategic plans, which respond to customers' needs, attitudes and behaviour. It has increasingly become cheaper to retain existing customers through provision of excellent service and development of long-term relationships.

Further, the marketing of financial services has developed rapidly over recent years. Management and marketing skills are considered crucial in the now very competitive world of financial services. Without a good reputation for understanding customer problems and requirements, a bank will lose existing customers and fail to attract at least its market share of new business. Typical research into the image and reputation of a bank, compared with its major competitors will involve exploring the responses and perceptions between key customers and non-customers to some of these topics;

- The banks' ability to make quick decisions
- Ability of the bank to administrate efficiently
- The degree to which the bank is seen to be helpful and friendly
- The professional level of skills and objectiveness exhibited by bank staff when giving financial advice
- Appreciation of customer problems shown by the bank and public perception of the degree of support they get when times are hard.
- Adaptability of services, approachability and general convenience factors both in terms of opening hours and branch location.

It should be recalled that the customer has become the centre of all business decisions right from conception of a product up to delivery. Customer centric approach to marketing policies and processes is critical. The antecedents of the recent status of the customer in marketing and business operations are the intense global competition, emergence of service driven economies, increasing customer awareness and sophistication and advancement in information technology. The success of any banking business hinges on how well services are delivered and perceived by customers. The value customers place on the service is vital for customer acquisition and retention.

In this respect, the customer centric marketing philosophy has been embraced by many business organisations today. Kotler and Keller observed that business organisations are now striving to understand their customers so that they could build long-term profitable relationships with them [13]. Several studies have been undertaken on customer satisfaction, customer retention and customer perceived quality in different industry sectors. Gronroos, Kotler and Keller have suggested the incorporation of customers view of what they need, want and dislike in the entire process of production [13,14].

Besides, the thrust of most bank marketing activities is to acquire and retain profitable customers. Reichheld has stated that it is believed that it is six times cheaper to retain existing customers than to acquire new customers in today's competitive banking business environment [15].

It should be noted that the retail banks are facing many challenges such as technological advancement, competitive products and services. In order to survive and compete effectively, banks must recognise the customer perceptions of service quality. There is lack of ample evidence of research on quality service in the banking industry in Zambia. Most research studies accessed are comparative studies of customer's perception of quality service of banks in other countries. The major limitation of this study may arise from the fact that it is only based on Finance Bank. The study may not give a thorough understanding of the antecedents and dimension of service quality that influence customer's perception of quality service.

The overall issue of customer's perception of quality service may still be unresolved. There is need to widen the understanding of service quality in the banking industry especially factors that drive customers' perception of quality service. This can only be achieved if a more encompassing study with large sample size and scope is conducted. It will be significant for banks to understand customers' perception of quality service in the banking industry and the drivers of such perceptions will be a sound basis for continuous improvement in the quality of service offered to customer, customer satisfaction and customer retention.

The bank under study

Finance Bank Zambia Plc (FBZ Plc) was incorporated in 1986 and was licensed to provide commercial banking services by the Bank of Zambia in that year. As one of the large local financial institutions in Zambia, FBZ Plc is one of the leading commercial banks that leverages on a strong nationwide presence to deliver a broad range of core banking and tailor made financial services to retail, SME and corporate customers. Moreover, Finance Bank Zambia Plc is a registered commercial bank and was incorporated on 23rd September 1986 as Leasing Finance Bank Limited. On 15th July 1988 the name changed to Finance Bank Zambia Plc.

It should be recalled that the operations of the bank commenced in 1987 with just two branches, one in Ndola and another in Lusaka. The number of branches has since increased over the years of which seven were acquired from Standard Chartered and four from Barclays. A total of 19 commercial banks currently operate in Zambia. It is a combination of local and foreign banks. All commercial banks offer the same range of standard facilities you would expect to find anywhere in the world. Selected banks also offer specialized unique accounts such as VIP, students or childrens accounts and electronic banking platforms.

The importance of service quality

Service quality has drawn the attention of researchers and managers because it is known to reduce costs and increase customer satisfaction, which are usually associated with customer loyalty which leads to increased economic returns for the company according to Buttle, McAdam, Seth, Edvardsson, Bontis and Booker [16-20]. Also, service quality was found to have a relationship with repeat purchase intention by Perez and Chen and consumption behavior by Dabholkar [1-3]. Therefore, service quality is a measure of the performance of an organization, which makes it important for both academics and practitioners to consider according to Karatepe [4]. According to Cook research indicates that companies with excellent customer service have reported a 72% increase in profit per employee compared to similar organizations that have poor customer service [5]; it is also five times costlier to attract new customers than to retain existing customers.

Further, Rust stated that service quality survey results can be used by managers to make important marketing decisions and to project the impact of different courses of action [6]. Firms might have to invest in finding new customers and/or retaining current customers, depending on the market situation according to Bridges and Freytag [7]. Offensive marketing involves attracting new customers, while defensive marketing involves keeping existing customers according to Athanassopoulos [8]. Having a defensive marketing strategy is better because it is cheaper to retain existing customers for many reasons, such as lower expenses for advertising to attract new customers with whom it takes time to establish loyalty. As discussed earlier, providing high levels of service quality is one way to keep customers both satisfied and loyal.

It should be noted that service quality has become prominent since the 1970s according to Lages and Fernandes because in many industrialized economies the service sector accounts for more than half of the GDP [9]; this represent the service sector without considering the manufacturing sector, which has also started to provide services according to Gupta [10]. According to Zeithaml employment in the service sector has been larger than in the manufacturing sector in the United States since 1929 [11], with 55% of the labor force working in the service sector; this increased to 82% in 2006, and services represent 80% of the GDP. This is an indication of the magnitude of the service industry and thus the need for high levels of service quality.

Rationale of the study

Bank customers are becoming more discerning consumers of their products. In the context of a competitive banking market, banks are beginning to recognize that customers increasingly deserve and will demand a voice that is listened to. Customers do have a definite stake in the banking process, are ideally placed to comment on issues and are core participants in the banking sector. Customer feedback has been recognized as a foundation on which to build any future quality assurance policy, recognizing the customer as the principal role player, with a voice that should be listened to and acted upon in order to enhance quality in the total banking experience.

As the question of quality has materialized and become the object of study, feedback from customers, as 'quality indicators' in the quality assurance process, has grown in acceptance.

Similarly, as banks continue to become more customer orientated, customer perceptions of bank facilities and services are becoming more important. It is, therefore, critical that banks develop some form of evaluating, tracking and managing the customer perceptions of service quality.

Service Quality and Related Literature

Newman has indicated that the literature featuring service marketing, mainly that of the 1990s has supported excellence in customer service and solutions to improve service quality as a means towards improving customer satisfaction and loyalty; thus, causing increased profitability and competitiveness [21]. Lewis and Arasli further state that service organizations are more and more viewing service quality as one of their fundamental strategic values [22,23]. Marla also stated that this is also manifested in the case of banks where the achievement of superior service quality levels has become a primary objective for retail banking operations [24].

In this respect, Parasuraman and Newman have indicated that several studies found a strong relationship between service quality and performance, market share, profitability, competitiveness, or word-of-mouth recommendation [21,25]. Lewis, Newman, Caruana and Arasli indicated that service quality entails a point of differentiation from competitors, leading to various opportunities to enhance long-term customer relations and corporate image [21,22,26,27], through customer satisfaction, and customer retention which cultivates favorable word-of-mouth. Accordingly, service quality is universally acknowledged as a victorious competitive strategy which is healthy for both service providers and their respective customers.

Moreover, in a study by Cronin and Taylor, service quality was found to be an antecedent of customer satisfaction refuting the suggestions of Bitner and Bolton and Drew that satisfaction is an antecedent of service quality [28-30]. Lee et al. [31] found further support to Cronin and Taylor's [28] conclusion in addition to that of Woodside, Oliver and Spreng and MacKoy [32-34]. Lee results revealed that service quality leads to satisfaction which in turn leads to purchase intention and the link between satisfaction and purchase intentions is stronger than the link between service quality and purchase intentions [31]. Their justification was that customers might not purchase services because of their high quality but because they lead to higher satisfaction. According to Cronin and Taylor (1992), factors like price, convenience, or availability may have an effect on satisfaction and consequently purchase intention [28]; but may not at all affect the perception of service quality. Lee suggests that because of this, service managers should not only focus on service quality improvement, but also try to locate and control variables that are related to customer satisfaction but not necessarily related to service quality [31].

Furthermore, Karatepe indicated that service quality has been the main focus of many studies in the field of services marketing nevertheless and Legcevic stated that there is no universally agreed upon definition of service quality although most of them are close in meaning [35,36]. Before presenting the different definitions of service quality, the term "quality" should be discussed. Quality has been generally defined as the customer's overall impression of the relative inferiority or superiority of the organization and its services. Whereas, service quality is considered the "perceived quality" of services [37,38] and a "complex construct" [35]. It is distinct from "objective or actual quality" since it is based on consumer judgment [37]. Parasuraman present Lewis and Booms' definition of service quality declaring that it is "a measure of how well the service level delivered matches customer expectations [39]. Delivering quality service means conforming to customer expectations on a consistent basis". However, according to Spathis [40], perceived service quality is a customer's "judgment on the overall service"; hence, it is an "attitude". Moreover, Fogli present a similar definition declaring that service quality is "a global judgment or attitude relating to a particular service" and add that service quality is "a cognitive judgment" [41]. Therefore, the focus in this study is on the subjective perception of service quality; that is, from the point of view of customers trying to understand their own perceptions and find a better way to serve them.

Researchers have defined customer perceptions as global judgments of customers relating to the superiority of a service, which is influenced by a number of factors including education level and social background [42-44], consumers' beliefs concerning the service received [38], consumer directed interactions with services [45], the evaluation of customers when interacting with the service at a specific moment in time [11,46], consumer judgment of the actual service performance [39], the process by which an individual selects, interprets and organizes stimuli into a coherent and meaningful image of the world [47], and customers' opinions of the service or product. More precisely, customer perceptions are consumer judgments on the actual service performance. This is connected to how customers see and assess the quality of service they actually receive. More significantly, their evaluation and judgment on it will determine their perception. For instance, if they are satisfied after evaluating and judging the service they have received then their perceptions should be high.

Based on the literature studies regarding the service quality concept, measuring service quality, a summary can be drawn that the literature review in this research starts by examining various definitions and meanings attributed to the concept of service quality, the importance of service quality, and how service quality can be improved. It also explored the measurement of banking service quality, and the outcomes seem to suggest that service quality levels in banks can be measured.

The rationale behind this research, focusing on the literature studies, is to enable the researcher to undertake quantitative research, aimed not only at examining the meaning of service quality and how service quality can be measured, but also to assist in exploring answers to research questions. To address research questions, the researcher explored issues set out within the main research aim and research objectives which are:

- What do retail customers perceive as quality service?
- Of these factors which ones are significant?
- What factors constitute quality service?

The broad objective of the study is to assess Retail customers perception of quality service using a modified Servqual scale and to determine relative influence of each dimension in determining overall service quality

The specific objectives are to:-

- Identify factors that influence customers perception of service quality
- To determine the significant factors that influence customer's perception of quality service.
- Define service quality through tracing out customers' expectations
- To provide suggestions and recommendations.

It can be seen that the research questions and objectives provide the need for exploring further studies on the issues associated service quality especially in Zambia.

The conclusions arising from this review are summarized below:

- Within the literature there are various definitions of service quality aimed at contributing to the meaning of service quality.
- By gathering the most commonly used definitions in the literature from the last four decades, it is possible to emphasize that service quality means meeting customer satisfaction, meeting customer expectations and meeting service specifications [42,48].

It was also found that there is an overlap between the three definitions that cannot be separated since they are dependent on each other, for example, by meeting service specifications, the customer expectations and satisfaction will be met. These three definitions are more acceptable to this research. More importantly, this research adopted the modified SERVQUAL scale to measure perception service quality.

- The review of various service quality models revealed that the models, in addition to their evident role in conceptualizing service quality, also provided key elements to service quality measurements and improvements. In other words, the models suggested a number of facets which can lead to an improvement in service quality levels such as a clear understanding of service quality and the factors influencing it, the measurement of service quality and feedback, clear market, customer focus, customer care, an effective processes and system and motivated staff.

- The theoretical framework of service quality can be described through two schools of thought. These are the North American School (Gap Analysis Model) and the Nordic School. The North American School is the most widely reported theoretical framework in the literature proposed by Parasuraman [38]. The model identified a set of gaps existing between customer perceptions and the tasks associated with service delivered. These gaps are measured by the difference between the two scores - performance-minus–expectation (P-E). While the Nordic School, proposed by Gronroos [12], suggests that service quality is conceptualized as the result of comparisons between perceived and expected service, with perceived service quality being influenced by technical and functional dimensions.
- To help conceptualize service quality, service quality models were classified into three types: multidimensional reflective models (hierarchal model); multidimensional formative models (SERVQUAL); and multidimensional formative-reflective models (Brady and Cronin's hierarchical model). This research adopted a multidimensional formative model based on SERVQUAL, as the most appropriate scale for measuring perception of service quality by retail customers at Finance Bank.
- The review of the literature also found that the SERVQUAL instrument had been replicated and modified specifically for the banking-service sector [49-51]. It was also found from the review that despite the widespread usage of the SERVQUAL instrument, it was questioned in terms of theoretical and operational criticisms which led researchers to agree on possible modifications of SERVQUAL based on the type of service industry under review [51-53]. The researcher selected a modified version of the original SERVQUAL scale and specifically suits research conducted within the banking sector. It includes five dimensions from the SERVQUAL scale (assurance, tangibles, responsiveness, empathy and reliability) and three additional dimensions related to banking (access, image, convenience and ATM effectiveness).
- The review of literature found that there have been negligible studies on service quality in Zambia even though some isolated studies were done in South Africa and Kenya.

Methodology

A preliminary study was undertaken to examine Finance Banks' retail customers' perception of service quality using a modified Servqual scale. Pilot studies have several advantages, the main one being providing warnings about where failures might occur in the research project and whether the instruments used are unsuitable or too complex The finding of the study revealed that most of the respondents rated all service dimensions namely-tangibility, responsiveness, empathy, assurance, image, convenience reliability, access and ATM effectiveness as critical. The preliminary study served as a base and suggested the direction to the current study to further study Finance Bank retail customer's perception of quality service.

To address this research issue, a research framework exhibited based on a modified SERVQUAL scale as the foundation of the theoretical basis has been used to probe customer's perception of service quality. In addition to the original variables of SERVQUAL scale, namely tangibility, responsiveness, empathy, assurance, reliability, other variables such as convenience image, access and ATM effectiveness were integrated into the model.

Other than that, the nine main variables of the modified SERVQUAL scale had their individual attributes outlined for each service dimension as exhibited under Annexure 1.

The study examined the nature of factors that influence customer's perception of quality service. The research problem was anchored at exploring retail customer's perception of quality service and the relative influence of each service dimension in determining overall service quality. Finance Bank Zambia Plc is a private sector indigenous bank in the country. It is now 25 years old and has 35 branches and 20 agencies throughout the country. This is an analytical study based mainly on the primary data collected through a scientifically developed questionnaire and Secondary information sources. Based on the outcomes originating from the literature review, this research has used a modified SERVQUAL scale. This approach was seen as the most suitable and helped in the comparison of retail customers with bank branch staff in terms of perception of service quality, thus addressing the research aims, questions and objectives (Figure 1).

The selected scale was piloted for scale validity and modification before the main data collection. After preparing the questionnaire in its final version, 540 questionnaires were administered to retail customers and branch staff based on the selected sampling procedure.

The questionnaire to customers was administered on a sample size of 357, chosen on a convenient basis across the branch network. The questionnaire to staff was e-mailed to a sample of 124 staff chosen on a convenient across the branch network. The nine independent variables are tangibility, responsiveness, empathy, assurance, image, convenience, reliability, access and ATM effectiveness. The dependent variable is customer satisfaction. A 4-point Likert type scale was used for rating of customers and staff perception of quality service. The scale is represented as follows: 1=unimportant, 2=some importance, 3=important and 4=very important. The influence of a particular factor was measured both by a mean index score and the percentage of customers indicating that a factor was either very important or important in their decision. A critical factor will be characterised by a mean index score of 2.0 or greater and for which 50% or more customers affirmed it to be very important or important. In order to test the hypotheses factors pertaining to a certain service dimensions were tested.

Statistical methods have been used to help address the research aims, questions and objectives. These statistical methods are as follows: frequencies - to describe the respondent's characteristics; means - to identify level of perception (questionnaire statements); Independent-Samples T-Test - to identify the significance of differences in the means of retail customers and branch staff perceptions of quality service; factor analysis: to identify the differences between customers and bank branch staff in terms of the degree of importance they attach to various dimensions of service quality and Cronbach's coefficient alpha test: to examine scale reliability and internal consistency.

Measurement of reliability

The SERVQUAL questionnaire was the instrument of choice in this research project and was originally developed in 1985 by Parasuraman, Berry and Zeithaml. Critics of the SERVQUAL instrument include Brown [54], who tested the instrument and showed strong reliabilities for both the expectation (0.94) and perception (0.96) component of the questionnaire using Cronbach's Alpha, suggesting high levels of reliability and internal consistency [54].

According to Zeithaml [55], published studies have used SERVQUAL and adaptations of it in a variety of service contexts

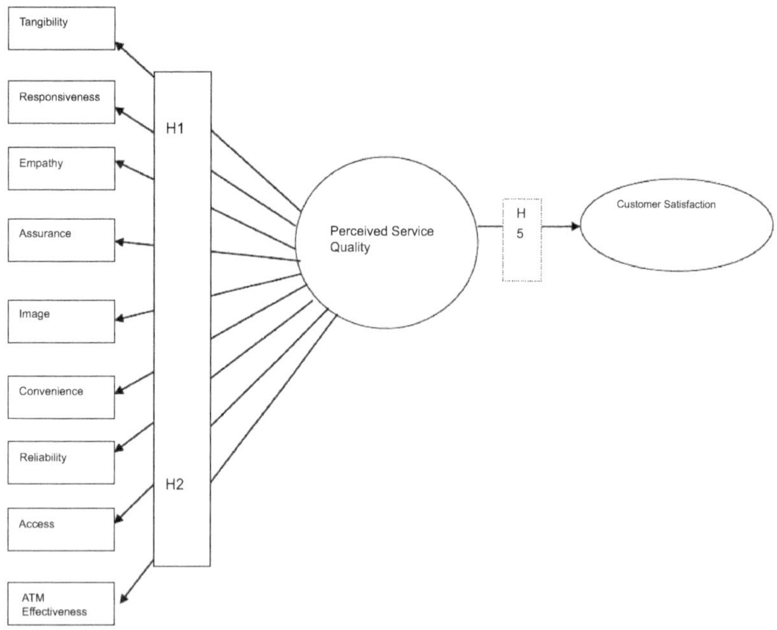

Figure 1: Theoretical framework.

including real estate brokers, hospitals, banks and higher education. Based on the fact that SERVQUAL has proven to be the most extensively utilized instrument in the service quality field of study, the researcher opted to use SERVQUAL modified manner with additional dimensions as the basis for measuring customers and staff perception of service quality at Finance Bank. However, a reliability test was carried out.

Empirical Findings

This section explains the empirical findings of the study based on the primary data analysis and second information to show the contribution of the study in the field of banking service quality issues and customer acceptability to the services provided by the bank under study.

Demographic profile of respondents

The questionnaire was designed to obtain information about the user groups, age, gender, education and their occupation. In total 383 questionnaires were distributed to branches for customers and 167 to staff. A total of 540 questionnaires were distributed of which 307 and 157 were for customers and staff respectively. The response rate for customers was at 80% and that of staff at 79%. The overall response rate stood at 80% as illustrated under table below. Annexure 2 shows the combined demographic profiles of respondents.

Gender - There was a total of 431 respondents of which male were 207 representing 48% and 224 female constituting 52%.

Age - The age distribution in year was that 18-25 age group, 119 respondents representing 28%, 26-35 age group, 113 respondents representing 26%, 36-45 age group,155 respondents representing 36% and 46-55 age group, 44 representing 10%.

Education – There were 270 respondents with college level education representing 63%, 72 respondents with Bachelor degrees representing 17%, 45 respondents had masters degrees representing 10% and 44 respondents had doctoral qualifications.

Occupation – Out of the 431 respondents, 44 were accounts representing 10%, professionals 212 representing 50%, 131 school teachers representing 30% and 44 self-employed representing 10%.

Discussion on descriptive statistics of customers' perception

The following are discussions on each of the parameters of retail customers and staff perception of service quality and refer to Annexure 3 for actual statistics:

- Tangibility is a critical factor as the mean index score was above rating of 2 and responses of 3=important and 4=very important were above 50%. There have been complaints raised in relation to state of branch infrastructure, poor internet banking channel and long queues at ATMs. The bank has put emphasis on tangibility issues as evidenced by renovations that are going, system upgrade and installation of ATMs in strategic locations. It is very important for the bank to invest in modern looking equipment especially those that interface with the customer such as ATMs. For visually appealing physical facilities, the bank has to invest in modern looking branch infrastructure. Distribution channels are keys and as such the physical branch foot print has continued to grow. The ATM foot print has equally continued to grow as this critical in reducing distance to bank and are usually installed in strategic locations that are easily accessible. There has been growth in additional self-service banking channels such mobile banking and internet banking that tends to promote remote banking.
- Responsiveness is a critical factor as the mean index score was above 2 and responses of 3=important and 4=very important were above 50%. The service attributes under it of Staff telling customers when services will be performed, prompt service, Staff willingness to help, ATMs responsive to financial requests and Reliable on line banking. This is consistent with customer complaints that have been received.
- Empathy is a critical factor as the mean index score was above 2 and responses of 3=important and 4=very important were above 50%. The service attributes under it of Bank employees

give customers individual attention, Bank employees deal with customers in a caring way, Bank employees have the customer's best interest at heart and Bank employees understand the needs of customers. This is consistent with customer complaints that have been received.

- Assurance-is a critical factor as the mean index score was above 2 and responses of 3=important and 4=very important were above 50%. The service attributes under it are Bank employees make customers feels safe in their transactions, Bank employees instil confidence in customer, Bank employees are consistently courteous, and Bank employees have knowledge to answer customer questions.
- Image is a critical factor as the mean index score was above 2 and responses of 3=important and 4=very important were above 50%. The service attributes under it are Bank highly reputable, Services of the bank by people I do business with and Services of the bank have a high image in the society.
- Convenience-Convenience is a critical factor as the mean index score was above 2 and responses of 3=important and 4=very important were above 50%. The service attributes under it are ATM conveniently located, Special services/counters for elderly /disabled, clear guidance on how to use banks services and facilities and convenient operating hours.
- Reliability-Reliability is a critical factor as the mean index score was above 2 and responses of 3=important and 4=very important were above 50%. The service attributes under it are No contradictions in decisions between staff and management, Delivering when promised, Feeling of security, Absence of errors in security, Good reputation, well trained staff, Precision of filing systems and Indication (communication) of quality.
- Access is a critical factor as the mean index score was above 2 and responses of 3=important and 4=very important were above 50%. The service attributes under it are waiting not to long, Queues that move rapidly, sufficient number of open tellers, No delays due to bureaucratic factors and procedures and sufficient number of ATMs per branch.
- ATM effectiveness is a critical factor as the mean index score was above 2 and responses of 3=important and 4=very important were above 50%. The service attributes under it are Safe to use ATMs, Easy to use and directions clearly provided, Always operating well, Always responding to financial requests and Services designed to serve best interest of customers.

Hypothesis testing

The hypothetical assumptions informed the basis of this research study, as this research measures retail customers and bank branch staff perception of service quality using a modified Servqual scale. The modified Servqual scale originating from the earlier discussion in Chapter Three of this research entails the service quality dimensions of tangibility, responsiveness, empathy, assurance, image, convenience, reliability, and access and ATM effectiveness. These nine service quality dimensions were used to determine and assess perception of service quality by branch staff and customers. Research hypotheses generated and developed based on the nine service quality dimensions of the modified Servqual scale. Additionally, the literature supported the view that addressing every service quality dimension was vital. The following hypotheses were therefore, subjected to statistical test and outcomes are stated below.

$H1_0$: The customer's perception of service quality is not dependent on tangibility, responsiveness, empathy, assurance, image, convenience, reliability, access and ATM effectiveness.

$H1_a$: Customers perception of service quality is dependent on tangibility, responsiveness, empathy, assurance, image, convenience, reliability, access and ATM effectiveness.

$H2_0$: There is no significant difference in influence of different factors on customer's perception of service quality.

$H2_a$: There is a significant difference in influence of different factors on customer's perception of service quality. In order to further examine other relationships, the following hypothesis needed to be tested.

$H3_0$: There is no difference between customer's perception of service quality and that of staff.

$H3_{a:}$ There is a difference in customer's perception of service quality and that of staff.

$H4_0$: There is a significant relationship between perceived service quality and customer satisfaction.

$H4_a$: There is no relationship between perceived service quality and customer satisfaction.

$H5_0$: There is a difference in perception of service quality based on gender.

$H5_a$: There is no difference in perception of service quality based on gender.

Hypothesis test results

The following measures will be used in the test of hypothesis.

- Statistical correlation was used to understand the relationship between research variables. It was used to understand whether the relationships were positive or negative and the strength of the relationship. Statistical correlation is measured by what is called coefficient of correlation (r). Its numerical value ranges from +1 to − 1. It gives an indication of the strength of relationship. In general, $r > 0$ indicates positive relationship, $r < 0$ indicates negative relationship while r=0 indicates no relationship (or that the variables are independent and not related). Here r=+1.0 describes a perfect positive relation and r=-1 describes a perfect negative correlation. Closer the coefficients are to +1.0 and -1.0; greater is the strength of the relationship between the variables. Correlation is suitable for examining the relationship between meaningful quantifiable data rather than categorical data.
- Independent-samples t-test is used to compare "the mean scores of two different groups of people", for example men and women, and check whether the difference between them is "real or statistically significant". Therefore, the objective of using the t-test is to test the "null hypothesis that two population means are equal". This method is used when the dependent variable, whose mean scores of two different populations are under investigation, is a continuous variable according to Pallant, like overall perceived service quality and customer satisfaction in the context of this study. The assumptions that need to be checked before using the independent-samples t-test is that all the observations are independent, and that the data is coming from a population with normal distribution if the sample is small, less than 40; otherwise there is no need to check the assumption of normality according to Norusis, which applies to this study having a large population of 431 respondents. The t-statistic is the "ratio of the difference between the two sample means divided by the standard error of the difference".
- Regression analysis is a statistical process for estimating the relationships among variables. It includes many techniques for

modeling and analyzing several variables, when the focus is on the relationship between a dependent variable and one or more independent variables (or 'predictors'). More specifically, regression analysis helps one understand how the typical value of the dependent variable (or 'criterion variable') changes when any one of the independent variables is varied, while the other independent variables are held fixed. Most commonly, regression analysis estimates the conditional expectation of the dependent variable given the independent variables – that is, the average value of the dependent variable when the independent variables are fixed. Less commonly, the focus is on a quartile, or other location parameter of the conditional distribution of the dependent variable given the independent variables. In all cases, the estimation target is a function of the independent variables called the regression function. In regression analysis, it is also of interest to characterize the variation of the dependent variable around the regression function which can be described by a probability distribution.

- Factor analysis attempts to identify underlying variables, or factors, that explain the pattern of correlations within a set of observed variables. Factor analysis is often used in data reduction to identify a small number of factors that explain most of the variance that is observed in a much larger number of manifest variables. Factor analysis can also be used to generate hypotheses regarding causal mechanisms or to screen variables for subsequent analysis (for example, to identify collinearity prior to performing a linear regression analysis).

Hypothesis 1

$H1_0$: The customer's perception of service quality is not dependent on tangibility, responsiveness, empathy, assurance, image, convenience, reliability, access and ATM effectiveness.

$H1_a$: Customers perception of service quality is dependent on tangibility, responsiveness, empathy, assurance, image, convenience, reliability, access and ATM effectiveness.

Using paired sample statistics and paired sample correlation the null hypothesis was rejected and alternative hypothesis retained implying that customer's perception of quality service was dependent on tangibility, responsiveness, empathy, assurance, image, convenience, reliability, access and ATM effectiveness (Table 1a).

Pair 1-9 is the list of variables. N is the number of valid (i.e., non-missing) observations used in calculating the t-test. Correlation - This is the correlation coefficient of the pair of variables indicated. This is a measure of the strength and direction of the linear relationship between the two variables. The correlation coefficient can range from -1 to +1, with -1 indicating a perfect negative correlation, +1 indicating a perfect positive correlation, and 0 indicating no correlation at all. (A variable correlated with it will always have a correlation coefficient of 1.) The correlation coefficient explains the extent to which you can guess the value of one variable given a value of the other variable. Sig - This is the p-value associated with the correlation. Here, correlation is significant at the .05 level (Table 1b).

Pair 1-9 is the list of variables. Mean are the respective means of the variables. N - This is the number of valid (i.e., non-missing) observations used in calculating the t-test. Std. Deviation - This is the standard deviations of the variables. Std Error Mean - Standard Error Mean is the estimated standard deviation of the sample mean. This value is estimated as the standard deviation of one sample divided by the square root of sample size. This provides a measure of the variability of the sample mean which in this case is zero.

Hypothesis 2

$H2_0$: There is no significant difference in influence of different factors on customer's perception of service quality.

$H2_a$: There is a significant difference in influence of different factors on customer's perception of service quality.

Using paired sample correlation test and factor analysis the null hypothesis was retained and alternative hypothesis was dropped implying there was no significant difference in influence of different factors on customer's perception of service quality (Table 1c).

Pair 1-9 is the list of variables. N is the number of valid (i.e., non-missing) observations used in calculating the t-test. Correlation - This is the correlation coefficient of the pair of variables indicated. This is a

		N	Correlation	Sig.
Pair 1	Perceived quality and Efficiency	307	0.824	0
Pair 2	Perceived quality and Access	307	0.975	0
Pair 3	Perceived quality and Reliability	307	0.955	0
Pair 4	Perceived quality and Convenience	307	0.922	0
Pair 5	Perceived quality and Image	307	0.948	0
Pair 6	Perceived quality and Assurance	307	0.741	0
Pair 7	Perceived quality and Empathy	307	0.844	0
Pair 8	Perceived quality and Responsiveness	307	0.846	0
Pair 9	Perceived quality and Tangibility	307	0.854	0

Table 1a: Paired samples correlations.

		Mean	N	Std. Deviation	Std. Error Mean
Pair 1	Perceived quality	3.3911208	307	0.4046426	0.0230942
	Efficiency	3.3	307	0.625	0.036
Pair 2	Perceived quality	3.3911208	307	0.4046426	0.0230942
	Access	3.356	307	0.4731	0.027
Pair 3	Perceived quality	3.3911208	307	0.4046426	0.0230942
	Reliability	3.4023	307	0.39583	0.02259
Pair 4	Perceived quality	3.3911208	307	0.4046426	0.0230942
	Convenience	3.371	307	0.5118	0.0292
Pair 5	Perceived quality	3.3911208	307	0.4046426	0.0230942
	Image	3.4375679	307	0.384891	0.0219669
Pair 6	Perceived quality	3.3911208	307	0.4046426	0.0230942
	Assurance	3.5049	307	0.37483	0.02139
Pair 7	Perceived quality	3.3911208	307	0.4046426	0.0230942
	Empathy	3.394	307	0.4337	0.0248
Pair 8	Perceived quality	3.3911208	307	0.4046426	0.0230942
	Responsiveness	3.451	307	0.3854	0.022
Pair 9	Perceived quality	3.3911208	307	0.4046426	0.0230942
	Tangibility	3.3013	307	0.56285	0.03212

Table 1b: Paired samples statistics.

		N	Correlation	Sig.
Pair 1	Perceived quality and Efficiency	307	0.824	0
Pair 2	Perceived quality and Access	307	0.975	0
Pair 3	Perceived quality and Reliability	307	0.955	0
Pair 4	Perceived quality and Convenience	307	0.922	0
Pair 5	Perceived quality and Image	307	0.948	0
Pair 6	Perceived quality and Assurance	307	0.741	0
Pair 7	Perceived quality and Empathy	307	0.844	0
Pair 8	Perceived quality and Responsiveness	307	0.846	0
Pair 9	Perceived quality and Tangibility	307	0.854	0

Table 1c: Paired samples correlations.

measure of the strength and direction of the linear relationship between the two variables. The correlation coefficient can range from -1 to +1, with -1 indicating a perfect negative correlation, +1 indicating a perfect positive correlation, and 0 indicating no correlation at all. (A variable correlated with it will always have a correlation coefficient of 1.) You can think of the correlation coefficient as telling you the extent to which you can guess the value of one variable given a value of the other variable. Sig - This is the p-value associated with the correlation. Here, correlation is significant at the .05 level.

Factor analysis was further undertaken as it identifies underlying dimensions within a list of separate variables was found suitable for the importance data though here also couple of items loaded heavily into more than one factor namely Tangibility and responsiveness. The extracted components explain nearly 95% of the variability in the nine original variables, so complexity can be reduced by using these components with only 5% loss of information. Principle component analysis was undertaken and the two underlying dimensions which emerged from the analysis are classified below (Table 1d).

The above table shows that the actual factors that were extracted. Under the column on 'Rotation Sums of Squared Loadings', it shows those factors that met the cut-off criterion (extraction method). In this case, two factors with eigenvalues greater than 1. The per cent of variance indicates how much of the total variability can be accounted for by each of the factors and this case Tangibility accounted for 78% and Responsiveness accounted for 95%.

Hypothesis 3

$H3_0$: There is a difference between customer's perception of service quality and that of staff.

H3: There is no difference in customer's perception of service quality and that of staff.

The Mann-Whitney U test was used to compare differences between two independent groups when the dependent variable is either ordinal or continuous, but not normally distributed. The Mann-Whitney U test is often considered the nonparametric alternative to the independent t-test although this is not always the case. This was done to determine whether there was a significant difference between staff and customers perception of service quality and the null hypothesis was rejected implying there was no difference between customer's perception of service quality and staff (Table 2a).

Hypothesis 4

$H4_0$: There is a significant relationship between perceived service quality and customer satisfaction.

$H4_a$: There is no relationship between perceived service quality and customer satisfaction.

Using a paired sample t-test and regression to determine whether there was a relationship between perceived service quality and customer satisfaction, null hypothesis was accepted implying there is a significant relationship between perceived service quality and customer satisfaction.

Through Kruskal-Wallis H test (sometimes also called the "one-way ANOVA on ranks") a rank-based nonparametric test that can be used to determine if there are statistically significant differences between two or more groups of an independent variable on a continuous or ordinal dependent variable. It is considered the nonparametric alternative to the one-way ANOVA, and an extension of the Mann-Whitney U test to allow the comparison of more than two independent groups. With a Sig .value of 0.855 associated with the correlation, the correlation was significant at the .05 level and the null hypothesis was retained (Table 2b).

Using regression (Table 3);

Model - SPSS allows you to specify multiple models in a single regression command. This tells you the number of the model being reported. R - R is the square root of R-Squared and is the correlation between the observed and predicted values of dependent variable. R-Square - This is the proportion of variance in the dependent variable (satisfaction) which can be explained by the independent variables (tangibility, responsiveness, empathy, assurance, image, convenience, reliability, access and ATM effectiveness). This is an overall measure of the strength of association and does not reflect the extent to which any particular independent variable is associated with the dependent variable. Adjusted R-square - This is an adjustment of the R-squared that penalizes the addition of extraneous predictors to the model.

The R square statistic represents how much of the variance in the response is explained by the weighted combination of predicators. The closer the R square to one, better the model fit. Regressing preference on the six predictors results in R square of 0.899 or 90% of variance in the preference rankings being explained by the predictor variables in the linear regression.

Hypothesis 5

$H5_0$: There is no difference in perception of service quality based on gender.

$H5_a$: There is a difference in perception of service quality based on gender.

Component	Initial Eigenvalues			Extraction Sums of Squared Loadings			Rotation Sums of Squared Loadings		
	Total	% of Variance	Cumulative %	Total	% of Variance	Cumulative %	Total	% of Variance	Cumulative %
1	7.042	78.244	78.244	7.042	78.244	78.244	4.585	50.943	50.943
2	1.506	16.739	94.983	1.506	16.739	94.983	3.964	44.04	94.983
3	0.293	3.26	98.243						
4	0.112	1.246	99.489						
5	0.035	0.393	99.882						
6	0.011	0.118	100						
7	4.42E-06	4.91E-05	100						
8	3.40E-15	3.78E-14	100						
9	-5.15E-16	-5.73E-15	100						

Extraction Method: Principal Component Analysis.

Table 1d: Total Variance Explained.

	Null Hypothesis	Test	sig.	Decision
1	The distribution of perceived quality is the same across categories of Staff/Customer	Independent samples Mann-Whitney U Test	.000	Reject the null hypothesis

Asymptotic significances are displayed. The significance level is 0.05.

Table 2a: Hypothesis test summary.

	Null Hypothesis	Test	sig.	Decision
1	The distribution of perceived quality is the same across of Satisfaction with services.	Independent samples Kruskal-Wallis Test	0.855	Retain the null hypothesis

Asymptotic significances are displayed. The significance level is 0.05.

Table 2b: Hypothesis test summary.

Using t-test to ascertain whether there was a difference in perception based on gender under model summary output below under model summary came out.

T-Test (Table 4a)

The above output shows that the average for Males is 68.10 and Females 70.30 (Table 4b).

The significance value of the statistic il 0.493 and because this is greater than 0.10, it can be assumed that both males and females have equal variance implying there are differences in perception of service quality arising from gender.

With the results presented thus far, this thesis is ready to evaluate on the hypotheses previously set upon in the beginning of section 3.3. The results of those hypotheses are listed in the table below (Table 4c).

Conclusion and Implications

The purpose of the study was to assess Finance Banks retail customers' perception of service quality using a modified Servqual scale. The findings of the study have revealed that most of the respondents rated all service dimensions namely-tangibility, responsiveness, empathy, assurance, image, convenience reliability, access and ATM effectiveness as important.

Based on statistical tests carried out it has been found that - customer's perception of service quality is dependent on tangibility, responsiveness, empathy, assurance, image, convenience reliability, access and ATM effectiveness.

There is no significant difference in influence of different factors on customer's perception of service quality and there is equally no difference in perception of service quality between customers and bank branch staff. There is a significant relationship between perceived quality and customer satisfaction and there is equally no difference in perception of service quality between male and female customers.

Based on the data collected from the 307 respondents a mathematical expression was formulated to determine the percentage level of satisfaction based on the data given.

To come up with the mathematical expression, the following was done:

- 'No' was represented by 1 while 'Yes' was represented by 2.
- The average score for all the nine attributes by each respondent were calculated.
- This score was then divided by four expressed as a percentage.
- For any respondent that gave a 'No' 30% was subtracted from the answer above. It was observed that respondents would give high score to the individual attributes but end up saying 'No'. By subtracting 30% bias and other attributes influencing the scores are adjusted for.
- For those that gave yes, no changes were made.

The answer above gives the level of satisfaction expressed as a percentage.

"Equation 5.1"

$$Y=-55.518+2.572X_1 +4.327X_2 - 0.731X_3+6.250 X_4+12.292 X_5 -0.350X_6+27.707X_7$$

Where X_1=Tangibility

X_2=Responsiveness

X_3=Assurance

X_4=Convenience

X_5=Reliability

X_6=ATM Effectiveness

X_7=Satisfaction

The model is 94.8% accurate as exhibited under Equation 5.1.

Predictive model results

Modern banking business is significantly influenced by the process of globalization. The impact is expressed, mainly, in financial market liberalization that, in turn, causes increased competition. To survive in a competitive struggle, banks should offer their customers affordable innovative products, because the competitive power of a bank is largely defined by the degree of its conformance to customer needs. In the information age, organizations require new capabilities for competitive success, such as customer relationships, product innovation, customized products, employee skills, motivation, and information technology (Table 5).

Many researchers believe that success of a bank depends directly on the bank's ability to capture and retain clients, as well as on intensity of relationships with clients. In turn, the human factors – bank employees – are the key instrument to enhance value of products and services perceived by customers. Thus, it is extremely important to determine factors affecting service quality, and to examine the gaps in customers' and employees' perceptions of these factors.

It is vital at this stage now to conclude on the main findings of the research. In order to facilitate this main findings are recapitulated below.

The findings of the study have revealed that most of the respondents rated all service dimensions namely-tangibility, responsiveness, empathy, assurance, image, convenience reliability, access and ATM effectiveness as important.

The research findings also support the following hypothesis.

$H1_0$: The customer's perception of service quality is dependent on tangibility, responsiveness, empathy, assurance, image, convenience, reliability, access and ATM effectiveness.

$H2_0$: There is no significant difference in influence of different factors on customer's perception of service quality.

H3a: There is no difference in customer's perception of service quality and that of staff.

Model	R	R Square	Adjusted R Square	Std. Error of the Estimate	Change Statistics				
					R Square Change	F Change	df1	df2	Sig. F Change
1	.948[a]	0.899	0.896	5.769	0.899	379.044	7	299	0

[a]Predictors: (Constant), Satisfaction, Reliability, ATM Effectiveness, Responsiveness, Tangibility, Assurance, Convenience.

Table 3: Model summary.

	Sex	N	Mean	Std. Deviation	Std. Error Mean
Satisfaction _level _percentage	1	175	68.1	19.542	1.477
	2	132	70.3	15.49	1.348

The above output shows that the average for Males is 68.10 and Females 70.30.

Table 4a: Group statistics.

		Levene's Test for Equality of Variances		t-test for Equality of Means						
		F	Sig.	t	df	Sig. (2-tailed)	Mean Difference	Std. Error Difference	95% Confidence Interval of the Difference: Lower	Upper
Satisfaction_level_percentage	Equal variances assumed	0.472	0.493	-1.067	305	0.287	-2.203	2.065	-6.267	1.861
	Equal variances not assumed			-1.102	304.228	0.272	-2.203	2	-6.139	1.732

Table 4b: Independent samples test.

Hypothesis	Description of Null hypothesis	Remarks
Hypothesis 1	The customer's perception of service quality is not dependent on tangibility, responsiveness, empathy, assurance, image, convenience, reliability, access and ATM effectiveness.	Rejected
Hypothesis 2	There is no significant difference in influence of different factors on customer's perception of service quality.	Retained
Hypothesis 3	There is no difference between customer's perception of service quality and that of staff	Retained
Hypothesis 4	There is a significant relationship between perceived service quality and customer satisfaction	
Hypothesis 5	There is no difference in perception of service quality based on gender	Retained

Table 4c: Hypothesis Evaluation Summary.

$H4_0$: There is a significant relationship between perceived service quality and customer satisfaction.

$H5_a$: There is no difference in perception of service quality based on gender.

As observed from the study, customer's expectations are high and calls for consistent delivery of high service quality. Service quality is an antecedent of customer satisfaction. There is obvious need to pay attention to quality.

In order, to manage service quality successfully, there is need to know the level of service customers expect. The bank should run surveys. Once what customers expect is known the position to deliver is solid. Frequently the easiest way to improve service quality is by providing front-line staff with more training. This gives customer contact a more solid background in solving problems and completing transactions more quickly. Another technique to improve quality is to provide additional automated equipment. It is very common now that service providers have websites, toll free phone lines, 24 hour automatic access to account data for this allows greater customization of service.

Satisfaction with services	Satisfaction with services	Level of satisfaction %	Expected level of satisfaction %(with model)
Yes	2	74.68	72.96
Yes	2	66.97	64.97
Yes	2	83.38	81.05
Yes	2	91.97	89.33
Yes	2	83.59	81.26
Yes	2	91.62	89.26
No	1	70	69.63
Yes	2	74.68	72.96
Yes	2	66.97	64.97
Yes	2	83.38	81.05
Yes	2	91.97	89.33
Yes	2	83.59	81.26
Yes	2	91.62	89.26
Yes	2	100	97.34
Yes	2	74.68	72.96
Yes	2	66.97	64.97
Yes	2	83.38	81.05
Yes	2	91.97	89.33
Yes	2	83.59	81.26
Yes	2	91.62	89.26
Yes	2	100	97.34
Yes	2	74.68	72.96
No	1	36.97	37.26
No	1	53.38	53.34
No	1	61.97	61.62
No	1	53.59	53.55

Table 5: Predictive model results.

Recommendations

Research of this nature is of great importance to the bank so that the institution can implement an appropriate set of processes to continuously review and refine customer service quality. Customer expectations based on perception are high based on the results from this survey and calls for customer service improvements to be put in place. The following recommendations are, therefore, made:

- With respect to service quality, branch managers should focus on improving all these nine dimensions.
- However, on the overall improvement of all nine dimensions of service quality, it is recommended that management invests in effective human resources programs to recruit, select, train, and support qualified employees. The selection process of employees should depend on finding certain qualities in potential candidates especially for reliability and empathy. For employees to be reliable, they should be ready to deliver on time, be sympathetic and understanding, reassuring and comforting, be dependable, and keep accurate records. To show the needed empathy, they need to have the ability to give personal attention, respond promptly to customer requests, attend accurately to customer needs, and be willing to help customers at any time. After selecting the right people with the basic qualities of reliability and empathy, managers should train these employees on providing better customer service and reveal their capabilities of being reliable and empathetic in the right way.
- Managers should provide adequate support to customer service employees especially when a problem arises.
- Front liners at the bank should be continuously trained and retained to improve their competency and on-the-job training is not enough; it has to be supported by training on soft skills, for instance, handling customer objections, service recovery, and effective communication skills.
- In addition to investing in reliable and empathetic employees, the bank should create a culture that focuses on quality customer service and customer satisfaction. Having a high-quality-supportive culture is extremely essential for service organizations. Members of the bank staff, from the highest to the lowest position, should have service quality and customer satisfaction at heart, and perform their jobs accurately to serve that purpose. With this culture instilled, the bank would be able to maintain a trust-worthy workforce that helps the customers feel safe when dealing with the bank.
- All channels operated by the bank should be easy and convenient to access since waiting is unsatisfying for customers. Therefore, the bank must think of innovative ways to create additional types of channels to connect with customers through exploiting new technological breakthroughs to reduce waiting time and service access effort for customers i.e. Internet Banking, Mobile Banking and Agency Banking.
- As for improving the tangibility dimension, bank management should invest in the interior design of the branches to portray a professional image. This is highly recommended in the sections where customers are most likely to visit, such as the front desk or counter, and managers' offices. Therefore, the physical facilities should be visually appealing and consistent with the type of service provided. In addition to that, all bank employees should maintain a professional look by dressing formally and neatly. The bank should maintain a network of enough and easily accessible ATMs and branches to serve the geographically dispersed target markets. Finally, the bank should make sure that each of the equipment used are also up-to-date, reliable and consistent.
- The bank should continuously and consistently review the service quality levels looking for discernments about what areas need more scrutiny for enhancement or retention. This would definitely aid banks in the process of formulating appropriate strategies and adapting quickly to the changing behaviour of bank customers. Moreover bank products/services should be designed using the customer perspective. This means that managers should first comprehend customer needs, wants, and desires to maximize customer satisfaction levels.
- Finally Branch Managers are advised to adopt FBSQPT1 questionnaire and use as a tool to collect customer feedback.

However, recommendations for improvements in the satisfaction gaps noticed include the following:-

- The bank should have measures of performance based on rigid measure of customer satisfaction. The measures should be regularly monitored and fed back to all internal stakeholders and a system of planning put in place to close all any gaps between actual performance and expectations;
- Teamwork should be encouraged to create the best influence of synergy by offering team building training and rewarding team efforts with group incentives;
- Winning the "hearts and minds" of employees and cultivating motivation and commitment amongst the staff should remain a key issue. The Senior Management Team must strive to share the bank's vision, mission and values and ensure that it becomes a reality, and also foster and promote an environment where people feel secure, trusted and respected;
- Timely and accurate data are a prerequisite of effective, quality-related decision-making. Quality information systems and quality databases need to be developed further in order to facilitate this accuracy. Feedback of internal and external data is a key issue;
- Most service quality problems are caused by poor communications. The bank needs to develop effective methods and channels which encourage open and honest communication between employees at all levels and customers; and
- Quality must start with education. The bank must invest to train employees at all levels in improvement skills in order to facilitate changes in behavior and attitude.

Limitations of the Study and Future Research

Limitations and constrictions exist within every field of study and research. This is simply because not one study is capable of comprehensively dealing with every aspect involved, studying all variables under all conditions and in all contexts, and using all different methodologies available. This research only adds a brick to the overall body of knowledge, thus it is only obvious that constraints exist. The following section presents all the possible limitations of the study; Limitations due to the constraint to a specific customer segment, Limitations due to the probability of having additional dimensions affecting service quality, Limitations due to the possibility of the presence of additional demographic-related differences and Limitations concerning the methodology followed.

Future research can build on this study's interesting findings and add further value through two approaches: research model consolidation and research model extension. Relative suggestions are put forward. The research model could be consolidated through eliminating or dealing with the limitations discussed above to reach a better understanding of perceived service quality and customer satisfaction in the banking industry. The research model could be easily broadened by including new ideas or variables thus transcending the research questions at hand (Annexures 1-4).

References

1. Perez M, Abad J, Carrillo G, Fernandez R (2007) Effects of service quality dimensions on behavioural purchase intentions: A study in public-sector transport. Managing Service Quality 17: 134-151.
2. Chen CF (2008) Investigating structural relationships between service quality, perceived value, satisfaction, and behavioural intentions for air passengers: Evidence from Taiwan. Transportation Research Part a: Policy and Practice 42: 709-717.
3. Dabholkar PA, Thorpe DI, Rentz JO (1996) A measure of service qualityfor retail stores: scale development and validation. Journal of the Academy of Marketing Science 24: 3-16.
4. Karatepe OM, Yavas U, Babakus E (2005) Measuring service quality of banks: scale development and validation. Journal of Retailing and Consumer Services 12: 373-383.
5. Cook S (2004) Measuring Customer Service Effectiveness. Hants: Gower Publishing Ltd.
6. Rust R, Danaher P, Varki S (2000) Using service quality data for competitive marketing decisions. International Journal of Service Industry Management 11: 438-469.
7. Bridges E, Freytag P (2009) When do firms invest in offensive and/or defensive marketing. Journal of business research 62: 745-749.
8. Athanassopoulos A, Gounaris S, Stathakopoulos V (2001) Behavioural responses to customer satisfaction: An empirical study. European Journal of Marketing 35: 687-707.
9. Lages LF, Fernandes JC (2005) The SERVPAL scale: A multi-item instrument for measuring service personal values. Journal of Business Research 58: 1562-1572.
10. Gupta A, McDanial J, Herath SK (2005) Quality management in service firms: sustaining structures of total quality service. Managing Service Quality 15: 389-402.
11. Zeithaml VA, Bitner MJ, Gremler DD (2009) Services Marketing. McGraw-Hill, New York.
12. Gronroos C (1984) A service quality model and its market implications. European Journal of Marketing 18: 36-44.
13. Kotler P, Keller KL (2006) Marketing Management. (13th edn), Upper Saddle River, Prentice Hall, NJ.
14. Gronroos C (2000) Service Management and Marketing: A Customer Relationship Management Approach. (2nd edn), Chichester: Wiley.
15. Reichheld F (1996) The Loyalty Effect. Harvard Business School Press, Boston, MA.
16. Buttle F (1996) SERVQUAL: Review, critique, research agenda. European Journal of Marketing 30: 8-32.
17. McAdam R., McLean J, Henderson J (2003) The strategic "pull" and operational "push" of total quality management in UK regional electricity service companies. International Journal of Quality and ReliabilityManagement 20: 436-457.
18. Seth N, Deshmukh SG, Vrat P (2005) Service Quality Models. An International Journal of Quality and Reliability Management 22: 913-949.
19. Edvardsson B (2005) Service quality: beyond cognitive assessment. Managing Service Quality 15: 127-131.
20. Bontis N, Booker L (2007) The mediating effect of organizational reputation on customer loyalty and service recommendation in the banking industry. Management Decision 45: 1426-1445.
21. Newman K (2001) Interrogating SERVQUAL: A critical assessment of service quality measurement in a high street retail bank. International Journal of Bank Marketing 19: 126-139.
22. Lewis BR (1991) Service quality: An international comparison of bank customers' expectations and perceptions. Journal of Marketing Management 7: 47-62.
23. Arasli H, Mehtap-Smadi S, Katircioglu ST (2005b) Customer service quality in the Greek Cypriot banking industry. Managing Service Quality 15: 41-56.
24. Marla S (1996) Demographic discriminators of service quality in the banking industry. The Journal of Services Marketing 10: 6-22.
25. Parasuraman A, Zeithaml VA, Berry (1991) Refining and reassessment of the SERVQUAL scale. Journal of Retailing 67: 420-450.
26. Caruana A (2002) Service loyalty: The effects of service quality and the mediating role of customer satisfaction. European Journal of Marketing 36: 811-828.
27. Arasli H, Katircioglu ST, Mehtap-Smadi S (2005a) A comparison of service quality in the banking industry. International Journal of Bank Marketing 23: 508-526.
28. Cronin Jr JJ, Taylor AS (1992) Measuring service quality: A re-examination and an extension. Journal of Marketing 56: 55-67.
29. Bitner MJ (1990) Evaluating service encounters: The effects of physical surroundings and employee responses. The Journal of Marketing 54: 69-82.
30. Bolton RN, Drew JH (1991) A Multistage Model of Customers' Assessments of Service Quality and Value. Journal of Consumer Research 17: 375-384.
31. Lee H, Lee Y, Yoo D (2000) The Determinants of Perceived Service Quality and its Relationship with Satisfaction. Journal of Services Marketing 14: 217-231.
32. Woodside AG, Frey LL, Daly RT (1989) Linking service quality, customer satisfaction, and behavioral intention. Journal of Health Care Marketing 9: 5-17.
33. Oliver RL (1993) Cognitive, affective and attributes bases of the satisfaction response. Journal of Consumer Research 20: 418-430.
34. Spreng RA, Mackoy RD (1996) An empirical examination of a model of perceived service quality and satisfaction. Elsevier 72: 201-214.
35. Karatepe O (2011) Service Quality, Customer Satisfaction and Loyalty: The Moderating Role of Gender. Journal of Business Economics and Management 12: 278-300.
36. Legcevic J (2008) Measuring Customer Satisfaction and Service Quality: The Case of Croatia. Journal of American Academy of Business, Cambridge 14: 123-130.
37. Lee MC, Hwan IS (2005) Relationships among Service Quality, Customer Satisfaction and Profitability in the Taiwanese Banking Industry. International Journal of Management 22: 635-648.
38. Parasuraman A, Zeithaml VA, Berry LL (1985) A conceptual model of service quality and its implications for future research. Journal of Marketing 49: 41-50.
39. Lewis BR (1989) Quality in the service sector: A review. International Journal of Bank Marketing 7: 4-12.
40. Spathis C, Pteridou E, Glaveli N (2004) Managing service quality in banks: customers' gender effects. Managing Service Quality 14: 90-102.
41. Fogli L (2006) Customer Service Delivery. Jossey-Bass, San Francisco.
42. Parasuraman A, Zeithaml V, Berry L (1988) SERVQUAL: A Multi-Scale for Measuring Consumer Perceptions of Service Quality. Journal of Retailing 64: 12-40.
43. Sureshchandar GS, Rajendran C, Anantharaman RN (2002) Determinants of customer-perceived service quality: A confirmatory factor analysis approach. Journal of Services Marketing 16: 9-34.
44. O'Neill M, Palmer A (2003) An exploratory study of the effects of experience on consumer perceptions of the service quality construct. Managing Service Quality 13: 187-196.
45. Bitner MJ, Brown SW, Meuter ML (2000) Technology infusion in service encounters. Academy of Marketing Science Journal 28: 138-149.
46. Cronin JJ, Taylor SA (1994) SERVPERF versus SERVQUAL: reconciling performance-based and perceptions-minus-expectations measurement of service quality. Journal of Marketing 58: 125-131.

47. Schiffman LG, Kanuk LL (1987) Consumer Behaviour. Englewood Cliffs NJ, Prentic-Hall.

48. Johnston R, Clark G (2005) Service Operations Management. (2nd edn), Prentice Hall.

49. Newman K (1996) Promoting service quality in British retail banking: the experience of two British clearing banks. International Journal of Bank Marketing 14: 1-9.

50. Jabnoun N, Khalifa A (2005) A customized measure of service quality in the UAE. Managing Service Quality 15: 374-88.

51. Bahia K, Nantel J (2000) A reliable and valid measurement scale for the perceived service quality of banks. International Journal of Bank Marketing 18: 84-91.

52. Guo X, Duff A, Hair M (2008) Service quality measurement in the Chinese corporate banking market. International Journal of Bank Marketing 26: 305-327.

53. Jabnoun N, Al-Tamimi HAH (2003) Measuring perceived service quality at UAE commercial banks. International Journal of Quality and Reliability Management 20: 458-472.

54. Brown TJ, Churchill GA, Peter JP (1993) Research note: Improving the measurement of service quality. Journal of Retailing 69: 127-139.

55. Zeithaml VA, Bitner MJ, Gremler DD (2003) Services marketing: Integrating customer focus across the firm. McGraw-Hill Companies.

Islamic Microfinance in Sudanese Perspective

Elsadig Musa Ahmed[1] and Anwar Ammar[2]

[1]*Faculty of Business, Multimedia University, Cyberjaya, Malaysia*

[2]*Faculty of Management, Multimedia University, Cyberjaya, Malaysia*

Abstract

Microfinance-providing affordable financial services to the poor- has been identified as an important tool in increasing the productivity of the poor and in enhancing economic development. Although conventional microfinance products have been very successful in Muslim countries the traditional microfinance contract which involves the payment of interest (riba) is strictly prohibited with the principles set forth in the Sharia of Islam. Sharia-compliant microfinance is one among many interventions designed to bring poor people into the formal financial mainstream. Islamic microfinance leaders have taken the initiatives to meet the increasing needs of the poor Muslim customers with the aim of alleviating poverty among poor Muslim people. While conventional microfinance institutions (MFIs) have expanded their operations in the last two decades, Islamic microfinance products are still quite small relative to the conventional microfinance sector. Sudan emerges as the most prominent market for Islamic banking in terms of number of Islamic banking providers. This is driven by the fact that the country requires full compliance with Sharia principles for the entire financial system. In this respect, the aim of this paper is to shed light on Islamic microfinance in Sudan.

Keywords: Islamic microfinance; Sharia-compliant; Sudan

Introduction

Sudan a country with a population of approximately 36.2 million, of which two-thirds is rural, holds abundant land and livestock, rich mineral resources and, solid manufacturing base. Despite these large endowments of natural resources, and its agricultural potential; Sudan is ranked the fifth hungriest nation in the world by the Global Hunger Index. "Much of this potential has not been realized due to long-running conflict and governance challenges; and the gains of the last growth decade have not advanced productive public investment that contributes to poverty reduction, or been widely shared [1].

The Sudanese economy is witnessing a crucial downturn since the separation of the south in 2011; Sudan loosed 75% of its oil revenue due to this secession. Growth rate of the country's GDP show declines from 3.5% in 2010 to -3.3% and -10.1% in 2011 and 2012, respectively (WDI) [2]. This is reflected on the livelihoods of many Sudanese in forms of increasing poverty statistics. Average rural poverty rates in Sudan are estimated at 58%, much higher than the national average and the urban poverty rate (47% and 27%, respectively) (National Baseline Household Survey [NBHS]. The main constraints on rural livelihoods are poor access to markets, lack of access to financial services. Unemployment is also high (19.8%) in rural than in urban (12.1%) areas (FAO 2015) Other factor contributed to the unemployment and poverty is longest civil wars and the internal conflicts across the regions.

Promotion of economic growth, reduction of poverty, achieving MDGs (Millennium Development Goals) and employment creation are among the first important policy priorities and strategy pillars of the Government of Sudan to address the challenges of high poverty, unemployment, an increase of inflation due to the secession of the South in 2011.Within this context and as articulated in theInterim Poverty Reduction Strategy Paper IPRSP for Sudan, microfinance is one of the major tools which is given due priority by the government to alleviate poverty particularly in marginalized and conflict areas [3].

Islamic Microfinance

Earlier studies of the application of Islamic finance in microfinance was carried by Rahul and Sapcanin cited by Khan [4] they demonstrate that Islamic banking, with its emphasis on risk sharing for certain products and collateral-free loans, is compatible with the needs of some micro-entrepreneurs. Islamic Microfinance is very effective and essential for creating hope for the poor and those above the poverty line as shown by the traditional microfinance, but also for the extremely poor in the community the Islamic microfinance, based on a partnership mode, is fair and does not require poor clients' payment, or lead to a loss of the livelihood of the poor in the case of project failure beyond the client's control. It also does not require strong guarantees [5]. Viable projects that are rejected by conventional lending institutions because of insufficient collateral might prove to be acceptable to Islamic banks on a profit-sharing basis. Poor Muslims remained excluded from traditional microfinance for several reasons, voluntarily due to the practices of the interest rate by conventional lending institutions which considered riba, can be excluded non-voluntarily due to inability to repay back the loan plus the interest rate accrued to it. Hence, Islamic microfinance can easily overcome these challenges due to its wide scope to cover various diversity of customer whether based on their expertise or sectorial dimension.

On the funding side, Islamic microfinance services providers can mobilize additional resources through zakat (Zakah is instruments of charity occupy a central position in the Islamic scheme of poverty alleviation) and waqf (Waqf is a trust or pious foundation), and on the lending side they mainly use financial instruments that are based on Profit and Loss Sharing (PLS) schemes such as mudarabah and musharaka (Musharaka and mudaraba are contracts which share risks and benefits) rather than loans. Qard-al-Hassan (Qard-al-Hassan is an interest-free loan that the Qur'an encourages Muslims to make to the needy) resources should be made available to Islamic microfinance

***Corresponding author:** Elsadig Musa Ahmed, Faculty of Management Multimedia University, Cyberjaya, Malaysia, E-mail: elsadig1965@gmail.com institutions to reduce the burden of high interest charges on their borrowers Zakat funds could be used to cover the default risk of microenterprises and to build capacity and skills. Takaful (Takaful is a mutual insurance) - micro-insurance – can be used for protection against unpredicted risks by borrowers. Murabaha (Murabaha is a "cost plus markup" sale contract) sale is used to finance goods. Salam is an advance payment in exchange of a future delivery, and istisna the exchange contract between a seller and a buyer.

Many studies show that poor Muslims refrain from taking interest-based microfinance products due to religious beliefs [4,6-8]. Salwana et al. [9] study revealed that traditional microfinance has failed to satisfy the Muslims communities because of its shift from poverty to focus on profit oriented business. Riwajanti [10] suggests that Islamic Microfinance should be considered contributing to poverty alleviation, financial development, and also financial inclusion because it offers unique characteristics with rich of values and human oriented. Shabrawy [11] favours the Islamic Microfinance because risk is shared between financial institutions and beneficiaries, allowing the entrepreneurs to concentrate on what they do best. A survey conducted in Azad Kashmir Pakistan by Al Huda Centre of Islamic Banking and Economics in 2011, exhibited that 99% of respondents showed strong demand for Islamic microfinance services [12].

Islamic microfinance in Sudan

Islamic microfinance is one of the essential unconventional outlets of lending that use by Islamic financial institutions to relieve the negative impact of the extreme poverty and unemployment among the people in Muslim countries. Being the majority are Muslims and more than 35 Islamic banks in addition to others non- banks Islamic financing providers, the country has become a suitable host for Islamic microfinance.

Microfinance existed in Sudan for decades as an informal economic activity. Traditionally villagers borrowed from local merchants in cash or in-kind consumption or emergency loans and paid back the loan when their anticipated funds become available. Microfinance was officially formalized by Bank of Sudan when it recognized Micro entrepreneurs and micro-enterprises in 1990 and included Artisan and skilled workers among the priority sectors to receive finance from commercial banks, especially for projects in rural areas. In 1994, micro-enterprises and low-income productive families were added together with agriculture, manufacturing, exports, mining, power generation, low cost housing, transport, and warehousing as priority sectors to receive finance from commercial banks. Social funds and donor supported programs have also been in operation for quite a while and many communities have benefited from their contributions. Islamic financial infrastructure has witnessed tremendous growth and improvement since 1989. The government transformed the existing dual economic system into Islamic financial system. This initiative has improved Islamic financial infrastructures and made enabling environment for Islamic microfinance.

Central Bank of Sudan (CBOS) in 2006, took the initiative of formulating a vision for developing and expanding microfinance sector in Sudan [13]. The vision detailed the creation of a conducive legal environment by: reviewing current law and policies of the CBOS to encourage banks to provide micro financing through i) monetary and flexible pricing policy, ii) restructuring and of some specialized bank like the Savings and Social Development Bank, and the Agriculture Bank of Sudan, iii) improving outreach of financial institutions though more bank branches and downscaling, iv) licensing of MFIs. The vision specified the requirements for a regulatory framework such as minimum capital requirements, capital adequacy, loan provisioning etc. in order to expand the financial resources. The vision also called for wholesale lending by banks to MFIs. Diversification of products and services including making use of traditional modes of finance and setting conducive modes of investments was emphasized in the vision. Institutionally; the vision called for the establishment of a MF Unit at the CBOS for regulating, supervising and promoting the development of micro finance and establishing an Apex institution outside CBOS to help in coordination among all stakeholders.

Since 2007, the policies issued annually by the CBOS incorporated specific section on microfinance. The CBOS started gradually to develop an enabling policy environment for microfinance adding elements that addresses constraints facing the sector from year to year. The major CBOS polices encompassed establishing a special MFU in CBOS to regulate, develop and supervise microfinance, encouraging banks to allocate specific resources to microfinance, resolving guarantees issues, allowing diversified Islamic modes of finance that are suitable for microfinance, developing wholesale financing and encouraging intermediaries and support services [14].

Microfinance providers

Total windows serving microfinance, both provisions of financial and non-financial services all over the country amount to 501 windows of which 466 are financial services windows and 35 windows are non-financial services. For financial services, it was found that micro are being provided by 21 banks (representing 54% of the operating banks) through 286 service windows, (i.e. 47% of the total branches providing banking services); a total number of 27 MFIs operating and under establishment through 37 windows; 18 mediators delivering their services through 87 windows (double number of the specialized MFIs windows); 33 windows of social security institutions and 23 supervision institutions. Non-financial micro financing services are provided by about 35 institutions of which: 4 are training and capacity building centres, 19 are technical support and development of small scale projects, 6 are consultancy firms and 6 are specialized collages. This is beside the informal sector spreading all over the country [3].

Outreach

Outreach is an important aspect of microfinance in view of the fact that the fundamental aim of microfinance is to reach the largest number of unnerved poor people who do not have access to financial services. Limited outreach can impact on the sustainability in terms of benefits linked to economies of scale.

The capacity of providers is very far from meeting the demand for this service. Potential microfinance customers in the country may exceed 8 million individuals, while coverage as shown by the number of clients of the microfinance services providers by this study hardly exceeds 350,000. Even discrepancies exist in the distribution between the state and between urban and rural. Most of the service providers are concentrated in the states with the lower poverty rates and are less in poverty stricken states, contrary to the policy and rationale that was behind the support for micro financing. Most windows are not in rural areas. There is only one rural micro finance service provider in all states out of 48 representing only 2% [14].

The number of clients (Banks and MFIs) increased from 244,000 in 2011 to 494,000 in 2012 and to 700,000 in 2013further to 970,000 in mid-2014, the banking MF portfolio increased from 1% in 2007 to 5% in 2013, MFIs increased from 3 in 2007 to 23 in 2013, The

MFIs' Non-Performing Loan NPL down from 6% in 2012 to 1.9% in 2013. According to IMF (2013) the number of MF borrowers went from 49,000 at end-2007 to 494,000 by 2012. The growth has occurred in both bank portfolios (49,000 to 300,000) and at the dedicated MF institutions (zero to 194,000) [15].

Penetration

UNICONS [16] study indicates that microloans are concentrated in urban areas; Microfinance Providers MFPs are far from achieving the CBOS directive for channelling 70% of their MF loans to rural areas. The Mapping (2012) shows that total windows serving microfinance, both provision of financial and non-financial services all over the country amount to 501 windows of which 466 are financial services windows and 35 windows are non-financial services. For financial services, it was found that microfinance are being provided by 21 banks (representing 54% of the operating banks) through 286 service windows, (i.e., 47% of the total branches providing banking services); a total number of 33 MFIs operating and under establishment through 37 windows; 18 mediators delivering their services through 87 windows (double number of the specialized MFIs windows); 33 windows of social security institutions and 23 supervision institutions. Non-financial microfinance services (Training and capacity building; Technical support, and consultation) are provided by about 35 institutions of which: 4 are training and capacity building centres, 19 are technical support and development of small scale projects, 6 are consultancy firms and 6 are specialized collages.

Sudan microfinance experience

The Sudanese experience showed that Islamic microfinance has a positive impact on income generating activities. Agricultural Bank of Sudan Microfinance Initiative (ABSUMI) Offer sharia-compliant credit, savings and micro insurance, particularly to women, ABSUMI was supported by three key stakeholders: the IFAD-funded Western Sudan Resources management Programme, ABS and the Microfinance Unit of the Central Bank of Sudan. As of May 2012, ABSUMI had reached 36,000 members of 6,000 households through 350 women's groups. It had mobilized savings worth US$72,000 with a client base of 4,500 borrowers and a loan portfolio of US$700,000. Its loans based on murabaha and musharaka are supporting small agricultural activities, livestock fattening and rearing, and a range of microenterprises such as petty trading, tea stalls and brick-making (IFAD [17]. Impact Evaluation (2013) study show that microfinance clients respondents reported an improvement in nutrition for their families (46.7% of clients), followed by better access to education (36.3%), better access to health services (33.8%), and purchase of property (30%). When compared to non-clients, less impact is reported by non-clients in all areas. Amira [18] study main findings revealed that participation of women in micro-credit program helps in promoting women's empowerment, in particular the economic and socio cultural dimensions of empowerment. The targeted women became economically empowered by (1) having their own income, (2) contributing to household purchases and (3) financing the education of their children; however, they did not manage to make savings to promote their micro-small operations. Fadul et al. [19] study impact of microfinance in North Kordofan, Sudan, results of the descriptive statistics show that there is a positive effect of microfinance on poverty reduction by 16%. Microfinance institutions enable poor low-income households to develop their microenterprises, which enhance their income earning capacity, and improve their living standard [20]. Maruod study was conducted to investigate the role of North Kordofan Rural Development Project (NKRDP) as a microfinance institution in women development, in Bara Locality. The results showed that 80%, 96.3%, 60%, 63.8% and 65% of the respondents mentioned that the project helped in providing education services, health services, water services, fuel services and handcrafts respectively. Results also showed that about 91.25% of the respondents had got profits from their investments.

Within the internal context, a survey for the collection of data on Islamic microfinance in the Arab region was conducted by Sanabel show that Sudan holds 70% of Islamic microfinance within the Arab region. CGAP [21], described Sudan Islamic microfinance model as: A laboratory for Islamic microfinance delivery where developments could shed light on effective Islamic microfinance practices. The IMF Sudan Article of Consultation, Sep. 2013, stated that "The microfinance sector is small but growing rapidly. The results of this push have been impressive to date. In terms of active clients, Sudan & Bangladesh are easily the global leaders in Islamic finance microfinance, with Sudan likely to take top spot given current growth rates". Issa et al. mapping exercise of Islamic banking/institutions in Africa, reveals that over 40% of these institutions are located in Sudan which imposes compliance with Shariah on the entire financial sector [22,23]. Within the three top countries with the highest Islamic microfinance outreach, two institutions dominate: (i) in Sudan the Agriculture Bank serves 75 percent of clients using Sharia-compliant products and (ii) in Bangladesh, the Islamic Bank of Bangladesh serves 67%. Task Team Leader Andres, Economist and Country Sector Coordinator with the World Bank say that "I have never seen a country so committed to microfinance as Sudan. The microfinance sector is growing in Sudan and it seems to be a healthy sector compared to other countries where the sector grows and then begins to drop."

Challenges of Islamic microfinance in Sudan

However, in spite of its successes, microfinance in Sudan has barely scratched the surface of need .Nonetheless late statistics show that the total number of clients in 2014 is 970,000 i.e. 8% coverage of total polemical clients (estimated at 7.2 mill.). Leaving more than 6 million individuals in Sudan have a need of microfinance services. This was also supported by the World Bank recent survey conducted in urban areas (state of Khartoum), showing that 1.5 million people-21% of the total population—expressed interest for such loans. Yet at the same time, 72% of the micro entrepreneurs surveyed said they had no access to formal or informal credit services [1]. In the same vein according to Asli Demirguc [24] 92% of the Sudanese adults who report having used mobile money in 2011do not have a formal account, 7% of adults have an account with formal financial institutions, 3% have saving with formal financial institutions, 2% get loans during 2011 from formal financial institutions, and only 1% have a credit card. This might be due to several reasons briefed below.

1. Sudan microfinance market maintains a high operating expense ratio at 56% (Situational Analysis 2006). Equally, for MFPs, the cost of reaching people is high. The lack of physical infrastructure increases the transaction costs for micro- and small enterprises. In addition, limited market information flows discourage market entry and formalization, particularly for subsistence farmers and rural micro entrepreneurs. Equally, for MFPs, the cost of reaching people is high. Distance of microfinance institutions [25]: is a variable that is always associated with high transaction costs. Time gaps to receive loans are 53, 59 and 86 days in Um Rwaba, Shiekan and Enuhud localities, respectively. These long time gaps have encouraged many borrowers to

drop out after one cycle of credit or not to ask for credit in the future [25].

2. There is no sustainable, i.e. profitable, microfinance model for the rural areas, which constitute about 90% of the geographical area of Sudan, mainly due to the lack of road and transportation infrastructure, lack of market access, lack of business skills and recurring conflicts [26]. Banks do not specifically target the rural poor [27]. The weakness on basic infrastructure represents big challenge, which hinders Islamic microfinance institutions to reach the poor in the very remote areas. the poor communication, and the weakness of the Sudanese basic infrastructures, microfinance providers deliberately ignoring the rural areas clients' because of the high risk/cost, only 20% of the available microfinance resources appear to be reaching the rural areas which have 80% of the microfinance market. Moreover, putting in mind the nature of Islamic finance such as Al-salam and Istisna'a in to consideration, the availability of warehouses and cheap in-land transportation are even more essential [28].

3. Limited range of microfinance products being focusing on micro loans for productive purposes only [29].

4. The diversity of Islamic microfinance beneficiaries in Sudan in terms of the geographical rural areas, climates, tribalism system, farms and non-farms based activities, livestock, trading, religious and the political climate need well trained microfinance providers staff to deal with different issues at the same times [28] most of Islamic microfinance providers currently active in Sudan are by international standards small and display serious weaknesses in operational, financial, managerial and strategic management capabilities [13].

5. Although there are many Islamic modes of finance, Murabaha seems to be the favoured mode for many providers, even though it might not be the most suitable for some clients and their projects. UNICONS (Situational analysis 2006) study show that the lending methods used by all organizations and institutions engaged in micro-credit are Murabaha (40%), Quardhasan (17.6%), hire-purchase (14.5%), Salam (10%) and Mudaraba (3.7%). Although CBOS directive places a ceiling of 30 per cent of the loan portfolio to be dedicated to murabaha and at the same time restricts the profit margin on murabaha contracts to a maximum of 9% [30]. Darfur [31] study revealed that the vast majority of microfinance loan products are traditional murabaha, Impact Evaluation [32] show that majority of clients (87.1%) have Murabaha as their Islamic mode of finance for their microfinance loan, while other modes of finance account for less than 5% each. As noted by Ibrahim in Crossfire [33] current practice of Islamic banking worldwide is heavy dependent on murabaha which is similar in practise, but not in principle to interest rate, might not be a suitable formula to combat poverty and profiting from the poor.

Conclusion and Implications

This study demonstrated Sudan's experience in implementing Islamic principles in developing Islamic microfinance. It has shown the financial models practiced in Sudan compared with the conventional microfinance models in general and those practice in the Muslim world in particular. The paper also, highlighted the Islamic microfinance implemented in Sudan and showed the shortcomings in these projects to be solved by taking the experiences of other countries into consideration.

Based on the aforementioned studies, this study concludes that there are a lot of opportunities for Islamic microfinance in Sudan and other Muslim countries if governments and regulators paid attention to the business model and profit and loss share products.

References

1. Banker Africa Issue (2014) 010.CPI Financial.
2. WDI (2013) World Development Indicators of the World Bank, Washington DC, USA.
3. (2012) Mapping, Capacity Assessment and Capacity Development of Microfinance Providers in Sudan.
4. Khan AA (2011) What role for Islamic finance in promoting development? Paper presented at the Institute of Social Studies, Netherlands.
5. Badr EDAI (2013) Islamic Microfinance-Why is it worth considering? Posted by Microfinance Nigeria, J Islam Banking Finance 30: 98.
6. IFC (2007) Syria Microfinance Market Assessment, Draft Report. Washington DC:IFC/The World Bank.
7. IFC/FINCA (2006) Business Plan for a Microfinance Institution in Jordan, Commissioned by IFC and FINCA.
8. (2006) Frankfurt School of Finance and Management (Bank akademia International), Access to Finance in Algeria, Final Report. Frankfurt: Frankfurt School of Finance and Management, Algeria.
9. Salwana H, Abdul Rahman R, Abu Bakar N, Mohd R, Muhammad AD, et al. (2013) Designing Microfinance Products for Islamic Banks in Malaysia, Middle-East Journal of Scientific Research 17: 359-366.
10. Riwajanti NI (2013) Islamic Microfinance as an Alternative for Poverty Alleviation: A Survey Afro Eurasian Studies 2: 254-271.
11. Shabrawy EA (2011) Innovation in Micro Entrepreneurship and Islamic Microfinance the model of Family bank in Bahrain, 10th International Entrepreneurship forum, Bahrain 1-18.
12. Mohsin S (2011) Overview of Microfinance. Education, Economy and Finance, Technology, International Conference on Islamic Microfinance, US.
13. Abukasawi MG, Hasssan AI (2006) Situational Analysis of the Microfinance Sector in Sudan Unicons.
14. (2013) Impact Evaluation Assessment MFI Sector in Sudan 2007-2012 Sudanese Microfinance Development Facility (SMDF) Draft Report, PACT, Sudan.
15. Badr EDAI (2014) Microfinance Sectors in two African countries-Sudan and Ethiopia, AEMFI 8th biennial conference, Hawassa, Ethiopia.
16. (2008) Unicons Evaluation of Implementation of the Strategy For Expansion and Development of The Micro Finance Sector In Sudan.
17. IFAD (2012) Islamic microfinance: Unlocking new potential to fight rural poverty From a market niche to a growing industry, Italy.
18. Amira YB (2013) The Role of Micro-credit System for Empowering Poor Women, Developing Country Studies 3: 71-84.
19. Elmola SF, Belal I (2013) The Impact of Microfinance on Rural Poor Households, Income and Vulnerability to Poverty: Case Study of North Kordofan State Tropentag 17-19.
20. Habeeb EEH, Maruod EM, Mohammed SE (2014) The Role of North Kordofan Rural Development Project (NKRDP) in Women Development in Bara locality, North Kordofan State. Int J Edu Res 2: 39-52.
21. CGAP (2008) Islamic Microfinance: An Emerging Market Niche, Focus Note No. 49.
22. Badr IEDA (2014) President, Microfinance Unit, Successful Models in Agricultural Microfinance Sponsored by the Central Bank of Sudan, (CBoSCTA-AFRACA) Revolutionizing finance for agri-chain 14-18.
23. Faye I, Triki T, Kangoye T (2013) The Islamic finance promises: Evidence from Africa. Review of Development Finance 3: 136-151.
24. Demirguc KA, Klapper L (2012) Measuring Financial Inclusion, The Global Findex Database. The World Bank Development Research Group Finance and Private Sector Development Team.
25. Ibrahim AH, Bauer S (2013) Access to Micro credit and its Impact on Farm Profit among Rural Farmers in Dryland of Sudan, Global Advanced Research Journal of Agricultural Science 2: 088-102.

26. (2006) Unicons: A Vision for the Development and Expansion of the Microfinance Sector in Sudan.

27. Sinha S (2007) Microfinance Consultant, IFAD-First National Consultative Forum on Microfinance in Sudan.

28. Ali ASE (2013) The Challenges of Islamic Trade Finance in Promoting SMEs In IDB Member Countries, Central banks of Sudan reports, J Eur Sci.

29. (2010) Evaluation report, The Savings and Social Development Bank SSDB-UNICONS, Sudan.

30. Laura A (2009) Government of Sudan Issues Directives Requiring Banks to Allocate 12 Percent of Portfolio to Microfinance, Sudan.

31. Badr IEDA (2014) Sudan-Enabling Policies, Supervisory and Regulatory Framework for Microfinance Sector, Roundtable Discussion on Regulatory and Supervisory Framework in Islamic Microfinance, Idb, Sudan University Of Science and Technology, Khartoum.

32. (2013) Country Programming Framework for Sudan "Plan of Action (2015-2019)" Resilient Livelihoods for Sustainable Agriculture, Food Security and Nutrition, FAO Representation in Sudan Khartoum.

33. (2013) Trends in Sharia-Compliant Financial Inclusion", Consultative Group to Help the Poor, CGAP, The World Bank, Focus Note.

Entrepreneurial Perceptions of Students of University of Central Punjab, Lahore and Also Finding the Hindrances They Perceive

Ambreen Khursheed*

FMS Faculty Office, University of Central Punjab, Lahore, Pakistan

Abstract

This study determines how students of University of Central Punjab, Lahore (UCP) perceive entrepreneurship as a career. The study considers four key factors that have the potential to influence the students' perception regarding entrepreneurship and thus contribute in determining their entrepreneurial intentions. The population consist of UCP students, out of which 40 students are selected by random purposive sampling who comprised of both male and female students. For collecting primary data open ended questionnaires are used. This study reveals that although majority of students have a positive perception of entrepreneurship as a career option, still there are various perceived hindrances which include fear of failure, fear of financial loss and lack of financial support. This study not only addresses the missing gap in current literature about entrepreneurship, but also provides implications for the university educators.

Keywords: Entrepreneurship; Entrepreneurial intentions; Perceptions

Introduction

Youth unemployment is one of the most severe socio-economic problems threatening developing and underdeveloped countries and Pakistan is not exceptional in this situation and this issue has become even much more bothersome in many parts of the world [1]. The solution to this problem is self-employment [2]. For developing countries entrepreneurship is the key basis of economic development [3]. Both educational research studies and economic procedures over the past two decade highlighted the significance of entrepreneurship as a profession [4-6]. The people engaged in entrepreneurism stated great advantages including independence in the choice making, high self-worth and more wisdom of manage [7].

Entrepreneurship is linked with the expansion of technological modernism and viable application and also with the enlargement of employment chances and competitiveness [5,8,9]. Haque further added that in developing countries, entrepreneurship is considered vital for enhancing employment opportunities. According to Qureshi and Sarfraz [10] limited concentration of policy makers and government has not flourished this field in Pakistan and this negligence towards entrepreneurship in the past has affected the student's intentions for selecting entrepreneurship as a career in Pakistan.

Previous research studies have established several generalizable reasons to the question that why some individuals decide to follow entrepreneurial endeavors whereas others do not. Carr and Sequeira described that by being grown in an entrepreneurial family unit extensively influences an individual's view towards entrepreneurship. On the other hand many experimental findings show that the students from underdeveloped countries have sharper and stronger entrepreneurial mind-set than those the students of developed countries. The results support the "Theory of Planned Behavior" in underdeveloped and developed countries [11]. Other research studies have examined and argued that the reason is the utility resulting from desiring self-employment over habitual career opportunities –as it is described by Kabui and Maalu that individuals will select self-employment as a professional opportunity if the value derived from this collection goes beyond the value resulting from employment.

But in the past no study has explored the entrepreneurial intentions of University of Central Punjab students by focusing on four major factors (entrepreneurial characteristics, risk perception, financial support and entrepreneurial education). So this exploratory study is conducted to fill the current gap in literature by finding the perception of students of UCP towards selection of entrepreneurship as a career option and the hindrances they perceive.

The outcomes of this research are vital for various reasons. First, awareness of desirability and feasibility of innovative venture can help public strategy decision-makers. Secondly, this study will provide a hopeful solution to joblessness youth of university alumni to become job supplier through entrepreneurial proposal than job seekers. Lastly, the findings will help in modifying strategies and educational activities carried by university accordingly.

The essential role of entrepreneurship in community is widely acknowledged by many researchers like Kuratko, Hisrich et al. Many scholars have investigated entrepreneurial intentions, interests, or tendencies of students in literature like Turker and Selcuk, Neck and Greene, Shariff and Saud [12-14]. All of them used different approaches to investigate entrepreneurship, some focus on personal background or personality characteristics of respondents, and their effect of decision of becoming an entrepreneur. Amentie et al. studied the perceived factors that affects undergraduates and specified entrepreneur as a modernizer who introduce new things and increases the growth of economy by getting benefited from the opportunities.

Naudéab et al. emphasized the importance of entrepreneurship and found that entrepreneurship involves the discovery, valuation and utilization of future goods and services. Byabashaija et al. studied entrepreneur's behavior and explained that entrepreneurs work to get achievements so they take the risks and bring innovations and the students who have strong financial background can easily

***Corresponding author:** Ambreen Khursheed, Research Associate, FMS Faculty Office, B-Building, 1st floor, University of Central Punjab, 1-Khayaban-e-Jinnah, Johar Town, Lahore, Pakistan
E-mail: ambreen.khursheed@ucp.edu.pk

run their business but those who don't have financial support face lots of problems. Many researchers focused on the importance of a persons' perception towards selection of entrepreneurship as a career. Manuere et al. studied the behaviors of youngsters and found that after graduation 30% students do not get jobs and they don't come into entrepreneurship. Because they are afraid of the criticism like what people might say that a good educated person running a shop on small scale.

Byabashaija et al. investigated the importance of education on the entrepreneurial decision and they highlighted that other than perception of a person, skills and attitudes also affects a person decision. Kabui and Maalu explored the nature of an entrepreneur by focusing on motivational aspects, personality characteristics and general thematic attitudes, habits and behaviors through word association. They concluded that a person should have some characteristics like personal control, self-confidence, independence and innovative ideas to be a successful entrepreneur.

Hong examined entrepreneurial spirits of two different university students, he found that personality characteristics and motivational factors effect entrepreneurial decision. On the other hand Wang and Wong, investigated entrepreneurial interest of students in Singapore on the basis of their personal background and discovered that willingness for going into entrepreneurship is high when an individual's family has a business experience and level of business education is high. Malebana and Swanepoel studied the relationship between the exposure of entrepreneurial education and entrepreneurial self-efficacy and found that self-efficacy is one of the primary factors for becoming a successful entrepreneur. Audretsch and Keilbach [4] highlighted the importance of entrepreneurial education by stating that the proper entrepreneurial education is basic remedy of unemployment and social crisis. From the literature following research questions are developed.

The central research question of this study is the determination of the factors that influences a student's decision of becoming an entrepreneur. The study develops four research questions, each of which will highlight four key factors affecting students' perception for becoming an entrepreneur.

- 1: What kind of entrepreneurial characteristics moves entrepreneurial intentions of students?
- 2: What is the role of risk perception in creating entrepreneurial intentions among students?
- 3: How strong financial background of students contributes in having entrepreneurial intentions among students?
- 4: How proper entrepreneurial education drives entrepreneurial intentions?

First research question addresses the issue that what kind of entrepreneurial characteristics drives a student's decision of selection entrepreneurship as a career. The second research question determines in what way risk perception of students moves entrepreneurial intentions of students. The third research question explored how financial assistance leads to any change in the decision of students of becoming an entrepreneur. As Pieters et al. explained that obtaining desired amount of finances for a new launch is an issue which leads possible entrepreneurs to join employment and concluded that finance directly affects entrepreneurial intentions. The last research question explored that how entrepreneurial education can derive an entrepreneurial intentions of students.

Research Methodology

This is a case study of University of Central Punjab which focuses at assessing the entrepreneurial intentions of potential last year students of MBA and M.Phil./MS program (accounting and finance department). A qualitative approach is selected for this study because it proposes the most appropriate technique to evaluate the intellectual illustration of entrepreneurial intentions as detained by individuals [15].

The population of this research comprise of all students of UCP (business school) and the data for this study is collected from 40 students selected by doing purposive random sampling (20 students from MS/M.Phil. and 20 students from MBA last year are selected). Out of 40 students 22 are female and 18 are male students. Self-administered open ended (40) questionnaires were delivered to the students randomly. Questionnaire included questions about selected four factors that are vital elements in determining a student's decision of becoming an entrepreneur and analysis of data is done to assess the entrepreneurial perceptions of students of UCP. The response rate is 100% in this study as all questionnaires are filled by the respondents.

Findings and Discussion

In response to the first research question that is about entrepreneurial characteristics. Majority (70%) of students of MBA program and (60%) students of MS/M.Phil. program have the opinion that an individual who possess entrepreneurial skills like confidence, self-efficacy and self-control can easily start a new venture. Few examples of student's perception are;

- "I am a focused person and I trust my abilities. I believe that a person with strong entrepreneurial characteristics like confidence, self-efficacy and self-control can easily become a successful entrepreneur."
- "Self-efficacy is one of the most important skill for starting and running a new venture."
- "In my view confidence and professional skills are the basic requirement for becoming an entrepreneur."

While minority of students responded that they lack confidence, professional skills and self-efficacy and they don't consider these skills are important for becoming an entrepreneur and they prefer job over running own business. While in response to the second question majority (80%) of students of MBA program and (65%) students of MS/M.Phil. program responded that they don't perceive risk as a hurdle in their career. Few examples of student's perception are;

- "I consider risk as a challenge and a key to success in entrepreneurial career."
- "I would take risk till the end in order to be a successful entrepreneur."
- "Risk is not a hurdle, it should be managed properly in order to become a successful entrepreneur."

While a small number of students responded that they would never take risk due to the fear of failure, fear of financial loss and they consider these risks as a biggest obstacle in their career. In answer to third question (55%) of MBA program students and (60%) students of MS/M.Phil. program have the opinion that strong financial background contributes a lot in starting a new venture as they think finance is one of the key element required for stating a new entrepreneurial project. Few examples of student's perception are;

- "Finance is blood of every business and no one can initiate its own venture without having adequate financial sources."
- "Without financial support no one can start and manage a new venture."
- "With adequate financial resources an entrepreneur can face any challenge in his career."

While 45% of students consider that strong financial background don't help in establishing a successful business because they consider having professional skills is the key of becoming a successful entrepreneur not the finance. In response to fourth research question (100%) students of MBA and MS/M.Phil. program expressed their opinion that proper entrepreneurial education helps a lot in becoming a successful entrepreneur. Few examples of student's perception are;

- "UCP is providing best entrepreneurial education by offering interesting courses, conducting different seminars and business plan competitions."
- "Entrepreneurial education grooms personality of an entrepreneur and also guides him that how he can practically start his own business."
- "An appropriate entrepreneurial education will boost students' skills and capability to start and run their own businesses."

From the results it can be inferred that majority of UCP students who have the opinion that possession of entrepreneurial characteristics and risk taking attitude is necessary for becoming a successful entrepreneur are highly inclined towards entrepreneurship and this result also supports the findings of Kabui and Maalu, Islam et al. and Lee and Poh-Kam Wong. Further the results also depicts that UCP students who considers that strong financial background and proper entrepreneurial education helps a lot in starting a new venture are more likely to have high entrepreneurial intentions and this outcome also supports the findings of Audretsch and Keilbach [4], Malebana and Swanepoel, AlaeGamar [16] and Wang and Wong. Thus, the outcomes of this study also support the statement made in Shapiro-Krueger model [17] which clarifies that perceived desirability is inclined towards expected outcomes of beginning a business and susceptibility to act is the tendency that encourages an individual who want to initiate a business.

Conclusion, Limitations and Future Research Directions

This is an exploratory study aimed to contribute in understanding of entrepreneurial perceptions of last year (40) students of UCP (MBA and M.Phil.) program in order to find what kind of factors effects a student's decision of becoming an entrepreneur. Open ended research questions are used to collect primary data for this study. The findings of this study revealed that majority of students from selected programs have high entrepreneurial intentions because they consider themselves to have strong entrepreneurial skills like self-efficacy, confidence and self-control, positive risk perception, strong financial background and attainment of proper entrepreneurial education.

This study is subject to some limitations. First of all this article is focused on only entrepreneurial intentions and these intentions may not convert into real behavior. Secondly this study is conducted in one of the private university (UCP) in Lahore so its results may not be generalizable for all universities in Pakistan. Finally, more research could further check the actual student's behavior for finding levels of correspondences between their intentions and impact.

This study contributes in entrepreneurship literature by enhancing the understanding of entrepreneurial intentions of UCP students and also provides a base of future research in this area. As majority of students' intensions are positively inclined towards selecting entrepreneurship as a career the findings of this study would also help UCP business school faculty to enhance students' perceived feasibility of self-employment by providing them relevant workshops and start up opportunities and they should consider more advanced teaching techniques that involve students to have enterprise experience as well as to exercise entrepreneurial directed approach in improving entrepreneurial mindset of students of UCP.

References

1. Akram S, Khan S, Nawab Khan M, Tufail M (2002) Unemployment Reasons and Its Impact on Pakistan Economy. City University Research Journal 3: 1-6.
2. Iqbal A, Melhem Y, Kokash H (2015) Readiness of the university students towards entrepreneurship in saudi private university: an exploratory study. European Scientific Journal 8: 109-131.
3. Karhunen P, Ledyaeva S (2008) Russian students' perceptions of entrepreneurship-Results of a survey in three St. Petersburg universities-Entrepreneurship Development Project. Helsinki School of Economics.
4. Audretsch D, Keilbach M (2004) Entrepreneurship and Regional Growth: An Evolutionary Interpretation. Journal of Evolutionary Economics 14: 605-616.
5. Versloot PH, Van Praag CM (2007) What is the Value of Entrepreneurship? A Review of Recent Research. Small Business Economics 29: 351-382.
6. Linan F, Rodríguez-Cohard JC, Rueda-Cantuche JM (2011) Factors affecting enterpreneurial intention levels: A role of education. International Enterpreneurship and Management Journal 7: 195-201.
7. McHugh JM, McHugh SM, Nickels WG (2010) Understanding Business Ninth Edition. McGraw-Hill Inc, NY.
8. Nystrom K (2008) Is Entrepreneurship the Salvation for Enhanced EconomicGrowth? CESIS, Royal Institute of Technology, Stockholm.
9. Thurik AR, Wennekeres A (2004) Entrepreneurship, small business and economic growth. Journal of Small Business and Enterprise Development 11: 140-149.
10. Qureshi S, Sarfraz MA (2010) Antecedents and Outcomes of Entrepreneurial Firms Marketing Capabilities: An Empirical investigation of Small Technology Based Firms. Strategic Innovation and Sustainability 6: 28-45.
11. Iakoveva T, Kolvereid L, Stephan U (2011) Entrepreneurial intentions in developing and developed countries. European Journal of Social Sciences 53: 353-370.
12. Turker D, Selcuk SS (2009) Which factors affect entrepreneurial intention of university students. European Industrial Training 33: 142-159.
13. Neck HM, Greene PG (2010) Entrepreneurship Education: Known Worlds and New Frontiers. Small Business Management 49: 55-70.
14. Shariff MN, Saud MB (2009) An attitude approach to the prediction of entrepreneurship on students at institution of higher learning in Malaysia. Business and Management 4: 1-7.
15. Roininen K, Arvola A, Lahteenmaki L (2006) Exploring consumers' perceptions of local food with two different qualitative techniques: Laddering and word association. Food Quality and Preference pp: 20-30.
16. AlaeGamar AD (2016) Entreprenuership and its link to corruption Assessment with the most recent world and country group data. African Studies and development 8: 13-20.
17. Elfving J, Brännback M, Carsrud A (2000) Toward A Contextual Model of Entrepreneurial. Journal of Risk Research 24: 23-33.

Accounting Conservatism and Corporate Performance: The Moderating Effect of the Board of Directors

Affes H and Sardouk H*

Faculty of Economics and Management of Sfax, University of Sfax, Tunisia

Abstract

The purpose of this article is to clarify the moderating effect of the board of directors in the relationship between the accounting conservatism and companies' performance. Previous studies have investigated the impact of corporate governance on the level of accounting conservatism. Our objective is to study the effect on the relationship between the level of accounting conservatism and performance of a central governance mechanism, namely, the board of directors. Using a sample of 60 French listed companies belonging to the SBF 120 index in all the period 2007-2012, we examine the effect of the size, the composition and the structure of such a mechanism on the relationship between the accounting conservatism and companies' performance. Therefore, most of our findings support the moderating impact of such a mechanism that has been ignored or left out by earlier studies.

Keywords: Board of directors; Moderating effect; Accounting conservatism; Performance

Introduction

We are currently witnessing a set of recommendations about governance and the quality of the accounting information disclosed by large companies. Such recommendations can detect the defects in order to deal with and control them [1]. In this context, accounting conservatism is a tool which is often used to assess the quality of the accounting standards. According to Cadbury and Mallin, the governance system needs a good quality of information to eliminate or reduce the information asymmetry between the company's executives and their stakeholders [2,3]. The governance systems can still counter balance the power and affect the relationship between the quality of the accounting information and performance. Its role is essential in terms of actors and tools. According to Gray, the accounting conservatism is a prudent accounting measure in the face of uncertainty of future events. This practice varies according to the European accounting or Anglo-Saxon systems [4]. Bebchuck and Roe identified two sources of dependency on corporate governance [5]. The first is guided by the structures that existed before, and the second is guided by the legal rules governing the relationships between the investors, the shareholders and the leaders. Deffains and Guigou tried to explain the persistent differences in the governance structures, especially, between the US and Europe and proposed different ways to be followed by the countries which are founded upon different legal systems [6].

According to Monks, corporate governance refers to the means by which the dominant decision makers (typically managers) are controlled by other stakeholders. The governance structure specifies the allocation of rights and responsibilities among the various participants in the corporation, such as the board, the managers, the shareholders and other stakeholders and clearly explains the rules and procedures required for decision making. It also describes the targets put in place and the necessary means to achieve these objectives and monitor performance (OECD 1999).

The empirical studies, which focused on the relationship between the governance structure and the information dissemination, concluded that there are links between some mechanisms of governance and voluntary information disclosure. Through these mechanisms, the information is involved in the alignment of the executive and stakeholders' interests. For Jacquillat, by means of the internal audit, the board ensures the control over the financial reporting [7]. On the other hand, John and Senbet and Fama argue that the characteristics of the board can have an effect on the quality of financial reporting [8,9]. Actually, the board is the main source of annual and quarterly information for the shareholders [10]. Its role main function is to actively supervise the management team and redirect it when necessary [11,12]. It comes directly from the shareholders' votes and can prompt the leaders to provide high quality information. According to Mizruchi, being a member of several boards provides administrators with an important source of information on practices and corporate policies [13]. It is a determinant positively associated with the directors' perception of their ability to contribute to board's debates [14].

Since the board is a supervisory body the effectiveness of which is essential, it would be interesting to analyze its impact on the relationship between the quality of the accounting information represented by the level of the accounting conservatism and the company's performance. In this sense, we seek to answer the following question: What is the contribution of the Board of directors to the relationship between accounting conservatism and corporate performance? For this purpose, it would be necessary to consider the moderating effect of this mechanism. Embedding this effect within our analysis helps improve the existing literature and complete the analyses dealing with this issue.

The remainder of the paper is structured as follows: we begin with a brief survey of the empirical literature. The description of the sample data and variables as well as the presentation and discusses of our empirical findings will be figured in a next part.

Literature Review and Hypothesis Development

As an internal mechanism of the governance system, the board

***Corresponding author:** Hadia Sardouk, PhD Researcher in Accounting Sciences, Faculty of Economics and Management of Sfax, University of Sfax, Tunisia, E-mail: hsardouk@ymail.com

of directors is viewed as a means of internal control that ensures the conflict resolution, the procurement and the allocation of resources as well as the determination of the strategic choices. The theoretical analysis of the board of directors, distinguishes, in particular, between the contractual (financial and partnership) and the strategic theories [15].

For the former strategies, the function of the board of directors is to discipline the leaders, whereas for the latter ones, it is rather a cognitive instrument which helps building skills. From a disciplinary perspective, the board's target is to protect the shareholders' interests [9,16,17]. It has the power to engage, assess, pay, and lay off the leaders, as well as ratify and control the strategic decisions. The intervention of the board of directors consists of the executives' incentive to be efficient either through remuneration systems (bonus, stock options...), or by threatening them with revocation. After non-quality financial communication, the board of directors can punish or consider a revocation that aims to penalize the incompetent or opportunist leaders [18].

In a spirit of a strategic perspective, the administrators' aim is rather to increase the shareholders' wealth by improving the company's competitive position. Its role is manifested by the involvement and commitment of the directors in the definition, selection and implementation of the strategies of the firm [19]. The obligation of the Council generally consists in the review and monitoring of the strategy of the undertaking [20].

Goodstein et al. defined the strategic role of the board as the major decision maker of the policy changes that will help the organization adapt to the environment significant changes [21]. The administrators are themselves elected by the general assembly [10]. They also play an ambivalent role between the shareholders' sovereignty expressed through the general assembly and the company's general direction on a daily basis [22]. The board of directors forces the leaders to unveil their strategies and limit their informational power when the information is communicated to the shareholders.

According to the major theoretical perspectives, it is clear that the quality of a board of directors is designed on the basis of its important role in the value creation. Its effect on the information quality and its corresponding empirical justifications can be summarized in the following Table 1.

However, the board of directors' effectiveness depends on its characteristics. According to John and Senbet and Fama, the size, structure and the combination of functions are the characteristics of the board of directors which may impact the information quality [8,9]. Several studies focused on the ability of the size of the board of directors to control the leader's discretion [23-25]. According to Jensen, adding an additional administrator tends to raise the control capacity of the board however its role is moderated by the marginal cost in terms of communication and decision making. Jensen proposed a moderate board size composed of 7 to 8 members [23]. The efficiency of a large board can still be limited by the communication and coordination difficulties of the board's members, which gives the leader a margin of extra freedom. For Lipton and Lorsh, the size of the board weighed down the communication process and makes it more difficult to decision making [26]. According to Zéghal et al. in a large-sized board, members often face coordination problems and a collusion risk between them [27]. Godard and Schatt found that large-sized boards are ineffective and may be fragmented after the emergence of coalitions and group conflicts and show difficulties regarding any consensus on the important decisions and generally characterized by the domination of the leaders, which reduces the protection of the interests of the shareholders [28]. Some other authors supported the idea that a small board may be more efficient [29,30]. Yermack and Eisenberg et al found that the Board's size is negatively correlated with the company's performance [24,31]. This can be explained by the coordination problems and the collusion risk which can occur between the Board's members, which complies with most of the studies [27,29,30]. On the basis of the group cohesion principles, other authors claimed that a small board can be more efficient [29,30]. Moreover, we should study the leadership structure so as to detect its impact on the information quality.

Klein showed that the structure of the board has a considerable impact on the disclosure of credible and relevant financial information [32]. According to Peasnel, Pope and Yeung and Weibach, the Board of Directors is a key mechanism to control the leadership opportunism [33,34]. It should include internal administrators and independent external directors, who can help with the decision ratification since they know the firm very well, and independent outside directors who can ensure the leaders' control. Tifafi and Dufour stated that the major role of the independent directors is to control the leaders so as to ensure the performance and safeguard the shareholders' interests [35]. In this context, the Board's effectiveness will be evaluated according to the degree of its independence from the leaders [36].

Moreover, Fama and Jensen claimed that a Board of Directors composed mainly of independent directors is deemed to be more inclined to monitor the executives [17]. Other authors found that the presence of independent outside directors on the Board reduced the agency conflicts and the opportunistic behavior proven by the leaders [37,38]. Rosentein and Wyatt argue that the presence of independent external directors positively affects the company's performance [39]. On the other hand, Weinbach, think that their presence can enhance the replacement of an ineffective leader [34]. For Charreaux, Daily and

Proposal	Hypotheses	Agency theory	Empirical justification
Board of directors	Size	Small	Abbot, Parker et Peters (2002) et Davidson et Dahalt (2002), Bedard, Coutreau et Chtourou (2001), Coulton, James et Taylor (2001), Peasnell, Pope et Young (1998), Beasley, (1996); Dechow, Sloan et Sweeney (1996); Lipton et Lorsh (1992).
Board of directors	Board of directors' independence	Large	Cormier (2007), Mezghani et Ellouze (2007), Cheng et Courtenay and Krishnamurti, (2005), Chtourou, Bédard et Courteau (2001), Chen et Jaggi (2000), Haniffa et Cooke (2000), Beasly (1996), Malone, Fries et Jones (1993), Williamson (1983), Leftiwich, Watts et Zimmerman (1981).
Board of directors	Board of directors' independence	Small	Eng et Mak (2003), Godard et Schatt (2000), Forker (1992).
Board of directors	Board of directors' independence	Neutral	Coulton, James et Taylor (2001), Wright (1996).
Board of directors	Combination of functions	Large	Labelle et Schatt (2005), Gul et Leung (2004), Wong (2001), Forker (1992).
Board of directors	Combination of functions	Small	Godard et Schatt (2004), Godard et Schatt (2003).
Board of directors	Combination of functions	Neutral	Coulton, James et Taylor (2001) et Hanifa et Cooke (2000).

Table 1: Impact of the board of directors on the information quality.

Dalton and Mizruchi and Stearns, the objective behind appointment the outside directors is to have a better control of the leader and provide the Board of Directors with skills and objective judgment, something which can only be ensured by the internal directors who are too much involved in management [40-42]. In this context, the studies of Haniffa and Cooke performed on some Malaysian listed companies stated that the presence of a positive relationship between the proportion of the independent directors and the quality of the annual report disclosure [43]. In short, internal administrators, too much involved in the company's internal management, do not have enough power to oppose the leaders' decisions. They can still be subject to their pressures to comply with their interests. Such pressure can be stronger when these administrators have some seniority within the company. In sum, the external directors are an effective tool to reduce the agency conflicts against the internal ones.

We must also study the cumulative impact of corporate executive positions and board of directors on the quality of information. In the literature on the separation of positions between the chief executive officer and the board's chairman, there are diverging opinions. In fact, some denounce this separation while others support it. According to the agency theory, to improve the monitoring level, the control and decision functions must be separated. Jensen also supports this idea and states that the dual function of the Board's leader and president helps strengthen the interest conflicts [23]. Moreover, for Jensen and Meckling and Jensen, the function duality can limit the effectiveness of the governance mechanisms and can also be a source of conflicts of interest between managers and shareholders [16,23]. Godard and Schatt found that the combination of functions allows managers to more easily defend the projects they have initiated, even if they do not create value for shareholders [28]. The separation of powers is therefore necessary to reduce the agency costs. For some researchers, such as Cannella and Lubatkin; Sridharan and Marsinko; the duality of functions is recommended since it helps avoid the miscommunication and the contradictions between the expectations and the actions and offers more flexibility to seize new opportunities [44,45]. By examining the accounting measures, Rechner and Dalton found that firms with separate management structure outperform those with combined management structure [46].

Based on the arguments cited above, we will assume that the Board of Directors and its characteristics have a moderator effect on the relationship between accounting conservatism and the enterprise's performance. Hence, the foregoing discussion suggests the following hypothesis:

H: Board of directors has a moderator effect on the relationship between accounting conservatism and the enterprise's performance.

Data and Sample Description

Study sample

Our study covers the period 2007-2012 and focuses on 60 French companies belonging to the SBF 120 index. Our choice of the study period is explained by the evolution of accounting conservatism level following the adoption of standards IFRS in 2005, particularly in the French context. Thus, our study focuses on a sample of 60 French firms observed over a period of 6 years. This will lead us to estimate panel data regression models that take into account the individual effects of companies and periods studied. In panel data, the model that takes into account the presence of heteroskedasticity and autocorrelation is the model Feasible Generalized Least Squares (FGLS) which explains our choice about using this search method. The bases "Thomson Financial", "Diane", "Worldscope" and "Dafsaliens" are the sources of our accounting data. Governance data were manually extracted from companies' annual reports available on the internet. We have eliminated the companies for which data was missing, those belonging to sectors presenting a particular functioning such as banks and those with accounting practices requiring a specific treatment. The final sample consists of 360 firm- years' observations.

Research model and measurement

To study the moderating effect of the Board of directors in the relationship between accounting conservatism and enterprise's performances, the following model will be tested:

$$PERF_{it} = \beta_0 + \beta_1 (C-SCRORE)_{it-1} + \sum \beta(1+h) X_{it-1} + \sum \beta(4+h)(C-Score)_{it-1} * X_{it-1} + \beta_8 TAILLE_{it-1}$$
$$+ \beta_9 ENDET_{it-1} + \beta_{10} Contentieux_{it-1} + \beta_{11} Verification_{it-1} + \varepsilon_{it} E$$

The indices i and t correspond, respectively to the company and the year (2007-2012).

PERF: enterprise's performance; C-Score: Accounting Conservatism; X: variables linked to the characteristics of the Board of directors.

Enterprise's performance: PERF: The review of existing empirical studies reveals the dominant place occupied by accounting measures of Performance Company's [47-50]. Our concern to compare our results with those of the majority of the research works led us to retain accounting nature indicator ROE (Return on Equity).

Accounting conservatism: C-Score: According to Khan and Watts, C-Score reflects the change in accounting conservatism between companies [51]. To estimate the conservatism level, authors fit the model of Basu [52]. The model of Basu adjusted by Khan, Watts, Ahmed and Duellman lead to the calcul of the conservatism level on each company and for each year [51,53].

Board of directors variables: X: According to Lobo and Zhou, companies are on average more conservative in their financial reports after the Sarbanes-Oxley Act [54]. For Bessieux-Ollier C, French and German companies have higher levels of conservatism that the US companies [55]. This can be explained by the characteristics of the Board of directors. In this regard, we can affirm that the agency problems lead to call for governance mechanisms as a regulator of the managers' opportunistic behavior. For the purpose of a more thorough, study of the characteristics of the Board of directors and their effect on the relationship between enterprises' performances and accounting conservatism becomes essential (Table 2).

Results and Discussions

In what follows we will discuss the obtained results about the moderator effect of the Board of directors in the relationship between conservatism and accounting performance of listed companies.

Descriptive analysis

At First, we will report the descriptive statistics belonging to the entirety of variables. We will present descriptive statistics over the period: 2007-2012 such as; Means, Median, Maximum, Minimum, Std. Dev Skewness, Kurtosis and Jarque-Bera (Table 3).

Then, we will present the descriptive statistics belonging to dichotomous variables as following Table 4.

We note that the average size of the board of directors is 12,55. Respectively, independent administrators' average is 6,380%. Indeed,

Variable	Abbreviation	Measures	Bibliographic references
		Measure of performance	
Performance	PERF	ROE=Net results/shareholders ' equity	Xu and Wang (1999), Jia et al. (2005) et Omran (2009)
		Conservatism variable	
Accounting conservatism	C-Score	C-SCORE i,t=λ0+λ1 (SIZE i,t)+λ2((M/B) i,t)+λ3 (LEV i,t)	Basu [52] adjusted by Khan and Watts [51], Ahmed and Duellman [53]
Ratio market-to-Book	M/B	Market value/book value	Khan and Watts [51]
Size	SIZE	value log of the equity market	Khan and Watts [51]
Leverage effect	LEV	Total debts/Equity market value	Khan and Watts [51]
		Board of directors variables	
Board of Directors' size	TCA	The overall number of administrators	Zahra and Pearce (1989); John and Senbet [8]
Independent administrators	ADM_IND	The proportion of independent administrators on the Board of Directors	Hermalin and Weisbach (2003)
Dual function	CUMUL	Binary variable=1 if the CEO is at the same time the Board's Chairman and 0 if not.	Baliga, and Moyer (1996); Rechner and Dalton [46]
		Control variables	
Firm's size	TAILLE	Debt ratio=total liabilities/total assets	Boubakri et al. (2005); Mak and Kusandi (2002); Villalonga (2000)
Leverage effect	ENDET	Binary variable=1 if the company is technological and 0 otherwise	Ng et al. (2009); Sun et al. (2002)
Litigation	Contentieux	Binary variable=1 if the firm is supervised by a large Board and 0 otherwise	Field et al. (2005)
Auditing	Vérification	Binary variable 1 if the company belong to CAC 40 and 0 otherwise	Watts (2003)

Table 2: Summary of variables definitions and measurements.

	Mean	Median	Max	Min	Std. Dev.	Skewness	Kurtosis	Jarque-Bera	Probability
PERF	10,705	10,097	1,43,244	-100,459	15,675	1,428	28,555	9863,516	0,000
C_SCORE	0,133	0,126	0,362	-0,162	0,100	-0,015	2,758	0,885	0,642
ADM_IND	6,380	6,500	13,000	0,000	2,750	0,067	2,407	5,515	0,063
ENDETT	0,319	0,235	7,605	0,005	0,512	10,463	1,36,154	271005,300	0,000
LEV	0,319	0,235	7,605	0,005	0,512	10,463	1,36,154	271005,300	0,000
M/B	1,833	1,457	28,423	0,000	1,950	7,914	1,00,055	144246,600	0,000
R	0,026	0,024	0,202	0,000	0,023	2,763	20,581	5066,105	0,000
SIZE	9,489	9,646	13,544	4,257	1,507	-0,079	3,202	0,987	0,611
TAILLE	9,489	9,646	13,544	4,257	1,507	-0,079	3,202	0,987	0,611
TCA	12,556	12,000	22,000	3,000	3,580	-0,182	3,008	1,983	0,371
X/P	2,837	2,608	9,986	-9,426	2,899	-0,416	4,760	56,489	0,000

Table 3: Statistics descriptive.

	Variables dichotomiques		
	Modalités	**effectifs**	**Fréquences (%)**
Cumul	0 1	159 201	44,2 55,8
Verification	0 1	180 180	50 50
Contentieux	0 1	324 36	90 10

Table 4: Variables dichotomiques

we notice a small percentage of independent directors in French companies. The average attributable to the combination of the functions corporate executive positions and board of directors is higher than the average of separation of the two functions, respectively, 55,8 and 44,2. Accordingly, there is not a significant disparity in the intensity of the quality of accounting information measured by the degree of accounting conservatism (0,133).

Correlation analysis

Before the estimation of any linear regression, it is advisable to ensure that there is no multicollinearity among the explanatory variables. Then, some tests, such as the heteroskedasticity and the error auto-correlation tests should be conducted to reach robust estimates. To check for this problem at the level of our sample, we will calculate Pearson correlation coefficients between these variables as well as the "Variance Inflation Factor" (Table 5).

The examination of the correlation matrix shows that all the correlation coefficients are below the 0.9 limit from which usually serious multicollinearity problems start to rise. In addition, according to this table, it can be noticed that all our explanatory variables have a value of the "variance Inflation Factor" below the 5, limit suggested by Gujarati and Kennedy [56,57]. These results make us conclude that there is no serious multicollinearity problem.

Regression analysis

Our study covers a sample of 60 French companies observed over several years, which, by definition, leads to estimate the regression model defined above on panel data. Given the particular nature of the panel data, the order of some econometric steps should be necessarily followed. At first, it should be noted that the fixed effect model was rejected since regression includes invariant dummy variables in the temporal dimension. Therefore, a random model estimation was used and subsequently the 'Breusch-Pagan' test, called the "Lagrange Multiplier test for random effect" was ordered to identify whether there are or not specific effects. In other words, this test helps identify which

	Perf	C-Score	TCA	ADM_IND	CUMUL	Verif	Cont	Taille	Endet	Vif
Perf	1.000									3.33
C-Score	-0.069	1.000								4.01
TCA	0.153	-0.555	1.000							3.05
ADM_IND	-0.443	-0.358	0.475	1.000						1.52
CUMUL	-0.068	0.330	0.108	-0.087	1.000					1.33
Verif	-0.059	0.378	0.472	0.562	0.072	1.000				3.54
Cont	-0.223	-0.056	-0.194	-0.155	0.091	-0.111	1.000			4.04
Taille	-0.099	0.239	-0.608	0.5079	-0.080	0.634	-0.331	1.000		1.56
Endett	-0.026	-0.047	-0.103	-0.098	0.049	-0.166	0.106	-0.212	1.000	1.77

Table 5: Correlation Matrix and VIF test.

model to be used: the "pooled" or the random-effect model. The result of this test (Table 5) is a significant Chi-square statistics (Prob>chi2 = 0.000), which makes us confirm the existence of individual effects. Therefore, the random effect model is retained for the estimation of the various regression models. Afterwards, heteroscedasticity was tested by conducting the Breusch-Pagan test. In the context of a heteroscedasticity test, the null hypothesis is homoscedasticity, which will be the case when all the residues in regression coefficients are zero. To carry out this test, we had to regress the squared residuals resulting from the random effect model with the explanatory variables of the various regression models. As a result of this test (see Table 5), there is a significant Fisher's statistics (prob>F=0.000). This makes us reject the null hypothesis and subsequently confirm the presence of a heteroscedasticity problem. In this case, the generalized least squares method (MCG or GLS) should be used, which enables the correction. However, to implement this method, we should first identify the form of heteroscedasticity. For this reason, a modified Wald test was conducted using the STATA program. This test checks whether heteroscedasticity is inter-individual. Under the null hypothesis, the test assumes that the error variance is the same for all the individuals and the statistics follows a Chi-square of N degree of freedom (60 in our case). On the basis of the assessment of the P-value associated with the Chi-square test, the null assumption cannot be accepted. The rejection of this hypothesis does not further specify the heteroscedasticity structure. The previous heteoscedasticity conclusion remains the same without any further specification. Afterwards, to test the error autocorrelation, we proceeded with the intra-individual autocorrelation test of Wooldrigde. The results of this test (see Table 5) confirm the presence of a serial autocorrelation (Prob>F is lower than 0.05). To sum up, we can say that there are heteroskedasticity and autocorrelation problems. In panel data, the model that takes into account the presence of heteroskedasticity and autocorrelation is that of the model Feasible Generalized Least Squares (FGLS) (Table 6).

In what follows, we will interpret the FGLS estimation results of the different regression models which test the moderating effect of the Board of Directors' characteristics on the relationship between the accounting information quality measured by the level of the accounting conservatism and the company's performance. We will try to check if the impact of the accounting conservatism on the company's performance is moderated by the characteristics related to the Board of directors. In other words, this point is to check if this impact varies with respect to the size of the Board of Directors, to the directors' independence and to the function combination of the Chief Executive Officer and the Chairman of the Board of Directors.

The following table presents the FGLS estimates of the various regression models including the various variables related to the Board of Directors. From models 2 to 4, we test the interaction effect of each variable taken alone with the level of the accounting conservatism on the company's performance. Model 1 includes simultaneously all the variables related to the Board of Directors and their interactions with the conservatism level.

Concerning the moderating effect of the Board of Directors' size, it is clear that the effect of the C-score * TCA interaction is negative and significant at 10 level % for model 1 and at 1% for model 2. Such a result suggests that Board of Directors' size has a negative effect on the moderation of the relationship between the level of the accounting conservatism and the company's performance. This thesis joins John, K. and Senbet, L and Lipton and Lorsch in their study [8,26]. Authors support the negative effect of the Board of Directors' size. According to John K and Senbet L the size of the board is negatively associated with its ability to work effectively. For Lipton and Lorsch the size of the board weighed down and hinders any communication process [8,26].

Models 1 and 3 of the following table indicates that the C-score * ADM_IND interaction term is positive and weakly significant (at 10% level). Such a result suggests that Board's independence has a positive impact on the relationship between conservatism and the company's performance. Therefore, the fact that the Board of Directors is pre-dominated by independent administrators leads to the improvement of performance. This is motivated by the fact that these independent administrators being free of any managerial influence are considered the best ones to control the leaders and limit their discretionary space. These administrators are essentially guided by the protection of the shareholders' interests and the maximization of the company's value. They actively participate in the decision-making process, the control and ratification of decisions taken by the leaders, in such a way that only the value-creator projects for the shareholders should be carried out [17,58].

The study of the effect of the combination of functions of the Chief Executive Officer and the Chairman of the Board of Directors on the relationship between thee accounting conservatism and the company's performance shows that this impact is negative and significant (at a level of 1%) according to the coefficient of the C-Score * CUMUL interaction term. This result suggests that the impact of the accounting conservatism on the company's performance is less favorable in companies where the function of the CEO and of the Chairman of the Board are performed by the same person compared to the companies where there is separation of both functions. Such a conclusion is also supported by the previous literature review [28,59,60]. This is in line with the input supported by the Agency theory which considers the combination of functions as a potential source of conflicts of interest.

We can finally point out that our achieved results appear to be consistent with the studies conducted by John K and Senbet L, Lipton and Lorsch, Fama and Jensen, Zahra, Godard and Schatt, and

Cross-sectional time-series FGLS regression Coefficients: Panel Feasible Generalized Least Squares Panels: Heteroskedastic with cross-sectional correlation Number of observations=360 Number of groups=60 Time periods=6 Dependent variable: PERF				
Independent variables	**Modèle 1**	**Modèle 2**	**Modèle 3**	**Modèle 4**
	Coeff. (z-stat)	**Coeff. (z-stat)**	**Coeff. (z-stat)**	**Coeff. (z-stat)**
Constante	21,175** (1,999)	32,048*** (3,5508)	25,26*** (2,8015)	21,97*** (0,2604)
C-score	20,038*** (2,0163)	69,339*** (2,84056)	4,8284 (0,1687)	10,6955* (1,9802)
TCA	-0,1638* (-1,9719)	-0,3911*** (-3,97432)		
C-score*TCA	4,078 (1,0274)	-5,3516** (-2,0629)		
ADM_IND	0,652*** (2,2671)		0,2362* (1,7624)	
C-score* ADM_IND	0,2934* (1,9645)		1,5516* (2,0896)	
CUMUL	-4,763*** (-2,2688)			-2,5551* (-1,8532)
C-score*CUMUL	-27,965*** (-2,4266)			-11,722** (-2,068)
VERIFICATION	0,08811 (0,02932)	-0,4442 (-0,16402)	-0,567 (-0,2057)	-0,9895 (-0,3659)
CONTENTIEUX	-9,3624** (-2,4269)	-10,3677*** (-2,9212)	-9,824*** (-2,7202)	-10,107*** (-2,8054)
TAILLE	-1,42319 (-1,2584)	-1,5622 (-1,6053)	-1,3455 (-1,3582)	-1,2322 (-1,3754)
ENDET	-0,24288 (-0,15673)	-0,0875 (-0,0594)	-0,11945 (-,08098)	-0,1421 (-0,0969)
Breusch-Pagan Lagrangian Multiplier Test for Random Effects				
Chi2 *Prob>chi2*	52,75 (0,000)	67,27 (0,000)	72,36 (0,000)	68,59 (0,000)
Breusch-Pagan Test for Heteroskedasticity				
F-statistic Prob>F	1104,35 (0,000)	906,66 (0,000)	666,43 (0,000)	587,66 (0,000)
Wald Test for Heteroskedasticity				
Wald chi2 *Prob>chi2*	304,35 (0,000)	33,02 (0,000)	43,02 (0,000)	43,82 (0,000)
Wooldridge Test for Autocorrelation				
F-statistic Prob>F	70,9553 (0,00000)	11,9592 (0,000808)	11,3087 (0,000985)	17,0685 (0,00003)
*Significant at 10% level ** Significant at 5% level *** Significant at 1% level				

Table 6: The results of FGLS estimates for the analysis of the moderating effects of the Board of Directors on the relationship between the accounting information quality and the company's performance.

Boyd which have demonstrates the impact of Board of Directors on the performance and accounting conservatism within companies [8,17,26,28,58-60].

Conclusion

In this paper, we tried to present the moderating effect of the Board of Directors on the relationship between the accounting conservatism and the company's performance. The objective of this work is twin. We have apprehended the effect of accounting conservatism on the performance of the company and identify the moderating effect of the board of directors on the relationship between the accounting conservatism and the performance of the company. The practical implication of our study consists in studying the effect of the interaction of the Board of Directors and the accounting conservatism on the company's performance. In this sense our moderating variable namely the board of Directors modulates the direction and the force of the effect of accounting conservatism on the company's performance. Identify the moderating effect of the board of Directors is of a great importance since moderation increases the significance of the relationship between accounting conservatism and company performance. Yet the ignorance of such effect may lead to the conclusion about the likely impact of the low level of accounting conservatism on the company's performance. An empirical study was conducted to test the validity of the assumptions which emerged from the previous literature to confirm or overturn the reached conclusions. Our results are in line with those of some previous studies. In fact, they enable to decide on the importance of the Board of Directors as a central mechanism of governance in the moderation of the relationship between the accounting conservatism and the company's performance. As a result, despite the found results, it seems that the recourse to the independent directors seems more effective in moderating the relationship between the accounting conservatism and the company's performance. Moreover, it would be more efficient to separate the CEO and the Board Chairman's to better moderate the relationship between the accounting conservatism and the company's performance. Similarly, small tips would be more effective in moderating the relationship between the accounting conservatism and the company's performance.

References

1. Wirtz P (2004) Meilleures pratiques de gouvernance, théorie de la firme et modèles de création de valeur: 0055ne appréciation critique des codes de bonne conduite. Université Lumière Lyon II, France.
2. Cadbury A (1999) What are the Trends in Corporate Governance? How will they affect your Company? Long Range Planning 32: 12-19.
3. Mallin C (2002) The Relationship between Corporate Governance, Transparency and Financial Disclosure. Corporate Governance: An International Review 10: 253-255.
4. Gray 0042 (1998) Collaboration: The constructive management of differences. IN Hickman GR (Ed) Leading Organizations: Perspectives for a new era. Sage Publications pp: 467-480.
5. Bebchuk LA, Roe MJ (1999) A Theory of Path Dependence in Corporate Ownership and Governance. Stanford Law Review 52: 127-170.
6. Deffains B, Guigou JD (2002) Droit, gouvernement d'entreprise et marchés de capitaux. Revue d'Economie Politique 112: 791-821.
7. Jacquillat B (2002) Les maillons faibles de la gouvernance. Sociétal 62-67.
8. John K, Sebnet LW (1998) Corporate governance and board effectiveness. Journal of Banking and Finance 22: 371-403.
9. Fama E (1980) Agency problems and the theory of the firm. Journal of Political Economy 88: 288-307.
10. Pigé B, Xavier V (2005) Financial reporting and corporate governance: the meaning of IFRS. EMS pp: 145.
11. Charreaux G (1997) L'entreprise publique est-elle nécessairement mois efficace? Revue Française de Gestion pp: 38-56.
12. Morck R, Shleifer A, Vishny R (1989) Alternative mechanisms for corporate control. American Economic Review 79: 842-852.
13. Mizruchi MS (1996) What Do Interlocks Do? An Analysis, Critique, and Assessment of Research on Interlocking Directories. Annual Review of Sociology 22: 271-298.
14. Carpenter MA, Westphal JD (2001) The strategic context of external network ties: Examining the impact of director appointments on board involvement in strategic decision making. Academy of Management Journal 44: 639-660.
15. Charreaux G (2000) Le conseil d'administration dans les théories de la gouvernance. Revue du Financier 20: 6-17.
16. Jensen M, Meckling W (1976) Theory of the firm: managerial behavior, agency costs and ownership structure. Journal of Financial Economics 3: 305-360.
17. Fama E, Jensen M (1983) Separation of ownership and control. Journal of Law and Economics 26: 301-325.
18. Ebondo Wa Mandzila (2006) Corporate governance: An approach by the audit and internal control. Management Business.
19. Judge W, Jr Q, Zeithaml CP (1992) Institutional and strategic choice perspectives on board involvement in the strategic decision process. Academy of Management Journal 35: 766-794.
20. Stiles P, Taylor B (2001) Boards at work: How directors view their roles and responsibilities. Oxford University Press, New York.
21. Goodstein J, Gautam K, Boeker W (1994) The Effects of Board Size and Diversity on Strategic Change. Strategic Management Journal 15: 241-250.
22. Pérez R (2003) la gouvernance de l'entreprise. Ed La Découverte.
23. Jensen M (1993) The modern industrial revolution, exit and the failure of internal control systems. Journal of Finance 48: 831-880.
24. Yermack D (1996) Higher market valuation of companies with small board of directors. Journal of Financial Economics 40: 185-211.
25. Patton A, Baker J (1987) Why do not directors rock the boat? Harvard Business Review 65: 10-12.
26. Lipton M, Lorsh J (1992) A modest proposal for improved corporate governance. Business Lawyer 48: 59-77.
27. Zéghal D, Marrakchi S, Makni Fourati Y (2005) Impact de la structure de propriété et de l'endettement sur les caractéristiques du conseil d'administration: étude empirique dans le contexte d'un pays émergent. 3rd International Finance Conférence, IFC3, Hammamet, Tunisie.
28. Godard L, Schatt A (2004) Les déterminants de la qualité des conseils d'administration français. Université de Franche-Comté, France.
29. Bantel KA, Jackson SE (1989) Top management and innovations in banking: Does the composition of the top team make a difference? Strategic Management Journal 10: 107-124.
30. Brown W, Mahoney M (1992) Acquisition performance and corporate board composition. Working Paper, Clemson University.
31. Eisenberg T (1998) larger board size and decreasing firm value in small firms. Journal of Financial Economics 48: 35-54.
32. Klein A (2002) Audit committee, board of director characteristics, and earnings management. Journal of Accounting and Economics 33: 375-400.
33. Peasnell KV, Pope PF, Yeung S (1998) Outside directors, board effectiveness and earning management. Working paper Lancaster University.
34. Weinbach RW (1998) The social worker as manager: A practical guide to success. Allyn and Bacon, Boston.
35. Tifafi F, Dufour D (2006) Une analyse de la présence d'administrateurs indépendants au sein du conseil d'administration.
36. Boujenoui, Ben Amar (2006) Qualité de la communication d'information au sujet des pratiques de gouvernance d'entreprise: le cas canadien. Working Paper, 5ième Congrès International de Gouvernance d'Entreprise: le cas Canadien, Mai pp: 1-20.
37. Dechow PM, Sloan RG, Sweeney AP (1996) Causes and consequences of earnings misstatement: An analysis of firms subject to enforcement actions by the SEC. Contemporary Accounting Research 13: 1-36.
38. Beasley MS (1996) An empirical analysis of the relation between the board of director composition and financial statement fraud. The Accounting Review pp: 433-465.
39. Rosenstein S, Wyatt JG (1990) Outside Directors, Board Independence, and Shareholder Wealth. Journal of Financial Economics 26: 175-191.
40. Charreaux G (1991) Structures de propriété, relation d'agence et performance financière Ownership structures, agency relationship and financial performance. Revue Economique 42: 521-552.
41. Daily CM, Dalton DR (1993) Board of Directors Leadership and Structure: Control and Performance Implications. Entrepreneurship Theory and Practice Spring pp: 65-81.
42. Mizruchi MS, Stearns LB (1993) Board composition and corporate financing: The impact of financial institution representation on borrowing. Academy of Management Journal 36: 603-618.
43. Haniffa R, Cooke T (2000) Culture, corporate governance and disclosure in Malaysian corporations. Document de travail.
44. Cannella A, Lubatkin M (1993) Succession as a socio-political process: Internal impediments to outsider succession. Academy of Management Journal 36: 763-793.
45. Sridharan, UV, Marsinko A (1997) CEO duality in the paper and forest products Industry. Journal of Finance and Strategic Decisions 10: 59-65.
46. Rechner P, Dalton D (1991) CEO duality and organizational performance: a longitudinal analysis. Strategic Management Journal 12: 155-160.
47. Megginson WL, Nash RC, Randernborgh MV (1994) The Financial and Operating Performance of Newly Privatized Firms: An International Empirical Analysis. Journal of Finance 49: 403-452.
48. Alexandre H, Charreaux G (2004) L'efficacité des privatisations françaises : une vision dynamique à travers la théorie de la gouvernance. Revue économique 55: 791-821.
49. Aussenegg W, Jelic K (2006) Operating Performance of Newly Privatized Firms in Central European Transition Economies. European Financial Management 13: 853-879.
50. Kang C (2009) Privatization and production efficiency in Taiwan's telecommunications industry. Telecommunications Policy 33: 495-505.
51. Khan M, Watts RL (2009) Estimation and validation of a firm-Year Measure of Conservatism. Journal of Accounting & Economics 48: 132-150.

52. Basu S (1997) The conservatism principle and the asymmetric timeliness of earnings. Journal of Accounting and Economics 24: 3-37.

53. Ahmed A, Duellman S (2013) Managerial overconfidence and accounting conservatism. Journal of Accounting Research 51: 1-30.

54. Lobo G, Zhou J (2006) Did conservatism in financial reporting increase after the Sarbanes- Oxley Act? Initial evidence. Accounting Horizons 20: 57-73.

55. Bessieux-Ollier C (2006) Les actifs courants. In: Missonier-Piera F, Dick W (eds.) Comptabilité financière en IFRS: 67-99.

56. Gujarati D (1995) Basic Econometrics. McGraw-Hill International Edition, New York.

57. Kennedy P (1998) A guide to econometrics. Blackwell, Oxford.

58. Zahra SA (1996) Governance, ownership, and corporate entrepreneurship: The moderating impact of industry technological opportunities. Academy of Management Journal 39: 1713-1735.

59. Godard L, Schatt A (2003) Faut-il limiter le cumul des fonctions dans les conseils d'administration? Gouvernance, à paraître.

60. Boyd BK (1995) CEO duality and firm performance: A contingency model. Strategic Management Journal 16: 301-312.

11

Micro Takaful Insurance as a Tool to Guaranteeing Financing and Protecting Micro Enterprises

Ahmed MH*

Risk Management & Insurance,Arab East Colleges, BusinessAdministration Department, KSA, SaudiArabia

Abstract

Micro Takaful insurance is considered an important incentive for the protection and financing of micro enterprise and low income families. Therefore, it encourages banks to finance these micro enterprises. Micro Takaful insurance mainly supports protecting micro enterprises by using Micro Takaful insurance to aid in financing these enterprises which results in higher return on investment and growth in developing countries.

Micro Takaful insurance should be the corner stone for development in developing countries since it provides the availability to finance catastrophe victims and supporting micro enterprises mainly in agriculture industry. Also, it targets the people living in isolated areas or in difficult living circumstances by supporting them in facing the risks they face, and as a result, it is an effective tools for facing poverty in developing countries.

It is fair to say that the success of micro finance- which is certainly supported by Micro Takaful insurance- is a positive indicator on the availability of protecting the poor people, saving their investments in an economical way, and supporting social security networks. We remind Takaful Insurance Companies that by practicing in Micro Takaful insurance, they are performing their social responsibility towards the society they live in.

We will study Micro Takaful insurance through the following sections:

Section One: Micro Takaful Insurance: its definition, origin, importance and benefits.

Section Two: Micro Takaful Insurance: covered risks and its characteristics.

Section Three: The importance of Micro Takaful Insurance for micro enterprise finance.

Section Four: Micro Takaful Insurance's international experience and its marketing methods.

Section Five: Micro Takaful Insurance's future, success requirements and challenges.

Section Six: Results and Recommendations.

Keywords: Micro insurance; Micro Takaful insurance; Micro finance; Micro enterprises; Economic development; Low income people

Introduction

Micro Takaful Insurance: Its definition, origin, importance and benefits

Definition of micro Takaful insurance: Micro Takaful insurance is a contract whereby the operator (insurer) undertakes as an agent of the participants (insured/policy holders) to pay the participant (insured) of the beneficiary a given sum of money or any other indemnity when the risk insured against occurs. The participant (insured) pays the contribution (premium) to the insurer on a donation basis.

Finally, it is the Shari 'a compliant version of Micro insurance.

The Main Differences between Takaful and Micro Takaful Insurance are:

1. Micro Takaful insurance provide protection mainly to the poor people,

2. Micro Takaful insurance provide protection mainly against specific risks,

3. Micro Takaful insurance help poor people to get finance,

4. Micro Takaful insurance is based on brotherhood and solidarity,

5. Micro Takaful insurance is sold through convenient and well-trusted delivery channels,

6. Micro Takaful insurance links with financial services and other services and purchases,

7. Micro Takaful insurance requires a large risk pool,

8. Micro Takaful insurance in most cases need subsidy from the government, charity organizations or the insurance companies (Corporate Social Responsibility) and can benefit from Zakat.

The concept and the origin of micro Takaful insurance: Micro Takaful insurance is not a new concept; it is a new name for a very old practice, a technique intended to provide protection against the risks, where the poor societies in the past developed informal insurance mechanisms to face the risks resulting from: selling assets, money transfers and diversifying crops. Also there was a form of group self-

***Corresponding author:** Mamdouh Hamza Ahmed, Professor of Risk Management and Insurance, Arab East Colleges, Business Administration Department, Fellow of The American Risk and Insurance Management Society (RIMS), KSA, Saudi Arabia, E-mail: nhassan230@yahoo.com

insurance in Africa and Muslim communities for wedding, death or any other unpleasant events [1].

Pro-poor Micro finance institutions (MFIs) have been came into existence in the early seventies to the semi-formal sector. Then Modern micro-insurance was developed to accompany the development of the MFI's and NGO's in developing countries; where their success has led to the recognition that poor people can and want to save.

The importance of micro Takaful insurance: There is an urgent, necessary and immediate need for Micro Takaful Insurance where a large portion of those who are below the poverty line live in Muslim countries and nearly 50% of the developing countries are located in countries with predominantly Muslim [2]. These countries characterized by low insurance penetration (which represents the ratio of insurance premiums to GDP), adding to that the religion plays an important and central role in the lives of the poor, and finally Takaful insurance in general, and by subsequently Micro Takaful insurance comply with the roles and teachings of Islam [3].

Keep in mind that micro Takaful insurance is so important that any funding can't be done without it, so it fills the existing gap in microfinance with respect to the need for the availability of security/collateral needed for poor segment on one hand- which represents an impediment to access to finance - and to provide adequate security to financing institutions against the risk of default on the other hand. Micro Takaful insurance encourage financial institutions to finance this category and thus contribute to the reduction of poverty on one hand and turning a large number of the unemployed poor and destitute segment to a working-one and well-off on the other hand. This will reduce the pressure on the state to provide financial assistance to this category forever. So micro Takaful insurance will helps to guarantee loan financiers and works to spread the culture of social responsibility and limit the economic risks and help to eradicate poverty.

The benefits of micro Takaful insurance

The main benefits of Micro Takaful Insurance are [4]:

1. Micro Takaful insurance help guaranteeing loans to financiers.

2. Micro Takaful insurance help reducing the cost of insurance and therefore low income people can afford its premiums.

3. Benefiting from the advantage of other insurance services (risk control and loss reduction).

4. Policyholders would participate in surplus in the event of it accomplished.

5. Limits the wasted economic energy of a large segment of society.

6. Helps in spreading the culture of social responsibility.

7. Contributes to the reduction of poverty and even improve the standard of living for the poor and low-income people.

8. Reinforcing cooperation and solidarity and its reference in all transaction would be the principles of Islamic law (Shari'ah), therefore it would be an alternative to traditional insurance.

The risks it covers and its distinctive characteristics

Members of the community are divided according to their income level and required type of insurance into three groups [2,5]:

First Group: Individuals with very low incomes (less than $ 1.25 per day according to the World Bank definition): They can buy micro insurance, whether private insurance or public insurance or private/public insurance. The number of this group reaches 1.4 billion people.

Second Group: Individuals with low income (1.25-$4 per day): They can buy commercial micro insurance (Press release Munich Re, ILO, 10th of April 2012).

Third: the rest of society: They can buy traditional insurance [6-9].

And bear in mind that there are approximately 4 billion potential customers for the insurance industry with estimated gross written premiums $ 40 billion (Sigma, Swiss Re 6/10), while the number of those who already have micro insurance is estimated to 500 million insured (Munich Re Foundation website: http://www.munichrefoundation.org/StiftungsWebsite/Topics/PovertyAndMicroinsurance/default.htm).

The most important risks that the poor people are exposed to: The poor people (less than $4 per day) and those who are below the poverty line (less than $1.25 per day) are exposed to many risks the most important of them are:

-Sickness, death or disability of the family breadwinner.

-Natural disaster, climatic changes (drought)

-Fire or theft of assets which represent the main source of income.

-Loss of job.

-Frequency of claims/disasters in some areas greater for this category.

The most important types of insurance needed by the poor people and provided by micro Takaful insurance:

a) Type I: Life Insurance:

-Term insurance [10].

-Credit insurance for small loans from the risk of death.

-Disability insurance.

-Savings insurance.

b) Type II: Medical Insurance:

-Treatment costs and hospital stay.

-Serious and chronic diseases.

-Loss of income due to illness.

c) Type III: Agricultural Insurance:

-Crops insurance.

-Animals and livestock.

d) Type IV: Assets and Property Insurance:

-Homeowners Insurance.

-Small and micro enterprises Insurance.

As availability of savings and credit facilities will help the poor to face and overcome unforeseen losses, but that due to the high recurrence of accidents and disasters in the areas where this category live, and a higher claims rate on one hand, and the ability to save or borrow is very limited or non-existent on the other hand. Beside the death or illness or disability of the head of household means inability to pay any outstanding balances of debt, so the insurance can play an important role, even it will be the only resort and the most effective way to confront risks to this category and at the same time maintaining optimum utilization of assets, savings and loans [11].

Takaful insurance is considered one of the economic services sectors that are expected to experience an increasing growth in the coming years at rates ranging between 20-25%, especially with the presence of a fertile environment for the growth. This sector is characterized by plenty of population and the increasing demand for Islamic financial products and services. Among the 100 poorest countries in the world there are 23 countries do not have any micro insurance activity, and out of the 2.5 billion poor around the world, there were only eight million beneficiaries of one form of micro insurance [12].

The following table shows the states that have at least one type of micro insurance [13-15] (Table 1).

The main characteristics of micro Takaful insurance: Takaful insurance is characterized as a mutual insurance as well as its commitment to Islamic Shari'ah/law, but micro Takaful insurance in addition to that is characterized by the following:

1. It focuses and concentrates on the poor and marginalized segment that is capable for production, but is not able to get the funding.

2. It targets a segment that represents a large segment of society that is dangerous to it and can be converted into positive and productive factor.

3. It needs and can benefit from grants, donations and Zakat.

4. It saves for the state a large part of aids and subsidies provided to this segment of society, which does not change its status and need help on an ongoing basis, but it will be turned into a productive and self reliant by benefiting from micro Takaful insurance and consequently from micro finance.

5. It meets the urgent need for Islamic countries, which is located mostly within the poorer countries as it helps her cope and reduce poverty states.

6. Its premium does not depend on just the cost as it is subsidized.

Types of Insurance	States
Life/Endowment	-India, Bangladesh, Sri Lanka, Nepal, Vietnam, Pakistan, Indonesia, Laos -East Africa, South Africa, West Africa -Colombia, Guatemala, Mexico, Nicaragua
Health/Critical Illness	-India, Bangladesh, Philippines, Cambodia, China -East Africa, South Africa, West Africa -Colombia, Mexico -Georgia, Russia
Crop/Weather	-India -East Africa, North Africa -Mexico, Nicaragua
Property/Asset/Livestock	-India, Nepal, Bangladesh -East Africa -Albania
Funeral	-East Africa, South Africa, West Africa -Colombia, Mexico
Integrated Package	India
Rural Insurance Schemes	India
Group Personal Accident	West Africa
Unemployment	East Africa
Flood	China

Table 1: The states that have at least one type of micro insurance.

7. It is often available and easily accessed by targeted segment, and it understands and takes into account the nature of this segment [16].

The main conditions to be met in micro Takaful insurance:

1. Simplicity: its products should be designed to suit different categories of this group.

2. Cost: it must be reasonable for financial capabilities of this group.

3. Ease: it must be easy to be accessed to for all categories of this segment.

The importance of micro Takaful insurance for micro finance

Micro Takaful Insurance represents lifeblood of micro finance, and we will clarify the relationship between them as follow:

The relationship between micro insurance and micro finance: Takaful insurance market is a promising one, especially if we take into account the existence of nearly one billion borrowers in the micro finance system, which is targeted by micro Takaful insurance.

The following diagram explains the relationship between micro finance and the micro Takaful insurance and the relationship between both of them and reduction of poverty and achievement of security, safety and development [17] (Figure 1).

It is clear from the above diagram that both micro finance and micro insurance are contributing in fighting poverty, reducing its effects and achieving security and development where:

-Micro finance: increase productivity, creates new jobs and composition of assets.

-Micro insurance: raise awareness, protect assets and manage them in well manner and indemnify losses when they occur.

The difference between traditional insurance and micro insurance: There are several differences between traditional insurance and micro insurance, the following table shows the most important differences between them [2] (Table 2).

The difference between Takaful insurance and micro Takaful insurance: There are several differences between micro insurance and micro Takaful insurance, the following table shows the most important differences between both of them [18-23] (Table 3).

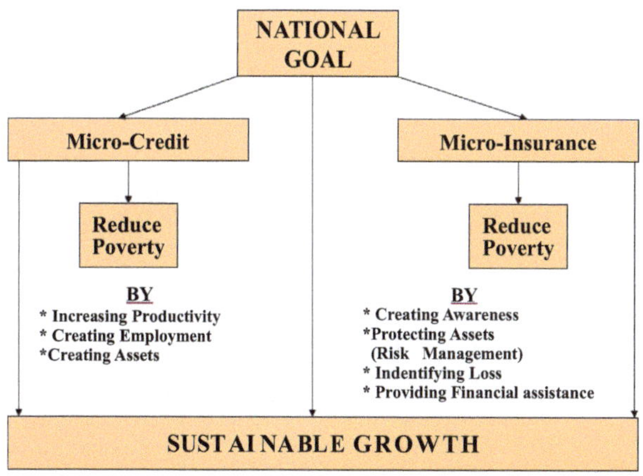

Figure 1: Relationship between micro finance and the micro Takaful insurance.

Consideration	Micro Insurance	Traditional Insurance
Target Market	- Low income individuals - Extremely limited insurance awareness/knowledge	- High and medium income individuals - market is largely aware of insurance benefits
Product design	- Simple product design with easy to understand features - Community of group pricing: limited actuarial data	- Multiple coverage and features - Risk based pricing driven by multiple parameters, good data quality
Marketing and Distribution	- Innovative distribution with multiple tie- up - Usually sold as combined product through microfinance institutions	- Employs conventional channels including agents, banks, internet - Insurance sold by licensed intermediaries
Underwriting	- Simple underwriting practices (often no screening), small sum assured - Simple policy language with minimal or no exclusions	- Comprehensive underwriting: large sum assured - Complex language with multiple exclusions and terms&conditions
Administration	- Irregular premium payments by cash or bundles with other products	- Regular payments paid by cheque, direct bank debit, credit card
Claims Handling	- Simple and quick claims turnaround process: limited documentation	- Comprehensive process: detailed documentation
Asset Management	- As per regulatory norms of investment rules of risk carrier	- As per regulatory norms of investment rules of risk carrier

Table 2: Difference between Traditional Insurance and Micro Insurance.

Consideration	Takaful Insurance	Micro Takaful Insurance
Can it cover high risks?	Normally excluded	Yes
Is it an extension of social insurance?	No	Yes
What about preexisting conditions?	Excluded	Difficult to exclude
Customer segmentation	Formal economy, mostly employed or self-employed	Informal economy, outside the social insurance coverage
Affordability considerations	Upper- to middle-income classes	Bottom of the income and social pyramid; subsidies needed from *zakat* funds, government, donor agencies
Underwriting considerations	Easier to mitigate adverse selection and exposure to fraud	Need to mitigate risk from adverse selection and fraud through links with economic benefits of microcredit, microfinance, or schemes for community and affinity groups
Distribution	Agency, brokers, commercial banks, direct, electronic	Microfinance institutions, rural banks, mosques; no brokers

Table 3: Difference between Takaful Insurance and Micro Takaful Insurance.

Micro insurance aims to reduce poverty and help those who are prone to confront it and not to fall into the clutches. It also provides service to a large segment of the society which no other one can provide it to them. In fact, this important producing segment of low-income which owns and/or works in small and micro-enterprises, which represent a large proportion of society in both developing and poor countries, could be protected by one of two methods [16]:

a) First: Commercial Insurance, which Aims to Profit.

b) Second: Micro Takaful Insurance which is based on Solidarity and takes into Account the Economic and Social Conditions for this Category.

In general, even though both methods are required, however, the first method is not suitable for this category because their inability to afford its cost because it depends on the degree of risk, which in turn is high for this category. As a result, this limits their ability to obtain the necessary funding because of the lack of adequate collateral and therefore they are neither able to get funding nor insurance.

The insurance sector is considered one of the most promising sectors for the national economy because it represents a significant volume of investments as well as it protects the ingredients of the national economy in one hand and adding jobs it's all various branches in the other hand.

At the same time, Takaful insurance contributes to the expansion of banks in financing several projects which result in achieving higher investment rate of return, especially in developing countries, as there is a positive and strong correlation between economic growth and both micro insurance and micro Takaful insurance. Takaful insurance is deemed one of the main tools of providing protection for microenterprises. At the same time, Takaful insurance market has a large segment of customers that is estimated at nearly one billion borrowers in the micro financial system, which is targeted by small micro Takaful insurance.

There is no doubt that there is a significant role lies on the insurance companies for the success of this insurance, where there must be innovation in the products creation and design and in the use of technology in marketing and distributing it. At the same time, it should be borne in mind that micro insurance will lead to an increase in the insurance companies' sales.

c) Small and micro enterprises in the Arab states: One of the positive indicators at the Arab states level is the increased attention to small and medium-sized enterprises such as the establishment of the Arab Union for Small Enterprises in May 31, 2004, which brings together all institutions, bodies, funds, unions, associations, societies, public and private and civil organizations that are engaged in the development, financing, taking care and supporting small enterprises. One of the positive actions, the decision of the economic summit in Kuwait in January 2009 to finance small and medium enterprises and the establishment of a fund for this purpose [16].

Available data for the Gulf Cooperation Council (GCC) indicates that the number of small and medium-sized industrial enterprises accounts for about 85% of the total industrial enterprises, and they occupy more than half of the industrial sector's employment with investments estimated at around 9% of the total investment in the manufacturing industry. It is expected for this project to be a locomotive for economic growth in the Arab countries in the coming decades, and to contribute to providing many jobs needed to meet population steady growth, where the role of small and medium enterprises sector in creating jobs is growing to meet the needs of the Arab countries to create 100 million jobs during the next twenty years.

The Arab Labor Organization report indicates that small and medium -sized enterprises account for more than 90% of the total workforce in the Arab countries' institutions, which employs about 60% of the workforce and its contribution is 50% of the GDP. So, it is considered one of the driving forces behind the growth of the national economy through creating jobs and opportunities for investment and exports. The Director-General of the Arab Labor Organization has announced that small and medium enterprises are the engine of development in the coming period, pointing out that the Arab world has about 12 million small enterprises employs about 30 million employees [22].

Micro, small and medium enterprises are considered the dominant pattern of investments in the Arab countries, they make up nearly 90% of the private enterprises in Kuwait, and small and medium enterprises accounted for about 94.3% of economic projects in UAE, and employs about 62% of the workforce and it contributes about 75% of the GDP [16].

In the Arab Gulf Countries, small and medium enterprises are the backbone of the industrial sector as it represents 85% of the total industrial enterprises, small and medium-sized factories reached (94%) of the volume of the UAE enterprises and (92%) of Qatar, Oman and Bahrain, (75%) of Saudi Arabia and (78%) of Kuwait. A study of the World Bank indicates that 25% of these enterprises in the Gulf Countries are women-owned [17].

In Saudi Arabia: small and medium enterprises, which their majority are led by young entrepreneurs recorded a marked increase, where about 90% of the registered companies in Saudi Arabia is small and medium enterprises (in terms of the total number of employees and turnover). Even though the contribution of small and medium enterprises is only about 15.5% of the GDP, however, Saudi Arabia is witnessing what was described as an explosion in the small and medium enterprises as much as the number is about 80,000 projects.

There are great efforts to find banks, mutual funds and financing companies that can guarantee loans to these enterprises, such as "Kafalah" (guarantee) program implemented by the Industrial Development Fund in Saudi Arabia, which covers part of the banks' risk in the event of small borrowers' default. Although the Kafalah program remains limited as described by the Saudi Shura's Council, but it is expandable.

Among the most important institutions working now in this area in Saudi Arabia are: Saudi Credit and Savings, Small Enterprises Development Denter, the General Organization for Technical Education, the Centennial Fund, Saudi Industrial Development Fund, the General Authority for Tourism and Antiquities, King Abdul Aziz City for Science and Technology, Human Resources Fund, the National Charity Fund, the General Authority for Investment, Saudi Chamber of Commerce and Industry, Abdul Latif Jameel Program for Community Services, Saudi Agricultural Bank, Abdullah Hamad Al Zamil Center for Community Service [16]. Examples from some Arab of countries are: the Tunisian Bank for Solidarity, the 21/21 Fund, the Export Credit Guarantee Company of Egypt, and Small and Medium Industries' loans guarantee in Algeria.

Banks started to use Islamic transactions such as risks sharing rather than the fixed rate. According to a survey conducted on a sample of 57 banks in the Arab Countries, it shows that 59% of the banks in the GCC are using Islamic transactions where only 30% in non GCC Arab Countries [12]. The reason behind this may be due to lack of care and interest of the Gulf Arab banks to finance these enterprises is that dealing with the large enterprises (more than 100 workers) is more profitable under normal circumstances [16].

Dr. Muhammad Yunus the founder of the Grameen Bank in Bangladesh in 1976 did not expect that his initiative will become a model for more than ten thousand program and micro finance bank around the world. So he deserved the Nobel Peace Prize in 2006 for his efforts in this area, as the many of the poor people have been benefited from the "Poor Banks" in more than 54 countries around the world in 2002, and culminated his efforts in the declaration of the United Nations the year 2005 as international year of micro-lending. As a result, it has been recognized its necessity in anti-poverty in micro-loans summit in Washington, 2 - 04/02/1997).

Gulf Fund (AGFUND) has cared of in the experience of Muhammad Yunus of Grameen Bank and even cooperates with him personally. UNFPA is working successfully in cooperation with governments and the private sector to create banks along the lines of the Grameen Bank to spread the culture of micro-finance and explore pilot projects, and honoring it by the award of the global (AGFUND) [16].

The Gulf Fund (AGFUND) has begun this project for the establishment of Poor Banks in 1997 and established the Hope Bank for micro finance in Egypt and Yemen, the National Bank for small enterprise in Jordan and the Creativity Bank in Bahrain, and has many projects in the near future in Sudan and Mauritania, Lebanon and Syria. The Grameen Bank initiative is considered a positive example of social responsibility of the for profit organizations as it makes a balance between the social aspect and the profit one without eliminating each other. At the same time, it has been proven that the repayment rates in this type of lending are high compared with other types of loans as the rate exceeds 90% [12].

Arab Fund for Economic and Social Development refers in his report for the year 2012 about microenterprises that the Arab region is characterized by less levels of access to micro-loans when compared to other regional groups, where the number of beneficiaries of these loans in 2010 is about 2.2 million, and the average value of the loan did not exceed micro $550. Studies show that the share of small and medium enterprise loans of the Gulf banks loans does not exceed 2%" [16].

The international experiences in the field of Micro-Takaful insurance and its methods of marketing

We clarify here the main methods of providing and marketing micro insurance:

Methods of Providing Micro-Takaful insurance: Micro Takaful Insurance can be provided through two models:

a) The first model, which focuses on the poor side that is:

- Focusses on reaching the poor people.

- Depends on its finance and success on subsidiaries (donations and Zakat).

- Delivered by not-for-profit organizations.

b) The second model, which focuses on the business side that is:

- Focusses on Continuity and self-financing (from the insureds' premium)

- Targeted capable people

- Delivered by for profits organizations

It should be noted that micro insurance has emerged before micro Takaful insurance and benefited from the development of conventional insurance and experience that has been gained, so micro Takaful insurance is considered to be in its initial stages.

The most important international practices and experiences in the field of Micro Takaful insurance: There are many successful experiences in the field of micro Takaful insurance in some countries, among them [23]:

a) Philippines: The Philippine government strives to make financial services, including insurance available to all citizens regardless of their income levels, including those with low-income levels. In 1997, the state has issued the necessary legislation to develop and implement a national strategy for microfinance, this led the financing institutions to finance poor people and therefore the savings and lending services became available to them, which let to increasing the number of these institutions from a handful in 1995 to more than 200 institutions in 2013, which provides services to more than 7 million low-income people.

These institutions are financing those articles of livelihood projects and simple activities, but these activities and these people are still exposed to the risks that may ruin their projects and even their lives and their families as a result of the risks of premature death, injury, illness, lose or damage of property etc. Here the state intervened not to provide micro insurance but to create the appropriate legislative environment and determining the risks that need to be covered and urged the private institutions to introducing the needed coverages, where these coverages are provided through commercial insurance companies and associations of cooperative insurance and reciprocal benefits societies in addition to the financial intermediaries (banks, cooperative societies and non-profit organizations and consumer outlets, all these parties participate in the process of underwriting, sales and distribution of the products of micro insurance). All these things lowered the cost of distributing and marketing of insurance in addition to increasing the number of beneficiaries and ease the access to them as a result of benefiting of a large network of financial institution intermediaries with its hundreds of thousands of members [11]. In addition, the state intervened in drafting and simplifying the policy wording and easing the required documents and conditions and adapted the number and methods of premium's payment to be commensurate with the financial flows of the insured in addition to determining the amount of insurance clearly. All these things have led to a boom in the micro insurance industry during the four years from 2009 to 2012.

So the Philippines experiment is considered a successful model in applying micro insurance, so all other countries should benefit from its model and identifying the elements of success particularly with regard to insurance companies and NGOs working in this area in addition to the identification of electronic payment and payment through the mobile service providers, which are used widely in the Philippines and all over the world. All the previous elements made the Philippines to be one of the highest percentage of the insurance coverage, where 20% of the population benefited from micro insurance through agricultural associations and banks.

b) Lebanon: the first type of micro Takaful insurance is appeared in Lebanon in 1997 where agricultural fund was created to submit micro Takaful medical insurance to cover the medical cost that is not covered by the government through the social security fund, which covers 85% of hospital costs. This micro Takaful insurance covers 5,000 families (approximately 23,000 beneficiaries) for monthly premium of $10 per a family, where the villagers and the policyholders bear the cost on behalf of those who do not have the financial ability to pay it. This insurance is available to all sectarians and religions, and there are preferential contracts between the Fund and among health service providers, where the fund members get up to 50% discount. This fund covers more than 180 villages in southern Lebanon and targets primarily the poor communities and weak economy regions. At the same time, the fund provides scholarships.

c) Indonesia: Indonesia is the largest Muslim country and at the same time it has tens of thousands of cooperative societies that are engaged in the field of Islamic microfinance. We can say that Indonesia is the most developed countries in the field of micro Takaful insurance. It goes back to 2006 when the United Nations Development Program-sponsored a study about microfinance in Indonesia resulted in two initiatives: the first represents a partner-agency model between Indonesia Takaful Company and Peramu company where there started Sakinah micro insurance program that is a credit Life Insurance program 2007 [13].

This initiative has introduced term mutual Takaful insurance for the same finance period ranging from six months to one year which was a mandatory group insurance for the Islamic micro finance institutions to secure the loans. These institutions have been established carefully and very close to the poor communities to make the collection of premiums per month very easy where the insurance premiums are paid as part of the finance payments and depending on the outstanding balance. At the same time there are no additional provisions of the insurance policy and the benefits are simple and easy to understand and, more importantly, any claim is settled within a week.

This type of insurance is marketing through conventional and Islamic financing institutions where they cooperate together to raise awareness of micro-insurance compliant with Islamic law. The used model is the agency with fees as the operator gets a fixed fee plus a share of both investment and underwriting surplus. The good thing is that Indonesia Takaful Insurance Company uses part of the Zakat amounts owed in launching and developing micro Takaful Insurance products. The company in partnership with the National Council of Zakat and charity has developed a micro Takaful insurance initiative to beneficiaries of Zakat and charity through a policy covering the risk of death as a result of accidents and natural disasters.

The second initiative was started in 2006 by Allianz, the German through offering micro Takaful insurance policies from a separate window as a copy of the Indonesian micro Takaful insurance, followed by a credit life insurance policy in 2007, with several options: the first option is to cover either the whole amount of finance or the outstanding balance, and the second one is that the beneficiaries get double the amount of insurance, and the third option is that the finance institution will get the benefits of the policy if the husband/wife dies (term insurance for the finance/loan period-mostly 20 months) . During that period, term insurance and natural disasters has been for more than 42,000 borrowers for micro enterprises for a premium of $0.66. An additional amount is paid off for the family as clients' need and the premiums are collected at the time of finance through a very simple procedures and the underwriting process is done by an external source [18].

d) Malaysia: despite the fact that Malaysia is one of the most advanced countries in the world in the field of Takaful insurance but the micro Takaful insurance is still in its early stages and is growing very slowly. In 2007 micro-Takaful Insurance was establishment with cooperation between Ikhlas Takaful Insurance company and the Farmers Malaysian Union (NGO Private not for-profit organization that taking care of the interests of the unemployed and the indigents). This insurance is compulsory, governmental-funded, offers compensation equivalent to $140 to cover the death expenses in lieu of $ 1.8 premium and covers nearly 100,000 farmers at this time. It also offers an optional personal accident insurance that provides compensation equivalent to $ 2,800 in the event of disability or death. The company signed an agreement with the Zakat Centre, which includes 10 agencies (including Post-Malaysian and the Commercial Bank of Malaysia) for the collection of zakat to form Takaful fund to be used to pay the premiums on behalf of the poor people and pays the benefits in case of death, disability, chronic diseases, costs of burial and the costs of hospitals.

e) Jordan: In 2007 it was inaugurated micro financing fund in cooperation with the Jordan Insurance Company to provide a compulsory insured funding for women's projects against the risks of death and partial and total disability for a premium of 0.11% of the loan.

f) Morocco: Microfinance began in the early nineties of the last century to finance small enterprises and to serve those who have been excluded from traditional bank loans. Amanah Foundation was established as the largest microfinance institution to serve nearly half a million clients in rural and urban areas and to provide them with many financial services, including insurance.

g) Egypt: the Credit Guarantee Company for small enterprise has been established by contribution of nine commercial banks and support from government to insure bank credit risks to develop and improve micro, small and medium enterprises by guaranteeing up to 100% of the loans that has been granted without guarantee or collateral by the banks that have an agreement with the company. This encouraged banks to extend loans and facilities for these projects which led to an increase in its number in the small and medium size and increase its contribution to the achievement of economic and social development and to as well as to ease the burden on the government and the public sector by absorbing manpower and forming a broad base of small investors [12].

The company has managed since the start of its activity in 1991 until the end of 2012 to issue of more than 10 billion pounds of guarantee to guarantee the credits that has been granted by banks for micro, small and medium enterprises operating in all economic sectors. Also, the central bank has encouraged banks to lend and develop this sector which allowed it to deduct these loans from their cash reserves that have to keep it.

This new law of the financial regulation of the insurance sector, which was issued in 2014 has allowed the establishment of companies that engage in micro insurance either life or property to have low capital to encourage and support this microfinance activity. Micro insurance is very important in Egypt because the number of small businesses (with fewer than 10 workers) represents 97% of the business volume and that 40% of the population lives below the poverty line.

h) Sri Lanka: Amana and Muslim Aid project was launched to cover 1000 beneficiary and is linked to microfinance (loans in the range of $100) where the annual cost is collected in a weekly base and gives indemnity in case of illness and accidents [22]. Also, Micro Takaful Support Center (MSC) has been established through the International Cooperative and Mutual Insurance Union (ICMIF) to provide micro-insurance products for low-income people.

The Takaful Insurance Company provides micro-Takaful insurance as a group insurance to pay the benefits in case of death, disability, and costs of burial education. And at the end of the year the company sponsor a concert for the group in which the surplus is distributed.

Pakistan: The Kashf company as an intermediary to provide Life Insurance and accidents linked to funding in collaboration with the insurance company, and the insurance is compulsory for anyone who wants funding.

i) Bangladesh: the beginnings of micro insurance go back to more than 25 years (where the first time the villages insurance is offered in 1988 and then the rural endowment insurance is offered. Micro insurance was not adopted in Bangladesh to cover death only but to collect the savings of the poor people, where these systems provide cash money unlike the other countries that provide term insurance with the right of renewal, which covers the risks of death and disability only.

The Bangladeshi experience is considered an extremely wealthy one, especially if we take into account the very low income levels (where the average income per family bread winner does not reach $ 100) and 40% of the population, i.e., more than 60 million people live below the poverty line. The Bangladeshi experiment can be understood from the Delta Insurance Company (a private insurance company), which serve the poor people where:

1. It provided life insurance to more than 80,000 insured.

2. The process of service delivery and the premiums collection is done by delegates from insured's homes.

3. The insured can get a loan using the insurance policy as collateral.

j) India: VIMO SEWA INDIA insurance company offers three types of integrated/composite insurance policies where:

1. It covers risks of death, illness and loss of property or assets.

2. Premiums are paid annually or through fixed periodic payments.

k) China: where the State in partnership with the People's Insurance Company deliver flood insurance as:

1. Compulsory insurance for all residents in the Yangtze River Basin area.

2. The government bears 70% of the premiums and the policyholders bear 30% with a maximum limit of indemnity.

l) South Africa: where there is a burial insurance as:

1. There are 100,000 service providers, whether they are officials or not.

2. The annual premium range between 7.5 - 50 dollars, and the average of indemnity range between 750-1500 dollars.

m) Malawi: where there was unemployment insurance which began in 2003 and which:

1. Launched in cooperation between the Bank of Malawi and a local insurance company

2. It covers three monthly installments in the event of default of the borrower due to unemployment

n) Trinidad and Tobago: in 1999, the Trinidad and Tobago Takaful insurance company has been founded by the Cooperative Islamic Credit Union that has more than 7,000 members and offers benefits for the burial costs in case of death by an Islamic investment fund. The members pay an annual membership of $20 that reduced to $5 for those who are less than 16 years old.

o) Sudan: Micro Takaful insurance experiment has begun in Sudan in 2008 through Shiekan Insurance Company, which provides credit insurance and Family Takaful insurance, property insurance, poultry and livestock insurance, fire insurance, burglary and agricultural insurance [6]. We can say that the micro projects finance system in Sudan consists of:

A) The organizer: The Central Bank of Sudan through the microfinance unit:

Based on Sudan's central bank instructions, the commercial banks allocate 12% of its loan portfolio to be allocated to micro-finance, which amounted to 3.6 billion Sudanese pounds (about 1.5 billion dollars).

B) The financiers: micro finance projects are financed through microfinance unit which consists of:

1. Banks: there are 30 commercial banks, out of them 20 banks financing micro enterprises.

2. Aman Fund to finance micro enterprises: its capital $75 million (200 million Sudanese pounds), 75% from banks and 25% from the Zakat Institution. It gives loans to microenterprises up to $ 4,000 (10,000 Sudanese pounds).

3. Social Fund: financed from the pension fund and Graduates Recruitment Project and others. It provides financial support for the poor and low-income people, including women and the elderly, graduates and retirees.

The most important supporters of microenterprises in the Sudan are:

1. The governments (central, province and municipality)

2. The banks

3. Insurance sector

4. Not for profit organizations

5. Private sector

6. Training centers and universities

Government support for financing micro-enterprises and micro-insurance on small micro enterprises:

1. The government pays 50% of the insurance premiums on crops to insurance companies.

2. The government pay 50% of the margin of speculation (interest) to the banks as an incentive for beneficiaries who repay the loan on time.

p) Ethiopia: in 2010 about 1,300 families have been insured from the risk of drought by micro insurance through cooperation between the two companies: Swiss Re and Oxfam America.

q) Haiti: micro insurance program has been established to help small women businesses to return to their activity after suffering from a natural disaster. Also, a Micro Insurance Authority has been established as a subsidiary of Munich Re.

Methods of marketing Micro Takaful insurance: It is known that Takaful insurance mirrors the investment of the Islamic religion because its underlying authority reference in transactions is the principles of Islamic law (shari'a) which makes it easier to market in Saudi Arabia in particular and in the GCC countries and Muslim countries in general. Therefore, it is the duty of the nation's scholars to raise the public awareness of the Takaful insurance and of its benefits.

With regard to the method of marketing Takaful insurance, mobiles can be used in distributing it to provide information, especially for farmers who know how to read and write. There is no doubt that it should not be the focus of this type of insurance to achieve faster returns but must rely on competitive pricing and innovative products in addition to the discovery of other segments through short- and long-term strategies.

As the micro Takaful insurance has its special characteristics with regard to the targeted segment and the covered risks, we demand to benefit from the high level of expertise available in the field of Takaful insurance and risk management for the deployment and development of micro Takaful insurance. In addition, it should to rely on social marketing, which provides service to the community and does not aim for profit. It also contributes to the development of both social and human factors of the company as opposed to commercial marketing, which focuses on increasing the company's sales only sales. In addition, the entry of multinational companies into the industry is a good addition which contributing to the development of this sector in order to achieve the desired goal. There is no doubt that there is a significant role that is expected from the insurance companies to the success of this type of insurance, where there must be an innovation in the design and creativity of its products and the use of technology in its marketing and distribution. Also, it should be borne in mind that micro insurance will increase the insurance distribution in general.

Who offers micro insurance: There are many key players who can provide micro insurance, such as:

1. Commercial insurance companies

2. Cooperative and Takaful insurance companies

3. Mutual insurance companies

4. Lending companies

5. State through Social insurance

Micro Takaful insurance: Its future, success requirements and challenges

The future of micro Takaful insurance: Takaful insurance is one of the economic services sectors that is expected to experience exponential growth in the coming years in most of the Islamic and Arab countries, at rates ranging between 20-25%, especially with a fertile environment for the growth of the sector which is characterized by abundant population and an increasing demand for Islamic products [12]. The micro insurance (Commercial or Takaful) is a promising market for the insurance sector that has to increase insurance awareness and introduce new products that fit this category, as is incumbent on the social responsibility of insurance companies towards this category.

There is no doubt that there is great hope in micro insurance (Commercial or Takaful) resulting from the concerted efforts and participation of both governmental and private sector, all other not for profits organizations that are interested in small and micro enterprises, the assistances provided by governments and international supporting institutions, grants, donations and Zakat to help this poor and important category at the same time.

The requirement for the success of micro Takaful insurance:

There are a set of requirements which must be met for the success of Micro Takaful Insurance, the most important are [20]:

1. Establishing an unofficially Micro Takaful Insurance System away from the administrative complexities

2. Interacting and communicating with the funder or donor (government, public or private) to raise awareness of the problem of the poor and low-income people

3. Takaful sector has to do an important and pivotal role at least in the following areas:

-Provide technical expertise

-Provide financial assistance

-Cooperation with Micro Takaful and Commercial Insurance providers and other agencies that deal with this layer

4. Issuing Micro Takaful insurance legislation to establish the legal framework for its practice

5. Establishing an independent regulatory body to control, organize and develop Micro Takaful Insurance.

6. Provide the necessary governmental support.

The most important challenges facing micro Takaful insurance: There is a dilemma related to this type of insurance with this layer that is the ability of the insurance companies to bring about a balance between providing the insurance service to a limited or no income layer which at the same time its exposure to risk is very high.

We can sum up the most important challenges that facing this type of insurance as follows [12]:

1. No attention or interest neither from states nor from the financial institutions to this poor layer, which due to:

- This layer does not have the required guarantees or collateral.

- High cost.

- Its success is not guaranteed.

- Its exposure to risk is high.

- Limited ability to meet the needs of this layer with special nature.

2. Failure of the traditional professional insurance institutions to provide insurance for this category has led it to resort to the organizations that are not-for-profit, loans donor agencies and cooperative insurance companies and Credit Unions which inherently suffer from many problems including:

- Lack of expertise in this area.

- Bureaucracy and lack of effective management systems.

- Weakness of the distribution and marketing style that rely on traditional systems that do not fit with this category.

- Unavailability of reinsurance.

- Low Level of education.

3. Absence of insurance awareness.

4. Lack of trust among the individuals targeted by this type of insurance.

5. Lack of an accurate insurance data for the targeted group.

6. Lack of credit information for the targeted group.

7. Lack of awareness of the majority of poor people in developing countries of the nature of micro insurance.

8. Delivering high quality services and credible commitment of the provision of insurance coverage and the speed of claims payment services.

We see that, a major effort must be made to convince the potential clients as borrowers to explain the legitimacy of these loans and at the same time discuss the expansion of the loans, which are described as Islamic as a practical alternative to commercial insurance. It should be understood that many of the young borrowers especially those who suffer poverty do not want to add to it what they may consider the divine disobedience to orders (conventional insurance).

Findings and Recommendations

Findings

Through this research, the researcher has reached the following set of results:

1. Large number of poor people in developing countries is not aware of the nature or even the presence of micro insurance.

2. Takaful insurance reflects the image of the Islamic investment because its underlying reference in dealing is the principles of Islamic law, making it easier to market.

3. The biggest challenge for Micro Takaful Insurance is the insufficient awareness of its importance and its nature in addition to the absence of accurate data, these two elements hamper its growth in developing countries.

4. Due to high risk of small and micro projects, financial institutions are reluctant to provide financing for this group.

5. The spread of micro insurance will lead to an increase of the insurance product' sales.

6. Micro Takaful Insurance contributing in the expansion of banks in financing small and micro enterprises that result in greater investment return and growth rates especially in developing countries as there is a strong positive correlation between economic growth in one hand and micro-finance and micro insurance on the other hand.

7. The entry of multinational companies to this industry is a good addition to contributing to the development of this sector in order to achieve its desired goals.

8. Takaful insurance companies have a great opportunity to take advantage of micro insurance as at the same time they fulfill their social responsibility to the communities in which they reside.

9. The financing conditions is the main problem that faces these small and micro enterprises, whether the scarcity of allocated financial resources from the governments or the tough conditions to borrow from traditional financial institutions.

10. There are some successful practices and experiences of some countries to resolve the problem of financing small and micro projects through creating a governmental body to guaranteeing the financing of commercial banks for these projects in the event of the default any of them. Some examples of the countries are carried out by the American and Indonesian governments as well as the Egyptian government, which established in 1991 The Export Credit Guarantee Company for

small enterprises with the contribution of nine commercial banks. Also, the Jordanian government has established in 1994 the Jordan Loan Guarantee Corporation with a capital of 10 million dinars, to guarantee 100% the financed projects by commercial banks. This experiment is characterized by developing tools to guarantee financing operations that are consistent with the provisions of Islamic Sharia law.

Recommendations

1. Activation of the initiatives of Micro-Insurance for supporting small and micro projects and reducing the cost of insurance for the poor people, especially in developing countries.

2. The legislature should pass laws and facilitate the procedures to allow poor people to take advantage of this type of insurance.

3. The need for strengthen cooperation between state institutions and insurance companies to provide financing for microenterprises.

4. Establishing a specialized body to provide microfinance for the most needed category in the developing countries.

5. Establishing a robust environment for Social Solidarity to benefit from its spread, growth and prosperity.

6. Risks should be management with a high degree of efficiency specially for the loans and life insurance.

7. Design, innovate and develop insurance products for this category and benefit from the use of technology especially the mobiles as channels for distribution and to provide information, especially for farmers and skilled craftsmen.

8. We recommend that Micro Takaful insurance shouldn't depend when setting the price on the actual cost, to be easily available to individuals and to take into account the nature of the targeted group.

9. The researcher recommends the nation's scholars to play an active role in raising awareness about Takaful insurance and its benefits because its reference in dealing is the principles of Islamic law and this will facilitate for them its spread and marketing.

10. We recommend all working Micro Takaful insurance companies to depend on the quality of services provided to customers and to follow a credible commitment of the provision of insurance coverage and in prompt and fair payment of claims when the risk occurs.

11. Developing and stimulating Takaful insurance activities and creating and developing new insurance products that conform to the needs and culture of our society, especially in the field of small, medium and micro enterprises, and adding to it the personal accidents and home insurance.

12. Paying more attention to human resource development for the insurance sector employees, where there is a clear shortage of specialized competencies which affects the provision of human resources to the practice of insurance in general and Micro Takaful insurance in particular.

13. We should rely on banks in the initial phase for the promotion of Micro insurance.

14. We recommend that the new products begin to cover the risks of micro, small and medium enterprises.

15. Relying on social marketing in marketing Micro Takaful Insurance as it offers a community service and does not aim for profit, in addition its contribution to the development of social, human and material elements of the company in the contrary from the commercial marketing, which aims to increasing the company's sales only.

16. Establishing a specialized body for providing Microfinance in developing countries that has among its structure a department for micro-insurance until it spreads, then establishing an independent and separate entity.

17. We recommend the service providers not to focus on achieving quick returns, but must rely on competitive pricing and innovative products in addition to reaching new segments through short- and long-term strategies.

18. Benefiting from the available expertise in the areas of Micro Commercial insurance, Micro Takaful Insurance and micro Takaful insurance and risk management for the deployment and development of Micro Takaful insurance.

19. Under the current situation and the difficulties, challenges and financing problems faced by small and micro enterprises and the tough terms to borrow from traditional financial institutions due to a high risk of these projects that has led to the reluctance of traditional commercial banks and Islamic banks to fund it. This problem can be solved through the establishment of specialized governmental institutions to guarantee these enterprises when the projects financed by the commercial banks in the event of default. We can apply this initiative with taking into account the successful experiences of some governments such as the United States, Indonesia, Egypt and Jordan.

20. We propose the establishment of an Arab institution with considerable capital to guarantee these loans from Arab Banks and Financing Institutions for these projects, which provides the required guarantee/collateral for the lenders, which will lead to expanding of the financing institutions in support this important sector.

References

1. Abdelhameed AA (2009) Micro Loans Management: Mechanism, Objectives and Challenges. Arab Management Magazine 29: 159-182.
2. Abouzaid C (2012) Challenges and Opportunities of Micro-Takaful and Micro-Insurance in Africa. 39th AIO Conference, Khartoum pp: 6-9.
3. Abdullah AJ, Eid A, Mousa Q (2004) Small Project Management. Dar Alyazouri for Publishing & Distribution, Amman pp: 46-47.
4. Ahmed, Habib, (2011) Waqf as Sustainable Social Enterprise: Organizational Architecture and Prospects. 4th World Congress of Muslim Philanthropists, Dubai pp: 8-14.
5. Ahmed OE (2012) How Shiekan Designed a Risk Controlled MicroTakaful Product. Case from Sudan, 2nd Annual Microinsurance Summit Latin America, Miami p. 25.
6. Ahmed OE (2013) Micro Takaful as a Stimulus for Islamic Microfinance: Sudan View. 7th International Takaful Summit, Cairo pp: 42-43.
7. Mortuza KMA (2011) Landscape of Micro Insurance In Bangladesh: Poverty Alleviation and Need for Mutual Micro Insurance. 4th World Congress of Muslim Philanthropists, Dubai pp: 12-14.
8. Almahrouq M, Moqabala E (2006) Small & Medium Enterprises: Its Objectives and Obstacles, Small and Medium Enterprises. Amman pp: 11-34.
9. Bhatty A (2010) Protecting the Forgotten through Micro Takaful. Middle East Insurance Review pp: 60-61.
10. Churchill C, Matul M (2012) Protecting the poor; A micro insurance compendium. Munich Re Foundation and International Labor Office (ILO) 2: 59-80.
11. Portula DO, Vergara R (2013) The Philippine experience on Microinsurance Market Development. Philippine Department of Finance – National Credit Council and The Insurance Commission, Manila, Philippines pp: 4-8.
12. Farouq O (2012) A Future Vision of Takaful Insurance: Takaful in a Changing

World and Micro Takaful Insurance for Developing Countries. 7th International Takaful Insurance Conference, Cairo.

13. Agus H (2007) Developing Micro Takaful in Indonesia. 2nd International Convention on Takaful and Re Takaful, Kuala Lumpur pp: 6-11.

14. Tashtoush AH (2012) The Role of Small Enterprises in Development. Small Enterprises Conference, Qasdi Mirbah University, Algeria pp: 62-84.

15. Khan MJA (2006) Micro Takaful: the Way Forward. Academy for International Modern Studies (AIMS), Institute of Islamic Banking and Finance pp: 3-14.

16. Alsibaiei NO (2013) The Role of Women Small Enterprises in Solving Unemployment Problem in Kingdom of Saudi Arabia. Arab Open Academy in Denmark, College of Management and Economics pp: 16-17.

17. Odierno HS (2013) Malaysian experience with Takaful and lessons for Africa, Actuarial Partners, Abuja pp: 6-11.

18. Odierno HS (2013) Takaful Innovation: Using Takaful to Solve Challenges in Microinsurance. Dhaka pp: 15-18.

19. Sabbirl P (2012) Micro Takaful: Meeting the Challenges of Change. 14th Global Conference of Actuaries, Institute of Actuaries of India, Mumbai pp: 23-29.

20. Takaful and Poverty Alleviation (2012), 8th International Microinsurance Conference, International Cooperative & Mutual Insurance Federation, Dares Salaam pp: 11-14.

21. Qadoumi T (2011) Financing Small Enterprises in Jordan: Obstacles and Challenges. Private University of Applied Sciences, Amman pp: 22-43.

22. Serap OG (2013) Takaful and Mutual Insurance: Alternative Approach to Meeting Risks. International Bank for Reconstruction and Development, The World Bank, Washington DC pp: 161-165.

23. Statistical Year Book (2013), Central Agency for Public Mobilization and Statistics (CAPMAS), Cairo.

12

Evolution of Corporate Governance Practices and Conventional Banks Profitability

Khan N* and Iqbal N

Management Sciences, Indus International Institute DG Khan, Pakistan

Abstract

This study has been conducted to discover the good governance practices influence on profit of conventional banking system. Prime aim is to discover the application of these practices in the corporation for betterment. This research based on mixture of primary and secondary data. Sample for primary data collection for study is different conventional banks of Pakistan. Observation method and structured questionnaires is used to obtain the data from respondents (banks employees). Obtained data is analyzed through statistical software SPSS. Regression analysis is done to check out the effects of corporate governance and its determinants on profitability of conventional financial institution. So findings possess that banks profit tend to be enhance with the espousal of ethical practices in corporate culture. Study concluded that if financial institution behave ethical manner, socially obliged and invest for well being of society after that they will get and enhance profit from social capital in addition to be considered as socially responsible corporations by adopting regulatory system aptly.

Keywords: Corporate governance; Profitability; Ethical practices; Regulatory system; Performance measures

Introduction

Corporate administration is known as mix of parameters, standards, regulation and business rehearses that lead the relationship among administration and all partners. This business technique or practice includes reasonable, translucent and productivity in organization which make them ready to get the sought and arranged results. Corporate administration works and controls an organization in precise way despite the fact that organizations animate and draw in the money related and human capital. Corporate administration framework is grasped a wide exhibit of business practices and organization since book keeping laws and standard which concern the financial admission and revelation towards administrative remuneration and in addition piece of corporate board.

First time in Pakistan corporate administration code was dispersed in March 2002. Prior to this it was noticed that present business college was accentuating on the improvement of solid corporate administration. Pakistan establishment of corporate administration was produced to put consideration on preparing of personnel of SECP and stock trade. In corporate world, that establishment was formed to add to a bridge or association among company and its regulation framework. In broad mind and wide view corporate administration is the reciprocal and relating arrangement of legal , social and money related organization that shield the enthusiasm of all partners of company.

In Anglo American framework, real shareholders known as proprietors and corporate chief acts as specialists so corporate administration origination expect an essential anxiety among shareholders and corporate directors. The two put exertion for their own particular intrigue so as organization set administrative bodies as Directors who are the adherents of stewardship hypothesis. The foundation and establishing of SEC security and Exchange Commission of Pakistan is spoken to an indispensable highlight for the advancement of domineering structure of capital marketplace. SEC performs operational exercises and be fruitful for CLA Corporate Law Authority known as government office appended to Ministry of Finance. In the first place it was concerned with administrative of capital business and corporate division. Commission has been ordered into distinctive areas like as protection, securities, HR and Administration and organization Law division and the greater part of that work for powerful administration.

Good corporate governance proves more supportive for the development of economic sustainability through maximizing corporation's performance and productivity as well as access to outside or exterior capital. It reduces liability and exposure of financial crises, reinforcing property rights and contributes to development of capital market. Corporate governance concerns to the linkage between major and minority shareholders, BOD's, top management and all other stakeholders. East Asian Financial crises capture the serious consideration and notice to the vitality of corporate governance in developing countries.

In 1999, OECD (organization for Economic Co-operation and Development) has developed a series of principles for corporate governance that have been proved core pattern to assess the country CG pact and arrangements. It provides composition by which company goals are set, means of accomplishing all those objectives and monitoring performance and quality standards. General approaches to corporate governance to defend and protect rights of investors. Initially delegates power to investors and shareholders through legal way and focus for minorities shareholders' rights and legal prohibition beside administrative self decision and dealing. The next major approach relates to concentrated ownership by major investors by matching considerable and significant cash flows and control rights. Large investors mostly rely on legal system and minimize the agency cost and issues as they do not have require many rights as minor shareholders needs to protect own rights, So Corporate governance is commonly exercised via major investors or shareholders.

***Corresponding author:** Nabila Khan, Management Sciences, Indus International Institute DG Khan, Pakistan, E-mail: Nabilakhan255@yahoo.com

Effective corporate governance leads to efficiency and high growth of companies, minimize risk and stabilized economic conditions by getting investors confidence in strategic way. Apart since all these financial development and modifications, corporate governance code has been executed to all listed firms of Pakistan in 2002, prime aim is to persuade good governance in whole dynamic business market.

The aim of this research paper is to find out the link among corporate governance and corporate performance for financial institutions. So in this study we try to recognize the relationship among corporate governance determinants and practices with conventional banking regulatory and profitability in dynamic competitive market.

Literature Review

This research paper is going to review the previous studies on corporate governance practices in various financial institutions of different developing and developed countries. Corporate governance makes sure that companies get the responsibility to manage, control and monitor all matters in systematic way by preserving the interest of stakeholders [1]. The facets of corporate governance deal with initiating the process by which core values are achieved and ethics known as behavioral guide [2-4].

According to Mallin [5] corporate governance is a mode through which companies administer and oversee their businesses by following its practices and reforms strategies and maximize profitability. Ineffective corporate governance mechanism in corporations proves as major factor to the current financial crises. Jamali, Safieddine, Rabbath [6] argued that ideas and suggestions for governance variables as corporate social responsibility is the advancement and evolution since benevolent activities toward applicable tactic for getting the trust of community and major clients at all. In accordance to Marcinkowska [7] corporate governance determines all factors that have significant influence on institutional procedures such as employing and appointing controllers and regulatory systems for organizing activities. The customers are the co-initiator of assessment and value thus corporate governance practices and social responsibility of corporations is incorporated similar to others firm capital and possessions that give strength to shareholders as well as all stakeholders. In accordance to Iqbal [8], study finding explored strong connectivity among fiscal performance of banking sectors of Pakistan and application of corporate governance. It covers up basically many gauges involving effectiveness and independence of board and audit committee for regulatory system. Khan et al. [9] explains that corporate governance practices and governance determinants and financial performance of Islamic financial institutions. Study revealed that significance link and connectivity among large board size and profitability because board protect the rights of major shareholders. They idealize the resource dependent theory which mainly emphasize on accountability, profitability and transparency for achieving corporate goals (Figure 1).

Determinants of governance and profitability and development of hypotheses

Corporate governance is used as independent variable measured through its component which is Ethical practices applicable in corporation. Banks profitability is measured through two determinants that is Return on equity and Return on Assets. Research Hypotheses is developed after review previous studies regarding corporate governance and financial performance of financial institutions and test by descriptive research device.

H1: There is a positive link among corporate governance Practices and conventional banks profit.

H2: There is a positive link among Ethical practices (business ethics and social obligations) and firm financial performance.

Research Methodology

For this study, descriptive research design is adopted that include questionnaires, observation method, individual interviews and case study but convenience method is structured questionnaires by using lickert scale method. Primary data is obtained by distributing questionnaires among bank's employees by hand and some through mails in different branches of conventional banks in Punjab. Response from electronic mode is less significance rather than by own visits and individual interviews from employees.

Data Analysis and Results

Statistical analysis is conducted by the help of statistical instruments SPSS. Various tools and techniques are availed for testing research hypothesis. Regression analysis is done to interpret the obtained data. To get confirmation the significance of governance variables and profitability measures through firm performance, ROA and ROE (Tables 1-4).

Results

In this study analysis shows that the goodness of research model, in accordance to ANOVA test results significance value is .000<. .005 and R SQUARE results = .992 which implies 99% variation come into dependent variable measures ROA is due to applying ethical practices in the financial institution R-SQUARE value for ROE .87 which explains by CG determinants. Social obligation of corporate Coefficient value is 2% and 8% which possess that if firms invest 1% for social work then it will become cause increase near about 8% increment

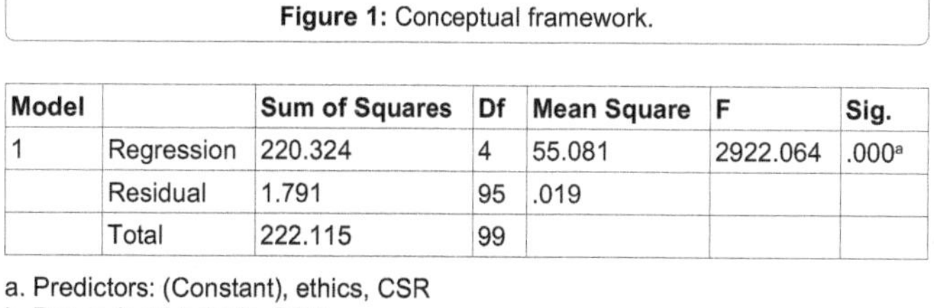

Figure 1: Conceptual framework.

Model		Sum of Squares	Df	Mean Square	F	Sig.
1	Regression	220.324	4	55.081	2922.064	.000ᵃ
	Residual	1.791	95	.019		
	Total	222.115	99			

a. Predictors: (Constant), ethics, CSR
b. Dependent Variable: ROA

Table 1: ANOVA[b].

Model		Sum of Squares	Df	Mean Square	F	Sig.
1	Regression	32013.365	4	8003.341	169.526	.000ᵃ
	Residual	4484.956	95	47.210		
	Total	36498.321	99			

a.Predictors: (Constant), business ethics, social obligations
b.Dependent Variable: ROE

Table 2: ANOVA[b].

Model	R	R Square	Adjusted R Square	Std. Error of the Estimate
1	.996[a]	.992	.992	.13730

a. Predictors: (Constant), Business ethics, Social obligation.

Table 3: Model summary.

Model	R	R Square	Adjusted R Square	Std. Error of the Estimate
1	.937[a]	.877	.872	6.87096

a. Predictors: (Constant), Business Ethics, Social Obligation

Table 4: Model summary.

IV	DV	β coefficient	p-value
Business Ethics	ROA	0.008	0.046
Business Ethics	ROE	0.039	0.038

Table 5: Regression results.

IV	DV	β coefficient	p-value
Social Obligations	ROA	0.020	0.043
Social Obligations	ROE	0.086	0.045

Table 6: Regression results.

in profitability. Regression results shows p value is significant at .04 for ROA and .03 for ROE for both predictors as social obligation and ethics. Business ethics coefficient results reveals no more change in profitability measures as in results of investing in ethical practices. So statistical results are quite different from previous study and discussed data in this research (Tables 4-6).

Conclusion and Discussion

By applying different statistical tool to interpret the obtained data and to test the research hypothesis, it is identified positive influence of governance practices on banks profitability. First hypothesis states positive relationship among governance practices and conventional banks profitability so statistically proved the significance of link among both variables. Profitability ratio is enhanced little bit way when banking system behave themselves as ethical manners. By performing these codes of conduct and principles, performance and profitability of financial institutions will lead to the development of corporations. Second hypothesis is analyzed statistically, all components of ethical practices like as business ethics and social obligations are positively associated with firm financial performance. If corporations behave ethically and maintain business decorum and socially obliged to perform for well being of society thus they will not consider as materialistic entity that only work for profit maximization. Since corporations act as socially responsible and enhance their social contacts with clients and customers subsequently they achieve their goals ultimately.

Direction for future research

Current study has revealed the significance influence and relationship among corporate governance and profitability of banks. Thus here researcher emphasize on governance variables or determinants like as business ethics and social obligations of the corporations so others ethical practices must have to be discussed and evaluated in terms of financial performance indicators. Corporate governance code should be essential for adoption for every firm because adequate application of this code will prove more opportunistic ways for getting maximum profitability.

References

1. Berghe LV, Louche C (2005) The link between corporate governance and corporate social responsibility in insurance. Geneva Papers on Risk and Insurance 30: 425-442.
2. Sullivan JD, Shkolnikov A (2006) Business ethics: The essential component of corporate governance. Economic forum feature service 1-16.
3. Berenbeim RE (2006) Defining an organization's ethics brand. In the conference board. Paper delivered to the ethics and compliance conference: Putting it all together 501-504.
4. Graafland J, Mazereeuw C, Yahia A (2006) Islam and socially responsible business conduct: an empirical study of Dutch entrepreneurs. Business Ethics: A European Review 15: 390-406.
5. Mallin CA (2007) Corporate Governance (2ndedn). New York, Oxford Press.
6. Jamali D, Safieddine AM, Rabbath A (2008) Corporate governance and corporate social responsibility synergies and interrelationships. Highfield Southampton, Blackwell Publishing Ltd 16: 443-459.
7. Marcinkowska M (2012) Corporate governance in banks: Problems and Remedies. Faculty of Arts, Masaryk University, FAI.
8. Iqbal QK (2015) Impact of corporate governance on firm financial performance in financial sector of Pakistan.
9. Khan HI (2015) Impact of corporate governance on firm financial performance in Islamic financial institution. International Letters of Social and Humanistic Science 51: 106-110.

13

Consumer's Satisfaction Level about Grameen Phone's (GP) Service in Bangladesh: A Case Study on Perception Analysis

Ullah A[1], Islam T[2*] and Rahman M[3]

[1]*Department of Business Administration, Port City International University, Chittagong, Bangladesh*
[2]*Faculty of Business Studies, University of Dhaka, Bangladesh*
[3]*Department of Business Administration, Northern University, Bangladesh*

Abstract

Grameenphone (GP) is the leader of Bangladesh telecommunication industry. Grameenphone (GP) not only provides voice service but also offers a number of value added services, in each on both a prepaid and contract bases. Service network, 3G, customer care, physical facilities, billing cost, information service, mobile banking, GP offers and studyline are included in the value added services. Our study discloses the customer's reaction about GPs services. This study investigates why customers are satisfied the GPs existing services and why they are not satisfied and their reaction about GPs services. The study recommends the customers approach and how Grameenphone (GP) retains its customers as a result gradually converted to the loyal customer with competing others operators in the marketplace.

Keywords: Brand image; Customer value; Value added services; Grameenphone

Introduction

By connecting 56.300 million subscribers, 15.7 million Internet subscribers and more than 43 thousand shareholders as of July 2016, giving people access to the internet and digital services, Grameenphone is enabling people to drive business, improve their lives and contribute to building a better future for society [1], the largest cellular operator in the country is GP. GP has nationwide 345,263 point of sales as a result it can easily serve the customer service to their optimal customers. Grameenphone offers innovative services in line with socio-economic conditions of Bangladesh. In 2006, Grameenphone introduced Healthline, a 24 h medical call centre manned by licensed physicians, Mobicash, for electronic purchase of train and lottery tickets and BillPay, which allows utility bill payments to be made by mobile phone. "Studyline", a call centre based service providing education related information, was launched in October 2009. Grameenphone has established approximately 500 Community Information Centers which aim to bring affordable Internet access and other information based services to people in rural areas of Bangladesh. In 2009, Grameenphone introduced branded plug and play USB Internet access modems and branded handsets at a very affordable price. Grameenphone won the GSMA Global Mobile Award for "Best use of Mobile for Social and Economic Development" for its Health Line. Grameenphone also won the GSMA "Green Mobile Award" jointly with Huawei Technologies for building an environment friendly network in Bangladesh [1].

The vision of Grameenphone is to provide the power of digital communication, enabling everyone to improve their lives, build societies and secure a better future for all. The mission of Grameenphone is to help existing customers get the full benefit of being connected. Our success is measured by how passionately they promote us. Everything which is produced by GP should be easy to understand and use. It should always remember that its try to make customers' lives easier. The work of GP should do perfectly. If it doesn't, GP put things right. GP try to delivery, not over-promising. It believes about actions, not words and tries to creative. We bring energy and imagination to our work. Everything GP produce should look fresh and modern. It acknowledges and respect local cultures. GP want to be a part of local communities wherever it operates. It wants to help customers with their specific needs in a way that suits way of their life best [1].

Objectives of the study

On the basis of significance of the study the researchers are motivated

(a) To overview the respondent demographics of Grameenphone users in Bangladesh.

(b) To evaluate the customers' expectation, reaction and satisfaction about GP's existing service in Bangladesh.

(c) To provide some recommendations and suggestions to increase the level of customer satisfaction about GP's existing service in Bangladesh.

Literature Review

Existing customers switch to other operators in order to get low call charges, wide and strong network coverage, and other service incentives [2]. Similarly, a quantitative study on university students in Ghana found that the basic reason for changing mobile service operators is cost savings and network reliability, followed by peer group influence and social reputation [3]. A study on Malaysian big city dwellers found that Malaysian telecom customers perceived price or call rate to be the most important factor, followed by service quality, service availability, and promotion [4].

Contents of strategic service

In the process of implementing the strategy, the organization should address some unique considerations to important factors, not

***Corresponding author:** Touhidul Islam, MPhil, Faculty of Business Studies, University of Dhaka, Bangladesh, E-mail: touhidpust@gmail.com

all at generic level [5]. Customer service is a system of activities that comprises customer support systems, complaint processing, speed of complaint processing, ease of reporting complaint and friendliness when reporting complaint [6]. Many studies have found a direct positive link between service quality perceptions and customer behavioral intensions [7]. According to Turel and Sereko [8] improved customer services are the focal point of the telecom service providers for social as well as for economic reasons. From a social view point, services should be available to the customers on reasonable terms.

Customer satisfaction

Customer satisfaction is a measure of how products and services supplied by a company meet or surpass customer expectation. Customer satisfaction is defined as "the number of customers, or percentage of total customers, whose reported experience with a firm, its products, or its services (ratings) exceeds specified satisfaction goals" [9].

Some other researchers suggest that customer satisfaction can be defined at two levels [10-12]. They are transaction-specific satisfaction and overall satisfaction (holistic). Transaction-specific satisfaction refers to the consumer's satisfaction with a discrete service encounter. It based on the individual level, they judgment customer satisfaction on a specific purchase occasion. Overall satisfaction refers to the consumer's overall subjective post-consumption evaluative judgment based on all encounters and experiences with particular organization. Like Wang, Yonggui et al. [13] said that the overall satisfaction is more fundamental and useful than transaction-specific consumer satisfaction in predicting subsequent consumer behaviors and a firm's past, present and future performance. Satisfaction may result from a very simple or a complex process involving extensive cognitive, affective and other undiscovered psychological and physiological dynamics [14]. Comparing the definitions of satisfaction, it can be found that satisfaction is stated to be a relative concept always judged in relation to a standard [15].

Value added services

A value-added service (VAS) is a popular telecommunications industry term for non-core services, or in short, all services beyond standard voice calls and fax transmissions. However, it can be used in any service industry, for services available at little or no cost, to promote their primary business. In the telecommunications industry, value-added services add value to the standard service offering, spurring the subscriber to use their phone more and allowing the operator to drive up their ARPU. For mobile phones, technologies like SMS, MMS and data access were historically usually considered value-added services, but in recent years SMS, MMS and data access have more and more become core services, and VAS therefore has begun to exclude those services.

Instant messaging, pay for me SMS, miss call alert, call block, mobile email, Facebook/twitter, voice SMS, voice mail, SMS, mms, voice chat, SMS chat, online mobile games, welcome tune, icche tune, music radio, video store , audio-video content, news alert, job alert, sports alert, election information, health tips, education tips matrimonial service, religious service, muktijuddho portal (SMS service), entertainment box, downloadable content infotainment, quick search, and business tune.

Customer value and brand image

Babin et al. [16] defined customer value as "value is a customer's perception of the subjective worth of some activity or object considering all net benefits and costs of consumption". In this research work, the applicable consumption act is the complete services received from Grameenphone. According to the Chang and Wildt [17], the perceived product quality will definitely effects brand value, whereas the price would harmfully influence the brand value. Rationally, higher product quality is not a precondition for brand value since a decrease in product quality can be counterbalance by lesser total price. Nevertheless, Andreassen and Lindestad [18] and Cronin et al. [19] research work showed a positive association between product quality and brand value.

Bitner [20] evaluated that brand image is an additional significant feature in the whole service assessment. Brand image is an acuity of firm detained in customer reminiscence and works as a sieve which influences the insight of the process of the firm [21,22]. Fazio and Zanna [23] find that the service assessments are the important reason of brand image according to the attitude model.

Conceptualization of hypotheses

For extensive review of literature the following hypotheses have been developed to examine the investigation for the purpose of determining customer satisfaction level about Grameenphone's (GP) service in Bangladesh.

H_1: Customer reaction about GP's Billing Cost is positive

H_2: Customer reaction about GP's Customer Care Services is positive.

H_3: Customer reaction about GP's Network is positive.

H_4: Customer reaction about GP's 3G service is positive.

H_5: Customer reaction about GP's Mobile Banking Platform is positive.

H_6: Customer reaction about GP's Information Service is positive.

H_7: Customer reaction about GP's Physical Facilities is positive.

Materials and Methods

It is descriptive research and designed to examine hypotheses. However, the main purpose of the study is to test the customer reaction GP's existing services factors leading to the customer satisfaction and loyalty. The hypotheses have been drawn based on the literature review and the empirical tests have been deployed for explaining the reaction GP's existing services and different variables. For collecting data the structured questionnaire sampling procedure has been applied. The survey is conducted during January 2014 to May 2015 and total 200 numbers of Grameenphone users at Pabna University of Science and Technology, Bangladesh at the graduate level has been taken for this study. This study is depended on raw data originating from a survey. A constructed questionnaire has developed for this purpose. Excepting the questions regarding demographic characteristics and user's value added service interface of the respondents and the issues relating to customers reaction, measured and investigated through 5 point Scale standardized by Brayfield and Rothe [24]. The scale consists of 71 statements, for each statement have five options/ points such as strongly agree- 5, agree- 4, undecided- 3, disagree- 2, and strongly disagree- 1. For statistical analysis SPSS Statistics software package version 17 is used. Reliability of data has been measured by using the Cronbach alpha [25]. Cronbach alpha was 0.910. Alpha is higher than that is suggested by Nunnally and therefore data collected can be considered reliable [26].

Results and Findings

Respondent's demographic

The questionnaires were distributed to the users (n=200) of Grameenphone among them 66.5% respondents thoroughly use GP, 17.0% users were Banglalink users, 6.0% users were Robi, 2.25% users were Airtel, 2.0% were Taletalk, 6.0% were Citycell users who currently use GP service. Among the respondents, 76.5% users use multiple operators' service and 23.5% use only the GP service. 33.5% users use GP below 3 years, 47.0% respondents use within 3-6 years, 29.5% use for 6 years and above. Respondents below 30 years using GP are 100%. 65.0% respondent's monthly expense below Tk 500, 27.0% incurs expense within Tk. 500-1000 and 8.0% respondents have above Tk 1000 monthly expense. All of the respondent's have bachelor degree comprises 100%. 100% respondents are student. 76.0% Male and 24.0% are Female respondents (Table 1).

Chi-square tests for customer reaction assessment

Opinion has been served in respect to satisfaction with GP's billing cost among two hundred (200) respondents. Among the respondent 18.5 % strongly disagreed, 31% disagreed, 14% remained undecided, 29.5% agreed, and 7% strongly agreed with Chi-Square value 41.850[a] (*df*=4) with *Asymp. Sig.* =.000. Therefore, it can be concluded that customers' reaction is negative impact or they are not satisfied about GP's billing cost (Tables 2 and 3).

Opinion has been served in respect to satisfaction with GP's customer care service among two hundred (200) respondents. Among the respondent 8.5% strongly disagreed, 18.5% disagreed, 13.5% remained undecided, 43% agreed, and 16.5% strongly agreed with Chi-Square value 71.800[a] (*df*=4) with *Asymp. Sig.* =.000. Therefore, it can be concluded that customers' reaction is positive or they are satisfied about GP's customer care service (Tables 4 and 5).

		Frequency	Percent	Cumulative percent
First Mobile Operators	GP	133	66.5	66.5
	Banglalink	34	17.0	83.5
	Robi	12	6.0	89.5
	Airtel	5	2.5	92.0
	Taletalk	4	2.0	94.0
	Citycell	12	6.0	100.0
	Total	200	100.0	
Current Operator	GP	200	100.0	100.0
Multiple operators Service	Yes	153	76.5	76.5
	No	47	23.5	100.0
	Total	200	100.0	
Year of Connection	below 3 years	47	23.5	23.5
	3-6 years	94	47.0	70.5
	6 years & above	59	29.5	100.0
	Total	200	100.0	
Age	bellow 30 years	200	100.0	100.0
Monthly Mobile Expense	bellow Tk 500	130	65.0	65.0
	Tk 500-1000	54	27.0	92.0
	above Tk 1000	16	8.0	100.0
	Total	200	100.0	
Education	Bachelor	200	100.0	100.0
Profession	Student	200	100.0	100.0
Gender	Male	152	76.0	76.0
	Female	48	24.0	100.0
	Total	200	100.0	

Table 1: Respondents demographics.

	Observed N	Percent	Expected N	Residual
Strongly disagree	37	18.5	40.0	-3.0
Disagree	62	31.0	40.0	22.0
Undecided	28	14.0	40.0	-12.0
Agree	59	29.5	40.0	19.0
Strongly agree	14	7.0	40.0	-26.0
Total	200	100.0		

Table 2: Satisfaction with GP's billing cost.

Chi-Square	41.850[a]
Df	4
Asymp. Sig.	.000
a. 0 cells (.0%) have expected frequencies less than 5. The minimum expected cell frequency is 40.0.	

Table 3: Test statistics - GP's billing cost.

	Observed N	Percent	Expected N	Residual
Strongly Disagree	17	8.5	40.0	-23.0
Disagree	37	18.5	40.0	-3.0
Undecided	27	13.5	40.0	-13.0
Agree	86	43.0	40.0	46.0
Strongly Agree	33	16.5	40.0	-7.0
Total	200	100.0		

Table 4: Satisfaction with customer care service.

Chi-Square	71.800[a]
Df	4
Asymp. Sig.	.000
a. 0 cells (.0%) have expected frequencies less than 5. The minimum expected cell frequency is 40.0.	

Table 5: Test statistics - GP's customer care service.

	Observed N	Percent	Expected N	Residual
Strongly Disagree	21	10.5	40.0	-19.0
Disagree	30	15.0	40.0	-10.0
Undecided	19	9.5	40.0	-21.0
Agree	85	42.5	40.0	45.0
Strongly Agree	45	22.5	40.0	5.0
Total	200	100.0		

Table 6: Satisfaction with GP's network.

Opinion has been served in respect to satisfaction with GP's network among two hundred (200) respondents. Among the respondent 10.5% strongly disagreed, 15% disagreed, 9.5% remained undecided, 42.5% agreed, and 22.5% strongly agreed with Chi-Square value 73.800[a] (*df*=4) with *Asymp. Sig.*=.000. Therefore, it can be concluded that customers' reaction is positive or they are satisfied about GP's network (Tables 6 and 7).

Opinion has been served in respect to satisfaction with GP's 3G service among two hundred (200) respondents. Among the respondent 12% strongly disagreed, 24% disagreed, 19% remained undecided, 35% agreed, and 10% strongly agreed with Chi-Square value 40.600[a] (*df*=4) with *Asymp. Sig.* =.000. Therefore, it can be concluded that customers' reaction is positive or they are satisfied about GP's 3G service (Tables 8 and 9).

Opinion has been served in respect to satisfaction with GP's mobile banking platform among two hundred (200) respondents. Among the respondent 8.5% strongly disagreed, 15% disagreed, 14% remained undecided, 44.5% agreed, and 18% strongly agreed with Chi-Square value 79.750[a] (*df*=4) with *Asymp. Sig.* =.000. Therefore, it can be concluded that customers' reaction is positive or they are satisfied about GP's mobile banking platform (Tables 10 and 11).

Chi-Square	73.800[a]
Df	4
Asymp. Sig.	.000
a. 0 cells (.0%) have expected frequencies less than 5. The minimum expected cell frequency is 40.0.	

Table 7: Test statistics - GP's network.

	Observed N	Percent	Expected N	Residual
Strongly Disagree	24	12.0	40.0	-16.0
Disagree	48	24.0	40.0	8.0
Undecided	38	19.0	40.0	-2.0
Agree	70	35.0	40.0	30.0
Strongly Agree	20	10.0	40.0	-20.0
Total	200	100.0		

Table 8: Satisfaction with GP's 3G service.

Chi-Square	40.600[a]
Df	4
Asymp. Sig.	.000
a. 0 cells (.0%) have expected frequencies less than 5. The minimum expected cell frequency is 40.0.	

Table 9: Test statistics - GP's 3G service.

	Observed N	Percent	Expected N	Residual
Strongly Disagree	17	8.5	40	-23
Disagree	30	15	40	-10
Undecided	28	14	40	-12
Agree	89	44.5	40	49
Strongly Agree	36	18	40	-4
Total	200	100		

Table 10: Satisfaction with GP's mobile banking platform.

Chi-Square	79.750[a]
Df	4
Asymp. Sig.	.000
a. 0 cells (.0%) have expected frequencies less than 5. The minimum expected cell frequency is 40.0.	

Table 11: Test statistics - GP's mobile banking platform.

	Observed N	Percent	Expected N	Residual
Strongly Disagree	22	11.0	40.0	-18.0
Disagree	33	16.5	40.0	-7.0
Undecided	31	15.5	40.0	-9.0
Agree	89	44.5	40.0	49.0
Strongly Agree	25	12.5	40.0	-15.0
Total	200	100.0		

Table 12: Satisfaction with GP's information service.

Opinion has been served in respect to satisfaction with GP's information service among two hundred (200) respondents. Among the respondent 11% strongly disagreed, 16.5% disagreed, 15.5% remained undecided, 44.5% agreed, and 12.5% strongly agreed with Chi-Square value 77.000[a] (*df*=4) with *Asymp. Sig.* =.000. Therefore, it can be concluded that customers' reaction is positive or they are satisfied about GP's information service (Tables 12 and 13).

Opinion has been served in respect to satisfaction with GP's physical facilities among two hundred (200) respondents. Among the respondent 10% strongly disagreed, 25.5% disagreed, 20.5% remained undecided, 34% agreed, and 10% strongly agreed with Chi-Square value 42.650[a] (*df*=4) with *Asymp. Sig.* =.000. Therefore, it can be concluded that customers' reaction is positive or they are satisfied about GP's physical facilities (Tables 14 and 15).

Hypotheses testing

According to the analysis of Chi-Square Tests we can go to conclusion of hypotheses test-in Table 16.

Recommendations and Conclusions

Grameenphone try to achieve optimal objective or goal it must be considered customer reaction and meet up their satisfaction. To ensure GP's goal as well as retain existing customer and capture new prospects it must be served the better services match with customers expectation due to customers are the king of market. If customer reaction is positive or favorable obviously it leads the GP's better position in the marketplace. GP try to provide better quality product performance to mesh with customer's desire in mind and satisfied customer become a loyal customer of Grameenphone who are the advocate of the organization. If customer reaction is not positive and GP can't consider the customer perception automatically they will not continue of using GP's service ultimately goes to others operator. It should be considered the customer reaction because the prosperity of Grameenphone depends upon the customer satisfaction.

- Customer reaction about GP's billing cost is negative or not

Chi-Square	77.000[a]
Df	4
Asymp. Sig.	.000
a. 0 cells (.0%) have expected frequencies less than 5. The minimum expected cell frequency is 40.0.	

Table 13: Test Statistics - GP's information service.

	Observed N	Percent	Expected N	Residual
Strongly Disagree	20	10.0	40.0	-20.0
Disagree	51	25.5	40.0	11.0
Undecided	41	20.5	40.0	1.0
Agree	68	34.0	40.0	28.0
Strongly Agree	20	10.0	40.0	-20.0
Total	200	100.0		

Table 14: Satisfaction with physical facilities.

Chi-Square	42.650[a]
Df	4
Asymp. Sig.	.000
a. 0 cells (.0%) have expected frequencies less than 5. The minimum expected cell frequency is 40.0.	

Table 15: Test statistics.

S. N.	Hypotheses	Accept/reject
	H1: Customer reaction about GP's Billing Cost is positive	Rejected
	H2: Customer reaction about GP's Customer Care Services is positive.	Accepted
	H3: Customer reaction about GP's Network is positive.	Accepted
	H4: Customer reaction about GP's 3G service is positive.	Accepted
	H5: Customer reaction about GP's Mobile Banking Platform is positive.	Accepted
	H6: Customer reaction about GP's Information Service is positive.	Accepted
	H7: Customer reaction about GP's Physical Facilities is positive.	Accepted

Table 16: Hypotheses testing.

favorable, so Grameenphone reset its billing cost which is matched with satisfactory level of customers.

- Customer reaction about GP's customer care service is favorable but not strongly agrees, so Grameenphone try to serve better customer care service for retaining existing customers and capture new customers.
- Customer reaction about GP's network is positive but not strongly agrees, so GP try to improve its network system.
- Customer reaction about GP's 3G service is positive but not strongly agrees, so Grameenphone serve the high speed of 3G service
- Customer reaction about GP's mobile banking service is favorable but not strongly agrees, so Grameenphone try to develop its mobile banking service.
- Customer reaction about GP's information service is positive but not strongly agrees, so Grameenphone try to deliver information services which are needed by customers.
- Customer reaction about GP's physical facilities is positive but not strongly agrees, so Grameenphone try to set up available physical facilities to serve the existing and optimum customers.

References

1. GP (2016) About Grameenphone. Grameenphone, Bangladesh.
2. Hasan MK, Yeasmin A, Dey P (2013) Factors Influencing to Bangladeshi Consumers' Mobile Phone Operators Choice and Change Behavior. Journal of Economics and Sustainable Development 4: 2222-2855.
3. Keelson S (2012) Factors Affecting Consumer Choice of Multiple Mobile Services, Global Journal of Business Research 6: 59
4. Rahman S, Haque A , Ahmad MIS (2010) Exploring influencing factors for the selection of mobile phone service providers: A structural equational modeling (SEM) approach on Malaysian consumers. African Journal of Business Management 4: 2885-2898
5. Marketing Plan (2015) Center for Business Planning.
6. Hanif M, Hafeez S, Riaz A (2010) Factors affecting customer satisfaction. International Research Journal of Finance and Economics 60: 44-52.
7. Zeithaml VA, Berry LL, Parasuraman A (1996) The behavioral consequences of service quality. The Journal of Marketing 60: 31-46.
8. Turel O, Serenko A (2006) Satisfaction with mobile services in Canada: An empirical investigation. Telecommunications policy 30: 314-331.
9. Farris, Paul W, Neil T, Bendle, Phillip et al. (2010) Marketing Metrics: The Definitive Guide to Measuring Marketing Performance. Upper Saddle River, New Jersey: Pearson Education, Inc.
10. Bitner MJ, Hubbert AR (1994) Encounter Satisfaction versus Overall Satisfaction versus Quality, Service Quality New Directions in Theory and Practices. London: Sage Publications, pp: 72-95.
11. Jones MA, Suh J (2000) Transaction-specific satisfaction and overall satisfaction: an empirical analysis. Journal of Services Marketing 14: 147-160.
12. Bodet G (2008) Customer satisfaction and loyalty in service: Two concepts, four constructs, several relationships. Journal of Retailing & Consumer Services 15: 156-163.
13. Yonggui W, Hing PL, Yongheng Y (2004) An integrated framework for service quality, customer value, satisfaction: Evidence from China's telecommunication industry. Information Systems Frontiers 6: 325-340.
14. Oh H, Parks CS (1997) Customer satisfaction and service quality: A critical review of the literature and research implications for the hospitality industry. Hospitality Research Journal 20: 36-64.
15. Yuksel A, Yuksel F (2001) Measurement and Management Issues in Customer Satisfaction Research: Review, Critique and Research Agenda: Part One. Journal of travel and tourism marketing 10: 47-80.
16. Babin B, Darden W, Griffin M (1994) Work and/or fun? Measuring hedonic and utilitarian shopping value. J Consum Res 20: 644-656.
17. Chang T, Wildt A (1994) Price, product information, and purchase intention: an empirical study. Journal of Academy Marketing Science 22: 16-27.
18. Andreassen T, Lindestad B (1998) Customer loyalty and complex services: the impact of corporate image on quality, customer satisfaction and loyalty for customers with varying degrees of service expertise. International Journal of Service Industrial Management 9: 7-23.
19. Cronin J, Brady M, Hult G (2000) Assessing the effects of quality, value, and customer satisfaction on consumer behavioral intentions in service environments. Journal of Retail 76: 193-218.
20. Bitner M (1991) The evolution of the services marketing mix and its relationship to service quality: A multidisciplinary and multinational perspective.
21. Gronroos C (1988) Service quality: the six criteria of good perceived service quality. Revenue Business 9: 10-3.
22. Keller K (1993) Conceptualizing, measuring, and managing customer based equity. Journal of Marketing, 57: 1-22.
23. Fazio R, Zanna M (1978) Attitudinal qualities relating to the strength of the attitude – behavior relationship. Journal of Exp. Social Psychology 14: 398-408.
24. Brayfield AH, Rothe HF (1951) An Index of Job Satisfaction. Journal of Applied Psychology 35: 307-311.
25. Cronbach LJ (1951) Coefficient Alpha and Internal Structure of Test. Psychometrika 16: 297-334.
26. Nunnally JL (1978) Psychometric Theory. New York: McGraw Hill Company, p: 640.

Firm Aggressiveness and Respective Performance Empirical Study under Pakistani Setting

Rehman OU*

Lecturer at CFCBE, CECOS University, Peshawar, Pakistan

Abstract

Policy makers Aggressiveness and conservativeness regarding designing optimal capital structure (especially working capital) is a debatable matter from last 50 years. The phenomenon is still vague especially in Pakistan because of the information asymmetry and failure of perfect market hypothesis. The study investigates capital structure of all non-financial listed firms on Pakistan Stock Exchange (PSX) for the period of 2008 to 2014. To test the relation between dependent (ROI and ROA) and independent variables (AIP and AFP), the study employ control variables (ROE, ROCE, GROWTH, SIZE and AGE) and uses exponential generalized least square regression. Results reveals that financial managers aggressiveness regarding financial policy negatively, while aggressiveness regarding investment policy positively effecting the firm's performance. The study also found that with the passage of time, firms in Pakistan devastating their performance. That's why study found negative relation between firms' age and dependent variables.

Keywords: Capital structure; Firm's performance; ROI; ROA

Introduction

Financial performance of firm and its value is greatly affected by the design of its capital structure. This issue is getting immense consideration after the MM hypothesis [1]. MM proposes the perfect market hypothesis, that under such circumstances the firm value is not affected by fluctuating in the capital structure. MM postulates that interest ratio provides tax advantage to the firm and because of that it is decidedly suggested that firms use more debts in their capital structure [1]. Various researcher work on this concept to reveal the main idea, which enrich literature in the following forms (Figure 1):

(a) MM proposes that capital structure design has no relation with firm value

(b) MM contended that interest expense is beneficial to the firm as it work as tax shield for the firm. So their study recommends high use of leverage in the capital structure.

(c) The point L in Figure 1 postulates the optimal capital structure position. If debt is furthermore boost from point L, financial distress cost increases compare to leverage benefits.

(d) This balanced association will supplementary be changed when taking into consideration the effect of other variables like agency conflicts, informational asymmetry, financial distress etc…

(e) The concluding concern of the study integrates the inclination of management towards financial preference selection. By doing this, there is not full control in the finance manager hands plus there's sufficient equity balance for firm's robust solvency position.

Key: W: firm value; L: leverage; L', L" and L'": optimal capital structure

Problem statement

The corporate level orthodoxy over the few decades is supposing finance manager doing well with running capital. The dilemma bits when managers second, third and/or so forth decision are not up to the mark that mostly deviating from the firm's goal. The study attempts to identify such aggressiveness of finance manager while dealing with working capital during the business course.

Research question

The study attempts to analyze the finance manager's aggressiveness regarding handling working capital of the company at corporate level.

Significance of the study

In Pakistan, there are many factors which play vital role in effecting the firm performance or are uncourageous to the business environment like financial constraints awarded by the govt. impoverished infrastructure, political instability, low transparency position etc. Because of noised and inefficient market structure, it is very difficult for the firms (non-financial) listed on PSX to maintained optimum capital structure. In such scenarios, the role of finance manager in any organization becomes tough as on one hand, he has to boost up the firm's worth by appreciated the firm's performance. The major intention of the research is to investigate the capital structure design effect on performance of the firm during the period of 2008 to 2014 in Pakistan.

Literature Review

Conceptual review

One of the major rationales of fluctuating firm performance is the design selection of capital structure. Major use of leverage yield tax shield but also hoisting insolvency cost distress. So there's a capital structure mix in which tax shield marginal benefit is more than its bankruptcy cost. Harris and Raviv contended that capital structure is associated to the balance between bankruptcy gain from both managers and shareholders and insolvency cost [2]. Therefore because of more benefit of highest leverage ratio, it is beneficial to both managers

***Corresponding author:** Obaid Ur Rehman, Lecturer at CFCBE, CECOS University, Peshawar, Pakistan, E-mail: bluechip1122@gmail.com

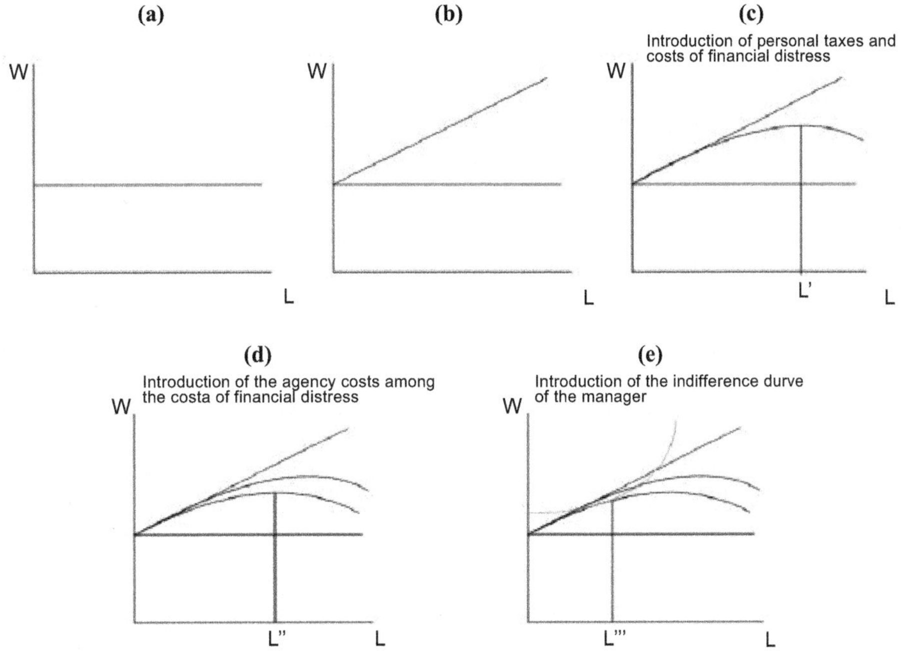

Figure 1: Taken from La Rocca, (2007).

and shareholders. Though literature take too lightly the liquidation overheads of bankruptcy or restructuring, or the united curiosity of shareholders and managers, which direct organizations to employs high leverage ratio than optimal in their capital structure.

Theoretical review

Irrelevant and relevant theory: Modigliani and Miller postulates that firm's worth is impassive under certain assumptions like efficient market hypothesis, no transaction or impoverishment cost and taxation is irrelevant [1]. It means choice of leverage is extraneous and external and internal finances are faultlessly alternate to each other.

Agency cost theory: Berle and Means contended the relation between principal (shareholders) and agent (manager) [3]. This relationship came into being when one or more principals hire one or more agents to work on their behalf in the company. This phenomenon creates opportunity for the manager to put their interest prioritized to principal's interest.

Pecking order theory: Developed by Donaldson assert that firm's financing needs decides the level of leverage. The theory postulates that typically companies used their retain earning at first in priority to sponsor their projects. Secondly company call for external debt and finally the alternative of issuing new share and generating equity is exercise to fuel their project engine. The theory is cited by Akhtar et al. in their research work [2,4].

Empirical literature

Literature exposes that many researcher work on working capital management but particularly the aggressiveness area is still vague in Pakistan. Gupta and Huefner and Gupta apply variant financial ratios in working capital management among industries [5]. Their study found variation among industry w.r.t. leverage, liquidity, profitability and performance. Johnson strengthens the previous work by indulging more samples using random effect test [6]. Pinches et al. categorize different financial ratios using FCA and concluded that they're constant over the longer period [7].

Various researchers contended that firm capital structure regarding current assets and current liability altered within industry eventually Soenen et al. [8]. The significance of capital structure arrangement especially working capital is analyzed by Filbeck and Krueger by considering manager policy of 32 non-financial listed companies in United State. Their study postulates a momentous variation found among industry sooner or later [9].

Association between conservative and aggressive working capital portion of capital structure is analyzed by Afza and Nazir by taking a total of 263 non financial listed firms on KSE for the period of 1998 to 2003 [10]. Researchers employed LSD and ANOVA test for data analysis. The result shows variant outcomes regarding working capital aggressiveness and conservativeness transversely diverse industries in Pakistan. Furthermore, correlation test corroborated that divergence across industry is significant over 6 years. Researcher found adverse association between firm's profitability and aggressiveness in working capital management policies (AIP and AFP).

The study on hand updates the literature regarding aggressiveness in working capital impact on profitability of the company measured by ROI and ROA.

Methodologies

Universe of the study

The study is conducted for the rationale to provide a complete review about the relationship of the capital Structure design and its effect on firm performance. For this purpose, the study uses all non financial listed companies domiciled at Pakistan Stock Exchange as universe of the study for the period of 2008 to 2014. A total of 527 firms are analyzed at first stage which is slimed to 209 firms after meeting the sample selection criterion which makes a total of 1869 observations. The whole population is taken as a census for the analysis.

Sampling design

At first stage, 527 non-financial listed firms on PSX are selected whose financial secondary data is available for the study period i.e. 2008-2014. Following firms are excluded from the sample:

1. Banks, investment companies, and insurance companies as their capital structure are different from the non-financial sector firms, which possibly distort our analysis.
2. Incomplete data for study period
3. Firms those are suspended or delisted during the study period.
4. Firms having standard deviation more than 3 at any variable (dependent or independent) (Table 1).

Data collection

Data is collected from the state bank of Pakistan publications, balance sheet analysis of joint stock companies listed on Karachi stock exchange, financial highlights and financial statements which exists in the annual reports downloaded from the company's respective websites of entire non-financial listed firms for the year 2008-2014 based on the subjective sampling.

Justification of variables

Degree of firm's aggressiveness (in working capital) and its marginal role on overall performance is the intent of the study. The study takes firm performance (ROI and ROA) as dependent while aggressiveness (AIP and AFP) as independent variables. In order to cop the more rationalization, the study employs major contributory variables to minimize standard error.

Dependent variable

$$\text{Return on Investment}\left(\text{ROI}\right)_{it} = \frac{\text{Average}(\text{EAT}_{it} + \text{EAT}_{it-1})}{\text{Average}(\text{Equity}_{it} + \text{Equity}_{it-1})}$$

$$\text{Return on Assets}\left(\text{ROA}\right)_{it} = \frac{\text{Average}(\text{EAT}_{it} + \text{EAT}_{it-1})}{\text{Average}(\text{Asset}_{it} + \text{Asset}_{it-1})}$$

Independent variable

$$\text{Return on Equity (ROE)}_{it} = \frac{(\text{Net Profit before Tax})_{it}}{\text{Average}(\text{Equity}_{it} + \text{Equity}_{it-1})}$$

$$\text{Return on Capital Employed (ROCE)it} = \frac{(\text{Net Profit before Tax})_{it}}{\text{Average}(\text{Capital Employed}_{it} + \text{Capital Employed}_{it-1})}$$

$$\text{Growth of the firm (GROWTH)}_{it} = \frac{(\text{Sales}_{it} - \text{Sales}_{it-1})}{(\text{Sales})_{it-1}}$$

$$\text{Size of the firm (SIZE)}_{it} = \text{Logarithm of total assets}$$

AGE = Firm's date of incorporation (Logarithm of Age)

Control variable

Several researcher uses control variable in their studies while measuring firm performance [11-14]. The study on hand employs the following control variables to cope the elucidating aspects of firm performance which eventually curtail standard error.

ROE and ROCE is taken as control variable because of scheming other than ROI and ROA variables [15,16]. GROWTH, SIZE and AGE are taken as control variable because of the modified industry nature.

Model specification

Analytical framework and empirical model specification: It's the strength of the study that it uses panel data for a longer period of time (2008-2014). In panel regression estimation, the data is doubly indexed (cross-sectional and time series) which making a huge data as sample of the study. Furthermore panel data has the characteristics of controlling the endogeneity and heterogeneity problems. So the panel regression model analyzes the individual specific factor in different cross sections and in different time series of dependent variable with the independent variables.

The fundamental structure of panel regression model is:

$$Y_{it}=\beta X'_{it} + \alpha Z'_{i} + \varepsilon_{it} \quad (1)$$

In the above equation (1), the endogeneity is denoted by X'_{it} and the individual effect or heterogeneity is expressed by Z'_{t} which postulates a stable and recognizable and non-recognizable variables. OLS evaluation supplies proficient and steady approximation of the original considerations (Kyereboah and Coleman, 2007) [17]. Except when Z'_{t} is non-recognizable and associated with X'_{it} then it need to use the other parametric tests because using of OLS in this situation will ultimately distort the fundamental objective of the analysis.

Model specification: From the literature, the study applies panel data analysis (fixed-effect, random-effect and OLS model) in order to analyse the depiction of capital structure on firm performance. The study has the following models in order to examine the hypothesis:

Firm performance=f (Aggressive Investment Policy, Aggressive Financial Policy, Return on Equity, Return on Capital Employed, Firm Growth, Firm Size, Firm AGE).

Firm performance measured by ROI

Pooled Regression Model

Fixed Effect Model

Random Effect Model

Firm performance measured by ROA

Pooled Regression Model

Fixed Effect Model

Random Effect Model

Data Presentation, Analysis and Interpretation

The study analyses the data on hand in two major parts. In first part, data is expressed using descriptive analysis. While in the second

Total indexed firms at first stage for the study period	527
Less: Firms having incomplete data for the study period	-162
Less: Firms with negative equity	-77
Less: Firms having standard deviation more than 3	-21
Study sample for non-financial listed firms:	267

Table 1: Study sample selection.

part, data is empirically examined using inferential analysis using variant statistical software packages.

Interpretation and analysis of data

Descriptive statistics: This part shows the general nature of data on hand for analysis purpose like mean, Std. Dev., minimum and maximum etc...

Standard deviation value of all the variables in Table 2, Appendix exposes that data used in the study is normally distributed. ROI and ROA values are asymmetrically distributed with a long tail moving towards left. It means firms in Pakistan are recurrently gaining little and few extreme losses. The Kurtosis values of ROI and ROA crossing the high degree of leptokurtic.

Correlation analysis: Table 3 exposes the correlation analysis among variables (dependent and independent) of the study. Correlation analysis (Table 3) postulates that there is high degree of association among return proxies of the study. The study found slight negative impact of aggressive financial policy on firms return. Growth has no concern with the firm performance (ROI and ROA) while Age is statistically significant with ROA while show no association with ROI.

Test of hypothesis

Regression analysis: This part of the study analyzes the panel data on hand to reveal the effect of explanatory variables on performance of the firm in Pakistan for the period of 2008 to 2014. The research work employs OLS model considering identical intercept overtime. The analysis also indulges the consideration of variant intercept for every firm in Pakistan by conducting fixed-effect model and random-effect model.

Capital Structure and firm performance measured by ROI: Table 4 exposes the relation between capital structure and firm's performance (ROI) in Pakistan for the period of 2008 to 2014. The p-value of F-statistics 645.68 (0.000<0.05), 245.93 (0.000<0.05) and 4287.58 (0.000<0.05) contended that all the independent variables are mutually statistically significant at pooled-model, fixed-effect model and random-effect model in explicating deviation in the firm's performance in Pakistan. The p-value of Hausman test (0.000) postulating that difference in fixed-effect and random-effect models coefficients is systematic. So the study accept the alternative hypothesis thus acknowledge and infer the fixed-effect model for data analysis, which contradicting the study of Lawal et al. [18,19].

Fixed effect model organize the lost variables that are variant in cases while constant overtime.

This let the data alter overtime and exposing independent variable impact on dependent variable.

For i cases within j group

Therefore αj is a separate intercept for each group

It is equivalent to solely at within group variations:

¯X-bar-sub-j means of X for group j, etc.

Model is within group because all the variables are centered on mean of each group.

Variables	Mean	Std. Dev.	Skewness	Kurtosis	Minimum	Maximum
ROI	0.068071	0.25162	-2.116738	19.616974	-2.08677	1.771462
ROA	0.041206	0.09953	-3.23484	50.811686	-1.65149	0.406255
AIP	0.462992	0.204154	0.177328	-0.27124	0.000874	0.999594
AFP	0.375796	0.170659	0.072003	-0.557938	0	0.892639
ROE	0.12765	0.320601	0.243567	13.056689	-1.95829	2.800278
ROCE	0.106261	0.229753	1.364374	18.46689	-1.94783	2.319279
GROWTH	1.067346	0.585424	6.05462	56.659875	0	8.369427
SIZE	6.479196	0.712418	0.091951	0.428504	3.841172	8.695685
AGE	1.438564	0.28394	-2.050464	8.197873	0	2.10721

Table 2: Descriptive statistics.

Description		1	2	3	4	5	6	7	8	9
ROI	Pearson	1	0.841	0.189	-0.053	0.829	0.744	0.089	0.238	0.045
(1)	Sig		0	0	0.023	0	0	0	0	0.051
ROA	Pearson	0.841	1	0.233	-0.15	0.684	0.729	0.098	0.268	0.103
(2)	Sig	0		0	0	0	0	0	0	0
AIP	Pearson	0.189	0.233	1	0.422	0.205	0.285	0.071	-0.051	-0.018
(3)	Sig	0	0		0	0	0	0.002	0.027	0.432
AFP	Pearson	-0.53	-.150	0.422	1	0.026	0.029	0.059	0.028	-0.076
(4)	Sig	0.023	0	0		0.269	0.206	0.011	0.219	0.001
ROE	Pearson	0.829	0.684	0.205	0.026	1	0.92	0.173	0.229	0.047
(5)	Sig	0	0	0	0.269		0	0	0	0.041
ROCE	Pearson	0.744	0.729	0.285	0.029	0.92	1	0.183	0.234	0.081
(6)	Sig	0	0	0	0.206	0		0	0	0
GRTH	Pearson	0.089	0.098	0.071	0.059	0.173	0.183	1	0.168	-0.016
(7)	Sig	0	0	0.002	0.011	0	0		0	0.502
SIZ	Pearson	0.238	0.268	-0.051	0.028	0.229	0.234	0.168	1	-0.02
(8)	Sig	0	0	0.027	0.219	0	0	0		0.399
AGE	Pearson	0.045	0.103	-0.018	-0.076	0.047	0.081	-0.016	-0.02	1
(9)	Sig	0.051	0	0.432	0.001	0.041	0	0.502	0.399	

Table 3: Pearson bivariate correlations analysis.

Variables	Pooled		Fixed Effect		Random Effect	
	ROI	ROA	ROI	ROA	ROI	ROA
AIP	0.120***	0.079***	0.291***	0.189***	0.126***	0.111***
AFP	−0.164***	−0.137***	−0.266***	−0.203***	−0.168***	−0.158***
ROE	0.766***	0.043*	0.680***	0.051*	0.760***	0.044***
ROCE	−0.204	0.231***	−0.253	0.154***	−0.205***	0.204***
GROWTH	−0.025***	−0.007**	−0.021***	−0.009***	−0.025***	−0.009***
SIZE	0.027***	0.018***	0.167***	0.084*	0.028***	0.022***
AGE	0.006	0.014*	−0.254	−0.178	0.007	0.012*
Const	−0.160***	-0.107**	−0.721****	−0.276	−0.167***	−0.134***
No. of Obs.			1869			
R2	0.7083	0.594	0.5191	0.4194	0.7083	0.589
F (*p*-value)	645 (0.00)	388 (0.00)	245 (0.00)	164 (0.00)	4287 (0.00)	1958 (0.00)
	Hausman (ROI)			212.33 (0.000)		
	Hausman (ROA)			934.94 (0.000)		

Note: *, ** and *** shows the significance level at 10%, 5% and 1% level of significance.

Table 4: Capital Structure Aggressiveness and Firm Performance (measured by ROI and ROA).

The results at Table 4 exposes that firm's aggressive policy regarding investment has statistically positive impact on firm performance. While aggressive financial policy negatively impacts the firm performance. It means firms in Pakistan if uses more fixed liability instead of current liability, it'll perform better. On the other hand, if firms put into practice high degree of current assets, it has positive impact on its performance. Furthermore; all the other control variables (except ROE and SIZE of the firm) negatively effecting the firm performance. ROCE and AGE shows negative and statistically non significance with respect to ROI in measuring firm performance [20].

Capital Structure and firm performance measured by ROA: Table 4 exposes the connection between capital structure design and firm's performance (measured by ROA) in Pakistan for the period of 2008 to 2014. The F-statistic p-value postulates that 388.96 (0.000<0.05), 164.56 (0.000<0.05) and 1958.97 (0.000<0.05) contended that all the independent variables are strongly statistically significant at pooled-model, fixed-effect model and random-effect model in explicating variation in the firm's performance in Pakistan. The p-value of Hausman test (0.000) postulating that difference in fixed-effect and random-effect models coefficients is organized. So the study accept the alternative hypothesis, which means fixed-effect model fit for data analysis, which is also contradicting with the study of Lawal et al. [18,21].

The results at Table 4, exposes that firm's aggressive policy regarding investment has statistically positive impact on firm performance. While aggressive financial policy negatively impacts the firm performance [22]. It means firms in Pakistan if uses more fixed liability instead of current liability, it'll perform better. On the other hand, if firms put into practice high degree of current assets, it has positive impact on its performance. Furthermore; all the other control variables (except GROWTH and AGE of the firm) has positively affecting the firm performance. AGE shows negative and statistically non-significance with respect to ROA in measuring firm performance.

Table 5 postulates the Levin-Lin-Chu panel unit root testing at level (1) and at first difference.

The hypothesis of unit root testing are:

H_0: Panels contain unit roots

H_1: Panels are stationary

The p-value of dependent and independent variables contended

Variables	*Levin-Lin-Chu*	*p*-value	*Hadri LM Stationary*	
	Statistics		Statistics	*p*-value
ROI	-34.2511	0	20.2354	0
D_ROI	-5.40E+02	0	0.3135	0.377
ROA	-44.9769	0	22.5098	0
D_ROA	-34.2511	0	3.9294	0
AIP	-47.254	0	18.4439	0
D_AIP	-1.30E+02	0	7.8984	0
AFP	-4.40E+03	0	19.9799	0
D_AFP	-6.60E+02	0	5.9114	0

Table 5: Unit root testing at level (1) and first difference.

that all the variables are stationary at level and first difference. While the Hadri LM stationary test postulates that ROI data contain unit root at level (1) and at first difference, it is stationary. After this, the study run the panel co-integration model because the pre-condition of panel co-integration model is the variable must unit root at level but when converted into first difference, then it will become stationary. Hadri LM test can fulfill the condition of panel co-integration model, so it can be considered as benchmark of the study. The result in Table 5 exposes that except D_ROI, all the other variables at level (1) and at first difference contains some unit roots because of the longer period of time and high number of cross sections [23].

Summary, Conclusion and Recommendations

Summary

The research is about to find the finance manager's aggressive and conservative behavior regarding restructuring the capital structure of the firm (esp. working capital). The study tries to find (in the context of Pakistani setting) that what style of manager's is successful in boosting the firm's performance.

The study found that finance manager's aggressiveness in working capital regarding investment policy shows favorable impacts. But with the passage of time, such policy need to be reconstructed otherwise it'll shows unfavorable outcomes in the long run.

On the other hand, finance managers aggressiveness in working capital holding financial policy shows unfavorable outcomes. But in the long run, such decision shows fruitful results. Concisely finance managers in Pakistan need to be aggressive in working capital regarding investments policy but for the short run. While finance manager need to be conservatives regarding financial policy for the long run. If the above hypothesis is followed by the finance manager's, they'll successful in their decision up to 51.91% in investment policy and 41.94% in financial policy.

Conclusion

The study discloses the relation between dependent variables (ROI and ROA) and independent variables (AIP and AFP). A sample of 267 non-financial listed firms from all sectors of PSX (after meeting the sample selection criterion) for the period of 2008 to 2014 making a total of 1869 observations. The R2 value in case of ROI is 51.91% and 41.94% in case of ROA (Table 4). Standard Deviation (Table 2) shows normality of data distribution in all variables (as their respective standard deviation is >1). However the Skewness and Kurtosis results (in case of dependent variables) data is negatively skewed and showing high degree of leptokurtic. Pearson correlation (2-tailed at 5% significance level) (Table 3) reveals that AFP is negative and significant while AIP is positive and significantly associated with dependent variables. All the control variables are positively and statistically significantly associated (at 5% level of significance) with the firm performance except AGE in case of ROI (Figures 2 and 3).

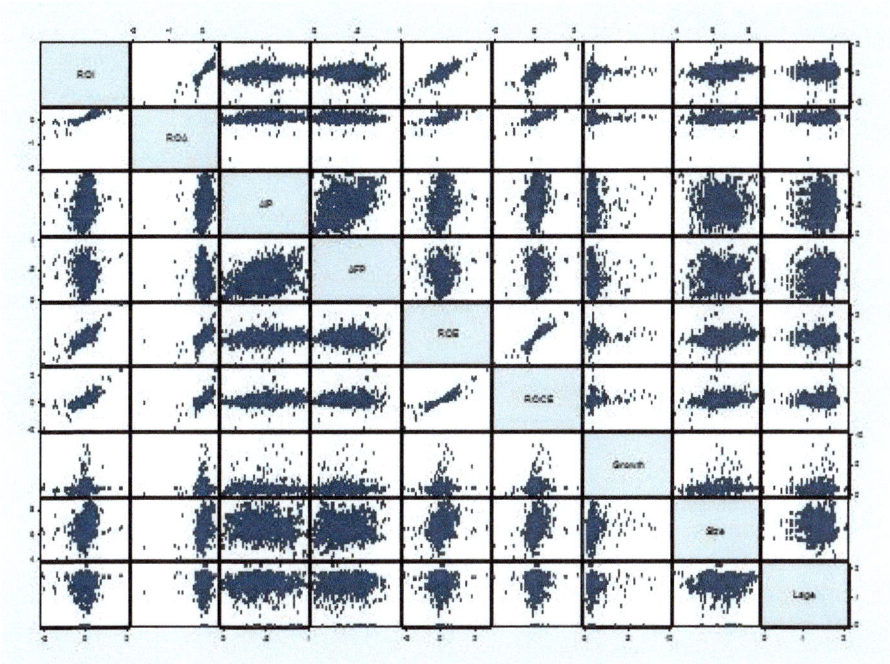

Figure 2: Data Normality Diagram.

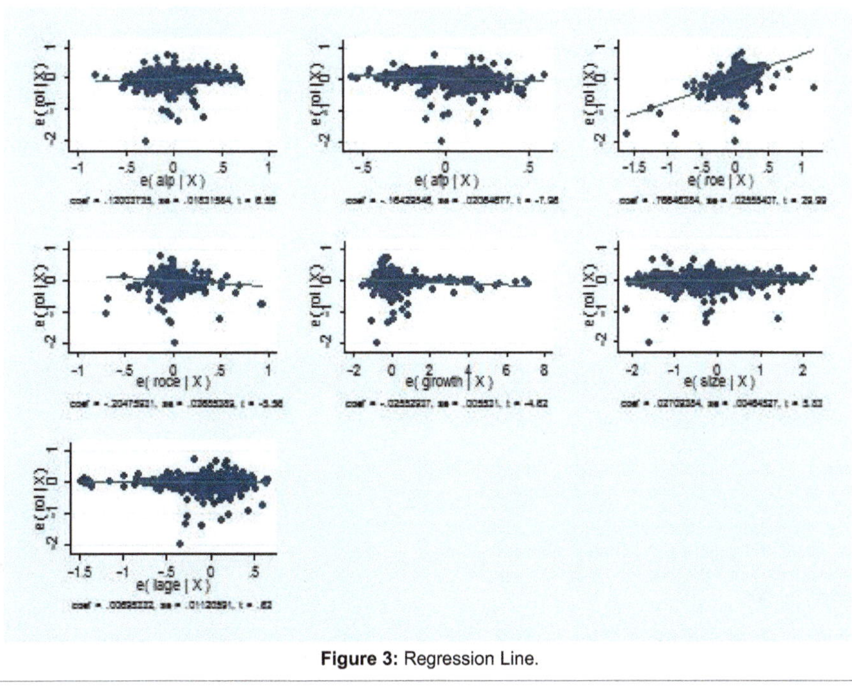

Figure 3: Regression Line.

Table 4 shows the degree of aggressiveness of finance manager on firm's performance. The results reveal that explanatory variable has significantly explaining its impact on firm performance measured by ROI and ROA. It has been concluded from the Hausman test in diagnostic analysis that fixed effect within regression test is appropriate for data analysis for both proxies of dependent variable (ROI and ROA). The findings of the study reveal that aggressiveness of the finance manager regarding current liability adversely affecting the firm's performance. It means in designing capital structure of Pakistani non financial listed firms on PSX, finance manager needs to be conservative regarding short term financial policy. Elaborately when increasing in the company's short term debt compare to its total assets yields negative results on firm's performance in Pakistan (−26.6% in case of ROI and −20.3% in case of ROA).

On the other hand, aggressiveness regarding firm's investment policy postulates a positive impact on overall performance of the firm (seen from AIP respective coefficient). It means Pakistani non financial firms when designing the capital structure employee the current assets on maturity financial policy basis, it yield fruitful results in the short run. It is also observed from the results in Table 4 that with the passage of time, firms in Pakistan devastating their performance. That's why study found negative relation between firms' age and ROI (−25.4%) and ROA (−17.8%).

Hausman test score favor to pick fixed effect model for data analysis (p-value=0.000 from Table 4) in case of ROA. The study found that ROA is adversely affected when firms in Pakistan increase their long term debt compare to capitalization or their leverage ratio. The study found that as the time passes, Pakistani firm's performing well which is displayed in the form of favorable statistical significance in the Table 4. Leverage ratio has little concern with the firm's performance (ROA).

Recommendation

From the above findings, the study recommends certain actions directing the corporate governance and finance manager of the companies in Pakistan. Most of the firms in Pakistan finance tangible fixed assets by short-term debts. Regarding short-term debt, this research work found unfavorable results with the firm performance (in both ROI and ROA cases). So the study recommends analyzing a scale on which aggressiveness of the finance manager regarding funding postulates negative impact on firm performance.

The research work gave direction to finance manager that if he want to create firm value and boost up its performance in the market, it need to design an optimal capital structure which congruence the firms current assets with the maturity matching policy.

Acknowledgement

First of all I owe my deepest gratitude to almighty Allah for his providential guidance and analytical wisdom to put my best possible efforts towards the accomplishment of this thesis.

I express my gratitude for my honorable supervisor Sir. Idrees Ali Shah at The University of Agriculture Peshawar for his support, insightful suggestions and endless patience in making this study possible. Indeed, it was his guidance that helped me overcome difficult phases in this research. I also extend my gratitude for all of my teachers for their kind contribution in my knowledge and expertise.

I also extend my thanks to all my colleagues and seniors for their moral and official support in my office during my Ms. Management Sciences (Finance) degree acquirement. I am also thankful to all my university friends for motivating me in completion of my studies and research work.

Last but not least I want to thank my parents, particularly my mother. She always feels my frequent physical or mental absences, while I have been working with my dissertation. I am proud of her.

References

1. Modigliani F, Miller MH (1963) Corporate income taxes and the cost of capital: A correction. The American economic review 53: 433-443.
2. Harris M, Raviv A (1991) The theory of capital structure. The Journal of Finance 46: 297-355.
3. Berle AA, Means GC (1932) The Modern Corporation and Private Property. Transaction puiblishers, London.
4. Shah A, Khan S (2007) Determinants of capital structure: Evidence from Pakistani panel data. International review of business research papers 3: 265-282.
5. Gupta MC, Huefner RJ (1972) A cluster analysis study of financial ratios and industry characteristics. Journal of Accounting Research 10: 77-95.
6. Carpenter MD, Johnson KH (1983) The Association between Working Capital Policy and Operating Risk. The Financial Review 18: 106-106.
7. Pinches GE, Mingo KA, Caruthers JK (1973) The stability of financial patterns in industrial organizations. The Journal of Finance 28: 389-396.
8. Soenen LA (1993) Cash Conversion Cycle and Corporate Profitability. Journal of Cash Management 13: 53-58.
9. Filbeck G, Krueger TM (2005) An analysis of working capital management results across industries. American Journal of Business 20: 11-20.
10. Nazir MS, Afza T (2009) Impact of aggressive working capital management policy on firms' profitability. IUP Journal of Applied Finance 15: 19.
11. Smith K (1980) Profitability versus liquidity tradeoffs in working capital management. Readings on the management of working capital 3: 549-562.
12. Lamberson M (1995) Changes in working capital of small firms in relation to changes in economic activity. American Journal of Business 10: 45-50.
13. Deloof M (2003) Does Working Capital Management Affect Profitability of Belgian Firms? Journal of Business, Finance and Accounting 30: 573-587.
14. Teruel PJG, Solano PM (2005) Effects of Working Capital Management on SME Profitability. International Journal of Managerial Finance 3: 164-177.
15. Murugesu T (2013) Effect of debt on corporate profitability (Listed Hotel Companies Sri Lanka). European Journal of Business and Management 5: 13-18.
16. Zhang Y, Toppinen A (2011) Internationalization and financial performance in the global forest industry. International Forestry Review 13: 96-105.
17. Kyereboah-Coleman A (2007) The impact of capital structure on the performance of microfinance institutions. Journal of Risk Finance 8: 56-71.
18. Drobetz W, Fix R (2003) What are the determinants of the capital structure? Some evidence for Switzerland. WWZ/department of finance pp: 1-37.
19. Graham JR, Harvey C (2001) The theory and practice of corporate finance: evidence from the field. Journal of Financial Economics 60: 187-243.
20. Jensen M, Meckling W (1976) Theory of the Firm: Managerial Behavior, Agency costs and Ownership Structure. Journal of Financial Economics 3: 305-360.
21. Jose ML, Lancaster C, Stevens JL (1996) Corporate Returns and Cash Conversion Cycles. Journal of Economics and Finance 20: 33-46.
22. Shin HH, Soenen L (1998) Efficiency of Working Capital and Corporate Profitability. Financial Practice and Education 8: 37-45.
23. Akerlof GA (1970) The Market for 'Lemons': Asymmetrical Information and Market Behavior. The Quarterly Journal of Economics 83: 488-500.

Contribution of ICT to Poverty Reduction among Women in Kilosa District

Khaliq IH[1*], Naeem B[2], Abbas Q[2] and Khalid S[3]

[1]Warid Telecom Pakistan & Pacific Western University, USA
[2]Department of Management Sciences, COMSATS Institute of Information Technology, Lahore, Pakisthan
[3]Lecturer, Department of Education, University of Sargodha, Sargodha, Pakistan

Abstract

This study examines the contribution of information communication technology to poverty reduction among women. The study assessed availability and accessibility of ICT infrastructures, the role of ICTs in poverty reduction among womenand determine factors that hinder accessibility of ICT tools among women. The study was done in kilosa Morogoro and involved a total of 50 respondent. The study used survey research methodology to collect data. Three instruments were applied to facilitate data collection, that is structured questionnaire for interview, observation and documentation (secondary data) collected from household as a base of data collection as well as ICT telecentre and other sources of data. The data was collected and analyzed using Statistical Package for Social Scientist. Findings show that male respondents were 38% while females were 62%. Of the sample population who use ICT 60% were females while 38% were males.

This study provided a first look on the role of ICTs to poverty reduction among women by identifying the benefits of ICT which are: job creation, banking services, improvement agriculture by ensuring availability of market, prevent middlemen exploitation, expanding and strengthening social networks and ensure accessibility and ownership of assets.

The conclusion of the study calls for increasing investment in education, creating awareness among women regarding the range of services provided, improvement of ICT infrastructure, reduces cost in ICTs services provision, public and private investment is a vital tool therefore maximization of employment opportunity, including physical infrastructure, and entrepreneurial skills.

The study suggests one area for further research: one is the extent to which ICTs infrastructures helps women in poverty reduction compared to those who do not use by specifying indicators of development brought by ICT tools.

Keywords: Contribution; ICT; Poverty reduction; Women

Introduction

Background information

No one can refute the fact that Information and Communication Technology (ICT) is a cross-cutting sector that plays great role in most sectors for human development including social, economic as well as political development. Recently days ICT has been proven to be commonly in many areas, and majority have access ICTs services [1]. Theseincludes Internets, radios, and mobile phones. These ICT toolsmake a world as a single village by guarantee communication. But despite of these development women are marginalized group hence less accessibility and use of ICT in all aspect of life including in economic development [2]. This has resulted to poor living standard of them.

Women make up half of the world's population and yet represent a staggering 70% of the world's poor [3]. For the millions of women living in poverty, their lives are a litany of injustice, discrimination and obstacles that get in the way of achieving their basic needs of good health, safe childbirth, education and employment [4].

Poverty in Africa is predominantly in rural area and it account more than 70 per cent of the continent's poor people live in rural areas who depend on agriculture for food and livelihood. In Sub-Saharan Africa more than 218 million people live in extremely poverty [3]. The incidence of poverty in Sub-Saharan Africa is increasing faster than the population. Overall, the pace of poverty reduction in most of Africa has slowed since the 1970s [3].

According to Yonna and Cons [5], poverty in Tanzania is characterized by low income and expenditure, high mortality and morbidity, poor nutritional status, low educational attainment, vulnerability to external shocks and exclusion from economic, social and political processes. The depth and severity of poverty is greatest in the rural areas as around 85 per cent of the poor women live in extream poverty [5]. Most of the rural poor are primarily engaged in Agriculture where the incidence of poverty is twice as high in rural areas as in urban areas [6].

Those who most at risk being likely to live under poverty are young children and youths, the elderly, women, who live in large households and those involved in subsistence agriculture, livestock production and small-scale fishing [7]. In Tanzania, 35.7 per cent of the population live below the "basic needs" poverty line and 18.7 percent living below the food poverty line. Women in Tanzania are subjected to live in abject poverty compared to men, this is due to the fact that women are lacking concern in development program /project and are voiceless in any

***Corresponding author:** Imran Hameed Khaliq, Pacific Western University (USA), Warid Telecom, Pakistan
E-mail: imranhameedkhaliq@gmail.com

aspect of development [8]. In most of the societies especially in rural areas women where limited access to education, limited access to control land, limited access to credit, agricultural extension services as well as being denied in decision-making. This is due to the fact that men have the final say in decision making in family level and community level.

Most of ICT firms in Tanzania focus on serving urban centers whereas 80% of the population is in sparsely populated rural [9]. ICT is concentrated in Dar es Salaam, the commercial capital with little deployment or access in other urban centers or in rural Tanzania. Recently landing of the fibre optical cable in Tanzania and the implementation of last mile project will reverse this situation [10]. According to UNESCO women's are marginalized from ICT based on the assumption that women will benefit less from new educational and employment opportunities [11]. Lack of access and use of ICT is probably sufficient to explain the low adoption rates of women. Contrary Dyson finds no evidence that indigenous people had any specific problems with learning and using technology, but there are major problems of access and awareness [12]. Access factors include cost, environmental constraints, as well as difficult in acquiring better computer skills thus many rural areas do not have structured local communication networks or access to information and knowledge barriers that compound and enhance poverty.

ICT has proven to bring about development in Tanzania including rural and urban area yet women in most of rural and urban societies face the same problem [13]. Thus there is need to understand how rural women can run out of poverty, it is necessary to examine the contribution of ICT on poverty reduction among women.

Government through Agricultural Sector Development Strategy (ASDS) emphasizes the importance to formulate a special program to enhance women's access to technology, training and credit [9]. The problem of poverty among women particularly in rural areas continues worse, although women are the main producers of cash crops and providers of food [1]. Supporting research confirms that women carry out 70-80 percent of all subsistence farming in Africa and that farming is a woman's principle duty [14]. Women participate not only in productive role but also most of household chores.

Women lack time in acessing and using new opportunities like accessibility of different information that ICT is opening up. This include market information for agriculture products and opportunities for entrepreneurship. This is important if all citizens are to be uplifted for meeting the goals of reduction of poverty.

Several studies have justified the need for paying attention to women on accessing and control to various issues in rural livelihoods as an entry point to address women discrimination in development towards poverty reduction [8,15].

The Tanzania Development Vision 2025 explains about the need to make a hub of ICT infrastructure and ICT solutions that enhance sustainable socio-economic development and accelerated poverty reduction both nationally and globally [16]. Tanzania Communications Commission (TCC) has licensed nine companies to provide public data communication services including Internet bandwidth [16].

Tanzania's Public Switched Telephone Network (PSTN), using fiber optic, microwave and satellite-based links, is now over 95% digital this paves the way for allowing the provision of new services enabled by ICT [9]. Similary David explain about the great increase in telephone ownership and use since the advent of mobile phones. Panos comment on mobile phone subscriptions rose from close to zero at the turn of the century to some 13 million by July 2009 [13]. But ICTs infrastructure is a great problem in rural areas and are more concentrated in urban areas, thus still there is a lack of telecommunications and other ICT infrastructures in rural areas.

Despite the fact that there is potential links between ICT and poverty reduction, in bring positive change on poverty reduction, but women face some limitations to access ICTs services in comparison with men. Women are excessive domestic workload, illiteracy and lack of formal education this factors prevent these groups from accessing information that can help them to create sustainable development.

Thus this study generated empirical information on which strategies should be emphasied on the development of ICT to women in Kilosa District. Findings would enable Government departments, institutions of higher learning and Non-Governmental Organizations (NGOs) to come to improve ICT solutions that would address women problems most appropriately. Findings from this study will also provide a base for reference in an academic arena especially in the field of community informatics [17].

Women has to know proper usage of ICT, its advantages offered by, and its potential in opening up window to outside world so as to bring about development hence eradicate poverty [18].

The general objective of this study is to investigate the contribution of Information and communication Technology to poverty reduction among women in Kilosa district.

Thus the specific objectives are:

i. To examine availability and accessibility of ICT infrastructures in Kilosa.

ii. To examine the role of ICTs to poverty reduction among women in Kilosa.

iii. To examine indicator for development of women who access and who do not use Information Communication Technology.

iv. To determine factors that hinder accessibility of ICT to women.

The chapter is organised as follows: the next section presents the background which outlines the theoretical fundamentals linking the digital divide and e-Government. Thereafter, the status and prospects of e-Government implementation in Zambia is discussed by presenting the different ICT initiatives that are being currently put in place. Following this, the recommendations and future research directions especially on what should be done regarding the development of e-Government in Zambia are presented. In conclusion, the chapter summarises the '*Achilles' heel*' of e-Government in the Zambian context.

Definition of concept

According to Scherba, communication is any act by which one person gives to or receives from person information about that person's needs, desires, perceptions, knowledge, or affective states. Communication may be intentional or unintentional, may involve conventional or unconventional signals, may take linguistic or nonlinguistic forms, and may occur through spoken or other modes. In business dictionary define communication as two-way process of reaching mutual understanding, in which participants not only exchange (encode-decode) information, news, ideas and feelings but also create and share meaning. In general, communication is a means of connecting people or places. In business, it is a key function of management an organization cannot operate without communication between levels, departments and employees.

According to URT (2003) [9], Information Technology embrace the use of computers, telecommunications and office systems technologies for the collection, processing, storing, packaging and dissemination of information.

According to URT (2007), ICT refers to forms of technology that are used for communication and to transmit, store, create, share or exchange information [19]. This broad definition of ICT includes technologies such as: radio, television, video, telephone (both fixed line and mobile), computer and network hardware and software; as well as the equipment and services associated with these technologies, such as electronic mail, text messaging and radio broadcasts.

Poverty is defined as a state of deprivation and prohibitive of decent life that results from many mutually reinforcing factors, including lack of productive resources to generate material wealth, illiteracy, prevalence of diseases, discriminative socio-economic and political systems, natural calamities, such as drought, floods, and HIV/AIDS (URT, 1999) [20].

Poverty is characterized by low income and expenditure, high mortality and morbidity, poor nutritional status, low educational attainment, vulnerability to external shocks like natural disasters (e.g. drought, pests, diseases and floods), and exclusion from economic, social and political processes. Poverty is particularly widespread in the rural areas, rather than in urban areas [5].

Poverty reduction is about how to empower the poor with knowledge and skills thus availing to them new opportunities to improve their livelihood in terms of income and expenditure this would mean increase in income, and hence capacity to afford food, health services, and other basic needs [5]. The focus of policy makers and development partners lays out the long-term development goals and perspectives against which the strategy for poverty reduction is emphasized. PRSP which was formulated in 2000 aims to combine macro-economic stability, sector strategies and decentralization and poverty reduction itself which is broken down into three goals: reducing income poverty, improving human capabilities and containing vulnerability (URT, 2000) [21].

ICT in tanzania

ICTs advances since the end of the 20th century have led to multiple convergences of content, computing, telecommunications and broadcasting (URT, 2003) [9]. They have brought about changes in other areas, particularly in knowledge management and businesses improvements [22]. ICT has further been empowered by the growth of a global network of computer networks known as the Internet. It has impacted the way business is conducted, facilitated learning and knowledge sharing, generating global information flows, empowering citizens and communities, creating significant wealth and economic growth [16].

There is the gap between those able, and those unable, to participate in the knowledge economy as currently termed "the digital divide". This is shown within a community as well as nation. The dangers created by the digital divide and the risk of being excluded further from the knowledge economy and social development, pushes the Government to put in place an ICT policy in 2003, through which coordinating mechanisms and harmonized strategies were stipulated (URT, 2003). The policy framework makes possible for enabling sectors such as telecommunications, information, or broadcasting to work together whereby enabled sectors such as education, health, governance, or agriculture can become further empowered through application of ICT.

Tanzania through development vision 2025, put emphases in ten main focus areas in connecting ICT in Tanzania which include; strategic ICT leadership, ICT infrastructure, ICT Industry, Human Capital, Legal and Regulatory Framework, Productive Sectors, Service Sectors, Public Service, Local Content, and Universal Access. The National ICT Policy is aligned to follow vision by stating that Tanzania to become a hub of ICT Infrastructure and ICT solutions that enhance sustainable socio-economic development and accelerated poverty reduction both nationally and globally (URT, 2003) [9].

Private sector has actively contributed to these achievements by investing much in different area through development and provision of facilities as well as improvement of ICT. The improvement are in many ICTs services including simple information centers with notice boards, books, brochures, posters and newspapers, telephone, fax, television, and radio. Also there is improvemnt on modern ICTs which include the Internet, email, computers, mobile phones as well as training centre.

The objective of the Tanzania ICT policy 2003 is to offer a national framework that will enable ICT to contribute towards achieving national development goals (URT 2003) [9].

Relationship between ICT and poverty reduction

There is direct relationship between ICT and poverty reduction [5]. Government of Tanzania has recognized that ICT can be used to meet the goals of the Vision 2025 as well as that of the Tanzania-Millenium Development Goals (TZ-MDG) on poverty reduction (http://www.povertymonitoring.go.tz/). Government realized the importance of ICT on poverty reduction nationality, hence it has formulated the National ICT Policy. In the ICT policy agenda, it explains clearly the contribution of ICT on national development and poverty reduction (URT, 2003) [9].

ICT promote and facilitate communication process which links individuals, communities, Non-governmental organizations as well as government, in shared decision-making which enable them to approach clear alternative and opportunity and thus increasing involvement in development.

ICT include simple information centers and modern ICT such as Internet, email, computers, mobile phones, engaged directly on educating people (knowledge and skills) hence promote development. Yonna and Cons demonstrates that ICTs is a set of tools for knowledge sharing, which is a proven powerful means for poverty reduction [5].

Contribution of ICT to poverty reduction

As a matter of emphasis, the role of ICT in poverty reduction not limited to reduction of income poverty, economic empowerment by address barrier and vulnerability that prevent women seeking opportunities and participate in sectors of the economy that require highly developed skills. ICTs contribute to poverty reduction among women as explained below.

ICTs contribute on facilitating and increasing productivity in agriculture through the usage of radios and phones. Farmer communication with technical experts on methods and strategies of farming and trading using ICTs help them to access improved information and knowledge hence contribute to higher agriculture productivity. Through radios programs farmers are able to acquire necessary knowledge on improvement of productivity as explain by Gerster and Sanga et al. [10,23]. Uganda's community radio programs had a significant impact on livelihood strategies of farming [23]. In Uganda, women are reported that have started their own small vegetable gardens as a result of information provided by Uganda Development Services.

ICTs contribute on job creation directly and indirectly, this is easily through telephones communication,where by people bargain for price through phones and reduce the need to meet face to face to conduct business. Ovum as quoted in Bhavinan found that the mobile telephone industry created about 3.6 million jobs in India directly and indirectly. This figure is expected to increase by 30% per year [24]. Also there is direct employment brought by through selling handsets, and SIM cards as well as sale of airtime and maintenance mobile phones.

ICTs contribute on information asymmetry, the use of mobile phones as well as radios as a means of passing information concerning prices and market place, increase information asymmetries which regulate variation of prices thus enabling users to access market or trade opportunities that they otherwise would have missed. Information asymmetry helps women to be in good contact of better market for production. According to Jensen as reported in Bhavinan a study of fishermen in the Kerala state in India has shown that the use of mobile phones by fishermen in Kerala to arbitrage over price information from potential buyers and coordinate sales has helped them to increase incomes and reduce wastage [24]. Also Yonna and Cons explain the role of ICT on making services previously difficulty to trade or non-traded at all to become easily tradable within countries and internationally [5].

ICTs contribute on preventing exploitation by middlemen. This is possible due to accessibility and availability of information through ICT. Community share common information including marketing, as well as prices of product whichhelp to the increase the bargaining power. Bhavian explain the importance of using mobile phones in businesses to correct market inefficiencies by readressing the balance of supply and demand. For example, affordable access to information is a way of correcting the market inefficiency [24]. Eardley explain on the uses of mobiles in poor rural areas concerning knowledge about market opportunities, arbitrating price information and coordinating sales, thereby increasing incomes and reducing wastage [25].

ICTs contribute to reduction of transport cost, this is possible through improvements in the information flows between buyers and seller which allows trading activities without traveling. This is commonly appeared in rural areas where traders needed to travel to urban areas to check for demand and negotiate on price. The business in some casesnow is conducted through mobile. According to Bhavian "traders are able to ensure demand exists for their products, before setting out on a journey", this can help to reduce transportation cost. According to Myhr mobile telephone can also substitute for transport in remote communities, reducing business transaction costs [7]. Increased contact via mobile telephone between clients and workers can have profound implications for homeless clients, as well as for social service delivery processes [26].

ICTs strengthen good governance and accountability through ICT tools. People are increasing knowledgable and demand necessities for sustainable development [23]. ICT can increase knowledge of human and constitutional rights, in making the leaders more accountable, and giving the poor a voice. Thus ICT can enhance the government accountability for rural women, hence facilitate poverty reduction.

ICTs increase relations and involvement in communities. Mobile phones enhance social inclusion and autonomy within the society among groups including; women, men and youth as well as older people. The social benefits from ICT has direct and indirect impacts to economic. Bhavnani provide a number of examples, including use of mobiles to aid disaster, relief and emergency communication, dissemination of locally-generated educational and health information, and maintenance of familiar and social contact [25]. ICT allow populations that are geographically isolated to become part of a global information community [27]. Also Dobransky argue ICTs have been viewed as tools that enable people with disabilities to escape the isolation and stigma that sometimes accompany their disabilities. Also through ICTs citizens are able to acquire better social services [28].

Factors that influence the use of ICT tools in rural areas

There are various factors influencing the use of ICT in communities; gender is one of the factors influencing the use of ICT tools (radio, television, mobile phone, etc). Hudson reported that women are more likely to use ICT tools if there is influential from staff in telecenter [29]. Also, shortage of telecommunication networks, limited types of services, costs of using services and lack of information and skills among users are factors affecting the use of ICT tools [30].

Dyson pointed out that another major problem is accessing and awareness associated with issues of cost, environmental constraints, as well as difficulty in acquiring better computer skills [12]. Similarly Mtega explain about limited information including means of electronic communication with the outside world are just one source that isolated rural communities and economies from the forces of national and global integration [31].

Limited information needed for decision making lead to them to difficulties in decision making concerning socio economic activities. This resulted to low level of awareness among farmers on agricultural innovations on the basis of scientific and technical information hence contributes to their poverty.

Theoretical perspectives of information and communication technology (ICT) and poverty reduction

Potential theoretical concepts developed to analyze and advance ICT is the concept of the new ICT Eco-system pioneered by Fransman [32]. It explains the relationships between technical, economic and social analysis within the sector system of ICT. The concept argues that each actor whether a person, firm or an entire nation, assumes a position and unique relationships in hierarchically organized ecosystem. Anyone desired to create and implement effective strategy within the system have to consider relationships with other actors to be viable or interdependent.

The new ICT Eco-system emerged to think and act about ICTs on social and economic issues. The aims is to offer a conceptual vehicle on analyzing and explaining changes in the digital countryside and support decision making in organizations, firms and government on the application and implementation of ICT as an engine for socio-economic and political development.

Thus application and implementation of ICT in the reduction of poverty requires careful consideration of local conditions and demand. This does not lead to fragmented approach, but create pressures to produce a major sound strategy for ICT distribution and effective coordination and progress monitoring of grass-root implementation activities [32]. One of its central points is that ICT are beneficial only if it is in effective uses.

Tanzania has identified ICT as one of the key areas, where science, technology and innovations are to contribute to the broader development of the society and address vital social problems [16]. Taking aim at the Millennium Development Goals, government has spearheaded several important reforms on ICT in an attempt to accelerate adoption and diffusion of new technologies. These reforms range from regulatory framework to privatization, to increased higher education and research, as well as to create a wide base adoption of ICT and information society technologies across the society [5]. In 2003 National Information and Communications Technologies Policy states its vision as to become a hub of ICT infrastructure and ICT solutions that enhance sustainable socio-economic development and accelerated poverty reduction both at national and global level.

Evidently numbers of mobile phone subscriptions approached 15 million in 2009 in a country of approximately 40 million inhabitants [16]. With total telephony penetration rate closing towards 36% of the population and the recently data of October 2011 reported by Tanzania Communications Regulatory Authority (TCRA) shows that number of mobile phone subscribers in Tanzania were 19 Million. Also it shows 11% of Tanzania's 42 Million population were accessing Internet, around 4.8 million accessing the Internet from Tanzania up from 1.6 million users in 2005. 2,663,200 were institutional users while 1,932,816 were households or individual users and 260,280 Internet café users. Level of communication has been revolutionized in Tanzania within the last 10 years [16]. This is amplified by the fact that during the last years, increasing number of mobile application services, such as e-Banking, agricultural information and micropayments has become available for citizens to take care of day-to-day activities in business and private life. It also makes the point that too much of ICT policies are formulated at the supply-side policies and too little attention is paid on the demand side, without considering that users are final beneficiaries.

Weaknesses of ICT on poverty reduction among women

The layer model proposed by Fransman mobile telephony were evidenced that majority of Tanzania are taking technology for their choices [32]. Mobile network providers and operators, as well as service providers, such as banks are actively innovating for the Tanzanian market. This is expected to have direct or indirect relationship with rural women in market services and production. Information obtained from this process will sustained agriculture production and businesses development, but experience show that rural areas are lagging behind to this development in information flow.

Internet is currently weak but it will improve in some coming years, as stated previous that around 4.8 million accessing the Internet out of Tanzania's 42 Million populations and most of them are under institution including Governmental institution and Non-Governmental institution in urban areas.

Training institution, education and research in ICT have been relatively low, it is clearly shown that training institutions is only concentrated in urban area within an institution rather than in rural area to strengthen capability to access and uses ICT in a very profitable way.

Lack of knowledge about the potential benefits of using ICT in society for better usefulness in economic sector for development it then causes communities to use phones and other means of communication in non-economic benefit (e.g. social).

Too little knowledge about how ICT alleviates poverty in rural areas is reported. The evidence about this is based on literature search [33]. Fransman explains that too much of ICT policies are formulated at the supply-side policies and too little attention is paid on the demand side [32]. This means in initialization of many ICT projects there is weak involvement of users in ICT strategies and programming [10]. Thus users are not participatory involved as final beneficiaries. This in turn led to poor adoption of some of innovations.

Conceptual Framework

This section explains the conceptual framework which used as guide in measuring the impact of ICT in poverty reduction among women in Kilosa. This framework conceptualizes a clear and direct relationship between the use of ICT and poverty reduction among women by undertaking assessment of corrected data on ICT accessibility and affordability by women. The essence is on determining the level of development both those who use and who do not use ICT and to come up with those factors that undermine women to access and use ICT in daily life (Figure 1).

The relationship between variables which are dependent variables and independent variables is evaluated. In this study independent variable are ICTs and in dependent variable is any initiative towards poverty reduction among women. There are indicators of independent variables which are increases use of computer, uses of mobile phones, uses of radio, TV and access to magazine (newspaper). Indicator of dependent variable are increases of information search, increases employment, reduces vulnerability, as well as increases income. This dependent and independent variable factors can be influenced by background variables which are age, sex and education level of the respondents.

According to Pannos [13], ICT has direct relationship on changes in women livelihood. It has been proven that many countries have seen a dynamic and rapid expansion in mobile telephony including provision of services to those far under services. According to TCRA, recent report shows that number of mobile phone subscribers in Tanzania has reached 19 Million.

ICT appears to benefit innovative in business such as the use of prepaid cards, the resale of airtime by small or informal sector operators in services offered and financed through drawing on microfinance e.g. Grameen Village Phone networks and financing [13]. According to Accascina as cited in Hassan the ICT has helped to decrease poverty and foster knowledge and trade [34]. Moreover through appropriate enabling environment, ICT can contribute in creation of and access to services, products, markets and employment.

Another important element has been a growing awareness of the communication needs of the poor and the willingness of poor people to pay for communication services. In this context, it has been proven by the rapid increase of telephones subscribers as stated above. Communities can access information and be able to use information on agriculture productivity [23].

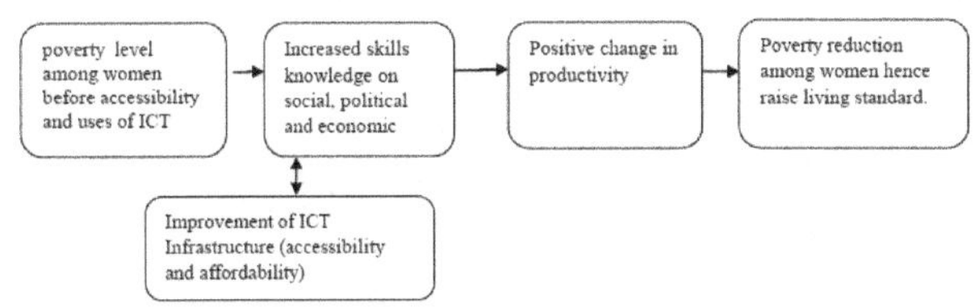

Figure 1: Conceptual framework.

Mobile phone remains the most commonly used ICT and very innovatively in many contexts hence become widely accessible and affordable by the poor [13]. The factors that has contributed to the rapid growth in mobile phone subscribers include the relatively low cost, the high best located on mobility of consumers, the strong presence of the private investors in mobile phone provision and easy way of adding new subscribers to the cellular network [34]. Also privatization of telecomunications companies and enactement of ICT and telecommunications policies.

Research Methodology

Overview

Description of the study area: Kilosa District Council is one of six districts that comprise Morogoro Region. It is located in East central Tanzania 300 km west of Dar es Salaam and is bounded by latitude 5°55' and 7°53' South and longitudes 36°30' and 37°30 East. Kilosa bounders Mvomero district to the East, Kilombero and Kilolo Districts to the South, Gairo (Morogoro region), Kiteto (Manyara region) and Kilindi (Tanga region) to the North; and Mpwapwa district (Dodoma Region) to the West. Population in Kilosa shows female population is higher than male, the District recorded 488,191 people where 243,329 are males and 244,862 are Females according to the population census of Movek [35].

The reason behind selecting Kilosa district as study area was that ICT infrastructure is much concentrated in urban area than rural areas which makes variability in development between rural and urban areas. This is opposite to the way ICT is advocated as cross-cutting sector for social, economic and political development.

Sampling procedure and sample size

The targeted respondents for this study were residents from Kilosa both owning and using and not owning ICT tools. They were chosen randomly taking into account different age groups and gender parity. A total of 50 individuals from selected households were interviewed. In order to ensure the reliability and validity of the instruments for data collection the multi stage sampling was used to obtain respondents for the study. The key informants included prominent business people.

Methods of data collection

Primary data: This study has made uses of primary data whereby qualitative and quantitative information were gathered directly by interviewing different respondents in the selected wards and from community records.

Secondary data: These data were obtained in order to complement primary data. The secondary data were collected from various sources including reviewing various literatures from the Sokoine National Agriculture Library (SNAL), official annual reports and publications. Research reports as well as other publications related to ICT tools for poverty reduction were also used.

Data collection tools: The study used survey research method to collect data. Three instruments were applied to facilitate data collection. These included a structured questionnaire for interview, observation and documentations. The instruments were used to collect data from household as a base of data collection as well as from ICT telecentre and other sources of data.

Questionnaire and Observation were used to collect primary and secondary data from different reports from library and telecentre. This was meant for the data collection of examination of availability and accessibility of ICT infrastructures in Kilosa, similarly, the same instruments were used to examine the role of ICT's in poverty reduction among women at Kilosa, to examine indicator for development for women who access and who do not use Information communication Technology and to determine factors that hinder accessibility of ICT to women.

Data analysis

The method of data analysis was conducted according to specific objective by using various variables. The variables included; age of respondent, gender, religion, level of education, major occupation of the family, ICT availabilities and accessibilty, ownership of ICT tools, role of ICT to poverty reduction, household assets, probleams of accessing and ICT services.

In order to examine availability and accessibility of ICT infrastructures in Kilosa, the data collected from the field and other sources include secondary data were coded and analyzed by using statistical package for social sciences (SPSS). Descriptive statistics such as frequencies, percentage were computed to draw conclusion and make relationship or comparison of the variables and interpretation of the data in order to ensure the reliability and validity.

On the second specific objective, to examine the role of ICTs in poverty reduction among women at Kilosa, the data collected from the field and other sources include secondary data and primary data were coded and analyzed by using the same method as indicated in first specific objective to ensure reliability and validity.

The third specific objective which wasto examine indicators for development for women who access and who do not use ICT involve the data collected from the field and other sources. This include secondary data which were coded and analyzed by using the same method as indicated in second specific objectives inorder to ensure reliability and validity.

The last specific objective was to determine factors that hinder accessibility of ICT to women. In order to answer this data were collected from the field and other sources. This include secondary data which were coded and analyzed by using the same method as indicated in third specific objective in order to ensure the reliability and validity.

Kilosa is an area which characterised with various economic activities, that needed to be interconected with other region to ensure socio-economic progress. ICT is an important sector that can bridge the gap of distances, thus there is need to develop and maintain ICT infrastructure in oder to ensure sectors and regional interconnection hence facilitate development.

Results and Discussion

Introduction

Conceptual framework analysis focuses on the relationships between concepts which are ICT and poverty reduction among women.The coding process directs the outcome of the study. Therefore in this study the main concept was to determine or understand the contribution of ICT to poverty reduction among women in Kilosa.

Socio-demographic characteristics of the respondents

This section deals with description of socio-demographic characteristics of the respondents interviewed in two communities or wards which were Mbumi and Mkatani in Kilosa District.

Age of respondents: The results show that 12% of the interviewed respondents were aged between 18 to 25 years, 30% were between 26 to 32 years, 24% were aged between 33 to 39 years, 18% were between 40 to 46 years, 10% were above 47 to 53 while 6%were aged 54 to 60 years. This implies that most of the respondents uses ICT Tools.

Sex of respondents: The sample of respondents interviewed comprised of 38% male and 62% female. Different number of men and women were used in research based on investigation of the access and availability of ICT tools to poverty reduction among women. This implies that women has ability and accessibility to the use of ICTs tools as Men.

Respondents' marital status: The results show that 58% of the interviewed respondents were married, 22% were single, 14% were widow and 6% were separated. This implies that married people had wide chance to overcome poverty reduction since there is possibility to combine labor force in production.

Household size: The results indicates that 42% of the interviewed respondents household member were between 1 to 4, 54% of the interviewed respondents were between 5 to 8 member , and 4.%of the interviewed respondents were 9 to 12 member. This imply that majority of household size had 5 to 8 members, that represent big family in relation to dependence ratio.

Level of education of respondents

The results indicates that 10% of the interviewed respondents as presented in Table 1 had no formal education, 6% of respondents had attained adult education, 30% of respondents completed primary education, 46% of the respondents had completed secondary education, 8% of respondents had post-secondary education, this imply majority of respondents had secondary education that lead the use of ICTs tool to poverty reduction (Table 1).

Characteristics	Values	Frequency	Percentage %
Age	18-25	6	12
	26-32	15	30
	33-39	12	24
	40-46	9	18
	47-53	5	10
	54-60	3	6
Sex	Male	19	38
	Female	31	62
Marital status	Married	29	58
	Single	11	22
	Widow	7	14
	separated	3	6
Household size	01-Apr	21	42
	05-Aug	27	54
	09-Dec	2	4
Education level	No formal education	5	10
	Adult education	3	6
	Primary education	15	30
	Secondary education	23	46
	Post-secondary education	4	8
Family occupation	Salary/wages	13	26
	Off farming	5	10
	Farming	32	64
TOTAL		50	100%

Source: Field data, 2013.

Table 1: Social-demographic characteristics of respondents.

Occupations of respondents: The results in Table 1 show 26% of the interviewed respondents were salaried or waged workers, 10% of interviewed respondents were off farming, 64% of interviewed respondents were farmers.This implied that most of respondents lack formal employment, that's why they are engaged in small business and directly in agriculture industry at least to sustain their basic needs (Table 1).

Availability and accessibility of ICTs infrastructures in Kilosa district

ICT infrastructure availability and accessibility in Kilosa: The results show that 58% of the interviewed respondents agreed that ICT Infrastructure are well equipped enough to reach everybody, while 42% disagreed on the availability of ICT Infrastructure.The main causes are lack of a policy and regulatory environment and poor availability of ICTs infrastructure [24]. Despite the fact that ICTs tools have been proven by many authors that play a great role in poverty reduction but in kilosa there is shortage of ICT infrastructure to reach every individual for his or her own demand, including agriculturalists, pastoralists, business men and women, and job seekers.

Availability and accessibility of ICT infrastructure in occupation areas: The results show that the interviewed who agreed on radio helping them in occupation were 92%, and those who disagreed 8%, who use mobile phones were 88% while 12% disagreed, who use Internet were 30% while 70% disagreed, 48% use newspaperswhile 52% disagreed and 50% agreed on the use of television while 50% disagreed. This imply that majority of interviewed respondents used much radio, mobile phones and sometimes were using television due to the accessibility and affordability of these services in terms of cost and awareness. According to Gester commented on radio and telephone are rather cheap, their use requires few skills while in terms of context and language, they enjoy great flexibility [23].

Ownership and uses of ICT: The results show that 76% of interviewed respondents agreed on the uses and ownership of radio, 24% disagreed, 70% of respondentsagreed the uses and ownership of mobile phones,30%, disagreed, 16% agreed on the uses and access Internet while 84% disagreed, 26% agreed on the uses and ownershipof television while 74% disagreed. Mittal el al. highlights the fast growth of mobile telephone in the emerging developing countries of Asia and Africa and their key role in reducing information search costs and information asymmetries [36]. Thus majority of people in Kilosa have access to radio and Mobile Phone in day to day activities due to affordability in expenses and awareness.

ICT tool easy to use and at low cost: The results indicates that 42% of the interviewed respondents house hold member were prefer radio, 50% of the interviewed respondents were prefer mobile phones, 2.% of the interviewed respondents were prefered internet, 2% interview respondent prefer newspaper, as well as 4% prefer television, Gerster comment on radio and telephony are rather cheap, their use requires few skills while in terms of context and language, they enjoy great flexibility.Majority of women in Kilosa have problem of money to buy credits and put on the phone [23]. This imply that majority of interviewed lacked access to consistent reliable information and also do not have single channel source that serve a comprehensive information needed (Table 2).

Characteristics	Values	frequency	Percentage
ICT infrastructures availability and accessibility	Yes	28	58
	No	22	42
Availability/accessibility of ICT infrastructures in occupation areas	Yes	47	94
	No	3	6
Radio	Yes	46	92
	No	4	8
Mobile phones	Yes	44	88
	No	6	12
Internet	Yes	15	30
	No	35	70
News paper	Yes	24	48
	No	26	52
Television	Yes	25	50
	no	25	50
Ownership and uses of ICT	Yes	45	90
	NO	5	10
Radio	Yes	38	76
	No	12	24
Mobile phone	Yes	35	70
	NO	15	30
Internets	Yes	8	16
	No	42	84
Newspapers	Yes	13	26
	No	37	74
Television	Yes	14	28
	No	36	72
ICT tool easy to use and at low cost Radio	Yes	21	42
	No	29	58
Mobile phone	Yes	25	50
	No	25	50
Internet	Yes	1	2
	No	49	98
Newspaper	Yes	1	2
	No	49	98
Television	Yes	2	4
	No	48	96
TOTAL		50	100%

Source: Field data, 2013

Table 2: Availability and accessibility Of ICTs infrastructures in Kilosa District.

The Role of ICTs in poverty reduction among women

ICT help in occupation area: The results show that 66% of respondents agreed that ICT can help them in agricuture productivity while 34% disagreed, 36% agreed in job creation while 64% disagreed, with information asymmety 50% agreed while 50% disagreed, 12% of respondents agreed that it strengthens good governance accountability while 88% disagreed, 20% of respondents agreed that ICT help prevention of exploitation by middlemen while 80% disagreed. Abraham commented on how mobile phones reduces risk to fishermen, they were able to communicate problems such as failed engines and bad weather quickly.In Kilosa, majority of the interviewed respondents were profited by increasing agriculture productivity as the main source of employment by ensuring availability and accessibility of agriculture inputs.

ICT enhancement livelihood: The results show that 96% of the interviewed respondents agreed that ICT Infrastructure help to enhance livelihood while 4% disagreed. Also among interviewed respondents who agreed ICT help accessing finance were 92%, also those who agreed on job creation were 38% and 26% agreed that it can help in mobile phone industry through selling air time, agent of mobile banking and running telephone kiosk. According to Abraham fisheries spent less time waiting for their boats since they adopted mobile phones, thus saved time working on other business and personal issues like footwear business and grocery store. Goodman reported that the impacts of telephones on peoples' livelihoods were more evident in emergencies, social networks, and saving costs and time. Thus women argued that there is an increase of accumulation of income that they used in day to day activities to enhance productivity for their livelihood.

How ICT help to own assets: The results show that 78% of the interviewed respondents agreed that ICT infrastructure helped to own assets. while 22% disagreed, those who agreed on the ownership of house were 60% while who disagreed were 40%, those who agreed on the ownership of land were 72% and who disagreed were 28%, also who agreed on the ownership of car were 2% and who disagreed were 98% as well as motorcycle were 20% and who do not own were 80%, and who own cattle were 12% and 88% do not own. This imply that majority of respondents own assets that help them to employ in directly investment in return to outputs, as well as used as collateral in accumulation of loans and grants that helped in improvement of economic activities.

Expanding and strengthening social networks: Expanding and strengthening social networks was the most important benefit of using ICTs tools.The results show that 90% of the interviewed respondents agreed that ICT helped strengthening social network while 10% disagreed. Radios and telephones play greater role in improvement and strengthening friendship by bringing about current information including market information. According to Mtega commented on adoption of phones that leads to greater social cohesion by decreasing the feeling of isolation and improving social relationships. Abraham explained that phones lowered a sense of isolation that fishermen felt, they were now able to stay in touch with their friends and family.Thus ICT could help women to access new markets for their various products hence increase income (Table 3) [31].

Indicator for development

Changes brought by ICT: Results show that 60% of the interviewed respondents agreed that ICT helped them to own houses while 40% disagreed, 72% agreed on the ownership of land while 28% disagreed,2% of the interviewed respondents agreed on the ownership of cars while 98% disagreed, 20% of interviewed respondents agreed on the ownership of motorcycles while 80% disagreed, and 12% agreed on the ownership of cattle while 88% disagreed. According to Sife et al. majority of people in Kilosa own bicycles, nearly two-thirds of households, other means of transport were very low, with regards to housing quality.This imply that ICT industry helped women to own assets that acted as collateral in loans acquization that helped them in business improvement hence ensure improved livelihood [33].

ICT help in mobile money servings: The results show that 92% of the interviewed respondents agreed that ICT tools help them in banking and 8% of the interviewed respondent were disagreed on the use of phone banking. Sife et al. comment on the uses of mobile services (m-services) for sending and receiving money [33]. This is the way of reducing the risk of sending money through buses. This imply

Characteristics	Values	Frequency	Percentage%
ICT help in occupation area	Yes	47	94
	No	3	6
Increase productivity	Yes	33	66
	No	17	34
Information asymmetry	Yes	25	50
	No	25	50
Job creation	Yes	18	36
	No	32	64
Prevention exploitation by middlemen	Yes	10	20
	No	40	80
CT enhancement livelihood	Yes	48	96
	No	2	4
ICT and ownership of assets	Yes	39	78
	No	11	22
ICT helping socio network	Yes	45	90
	No	5	10
TOTAL		50	100%

Source: Field data, 2013.

Table 3: The Role of ICTs in poverty reduction among women.

that majority of women were benefited by ICT banking specifically mobile banking and easier the process of savings. Thus using savings it improved their business as well as agriculture. Through phones money accumulated in various relatives as remittances and grant.

ICT and employment: ICT is an industry of employment, results show that 26% of the interviewed respondents women agreed that ICT industry provided employment to them, 74% of the interviewed respondent disagreed on direct employment in ICT industry. According to Sife et al. some people earn money through selling mobile phone-related goods and services such as recharge voucher, making phone calls and sending SMS, charging phone batteries and repairing mobile phones [33]. Despite the fact that interviewed respondents were few compared to those who engage in other businesses but ICT industry play a great role to employ women including selling airtime, running telephone kiosks, agents of M-banking, and radio presenters. But on the other hand ICT brings about employment in other businesses such as agriculture and small shops (kiosk). Thise help women to earn income (Table 4).

Factor that hinder accesssibility and availability of ICT

The results show that 66% of the interviewed respondents agreed on the limitation that hinder women to access ICT services while 34% disagreed on the limitation that hinder women to access ICTs services. 54% of the interviewed agreed on the shortage of time, while 36% disagreed, 38% of the interviewed agreed on lack of awareness while 62% disagreed, 62% of respondents agreed on shortage of infrastructure and while 48% disagreed. Mittal commented on those having resources and skills benefit more than those who lack [36]. Bhavnani et al. explain the main causes are lack of a policy and regulatory environment and poor availability of ICT and mobile infrastructure. Effort is needed to overcome factors that hinder women to access ICTs services for development on different information that help women who are striving and willing to break abject poverty (Table 5) [24].

Accessibility of ICT infrastructure to women and men: The results show that 38% of the interviewed respondents agreed that ICT infrastructure and services are accessed equally to both women and women while 62% disagreed. According to Gester in many countries women are among the most disadvantageous, hence highlight the concern of gender inequality in access of ICT [23]. This imply that there is existance of gap among women and men in accessing ICTs services. This is due to the fact majority of the interviewed respondents agreed on the gap resulting to poor economic growth among women compared to men since ICTs is the sector that cut across all other sectors for development (Table 5).

Roles played by Government and Non Governmental Organizations on provision of ICTs education among women: The results show that 24% of the interviewed respondents agreed with the response shown by the government and NGOs on provision of ICTs education to women, while 76% disagreed on the contribution played by Government and NGOs on provision of ICTs education among Women. Most of the interviewed respondents appreciate the role played by Radio Jamii in organizing women (Ukumbi wa wanawake) that allows them to discuss different issues concerning Socio- economic development. Hence helping advertisements of different commodities for market, women acquiring knowledge and skills that helps them in their socio-economic activities and ensuring poverty reduction.

Characteristics	Values	Frequency	Percentage%
ICT Infrastructure help to brought about change	Yes	42	84
	No	2	4
	undecided	6	I2
ICT helps in ownership of assets	Yes	39	78
	No	11	22
House	Yes	36	72
	No	14	28
Land	Yes	30	60
	No	20	40
Cattle	Yes	6	12
	No	44	88
Motorcycle	Yes	10	20
	No	40	80
Car	Yes	1	2
	No	49	98
ICT help in mobile moneyservices	Yes	46	92
	No	4	8
ICT and employment	Yes	13	26
	No	37	74
Total		50	100%

Source: Field data, 2013

Table 4: Indicator for development.

Characteristics	Values	Frequency	Percentage%
Factor that hinder women to access ICTs Cost full	Yes	33	66
	No	17	34
Shortage of time and domestic chores	Yes	27	54
	No	23	46
Lack of awareness	Yes	19	38
	No	31	62
Shortage of ICT tools	Yes	31	62
	No	19	38
Equal accessibility of ICT Infrastructure to women and men	Yes	31	62
	No	19	38
TOTAL		50	100%

Source: Field data, 2013.

Table 5: Factor hinder accesssibility, availability and adoption of ICT to women.

Conclusion and Recommendation

ICT is the cross cutting sector that enhances transparency and accountability of Governments. It contribute to an enabling environment of good governance and support the mobilisation and empowerment of people in poverty reduction. ICT enables people to gain access to decision making processes and put crucial issues on the agenda for decision making in development. Thus there is a need to put effort to improve ICT so as to ensure genuine development in Kilosa and other Districts of Tanzania.

Overview

This section presents the conclusion and recommendation in which the conclusion is basing on the study objectives in relation with conceptual framework while the recommendation is basing on the way forward on what Government and Non-Government should do to improve ICTs industry as a cornerstone of development in all sectors.

Conclusion

This study found evidence that ICT tools are being used in ways which contribute to poverty reduction among women. This study provided an investigation on the role of ICTs (e.g. mobile telephony, radios, television, newspaper and Internet) to poverty reduction among women in raising productivity in the agricultural sector. The study specified many examples of benefits which are: job creation (directly and indirectly), improved means of banking, improvement in agriculture by ensure availability of market, expanding and strengthening social networks. Also the result show benefit that women acquired directly such as ownership of assets which are not limited to land, house, cattle, motorcycle, as well as car.

In Kilosa District, ICTs infrastructure are not well equipped enough to reach every citizen in place for everyday activities as shown in Table 2. Results show that 58% of the interviewed respondents agreed that ICT infrastructure are well equipped enough to reach everybody while 42% were disagreed. Most of women own and use radio, mobile phone and also were using television. This is due to the accessibility and affordability of these tools in terms of cost and awareness.

The findings indicate that ICT tools such as radios, television and mobile phones contribute much to reduce poverty and improvement of livelihoods to women by expanding and strengthening social networks; cut down travel costs; and facilitate efficiency of activities in businesses and agriculture. The use of mobile phones also is helping rural farmers (women) to prevent exploitation by middlemen hence secure better markets and prices. Also promptly business related information enable them to generate some income through mobile phone services including selling of air time; running telephone kiosk; agent of mobile banking as well as employment in communication services provider. Thus ICT tool contributing greatly in reducing poverty to women and fasting and easy means or system of communication.

Also findings highlighted infrastructure gaps that affected women ability to realize development by ensure poverty reduction through improve productivity by maximize yields and assured higher prices of agriculture product; job creation; strengthen good governance and accountability and necessary information like health services. Thus in order women realize the full potential of access of ICT tools, they must be able to use it effectively. We found, consistently, that inadequate ICTs infrastructure, higher cost, lack of skills and awareness, socio-culture aspect (domestic chores) and time shortage prevented this effort towards poverty reduction among women.

In order for the citizens to benefit fully the potential of ICT services ICT services providers and Government need improvements in supporting ICT infrastructure and capacity building among women.

Recommendation

Creating awareness among women regarding the range of services provided, fully informed about the existing services and various facilities under these services may help women to use ICT services as well as ICT service providers to increase their subscribers' base.

Improvement of ICT infrastructure is needed in order that majority of people in many areas access these services easily those not limited to radios,Internet, mobile phones, television and newspaper, in order to help them to access current information that helps their day to day activities.

Reduced cost of ICTs services provision is also needed. ICT services provider have to reduce cost of using this services in order that majority of people have to own and access those necessary ICTs services in order to have necessary and current information that required to improve women in their day to day socio- economic activities.

Additional interventions may be required including physical ICT infrastructure, and entrepreneurial skills. This can help to improve agricultural growth as a key sector for development to rural people. Increased public and private investment is also important so that there is maximization of employment opportunity.

Future study

There are some important questions that were not covered in this study. One is the extent to which ICTs infrastractures helps women in poverty reduction compared to those who do not use by specifying indicators of development brought by ICT. Further research may Also look at the contribution of ICTs in helping other marginalized groups such as people with disability. There is quite a number of challenges associated with ICTs to support people with diasabilities. Gender digital divide is another area for study [2].

References

1. Wamala C (2012) Empowering Women through ICT. Stockholm University, Sweden.
2. Liff S, Shepherd A, Wajcman J, Rice R, Hargittai E (2004) An evolving gender digital divide? OII Internet Issue Brief 2: 1-17.
3. New Dawn (2001) Looking inside from outside: Rural Poverty in Africa.
4. Singer ER (2012) Women and poverty. New York University, New York.
5. Yonnah OZ, Cons R (2005) ICT as a tool for poverty reduction. AED, Tanzania Telecommunications Company Limited.
6. World Bank (2000) Agriculture in Tanzania since 1986: Follower or leader of growth.
7. Myhr J (2006) Livelihood Changes Enabled by Mobile Phones; the Case of Tanzanian Fishermen. Department of Business, Uppsala University, Uppsala.
8. WDR (2012) Gender equality and development.
9. URT (2003) The national information and communication Technology policy; ministry of communication and transport.
10. Sanga C, Kalungwizi V, Msuya C (2013) Building agricultural extension services system supported by ICTs in Tanzania: Progress made, Challenges remain. International Journal of Education and Development using ICT 9: 80-99.
11. UNESCO (2005) Women poverty and ICT: Mediating social change. Communication and Information Resources, Paris.
12. Dyson L (2004) Cultural issues in the adoption of information and communications technology. In: Sudweeks F, Ess C (eds), Proceedings of

the Cultural Attitudes towards Communication and Technology Conference, Murdoch University pp: 58-71

13. SDC/Panos (2005) Information and communication technology and large scale poverty reduction. Lesson from Asia, Africa, Latin America and the Caribbean, Panos London.
14. UNICEF (1990) The situation analysis of women and children in Tanzania. Research on Poverty Alleviation (REPOA), The government printer.
15. URT (1997) National Enviloment policy.
16. Sanga C, Churi A, Tumbo S (2007) Status, Opportunities, Potential and Challenges of Technology-Mediated Open and Distance Education (Tech-MODE) for Agricultural Education and Improved Livelihoods: A Case Study of Tanzania. Country case studies pp: 113-134.
17. Larry S, Henry L (2009) Community Informatics and Information Systems: Can They Be Better Connected? The Information Society: An International Journal 25: 255-264.
18. Obayelu A, Ogunlade I (2006) Analysis of the uses of information communication technology (ICT) for gender empowerment and sustainable poverty alleviation in Nigeria. International Journal of Education and Development using ICT.
19. URT (2007) Information and communication Technology ICT Ministry of education and vocation training.
20. URT (1999) Poverty and Welfare Monitoring Indicators.
21. URT (2000) Poverty reduction Strategy Paper (PRSP). Washington, DC
22. Chilimo WL, Sanga C (2006) Towards effective knowledge management practices for agricultural information specialists in Tanzania. SCECSAL XVII.
23. Gerster (2003) ICTs for poverty reduction? Swiss Agency for Development and Cooperation (SDC), ICT4D Consulting, CH-8805 Richterswil, Switzerland.
24. Bhavnani A, Won-Wai Ciu R, Janakiram S, Silarszky P (2008) The Role of Mobile Phones in Sustainable Rural Poverty Reduction. ICT Policy Division, Global Information and Communications Department, Washington DC.
25. Eardley T, Bruce J, Goggin G (2009) Telecommunications and Community Wellbeing: A review of the literature on access and affordability for low-income and disadvantaged groups. Telstra Low Income Measures Assessment Committee (LIMAC), Social Policy Research Centre, University of New South Wales, Sydney.
26. Bure CE (2005) Digital inclusion without social inclusion: The consumption of information and communication technologies (ICTs) within homeless subculture in Scotland. The Journal of Community Informatics 1: 116-133.
27. Ling C, Hwang W, Salvendy G (2006) Diversified users satisfaction with advanced mobile features. Universal Access Information Society 5: 239-249.
28. Dobransky K, Hargittai E (2006) The disability divide in internet access and use. Information, Communication and Society 9: 313-334.
29. Hudson HE (2000) From African village to global village: lessons in bridging the African digital divide. Semantic scholar pp: 1-15.
30. Ellen D (2003) Telecenters and the provision of community based access to electronic information in everyday life in the UK. Information Research, The open university, UK.
31. Mtega W (2009) Analyzing the usage patterns and challenges of telecasters among rural communities: Experience from four selected telecasters in Tanzania. International Journal of Education and Development 5: 68-87.
32. Fransman M (2007) The New ICT Ecosystem. Implications for Europe, Kokoro.
33. Sife A, Kiondo J, Macha L (2010) Contribution of mobile phones to rural livelihoods and poverty reduction in Morogoro region. Tanzania, EJISDC 42: 1-15.
34. Hassan Ak (2011) The role of mobile phones on sustainable livelihood: The economic and social research foundation. The Economic and Social Research Foundation (ESRF), Tanzania.
35. Movek DS (2008) Small Farmer Productivity through Increased Access to Draught Power Opportunities. Consultancy Report Stakeholder mapping in Morogoro region.
36. Mittal S, Ganjay S, Praduman K (2000) Socio-Economic Impact of Mobile Phones on Indian Agriculture. Indian Journal of Agricultural Economics.

Nordic Management and Sustainable Business

Björn Preuß*

Department of International Management and Economics, Copenhagen Business School, Denmark Department of Economics, Radboud University Nijmegen, The Netherlands

Abstract

The Nordics have been since a longer time a role model for a social and reliable management style. However, this statement was in the last just proven by doing few case studies with top executives. This study wants to describe the corporate culture and management style in the biggest companies of the Nordics and from that wants to answer if this management approach fosters a sustainable business culture. For defining the management and cultural approach applied in Nordic companies, the method of text mining in relation with machine learning will be used. Among European companies, the Nordic companies show a higher focus on sustainability. The cultural dimensions which describe the uniqueness of the Nordic business culture are to a high degree predictors of a more sustainable business.

Keywords: Management; Nordic; Sustainability; Culture; Corporate; Leadership

Introduction

The Nordic countries are from a historical perspective closely related to each other. Not just from their relation due to trading but also from a cultural perspective. Nearly all countries of the region including Norway, Finland, Denmark and Sweden belonged at one point in time together [1]. Management principles and cultural similarities among companies in the Nordic countries have been proved over the last decades by many scholars [2-6]. The corporate culture is mainly influenced by the national culture and companies exist surrounded by this. Due to this fact, the corporate culture can be better understood by looking at the national culture [7]. Studies have shown that the Nordic countries have, when it comes to leadership styles, similarities that have an impact on their market orientation [7].

The goal of researching the impact of culture might be to draw conclusions in which way the cultural factors influence the sustainability of corporate management. In fact, research faces in this way some difficulties that arise from the nature of culture. The hidden nature of cultural behavior causes some difficulties in measurement and defining these Smith [1]. In order to cope with this difficulties, researchers from outside the region have developed measurements that measure culture on a general scale in order to compare differences among cultures and management styles [2,8]. These results can be used in order to define similarities in a region and or differences to other regions. Not just on country level but also on corporate level might the culture and their difference play a role in the way on how companies react on the development of the world's economy. The fact that current research showed the stakeholder orientation from Nordic companies lead to the consequences that they are more concerned about factors beside the shareholder value [9], according to Freeman who's main research was contributing to the development of the stakeholder approach which is mainly taught by Nordic scholars and has therefore a big influence on the development of Nordic management styles [10,11]. However, beside this logical assumption, current research took this fact more as granted and did not researched on this relation between the long-term stability and the cultural and leadership approach in the Nordic countries.

Due to this fact, the following paper aims to analyze the relation between the Nordic corporate culture and the long term sustainable development of companies. In this connection the study aims to look on the sustainability of management actions and how the corporate culture might influence this. The study collects data from the blue chip companies of the Nordic countries listed in the large cap indices of Denmark, Sweden, Norway and Finland. In order to present differences to other European companies and in order to show the impact of a specific corporate culture a peer group from companies of other European countries was selected. These are listed in the Euro Stoxx 50 index. From this the study uses text mining in order to process an extensive amount of text describing the cultural and management practices in the target companies. Software for text mining and principles or language processing allows to process and quantifies the information and throughout this link it to the economic data which will be collected for each of the countries and companies.

Furthermore, methods from machine learning will be used in order to describe patterns in the linked data and with that present a significant relation between the sustainability of companies in the Nordics and their specific management approach. The models being used for this will be described in more detail under the method selection topic.

The Nordic management approach

The four countries Denmark, Sweden, Norway and Finland can be summarized under the name Nordic region. These country group shares according to current research an equal approach to management that differentiates them from other countries [12,13]. Corporate culture is according to Weber a system of believes [1,14], values and assumptions that are shared among the managers of an organization and that are influencing the way how the organization is managed [15]. Gjølberg showed that in Scandinavia cultural norms and institutional structures that encourage the relationship between stakeholders and the companies are dominant [16]. The structures in companies from the Nordics follow mainly a participative culture [17]. The organizations follow an approach of a high degree of employee engagement and flat hierarchies [13,18]. According to Midttun et al. companies from the

***Corresponding author:** Björn Preuß, Department of Int. Management and Economics, Copenhagen Business School, Denmark Department of Economics, Radboud University Nijmegen, The Netherlands, E-mail: bp.int@cbs.dk

Nordics follow a culture of combining economic interests within a broader societal interest [19]. Furthermore, Scandinavian companies show an involvement of the employees in the management by having participations from the employee side in the board [20]. The whole corporate governance in the Nordics is stakeholder orientated and the corporate ownership is concentrated [9,21]. A high percentage of owners are the state by foundations and families [9,22]. Research showed furthermore that owners in this case behave not as individuals who are just hunting for the short term profit rather than having a long-term interest in the company [11]. This can be backed up by findings that state that Nordic management seems to be more stability orientated. [23,24]. Mintzberg et al. showed that in the Nordics is a high conformity what theory of stakeholder management says and what is done in the practical world [25]. Researchers like Kakabadse et al. claimed that the stakeholder approach nearly dominated the teaching at universities in Scandinavia as well as that the approach has an important status in Scandinavian management since the 1960s [26].

According to the Globe study, the following dimensions can be used to classify the management style in Sweden. Inspirational integrity, visionary, team integration, performance orientation, collaboration. The level of top and middle management is on the same high [27]. This is due to a low level of hierarchy in Scandinavia and in particular Sweden. This participative style in leadership comes in connection with egalitarism and status conscious [28]. There are according to current research certain factors that inhibit leadership in Sweden [27]. These are according to Jagdeep et al. Autocratic, face saver, self-centered, malevolent. As a challenge for the Swedish leader can be seen to balance these factors for good leadership with some of the in depth values of the culture as for example equality [27].

Working in Denmark is characterized by a relatively liberal labor market which means that it is based on self-regulatory mechanisms [29]. In order to provide stability beside this flexible set up, there is a high level of social security provided [30]. This set up of the labor market can also be found in a way in the management style in Danish companies. The focus lies on worker involvement, autonomy and corporation. This had in the latest decade's influence on a positive development of productivity, higher quality and innovativeness [31-33]. Practice in Denmark has shown that practices which create management involvement a positive internal working climate and less repetitive jobs have a positive on the financial performance in Danish companies. In the same, Danish work life can be described as trust in employees and corporation. This had according to current research a positive influence on creating less absenteeism and less strikes [31-33]. In general Danish employees feel adequately informed regarding management decisions. This is due to good information policy in companies as well as a high level of flat hierarchies [34].

One main reason for the economic development of Norway is the increasing democracy both in the public as well as in the management style [35]. Norway did not take part in the Globe project. However, there is research that adapted the questionnaire from this project to Norway [36]. The results have shown that Norway similar to Denmark scores low in power distance and very high in human orientation and collectiveness. In these high score categories, it outperforms all other Nordic countries by far [36]. When it comes to uncertainty avoidance, Norway scores much lower as Sweden which is the highest scoring country in this measure of the Nordic cluster.

In Finland the situation looks a bit like in Sweden. The importance of non-hierarchical dialogue and participative leadership are established values in the Finish management practice [37-39]. Advances in productivity of Finish companies can be related to team tasks, the structure and processes of organizations as well as the creation of social workspaces [40]. The individualistic behavior as well as the high equality between men and women is in Finland same as in Sweden an important element of the culture in companies and society [27]. Another factor that influences the working life as well as the management style is that according to Jagdeep et al. the power distance in Finland can be described as low. This creates equality among the employees. An interesting point that can be found in Finland and differentiate the country in some way from other Nordic societies is that there is a low performance orientation according to the Globe study [41]. Beside this which can have an effect on the performance and reward system in companies, the future orientation is higher as the average country in the Globe study [27].

Sustainability is not just environmental friendliness

In the past year's research has shown that the industrialization had negative effects on the environment [42]. However, the economic output is to a high proportion dependent on the natural system [43]. This leads to more sustainability and environmental friendliness in business. Furthermore, the economic environment is unstable so that business needs to adapt fast to this condition in order to reduce risk of failure [44].

In the 21st century the environment is an important factor that should be preserved for upcoming generations. In order to measure the impact that company have on the environment multiple methods and measures have been developed [45]. One prominent measure of companies' environmental impact is the ESG ratings. The available ESG scores cover a multiple factor that describe company's social responsibility and combine them in one score. These social factors relate to treatment of employees, labor conditions, human rights, supply chains, and treating stakeholders in society fairly. The last factor, governance, covers abuses in executive pay, diversity on boards, equal employment opportunities, business transparency and disclosure, and corruption inter alia [46]. However the principles of score calculation are not transparent. Butz and Pictet argue that ESG scores have become commodities [47], which has led to firms proactively adopting ESG strategies that live up to these rating criteria. Thereby, adopting ESG strategies on a firm level can increase the potential investor base and potentially lead to a higher share price [48]. Beside the impact on the environment a company can also be defined as sustainable from a business perspective. Porter defined a company as sustainable when it creates long term sustainable value for its stakeholders [49].

The Nordic companies score especially high in responsibility measures [15,19,50,51]. This might be due to the fact that shareholder value is teached extensively in business schools as well as used in business [11,52]. In current research, Harrison et al. provided in his work a demonstration that managing stakeholders leads to stakeholder trust and with this to additional value creation.

Method and Sample Selection

In this section we describe the method that was used in order to analyze big data of cultural statement document corpus. The corpus contained 3000 documents with single statements about the corporate culture, the management and leadership style in Scandinavian and European companies. The text extraction in order to apply text mining and machine learning was done from txt files. For doing both the extraction, mining the software rapid miner was used. The machine learning algorithms were optimized by using the R extension of rapid miner.

Sample: A company selection

The sample size selection for this paper was made by choosing companies from the blue chip indices from the Nordic companies and the European Union. See for detailed information the following table. The selection was made in align with the fact that the companies in the analysis represent the main economic activity in the selected regions. With that it will be possible to draw conclusions about the corporate culture in the target countries and companies (Table 1).

The data were collected from websites which give employees a platform to comment on the management and leadership style as well as the corporate culture of their current or former employees (e.g., glassdoor.com, indeed.com). This post gives in their total a realistic view on the culture in the various firms. Although the way of data collection makes this study less dependent on the companies and also has a lower level influence through participants [52,53].

The sample consists of in total 3.000 attributes where each describes the culture of a specific company. For each company ca. 2030 of such descriptions were collected.

Text mining for data collection

Text mining is a method to process and analyse unstructured textual data. It uses techniques from data mining and machine learning in order to extract knowledge from multiple documents. Clustering trend analysis or association rules are common fields in which text mining is applied [54]. The method of text mining finds in multiple research areas of social science and application [55-57]. In this paper the software Rapidminer® was used in order to process the text with the goal to get the text data in a structured for which can be analyzed by a statistics program. This was necessary in order to use machine learning and also for later linking the findings to the economic data. Furthermore, this method allows drawing also a picture of the cultural set up in each of the companies which makes it different to the current studies on culture and for the purpose of this study necessary.

The text mining process is presented in Figure 1 and contains different steps that lead to a list of words that mainly describe the underlying text and with that includes the core information of the text. The first step is that the words get tokenized. That means that the text will be split into the single words. After that the words were filtered by length. In this case words with less than 4 and with more than 25 characters where excluded. The words got also filtered by English stop words so that words like "and" and "then" etc. were excluded from the sample since they do not contain specific content information. The next step that was performed was stemming. The used operator (written in the snowball language) stems the words in the documents based on their English word stem. This is necessary in order to not have multiple words with just different forms in the output of the text mining process. After all the words were transformed to a homogeneous case (here lower case), the result was then written into an excel document for further analysis.

Country	Index	Num. Companies
Norway	OBX 26	26
Denmark	OBX 26 OMX Copenhagen 20	20
Sweden	OMX Stockholm 30	30
Finland	OMX Stockholm 30 OMX Helsinki 25	25
EU	EUROSTOXX 50	49[2]

Table 1: Covered indices.

The outcome is a list of words that each of the documents contain and the number of it. Each document is linked to the company it belongs to and it can therefore easy be linked to data from the country or the company.

Machine learning to predict defined patterns

As a part of the method, machine learning algorithms were applied on the text corpus in order to classify the text. The text classification uses a supervised machine learning approach and can be seen as a process were the machine as signs predefined labels to new documents. This is done by using a probabilistic measure of likelihood using a training set of documents that where labelled before [58].

First sample data sets were defined. This was done for each of the cultural dimensions. The sample data were statements that described for example a more future oriented culture or a less future oriented culture. After that, a linear support vector machine (SVM) was used as a classifier [59]. The SVM groups the data points into classes by designing a hyper plane between these.

There can be multiple hyper planes be designed but the algorithm choses the one which leaves the maximum margin between both classes. The hyper plane delivers for each class different value: With minimizing the distance, the algorithm minimizes the reparability of the classes. This is done by using a nonlinear optimization task using the KKT method and Lagrangian multipliers λ [60,61].

The vector that describes distance between the hyper plane and the data point's is also named support vector. The hyper plane is the used for classifying the data. This process was repeated for each of the cultural dimensions. The resulting data was then saves as .xlsx file. This process can be described in the following rapidminer processes (Figure 2).

After training the model with a split of the sample, the model was applied to classify the rest of the data set. This process is described in the following (Figure 3).

This was done several times in order to classify the corpus with different labels for each of the cultural dimensions defined by the Globe project as well as for sustainability.

The data that results from the text mining and machine learning operations will be analyzed with descriptive statistics and regression modelling. Based on a selection made by the descriptive statistics, the main cultural dimensions will be analyzed by simple regression models and together in a multiple regression model which can be described by the following formula. In the descriptive statistics the scores for the Nordic countries and the other EU countries will be described and compared with each other.

Nordic management on top of Europe

The management of the Nordic countries was in the past extensively studied on country level. This study examines the leadership culture on company level in order to bring it into relation with the companies' actions related to sustainability.

The difference in leadership between the Nordics and rest of Europe

The first step in order to define the leadership styles in each of the companies that are contained in the sample size was to extract the word list by using the above described algorithms in rapid miner. The resulting word count list can be requested from the author but will not be displayed in this paper due to limited space for the rich data. In the

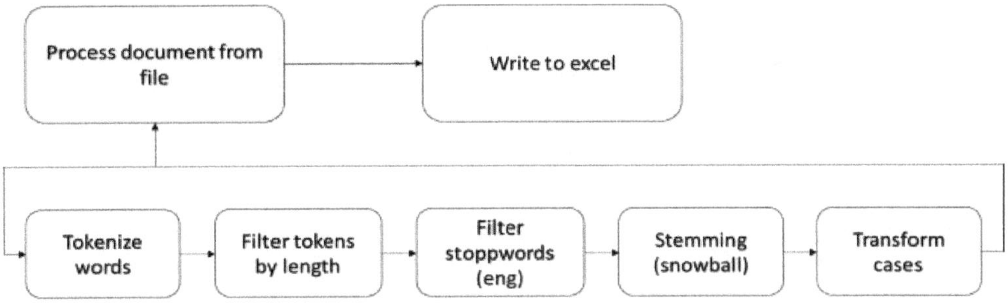

Figure 1: Text mining process.

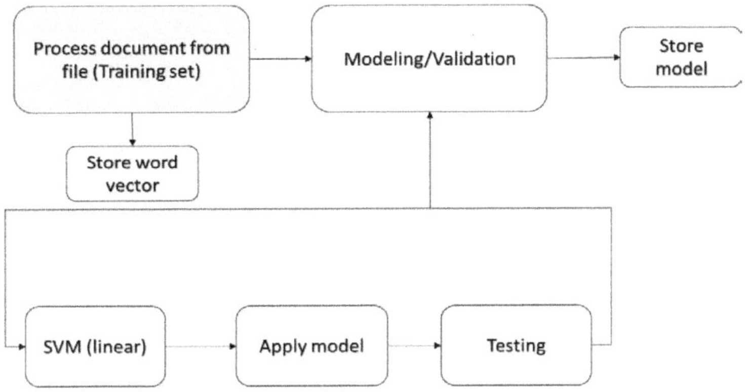

Figure 2: Building and testing SVM model.

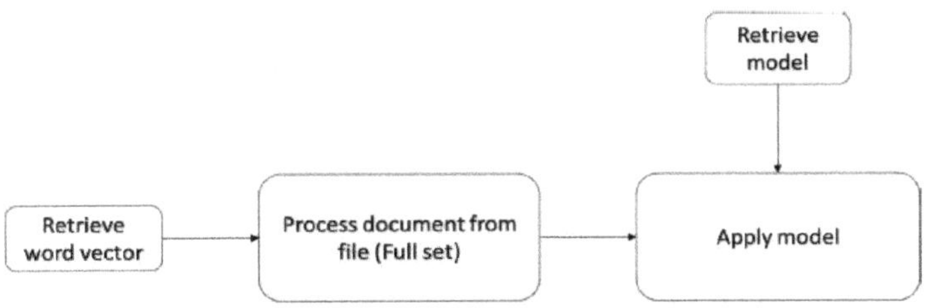

Figure 3: Applying VSM model on data set.

first step of the analysis an exploratory factor analysis was performed. The number of factors was distinguished by theory and the definitions of the GLOBE study were chosen since they were more detailed and it allowed making the model more precise.

The following graphs show how the Nordic countries differ in terms of management approach based on the Globe study dimensions (Figure 4).

It is from the graphs clear to see that companies in the Nordics score lover then in the rest of Europe when it comes to the dimension's collectivism, uncertainty avoidance, power distance and masculinity. In Human and future orientation have the Nordic companies higher scores then I the rest of Europe. These findings out of the text mining process is in align with the findings of previous research related to the Nordic culture.

Impact of Nordic corporate culture on stability

The first look on the difference of sustainability of the Nordic countries compared to the other Europeans shows that there is not a huge difference in how they talk about sustainability. However, all the Nordic companies score slightly higher as the average European company (Figure 5).

The data analysis shows that the average European company scores lower as companies from the Nordic countries. This is in aligning with the findings from current research regarding the social and environmental friendly orientation of Nordic companies. However, these descriptions show just the current situation and do not focus on the question whether there is a relation between the Nordic leadership and the higher sustainable orientation of the Nordic countries. In order to discover this multiple regression models were performed. To oversee the relations between the sustainable orientation and the corporate culture see the following scatter plots (Figure 6).

The strongest relationship is between sustainability and the cultural dimension's future orientation, masculinity and human orientation. This can be also seen in the correlation matrix in the appendix of this paper. Therefore, the further analysis will have a more in depth look on these. The sustainability measure is for all following in depth analysis the same and can be described by the following descriptive statistics (Table 2).

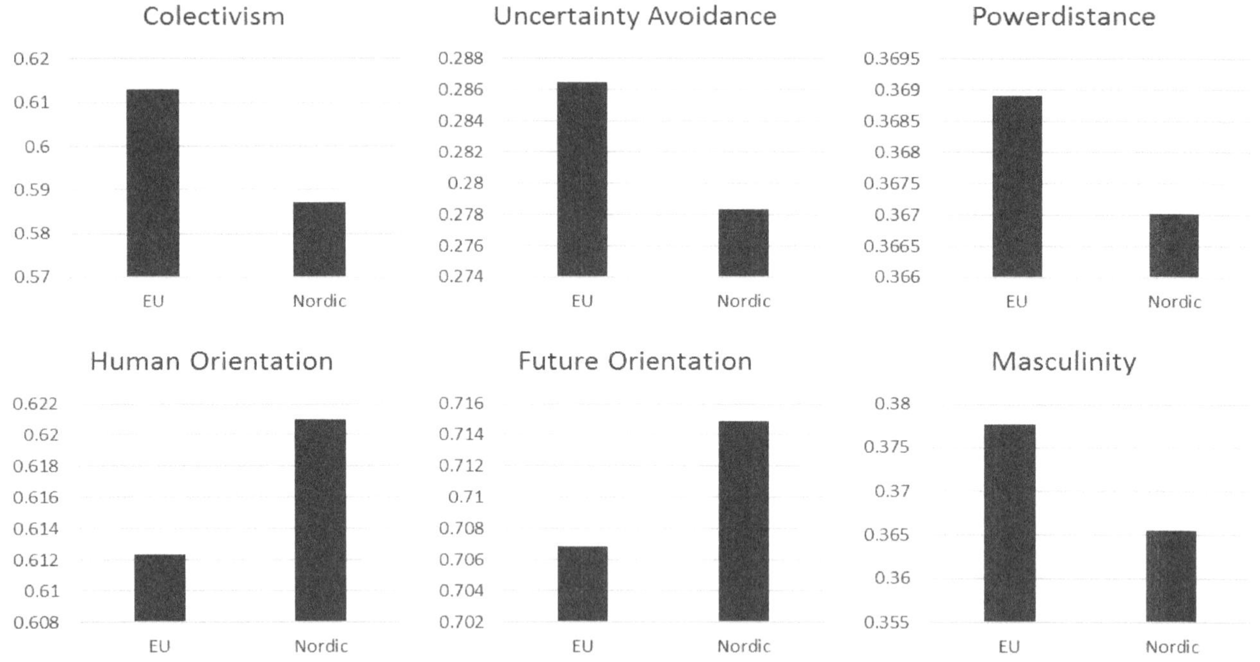

Figure 4: Graphs cultural dimensions.

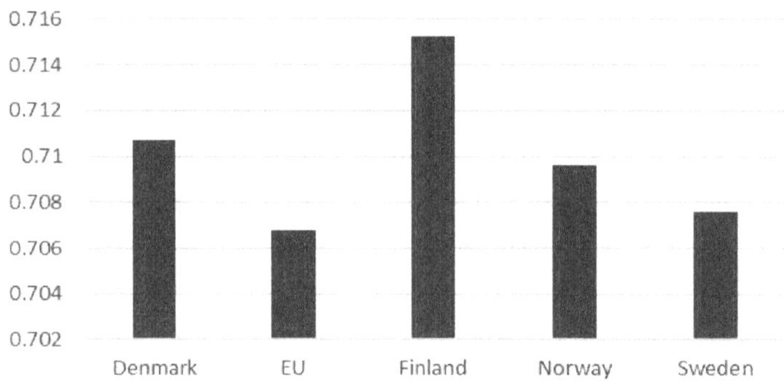

Figure 5: Sustainability score.

Sustainability	
Mean	0.7094
Standard Error	0.0013
Median	0.7095
Standard Deviation	0.0149
Sample Variance	0.0002
Kurtosis	0.8843
Skewness	0.0090
Range	0.0887
Minimum	0.6677
Maximum	0.7564
Sum	97.1873
Count	137

Table 2: Summary descriptive statistics Sustainability.

It can be said that the median and the mean are nearly the same which indicate a normal distribution. The regression model with the highest prediction power is between Sustainability and Masculinity (Table 3).

Also for this dimension is the mean close to the median. However, over all, this dimension is wider spread then the dimension describing sustainability which indicates for a higher variety among the data set. The regression statistics in the following table highlight that the model has a maximum prediction power of ca. 25%. This is for just one cultural dimension high. The R square as well the adjusted R square is much lower but this can be in this case neglected since it accounts for a small sample size. However, since the number of companies is given, this can't be adjusted (Table 4).

Also the ANOVA table supports the hypothesis that a higher masculinity has a negative impact on the sustainability of a company. And with that accounts this for a higher sustainable management in Nordic companies which have in average a lower masculinity then the average European company (Table 5).

The significance of the model is below 0.005 so it can be used as a predictor for the outcome of the model. The second cultural dimension which has a high impact on the sustainability based on the regression model is the future orientation. This is also logic and was proven my current research that a more towards the future oriented company searches also for more innovative and sustainable solutions.

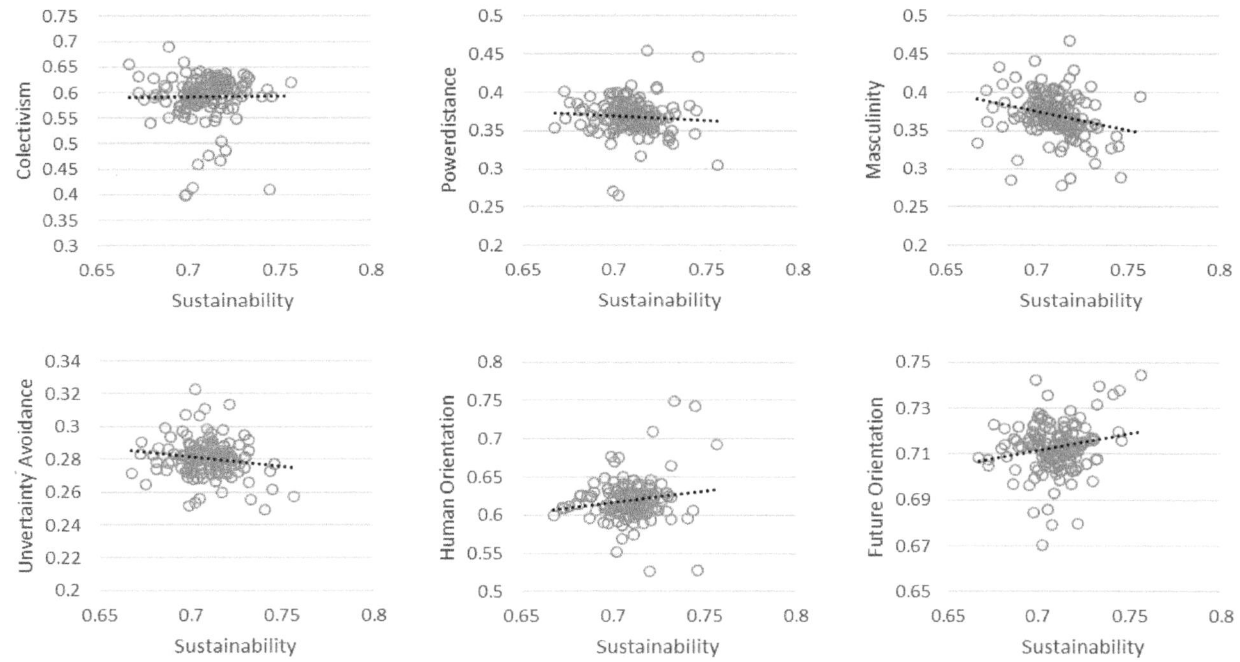

Figure 6: Scatter plots - relation sustainability and cultural dimensions.

Masculinity	
Mean	0.3705
Standard Error	0.0025
Median	0.3702
Standard Deviation	0.0293
Sample Variance	0.0009
Kurtosis	1.7119
Skewness	-0.3237
Range	0.1897
Minimum	0.2781
Maximum	0.4678
Sum	50.7625
Count	137

Table 3: Summary descriptive statistics masculinity.

Regression Statistics	
Multiple R	0.247168228
R Square	0.061092133
Adjusted R Square	0.05413726
Standard Error	0.014458545
Observations	137

Table 4: Regression statistics masculinity-sustainability.

	df	SS	MS	F	Significance F
Regression	1	0.001836307	0.00183631	8.78407589	0.003593041
Residual	135	0.028221687	0.00020905		
Total	136	0.030057994			

Table 5: ANOVA statistics regression model masculinity-sustainability.

The dimension can be described by the following descriptive statistics (Table 6).

The dimension is like the sustainability not wide spread across the companies as well as has a median which is near to the mean. The regression model between future orientation and sustainability can be described by the key figures in the following (Table 7).

Future Orientation	
Mean	0.7129
Standard Error	0.001
Median	0.7137
Mode	n/a
Standard Deviation	0.0113
Sample Variance	0.0001
Kurtosis	2.3612
Skewness	-0.4369
Range	0.0742
Minimum	0.6704
Maximum	0.7445
Sum	97.6695
Count	137

Table 6: Descriptive statistics future orientation.

Regression Statistics	
Multiple R	0.199037629
R Square	0.039615978
Adjusted R Square	0.032502022
Standard Error	0.01462297
Observations	137

Table 7: Regression statistics future orientation-sustainability.

The prediction power of the future orientation is slightly lower as the one of masculinity which is could have been based on current research the other way around. However, both R's are with 25% and 20% close to each other. The ANOVA table for this model can be seen in the following (Table 8).

With ca 0.02 is the significance much higher as for the masculinity but still can be accepted since the model contains just one cultural dimension which is only a piece of the whole corporate culture and management style of a company. The last dimension which has a major impact on how sustainable a company is managed is the human orientation. The more human a company is oriented the more sustainable is the company managed. This is in align with current research and also logic since how a company interacts with employees as well as other human is also a factor for how sustainable a company (Table 9).

Also hear is the mean close to the median. But the maximum and minimum are wider spread then at the future orientation ore the sustainability (Table 10).

The prediction power of the model is with ca. 15%, 5% points lower as the other two dimensions but still one of the most important once (see scatter plots) (Table 11).

Parallel with the prediction power of the model is also the significance changed. With 0.07 is it the highest out of the main predictors. If these three cultural dimensions are put together in a multiple regression model, then then culture defined by this dimensions can predict 32.6% of the outcome of the sustainability. The regression model can be seen in the appendix of this paper (Tables 12 and 13).

Result and Discussion

The results of this research present the relation between cultural dimensions and the sustainability of the companies. For the four Nordic countries Denmark, Sweden, Norway and Finland as well as the biggest European companies (Euro Stoxx50). However, the picture remains incomplete and the question regarding how to in detail influence the cultural dimensions remains unanswered by this analysis. Methodological limitations should also be considered when drawing conclusions from these findings.

df		SS	MS	F	Significance F
Regression	1	0.001190777	0.001190777	5.568769207	0.019715952
Residual	135	0.028867217	0.000213831		
Total	136	0.030057994			

Table 8: ANOVA future orientation-sustainability.

Mean	0.6193
Human Orientation	
Standard Error	0.0024
Median	0.6168
Mode	n/a
Standard Deviation	0.0283
Sample Variance	0.0008
Kurtosis	6.8426
Skewness	1.1802
Range	0.2220
Minimum	0.5273
Maximum	0.7493
Sum	84.8414
Count	137

Table 9: Descriptive statistics human orientation.

Regression Statistics	
Multiple R	0.153911585
R Square	0.023688776
Adjusted R Square	0.016456841
Standard Error	0.014743726
Observations	137

Table 10: Regression statistics human orientation-sustainability.

df		SS	MS	F	Significance F
Regression	1	0.000712037	0.000712037	3.275579221	0.072542563
Residual	135	0.029345957	0.000217377		
Total	136	0.030057994			

Table 11: ANOVA table regression model human orientation-sustainability.

	SUST	PWD	MAS	UAV	HUO	FUO	COL
SUST	1						
PWD	-0.08089	1					
MAS	-0.24717	0.11903	1				
UAV	-0.15705	0.15732	0.02017	1			
HUO	0.15391	-0.27789	-0.04053	-0.0625	1		
FUO	0.19904	-0.19779	-0.09384	-0.9376	0.1580	1	
COL	0.00607	0.05450	-0.27281	0.3228	-0.0783	-0.2198	1

Table 12: Correlation matrix sustainability and cultural dimensions.

In the first step it can be summarized that the findings about the Nordic corporate culture can support the current research. The management style in the Nordic companies is in contrast to the rest of European companies defined by flat hierarchies. The broader social interest of companies in Denmark, Sweden, Norway and Finland can be found respectively in the score of the human orientation. Nordic companies are focused on social values and highly future orientated. This future orientation is in align with the visionary set up that is especially in the Swedish corporate set up the case.

When connecting this score to the sustainability, the analysis showed that the cultural dimension's masculinity, future orientation and human orientation have the highest impact on how high the firm scores in sustainability. Masculinity has a negative impact and the other two dimensions have a positive impact on the sustainability. When comparing the Nordic companies with other European companies they score in these dimensions in exactly the supporting direction. The way how the Nordic companies in average differentiate themselves against the rest of Europe is in align with current research. The companies in the Nordic countries have a culture that can be defined by higher individualism and lower uncertainty avoidance. They account for a low power distance and a higher future and human orientation. Furthermore, they have a less masculine culture which can also be seen by the role of women in those societies.

Managerial Implications

Since certain studies showed already a correlation between sustainability and corporate financial performance [62-64]. Managers are good advised to focus on responsibility activities. This paper showed that by adopting a management style similar to the Nordic countries, the sustainability of business operations can be increased. The Nordic approach is more future orientated, focus on the human capital and increases the flexibility by giving the employees more freedom to act.

Future Research

The method of text analytics and machine learning is rather new in the field of social science research. Therefore, it gives further research the possibility in finding more suitable algorithms for certain data sets. Furthermore, the paper used also for the discovery of firm's responsibility a text mining approach. Also if the results of this are in align with current research it can be enriching to analyze how the assessment of social responsibility with this method scores in combination with other established rating methods (e.g., sustain alythics' ESG rating). There might be a slight difference in the outcomes of certain methods given by the underlying data.

Regression Statistics								
Multiple R	0.3259							
R Square	0.1062							
Adjusted R Sq.	0.0860							
Standard Error	0.0142							
Observations	137							
ANOVA								
					Significance			
	df	*SS*	*MS*	*F*	*F*			
Regression	3	0.0031	0.0010	5.2692	0.0018			
Residual	133	0.0268	0.0002					
Total	136	0.0300						
		Standard				*Upper*	*Lower*	*Upper*
	Coefficients	*Error*	*t Stat*	*P-value*	*Lower 95%*	*95%*	*95.0%*	*95.0%*
				2.07E-				
Intercept	0.5637	0.08187	6.8846	10	0.4017	0.7256	0.4017	0.7256
MAS	-0.1152	0.0417	-2.7610	0.0065	-0.1977	-0.0326	-0.1977	-0.0326
FUO	0.2096	0.1100	1.9053	0.0588	-0.0079	0.4273	-0.0079	0.4273
HUO	0.0628	0.0436	1.4402	0.1521	-0.0234	0.1490	-0.0234	0.1490

Table 13: Multiple regression model.

References

1. Smith PB (2003) In search of Nordic management styles. Scandinavian Journal of Management 19: 491-507.
2. Hofstede G (1980) Culture's Consequences. Beverly Hills: Sage Publications.
3. Hofstede G (1991) Cultures and Organizations; Software of the Mind. McGraw-Hill, London.
4. Ronen S, Shenkar O (1985) Clustering countries on attitudinal dimensions: A review. Academy of Management Review 10: 435-454.
5. Grenness T (2000) Management in Norway. In: Regional Encyclopedia of Business and Management: Management in Europe. Business Press Thomson Learning.
6. Grenness T, Joynt P (1996) Management in Scandinavia. International Encyclopedia of Business and Management London: Routledge, pp: 3021-3029.
7. Selnes F (1996) Market orientation in United States and Scandinavian companies: A cross cultural study. Journal of Scandinavian Management 12: 139-157.
8. House RJ (2003) Culture, Leadership, and Organizations: A 62 nation GLOBE study. Sage in press, CA.
9. Carlsson RH (2007) Swedish corporate governance and value creation: Owners still in the driver's seat. Corporate Governance: An International Review 15: 1038-1055.
10. Freeman RE (1984) Strategic Management: A Stakeholder Approach. Pitman, Boston.
11. Strand R, Freeman RE (2013) Scandinavian cooperative advantage: The theory and practice of stakeholder engagement in Scandinavia. Journal of Business Ethics 127: 65-85.
12. Nordstrom B (2000) Scandinavia since 1500. Mineapolis: University of Mineapolis Press.
13. Bonderson U (2003) Nordic moral Climates: value Continuities and Discontinuities in Denmark, Finland, Norway and Sweden. New Brunswik: Transaction Publishers.
14. Nielsen SJ, Sivesind KH, Lawrence P (2004) Management in Scandinavia: Culture, context and change. Edward Elgar, Cheltenham.
15. Weber Y (1996) Corporate culture fit and performance in mergers and acquisitions. Human relations 49: 1181-1202.
16. Gjølberg M (2010) Varietes of corporate social responsibility (CSR): CSR meets the Nordic Model. Regulation and Governance 4: 203-229.
17. Grenness T (2003) Scandinavian Managers on Scandinavian Management. International Journal of Value-Based Management, 16: 9-21.
18. Morsing M, Midttun A, Palmas K (2007) Corporate Social Responsibility in Scandinavia - a turn towards the business case?. In: May S, Cheney G, editors. The Debate over Corporate Social Responsibility. London: Oxford University Press 98-127.
19. Midttun A, Gautesen K, Gjølberg M (2006) The political economy of CSR in Western Europe. Corporate Governance: The international Journal of Business in Society 6: 369-385.
20. Sinani E (2008) Corporate governance in Scandinavia: Comparing networks and formal institutions. European Management Review 5: 27-40.
21. Carlsson RH (2002) Ownership and Value Creation: Strategic Corporate Governance in the New Economy. New York: John Wiley and Sons pp: 320.
22. Porta R, Lopez-de-Silanes F, Shleifer A (1999) Corporate ownership around the World. Journal of Finance 54: 471-517.
23. Lindoe PH, Engen AO (2007) Behaviour based safety and the nordic model. In: Proceedings and Monographs in Engineering. Water and Earth Sciences. s.l.s.n.
24. Kvande E, Brøve HE (2012) The nordic model in a global company situated in norway: challanging institutional orders? Nordic Journal of Life Studies 2: 117-134.
25. Mintzberg H, Ahlstrand B, Lampel J (2009) Strategy Safari: The Complete Guide Through the Wilds of Startegic Management. London: Financial Times/ Pearson Prentice Hall.
26. Kakabadse NK, Rozuel C, Lee-Davis L (2005) Corporate Social Responsibility and Stakeholder Approach: A Conceptual Review. Journal of Business Governance and Ethics 11: 277-302.
27. Jagdeep S, Chhookar FC, Brodbeck F, House J R (2007) Culture and Leadership Across the World. The GLOBE Book of in-depth studies of 25 societies, s.l. Lawrence Erlbraum Ass.
28. Tollgerdt-Andersson I (1989) Ledarskapsteorier, företagsklimat och bedömningsmetoder, Stockholm: Doctoral Dissertation SSE.
29. Due J, Madsen JS (2008) The Danish model of industrial relations: Erosion or renewal? Journal of Industrial Relations 50: 513-529.
30. Sørensen OH, Hasle P, Navrbjerg SE (2009) Local Agreements as an Instrument for Improvements as an Instrument of Improvement of Management - Employee collaboration on Occupational Health and Safety. Economic and Industrial Democracy 30: 643.
31. Hvid H, Hasle P (2003) Human Working Life. (1st ed) Aldershot: Ashgate Publishing LTD.
32. Hansen NJ (2007) Skaber lean bedre arbejdsmiljø? DTU.
33. Cottini E, Kato T, Westergaard-Nielsen N (2011) Adverse workplace conditions, high-involvement work practices and labor turnover: Evidence from Danish linked employer-employee data. Labor Economics 18: 872-880.

34. Lund HL (2004) Strategies for Sustainable Business and the Handling of Workers Interests: Integrated Management Systems and Work Participation. Economic and Industrial Democracy 25: 41-74.

35. Levin M, Nilssen T, Ravn J E, Øyum L (2012) Demokrati i arbeidslivet: Dennorske samarbeidsmodellen som konkurransefortrinn. Bergen: Fagbokforlaget.

36. Warner-Søderholm G (2010) Understanding Perceptions of Cultural and Intrarcultural Societal Practices and Values of Norwegian Managers. University of Reading.

37. Jones DC, Kalmi P, Kauhanen A (2010) How does employee involvement stack up? The effects of human resource management policies on performance in a retail firm. Industrial Relations 49: 1-21.

38. Fey CF, Morgulis-Yakushev S, Park HJ, Björkman I (2009) Opening the black box of the relationship between HRM practices and firm performance: A comparison of MNE subsidiaries in the USA, Finland and Russia. Journal of International Business Studies 40: 690-712.

39. Andreeva T, Kianto A (2012) Does knowledge management really matter? Linking knowledge management practices, competitiveness and economic performance. Journal of Knowledge Management 16: 617-636.

40. Bosch-Sijtsema PM, Ruohomäki V, Vartiainen M (2009) Knowledge work productivity in distributed teams. Journal of Knowledge Management 13: 533-546.

41. House R, Hanges PJ, Javidan M, Dorfman PW, Gupta V, et al. (2004) Culture, leadership, and organizations: The GLOBE study of 62 societies. Sage Publications.

42. World Ressource Institute (2004) World Resources 2002-2004: Decisions for the Earth: Balance, voice, and power. World Resource Institute, Washington DC.

43. Constanza R, Ralph d'arge, Groot R, Farber S, Grasso M, et al. (1997) The value of the World's ecosystem services and natural capital. Nature 387: 253-260.

44. Miller KD (1992) A framework for integrated risk management in international business. Journal of International Business Studies 311-331.

45. Verfaille H, Bidwell R (2000) Measuring Eco-Efficiency: A Guide to Reporting Company Performance. World Business Council for Sustainable Development, Geneva.

46. Charles A, Darne O, Fouilloux J (2015) ESG Indices Financial Risk: Performance measures based on Value-at-Risk approach, pp: 1-34.

47. Butz C, Pictet O (2008) The SRI Performance Paradox. Geneva: Pictet & Cie.

48. Monika K, Erzsebet S (2014) Challenges in Performance Metrics in Socially Responsible Investments. Annals of the University of Oradea: Economics Science Series 23: 919-927.

49. Porter ME (2010) On competition. Harvard Business Press, Boston.

50. Campell JL (2007) Why would corporations behave in socially responsible ways? An institutional theory of corporate social responsibility. Academy of Management Review 32: 946-967.

51. Broberg MP (1996) Corporate social responsibility in the European communities-The scandinavian viewpoint. Journal of Business Ethics 15: 615-622.

52. Pettersen IJ, Rotefoss B, Jönsson S, Korneliussen T (2002) Nordic Management Business Administration Reserach - Quo Vadis, Göteburg: Gothenburg Research Institute.

53. Bryman A, Bell E (2015) Business research methods. New York: Oxford University Press.

54. Feldman R, Sanger J (2007) Text mining handbook: Advanced methods in analysing unstructured data. Cambridge: Cambridge University Press.

55. Torvaten H, Sörensen O, Talja H, Eriksen B (2015) Good Nordic management practices - State of the art. Oslo: Norden - Chamber of nordic ministers.

56. Kinra A, Vatrapu R, Mukkamala RR (2016) Methodological Demonstration of a Text Analytics Approach to Country Logistics System Assesment. Copenhagen: non published.

57. Hippner H, Rentzmann R (2006) Text mining. Informatik-Spektrum 29: 287-290.

58. Yang Y, Liu X (1999) A re-examination of text categorization methods. ACM SIGR conference on Research and development in information retrieval.

59. Ben-Hur A, Hom D, Siegelmann H, Vapnik V (2001) Support vector clustering. Journal of Machine learning research 2: 125-137.

60. Mangasarian OL, David RM (2001) Lagrangian support vector machines. Journal of Machine Learning Research 1: 161-177.

61. Wu HC (2009) The Karush-Kuhn-Tucker optimality conditions in multi objective programing problems with interval-valued objective functions. European Journal of Operations Research 196: 49-60.

62. Luo X, Bhattacharya C (2009) The Debate over Doing Good: Corporate Social Performance. strategic Marketing Levers and Firm-Idosocratic Risk. Journal of Marketing 73: 198-213.

63. Margolis J, Walsh J (2003) Misery Lovers Companies: Rethinking Social Initiatives by Business. Administartive Science Quarterly 48: 268-305.

64. Sen S, Bhattacharya C, Korschun D (2006) The role of corporate social responsibility in strenthening multiple stakeholder relationships: A field experiment. Journal of Academy of Marketing Science 34: 158-166.

The impact of capital structure on Financial Performance of the firms: Evidence From Borsa Istanbul

Nassar S*

Marmara University, Institute of social science, Accounting and Finance Department, Istanbul/Turkey

Abstract

The paper tries to examine the impact of capital structure on the financial firm performance of industrial companies in Turkey. the annual financial statements of 136 industrial companies listed on Istanbul Stock Exchange (ISE) were used for this study which covers a period of 8 years from 2005-20012. A multivariate regression analysis is applied to test the relationship between capital structure and firm performance. To measure firm performance used indicators such as Return on Asset (ROA), Return on Equity (ROE) and Earning per Share (EPS) as well as Debt Ratio (DR) as capital structure variable. The results show that there is a negative significant relationship between capital structure and firm performance.

Keywords: Capital structure; Firm performance; Return on asset; Return on equity; Earning per share; Debt ratio

Introduction

The main objective of the firms is to maximize its profits and in the same time minimize its costs, when companies search about resources to finance its investments they take this objective in consideration.

The main sources that firms could use to provide the necessary finance are the internal finance which is equity, and the external finance which is debt. Most of companies use a mix between equity and debt which form the capital structure.

Capital structure was defined firstly by Modigliani and Miller as the mix between debt and equity that the company uses in its operation. The paper that published by Modigliani and Miller refers to the impact of capital structure on firm value under many restrictive assumptions that have been modified by them five years later in (1963) [1].

After Modigliani and Miller, Jensen and Meckling discussed the agency cost theory which refers to the potential conflict between managers and shareholders in one side, and between shareholders and debtors in another side.

Since Jensen and Meckling's argument the relationship between capital structure and firm performance, many researchers have begun to study the relationship between capital structure and firm performance.

The main objective of this paper is to examine the impact of capital structure measured by debt ratio (DR) on financial performance measured by earning per share (EPS), return on equity (ROE), and return on assets (ROA). Data of 136 firms listed as industrial sector companies on Istanbul stock exchange (ISE) during the period 2005-2012 will be used.

The paper proceeds along the following lines. Section-2 presents the theoretical framework, Section-3 discusses review of literature, Section-4 discusses the research methodology, hypothesis, data, and variables, Section-5 discusses data analysis and results and Section-6 offers findings and conclusions.

Theoretical Framework and Literature Review

Capital structure has been defined by many authors and scholars. However, these definitions are explicit and have the same meaning. This research work adopts that of Pandey which says "a company's capital structure refers to its debt level relative to equity on the balance sheet [2]. It is a snapshot of the amounts and types of capital that a firm has access to, and what financing methods it has used to conduct growth initiatives such as research and development or acquiring assets".

From this definition, we can say that capital structure is a trend at how a company finances its assets through a combination of debt, equity or mixture between securities and that a company's capital structure is then the figuration or structuring its liabilities.

Capital structure theories

The following capital structure theories have evolved from capital structure literature:

Modigliani and miller (mm) theory (1958, 1963): In Modigliani and Miller provided the seminal in capital structure under certain assumptions include no taxes, homogenous expectations, perfect capital markets, and no transaction costs [1]. This theory which called "capital structure irrelevance" states that the relationship between capital structure and cost of capital is irrelevant, that mean the increases in debt does not effect on cost of capital. In a result, the investor's expectations of future benefits are totally effect on firm value and cost of capital.

Latterly, Modigliani and Miller introduced new evidence that cost of capital effect on capital structure, and thus effect on firm value with taking taxes as assumption into consideration, which refer that borrowing give tax advantage, because the interest will deduct from the tax which result what is known as tax shields, which in turn reduce the cost of debt and then maximize the firm performance [3].

Pecking order theory: Pecking order theory is the result of Asymmetric information. The pecking order model does not discuss

***Corresponding author:** Sedeaq Nassar, Accounting and Finance Department, Marmara University, Institute of social science, Istanbul/Turkey
E-mail: Sedeaq.nassar@gmail.com

the optimal capital structure as significant point, but states that firms have two main sources to fund its financial needs which are internal and external finance; the theory claims that firms prefer to use firstly internal finance such as excess liquid assets or retained earnings then external finance. If internal financing is not enough to fund investment projects, firms may or may not obtain external financing, and if they do, In order to minimize additional costs of asymmetric information, the managers head for choosing between the different sources of external finance, firms prefer to use debt leverage firstly, secondly issuance of preferred stock and finally issuance of common stock [4,5].

Trade-off theory: Trade off theory is an extension of the MM theory developed by Miller. The theory proposes that the firm's optimal capital structure include the tradeoff among the influences of firms and personal taxes, agency costs and bankruptcy costs, etc. Trade-off theory expect that corporations choose levels of debt in order to achieve a balance among the benefits from the interest tax shield with the costs related to a future financial distress or with current financial inflexibility.

The agency theory: Agency cost theory which provided by Jensen and Meckling is discussing the conflict of interest between principals (shareholders) and decision makers (agents) of firms (managers, board members, etc), this conflict stems from the differences in behavior or decisions by point out that the parties (agents and shareholders) often have different goals, and different tolerances toward risk. In this case, the managers whom are responsible of guiding the firm toward to achieve them personal goals rather than maximizing benefits to the shareholders. Hence, the main conflict that shareholders face is to ensure that managers (agents) do not invest the free cash flow in unprofitable projects. In another hand, increasing the debt to equity ratio would assist firms to make sure that managers are running the firm more efficiently [6].

Literature review

Since Modigliani and Miller's theory has been published many of the researchers are still studying the relationship between capital structure and firm performance, some of them found that there is a negative relation between capital structure and firm performance, while others found a positive relation between capital structure and firm performance. In another hand many papers referred to a significant relation between structure and firm performance, while some of them referred to an insignificant relation between structure and firm performance.

In this study we will browse the newest published papers in this aspect, because its will be closer to reality, in addition these papers applied in an emerging markets which have similar characteristics with Turkish market.

Badar and Saeed study showed the impact of using leverage in firm's capital structure on firm's performance [7]. They applied study on all firms of food sector listed on Karachi stock exchange. The paper covered a period of five years from 2007-2011. The capital structure variables were three variables, long term debts to total assets (LTDTA), Total debt to Equity (TDE), and Short-term debts to Total assets (STDTA). and they measured firm performance by Return on Assets (ROA) and Assets Turnover Ratio (ATO), they found that long term debts has a positive and significant impact on firm performance, while, short term debts has negative significant impact of on firm performance.

Mumtaz study seeks to investigate the relationship between capital structure and firm performance in the context of large private companies in Pakistan [8]. To measure capital structure they used Debt to Equity ratio (DR), while ratios such as, Return on Asset (ROA), Earning per Share (EPS), Return on equity (ROE), Operating profit Margin, Price to Earnings Ratio are used to measure firm performance. Moreover, the relationship between capital structure of a firm and market value of the firm is significant and negative.

Le and Phung study investigates the impact of capital structure on firm performance in all firms listed in Vietnamese Stock Exchange during the period from 2007 to 2011 [9]. They used return on assets (ROA), return on equity (ROE), and Tobin Q to measure firm performance, while to measure capital structure they used short-term debt, long term-debt, and total debt ratios. They found that capital structure has a significant negative impact on firm performance.

Salteh paper explores the impact of capital structure on firm performance in Iranian corporations listed as a vehicles and parts manufacturing economic sector in Tehran Stock Exchange (TSE) [10]. To measure firm performance they used five variables including, Return on Assets (ROA), Return on Equity (ROE), Tobin's Q, Earning per Share (EPS), and equity market value to equity book value (MB/VR). While they measure capital structure by, Long-Term Debt, Short-Term Debt and Total Debt to Total Assets, and Total Debt to Total Equity. The findings referred to a positive and significant relation between capital structure and ROE, MB/VR, and Tobin's Q, while, showed a negative relation with ROA, and EPS.

Ahmad study discussed the influence of capital structure on firm performance of Malaysian firms listed as consumers and industrials sectors in Malaysian equity market from 2005 to 2010, to measure firm performance they use return on equity (ROE) and return on asset (ROA), and to measure capital structure they use long-term debt (LTD), short-term debt (STD), and total debt (TD). The study results that each of debt level has significant negative relationship with ROE, while ROA has significant positive relationship only with STD and TD [11].

Iorpev and kwanum study investigates the relationship between capital structure and firm performance of manufacturing companies listed on the Nigerian Stock Exchange [12]. They covered a period of five (5) years from 2005-2009. The study used multiple regression analysis to examine firm performance indicators such as Profit Margin (PM) and Return on Asset (ROA), while, the capital structure variables were, Long term debts to Total assets (LTDTA), Short-term debts to Total assets (STDTA), and Total debt to Equity (TDE). They found that STDTA and LTDTA have insignificant negative relationship with ROA and PM; while TDE has positive relationship with ROA and negative relationship with PM. STDTA is significantly related with ROA while LTDTA is significantly related with PM. The study concludes that capital structure is not a main determinant of firm performance.

Onaolapo and Kajola study investigates the influence of capital structure on financial firm performance, applied on non-financial firms listed in Nigerian Stock Exchange according the period from 2001 to 2007 [13]. To examine capital structure they used Debt Ratio (DR), while used Return on Assets (ROA), and Return on Equity (ROE) to examine firm performance. They found that capital structure has a significantly negative impact on financial firm performance.

Comments of literature review: Since Modigliani and Miller's theory has been published many of the researchers are still studying the relationship between capital structure and firm performance [1], some of them have been found a negative relation between capital structure and firm performance such as Mumtaz, Le, Phung, Salteh, Ahmadand

Onaolapo, Kajola [8-11,13] while; Badar and Saeed found a significant positive relation between capital structure and firm performance [7], As well as Iorpev and kwanum found that capital structure and firm performance have insignificant negative relation [12].

Research Methodology, Hypothesis, Data and Variables

Conceptual framework

This paper aims to find if there is an Impact of Capital structure on Performance evidence from all industrial firms listed in Amman stock exchange.

Variables measurement and empirical model

Variables of the study illustrated in the following Figure 1, which was designed by the researcher.

Capital structure (independent variable): Capital structure of a firm is measured by different accounting based methods like short term liability to total assets, long term liability to total assets and total debt to total assets [7,9-12]. This study takes total debt to total assets as a proxy for capital structure of a firm based on Onaolapo, Kajola and Mumtaz [8,13].

$$\text{Debt Ratio}(\text{DR}) = \frac{\text{Total Debt}}{\text{Total Assets}}$$

Firm performance (dependent variables): A number of variables measuring firm performance are commonly accounting based measures of performance calculated from financial statements as ROE, ROA, EPS and Net Profit Margin [3], while stock market return and volatility in returns are also used as performance measures of firms. Tobin's Q measurement of performance is also used by some studies which are a mix of market performance and accounting measurement. This study adopts the three accounting based measure of performance including earning per share (EPS), return on equity (ROE), and return on assets (ROA) computed as follow:

$$\text{Earning per Share}(\text{EPS}) = \frac{(\text{Net income - Dividends on preffered stock})}{\text{Average outstanding share}}$$

$$\text{Return on Equity (ROE)} = \frac{\text{Net Income}}{\text{Equity}}$$

$$\text{Return on Assets (ROA)} = \frac{\text{Net Income}}{\text{Total Assets}}$$

Hypotheses

The following hypothesis is formulated for the study:

H_1: There is a negative relationship between capital structure (DR) and financial performance (ROE).

H_2: There is a negative relationship between capital structure (DR) and financial performance (ROA).

H_3: There is a negative relationship between capital structure (DR) and financial performance (EPS).

Data collection

Data for this study is taken from annual financial statements of firms. Ratios of firms are collected from annual firm analysis reports which available on Fin net program, and stockeys website. This study is conducted on firms listed as industrial companies under (UXSIN) index on Istanbul Stock Exchange (ISE), 136 firms are taken from 290 firms form the period of 2005-2012.

Criteria for selected the sample: The sample of firms is selected on the basis of following criteria.

- Firms with missing data for any factor in the model during study period are dropped.
- Firms having extremist values for any of capital structure are also dropped.
- Firms having extremist values for any of performance variables are also dropped.

Results and Discussions

Descriptive statistics

Table 1 gives the detail of descriptive statistics of the variables used in this paper. First row of the table shows the mean of the variables including debt Ratio (DR), earnings per share (EPS), return on assets (ROA), and return on equity (ROE). The respective mean values are 46.528, 0.619, 4.455, and 7.881 (Table 1).

Correlation analysis

Correlation is concern describing the strength of relationship between two variables. In this study the correlation co-efficient analysis is under taken to find out the relationship between capital structure and financial firm performance. It shows the degree of relationship exist between capital structure and financial performance.

Capital structure correlated with Performance variables: The Table 2 above shows the relationship between Performance variables (EPS, ROE, and ROA) and capital structure variable (DR). There are a weak negative relationship between independent variable (capital structure DR) and all dependent variables (performance variables).

The correlation between DR and EPS is -0.088. Significant level is 0.01. The co-efficient of determination is 0.0077. That is 0.7% of variance in the capital structure is accounted by the EPS.

The correlation between DR and ROE is -0.287. Significant level is 0.01. The co-efficient of determination is 0.015. That is 1.5% of variance in the capital structure is accounted by the ROE.

The correlation between DR and ROA is -0.124. Significant level is

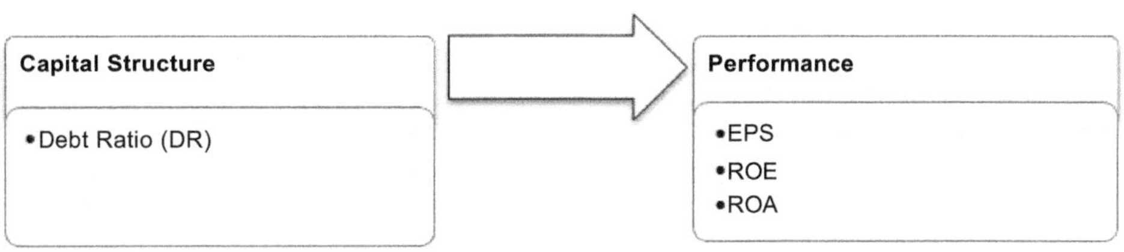

Figure 1: Variables of the study.

	DR	EPS	ROA	ROE
Mean	46.528	0.619	4.455	7.881
Median	44.645	0.263	4.441	8.593
Maximum	87.878	27.898	38.040	54.123
Minimum	15.073	-12.180	-32.760	-61.843
Std. Dev.	16.433	1.716	7.438	15.501
Jarque-Bera	50.991	389892.004	323.448	397.221
Probability	8.5E-12	0	0	0

Table 1: Descriptive statistics.

Variables	Performance variables		
	EPS	ROE	ROA
Capital structure variable (DR)	-0.088	-0.287	-0.124
R^2	0.0077	0.0153	0.0824

Table 2: Correlation result between capital structure variable (DR) and performance variables (EPS, ROE, ROA).

Variables	Financial Performance					
	EPS		ROE		ROA	
Constant	1.046	0.000	13.31	0.00	10.502	0.00
DR	-0.009	0.003	-0.12	0.00	-0.129	0.00
R2	0.007		0.015		0.082	
F value	8.488		16.893		97.61	
Sig	0.003		0.000		0.000	

Table 3: Regression result between capital structure variable (DR) and Performance variables (EPS, ROE, ROA).

0.01. The co-efficient of determination is 0.082. That is 8.2% of variance in the capital structure is accounted by the ROA.

Regression analysis

Regression analysis is used to examine the impact of capital structure on financial performance of the listed companies traded in Istanbul stock exchange (Table 3).

The table above shows the regression result used to verify the association between independent variable (DR) and dependent variables (EPS, ROE, and ROA). The result indicates a negative significant relation between DR and all financial performance variables (EPS, ROE, and ROA). This means an increase in DR by one dollar will increase EPS, ROE, and ROA by 0.009, 0.12, 0.12 dollar respectively. R^2 in average is 3.4%; means only 3.4% of variance of performance variables is accurate by these factors. But, remaining 86.60% of variance with performance variables is attributed to other factors.

Findings

Based on the empirical results of this study, we accept all of three hypotheses (H1, H2, and H3) which referred to a negative relationship between capital structure and financial firm performance (EPS, ROE, ROA). These results are consistent with Mumtaz, Le and Phung, Salteh, Ahmad and Onaolapo, Kajola [8-11,13], who pointed to the negative relationship between capital structure and financial firm performance, While inconsistent with Badar and Saeed who found a significant positive relation between capital structure and firm performance [7], As well as Iorpev and kwanum, who found that capital structure and firm performance have insignificant negative relation [12].

Conclusion

This study investigates the impact of capital structure on firm performance in Istanbul's stock market, particularly on industrial sector companies listed under XUSIN index. Our results suggest that firm's capital structure is negatively and significantly associated with financial firm performance which defined by (EPS, ROE, and ROA variables). That mean using a high level of debt negatively affects a firm's return on assets, earnings per share, and return on equity.

There are three main limitations of this study; it studies the data of only one market of developing economy so it cannot represent all the markets of transition economies. Secondly this study includes only 8 years data. To explore consistent results long time series of data could be required. Thirdly we can find the impact of capital structure on firm's performance by sector and then compare the results to know the real picture of the relationship.

Capital structure is a puzzling concept especially so in emerging markets like Turkey. Further study can be conducted by adding sales growth and business risk as independent variables. To clarify the results of our study more variables for performance measurement may be useful. Data of long time series could also be used for credibility of results. Future research can be can be processed by comparing the capital structure and firm performance of small and large firms.

References

1. Modigliani F, Miller MH (1958) The cost of capital, corporation finance and the theory of investment. The American Economic Review 48: 261-297.
2. Pandey IM (1999) Financial Management. (7th ed), Vikas Publishing House Pvt Ltd, New Delhi, India.
3. Abor J (2005) The effect of capital structure on profitability: an empirical analysis of listed firms in Ghana. Journal of Risk Finance 6: 438-445.
4. Ahmadinia H, Javad A, Elham H (2012) A Comprehensive Review on Capital Structure Theories. The Romanian Economic Journal 15: 3.
5. Abosede (2012) Pecking Order Theory of Capital Structure: Another Way to Look At It. Journal of Business Management and Applied Economics.
6. Roshan B (2009) Capital Structure and Ownership Structure: A Review of Literature. The Journal of Online Education, New York, India.
7. Badar R, Saeed A (2013) Impact of Capital Structure on Performance Empirical Evidence from Sugar Sector of Pakistan. European Journal of Business and Management 5: 78-86.
8. Mumtaz R, Rauf SA, Ahmed B, Noreen U (2013) Capital Structure and Financial Performance: Evidence from Pakistan (Kse 100 Index). Journal of Basic and Applied Scientific Research 3: 113-119.
9. Le TPV, Phung DN (2013) Capital Structure and Firm performance: Empirical evidence from Vietnamese listed firms.
10. Mohammadzadeh SH, Elham G, Taghizadeh KV, Akbari KM (2012) Capital Structure and Firm Performance: Evidence from Tehran Stock Exchange. International Proceedings of Economics Development & Research 43: 225.
11. Ahmad Z, Abdullah NMH, Roslan S (2012) Capital Structure Effect on Firms Performance: Focusing on Consumers and Industrials Sectors on Malaysian Firms. International Review of Business Research Papers 8: 137-155.
12. Iorpev, Kwanum, (2012) Capital Structure and Firm Performance: Evidence from Manufacturing Companies in Nigeria. International Journal of Business and Management Tomorrow.
13. Onaolapo AA, Kajola SO (2010) Capital structure and firm performance: evidence from Nigeria. European Journal of Economics, Finance and Administrative Sciences p: 70.

Personality Traits of Micro Enterprises Runs by Women Self Help Groups in Madurai, Ramnad and Dindigul Districts of Tamil Nadu

Selvaraj N*

Saraswathi Narayanan College

Abstract

Micro enterprises make an important contribution to economic output and employment in Micro enterprise faces many problems in raising finance, as the provider of finance may not find the return on investment interesting as compared to large enterprise, and also investor is more skeptical about repayment. Entrepreneurship gives women the chance to own property and help commodity production in the state, which in turn would help sustain the social sector. Unlike in a paid job scenario, women can have personal freedom and decision-making authority. This will help them get empowered and create a better image and place for women in the society, an attempt has been made in the personality traits of women entrepreneurs in order to identify whether they have the requisite personality dispositions to undertake activities which are independent and self-sustaining, there by contributing to entrepreneurship.

Keywords: Personality traits; Micro-enterprise; Constraints; Women Entrepreneurs.

Introduction

Micro enterprises make an important contribution to economic output and employment in developing economies. While estimates vary greatly depending on definitions, recent work by the World Bank suggests that almost 30% of employment in low-income countries is generated by the informal economy, while an additional 18% is provided by (formal) small and medium enterprises [1]. Together these two groups contribute 63% of the GDP. Finance is the lifeblood of any enterprise irrespective of its size. Micro enterprise faces many problems in raising finance, as the provider of finance may not find the return on investment interesting as compared to large enterprise, and also investor is more skeptical about repayment.

In India, 41% of the rural population lives below poverty line [2]. Most of them are agricultural labourers who get employment during agricultural season; more than 80% of the women work in agriculture. Agriculture is not able to provide employment for all these people throughout the year. Women and children suffer from penury as men migrate from rural to urban areas in search of jobs.

In recent years, women have come to the forefront in different walks of life and are competing successfully with men despite social, psychological and economic barriers. This has been possible because of education, political awakening, legal safeguards, urbanization and social reforms. Today in India, some of the women have distinguished themselves in many unconventional fields. They are leading consultants, eminent scientists and mathematicians distinguished doctors, interior decorators, artists, educationists, managers, administrators and business entrepreneurs [3].

Entrepreneurship gives women the chance to own property and help commodity production in the state, which in turn would help sustain the social sector. Unlike in a paid job scenario, women can have personal freedom and decision-making authority. This will help them get empowered and create a better image and place for women in the society. The status of women can be improved in the form of higher savings, enhanced buying power capacity and increased social status by helping them to become economically independent.

Personality traits

Some psychologists, such as Albert Ellis, suggest that it is important to understand the way of a person views or thinks about life. Others, like B.F.Skinner and William Glomi, take the position that the most appropriate means of understanding a person is to observe that person's behaviour and actions. Rogan suggests the need to be aware of emotions or feeling of a person [4-6].

An attempt has been made in the this paper to assess the personality traits of women entrepreneurs in order to identify whether they have the requisite personality dispositions to undertake activities which are independent and self-sustaining, there by contributing to entrepreneurship. Even though the personality factors are too many, the present study is confined to only 14 personality factors, namely, information seeking, mass media exposure, social participation, cosmopolitanism, level of aspirations, attitude towards self-employment, scientific orientation, decision making ability, economic motivation, managerial ability, problem recognition, risk orientation, urban pull and extension contact.

Statement of the problem

A self-help group (SHG) is a voluntary association of people with common goal. The concept of 'Self Help Group' appears to be a good alternative strategy to involve people in the development process. In these circumstances it is felt important and necessary to study personality traits of empowerment acquired by women [4].

Hence, the present study is undertaken to analyse the entrepreneurship

***Corresponding author:** Selvaraj N, Assistant Professor of Commerce, Saraswathi Narayanan College, Madurai, Tamilnadu, India
E-mail: selvaraj_narayanan@yahoo.com

of women for Madurai, Ramnad and Dindigul districts of Tamil Nadu.

Period of study

The field survey was conducted from September 2014 to March 2015 for the collection of primary data. The reference period of the survey was 2014-2015.

Objectives of the Study

The basic objectives of the study are to learn about the personality traits of the micro entrepreneurs (Women).

Sampling design

For the purpose of primary data collection, three districts namely Madurai, Ramnad and Dindigul have been selected the main reason for selecting these districts is that the former are a developed district, the middle is backward one and the last is developing district [6,7]. Keeping in view of the objectives of the study, the research has identified with the help of the concerned persons (officers and leaders of SHGs) women those who are engaged in running Micro enterprises for selecting the sample. Out of the total of 450 sample women Micro entrepreneurs each 150 from the districts were randomly selected from SHGs functioning under NGOs and Mahilar Thittam Schemes in each block of three districts by using proportionate sample method.

Tools for analysis

For analysis the data collected during the investigation the following statistical tools were used based on the nature of data and relevance of information required.

Percentage analysis

The conventional percentage analysis has been carried out to fulfill the objectives of the study.

T-test

In order to discuss the objective T-test has been used.

The analytical framework

The fourteen personality factors mentioned above are assessed on a four – point scale, which are assigned 4, 3, 2 and 1 score according to the order of personality traits. The following formula is used to measure the personality index of women entrepreneurs.

$$PI = \frac{\sum_{i=1}^{n} Psi}{\sum_{i=1}^{n} MsPi} \times 100 \qquad (1)$$

Where,

P1 = Personality index

Ps = Personality factor score

Msp = Maximum score of the personality factor

i = 1 --- n = number of personality factors

Average score of personality factors: The average scores of the different personality factors calculated for the entrepreneurs in the study area are presented in Table 1.

From the Table 1 it has been observed that in the case of women entrepreneurs in Madurai, the entrepreneurs are very good in information seeking, decision making ability, social participation and managerial ability since the mean values of these personality factors are as high at 4.42, 4.30, 4.02 and 3.94 respectively. In total, the average score of the personality traits among the women entrepreneurs in Madurai District is 3.46. Whereas, in the case of women entrepreneurs in Ramnad, the entrepreneurs are very good decision making ability, problem recognition and social participation since the mean values of these personality factors are as high at 4.21, 3.96, and 3.87 respectively [8]. In total, the average score of the personality traits among the women entrepreneurs in Ramnad is 3.30. In the case of Dindigul district, decision making ability (4.26) information seeking (4.40) managerial ability (3.91) and problem recognition (3.91) are good. In total, the average score is 3.39. Thus it may be inferred from the analysis that decision making ability was found high among women entrepreneurs in all three districts.

Personality index: The personality index of women entrepreneurs is calculated by the formula (1). The personality index in the present study is classified as less than 20, 20-40, 40-60, 60-80 and above. The distribution of entrepreneurs according to the personality index is presented in Table 2 and Figure 1.

It has been inferred from the Table 2 that in the case of Women entrepreneurs in Madurai district, maximum of 50 (33.33%) of the entrepreneurs have personality index of above 20-40 followed by 52 (34.67%) and 52 (35.33%) in Dindigul and Ramnad district. Whereas in the case of women entrepreneurs in Ramnad, maximum of 47 (31.33%) of them have personality index of 40 to 60 followed by 46 (30.67%) and 45 (30%) in Dindigul and Madurai district. The maximum of 53 (35.33%) have personality index of 20 to 40 in Ramnad. It is followed by Dindigul (34.67%) and Madurai (33.33%).

Personality Traits	Name of the District / Average score			Total
	Madurai	Ramnad	Dindigul	
Information seeking	4.42	3.81	4.40	4.21
Mass media exposure	3.65	3.16	3.63	3.48
Cosmopolitanism	3.28	3.16	3.16	3.20
Level of aspiration	2.70	2.63	2.68	2.67
Attitude to self-employment	2.38	2.27	2.39	2.35
Scientific orientation	3.81	3.78	3.71	3.77
Decision making ability	4.30	4.21	4.26	4.26
Economic motivation	2.86	2.27	2.73	2.62
Managerial ability	3.94	3.92	3.91	3.92
Problem recognition	3.72	3.96	3.91	3.92
Willingness to take risk	3.35	3.34	3.18	3.29
Urban pull	2.87	2.91	2.67	2.82
Social participation	4.02	3.87	3.91	3.93
Extension contact	3.18	2.92	3.12	3.07
Overall	3.46	3.30	3.39	3.38

Table 1: Personality traits of women entrepreneurs in Madurai, Ramnad and Dindigul districts.

Personality Traits Index	Number of Respondents / Name of the District			Total
	Madurai	Ramnad	Dindigul	
Less than 20	17 (11.33)	20 (13.33)	18 (12.00)	55 (12.22)
20 – 40	50 (33.33)	53 (35.33)	52 (34.67)	155 (34.44)
40 – 60	45 (30.00)	47 (31.33)	46 (30.67)	138 (30.67)
60 – 80	18 (12.00)	20 (13.33)	21 (14.00)	59 (13.11)
Above 80	20 (13.33)	10 (6.67)	13 (8.67)	43 (9.56)
Total	150 (100.00)	150 (100.00)	150 (100.00)	450 (100.00)

Source: Primary data.
Note: Figures in brackets are percentage to total

Table 2: Personality traits index of women entrepreneurs in Madurai, Ramnad and Dindigul Districts.

Organisation profile among the respondents

Organization represents the units run by the respondents in the present study. The profile of the organization may show its own impact on the performance of the organization. Even though, the profiles of the organization are too many, the present study confines these variables into nature of enterprises, years of experience, monthly turnover, monthly profit and number of employees engaged in work.

Nature of business: The women entrepreneurs may run the enterprises according to their capability relating to finance, management, marketing and risk taking ability. The nature of enterprise selected by them is influenced by the scope of business, profitability and other aspects. The nature of enterprise may be related to milch animals [9].

The details of activities undertaken by the selected women entrepreneurs are given in Table 3.

The Table 3 shows that manufacturing of food products accounts for Madurai and Dindigul district for 24.00% and 24.67% of the total respondents respectively. Among the respondents in Ramnad maximum of 22.67% and engaged in Mini dairy. Among the respondents in Madurai district, tailoring, mini dairy constitute 18.67% and 18.00% total. In Ramnad district, manufacturing of food products, vermi compost and seashell ornaments constitute 14.67%, 12% and 12%. Mini-dairy and tailoring constitute 21.33% and 17.33% respectively in Dindigul district.

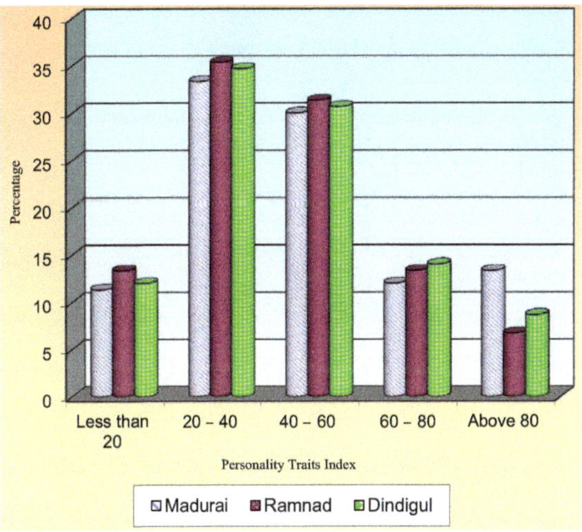

Figure 1: Personality traits index of women entrepreneurs in Madurai, Ramnad and Dindigul districts.

Years of experience: Years of experience represents the number of years the respondents have gathered through enterprising. Since the experience of the respondents may have its impact on enterprising, it is included in the present study. The more experience a person has, the more will be his knowledge in his trade and he will manage the business well. Consequently, his performance in the respective business will be enriched. In the present study, the years of experience among the respondents are confined to 'upto 3 years', '4 to 6 years', '7 to 10 years', '11 to 14 years' and above 14 years. The distribution of respondents on the basis of their experience is presented below in Table 4.

It is inferred from the Table 4 that 26.44% of the respondents have 7 to 10 years of experience in their own business followed by 23.78% with an experience of 11 to 14 years. The number of respondents with an experience of less than 6 years constitutes 34.00% of the total. Among the respondents, 11 to 14 years and above 14 years rank first and second in Madurai and Dindigul districts, whereas among the respondents in Ramnad, 7 to 10 years and 4 to 6 years occupy the first two places. The analysis reveals that experience in business among the respondents in Madurai and Dindigul districts is less than that among the respondents in Ramnad (Figure 2).

Monthly turnover: 'Turnover' in the present study represents the sales turnover achieved by the respondents per month during the study period. The sales turnover is one of the important factors which determine the ability of the enterprise regarding its performance. It also shows the marketability of the unit. In the present study, the monthly turnover is classified into 'less than Rs.15,000', Rs.15001 to 30,000, Rs.30001 to 45,000, Rs.45001 to 60000, and above Rs.60000. The distribution of the respondents according to their monthly turnover achieved in their business is illustrated in Table 5.

The first two important ranges of monthly turnover among the respondents are Rs.15001 to Rs.30,000, Rs.30001 to 45000 which constitute 28.44 and 25.77% to the respective totals. The number of respondents whose turnover is above Rs.60000 constitutes 15.34% to the total whereas the respondents with a monthly turnover of less than Rs.15,000 constitute 13.33%. The most important monthly turnover category among the respondents in Madurai and Dindigul are Rs.30001 to 45000 and Rs.15001 to 30000 respectively whereas in Ramnad, it is Rs.15001 to 30000 and 30001 to 45000.

Sl. No.	Nature of Enterprise	Madurai		Ramnad		Dindigul	
		No. of Respondents	%	No. of Respondents	%	No. of Respondents	%
1.	Readymade Garments	12	8.00	3	2.00	8	5.33
2.	Mini dairy	27	18.00	34	22.67	32	21.33
3.	Tailoring	28	18.67	12	8.00	26	17.33
4.	Manufacturing of food products	36	24.00	22	14.67	37	24.67
5.	Pickles making	14	9.33	11	7.33	12	8.0
6.	Vermi compost	15	10.0	18	12.0	10	6.67
7.	Bamboo baskets	2	1.33	12	8.00	18	12.0
8.	Candle and Sampirani manufacturing	16	10.67	4	2.67	7	4.67
9.	Dry Fish	--	--	16	10.67	--	--
10.	Seashell ornaments	--	--	18	12.00	--	--
	Total	150	100.00	150	100.00	150	100.00

Source: Primary data.

Table 3: Nature of business among the respondents.

Years of Experience	Number of Respondents /Name of the District			Total
	Madurai	Ramnad	Dindigul	
Upto 3 years	18 (22.00)	28 (18.67)	21 (14.00)	67 (14.89)
4 – 6	21 (14.00)	39 (26.00)	26 (17.33)	86 (19.11)
7 – 10	31 (20.67)	61 (34.00)	37 (24.67)	119 (26.44)
11 – 14	45 (40.00)	23 (15.33)	39 (26.00)	107 (23.78)
14 and above	35 (23.33)	9 (6.00)	27 (18.00)	71 (15.78)
Total	150 (100.00)	150 (100.00)	150 (100.00)	450 (100.00)

Table 4: Years of experience in business.

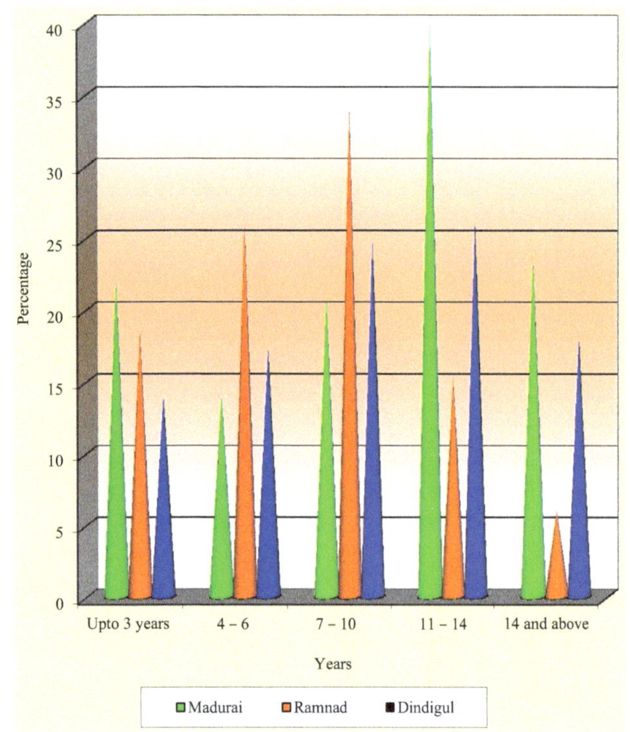

Figure 2: Years of experience in business.

Monthly Turnover (in Rs.)	Number of Respondents / Name of the District			Total
	Madurai	Ramnad	Dindigul	
Less than 15000	18 (12.00)	20 (13.33)	22 (14.67)	60 (13.33)
15001- 30000	33 (22.00)	56 (37.33)	39 (26.00)	128 (28.44)
30001- 45000	36 (24.00)	46 (30.67)	34 (22.66)	116 (25.77)
45001 – 60000	31 (20.67)	18 (12.00)	28 (18.67)	77 (17.11)
Above 60000	32 (21.33)	10 (6.67)	27 (18.00)	69 (15.34)
Total	150 (100.00)	150 (100.00)	150 (100.00)	450 (100.00)

Table 5: Monthly turnover among the respondents.

Monthly Profit: 'Profit' is the difference between the total revenue realized in business and the expenses incurred in business [10]. All entrepreneurs aim at maximum profit. They want to increase their profit consistently. Since profit is one of the important measuring yards of the performance of the unit, it is included in the present study. The monthly profits are classified into 'less than Rs.1000', 'Rs.1000 to 2000', 'Rs.2001 to 3000', 'Rs.3001 to 4000' and 'above Rs.4000' (Table 6).

Table 6 exhibits the distribution of respondents according to the profit achieved by them in business. A maximum of 30.89% of the respondents have earned a profit Rs.2001 to 3000 followed by 28.00% showing the profit performance of Rs.3001 to 4000. The numbers of respondents who earn a monthly profit of above Rs.4000 per month constitute 16.44%. The important profit range among the respondents is Rs.2001 - 3000 in all the three districts (Figure 3).

Extent of employment provided: The purpose of entrepreneurship is to promote self-employment and to create employment opportunities. Even in the case of micro enterprises, employment opportunities are visible. In order to analyze this aspect, the number of employees engaged in business units have been taken into account and classified into nil, one, two, three and above three. The 'nil' category represents self-employment in the business (Table 7 and Figure 4).

Table 7 explains the number of employment opportunities provided by the respondents through their business units. 27.11% of the respondents are self-employed. It is followed by 26.44% of the respondents providing employment for one person. The number of respondents engaging more than three employees in their business units constitutes 11.34% to the total. Majority of the respondents are

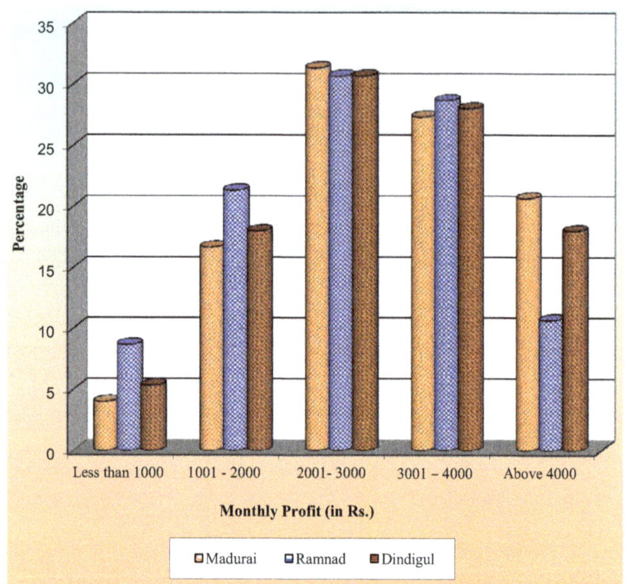

Figure 3: Monthly profit achieved among the respondents.

Monthly Profit (in Rs.)	Number of Respondents / Name of the District			Total
	Madurai	Ramnad	Dindigul	
Less than 1000	6 (4.00)	13 (8.67)	8 (5.33)	27 (6.00)
1001 - 2000	25 (16.67)	32 (21.33)	27 (18.00)	84 (18.67)
2001- 3000	47 (31.33)	46 (30.67)	46 (30.67)	139 (30.89)
3001 – 4000	41 (27.33)	43 (28.66)	42 (28.00)	126 (28.00)
Above 4000	31 (20.67)	16 (10.67)	27 (18.00)	74 (16.44)
Total	150 (100.00)	150 (100.00)	150 (100.00)	450 (100.00)

Table 6: Monthly profit achieved among the respondents.

Number of Employees	Number of Respondents /Name of the District			Total
	Madurai	Ramnad	Dindigul	
Nil	35 (23.33)	48 (32.00)	39 (26.00)	122 (27.11)
One	41 (27.33)	38 (25.33)	40 (26.67)	119 (26.44)
Two	24 (16.00)	29 (19.33)	25 (16.67)	78 (17.33)
Three	28 (18.67)	24 (16.00)	28 (18.66)	80 (17.78)
Above Three	22 (14.67)	11 (7.34)	18 (12.00)	51 (11.34)
Total	150 (100.00)	150 (100.00)	150 (100.00)	450 (100.00)

Table 7: Number of employees engaged in business.

self-employed in their enterprises at Ramnad. Other two districts namely Madurai and Dindigul provide employment to one person. Relatively, the rate of employment provided by the respondents in Madurai district is higher than the employment provided by the respondents in Ramnad and Dindigul.

Source of inspiration to start enterprise

Competitiveness always brings the best out of people. The incidence of increasing competition in the present global scenario has forced many people to find out ways and means to innovate. The entrepreneurship is generally understood as a pursuit of opportunity without limiting oneself to the accepted existing norms and confines to an organization. The sources of inspiration to start the enterprise were developed by Gasse and Robinson [5]. Based on the reviews, eighteen variables are created with respect to sources of inspiration. The respondents were asked to rate all these 18 variables at five points scale namely 'highly important', 'important', 'moderate', 'not important' and 'not at all important'. The scores assigned on these ratings are 5, 4, 3, 2 and 1 respectively.

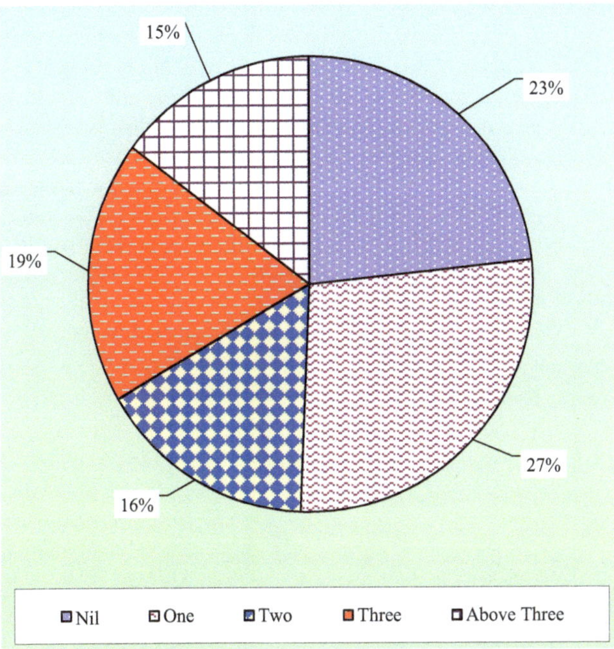

Figure 4: Number of employees engaged in business.

S. No	Psychological Constraints	Good Performers	Poor Performers	T-statistics
1.	Lack of resource sharing ability	2.6017	3.9201	-3.0742*
2.	Lack of communication skills	3.0366	3.8267	-2.6471*
3.	Lack of net works	2.5171	2.8711	-0.7141
4.	Fear on future	2.4034	3.5411	-3.0471*
5.	Lack of self motivation	2.5712	3.6121	-2.7948*
6.	Unbelievable attitude towards others	2.8342	2.6712	0.7121
7.	Lack of faith on personal skills	2.9691	2.0121	3.1471*

*Significant at 5% level.

Table 8: Psychological constraints among the respondents in Madurai district.

S. No	Psychological Constraints	Good Performers	Poor Performers	T-statistics
1.	Lack of resource sharing ability	2.5178	2.4711	0.1472
2.	Lack of communication skills	2.6711	3.8471	2.7241*
3.	Lack of net works	2.4678	2.7421	-0.8421
4.	Fear on future	2.3041	2.4712	-0.7412
5.	Lack of self motivation	3.6121	3.7069	-1.0127
6.	Unbelievable attitude towards others	2.8134	2.4371	0.5871
7.	Lack of faith on personal skills	3.0412	2.0714	3.1741*

*Significant at 5% level.

Table 9: Psychological constraints among the respondents in Ramnad district.

Table 7 exhibits the mean score of all eighteen sources of inspiration to start the enterprises. The important sources of inspiration among the respondents in Madurai district are self-employment, leading an independent life and financial crisis and their respective mean scores are 3.9491, 3.8511 and 3.7432. Among the respondents in Ramnad, the important sources of inspiration are family upliftment, family problem and supporting the spouse and the respective mean scores are 3.7211 and 3.3841. The sources of inspiration which have the highest score among the respondents in Dindigul, family upliftment and financial crisis. Thus the analysis reveals that the family upliftment and financial crisis are the prime factors to induce the respondents to start the enterprise in all the three districts. In order to analyze the important source of inspiration to start enterprise, the mean score on each variable is measured (Table 8).

Psychological constraints

Psychological constraints indicate lack of faith and confidence among the respondents. These types of constraints are purely personal and also psychological. A strong mind is highly needed for the entrepreneurs to face the risk and uncertainty involved in business. It is also required for the purpose of the innovativeness and scientific orientation among the respondents. In the present study, the psychological constraints among the respondents are confined to lack of resource sharing ability, lack of communication skills, lack of networks, fear about future, lack of self-motivation, unbelievable attitude towards others and lack of faith on personal skills. The respondents are asked to rate the above said seven constraints at five point scale namely agree, moderately agree, not agree and not at all agree. The assigned marks are 5, 4, 3, 2 and 1 respectively. In order to exhibit the importance of social constraints among the respondents, the mean score on the psychological constraints has been computed. The 'T' test has been administered to find out the significant difference among good and poor performers respondents regarding the perception on these psychological constraints. The resultant mean scores of the psychological constraints and for Madurai district the respective't' statistics are shown in Table 8.

Table 8 shows that the highly perceived psychological constraints among the good performers are lack of communication skills and lack of faith on personal skills since the respective mean scores are 3.0366 and 2.9691. Among the poor performers, the high scoring two constraints are lack of resource sharing ability and lack of communication skills since the respective mean scores are 3.9201 and 3.8267. The significant difference among good and poor performers regarding the perception on psychological constraints are found in lack of resource sharing ability, lack of communications skills, fear on future, lack of self-motivation and lack of faith on personal skills since the respective 'T' statistics are significant at five percent level.

The mean scores of the psychological constraints and the respective't' statistics for Ramnad district are shown in Table 9.

The highly perceived psychological constraints among the good performers are lack of self-motivation and lack of faith on personal

S. No	Psychological Constraints	Good Performers	Poor Performers	T-statistics
1.	Lack of resource sharing ability	2.5272	3.7678	3.7814*
2.	Lack of communication skills	3.0471	3.6927	-2.7211*
3.	Lack of net works	2.4121	2.5611	0.6911
4.	Fear on future	2.2216	2.2618	0.6972
5.	Lack of self motivation	3.8147	3.7421	0.7841
6.	Unbelievable attitude towards others	3.6712	2.3742	3.7214*
7.	Lack of faith on personal skills	2.7611	2.6811	0.7818

*Significant at 5% level.

Table 10: Psychological constraints among the respondents in Dindigul district.

skills since the respective mean scores are 3.0266 and 3.0472. Among the poor performers, the high scoring two constraints are lack of communication skills and lack of self-motivation since the respective mean scores are 3.8471 and 3.7069. The significant difference among good and poor performers regarding the perception on psychological constraints are found in lack of communications skills, and lack of faith on personal skills since the respective 'T' statistics are significant at five percent level.

The mean scores of the psychological constraints for Dindigul district and the respective't' statistics are shown in Table 10.

Table 10 reveals that the highly perceived psychological constraints among the good performers are lack of self-motivation and unbelievable attitude towards others since the respective mean scores are 3.8147 and 3.6712. Among the poor performers, the high scoring two constraints are lack of resource sharing ability and lack of communication skills since the respective mean scores are 3.7678 and 3.6927. The significant difference among good and poor performers regarding the perception on psychological constraints are found in lack of resource sharing ability, lack of communications skills and unbelievable attitude towards others since the respective 'T' statistics are significant at five percent level.

Summary of Findings

The present research was carried out with objectives of studying the personality traits among women members to start enterprises as good and poor performers encountered by women and offering suggestions for promoting women entrepreneurship.

The important sources of inspiration to start the enterprises among the male respondents are self-employment, leading an independent self-employment, leading an independent life and financial crisis whereas among the female respondents, these are family upliftment, family problem and supporting the spouse. The significant differences among the male and female respondents are identified regarding the perception on the sources of inspiration namely unemployment, financial crisis, previous experience, self-help groups, family problem and social recognition.

The sources of inspiration to start an enterprise are categorized into three factors namely personal, family and environmental factors. The most important factor of inspiration is the personal factor which consists of seven sources of inspiration. It is followed by the family factor which consists of six sources and the environment factor which consists of five sources of inspiration.

The important psychological constraints among the good performers are lack of communication skills, lack of self-motivation for Madurai, Ramnad and Dindigul districts. There is lack of resource sharing ability in Madurai district, lack of communication skills in Ramnad and lack of resource sharing ability in Dindigul district. Regarding the perception on psychological constraints, the significant difference among the good and poor performers is noticed in the perception on lack of resource sharing ability and lack of communication skills.

Suggestions

As observation from the analysis majority of the women entrepreneurs did not like to move out from their native places and wished to develop themselves within the areas of their business location. It is suggested that in Madurai, Ramnad and Dindigul districts women should be motivated to be ready to include themselves in the self-help groups' federations and willing to step on to virgin territories for reaping the benefits of rewarding business opportunities. This could be achieved only by enlightening them on business avenues. The seminars, audio-visual aids, tours, booklets, etc., could help in this respect.

References

1. Das A (1998) Women in Business.
2. Bales R (1965) The Equilibrium Problem in Small Group. In: Hare A, Boregotta E, Bales R (eds.) Small Groups: Studies In Social Interaction, Knoff, N.Y.
3. Singh K, Gain R (2002) Management of Micro-enterprises for Rural Women. National Institute of Rural Development, Rajendra Nagar, Hyderabad, India.
4. Ambigadevi DP (2003) Share of Women in total family Income: A two Group Discriminate Analysis. Asian Economic Review 45: 373-378.
5. Das K (2008) Micro Small and medium Enterprises in India: Unfair Fare. Gujarati Institute of Development Report Working Paper Series.
6. Purushotham P (2003) Micro Enterprise Opportunities in Food Industry. SEDME.
7. Rjajustus E, Mahiba M (2000) Participatory Micro Enterprises. Indian Journal of Rural Development.
8. Sheriff RL (2008) Micro Enterprises give California's Economy a Boost. Policy Briefs.
9. Ejigie, Abebaw D (2008) Eastern Africa Social Science Research Review.
10. Psaila K (2007) Constraints and Opportunities for Micro enterprises in Malta. Bank of Valletta Review 35: 25-38.

Role of Assets Holding of the Availing Micro Credit of Women: A Study With Reference to Madurai District of Tamil Nadu

Selvaraj N*, Balajikumar P and Alagukanna AS

Saraswathi Narayanan College, Madurai, Tamilnadu, India

Abstract

Micro-credit is a critical antipoverty tool, a wise investment in human capital. When the poorest especially women receive credit, they become economic actors with power to improve not only their own lives, but in a widening circle of impact, the lives of their families, their communities and their relations. Microfinance helps the NGOs all over the world in alleviation of urban and rural poverty through promoting micro enterprises as a solution to the problem of unemployment and underemployment among the poor. In India also NGOs use this methodology for financing the poor. MYRADA in Karnataka and SEWA in Gujarat are the forerunners in the field in India. SEWA has promoted a cooperative bank exclusively for women and is engaged in financing income generating activities of women. Friends of WWB (FWWB) Ahmedabad, an affiliate of Women's World Banking, New York, networks with NGOs giving financial assistance to women groups. The total value of assets includes movable and immovable assets owned by the respondents and their family members. The assets indicate the financial background of the respondents before availing credit. Assets of the respondents increased due to the additional income earned through new activities and savings.

Keyword: Micro-Credit; Assets; Agricultural; Manufacturing and trading

Introduction

Micro-credit is a critical antipoverty tool, a wise investment in human capital. When the poorest especially women receive credit, they become economic actors with power to improve not only their own lives, but in a widening circle of impact, the lives of their families, their communities and their relations.

Today in India, there are 15,000 registered NGOs and many more non-registered informal groups. These organizations have touched the lives of an estimated number of 15 million persons. According to an international estimate, 100 million persons have been helped worldwide by NGOs of one sort or another. NGOs follow different methods to reach the poor. Those who follow the 'grassroots' or the 'barefoot' approaches have attracted a good deal of admiration [1].

Microfinance helps the NGOs all over the world in alleviation of urban and rural poverty through promoting micro enterprises as a solution to the problem of unemployment and underemployment among the poor. NGOs undertake the responsibility of forming self-help groups, give training to members, and monitor business performance and promptness in repayment.

In India also NGOs use this methodology for financing the poor. MYRADA in Karnataka and SEWA in Gujarat are the forerunners in the field in India [2]. SEWA has promoted a cooperative bank exclusively for women and is engaged in financing income generating activities of women. Friends of WWB (FWWB) Ahmedabad, an affiliate of Women's World Banking, New York, networks with NGOs giving financial assistance to women groups. The Working Women's Forum (WWF), Chennai has organized women cooperative societies for pursuing income generating activities and facilitated empowerment of women. Attempts have also been made to replicate Bangladesh Grammen Bank model by SHARE in Andhra Pradesh and RDO in Manipur [3,4].

Objectives of the Study

To evaluate the impact of micro-credit on women empowerment with reference to Assets holding and to offer suitable suggestions based on the findings.

Period of Study

The present study is based on the primary. The primary data have been collected from the respondents directly for the period of study is impounded to one year (i.e., 2014-2015).

Analytical Framework to Test the Factors

Impact on assets

Assets holding of the respondents (Pre-credit): The total value of assets includes movable and immovable assets owned by the respondents and their family members. The assets indicate the financial background of the respondents before availing credit. In the present study, the assets of the respondents before availing credit are computed and classified as Nil, Below Rs 10000, Rs 10000 to Rs 15000, Rs 15000 to 20000, and above Rs 20000.

Table 1 presents the assets holding of the respondents before availing micro credit in various sectors.

In the study area, before availing the credit, the value of asset holding of the respondents accounts only a meager amount. About 82 respondents had no assets. Majority of the respondents that is 28.00 per cent of the respondents had assets value below Rs 10000–15000. 26.67 per cent of the respondents had assets value in the range of below Rs 10000. 11.67 per cent have assets value of Rs 15000 to Rs 20000. A very low percentage constituting 6.33 per cent of the respondents had assets value of Rs 20000 and above.

***Corresponding author:** Dr. Selvaraj N, Assistant Professor of Commerce, Saraswathi Narayanan College, Madurai, Tamilnadu, India
E-mail: selvaraj_narayanan@yahoo.com

Assets holding of the Respondents	Manufac-turing Sector	Service Sector	Trading Sector	Total
Nil	25 [30.86]	26 [25.49]	31 [26.50]	82 [27.33]
Below Rs.10000	18 [22.22]	25 [24.51]	37 [31.62]	80 [26.67]
Rs.10000 - 15000	21 [25.93]	31 [30.39]	32 [27.35]	84 [28.00]
Rs.15000 - 20000	9 [11.11]	16 [15.69]	10 [8.55]	35 [11.67]
Above Rs.20000	8 [9.88]	4 [3.92]	7 [5.98]	19 [6.33]
Total	**81 [100.0]**	**102 [100.0]**	**117 [100.0]**	**300 [100.0]**

Table 1: Assets holding of the respondents (pre-credit).

Assets holding of the respondents (Post-credit): Assets of the respondents increased due to the additional income earned through new activities and savings. The assets after availing credit are measured and classified as Nil, Below Rs 10000, Rs 10000 to Rs 15000, Rs 15000 to 20000, and above Rs 20000. Table 2 presents the assets holding of the respondents after availing credit in various sectors [5,6].

Table 2 clearly shows that, out of 81 respondents in manufacturing sector, 1 (1.23 per cent) respondent had no assets, 5 (6.17 per cent) of them belong to the holding of assets below Rs 10000, 18 (22.22 per cent) of them belong to the assets holding of Rs 10001 to Rs 15000, 14 (17.29 per cent) of them belong to the assets holding of Rs 15001 to Rs 20000, and 43 (53.09 per cent) of them belong to the assets holding of Rs 20001 and above after availing the credit.

Out of 102 respondents in service sector, 12 (11.76 per cent) of the respondents belong to below Rs 10000, 19 (18.63 per cent) of the respondent's family come under the value of assets holding in the range of Rs 10001 to Rs 15000, 18 (17.65 per cent) of the respondents come under assets holding of Rs 15001 to Rs 20000, and 53 (51.96 per cent) of the respondents belong to the assets holding Rs 20001 and above, after availing credit [7].

It is further inferred from the table, out of 117 respondents in trading sector, 3 (2.56 per cent) of them come under the value of assets holding below Rs 10000, 26 (22.22 per cent) of them belong to the value of assets holding of Rs 10001 to 15000, 30 (25.64 per cent) of them belong to the value of assets holding of Rs 15001 to Rs 20000, and 58 (49.58 per cent) of them belong to the value of assets holding of Rs 20001and above after availing the credit [8,9].

Thus it could be concluded from the table that after availing credit, the value of the assets holding of the respondent and her family has increased in the study area. 0.33 per cent respondent had no assets, 6.67 per cent of the respondents had the assets value of below Rs 10000, 21.00 per cent of the respondents and their family had the assets value of Rs 10001 to Rs 15000, 20.67 per cent of the respondents and their family had assets value of Rs 15001 to Rs 20000, and 51.33 per cent of the respondents and their family had the assets value of above Rs 20001 [10].

The null and alternative hypotheses are framed and tested in this study:

Null hypothesis (H_0): There is no relationship between assets holding of the respondents and the various sectors.

Alternative hypothesis (H_1): There is a relationship between asset holding of the respondents and the various sectors.

As the calculated value of χ^2 is greater than the table value at 5 per cent level of significance, the investigator rejects the null-hypothesis (H_0). Therefore, there exists a relationship between the assets holding of the respondents after joining the self-help groups and the various sectors (Table 3).

Mean value of asset holding: The micro-finance program might have a major impact of the activities undertaken beneficiaries. Sector-wise analysis of the mean value of asset holdings of the respondents is shown in Table 4.

Table 4 reveals that, the manufacturing sector has the highest mean value in the assets holding amounting Rs 24241.31, followed by the service sector with Rs 21433.26. Next is followed with the trading sector amounting to Rs 21411.61.

Association between family size of the respondents and their assets (post-credit) in various sectors

Null hypothesis (H_0): There is no association between family size of the respondents and their assets (post-credit) in various sectors.

Alternative hypothesis (H_1): There exists association between family size of the respondents and their assets (post-credit) in various sectors.

In order to find out whether there is any correlation between the family size of the respondents and their assets in various sectors, chi-square test has been applied. The results of the chi-square test are furnished below.

As the calculated value of χ^2 is greater than the table value at 5 per cent level of significance, the investigator rejects the null-hypothesis (H_0) and accepts the alternative hypothesis (H_1). Therefore there exists an association between family size of the respondents and their assets after availing credit in various sectors (Table 5) [11,12].

Association between family income (post-credit) of the respondents and their assets (post-credit) in various sectors

Null Hypothesis (H_0): There is no association between family income of the respondents and their assets (post-credit) in various sectors.

Alternative Hypothesis (H_1): There exists association between family income of the respondents and their assets (Post-Credit) in various sectors.

Assets holding of the Respondents	Manufacturing Sector	Service Sector	Trading Sector	Total
Nil	1 [1.23]	0 [0.0]	0 [0.0]	1 [0.33]
Below Rs.10000	5 [6.17]	12 [11.76]	3 [2.56]	20 [6.67]
Rs.10000 - 15000	18 [22.22]	19 [18.63]	26 [22.22]	63 [21.00]
Rs.15000 - 20000	14 [17.29]	18 [17.65]	30 [25.64]	62 [20.67]
Above Rs.20000	43 [53.09]	53 [51.96]	58 [49.58]	154 [51.33]
Total	**81 [100.0]**	**102 [100.0]**	**117 [100.0]**	**300 [100.0]**

Table 2: Assets holding of the respondents (post-credit).

Test	Value	d.f	Asymp.Sig. (2-Sided)	Table Value	Result
Pearson Chi-square	26.311	12	.006	21.0	Rejected

Table 3: Result of chi-square test – asset holding of the respondents and various sectors.

Sectors	Mean Value of Assets	Total	Std. Deviation
Manufacturing Sector	24241.31	81	9961.25
Service Sector	21433.26	102	7621.43
Trading Sector	21411.61	117	5761.45
Total	18634.41	300	7201.22

Table 4: Mean value of asset holding of the respondents in various sectors.

Family Size	Assets (Post-Credit)					Total
	Nil	Below Rs.10000	Rs.10001-Rs.15000	Rs.15001-Rs.20000	Above Rs.20001	
Below 5	1 [100.00]	8 [40.00]	29 [46.03]	28 [45.16]	62 [40.26]	128 [42.67]
5 – 8	0 [00.0]	7 [35.00]	23 [36.51]	21 [33.87]	54 [35.06]	105 [35.00]
9 and above	0 [0.0]	5 [25.00]	11 [17.46]	13 [20.97]	38 [24.68]	67 [22.50]
Total	1 [100.0]	20 [100.0]	63 [100.0]	62 [100.0]	154 [100.0]	300 [100.0]

Table 5: Contingency table – family size of the respondents and their value of assets (post-credit) in various sectors.

In order to find out whether there is any correlation between the family income after availing the micro credit of the respondents and their assets in various sectors, chi-square test has been applied. The results of the chi-square test are furnished in Table 6.

As the calculated value of $\chi 2$ is greater than the table value at 5 per cent level of significance, the investigator rejects the null-hypothesis (H_0) and accepts the alternative hypothesis (H_1). Therefore, there exists an association between family income after availing the credit of the respondents and their assets of the respondents in various sectors (Table 7).

Association between savings (post-credit) of the respondents and their assets (post-credit) in various sectors

Null Hypothesis (H_0): There is no association between savings of the respondents and their assets (post-credit) in various sectors.

Alternative Hypothesis (H_1): There exists association between savings of the respondents and their assets (post credit) in various sectors

In order to find out whether there is any correlation between the savings of the respondents and their assets in various sectors, chi-square test has been applied. The results of the chi-square test are furnished in Table 8.

As the calculated value of χ^2 is less than the table value at 5 per cent level of significance, the investigator accepts the null-hypothesis (H_0) and rejects the alternative hypothesis (H_1). Therefore there is no exists an association between savings after availing the credit of the respondents and their assets in various sectors (Table 9).

Variation in asset holding of the respondents and their family size among the various sectors

In this section, an attempt has been made to examine the variation in asset holding of the respondents among the various sectors, such as manufacturing, service and trading sectors. For this one way ANOVA is applied separately and the results are presented in Table 10.

Table 11 revealed that there was a significant variation in the asset holding of the respondents among the various sectors and their family size at 5 per cent level of significant. Hence, it may be concluded that the asset holding of the respondents and their family size varied significantly among the various sectors such as manufacturing sector, service sector and trading sector.

Summary of Findings

While the analyzing the assets holding pre-credit, the value of assets holding of the respondents accounts only a meagre amount. About 82 respondents have no assets. Majority of the respondents, that is 26.67 per cent of the respondents, have assets value below Rs 10000, 28.00 per cent of the respondents possess assets to the value Rs 10000 to Rs 15000, and 11.67 per cent have assets about value Rs 15000 to Rs 20000. A very low percentage constituting 6.33 per cent of the respondents have assets worthy of Rs 20000 and above.

It is observed that the assets holding of the respondents and their family, post-credit member has increased in the study area. 0.33 per cent of respondents have no assets, 6.67 per cent of the respondents have the assets, below Rs 10000, 21.00 per cent of the respondents have assets, to the value of Rs 10001 to Rs 15000, 20.67 per cent of the respondents have assets in the range of Rs 15001 to Rs 20000, and 51.33 per cent of the respondents and their family have the assets above Rs 20001.

ANOVA test reveals that there is a significant variation in the assets holding of the respondents among the various sectors and their family size at 5 per cent level of significant. Hence, it may be concluded that the assets holding of the respondents and their family size varies significantly among the various sectors such as manufacturing sector, service sector and trading sector.

The paired 't' test shows there is some significant difference in the assets holding of the respondents pre-credit and post-credit. The mean assets holdings of the respondent pre-credit are Rs 18611.241 and post-credit it is Rs 14321.731 and the difference Rs 14321.731 is statistically significant.

Test	Value	d.f	Asymp. Sig. (2-Sided)	Table Value	Result
Pearson Chi-square	122.5683	8	0.000	15.5	Rejected

Table 6: Result of chi-square test – family size of the respondents and their value of assets (post-credit) in various sectors.

Family Income (Post – Credit)	Assets (Post-Credit)					Total
	Nil	Below Rs.10000	Rs.10001-Rs.15000	Rs.15001-Rs.20000	Above Rs.20001	
Below Rs.25000	1 [100.0]	3 [15.00]	5 [7.94]	5 [8.06]	24 [15.58]	38 [12.67]
Rs.25001–Rs.35000	0 [0.0]	5 [25.00]	18 [28.57]	21 [33.87]	38 [24.68]	82 [27.33]
Rs.35001–Rs.45000	0 [0.0]	6 [30.00]	29 [46.03]	26 [41.94]	48 [31.17]	109 [36.33]
Above Rs.45001	0 [0.0]	6 [30.00]	11 [17.46]	10 [16.13]	44 [28.57]	71 [23.67]
Total	**1 [100.0]**	**20 [100.0]**	**63 [100.0]**	**62 [100.0]**	**154 [100.0]**	**300 [100.0]**

Table 7: Contingency table– family income of the respondents and their value of assets (post–credit) in various sectors.

Test	Value	d.f	Asymp.Sig. (2-Sided)	Table Value	Result
Pearson Chi-square	1861.6662	12	0.000	21.0	Rejected

Table 8: Result of chi-square test – family income of the respondents and their value of assets (post-credit) in various sectors.

Assets (Post – Credit)	Savings (Post – Credit)					Total
	Below Rs.1200	Rs.1201-Rs.2400	Rs.2401-Rs.3600	Rs.3601-Rs.4800	Above Rs.4801	
Nil	1 [1.23]	0 [0.0]	0 [0.0]	0 [0.0]	0 [0.0]	1 [0.33]
Below Rs.10000	5 [6.17]	4 [6.45]	4 [5.19]	6 [9.23]	1 [6.67]	20 [6.67]
Rs.10001–Rs.15000	16 [19.75]	13 [20.97]	14 [18.18]	16 [24.62]	4 [26.66]	63 [21.00]
Rs.15001–Rs.20000	17 [20.99]	12 [19.35]	15 [19.48]	11 [16.92]	7 [46.67]	62 [20.67]
Above Rs.20001	42 [51.85]	33 [53.23]	44 [57.15]	32 [49.23]	3 [20.00]	154 [51.33]
Total	**81 [100.0]**	**62 [100.0]**	**77 [100.0]**	**65 [100.0]**	**15 [100.0]**	**300 [100.0]**

Table 9: Contingency table– savings (post-credit) of the respondents and their value of asset holding in various sectors.

Test	Value	d.f	Asymp.Sig. (2-Sided)	Table Value	Result
Pearson Chi-square	6.2534	16	0.000	26.3	Accepts

Table 10: Result of chi-square test – savings (post-credit) of the respondents and their value of asset holding in various sectors.

Assets Variation	Sum of Squares	Df	Mean Square	F-ratio	Sig.	Table $F_{0.05}$
Between Groups	3.32E+09	2	176231142	41.211*	0.000	
Within groups	1.49E+11	297	42562341.31			
Total	1.82E+11	299				

Table 11: One-way ANOVA test results of asset holding of the respondents and their family size in various sectors.

Suggestions

In the light of the above discussion and findings, the following suggestions are made:

It is suggested that the NGOs should be prevented from interfering with the SHG movement. Steps should be taken to keep them as voluntary organizations. They should not be allowed to use extraneous influences.

SHG women are more concerned with poverty and its effect on society. Since they themselves fight against poverty by being members of SHG and move upwards from below poverty line, in future, the poverty alleviation programs can be implemented through SHGs, They can monitor themselves effectively, with all enthusiasm and involvement.

Institutional credit facility must be extended to women to develop their managerial skill for prompt repayment consciousness.

Micro-Finance should be used to meet the immediate demand of the poor women - for Health, Education or consumption purposes. This will improve the quality of their life and will be ready to take active participation in economic activities.

The NGOs can provide some common services to the Self-Help Groups for procurement of raw materials, marketing etc.

Though, these groups have made a positive impact on SHG women, SHG members suffer from lack of motivation, backward and forward linkages, inadequacy of infrastructure, insufficient loan, inadequate provision of marketing, non-availability of inputs, lack of systematic monitoring and follow up activities etc,. Thus there is need to evaluate the SHGs annually to assess the progress of different income and employment generating schemes.

References

1. Noponen H (2002) Micro Finance, Rural Livelihoods and Women's Empowerment- a Participatory Learning System to Access and Enhance Impact. In: Guérin I, Palier J (eds.) Micro finance challenges: empowerment or disempowerment of the poor? Institut Francais de Pondichery.
2. Kaladhar K (1997) Micro Finance in India. Economic and Political Weekly.
3. Kulshrestha LR (2000) Micro-Finance: The New Development Paradigm for Poor Rural Women. Kurushetra.
4. Karmakar KG (1990) Rural Credit and Self-Help Groups: Micro-Finance Need and Concepts in India. Sage, New Delhi.
5. Manimekalai N (2006) Impact of Micro Financing in Promoting Women Micro Entrepreneurship- An Analysis. Women Empowerment Issues and Challenges, Souvenir.
6. Mishra RK (2002) Self Help Groups and Micro Credit Movements in Orissa: Issues and Options, Indian Co-operative Review p. 34.
7. Morduch J, Haley B (2001) Analysis of the Effects of Micro Finance on Poverty Reduction. CIDA, Ottawa.
8. Muniyandi B (2006) Credit linkage of Self Help Groups through Micro Finance in Villupuram District, 27th Annual Conference of the Association of Economists of Tamil Nadu p. 93.
9. Marguerite RS (1994) Savings Mobilization and Microenterprise Finance: The Indonesian Experience. In: Otero M, Rhyne E (eds.) The New World of Micro Enterprise Finance. Kumarian, USA.
10. Sarma RH (1999) Micro financing through Self-Help Group and Non-Government Organizations by Commercial Banks. The Journal of the Indian Institute of Bankers 70: 19-23.
11. Thanuja M (2005) Relevance of Micro Finance and Empowerment in tribal areas: a case study of the Konda Reddis. In: Guérin I, Palier J (eds.) Micro Finance challenges: empowerment Disempowerment of the poor, Institut Francais de Pondichery p. 63-72.
12. Tripathy KK (2006) Micro-Credit Intervention and Poverty alleviation, Kurukshetra.

Strategies for Retaining a Multigenerational Workforce

Jones LM*

Walden University, College of Management andTechnology, 100 Washington Avenue South, Suite 900, Minneapolis, Minnesota, USA

Abstract

As organizations become more age diverse, some business leaders face challenges managing a multigenerational workforce. The purpose of this single case study was to explore strategies that leaders at a university in Northwest Florida implemented to retain their age-diverse workforce. The targeted population was higher education business managers who had success with retaining an age-diverse staff. The conceptual framework of the study was Herzberg's 2-factor theory of motivation. A significant tenet of this theory is employees explain satisfying and dissatisfying experiences based on intrinsic and extrinsic factors related to their job functions. The data collection process included face-to-face interviews with 4 participants and a review of company documents, including the university's strategic plan and diversity and inclusion initiatives. Through coding and thematic analysis, 7 themes emerged that could help leaders retain a multigenerational workforce: foster a diversity-friendly workplace culture, implement effective interpersonal communication strategies, employ a formal approach, encourage a healthy work-life balance, value employees and their differences, offer professional growth opportunities, and eliminate negative generational stereotyping. Developing and cultivating retention strategies may contribute to social change by helping managers and leaders enrich retention rates, thereby increasing employment stability, improving productivity, and enhancing organizational and community relations.

Keywords: Generational cohort; Traditionalists; Baby boomers; Generation X; Generation Y

Introduction

Background of the problem

The four generations that constitute today's workforce include traditionalists (born between 1925 and 1945), baby boomers (born between 1946 and 1964), Generation X (born between 1965 and 1981), and Generation Y (born between 1982 and 2000), also known as millennials [1]. According to Cloutier et al. [2], differences among the four generational cohorts can cause challenges for business leaders to develop successful strategies to retain a multigenerational staff. The generational differences that managers find challenging includes attitudes, beliefs, values, work ethics, workplace perceptions, and workplace expectations [3]. Additionally, intrinsic and extrinsic factors can affect the motivation levels of generational employees, which can strongly influence their workplace expectations [4].

Gaining a keen understanding of how to manage differences among multigenerational employees is vital to an organization's success [5]. Leaders of multigenerational staff tend to treat all workers the same, regardless of their cohort classification, instead of focusing on individual characteristics and traits of generational employees and treating them according to their needs [6]. Establishing a workplace environment that is diversity friendly can encourage innovation and teamwork between generational employees, which could have a positive effect on productivity and retention [7]. Al-Asfour and Lettau [8] asserted that it is essential for organizations to examine their leadership styles and level of understanding of the differences that exist among generational workers so that leaders can address workplace diversity, which can reduce generational conflict and improve employee retention.

Problem statement

Diversity in the workplace increases as baby boomers delay retirement and join the other generations in the labor force [5]. Differences in age, intrinsic and extrinsic motivator preferences, and characteristics of generational workers can lead to challenges for business managers in retaining their multigenerational staff [9]. By 2023, the workforce will reach an estimated 163.5 million people with the traditionalists representing 8% of the workforce, the baby boomers representing 22% of the workfore, Generation X representing 20% of the workforce, and Generation Y representing 50% of the workforce [10,11]. The general business problem is that some business managers do not recognize the differences among multigenerational workers, which can adversely affect employee retention. The specific business problem is that some business managers lack strategies to retain a multigenerational workforce.

Purpose statement

The purpose of this qualitative single case study was to explore retention strategies business managers use to retain their multigenerational workforce. The targeted population consisted of department managers from an education institution located in Northwest Florida who had success in retaining a multigenerational workforce. According to Hannay and Fretwell [12] and Matz-Costa and Pitt-Catsouphes [13], academic administrators can experience workplace conflict and retention dilemmas if managers do not identify and address the differences that exist among multigenerational workers. Therefore, an academic population was suitable for this study. The implications for positive social change include the opportunity to share strategies that could help organizations increase their retention rates of generational workers, as well as promote organizational unity across generations. Managers, administrators, and other individuals who hold authoritative positions could use the findings of this study to increase the retention rates of generational workers, thereby creating employment stability, improving productivity, and enhancing both organizational and community relations.

***Corresponding author:** Laurita M Jones, College of Management and Technology, Walden University, 100 Washington Avenue South, Suite 900, Minneapolis, Minnesota, 55401, USA, E-mail: Laurita.Jones@Waldenu.edu

Research question

The central research question was the following: What retention strategies do business managers use to retain their multigenerational workforce?

Interview questions

1. What strategies do you use to retain your multigenerational workforce?
2. What specific procedures or business practices have you implemented to ensure the retention of your multigenerational workforce?
3. What strategies have you found to be most effective in retaining your multigenerational workforce?
4. What strategies have you found to be the least effective in retaining your multigenerational workforce?
5. What challenges did you encounter when you implemented the strategies, and how did you overcome the challenges?
6. What advice would you share with other business managers about developing and implementing strategies to help retain their multigenerational workforce?

Conceptual Framework

Herzberg's two-factor theory of motivation, from an intrinsic motivator and extrinsic motivator perspective, was the conceptual framework for this study. The two-factory theory came about when Herzberg [14] collected data from interviews of 200 accountants and engineers from several industries in the Pittsburgh area. During the data collection process, Herzberg [14] asked his participants to explain periods of satisfaction and dissatisfaction on their jobs. The results of the study revealed that job satisfaction and dissatisfaction derives from two factors that he labeled motivation factors (intrinsic elements) and hygiene factors (extrinsic elements). According to Herzberg [15], the intrinsic factors of motivation that can lead to increased retention are job satisfaction and enhanced motivation. Herzberg [15] further stated that job satisfaction and motivation could encourage superior work performance and increased efforts from employees. Intrinsic motivators tend to represent more emotional but less tangible needs, such as project accomplishments, recognition for achievement, level of responsibility, growth and advancement opportunities, and the work itself [16]. Extrinsic factors of motivation correlate with job dissatisfaction and can lead to an increase in turnover, which will negatively affect retention rates [15,17]. Extrinsic factors are those that employees expect to be present and, if absent, can cause high levels of dissatisfaction. Examples of extrinsic factors include working conditions, authority or status, job security, company policies, leadership, and interpersonal relationships [16]. Herzberg [16] concluded that intrinsic motivators are the primary cause of job satisfaction, and extrinsic motivators are the main cause of unhappiness in the workplace. To improve job attitudes, increase productivity, and lengthen employee commitments, it is essential for managers to identify and apply intrinsic and extrinsic elements of Herzberg's two-factor theory of motivation [18].

Due to four generations simultaneously constituting the workforce, such diversity requires an in-depth comprehension of what motivates workers of differing ages and characteristics so that organizations can successfully retain them [19]. Hyun and Oh [20] suggested that motivation factors affect the actual job tasks that workers do; therefore, the jobs should consist of intrinsic and extrinsic factors to cultivate motivation within the workforce. Developing and implementing strategies that incorporate a balance of intrinsic and extrinsic motivation factors based on the needs and characteristics of their staff could help managers mitigate turnover and enhance workplace retention [21].

Operational definitions

Generational cohort: A generational cohort is a group of individuals who experience identical social, economic, political, and cultural events, and who share similar values and attitudes about life, work, and education [22].

Traditionalists: Traditionalists are individuals born between 1925 and 1945 who compose approximately 5% of today's workforce [1,23].

Baby boomers: Baby boomers are people born between 1946 and 1964 who compose approximately 30% of the population [1,23].

Generation X: Generation X constitutes nearly 34% of the population and includes individuals born between 1965 and 1981. The Generation X population is also known as the Xers, the 13th generation, and the latchkey generation [1,24].

Generation Y: Generation Y, also known as the millennials, consists of individuals born between 1982 and 2000. These individuals compose almost 12% of the population [1,25].

Literature Review

Background on generations

In the 1920s, Karl Manheim introduced the concept of generation as a realistic addition to the examination of social stratification in modern sociology [26]. The sociology of generations can directly arrogate theories that surround the idea of social class, yielding a range of ideas such as generational conflict, generational mobility, and generational ideologies [26]. Eyerman and Turner [26] defined a generation in terms of years and origination. The meaning of generational cohorts improves generational sociological substance, which could place emphasis on the problem of the final dissolution of a generational cohort as its members evolve through retirement and physical decline. Time identifies multigenerational variances because periodization encapsulates the strategic opportunities and complications that relate to precise generations [26]. The researchers indicated that different generations survive by preserving collective memory of its origins, historic struggles, political and historical events, and ideologists and leading characters.

Generational cohorts and age groups

Becton et al. [27] found that a generation, often referred to as a cohort, is a similar group of individuals that share birth years, age, and meaningful life events at critical stages of development. These people within the different cohorts acquire similar personalities and characteristics because of their shared experiences [28,29]. Society delegates these generational personalities and characteristics into stereotypes, which align with the environmental influences that affect their beliefs, values, personalities, and expectations. The generational cohort that individuals affiliate with can influence the views and attitudes related to leadership, management, work values, intrinsic and extrinsic motivators, and work ethic [30]. Colette and Stein [30] further highlighted how multigenerational workers view the workplace as well as the motivation influences that can promote retention and productivity. With the level of diversity in the business environment, it is essential for managers to identify and comprehend the rudiments that keep employees motivated to promote loyalty and increase retention.

With the changing structure of the workplace, multiple generations are now working side by side instead of operating as separate units [31]. The difference in values, beliefs, historical experiences, and social experiences that generational cohorts working simultaneously bring to the workplace will affect their professional interactions. These interactions can have an undesirable effect on individual performance and retention rates [32]. Wang and Peng [33] revealed that generational classifications utilize a categorical approach, creating subjective instead of scientific timelines to identify the cohorts. The subjectivity of categorizing the generations will not be an issue for the current study because the minimal variation of the birth years has no bearing on the generational descriptions.

The current business environment primarily includes four generational cohorts: (a) traditionalists, born between 1925 and 1945, (b) baby boomers, born between 1946 and 1964, (c) Generation X, born between 1965 and 1981, and (d) Generation Y (millennials), born between 1982 and 1999 [34]. Individuals within these cohorts share external historical events or life experiences that took place during their formative years [35]. In sharing significant life events, the four generations are susceptible to certain values and expectations that will contribute to how they perceive their work environment [36]. Workplace diversity is now custom in most companies due to the four generational cohorts coexisting in the workforce. The members of the four cohorts establish and determine their workplace beliefs, behaviors, attitudes, and expectations based on shared generational qualities [37].

Some organizations are modifying their processes and expectations due to baby boomers remaining in the workforce [38]. Younger generations joining the baby boomers in the workplace change the demographics of the business environment as the baby boomers become the subordinates of the younger generation of workers [39]. To remain in alignment with the presented literature about generations, I will apply descriptions discussed in the following sections to explain each cohort.

Traditionalists (1925-1945)

The traditionalist cohort includes individuals born between 1925 and 1945. Although the majority of the traditionalists have retired since reaching retirement eligibility, a small percentage remains in the workforce [40]. The Great Depression, World War II, and Pearl Harbor are the events that help shape and influence the lives of the traditionalist generation in the United States [7]. Reinbeck and Fitzsimons [41] informed that traditionalists currently hold three-quarters of the nation's wealth and helped shape the United State's military and economic power. They are or have been executive leaders of some of the most prosperous United States companies, and are not quick to speak up or share their ideas. Traditionalists are hardworking and tend to favor military-like management that follows a top-down or chain of command style [41]. This generation sacrifices and follows authoritative commands without question [42]. Individuals of this generation are loyal to their employer and will often work for the same organization for much of their career [43]. Additionally, traditionalists have respect for tradition and do not waiver from established rules. Their Great Depression experience caused the traditionalist generation to plan for financial security, and they are monetarily conservative, making them the wealthiest of the four generations [7].

Baby boomer generation (1946-1964)

The baby boomers are the largest and most popular generation in United States history, with a surge of their births taking place during and after The Great Depression and World War II [44,45]. Loroz and Helgeson [46] reported that approximately 76 million boomers were born between 1946 and 1964. Also known as the forgotten generation or the Woodstock generation, the boomers experienced postwar stress and radical social changes such as the Civil Rights movement and the Women's movement [47]. Kaifi et al. explained that parents of baby boomers raised them up in two-family households during a time of prosperity [48]. Kaifi et al. [48] also posited that the main events that significantly influenced this generation are the assassinations of John F Kennedy, Robert F Kennedy, and Dr. Martin Luther King, Jr. Srinivasan [47] stated that baby boomers are self-absorbed, less loyal, lack respect for authority, and that money and self-realization are their primary motivators. The geographical dynamics of the workforce is changing due to baby boomers choosing to remain in the workforce beyond retirement age and eligibility [49]. Understanding desired career paths of the baby boomer generation is important because this segment of the generational population will continue to impact the economy [50]. Rice advised that the baby boomer generation has the desire for promotions in the workplace but experience restrictions because they lack technology skills. Nevertheless, some managers prefer to retain older workers, such as baby boomers, because organizations can benefit from their wealth of knowledge and professional expertise [51].

Generation X (1965-1981)

Generation X, also acknowledged as the X'ers and the 13th generation, are currently between the ages of 35 and 51 as of 2016. Organizational downsizing, industrial restructuring, and increasing rates of temporary and part-time employment are events that fostered members of the Generation X cohort [52]. They also endured the country's political problems as well as the rejuvenation of the economy [53]. DeVaney [34] mentioned that Gen X members lived in single parent households or households with dual income earners that alternated childcare responsibilities. Generation X'ers are known as *latchkey* people because they would normally let themselves into the house after school, did their homework by themselves, and watched television unsupervised until a caregiver returned home [34]. The lifestyle preferences and attitudes of Generation X'ers shows that they tend to favor the ability to balance work with their family and life interests. Al-Asfour and Lettau [8] articulated that individuals of this generation have a more progressive outlook on life, and are tech-savvy because of their experiences with technology advancements such as the rise of the Internet. With the Generation X population having a strong focus on maintaining a work-life balance, being familiar and comfortable with technology can help empower them to realize and enhance the balance between work, family, and lifestyle [8].

Researchers often depict Generation X characteristics from a negative viewpoint; however, the elements that make them distinctive emphasize a more positive perspective. The Generation X cohort is skeptical about politics, and are independent, self-reliant, teamwork oriented, and values workplace flexibility. Additionally, authority does not intimidate them, they are outspoken, results and goal oriented, prefers multiple work assignments to keep them motivated and engaged, and desires consistent training and development opportunities to enhance their skills [54].

Generation Y (1982-2000)

Bolton et al. [55] stated that both managers and academics are curious and fascinated about the Generation Y cohort. Society perceives Generation Y or the *Millennials* as digital natives because they are the first generation to spend their entire lives in the digital era [55]. In 1982, 3.7 million members of Generation Y were born making them the second largest generational cohort in American history [25]. Of the four generations, members of Generation Y will most likely suffer the most from the housing market collapse and higher college tuition costs, which are aftereffects of the September 11 terror attacks [25]. Kamau et al. [56] posited that in addition to Millennials having an entitlement mentality, they are also the most ethnically diverse, creative, and multitasking generation ever to exist. Although they are the most educated cohort to exist and are selfish and narcissistic, they are also very optimistic and technology savvy [57]. Generation Yer's experienced very structured type lifestyles and experienced helicopter-style parenting (terms used to describe parents that are overly involved and hover over their children) as parents became as actively involved as possible in their children's lives [58]. Holt et al. [59] advised that the 75 million members of the millennial generation will most likely lead the global labor force through the complexities and chaos of cyber-socialization.

The Millennials acquire their knowledge and capabilities by using networks and technology, and are more challenging in the workplace than the older generations [60,61]. Over 90% of this generation is involved in online networks and social outlets due to their high comfort levels with technology, and they welcome new and challenging opportunities and finding ways to develop their skill sets [62]. Murray [63] suggested that millennials' can-do attitudes are like a breath of fresh air to the workforce. This generation is goal-driven and innovative, and prefers to work jobs that are meaningful with companies that value them [63]. Members of Generation Y are not fond of companies that have a culture based on a need-to-know basis and prefer to work for transparent business entities that share the organization's values, mission, expectations, goals and objectives, and workplace conflicts with all employees [64]. Work values are essential to learning and understanding how best to manage Generation Y because their work values are what make them unique and different from the older generational cohorts [65]. The Generation Y cohort is known as the trophy generation or the trophy kids because of the emerging trend in competitive sports and other events that give rewards for participating rather than for winning [48]. Many of the Generation Y'ers watched their parents suffer stress caused by the dot.com downfall and increased rates of layoffs and divorces, which shaped the generations views on long-term commitments and flexible careers [48].

Generational diversity

Some employees have made a habit of recruiting and hiring young people. Still, retaining experienced and knowledge-rich employees is of increasing importance in a globalized economy [66]. Retaining employees with knowledge and experience could be of mutual benefit to hiring older workers along with younger workers, and doing so could help develop a positive business stance that is not politically driven. A specific benefit of age diversity is the massive amount of skill sets acquired by employees. Swan [66] revealed that companies that employed primarily young workers found it to be detrimental to the business. Organizational leaders felt that hiring older workers could provide better emotional intelligence in handling business-client relationships.

The demographical changes of the workforce, along with high ethical standards and the pressure of maintaining a competitive advantage in a global marketplace are inducing more businesses to address employee diversity [67]. Heyler and Lee [68] stated that education, training, and employment providers would need to respond to generational differences by investigating the attributes of all parties, their development and life needs, the requirements of potential employers, and what the employers can offer to workers. Some business leaders are embracing the multigenerational workforce and are taking advantage of the benefits that the cross-generational workforce brings. DeMeulenaere et al. [69] suggested that age diversity could have both positive and negative effects on labor productivity. The positive aspect of age diversity is the large amount of knowledge that exists between the different generation of employees, and the negative aspect is the lack of unity and collaboration that age-related differences can cause, which can hinder performance. Organizations are establishing ways to harness the skills of their older workers to develop the skills of their younger generation of employees [68]. Comprehending that a multigenerational workforce can increase a company's competitive edge is the key to persuading businesses to take it seriously.

Generational stereotypes

Riggio and Saggi [70] affirmed that the belief in generational differences has been around since the twenty-fifth century, BC. Even during the twenty-fifth century, BC, the perception was that variances among generations could cause threats to production, so the older generations worked to mold the young generation to mirror their image [70]. Although a person is aware of the similarities and differences that exist within the generational cohort that he or she identifies with, such diversity may not be as obvious to individuals from other generations which can lead to age-related stereotyping and assumptions [71]. However, Constanza and Finkelstein [72] asserted that limited empirical evidence exists to support generational-based differences. Riggio and Saggi [70] suggested that the dominant belief in generation based variances is due to systematic predispositions in social perception. The social identity theory, developed by Tajfel and Turner [73], strengthens the significance of inter-cohort awareness of values between generations. The social identity theory purports that a person's view changes based on identified social categorizations across several constructs (e.g., beliefs, values, occupational types), which defines essential aspects of the individual [74]. For the social identity theory to apply to research regarding values and generational cohorts, it is essential for individuals to comprehend the way that generational cohorts perceive the value preferences of other generational cohorts [74]. In-group and out-group (social categorizations) biases can cause each generational cohort that has power and control in the workforce (today would be the baby boomers) to look at succeeding generations from a primarily negative perspective [70]. Consequently, the younger generations perceive work-related behaviors from a problematic viewpoint and are seen as distracted, unmotivated, lacking work ethic, and disloyal. Riggio and Saggi mentioned that members of the dominant generation pursue and decipher evidence that is consistent with stereotypes due to confirmation biases [70]. Stereotypes are difficult to disregard because it is simple to see substantiation of what is accurate, but this could be the result of how generational cohorts process inherent biases and social information [70]. Actual and perceived generational differences are present among older and younger generational cohorts. Zacher stated that because there is a lack of generational theory and methods available, it could be useful to organizational managers to further invest in the investigation of generational differences in the workplace [75].

Stereotypes regarding boomers, Generation X and Generation Y are highly common [76]. Numerous stereotypes, such as the credence that baby boomers are worriers and avaricious and that members of Generation Y are disparaging but tech-savvy, do exist. These traits emerged from experiences that generational cohorts have within their historical context, which creates steady individual differences that characterize generational cohort members [76].

Generational differences in work-related values and attitudes

Work values are the primary source of significant differences among generations, as well as the reason for conflict in the workplace. However, research indicates that if properly managed, those differences can help determine strengths and opportunities [39]. Gursoy et al. [39] argued that it is essential for managers to comprehend the foundation of each generation and their value differences if management wants to establish and maintain a work environment that promotes leadership, motivation, communication, and generational synergy. Additionally, the results of studies suggest that understanding the work values of a multigenerational workforce can help managers identify motivators to combine with the strategies they implement to retain employees [39].

The array of differences that exist among generations in the workplace has gained interest with organizations, researchers, and practitioners [77]. As the generational workforce continue to shift, organizations will experience predictable and evolving issues related to the differences that exist among generational cohorts [78]. The characteristics and experiences that generational cohorts share are what interest researchers and professionals because comprehending such information can help administrators manage generational workers more effectively [77]. Many organizations have executed programs and interventions to help capitalize on generational differences. Constanza et al. posited that such programs and interventions could cause detrimental outcomes instead of positive results if prematurely implemented [77]. Constanza and Finkelstein affirmed that a more useful approach might be to conduct needs assessments that will address generational differences among individuals, and to establish interventions based on characteristics identified through the assessment process [72]. Reis and Braga added that the motivation and preferences regarding work could differ for each generation, and might require modifications to recruitment and retention management practices [79].

Campbell et al. posited that there is a dynamic and mutually constitutive relationship between generations and culture [80]. Categorizing a person as a member of a generation is simple because all you need is the person's birth year; however, the challenge is defining the generational boundaries. Campbell et al. stated that there are a couple of ways to measure generational differences: (a) compare generations cross-sectionally on any variable in a survey, and (b) compare generations cross-temporally using samples of people at the same age and at different times [80]. Research tends to emphasize dissecting the different variances that underlie the generational differences found by using generational cohorts and generational factors [80]. The period and the cohort variance are meaningful for comprehending generational change, therefore, considering generational change as a combination of time plus cohort effects.

Campbell et al. [80] suggested that time and generational effects likely drive the majority of cultural change. Three popular models of generational change are the Strauss and Howe's cyclic model, the modernization model, and the rising extrinsic individualism model [80]. To understand generational change is to understand cultural change, because as culture changes so do the generations of people that are born into that culture. Campbell et al. further implied that the three things that alter culture are technology, cultural contracts, and economic changes.

The diversity of today's workforce has enhanced greatly due to the simultaneous presence of four different generations of workers. Some organizational leaders managing an age diverse workforce tend to treat their employee population the same regardless of their generational membership [6]. Managers will need first to identify and comprehend generational differences and then implement strategies and policies to improve communication and inclusion among generational staff [81]. These efforts can also significantly improve retention and productivity. Corporate leaders should review their leadership styles and understanding of generational differences to ensure that they are adequately ready to address the generational diversity of their staff to mitigate miscommunication and conflict [8]. Conflicts among the generational cohorts are a result of generational diversity. Leaders must comprehend the different generational characteristics, so the workplace environment can be one that exhibits high job satisfaction, work performance, productivity, attendance, and retention [6].

Retaining and motivating a multigenerational workforce

The role of management in retaining employees is to encourage the talent to stay. Understanding why people leave organizations is imperative, but it is more critical to determine the organizational characteristics that make people stay with business entities [82]. It is essential for corporations to retain the best professional talent as it eliminates the recruiting, selection, and hiring costs replacing key employees [82]. James and Mathew [83] defined workplace retention as a deliberate move by an agency to establish an environment that promotes long-term employee engagement. George shared that a favorable work environment, as well as management and leadership styles, social support, development opportunities, autonomy, compensation, and work-life balance, are critical factors in employee retention [82].

Implementing a flexible workplace for employees is necessary for managing talent across all four generations. Eversole et al. explained that for a flexible workplace program to work favorably for the employees and the organization, managers must be competent in the mechanics of work and family programs to operate the programs efficiently and to enforce the rules and guidelines [84]. Organizations that can recruit and retain top performing employees will enhance workplace motivation and reduce turnover.

The main responsibility of a manager is to have a business that function effectively by the subordinates working efficiently, and producing results that are beneficial to the organization [85]. Pandta et al. stated that motivation is one of the primary factors that determine the employees work performance and intentions to stay with the organization [85]. One of the most influential theories of motivation, which can help improve employee retention and productivity, relates to Maslow's Hierarchy of Needs where Maslow articulated that only an unsatisfied need can motivate the behavior with the dominant need being the primary factor for behavior motivation [86]. Factors that convey the importance of employee retention includes costs associated with turnover, company information loss, interruption in customer service, and a company's good will [87]. By maintaining higher employee retention rates, organizations can motivate talented employees to join the company by establishing a secured environment. Sandhya and Kumar mentioned that employee motivation is important factors that can help organizations enhance employee retention and organizational performance [87].

According to Kuyken [88], there is a specific economic impact with an organization when critical employees leave an organization;

especially taking into consideration the knowledge lost when employees depart. The concept of knowledge management is that people have critical skills, experience, and knowledge, and therefore, hold a significant amount of organizational value. Herzberg [15] discovered that employees tend to describe satisfying experiences regarding intrinsic factors about the job itself. Herzberg identifies these factors as motivators [20]. There is more to motivating employees other than compensation and proper working conditions. Hyun and Oh suggested that for an employee to be retainable and truly motivated, the employee's job must contain some fulfillment by providing the worker with opportunities for achievement, recognition, advancement, and responsibility [20].

High employee turnover results in increased costs of resources, recruiting, and time when replacing vacant positions. Employee retention strategies are a crucial element of an organization's vision, mission, values, and their policies, and should be a part of an organization's principles and operations [2]. Many organizational leaders fail to comprehend the reason for their high turnover rates, and only contribute turnover to poor relationships with subordinates and leadership [2]. However, studies show that the main reasons for low retention rates are the lack of opportunities for professional growth, unfair treatment, poor work and life balance, and low wages. Leaders are failing to recognize diversity in the workplace, thereby, adversely affecting production and retention rates among multigenerational workers. Cloutier et al. posited that training and development opportunities motivate employees and influence them to remain loyal to the organization [2]. Rahman and Nas advised that necessary training and development practices are significant to the success of business entities and that employees serve as the essential sources of consistent competitive advantage [89]. When organizations provide employees with development opportunities, the workers will usually reciprocate in positive ways by exhibiting job attitudes that commensurate with the amount of obligation that the companies offer in return [89]. Employee development programs can provide immediate benefit to organizations by increasing motivation and reducing employee turnover.

Therefore, organizations need to develop specific reward strategies to promote, attract, and motivate staff [90]. Establishing a one-size-fits-all approach to reward strategy can be detrimental to organizations because this can lead to direct or indirect financial implications for businesses. Bussin and van Rooy articulated that most managers feel that the most effective way to attract and retain staff is to offer rewards with greater benefits. Rewards can be financial and non-financial and the values of generational workers will determine what motivates them from a reward perspective [90]. The generational mix that plagues most businesses today requires managers to adapt and reinvent their retention and compensation strategies to take into consideration the different values, needs, and work ethics of the generational workforce. It is imperative for managers to consider the preferences and motivations of generational workers to attract and retain good quality employees and to enhance productivity [90]. It is beneficial for organizations to find a way to segment the workforce based on reward preference in a way that will provide a balance between the worker's needs and organizational efficiency.

One of the most vital and emerging issues that inundate the field of human resource development is how to assist organizations with changing workforce demographics successfully and effectively [84]. It will be difficult for businesses to retain a competitive advantage if they are unable to recruit and retain talented workers. Comprehending the needs of employees and creating or modifying organizational cultures are essential tools in talent management. Dwyer and Azevedo asserted that to encourage an organizational culture that embraces a multicultural approach, adopting programs that emphasize diversity as well as including diversity in an organization's mission statement are necessary [91]. The newer generation of workers entering the workplace is different from the older generations that are leaving the workforce due to retirement; therefore, leadership needs to focus on retaining workers of all generations for organizations to remain successful in the future [91].

Participants

This study included a purposeful sample of four managers of a higher education institution. The selection of participants took place irrespective of race and gender. Purposeful sampling is a widely-used technique in qualitative research and involves identifying and selecting research participants who are knowledgeable of and experienced with particular occurrences and interests [92]. The participants for this study included four managers of academic and nonacademic units or departments from an educational institution located in Northwest, Florida. The traditionalist generation constitutes a small percentage of the workforce due to aging and retirement [23]. To account for this, participants could take part in the study if they had experience with managing and retaining employees of the baby boomer, Generation X, and Generation Y cohorts. Participants included managers who had a minimum of 2 years of experience in a management position, and who managed a staff including three or four of the generational cohorts (traditionalists, baby boomers, Generation X, and Generation Y) for at least 2 years. Cleary et al. posited that researchers use purposeful sampling to pursue information by conducting an in-depth examination of the data [93]. I used purposeful sampling to select managers who had experience retaining several generations in the workplace so I could answer the research question.

I used information provided by the Department of Institutional Research to determine potential participants who met the requirements for the study. I adhered to the organization's process for receiving permission and consent for participants to take part in the study. Participants who met the requirements to take part in the study received the consent document and an explanation of confidentiality before the interview. I provided the consent form to each participant via an invitation email to ensure that the participants comprehended the process before they confirmed and signed the agreement. In addition to being knowledgeable and experienced, participants must be available and willing to take part in the study [92]. Participants responded to the email using the words *I consent* to confirm their willingness to take part in the study, and I made sure that each participant understood the purpose of the study and the interview protocol that I would follow. Additionally, I had frequent dialogue with participants to determine a convenient time for the interview. I interviewed the participants at their personal office space to ensure confidentiality, convenience, accessibility, and limited disruptions. Bristowe et al. articulated that keeping the information shared by participants confidential is vital to the integrity of a study [94].

Research Method and Design

Qualitative, quantitative, and mixed methods are three common types of research used to develop a thesis or dissertation [95]. I chose a qualitative method and a case study design based on the conceptual theory of constructivism. Boblin et al. asserted that case studies allow the researcher to investigate a phenomenon while focusing on the dynamics of the case within its real-life context [96]. Bailey suggested that researchers use a qualitative methodology when looking to explore and explicate human behavior [97]. The method and design chosen were appropriate to help me achieve the goal of this study, which was to explore strategies that managers use to retain a multigenerational workforce.

Data collection instruments

Neuman asserted that the individual using a qualitative method of research is the primary person that collects data [98]. I was the primary data collection instrument for the current qualitative case study, and I used semistructured face-to-face interview questions to gain knowledge of strategies higher education managers use to retain their multigenerational staff. The four participants for this study had experience managing three or four of the dominant generations in the workforce, which included traditionalists, baby boomers, Generation X, and Generation Y. Yin advised that interviews are beneficial in research because they help the investigator comprehend participants' experiences and perceptions about certain actions or events [99]. Drew articulated that conducting semistructured interviews is the most efficient approach to explore experiences because interviewees are then able to explain their experiences and perspectives honestly [100].

Data analysis

Data analysis is the most significant phase in qualitative research [101]. Qualitative data analysis provides the investigator with the opportunity to gain information and gather insights that otherwise could overlook traditional data analysis techniques. Lawrence and Tar posited that data analysis in qualitative research entails working with data, organizing it, synthesizing it, and searching for themes and patterns [102]. Thematic analysis, as defined by Percy et al. is the most known form of qualitative analysis and the process involves identifying patterns and themes of data [103]. Mabuza et al. [104] shared five stages of qualitative case study data analysis: (a) familiarization of qualitative data, (b) coding the data, (c) grouping the data into themes and categories, (d) interpreting the themes and categories, and (e) present research findings. I used a thematic analysis method based on Mabuza et al.'s (2014) data analysis process to analyze and organize the research data into categories and themes concerning retention strategies [104]. I first collected the data using face-to-face semistructured interviews. I then transcribed the data, transferred the data into NVivo software to help me group and regroup the data into themes and patterns, assessed the information, and developed conclusions to establish research results. I employed methodological triangulation by retrieving and reviewing electronic documents from the participants' employer's HR website about diversity and inclusion initiatives, strategies, and policies that managers could integrate into their managerial practices to help them retain multigenerational workers.

Presentation of the findings

The central research question for this qualitative single case study was the following: What retention strategies do business managers use to retain their multigenerational workforce? To help me answer the research question, I conducted semistructured interviews with four business leaders purposefully selected based on their success with developing and implementing strategies to retain a multigenerational workforce. In preparation for the interviews, I had the participants decide on a convenient date, time, and location to share information with me about their retention strategies without interruptions. I used my interview protocol to guide the interview process. Participant interviews consisted of six open-ended interview questions, and each interview took place within the allotted 60 minutes. Each participant provided informed consent agreeing to take part in the study prior to participating in the interview process. For the coding process, I used NVivo to aid in the development of themes and categories. I followed Mabuza et al.'s five-step process for reviewing and analyzing qualitative case study data [104]. I used a Sony digital voice recorder to record the interviews. I incorporated member checking into the interview process to allow each participant to validate their responses to ensure that I understood their responses and that I accurately represented each participant's views and perceptions. Harvey explained that using the member checking process improves the credibility and validity of research data [105].

After analyzing and coding data from the participant interview responses and electronic university documents, I identified seven themes (assembled into three thematic categories) that could help leaders retain a multigenerational workforce. I provided an analysis of the correlation between the developed themes and the conceptual framework. The conceptual framework for the current doctoral study was Herzberg's two-factor theory of motivation. Figure 1 shows the first thematic category and three themes (themes 1 through 3) for strategies to retain a multigenerational workforce, Figure 2 depicts the second thematic category and the three themes (themes 4 through 6) for procedures or business practices that can improve retention of a multigenerational workforce, and Figure 3 contains the third thematic category and the theme (theme 7) of a primary challenge that leaders experience when employing strategies for retaining a multigenerational workforce.

Themes 1 through 5 and Theme 7, along with the respective research findings for strategies that managers use to retain a multigenerational workforce, relate to the hygiene tenets (extrinisic)

Thematic Category 1: Strategies to retain a multigenerational workforce		
Theme 1: Foster diversity friendly workplace culture	Theme 2: Effective interpersonal and communiation strategies	Theme 3: Adopt and employ a formal approach

Figure 1: Thematic Category 1 and related themes.

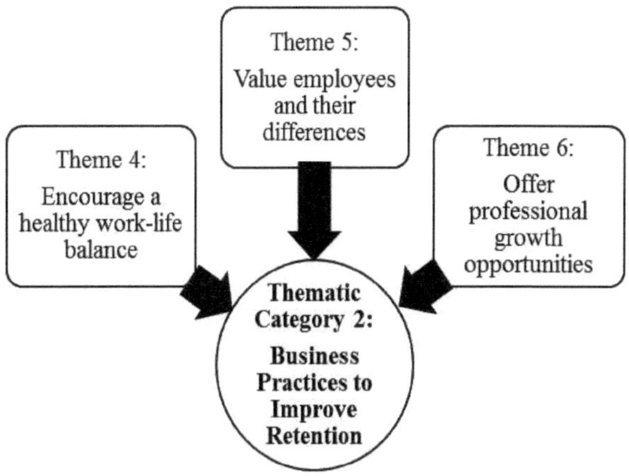

Figure 2: Thematic Category 2 and related themes.

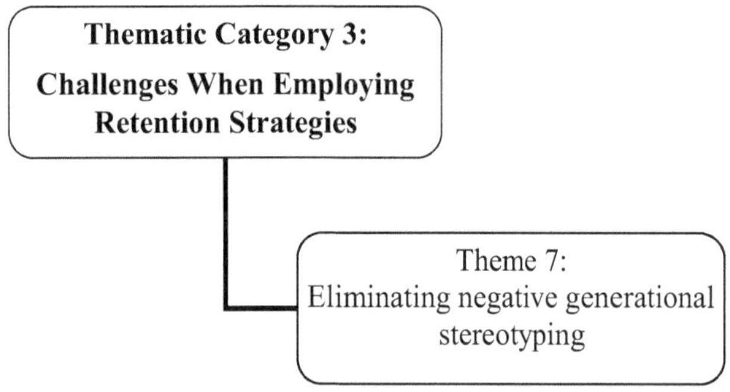

Figure 3: Thematic Category 3 and related theme.

of Herzberg's two-factor theory. Theme 6 and the corresponding findings on strategies that managers use to retain a multigenerational workforce relate to the motivation (intrinsic elements) factors of Herzberg's two-factor theory. Theme 1, fostering a diversity friendly workplace culture, correlates with the work cultures and environments hygiene factor; Theme 2, effective interpersonal and communicaiton strategies, links to the communication and interpersonal techniques hygiene factor; Theme 3, adopting and employing a formal approach to managing and retaining a multigenerational workforce has a parallel relationship to the company and administrative policies hygiene factor; Theme 4, encouraging a healthy work-life balance, correlates with the work cultures and environments hygiene factor; Theme 5, valuing employees and their differences, have a direct relationship to the value from leadership hygiene factor; Theme 6, offer professional growth opportunities, relates to the professional growth and learning opportunities motivation factor; and Theme 7, eliminate negative generational stereotyping, relates to the work cultures and environments hygiene factor.

Business leaders who want to manage workplace challenges caused by the rapid increase in generational diversity in the workforce might benefit from the findings of this study. The results of the current study provided strategies that leaders of higher educational institutions and other business entities can develop and implement to retain a multigenerational workforce. The research findings based on interview responses and unversity documents about diversity and inclusion confirmed and added to the information and knowledge about managing and retaining a multigenerational workforce.

Applications to professional practice

The purpose of this qualitative single case study was to explore retention strategies business managers use to retain their multigenerational workforce. The targeted population consisted of department managers from an educational institution located in northwest Florida who had success in retaining a multigenerational workforce. The population chosen for this study substantiated strategies on how to sustain or improve retention of a multigenerational workforce.

An abundance of older research exists about organizational leaders acknowledging the increase in workplace diversity, and the coexistence of generations in the workforce that offer reasons for better management and retention of an age-diverse workforce. However, minimal research studies exist on effective strategies that leaders can develop and implement to aid in the maintenance and retention of a multigenerational workforce. The dynamics of employment is changing due to an upsurge in diversity in the workforce [106]. Soto and Lugo posited that the increase in workplace diversity can cause leaders to experience challenges with managing diversity and retaining an age-diverse workforce [107]. Business managers and leaders at higher education institutions and other business entities can apply the findings, recommendations, and information about the generational cohorts included in this study to manage workplace diversity, enhance their knowledge base of generational differences, improve workplace cultures and environments, and to reduce negative generational stereotyping in the workplace. The themes that emerged throughout the data analysis process are applicable to higher education institutions and other business entities, and can be beneficial in helping managers develop and employ strategies to retain a multigenerational workforce. Additionally, business managers and leaders at higher education institutions and other organizations can utilize the knowledge and information included in this study to enhance retention, equality, and inclusion of a multigenerational workforce.

Implications for social change

The information that participants shared may help managers and leaders in all business industries identify and comprehend the differences that exist among generational workers, as well as acknowledge the intrinsic and extrinsic factors that the generational cohorts value and prefer. Leaders and managers of higher education institutions and other business entities may find the results of the study helpful in developing and cultivating strategies to manage and retain a multigenerational workforce. The implications for social change includes the potential for business managers and leaders to (a) enrich or increase retention rates of a multigenerational workforce, (b) create employment stability, (c) improve motivation and productivity, (d) and enhance both organizational and community relations.

Recommendations for further research

Recommendations for further research include retention strategies of a multigenerational workforce of other types of business entities other than higher education institutions. Conducting a study inclusive of several organizations in different business industries can offer leaders of non-education institutions effective strategies and business practices to retain an age-diverse workforce. Future research should consider a quantitative or mixed methods approach to examine or explore the retention strategies to determine which are most and least effective. Additionally, I recommend that researchers explore geographical locations outside of northwest Florida, and to use a sample size of more than four participants. Enlarging research efforts to cover a greater geographical area and increasing the number of research participants could generate more in-depth and efficient strategies that leaders in all industries can use to retain a multigenerational workforce.

Managers, administrators, and other individuals who hold authoritative positions could use the information, research findings, and recommendations in this study to mitigate turnover of multigenerational employees. Leaders at higher education institutions and other types of businesses can use the knowledge gained from the information in this study to (a) foster a diversity friendly workplace culture, (b) develop effective interpersonal communication strategies, (c) value generational employees and their differences, (d) develop professional learning and growth opportunities for generational workers, and (e) eliminate negative generational stereotyping in the workplace. By implementing these strategies and business practices, managers and leaders could improve retention, motivation, and productivity of a multigenerational workforce.

Conclusions

A significant and emerging issue that some business entities have difficulties with is successfully and effectively managing workplace diversity because managing diversity requires a wealth of skills and knowledge [84]. Differences in the age, intrinsic and extrinsic motivator preferences, and the characteristics of generational workers can lead to challenges for business managers in retaining their multigenerational staff [9]. After analyzing and coding the data, seven themes emerged through thematic analysis. The key themes included: (a) fostering a diversity friendly workplace culture, (b) developing and employing effective interpersonal communication strategies, (c) valuing generational employees and their differences, and (d) adopting and employing a formal approach to retaining a multigenerational workforce. Business leaders may use the themes identified in this research study to guide their efforts in gaining additional insight on the challenges of managing and retaining an age-diverse workforce, and to establish effective strategies to improve retention, motivation, and productivity of a multigenerational workforce.

The findings of the current research study may contribute to an enriched comprehension of the varying and distinctive values, characteristics, preferences, attitudes, and beliefs of a multigenerational workforce. Successful strategies for retaining an age-diverse workforce in a continuous altering business environment are imperative to the success and survival of most companies. Thus, deploying the retention strategies and recommendations identified in this study may assist business leaders with retaining and managing a multigenerational workforce, improving employee motivation, and enhancing workplace productivity.

References

1. Schullery N (2013) Workplace engagement and generational differences in values. Business and Professional Communication Quarterly 76: 252-265.
2. Cloutier O, Felusiak L, Hill C, Pemberton-Jones E (2015) The importance of developing strategies for employee retention. Journal of Leadership, Accountability and Ethics 12: 119-129.
3. Moore S, Grunberg L, Krause A (2015) Generational differences in workplace expectations: A comparison of production and professional workers. Current Psychology 34: 346-362.
4. Lester S, Standifer R, Schultz N, Windsor J (2012) Actual versus perceived generational differences at work: An empirical examination. Journal of Leadership & Organization Studies 19: 341-354.
5. Bennett J, Pitt M, Price S (2012) Understanding the impact of generational issues in the workplace. Facilities 30: 278-288.
6. Nelsey L, Brownie S (2012) Effective leadership, teamwork and mentoring – Essential elements in promoting generational cohesion in the nursing workforce and retaining nurses. Collegian 19: 197-202.
7. Bourne B (2015) Phenomenological study of generational response to organizational change. Journal of Managerial Issues 27: 141-159.
8. Al-Asfour A, Lettau L (2014) Strategies for leadership styles for multi-generational workforce. Journal of Leadership, Accountability and Ethics 11: 58-69.
9. Zemke R, Raines C, Filipczak B (2013) Generations at work: Managing the clash of boomers, gen Xers, and gen Yers in the workplace. AMACON, New York.
10. Bureau of Labor Statistics (2013) Labor force projections to 2022: The labor force participation rate continues to fall. U.S. Department of Labor, USA.
11. Willyerd K (2012) The 2020 workplace.
12. Hannay M, Fretwell C (2011) The higher education workplace: Meeting the needs of multiple generations. Research in Higher Education 10: 1-12.
13. Matz-Costa C, Pitt-Catsouphes M (2009) Workplace flexibility as an organizational response to the aging of the workplace: A comparison of nonprofit and for-profit organizations. Journal of Social Service Research 36: 68-80.
14. Herzberg F (1964) The motivation-hygiene concept and problems of manpower. Personnel Administration 27: 3-7.
15. Herzberg F (1966) Work and the nature of man. Cleveland: World Publication Company.
16. Herzberg F (1986) One more time: How do you motivate employees? Harvard Business Review, Boston.
17. Sankar M (2015) Impact of hygiene factors on employee retention: Experimental study on paper industry. Indian Journal of Management Science, pp: 58-61.
18. Herzberg F (1959) Work and the nature of man. OH: World Publishing Company, Cleveland.
19. Catania G, Randall R (2013) The relationship between age and intrinsic and extrinsic motivation in workers in a Maltese cultural context. International Journal of Arts & Sciences 6: 31-45.
20. Hyun S, Oh H (2011) Reexamination of Herzberg's two-factor theory of motivation in the Korean army foodservice operations. Journal of Foodservice Business Research 14: 100-121.
21. Kim J (2015) What increases public employees' turnover intention? Public Personnel Management 44: 496-503.
22. Fernandez-Duran JJ (2016) Defining generational cohorts for marketing in Mexico. Journal of Business Research 69: 435-444.
23. Wiedmer T (2015) Generations do differ: Best practices in leading traditionalists, boomers, and generations X, Y, and Z. Delta Kappa Gamma Bulletin 82: 51-58.
24. Eastman J, Liu J (2012) The impact of generational cohorts on status consumption: An exploratory look at generational cohort and demographics on status consumption. Journal of Consumer Marketing 29: 93-102.
25. Allison S (2013) Employment and the millennials. Youth Studies Australia 32: 81-84.
26. Eyerman R, Turner BS (1998) Outline of a theory of generations. European Journal of Social Theory 1: 91-106.
27. Becton JB, Walker JW, Jones-Farmer A (2014) Generational differences in workplace behavior. Journal of Applied Social Psychology 44: 175-189.
28. Kupperschmidt B (2000) Multigenerational employees: Strategies for effective management. The Health Care Manager 19: 65-76.
29. Lyons S, Schweitzer L, Ng E, Kuron L (2012) Comparing apples to apples: A qualitative investigation of career mobility patterns across four generations. Career Development International 17: 333-357.
30. Colette T, Stein L (2014) Stories of generational leadership: Women higher education administrator's voices. Advancing Women in Leadership 34: 1-10.
31. Jora R, Khan S (2014) Motivating multigenerational human resource. International Journal of Organizational Behaviour & Management Perspectives 3: 1276-1281.
32. Ledimo O (2015) Generational differences in organizational justice perceptions: An exploratory investigation across three generational cohorts. Foundation of Management 7: 129-142.
33. Wang Y, Peng Y (2015) An alternative approach to understanding generational differences. Industrial and Organizational Psychology 8: 390-395.
34. DeVaney S (2015) Understanding the millennial generation. Journal of Financial Service Professionals 69: 11-14.
35. Duh H, Struwig M (2015) Justification of generational cohort segmentation in South Africa. International Journal of Emerging Markets 10: 89-101.
36. Bell J (2013) Five generations in the nursing workforce. Journals for Nurses in Professional Development 29: 205-210.
37. Hendricks J, Cope V (2012) Generational diversity: What nurse managers need to know. Journal of Advanced Nursing 69: 717-725.
38. Wok S, Hashim J (2012) Communicating and sharing working relationships with older employees. Journal of Communication Management 17: 100-121.
39. Gursoy D, Chi C, Karadag E (2013) Generational differences in work values and attitudes among frontline and service contact employees. International Journal of Hospitality Management 32: 40-48.

40. Coulter JS, Faulkner DC (2014) The multigenerational workforce. Professional Case Management 19: 46-51.

41. Reinbeck D, Fitzsimons V (2014) Bridging nursing's digital generation gap. Nursing Management 45: 12-14.

42. Ferri-Reed J (2013) Leading a multigenerational workforce. The Journal for Quality and Participation 35: 12-14.

43. Hansen J, Leuty M (2012) Work values across generations. Journal of Career Assessment 20: 34-52.

44. Benson K, Connell K (2014) Fair trade consumption from the perspective of US baby boomers. Social Responsibility Journal 10: 364-382.

45. Tavener M, Byles J, Loxton D (2014) Research expert perceptions of the popular baby boomer image. Australasian Journal on Ageing 33: E31-E35.

46. Loroz P, Helgeson J (2013) Boomers and their babies: An exploratory study comparing psychological profiles and advertising appeal effectiveness across two generations. Journal of Marketing Theory and Practice 21: 289-306.

47. Srinivasan V (2012) Multigenerations in the workforce: Building collaboration. IIMB Management Review 24: 48-66.

48. Kaifi B, Nafei W, Khanfar N, Kaifi M (2012) A multigenerational workforce: Managing and understanding millennials. International Journal of Business and Management 7: 88-93.

49. Roodin P, Mendelson M (2013) Multiple generations at work: Current and future trends. Journal of Intergenerational Relationships 11: 213-222.

50. Boveda I, Metz AJ (2016) Predicting end-of-career transitions for baby boomers nearing retirement age. The Career Development Quarterly 64: 153-168.

51. Salb D (2015) Using technology to retain baby boomers in the workforce. Computer and Information Science 8: 180-185.

52. Krahn H, Galambos N (2014) Work values and beliefs of Generation X and Generation Y. Journal of Youth Studies 17: 92-112.

53. Zopiatis A, Krambia-Kapardis M, Varnavas A (2012) Y-ers, X-ers and boomers: Investigating the multigenerational (mis)perceptions in the hospitality workplace. Tourism and Hospitality Research 12: 101-121.

54. Hernaus T, Vokic N (2014) Work design for different generational cohorts. Journal of Organizational Change Management 27: 615-641.

55. Bolton R, Parasuraman A, Hoefnagels A, Mighels N, Kabadayi S, et al. (2013) Understanding Generation Y and their use of social media: A review and research agenda. Journal of Service Management 24: 245-267.

56. Kamau J, Njau M, Wanyagi J (2014) Factors influencing work attitude among 'Y' generation (a case of Africa Nazarene University). European Scientific Journal 1: 636-640.

57. Towns M (2013) Millennials-The new normal. The Canadian Nurse 109: 32.

58. Hutchinson D, Brown J, Longworth K (2012) Attracting and maintaining the Y Generation in nursing: A literature review. Journal of Nursing Management 20: 444-450.

59. Holt S, Marques J, Way D (2012) Bracing for Millennial workforce: Looking for ways to inspire Generation Y. Journal of Leadership, Accountability & Ethics 9: 81-93.

60. Akkucuk U, Turan C (2016) Mobile use and online preferences of the millenials: A study in Yalova. Journal of Internet Banking and Commerce 21: 1-11.

61. Kian TS, Fauziah W, Yusoff W, Rajah S (2013) Relationship between motivations and citizenship performance among generation X and generation Y. International Journal of Academic Research in Business and Social Sciences 3: 53-68.

62. Young AM, Hinsley MD (2012) Identifying millennials key influences from early childhood: Insights into current consumer preferences. Journal of Consumer Marketing 29: 146-155.

63. Murray K (2015) Leadership Q&A. Journal of Nursing Management 47: 56.

64. Ferri-Reed J (2014) Millennializing the workplace. The Journal for Quality and Participation 37: 13-14.

65. Winter RP, Jackson BA (2016) Work values preferences of Generation Y: Performance relationship insights in the Australian Public Service. The International Journal of Human Resource Management 27: 1997-2015.

66. Swan J (2012) Why are multigenerational workplaces important, and what benefits can they bring? Quality in Ageing and Older Adults 13: 270-274.

67. Ravazzani S (2016) Understanding approaches to managing diversity in the workplace. Equality, Diversity and Inclusion: An International Journal 35: 154-168.

68. Heyler R, Lee D (2012) The twenty-first century multiple generation workforce. Education + Training 54: 565-578.

69. DeMeulenaere K, Boone C, Buyl T (2016) Unraveling the impact of workforce age diversity on labor productivity: The moderating role of firm size and job security. Journal of Organizational Behavior 37: 193-212.

70. Riggio RE, Saggi K (2015) Belief in generational stereotypes: Why there is a there. Industrial and Organizational Psychology 8: 340-342.

71. Dow B, Joosten M, Biggs S, Kimberley H (2016) Age encounters: Exploring age and intergenerational perceptions. Journal of Intergenerational Relationships 14: 104-118.

72. Constanza DP, Finkelstein LM (2015) Generationally based differences in the workplace: Is there a there there? Industrial and Organizational Psychology: Perspectives on Science and Practice 8: 308-323.

73. Tajfel H, Turner JC (1979) An integrative theory of intergroup conflict. The social psychology of intergroup relations, Monterey, Brooks/Cole, CA, pp: 33-47.

74. Heritage B, Breen L, Roberts L (2016) In-groups, out-groups, and their contrasting perceptions of values among generational cohorts of Australians. Australian Psychologist 51: 246-255.

75. Zacher H (2015) Using lifespan developmental theory and methods as a viable alternative to the study of generational differences at work. Industrial and Organizational Psychology 8: 342-346.

76. Cox CB, Coulton G (2015) Fire all the boomers: How generational labeling legitimizes age discrimination. Industrial and Organizational Psychology 8: 372-376.

77. Constanza DP, Badger JM, Fraser RL, Severt JB, Gade PA (2012) Generational differences in the work-related attitudes: A meta-analysis. Journal of Business Psychology 27: 375-394.

78. Na'Desh F (2015) Revising culture to meet shifting multigenerational workforce needs. Organization Development Journal 33: 65-79.

79. Reis GG, Braga BM (2016) Employer attractiveness from a generational perspective: Implications for employer branding. Revista De Admistracao 51: 103-116.

80. Campbell WK, Campbell SM, Siedor LE, Twenge JM (2015) Generational differences are real and useful. Industrial and Organizational Psychology 8: 324-408.

81. Phillips M (2016) Embracing the multigenerational nursing team. MedSurg Nursing 25: 197-199.

82. George C (2015) Retaining professional workers: What makes them stay? Employee Relations 37: 102-121.

83. James L, Mathew L (2012) Employee retention strategies: IT industry. SMS Journal of Indian Management 9: 79-87.

84. Eversole B, Venneberg D, Crowder CL (2012) Creating a flexible organizational culture to attract and retain talented workers across generations. Advances in Developing Human Resources 14: 607-625.

85. Pandta J, Deri L, Galambos A, Galambos T (2015) Two-factor analysis of employee motivation at postal traffic department in Novi Sad. European Journal of Economic Studies 12: 101-111.

86. Sandrick C, Contacos-Sawyer TB (2014) Effects of Long term care insurance on employee motivation, satisfaction, and retention. Competition Forum 12: 228-233.

87. Sandhya K, Kumar D (2011) Employee retention by motivation. Indian Journal of Science and Technology 4: 1778-1782.

88. Kuyken K (2012) Knowledge communities: Towards a re-thinking of intergenerational knowledge transfer. Vine: The Journal of Information and Knowledge Management Systems 42: 365-381.

89. Rahman BW, Nas Z (2013) Employee development and turnover intention: Theory validation. European Journal of Training and Development 37: 564-579.

90. Bussin M, van Rooy DJ (2014) Total rewards strategy for a multi-generational

workforce in a financial institution. Journal of Human Resource Management 12: 1-11.

91. Dwyer RJ, Azevedo A (2016) Preparing leaders for the multi-generational workforce. Journal of Enterprising Communities 10: 281-305.

92. Palinkas LA, Horwitz SM, Green CA, Wisdom JP, Duan N, et al. (2015) Purposeful sampling for qualitative data collection and analysis in mixed method implementation research. Administration and Policy in Mental Health and Mental Health Services Research 42: 533-544.

93. Cleary M, Horsfall J, Hayter M (2014) Data collection and sampling in qualitative research: Does size matter? Journal of Advanced Nursing 70: 473-475.

94. Bristowe K, Selman L, Murtagh F (2015) Qualitative research methods in renal medicine: An introduction. Nephrol, Dialysis, Transplantation 30: 1424-1431.

95. McCusker K, Gunaydin S (2015) Research using qualitative, quantitative or mixed methods and choice based on the research. Perfusion 30: 537-542.

96. Boblin S, Ireland S, Kirkpatrick H, Robertson K (2013) Using Stake's qualitative case study approach to explore implementation of evidence-based practice. Qualitative Health Research 23: 1267-1275.

97. Bailey LF (2014) The origin and success of qualitative research. International Journal of Market Research, 56: 167-185.

98. Neuman D (2014) Qualitative research in educational communications and technology: A brief introduction to principles and procedures. Journal of Computing in Higher Education 26: 69-86.

99. Yin RK (2012) Applications of case study research. (3rd edn.), Thousand Oaks, Sage, CA.

100. Drew H (2014) Overcoming barriers: Qualitative interviews with German elites. Electronic Journal of Business Research Methods 12: 77-86.

101. Potestio ML, Boyd JM, Bagshaw SM, Heyland D, Oxland P, et al. (2015) Engaging the public to identify opportunities to improve critical care: A qualitative analysis of an open community forum. Plos ONE 10: 1-11.

102. Lawrence J, Tar U (2013) The use of grounded theory techniques as a practical tool for qualitative data collection and analysis. Electronic Journal of Business Research Methods 11: 29-40.

103. Percy WH, Kostere K, Kostere S (2015) Generic qualitative research in psychology. The Qualitative Report 20: 76-85.

104. Mabuza LH, Govender I, Ogunbanjo GA, Mash B (2014) African primary care research: Qualitative data analysis and writing results. African Journal of Primary Health Care & Family Medicine 6: 1-5.

105. Harvey L (2015) Beyond member-checking: A dialogic approach to the research interview. International Journal of Research & Method in Education 38: 23-38.

106. Holian R (2015) Work, career, age and life-stage: Assumptions and preferences of multigenerational workforce. Labour & Industry 25: 278-292.

107. Soto M, Lugo M (2013) Multigenerational differences in the Puerto Rican workforce. Journal of Business Diversity 13: 65-82.

Performance of Micro Enterprises Run by Women Self Help Groups in Madurai, Ramnad and Dindigul Districts of Tamil Nadu

Selvaraj N*

Saraswathi Narayanan College, Madurai,Tamilnadu, India

Abstract

Women can find gainful employment through entrepreneurship they will not become a social burden and the parents may not compel them to get married early. Once they find their way to entrepreneurship and earn for themselves, they become active members of the Society having courage to correct the faults of their male counterparts. Women are increasingly being conscious of their existence, their rights and their work situation. The performance of enterprises depends on the degree to which the women are involved in managing their enterprises. If women involve themselves in various managerial decisions, it would have a positive impact on their enterprise. The Tamilnadu's Women Development Project conceptualized the Self Help Groups under the name of Mahalir Thittam. This scheme is a replication and phased up scaling of Tamilnadu Women Development Programme successes. Keeping in view of the objectives of the study, the research has identified with the help of the concerned persons (officers & leaders of SHGs) women those who are engaged in running Micro enterprises for selecting the sample.

Keywords: Micro enterprises; Performance; Investment; Capital; Return

Introduction

Micro-enterprises represent the earliest stage of business development - a stage where the owner-founder is typically also the manager of the firm. At this stage, the management decisions of the founder or entrepreneur, his/her intentions about the business, and his background and aspirations are intrinsically linked with the success of the business itself.

The hidden entrepreneurial potentials of women have gradually been changing with the growing sensitivity to the role and economic status in Society. Women are increasingly being conscious of their existence, their rights and their work situation. And yet, the middle class strata women have accepted their role and are not ready to alter for fear of a social backlash. Today, women entrepreneurs represent a group of women who have broken away from the beaten track and are exploring new avenues of economic participation. Among the reasons for women to run organized enterprises are their skill and knowledge, their talents and abilities in business and a compelling desire of wanting to do something positive.

If women can find gainful employment through entrepreneurship they will not become a social burden and the parents may not compel them to get married early. Once they find their way to entrepreneurship and earn for themselves, they become active members of the Society having courage to correct the faults of their male counterparts [1].

With the increase in the number of educated women, there is considerable awareness among women to be self-reliant, thereby changing the role of women in the Society. Entrepreneurship offers an excellent scope for women to give expression to their urge for empowerment, to prove themselves as a potent economic factor contributing their best to the growth of economy by participating in decision making at all levels.

The major focus of this Tamilnadu Women Development Corporation has been to provide support to economically disadvantaged women. However, the Board of Directors viewed that for development of entrepreneurship among women and to encourage them to set up their own business ventures, exclusive adherence to poverty criteria would be unsuitable. Therefore the Corporation will be funding entrepreneurial programmes, which will be open to all potential women entrepreneurs, preferably first generation.

The Tamilnadu's Women Development Project conceptualized the Self Help Groups under the name of Mahalir Thittam. This scheme is a replication and phased up scaling of Tamilnadu Women Development Programme successes. Initially, it was proposed to cover about 10 lakh poor women of the State over the project period. This scheme was announced by the year 1996-97 and started its full swing operation in 1997-98. This scheme is projected to women who belong to the class of poverty line. These women join in a cluster to promote their social and economic empowerment. Social empowerment is acquired by their equal status, participation and powers of decision making at the community and village levels.

The performance of enterprises depends on the degree to which the women are involved in managing their enterprises. If women involve themselves in various managerial decisions, it would have a positive impact on their enterprise. An attempt has been made in this paper to discuss enterprising, enterprise involvement and enterprise management among the women SHG in the study area. The relationship between the degree of enterprise management and the performance in enterprise is also analyzed to reveal the importance of the enterprise management among the women SHGs.

Statement of the Problem

A self-help group (SHG) is a voluntary association of people with

***Corresponding author:** Selvaraj N, Assistant Professor of Commerce, Saraswathi Narayanan College, Madurai, Tamilnadu, India
E-mail: selvaraj_narayanan@yahoo.com

common goal. The concept of 'Self Help Group' appears to be a good alternative strategy to involve people in the development process [2]. In these circumstances it is felt important and necessary to study the performance of empowerment acquired by women.

Hence, the present study is undertaken to analyse the entrepreneurship of women for Madurai, Ramnad and Dindigul districts of Tamil Nadu.

Period of Study

The field survey was conducted from September 2014 to March 2015 for the collection of primary data. The reference period of the survey was 2014-2015.

Objectives of the Study

The basic objectives of the study are to learn about the performance of the micro entrepreneurs (women).

Sampling design

For the purpose of primary data collection, three districts namely Madurai, Ramnad and Dindigul have been selected the main reason for selecting these districts is that the former are a developed district, the middle is backward one and the last is developing district. Keeping in view of the objectives of the study, the research has identified with the help of the concerned persons (officers & leaders of SHGs) women those who are engaged in running Micro enterprises for selecting the sample [3,4]. Out of the total of 450 sample women Micro entrepreneurs each 150 from the districts were randomly selected from SHGs functioning under NGOs and Mahilar Thittam Schemes in each block of three districts by using proportionate sample method.

Percentage analysis

The conventional percentage analysis has been carried out to fulfill the objectives of the study.

This paper discusses the nature of enterprise owned by women SHGs in the study area, sources of capital and return on investment.

Nature of enterprise

The women SHGs may run the enterprise according to their capability relating to finance, management, marketing and risk - taking ability [5]. The nature of enterprise selected by them is influenced by the scope of business, profitability and other aspects. The nature and number of enterprises are presented in Table 1.

It is understood from the Table 1 that in the case of women SHGs in Madurai district, the dominant enterprises of women SHG relate to Catering, Edible items, Milch animals, handicrafts and Lamination which constitute 48 (32.00%), 36 (24.00%), 32 (21.33%), 21 (14.00%) and 13 (8.67%) respectively, whereas in the case of women SHG in Ramnad district, the dominant enterprises relate to palmleaf products, bricklin, fishnet making, dry fish and masala powder manufacturing which constitute 52 (34.67%), 35 (23.33%), 23 (15.33%), 22 (14.67%) and 18 (12.00%) to the total respectively. In the case of Dindigul district, the dominant enterprises are Sari textile (96), coir making (21), Tamrind preservation (12) Handicraft (14) and catering (7).

Years of experience in SHG

The year of experience of the unit shows the number of years the unit has been working since its establishment. It indicates the life period of the business unit completed. It may influence the profitability and also the perceptions of various problems encountered in running the enterprise. The years of experience in the present study, is classified as less than 2 years, 2 to 5 years and 5 years and above. The distribution of enterprises according to the years of experience is shown in Table 2.

It has been revealed from the Table 2 that in the case of women entrepreneurs in Madurai district, maximum of 83 (55.33%) of them have 2 to 5 years of experience followed by 49 (32.67%) of them have more than 5 years of experience and 18 (12.00%) of them have less than 2 years of experience, where as in the case of women entrepreneurs in Ramnad district, maximum of 91 (60.67%) of them have 2 to 5 years of experience followed by 47 (31.33%) of them have less than 2 years of experience. Similar trend was also found in Dindigul district. Out of 150, majority of them (56.67%) have 2 to 5 years of experience.

Investment in the enterprise

Investment is essential for purchasing capital goods and also for working capital needs. The capital invested at the time of starting the production is called initial capital. But the capital requirements

Sl. No.	Nature of Enterprises	Madurai		Ramnad		Dindigul	
		No. of Respondents	Percent age	No. of Respondents	Percent age	No. of Respondents	Percent age
1.	Milch Animals	32	21.33	--	--	--	--
2.	Handicrafts	21	14.00	--	--	--	--
3.	Lamination	13	8.67	--	--	--	--
4.	Catering	48	32.00	--	--	--	--
5.	Edible items	36	24.00	--	--	--	--
6.	Palm Leaf Products	--	--	52	34.67	--	--
7.	Bricklin	--	--	35	23.33	--	--
8.	Fishnet making	--	--	23	15.33	--	--
9.	Dry fish	--	--	22	14.67	--	--
10.	Masala Product manufacturing	--	--	18	12.00	--	--
11.	Sari Textile	--	--	--	--	96	64.00
12.	Coir Making	--	--	--	--	21	14.00
13.	Tamrind Preservation	--	--	--	--	12	8.00
14.	Handicrafts	--	--	--	--	14	9.33
15.	Catering	--	--	--	--	7	4.67
	Total	150	100.00	50	100.00	50	150.00

Source: Primary data.

Table 1: Nature of enterprises of women shgs.

Experience (in years)	Madurai		Ramnad		Dindigul	
	Number of entrepreneurs	Percentage	Number of entrepreneurs	Percentage	Number of entrepreneurs	Percentage
Less than 2 years	18	12.00	12	8.00	16	10.67
2 – 5 years	83	55.33	91	60.67	85	56.67
5 years and above	49	32.67	47	31.33	49	32.66
Total	150	100.00	150	100.00	150	100.00

Source: Primary Data.

Table 2: Years of experience and number of women entrepreneurs.

Investment (in Rupes)	Madurai		Ramnad		Dindigul	
	No. of enterprises	Percentage	Number of enterprises	Percentage	Number of enterprises	Percentage
Less than 10000	15	10.00	7	4.66	9	6.00
10000 to 20000	16	10.67	9	6.00	15	10.00
20000 to 30000	28	18.67	18	12.00	37	24.67
30000 to 40000	41	27.33	22	14.66	54	36.00
40000 to 50000	36	24.00	53	35.34	11	7.33
50000 and above	14	9.33	41	27.34	24	16.00
Total	150	100.00	150	100.00	150	100.00

Source: Primary Data.
Note: Mean Investment is Rs.4153.

Table 3: Investment pattern in the enterprises.

Source of Capital	Madurai			Ramnad			Dindigul		
	*No. of Enterprises	Percentage	Rank	*No. of Enterprises	Percentage	Rank	*No. of Enterprises	Percentage	Rank
Own /spouse/ parent	106	70.66	IV	131	87.33	III	123	82.00	V
Friends/ Relatives	140	93.33	III	115	76.67	IV	140	13.33	II
Private money lenders	56	37.33	V	38	25.33	V	136	90.67	IV
SHG	146	97.33	II	148	98.67	II	146	97.33	II
Commercial bank	150	100	I	150	100	I	150	100.00	I

Source: Primary Data.
*multi-Response

Table 4: Source of capital of the entrepreneurs.

grow day by day as the business activities start growing. Usually, demand for goods, cost of raw materials and the like would require additional investment to manage the enterprise. The investment made, as measured at the time of survey, is classified as less than Rs.10000, Rs.10000 to Rs.20000, Rs.20000 to Rs.30000, Rs.30000 to Rs.40000, Rs.40000 to Rs.50000, and Rs.50000 and above. The distribution of enterprises according to the amount of investment made is shown in Table 3.

It has been revealed from the Table 3 that in the case of women entrepreneurs in Madurai district, maximum of 41 (27.33) of them had investment of Rs.30000 to Rs.40000, followed by 36 (24.00) of them had investment of Rs.40000 to Rs.50000, 28 (18.67%) of them had investment of Rs.20000 to Rs.30000, 16 (10.67%) of them had investment of Rs.10000 to Rs.20000, 15 (10.00) of them had investment of less than Rs.10000 and 14 (9.33) of them had investment of more than Rs.50000 whereas in the case of women entrepreneurs in Ramnad district, maximum of 53 (35.34) of them had investment of Rs.40000 to Rs.50000, followed by 41 (27.34) of them had investment of above Rs.50000, 22 (14.66) of them had an investment of Rs.30000 to Rs.40000, 18 (12.00) of them had investment of Rs.20000 to Rs.30000, 9 (6.00) of them had investment of Rs.10000 to Rs.20000 and 7 (4.66) of them had investment of less than Rs.10000 [6]. In the case of Dindigul district, majority of the respondents (36.00%) had investment of Rs.30000 to 40000 followed by Rs.20000 to 30000 (27.00%).

Sources of capital

The sources of capital indicate from where the enterprises mobilized the capital. The source of capital determines the cost and profitability of the enterprise. In general the enterprise may mobilize their capital from one or more sources. So, in the present study, the entrepreneurs are allowed to make multi-responses in the sources of capital is classified as own/spouse/parents, friends and relatives, private money lenders, chit funds and commercial banks. In order to analyze the important sources of capital among the women entrepreneurs, the number of source are taken in to account, the percentage to the total for each source indicates the importance of the source details and they are presented in Table 4.

From the Table 4 it has been observed that in the case of women entrepreneurs in Madurai district, the important source of capital among the women entrepreneurs are Commercial banks, SHGs, friends and relatives, own/spouse/parent and private money lenders, since the percentage to the total are 100, 97.33, 93.33, 70.66 and 37.33 respectively, whereas in the case of women entrepreneurs in Ramnad, the important sources of capital among the women entrepreneurs are commercial banks, SHGs, own/spouse/parents friends and relatives and private money lenders, since the respective percentage to the total are 100, 98.67, 87.33, 76.67 and 25.33. Similar trend was found in Dindigul district also.

Monthly return from the enterprise

The performance of the enterprise is decided from the return received by the enterprises. The return indicates the total net income drawn from the enterprises by the women entrepreneurs. The net income is calculated per month by word of mouth among the entrepreneurs. They were allowed to mention the average monthly return from the enterprise at the time of survey. The average monthly return from the enterprise is classified as less than Rs.500, Rs.500 to Rs.1000, Rs.1000 to Rs.1500, Rs.1500 to Rs.2000 and Rs.2000 and above. The distribution of the enterprises according to the average monthly return is shown in Table 5.

It has been inferred from the Table 5 that in the case of women entrepreneurs in Madurai district, out of 150 respondents, 43 (28.67%) of them are earning an income of Rs.500 to Rs.1000, followed by 30 (20.00%) of them are earning an income of Less than Rs.500 and 29 (19.33%) of them are earning an income of Rs.1000 to Rs.1500 whereas in the case of women entrepreneurs in Ramnad maximum of 41 (27.33%) of them are earning an income of Rs.1000 to Rs.1500 followed by 30 (20.00%) of them are earning an income of Rs.500 to Rs.1000, 29 (19.33%) of them are earning an income of Rs.1500 to Rs.2000 [7,8]. In the case of Dindigul district, out of 150 respondents, maximum of 46 respondents of them an earning Rs.500 to 1000 followed by less than Rs.500 (31%) and Rs.1000 to Rs.1500 (29%).

Return on investment

The return on investment is the ratio, between the return and investment of enterprises. It is calculated by the annual return and annual investment during the period of the year. The return on investment is the real indicator of the profitability of units. In the present study, the return on investment is as told by the women entrepreneurs. The return on investment is only an average of various returns on investment in a unit during its performance. The average rate of return on investment in the study is classified as less than 5%, 5% to 8%, 8% to 11%, 11% to 14%, 14% to 17%, and 17% and above [9].

It has been inferred from the Table 6, in the case of Madurai district, maximum of 44 respondents have earned 8 to 11% of return on investment followed by 11 to 14% (36%), less than 5% (29%) and 5 to 8% (24), whereas in the case of women entrepreneurs in Ramnad, maximum of 43 (28.67) of them earned an average return on investment of 5% to 8%, followed by 32 (21.33) of them earned an average return on investment of 8% to 11%, 29 (19.33) of them earned an average return on investment of less than 5%, 17 (11.33) of them earned an average return on investment of 11% to 14%and 3 (2%) of them earned an average return on investment of above 17% [10]. In the case of women entrepreneurs in Dindigul district, 54 (36.00) of them earned an average return on investment of 8 to 11%, followed by 37 (24.67%) of them earned an average return on investment 11 to 14%, 21 (14.00%) of them earned an average return on investment 5% to 8% and 19 (12.67%) of them earned an average return on investment of less than 5%.

Summary of Findings

It is revealed from the analysis that in Madurai district a majority of women entrepreneurs (28.67%) are getting an average monthly return of Rs.500 to Rs.1000 on their investment followed by 20.00% earning an average monthly return of less than Rs.500. Only 19.33% of the entrepreneurs earn an average monthly return of Rs.1000 to 1500.

It is understood from the analysis that in Ramnad district the majority of women entrepreneurs (27.33) are getting in an average monthly return of Rs.1000 to Rs.1500 on their investment, followed by 20.00% earning an average monthly return of Rs.500 to Rs.1000. Only 19.33% of the entrepreneurs earn an average monthly return of Rs.1500 to Rs.2000.

In the case of Dindigul district, the majority of women entrepreneurs (30.67%) are getting an average monthly return of Rs.500 to Rs.1000 on their investment, followed by 20.67% earning an average monthly return of less than Rs.500. Only 19.33% of the entrepreneurs earn an

Monthly Return (in Rupees)	Madurai		Ramnad		Dindigul	
	No. of enterprises	Percentage	Number of enterprises	Percentage	Number of enterprises	Percentage
Less than 500	30	20.00	21	18.00	31	20.67
500 to 1000	43	28.67	30	20.00	46	30.67
1000 to 1500	29	19.33	41	27.33	29	19.33
1500 to 2000	26	17.33	29	19.33	23	15.33
2000 and above	22	14.67	23	15.34	21	14.00
Total	150	100.00	150	100.00	150	100.00

Source: Primary data.

Note: Mean investment is Rs.1243.

Table 5: Monthly return from the enterprises.

Return on Investment (in percentage)	Madurai		Ramnad		Dindigul	
	No. of enterprises	Percentage	Number of enterprises	Percentage	Number of enterprises	Percentage
Less than 5	29	19.33	29	19.33	19	12.67
5 to 8	24	16.00	43	28.67	21	14.00
8 to 11	44	29.33	32	21.33	54	36.00
11 to 14	36	24.00	17	11.33	37	24.67
14 to 17	10	6.67	26	17.00	11	7.33
17 and above	7	4.67	3	2.00	8	5.33
Total	150	100.00	150	100.00	150	100.00
Average Return Investment (%)	9.20		8.85		9.35	

Source: Primary Data.

Table 6: Average return on investment and the number of entrepreneurs.

average monthly return of Rs.1000 to Rs.1500.

Suggestions

The study highlights that some of the NGOs and banks in the selected districts have realized their crucial role in entrepreneurial development. However, the performance of many of the NGOs is far from satisfactory in this direction. So the Government should monitor them to check the registering of fake entrepreneurs and misuse of funds and incentives received from Government and foreign agencies and they may be encouraged in taking up the real women issues.

References

1. Das A (1998) Women in Business.
2. Bales R (1965) The Equilibrium Problem in Small Group. In: Hare A, Boregotta E, Bales R (eds.) Small Groups: Studies In Social Interaction, Knoff, N.Y.
3. Singh K, Gain R (2002) Management of Micro-enterprises for Rural Women. National Institute of Rural Development, Rajendra Nagar, Hyderabad, India.
4. Ambigadevi DP (2003) Share of Women in total family Income: A two Group Discriminate Analysis. Asian Economic Review 45: 373-378.
5. Das K (2008) Micro Small and medium Enterprises in India: Unfair Fare. Gujarati Institute of Development Report Working Paper Series.
6. Purushotham P (2003) Micro Enterprise Opportunities in Food Industry. SEDME.
7. Rjajustus E, Mahiba M (2000) Participatory Micro Enterprises. Indian Journal of Rural Development.
8. Sheriff RL (2008) Micro Enterprises give California's Economy a Boost. Policy Briefs.
9. Ejigie, Abebaw D (2008) Eastern Africa Social Science Research Review.
10. Psaila K (2007) Constraints and Opportunities for Micro enterprises in Malta. Bank of Valletta Review 35: 25-38.

Viewing the Purchase of Dental Practices in Australia through a Finance Lens

Narayana T[1] and Ramiah V[2*]

[1]*School of Commerce, University of South Australia, Australia*
[2]*Associate Professor of Applied Finance, UniSA Business School, Australia*

Abstract

Most private dentists are faced with the decision to purchase a dental practice at some point in their career, and are usually ill equipped to undertake the necessary capital budgeting decisions, including the valuing of the practice. Valuations of dental practices are usually done according to industry rules of thumb by the dentists themselves or according to accounting principles by accountants who often have little knowledge of the industry. These traditional techniques tend to value practices as a sum of their tangible and intangible assets, rather than in terms of what a prospective buyer is interested in: the potential to generate an income stream. Finance principles can be used to value a practice according to its cash flow potential and to help decide whether the investment in a particular practice should be undertaken. This paper proposes the use of net present value analysis to calculate the value of a dental practice using recent developed asset pricing models, and to evaluate its potential as a future investment, and also examines trends in the Australian market through a finance perspective.

Keywords: Dentistry; Net present value; Discount rate; Risk; Return; Valuation

Introduction

The dental landscape in Australia is still dominated by private practices owned by individual dentists or small groups of dentists. Most young private dentists eventually find themselves considering whether to purchase a dental practice, or a share in one, at some point in their career. This incredibly important career decision is often made out of the desire for clinical and managerial autonomy, as well as the desire for greater financial reward. Dentists often have little finance training and are usually ill equipped to undertake the rigorous financial analysis that would be required in such an important capital budgeting decision. In order to guide them through the process, especially the valuation of the target practice, dentists often turn to accountants or industry experts who use traditional accounting techniques or industry rules of thumb. These methods usually fail to truly value the practice in terms of what the buyer ultimately wants, a future income stream, and are also deficient in evaluating the risk considerations of the investment. This paper examines these considerations, discusses the various practice valuation methods in use, and proposes a method, based on finance principles, to help young dentists decide whether to invest in a dental practice.

Methodology

Risk and return considerations

Young dentists would usually consider practice ownership if they had limited employment opportunities as an employee or contractor, or if they were dissatisfied with working under such arrangements and sought the financial rewards and potential for autonomy that come with practice ownership. Having decided to become one, they must first determine whether to start a practice or buy an existing one, and from a finance perspective, must consider how quickly the cash flow of an existing practice can be replicated by a start-up [1]. Buying an existing practice is usually the less risky option in terms of guaranteeing cash flow, provided the buyer's billing and managerial capabilities are similar to the vendor's [2]. This is because dental patients usually tend to remain at a practice even after a change in ownership, provided there aren't significant changes in the nature of the new dentist and style of the treatment offered [2]. Given that the cost of starting a practice is often equivalent to purchasing an existing one, the latter option offers greater financial return on investment, especially in the time period immediately after the purchase, particularly if young dentists purchase from vendors with similar styles and values [2].

If the decision is madc to takc thc lcss risky option and buy an existing practice, the prospective purchaser must choose a suitable target based on factors such as its location, the type of dentistry offered, the values of the vendor, the demand for dental services in the practice service area, the number and demographics of the patient base, and any existing affiliations with health insurance companies [1,3,4]. As well as these external characteristics, the potential buyer would have to assess his or her billing and managerial capability and compare it to the vendor's [5]. Collectively, these external and internal characteristics will determine the risks associated with investing in the practice, specifically, the risk that the continuous stream of cash flow desired by the purchaser would not be realised. Finance principles dictate that the level of risk associated with an investment option should be matched by the return, or financial reward associated with it [6]. In the case of a capital budgeting decision, a buyer would wish to pay less for a risky investment to compensate with the risk of future financial reward not being realised. Thus according to these principles, young dentists should be willing to pay more for practices with large, secure patient bases run by dentists with similar clinical abilities to themselves, and less for practices that have small patient bases that are maintained by affiliation with insurance companies or that are operated by clinicians with very different styles and abilities to themselves.

***Corresponding author:** Vikash Ramiah, Associate Professor of Applied Finance, UniSA Business School, 37-43 North Terrace, City West, Adelaide, South Australia 5000, Australia, E-mail: vikash.ramiah@unisa.edu.au

Current practice valuation methods

The value of a practice can be calculated according to a number of different techniques, but the ultimate sale price depends on whether the market forces at the time favour buyers or sellers, and thus, may not correspond to the value calculated [7]. The current over supply of dentists, especially in urban areas, favours sellers, and prospective buyers are being asked to pay larger amounts of money than their predecessors - the dental paradox. Given this fact, it is prudent for young dentists to familiarise themselves with the techniques used to determine where the value in the practice lies, and what it equates to in numerical terms. The following methods are the most commonly used in the industry.

Gross revenue composite multiplier method or summation of assets method: This method values a practice as the sum of its tangible and intangible assets [2]. The tangible assets are the office and dental equipment and the intangible assets are the quality of the staff, existing protocols and policies, as well as goodwill, which is the propensity of patients to return to the practice [8,9]. The numerical value of the office and dental equipment can be difficult to determine, as it can be calculated according to acquisition price, book value, replacement value, or street value, leading to difficulties in calculation [10]. Calculating the numerical value of intangible assets can be even more difficult, particularly the value of the goodwill, which is specific to a certain clinician and thus cannot really be sold [8,10]. Because of this difficulty, multipliers of gross annual billings are often used to calculate the intangible asset value [11]. The inaccuracies of this method are well documented [10,12].

Income capitalisation method or excess earnings method: Here the intangible asset value is calculated by dividing the earnings of the dentist by a capitalisation rate, often expressed as a percentage that measures the risk of the venture [9,13]. The potential risk of the investment is thus considered in this method when arriving at a value. The capitalisation rate is calculated as the sum of the risk free rate, the percentage risk of the business cash flow not being realised and a percentage for managerial burden [13]. Practice capitalisation rates can range from 20-30% but the rate to be applied to an individual practice would depend on the risk factors associated with it [9,13]. In the excess earnings method, the intangible value is calculated using the earnings less a nominal dentist salary, that is, the final accounting profit of the practice. The value of the plant and equipment, calculated according the methods previously described, is then added to give the final practice value.

Market approach: This compares the practice to others that have recently sold and that are perceived to be similar. A price/gross billings ratio is then applied to the billings of the practice to obtain a price [13]. This relies on being able to make a fair comparison of practice similarity, which is nearly impossible as two practices with similar annual billings could have extremely different expense profiles and long term growth potential [10]. While commonly used, this method is also inaccurate from a finance perspective and again, provides little information to the buyer about the possibility of a future income stream.

Discounted cash flow (DCF) method: The discounted future earning method takes into account projected future cash flows. It totals the future earnings, discounted back to the present value, at a discount rate appropriate to the risk of the venture [9]. Often the discount rate is calculated as the capitalisation rate, with an allowance for growth [13]. The discount rate has to factor in the time value of money, where money is worth less in the future, and also the risk of the business, which factors in the possibility that future profits are never realised at all [14]. Likewise, the cash flow projections have to accurately portray the billing capacity of the dentist, and allow for increasing expenses and capital expenditure [14]. Most authors advise a time period of five to ten years for the time projection due to the diminishing returns over time [13,14]. Using a DCF method usually produces a higher value than the other methods described above [14]. It can therefore represent the highest possible value that a buyer may be willing to pay. In our opinion, while this method often produces the largest figures, it is the most accurate from the buyer's perspective, as the value is determined in terms of future cash flow potential, which is the ultimate concern. Nonetheless, we criticise this approach for failing to consider other asset pricing models such as the Fama and French three-factor model, the Carhart four-factor model and the Fama and French five-factor model as dental practices tend to be small (size factor), well established practices with more experienced dentists continue to perform better (momentum factor) and is experiencing a trend whereby firms are merging (trend factor is discussed later).

Proposed method for valuing a practice and evaluating the risk of the investment

The flaws in all of the valuation methods are well documented [15]. However, from a finance perspective, valuation based on the cash flow of the business is the most accurate, as all the goodwill of the practice ultimately translates to cash, which is the main consideration of a potential buyer [1,15]. A method to determine whether to invest in a practice, based on a net present value (NPV) analysis, is proposed below. NPV analysis states that an investment should be made if the value of future cash flows, adjusted for risk at an appropriate discount rate, is greater than the cost of the initial outlay [6]. Thus, an investor should proceed if the $NPV>0$, and reject it, if $NPV<0$.

Step 1: Calculate the value of the practice using the discounted cash flow method, using the formula

NPV= -(Initial cash outflow)+(sum of all future cash inflows, discounted to present value using a discount rate of ten percent)

At $NPV=0$, the initial cash outflow would equal the present value of all future cash inflows. Thus the cost of a practice, or the value that a buyer should pay, is equal to the present value of the future cash inflows.

It is proposed that the discounted cash flow analysis should use the projected billing and expense profiles of the vendor, and not the buyer, as the purchaser should pay for the practice in its current situation rather than for its future potential. If buyers suspect that they are capable of bettering the billing of the vendor, it would be unwise to use their own figures and thus pay for what the practice may generate. Careful examination of the vendor's financial documents is required to obtain an understanding of cash flow fluctuations, supply costs, equipment replacement frequency and other expenses [16]. Given that most buyers aim to own the practice they buy for an extended period of time we propose that the buyer use the intended time period in the analysis. Thus if the buyer intends to keep the practice for twenty years, this time period should be used in the analysis. In calculating a discount rate, one needs to start with the risk free rate (around 3%), add a premium for investment alternative, and a company specific premium [8]. A discount rate of ten percent has been advised for dentistry as it is a relatively low risk business, and the receipt of cash payments is usually immediately at the time of billing [14]. Given that this step calculates the value of the practice under the current owner, this discount rate is suitable, as the risk of future cash receipts not being realised under the existing owner would be low.

Step 2: Once the value of the practice has been determined, and agreed upon by the vendor and potential buyer, the buyer would usually seek finance for the purchase, usually in the form of a loan. Prior to the purchase, it is then prudent for the potential buyer to calculate the monthly repayments on the loan, and check whether he or she can afford the repayments by performing a top down personal cash flow analysis. The verification analysis should assume that the repayments are purely to be made from the cash flow of the business, and should ensure that the buyer would be left with what they consider to be a sufficient income after the loan repayments are deducted from the practice profit [9]. It is suspected that many young dentists focus too much on the asking price of the practice, rather than whether they or not they can service their purchase and end up struggling to meet their loan repayments or do so at considerable cost to their personal comfort.

Step 3:Finally, it is proposed that the buyer conduct an NPV analysis using the formula,

NPV=- (Cost calculated in Step 1)+(sum of all future cash inflows under the potential, discounted to present value using a discount rate of twelve percent)

We advocate a two percent increase in discount rate in this step to allow for the increased risk of cash flows not being realised under the potential buyer due to the possibility of patients and staff leaving the practice. The increased discount rate also accounts for the increased difficulty dentists experience in acquiring new patients and growing their patient base in the current competitive climate. The current owner would likely not depend on practice growth to maintain their cash flows as they could rely on their existing patients, but a new buyer would likely be dependent on growing their patient base to compensate for any losses in existing patients. The time period used should be the period that the buyer expects to own the practice, and thus the same as that used in Step 1.

From here, if the NPV analysis provides a result greater than zero, the buyer can feel comfortable proceeding with the practice purchase. While traditional accounting techniques might value the tangible and intangible assets more accurately, these assets are only of value to a buyer if they translate to cash flow, and it is for this reason that we propose that a net present value analysis using the DCF technique be used. It is also worth noting that value is distinctly different from price, as it is completely subjective, and the future success of the practice ultimately comes down to the clinical and managerial skill of the purchaser compared to the vendor. The NPV analysis technique, being forward looking, thus allows potential buyers to see the target practice as something that can be moulded to create future financial value.

The obvious flaw with using projected cash flow techniques is that it is impossible to accurately predict cash flow far into the future. However, the best indicator of future financial performance is immediate past performance, and thus using cash flow projections in Step 1, based on the vendor's billings into the future, is probably the most realistic way in measuring value in terms of cash, which is ultimately what the buyer wants. It is also impossible also for the buyer to project his or her own cash flow projections into the future. While the buyer may have knowledge of their billing capacity, the loss of patients due to the sale of the practice and the resultant drop in revenue, cannot be accurately predicted. Usually, these losses occur only in the first year or two, and if this is accounted for, along with foreseeable expenditure on increased marketing and practice refurbishment as a new owner, a reasonably accurate projection can be made in Step 3.

Current trends in the market

Australia is currently experiencing a wave of corporatisation in the dental landscape. Corporate entities, often private health insurance companies, are purchasing practices at a premium and employ clawback techniques such as requiring vendors to work for five years after the sale, in order to secure cash flow [5]. From a finance perspective, the purchase of practices by corporate entities appears to be an example of synergy in acquisitions. It can be assumed that the synergy comes from acquiring market share of the practice landscape, which can provide long term reduction in capital expenditure and other costs, and the ability to control prices if monopoly is achieved. Private health insurers may also use the provision of dental practices owned by them to attract new members, and thus increase shareholder value. However, it can also be argued that the increased prices paid by these entities are a more accurate reflection of their true worth. It is clear that an analysis based on future cash flow reveals a higher value than traditional accounting or industry rule of thumb methods, and it may be that the apparent synergy is actually the result of practices being valued according to finance principles by corporate entities that see the true potential of their investment. We argue that dental practices in Australia are actually under-valued when examined through a finance lens, and that market sale figures do not reflect their true worth.

Conclusion

The purchase of a dental practice is a major decision in the life of a dentist and not to be taken lightly. From a finance perspective, the decision to purchase a dental practice is a decision to purchase an income stream that ensures future financial security. While numerous accounting based techniques exist to value practices, we argue that discounted cash flow analysis offers the most realistic picture of the practice's worth in terms of its ability to deliver the desired income stream. Dentists are usually not well trained in finance, and often fixate on the cost of the purchase rather than seeing it in finance terms as an investment with risks and associated potential for return. The proposed capital budgeting method can be used by young dentists to methodically work through this decision making process. It is hoped that the proposed methodology and reflections on the current climate in Australia builds on the existing literature on dental practice valuation, and offers insights into how the investment process should be viewed.

References

1. Dolansky B (2001) Practice Management: Where's the value in a dental practice. Dental Practice Management, pp: 20-23.
2. Nunes E, McKinnon L (2013) Lending to Dental Professionals (Part 2) How to Value a Practice. The RMA Journal 96: 32-39.
3. Middleton G (2011a) More pitfalls in buying and selling dental practices. Synstrat Dentist Articles.
4. Middleton G (2011b) Determining the value of your dental practice. Synstrat Dentist Articles.
5. Middleton G (2010) Issues in buying, selling and valuing dental practices. Synstrat Dentist Articles.
6. Ross S, Westerfield R, Jaffe J (2013) Corporate Finance (10th edn.), McGraw-Hill Irwin.
7. Middleton G (2005) Dental practice valuations – facts and fantasies. Synstrat Dentist Articles.
8. Cimasi R, Zigrang T (2009) The valuation of healthcare professional practices.

In: Thomas R, Gup B editors. The valuation handbook: valuation techniques from today's top practitioners (1st edn.), Wiley Finance.

9. Prescott W (2001) Calculating practice value in a changing market. In Prescott (2nd edn.), Business, Legal and Tax Planning for the Dental Practice, Pennwell Books.
10. Douglas E (2009) How to appraise a dental practice. Dental Economics 99: 78.
11. Giroux TG (2011) Purchasing a practice: Getting a great value at a reasonable price ensures success. Dental economics 101: 98.
12. Cahill J (2012) Rules of thumb beware. Dental Economics, p: 48.
13. Pollock S (2009) Valuing Dental Practices. In: Thomas R, Gup B editors. The valuation handbook: valuation techniques from today's top practitioners (1st edn.), Wiley Finance.
14. Tanzi G, Tanzi J (2006) Practice valuation – using discounted cash flow methodology. Dental Economics 96: 116.
15. Brizedine J (1993) What is your practice really worth? Dental Economics 83: 79.
16. Middleton G (2004) The cost of having an uninformed accountant when buying a practice. Synstrat Dentist Articles.

Role of Knowledge Management in Safety of the Employees of the Electric Distribution Companies

Taghi Vahidi*

The Branch of Marketing Managemen, IslamicAzad University of Shahrood, Shahrood, Iran

Abstract

In the first wave of human life that all people had to continue living through the agriculture and husbandry jobs, the tangible assets like lands and number of family members were considered as important criteria for success. After the first wave, the second wave was commenced by working in factories and focusing on products and selling them in the market. In other words, the product-oriented and market-oriented stages were signs of industrial age; meanwhile, tangible assets were taken into account as important factors in the factories or organizations. The third wave in human life was started when the human found that by inventing computer and vast usage of computer and internet in changing traditional jobs, only knowledge and talent will be important in digital era. Thus, the human became familiar with the subjects such as knowledge-based organizations, learning organizations, knowledge management, talent management, and so on. After that, a belief gradually formed in the minds of most managers and even some employees at the different organizations that their success will be achieved by relying on knowledge and talent as intangible assets. Therefore, the human found out that tangible assets are not the only key for productivity and profitability and focusing on intangible assets will be helpful for future business. So, the paradigm shift and change in approaches was commenced more than before.

Although there are many advances in technology and science in different areas of knowledge, there are many hazards for the employees of the electric distribution companies especially those who work on the electric overhead lines and/or underground cables, this study aims to reveal the role of knowledge management in identifying the hazards, and by documenting the experiences resulting in the accidents, better recommendations on working the medium and low voltage networks have been presented in the current research.

Keywords: Safety; Knowledge; Management; Employees

Introduction

The current world is called the knowledge age. It is also full of uncertainty; meanwhile, huge communications and interaction have been emerged due to the Information Technology (IT). The communications are so increasing that the traditional approaches are not trustable but inefficient and therefore, together with changes resulted in social and industrial developments, there is a need in changing the employees' attitudes.

Nowadays, the world society has entered the age that knowledge is its main capital as well as a fundamental factor for growth and development of a society so that the expression "knowledge is power" is the main slogan of this era. One of the important subjects that managers of electric distribution companies need to focus in this era is the essence of considering physical and mental safety of the personnel. Thus, the study aims to analyze the experiences relating to safety from the aspect of knowledge management and give some recommendations for epitomize the mentioned experiences.

Group contribution in the current world for operating intra-organizational and extra-organizational knowledge via educating personnel may create a fundamental change in organization and manpower and it will have a key role in physical and mental safety of the employees. The important point relating to the knowledge management is that some current employees of the electric distribution companies are going to be retired and lack of documentation of their experiences on individual and group safety and also observing safety in utilizing electric equipment will be opposed many costs on the aforesaid companies.

Knowledge management emphasizes on tacit knowledge and notifies the essence of changing the tacit knowledge to explicit knowledge. Tacit knowledge is like an intangible treasure which is located in the minds of people and when the employees are retired, this kind of knowledge will be removed from the organization. Unfortunately, most companies do not notice on losing the invaluable experiences and this will threaten them in near or distant future. For instance, most of acquired experiences in connection with people's safety, electrification incidents, encountering the damaged people, and the acquired knowledge for observing safety (during working with equipment, working on electric hot lines, and erecting new low-voltage and medium-voltage electric distribution networks) will be removed after retiring the personnel from the electric distribution companies or in a general term, from the eclectic power industry. Thus, much time and expenditures will be consumed for preparing, educating, and training the new-comers in order to persuade them to follow the required activities in electric power industry. If no attention is paid to knowledge management after the mentioned expenditures, the cycle of consuming money will be repeated reciprocally.

Another challenge that the electric distribution companies are faced with is how to control the liquidity and utilize the cost management. So, consuming money to prepare the personnel does not have any

***Corresponding author:** Taghi Vahidi, PhD Student in Business Management - The Branch of Marketing Managemen, Islamic Azad University of Shahrood, Shahrood, Iran, E-mail: taghivahidi@yahoo.com

economical and technical justification because it will be possible to extract the tacit knowledge in the minds of personnel and document them and deploy it to the personnel without any need to extra costs.

Research background

According to Aliahmadi et al. [1] the evolution of planning has happened by passing through three eras of Product - Oriented, Market - Oriented, and Post – Industrial so that Knowledge Management is one of the issues which has been emphasized on it in this period. On the other hand, knowledge management is a systematic process of finding, selecting, organizing, distilling and presenting information in a way that improves an employee's comprehension in a specific area of interest [2]. Knowledge Management causes the personnel to disclose their hidden knowledge. According to Mehdivand [3], if the organizations notice utilizing knowledge in their processes, they will find out that the rate of knowledge in their organizations will be more than they diagnose.

In the research [4], the importance of Knowledge Management has been addressed and then it has been recommended that the Knowledge Management must be considered as organizational strategies and then the researchers believe that lack of registering the existing experiences in the organization will cause retraining of the personnel and this kind of training is not a kind of investment but a type of cost for the organization.

Based on the above comments, it will be reasonable to conclude that documentation of executive operations and the task of personnel will be the best educational sources for the employees of the above-mentioned companies. It will not only prevent the incidents, but also will hinder the loss of capitals in the organization. It should be notified that all the incidents are recorded in electric distribution companies and the employees are able to refer to them. Although these documents are referable for technical and administrative staff, the most important point is to prevent the incidents before they happen. The experiences of the personnel who have faced with the incidents and their solutions together with the safety points in working with electrical equipment and the essence of mental preparedness of the personnel are the invaluable sources in the companies that must be deployed; meanwhile, the mentioned experiences must be disclosed via the companies' websites.

There are many researches about Knowledge Management so that it's not possible to mention all of them, but Table 1 is a sample of researches stated in ref. [5]:

It will be possible to consider various methods for recording the experiences of the personnel in the field of knowledge management; however, each method which facilitates the recording of tacit and explicit knowledge will be efficient. Followings are some applicable methods for recording the knowledge management:

1. Persuading the employees to record their experiences in the field of safety as PDF files and uploading them in the websites of the companies. Attention must be paid that backup files will be essential.
2. Encouraging the employees to present monthly reports on incidents or some measures which could result in hazards.
3. Observing individual and group safety in working with the electrical equipment and networks based on ISO quality system together with updating the instructions and safety standards.
4. Holding annual seminars on safety which has been performing in the Khorasan-Razavi Electric Distribution Company (KEDC) as a routine event for ages.
5. Presenting the reports of taking part in other seminars and conferences and sharing them with all staff inside and outside of the organization.

Literature Review

Knowledge management

According to De Jarnett [6], knowledge management includes creating, interpreting, distributing, applying, keeping, and correcting knowledge. On the other hand, Quintas [7] believes that knowledge management is a process of meeting the existing requirements in order to identify and extract the gathered knowledge and develop the new opportunities.

There are two kinds of knowledge called Explicit Knowledge and Tacit Knowledge. Based on Keshavarzi [8], the explicit knowledge is recordable and recoverable form individuals' minds, but, the basis of tacit knowledge is theoretical and applicable experiences together with the employees' learning. In addition, King [9] argues that explicit knowledge can be observed as words, sentences, documents, organized data, computerized programs, and other forms of disclosing knowledge. Moreover, the researcher Abidi [10] addresses that tacit knowledge relates to the problem-solving skills, judges, and the individuals' intuition.

The essentials of knowledge management

According to Emami and Keihani [11], the hierarchy of the knowledge management includes four stages: data, information, knowledge, and wisdom. In addition, the researchers Asadzadeh and Jalalian [12] believe that there are four fundamental elements

Researchers	Field of research
Polyani (1966); Nonaka and Takeuchi (1995)	Difference between tacit and explicit knowledge
Tsoukas (1996)	Classified knowledge
Wiig(1993); Liebowitz (1999)	Fundamentals of knowledge management
Holsapple and Joshi (1997); Rubenstein et al. (2001)	Knowledge management models
Davenport et al. (1998)	Successful projects in knowledge management
Fowler (2000); Liebowitz (2001)	Knowledge management and artificial intelligence
Courtney (2001); Bolloju et al. (2002)	Knowledge management and decision support
Liao (2003); Kakabadse et al. (2003)	Researches on knowledge management
Tyndale (2002)	Knowledge management software
McAdam and Reid (2001); Wickert & Herschel (2001)	Knowledge management and small economical foundations
Rowley (2000); Metaxiotis and Psarras (2003)	Knowledge management and higher education
Weber et al. (2002)	Knowledge management standards

Table 1: A sample of researches in the field of knowledge management.

for knowledge management: knowledge, management, Information Technology (IT), and organizational culture. Moreover, Bixler [13] mentions four pillars for knowledge management that are: leadership, organization, technology, and learning. Furthermore, based on Salimi [14], knowledge management in an organization is responsible for the following items:

1. Disclosing the customer's needs inside and outside of the organization
2. Identifying the customer's laws
3. Identifying the customers
4. Diagnosing the interests and styles of the customers
5. Deploying knowledge transfer inside the organization and as an organizational culture
6. Deploying knowledge transfer to the customer inside the organization
7. Deploying the culture of disclosing customer laws inside the organization
8. Informing the customers about the product quality, service, solving the complaints, and product price
9. Identifying the media which transfer messages to the customers
10. Specifying the reasons for lack of customer willing toward the competitor
11. Following the implementation of Total Quality Management (TQM), Business Process Reengineering, and Research & Development (R&D)
12. Mitigating hazards and rebuilding the affairs as well as decreasing the costs via preventing the unnecessary measures
13. Preventing the leakage of information and empowering the business competitors via creating a knowledge participative space

Models of knowledge management

The researchers Asadzadeh and Jalalian [12] have named two famous models for stating the knowledge current. One of the models is called Knowledge Life Cycle and the other is General Knowledge Model. Theses model have been shown in Figures 1 and 2, respectively.

According to Abbasi [15] there is another model named Lustri Model which focuses on individual knowledge as the first item for creating organizational knowledge. So, it will be possible to notice the importance of knowledge in every person in an organization. There are many models on knowledge management so that it will not be possible to declare all of them in this study. On the other hand, based upon the research [16], the primitive frameworks for implementing knowledge management in private sector is much more than the governmental sector. Therefore, one can conclude that private companies like electric distribution companies will be able to refer to many models for development and deployment of knowledge management and find the best model which meets their requirements or present a combined model based on the existing and appropriate models.

Safety and its essence

The factor "risk" may be found in every human activity. Identifying the risks systematically and removing them will require implementing a managerial system based on the needs of each organization and this goal will be attained in different levels of organization such as staff, contractors, stakeholders, and other people and of course by considering the top managers of the organization [17].

One of the factors which threaten the employee safety is the mental stress which acts as a potential factor in happening the incidents. In the

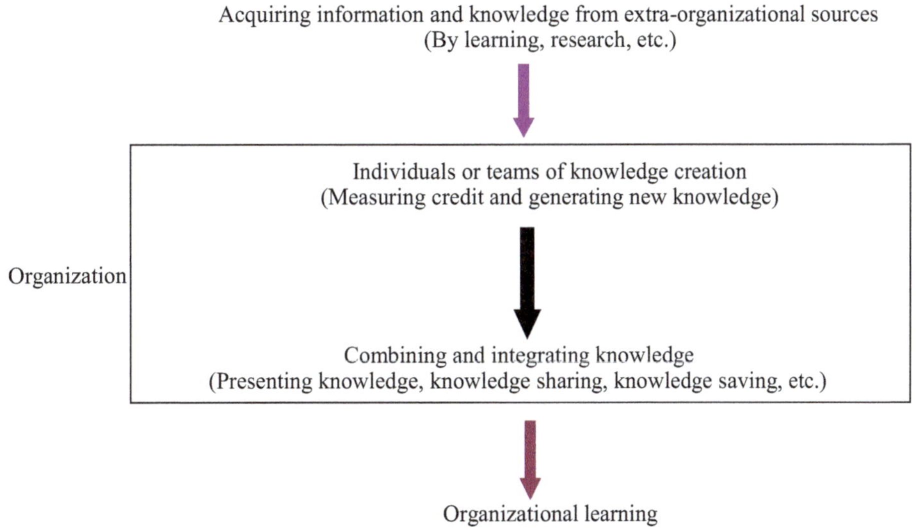

Figure 1: Knowledge life cycle.

Figure 2: General knowledge model.

study of Iravani [18], the stress phenomenon has been specified as the most critical issue in personnel's work life and it's a reason for most of mental and even physical disorders; meanwhile, stress is a reason for many diseases and it's also the disease of the current century.

The researcher Haji-Hosseini [19] addresses the process of acceleration in privatization and presence of contracting companies in electric power industry including Electric Regional Companies, Generation Management Companies, and Electric Distribution Companies and concluded that the result of such measures is a non-centric management in electric power industry; meanwhile, the required interactions in the field of mitigating losses and continuation of servicing as well as decrease in incidents by increasing safety factor has been specified in this paper.

Job diseases are called a group of diseases that are created due to the works and they create some spiritual and physical losses for all people in as society as well. A reason for such a disease is the lack of notice on safety knowledge in all organizational levels and it's the origin for most of diseases [20].

Proposed model for deploying safety in electric power industry

The proposed model for internalizing the safety knowledge in all Electric Distribution Companies is as shown in Figure 3.

Creating safety knowledge via:

- The commitment of the CEO
- Persuading the personnel to observe safety in all organizational units

Developing knowledge through:

- Intra-organizational safety experiences together with the experiences of other companies
- Investigating the new methods of safety via R&D as well as focusing on innovations

Capturing safety knowledge through:

- Documenting the experiences
- Expanding knowledge and sharing the ideas and safety knowledge

Cooperation and collaboration in the field of spreading the safety knowledge.

Conclusion

Focus of Electric Distribution Companies on knowledge management in the field of safety means that the managers invest for their development and preparedness in order to prevent risks and hazards and also hinder the intellectual and physical assets. In the current situation that the experienced personnel are being retired, the importance of transferring knowledge and experiences are specified more than before. On the other hand, the new manpower will be able to acquire the experiences and add their knowledge via utilizing the modern technologies and share what they know with others in their organizations. So it will be a clear reason why knowledge management has a key role in safety of the personnel in Electric Distribution Companies.

Suggestions

Some suggestions for epitomizing the safety knowledge in Electric Distribution Companies have been presented as follows:

1. Creating belief in company managers relating to the essence of implementing knowledge management in safety affairs
2. Recording the past experiences of the companies including writing the applicable reports and safety instructions for work with electric equipment
3. Recording the reports of participating in safety seminars and also having technical and scientific visits and make them available for all employees
4. Motivating the personnel to transfer their safety knowledge to their affiliated manpower aiming the succession management and prepare them to accept responsibilities and follow their tasks appropriately.

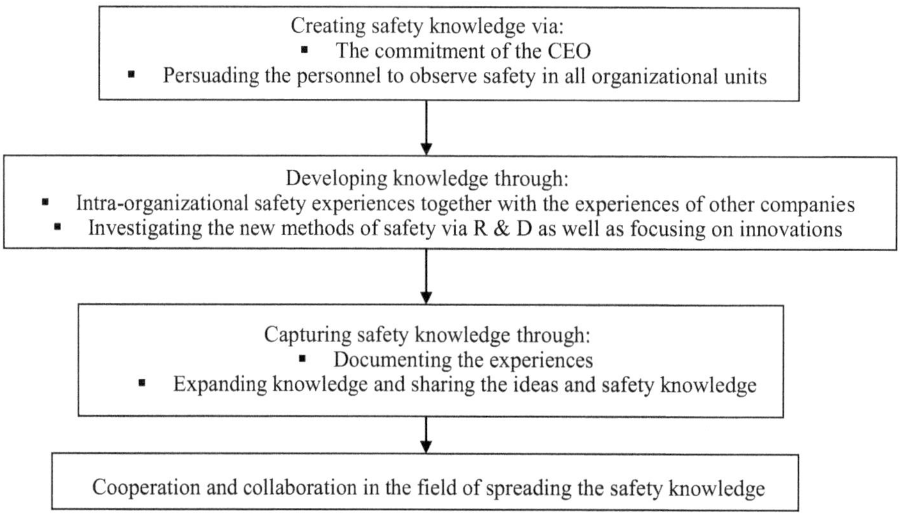

Figure 3: Proposed model of deploying knowledge in all electric distribution companies.

5. Reinforcing the loyalty and organizational interest in all employees especially the new employees in order to persuade them to learn knowledge from the experienced personnel and then attempt to share them with others.
6. Enhancing the cooperative atmosphere for scientific and innovative affairs and share the ideas relating to safety.

References

1. Aliahmadi A, Fathollah M, Taj-ol-din I (2010) A comprehensive Perspective on Strategic Knowledge. Tolid-e-Danesh Publication, Tehran.
2. Salehi Sadeghiyani J, Tavallaee R (2011) Review different knowledge strategy models and designing a new model. International Conference on Innovation, Management, and Service. IPEDR, Singapore 14: 271-275.
3. Mehdivand MM (2010) Examining the concept of Knowledge Management and its impact on human resource management. MA dissertation on business management, University of Mazandaran.
4. Vahidi T, Khani F (2012) A survey relating to the role of Knowledge Management on optimal consumption of energy by the customers at the Electric Distribution Companies. 17th Iranian conference on electric distribution networks.
5. Khatamian-Far P, Rahimi M (2007) Discovering the world of knowledge management: The agreements and disagreements among the researchers and scientists. Iranian e-journal of scientific documents and information research center 6: 2.
6. De Jarnett L (1996) Knowledge – the latest thing. Information Strategy. The Executive's Journal 12: 3-5.
7. Quintas P, Lefrere P, Jones G (1997) Knowledge management: A strategic agenda. Journal of Long Range Planning 30: 385-391.
8. Keshavarzi AH (2008) Obstacles and facilitators of sharing knowledge in organizations. The first Iranian conference on knowledge management, Tehran.
9. King WR (2009) Knowledge Management and Organizational Learning. Annals of Information Systems.
10. Abidi SSR (2008) Healthcare Knowledge Management: The Art of the Possible. Knowledge Management for Health Care Procedures, pp. 1-20.
11. Emami S, Keihani M (2008) A seminar on knowledge management systems. Iranian society for informatics.
12. Asadzadeh A, Jalalian M (2004) Knowledge Management.
13. Bixler C (2002) Applying the four pillars of Knowledge Management. KMWorld 11: 1-2.
14. Salimi MN (2008) Knowledge Management and customer relationship. Persian journal of Shoe Industry 14.
15. Abbasi Z (2008) A review on implementing knowledge management model at the organizations. The first Iranian conference on knowledge management, Tehran.
16. Hosseini S, Mazaheri N (2008) Application of knowledge management in electric distribution activities. Persian monthly report of electrical industry.
17. Baghsheini V, Hosseini SJ (2009) Risk Management and Evaluation by three-dimensional method together with its results at the North Khorasan Electric Distribution Company. The 13th Iranian Conference on Electrical Distribution Networks, Gilan Province.
18. Iravani GH (2008) Identifying the stressful organizational and occupations factors for the employees working in customer service department at Isfahan Electric Distribution Company. The 12th Iranian Conference on Electrical Distribution Networks, Tehran.
19. Haji-Hosseini A (2009) Design, implementation, and establishment of safety management system in Yazd Electric Regional Company. The sixth International Management Conference, Tehran.
20. Mousavi-Rad SH, Mousavi-Rad SM, Ghazanfari M (2009) The role of knowledge management in preventing occupational diseases. The first International conference on safety, health, and environment position in organizations, Isfahan.

The impact of Information Technology on Job Related Factors like Health and Safety, Job Satisfaction, Performance, Productivity and Work Life Balance

Ratna R[1] **and Kaur T**[2*]

[1]*PhD Scholar (IIT Kharagpur) and Assistant Professor (HR and OB), Amity Business School, Amity University, Noida-201301, Uttar Pradesh, India*
[2]*Academic Co-ordinator, Quality Assurance and Enhancement Cell, Amity University, Amity Lucknow Campus, Uttar Pradesh, India*

Abstract

The impact of Information Technology on workplaces, individuals and society as a whole has increased dramatically during the last two decades of the 21st century. This period has seen maturation in the field of digital computing, combined with the use of telecommunications technology, in order to link many computers into what is 'virtually' a very large single network, the Internet. Data has become widely accessible, and readily inter-related. Implementation of new technology has lead to many changes in the workplace. This paper aims to study the impact of technology on various Job related factors, 5 shortlisted for the study i.e. Health and Safety, Job Satisfaction, Performance, Productivity and Work Life Balance. Which Job factor is getting affected to maximum extent with the introduction of technology? The study was done with the help of questionnaire based on Likert scale. Data was collected from 100 employees of Barco and CMC Ltd. Convenience sampling method was used. Data was analyzed through SPSS Software and excel to find out that Performance is the most impacted factor by introduction of new technology, followed by Job Satisfaction, Health and Safety, Productivity and work life balance. The factor analysis converted them into three components in which component 1 contributed more towards the impact of technology.

Keywords: Information technology; Workplace; Digital computing; Internet; Health and safety; Job satisfaction; Performance; Productivity; Work life balance

Introduction

Introduction to information technology

IT, short for Information Technology, and pronounced as separate letters, Information Technology is the application of computers and various techniques, to handle masses of data. This broad subject is concerned with all aspects of managing and processing information, especially within a large organization or company. Computers and communications technologies form the backbone of Information Technology (IT). To a large extent it underlies the rise of modern business and economy.

Constantly, such a technology forces an industry to learn, to acquire, to adapt and to change its very mindset, let alone its technical knowledge. The impact of IT on workplaces, employment relations, individuals and society as a whole has increased dramatically during the last two decades of the 21st century. This period has witnessed maturation in the field of digital computing, with the combined usage of telecommunications technology, in order to link many computers, into what is 'virtually' a very large single network, the Internet. It is invading the very core of the way things are being done including industrial relations.

As stated by Peter Drucker, recognized management guru:

"Management has to recognize that there is no one technology that pertains to any industry, on the contrary, all technologies are capable to have an impact on any industry."

Data has become widely accessible, and readily inter-related. This matrix of widely inter-connected computers is being slowly but steadily augmented by the incorporation of robotics and artificial intelligence. This phenomenon can best be described as "digital business" or "digital economy", embracing e-commerce and the Internet, but extends much further. This makes IT a sole object that has the most pervasive effect on the modern society today. Organisations at global level are changing the way they do business in adopting the information revolution. Its impact can be seen in terms of:

- Changing relationships between companies and their customers and suppliers.
- The way they organize themselves.
- The very core of the business itself – the labour force.
- Its internal processes as well.

Impact of technology on health and safety

Occupational health and safety is a discipline with a broad scope aiming at "Promotion and maintenance of the highest degree of physical, mental and social well-being of workers that is the "whole person" in all occupations; prevention among workers of adverse effects on health caused by their working conditions; the protection of workers in their employment from risks resulting from factors adverse to health; the placing and maintenance of workers in an occupational environment adapted to physical and mental needs; the adaptation of work to humans.

***Corresponding author:** Tanpreet Kaur, Academic Co-ordinator, Quality Assurance and Enhancement Cell, Amity University, Amity Lucknow Campus, Sector 125, Noida, Lucknow-226028, Uttar Pradesh, India
E-mail: ktanpreet@gmail.com

Successful occupational health and safety practice requires the collaboration and participation of both employers and workers in health and safety programmes, and involves the consideration of issues relating to occupational medicine, industrial hygiene, toxicology, education, engineering safety, ergonomics, psychology, etc. With the introduction of new technology human health and safety can be well protected against:

- Communicable Diseases - Vector borne diseases (e.g. malaria), sanitary hygiene diseases, risk associated with handing of infectious wastes;
- Injury - Risk of accidents from traffic, explosions, falls, heat stress, operation of machinery, handling of physically hazardous wastes and resources (e.g. sharps), minimize loss of hearing; and
- Exposure to hazardous chemicals - Inhalation (e.g. air pollution), avoid dermal contact, ingestion of contaminated food and water (e.g. pesticide residue) of hazardous chemicals and of radioactive material.

Impact of technology on job satisfaction

Job Satisfaction is the favourableness or un-favourableness with which the employee views his work. It expresses the amount of agreement between one's expectation of the job and the rewards that the job provides. The nature of one's job environment is an important part of life because ultimately Job Satisfaction influences one's general life satisfaction. Job Satisfaction, thus, is the result of various attitudes possessed by an employee. In a narrow sense, these attitudes are related to the job under condition with such specific factors such as Wages, Employment Supervision, Working conditions, Social/Human relation on the job, Prompt settlement of grievances and Fair treatment by employer. However, more comprehensive approach requires that Inter and Intra Personal factors to be included before a complete understanding of job satisfaction can be obtained. Such factors as employee's age, health temperature, desire and level of aspiration should be considered. Further his family relationship, social status, recreational outlets, activity in the organizations etc. contribute deeply to job satisfaction.

Information Technology (IT) has played an important role in business since the 1950s and the use of technology to reduce costs, improve operations, enhance customer service, and improve communications has progressed rapidly over the past four decades.

Job satisfaction is an important criterion for the success of an organization where it is closely associated with job turnover and life satisfaction. Using new technologies such as Computer-Aided Manufacturing (CAM), Virtual Reality (VR), Expert Systems (ES), and the Internet can give companies an edge. New technologies can result in employees "working smarter" as well as providing high-quality products and more efficient services to customers. Companies that have realized greatest gains from new technology have human resource management practices that support the use of technology to create what is known as high-performance work systems. Work, training, programs and reward systems often need to be reconfigured to support employees' use of new technology.

Impact of technology on performance

Performance is the accomplishment of a given task measured against preset known standards of accuracy, completeness, cost, and speed. Use of technology within the ethical limits definitely benefits the organisation, along with improvisation in individual and group performance. On one hand, employee workload reduces through technological advancement; on the other number of employees to perform a task is also reduced, thus reducing job opportunities. Companies use advanced technologies to check and evaluate employee's performance via Human resource management department. To drive productivity and manage human capital, HR department leverages emerging technology to keep up with the market trend. Current technology trends impacting HR are Outsourcing and focus on value that HR brings to the organisation. The demand for better service performance has driven a technological trend towards more powerful, integrated and scalable system components.

Impact of technology on productivity growth

Productivity is one of the most closely watched indicators of long-term economic prospects. Rising productivity is the key to making possible permanent increases in the standard of living. Changes in technology are the only source of permanent increase in productivity, but a number of transient factors can affect both true and "measured" productivity. For example, workers may work harder during periods of high demand and firms may use their capital assets more intensively by running factories for extra shifts; both factors can lead measured productivity to be too high relative to actual technological progress. Similarly, during periods of high demand, productivity can rise because firms take advantage of increasing returns to scale; however some people argue that this effect is not permanent and should be discounted when measuring long-run technical change.

Impact of technology on work-life balance

Work- Life Balance is a comfortable state of equilibrium achieved between a person's primary priorities of their employment position and their personal lifestyle. To put it in simple words demands of a working individual's career should not overwhelm his ability to enjoy a satisfying personal life beyond the business environment. These days, we have so many potentially labour saving technological devices, which we have deeply inculcated in our daily practices but with a logical question: to what extent do such advances increase rather than decrease workload and stress? New technology can clearly enable us to work faster and more efficiently, and it facilitates flexible and remote working e.g. work from home, preparing quick presentations and reports with use of cell phones besides computers and laptop but it can also mean that we cannot ever really get away and switch off.

Literature Review

Derks et al. examined the impact of work related smartphone use on daily recovery from work-related efforts to which work-home interference (WHI) is an important inhibitor. Contrary, to their hypothesis it was found out that smartphone user did not experience more overall work-home interference (WHI) than non-users. For control group WHI was positively related to psychological detachment, relaxation, mastery and control activities, implying that being connected to work in evening hours through smartphone's had consequences only to the extent to which employees succeed in recovering [1].

Mazmanian et al. studied how wireless e-mail devices specifically the Blackberry were incorporated into daily lives of professionals and its consequent social impact. Findings suggested these Blackberry communication entailed 3 important dualities having conflicting consequences for work and lives of plymouth members: continuity and asynchronicity, engagement and withdrawal, autonomy and addiction, making it diffcult for memebers to dis-engage from work and blending among people [2].

Ali analysed employment relation systems of three Asian countries-China, India, and Korea. He made a case for diversion in employment relation systems that technological advances, improved communications, economic liberalization, and increased international competition has brought in an era of economic, institutional and cultural integration. Under globalization the workplace practices are under a constant state of movement. Academicians not only analysed the benefits and the deleterious effects of this phenomenon on the employment relations of developed and under-developed nations, but also stirring up the debate whether the industrial relations systems of countries are converging or diverging [3].

Bakker gives an overview of research on the impact of e-mail provided by personal computers and smart phone devices based on Job-demands resources (JD-R) model as a framework. The results of the studies were interpreted to show which aspects of e-mail communication can be considered as demands and resources, and hence complicate or facilitate our working life. Increasing pressure of excessive amounts of e-mail and prompt reply seems to be disproportionally loading the recipient, moreover a smart phone on one hand increases the flexibility of an employee on the other hand facilitates long working hours with a risk of disturbed work-home balance [4].

Bill identified contributing influences of an individual's attitude towards a technological innovation/ improvisation in the workplace. Multiple factors stemming from individuals knowledge, beliefs, values, cognitive/ mechanical ability, gender, organisational culture and social information processing tend to influence an individual's attitude. Now, since an organisation comprises of many individuals with various combination of above, careful consideration must be given before introducing any innovation. The study observes higher adoption rates where employees have control over the innovation and its implementation therefore the organisation must provide information sharing, risk-free environment and evolve a system of learning [5].

Morris and Dillon focussed on understanding the factors which influence user acceptance of information technology. They reviewed literature that demonstrates the nature of technological acceptance, which is mediated by distinct factor groups related to: the psychology of the users, the design process of information technology, and the quality of the technology in user terms. The research offered insights that could support the derivation of reliable predictions of user acceptance. However, potentially overlapping theories seem to exist, though independent of each other creating possibilities for unifying this framework to extend innovation diffusion concepts and systems design models (particularly user-centered design) into a formal theory of user acceptance of information technology [6].

Gudmundsdottir investigated that great changes have been discovered with the introduction of technology in the last decade, regarding the organization of work. The results show that when dividing fishing factories into three technological stages; low technology, middle technology and high technology, the job strain was highest and the decision authority by the employee was lowest in the high technological factories. This even had an impact on health and atmosphere at the workplace, where the employees in the high technological factories were more likely to complain about several health problems as well as about low degrees of cheerfulness at the workplace and tiresome jobs. However, initially these same people were most positive towards the implementation of the high technology and the new way of organizing their job that the technology introduced. This effect has made the psychosocial and physical working environment tougher, especially for women [7].

Bresnahan investigated that information technology (IT) and associated changes in work organization were important causes of shift in labour demand in favour of high-wage, high-skill work, which contributed to a substantial rise in income inequality in the United States. Specifically, it was found out that IT use is correlated with a new workplace organization that includes broader job responsibilities for line workers, more decentralized decision-making and more self-managing teams. Therefore, both IT and new organization are correlated with worker skill, measured in a variety of ways. Significantly, firms which attempt to implement only one of the hypothesized complements without the others are less productive than firms which invest in all the complements. Taken together, the results highlight the importance of organizational changes stimulated by IT in the changing demand workers of different types [8].

Vintangcol stresses on the importance of Information Technology (IT) and that computers and communication technologies form the backbone of IT. To a large extent it underlies the rise of modern business and economy; however on a continuous basis such a technology forces an industry to learn, to acquire, to adapt, to change its very mindset, let alone its technical knowledge. IT has invaded the very core of the way things are done - including industrial relations, which is grooming the work place as well as the employment relations [9].

Materials and Methods

Objectives

a) To study the impact of technology on various job related factors 'Job Satisfaction', 'Productivity', 'Performance', 'Health and Safety' and 'Work Life Balance' respectively via correlation.

b) To study which factor is most affected by the implementation of new technology via Factor Analysis.

Rationale of the study

The significance of the study is to understand the impact of technology on various factors like job satisfaction, productivity etc. and which factor is the most affected by the implementation of new technology.

Questionnaire design

The questionnaire measures the impact of technology on various factors like Performance, Job Satisfaction, Productivity, Health and Safety, Work Life Balance. Questionnaire is based on Likert Scale and designed according to the objectives of the present study.

Research design

Descriptive Research: Through Survey Method

Statistical tools

Sample size: The overall sample size in this study is one hundred (100).

Sampling technique: The sampling technique used is convenience sampling.

Sample description: The employees working with IT sector.

Data collection techniques

Primary data: It was collected by personally interviewing the employees with the help of the questionnaire made for the purpose.

Secondary data: It was collected from newspapers, magazines journals, online resources etc.

Pilot test

A pilot study was done on 40 samples to analyze the process and the possible outcomes of the questions to be asked.

Reliability

The data collected by the employees working in IT sector was analyzed with the help of SPSS (Tables 1 and 2).

Results

Analysis part-1

The new technology implemented in the organisations was found with the help of personal interviews of HR Managers of various companies like CMC and Barco. The various new technologies implemented were:-

- New software like Taleo, SAP etc
- Introduction of HRIS

Analysis part-2

The questionnaire was broken into 5 major sections each having 25 questions. The first five questions determined the impact of technology on 'Job Satisfaction', then 'Productivity', 'Performance', 'Health and Safety' and 'Work Life Balance' respectively.

The answers to the questions of 100 employees were analysed based on Likert Scale, where answers were graded as per the following Table 3.

Thereafter, average of the sections was taken into consideration and a correlation between the sectional average and the overall average was calculated.

Here we are assuming that if the sectional average is higher, the impact of technology is going to be much higher. For e.g. if the sectional average of 'Job Satisfaction' is 4 and the overall average is 3.6, then we infer that Job Satisfaction is much higher that Productivity of the employee (Table 4).

Interpretation: it is observed that the correlation numbers for each of the sections were very much similar, showing strong correlation between 'Job Satisfaction', 'Productivity', 'Health and Safety' and 'Work Life Balance' as compared with the total sum of all the answers, except 'Performance' which is showing a stronger correlation against

		N	%
Cases	Valid	40	72.7
	Excluded[a]	15	27.3
	Total	55	100.0

[a]Listwise deletion based on all variables in the procedure.

Table 1: Case processing summary.

Cronbach's Alpha	N of Items
0.825	25

Table 2: Reliability statistics.

	Score
Strongly Disagree	1
Disagree	2
Neither Agree nor Disagree	3
Agree	4
Strongly Agree	5

Table 3: Likert scale.

Job Satisfaction	Productivity	Performance	Health and Safety	Work Life Balance	Average All
1.4	1.6	2.4	1	1.8	1.64
1.4	1.6	2	2	1.2	1.64
1.4	1.6	2.8	2	1.2	1.8
1	1	2.8	2	2.8	1.92
1	1	3.8	3	3.8	2.52
1.6	1.4	3	3	3	2.4
1.6	1.4	3.2	4	4	2.84
1.6	1.4	2.4	1	1	1.48
2.6	2.4	2.8	2	1.2	2.2
1.4	1.6	3.2	1	1.8	1.8
1.6	1.4	2.4	1	1.8	1.64
1.6	1.4	2	2	2	1.8
1.6	1.4	3	3	1.4	2.08
1.4	1.6	2.8	2	1.2	1.8
1.4	1.6	2	2	1.2	1.64
1.6	1.4	2	2	1.2	1.64
1	1	3	3	2.2	2.04
1	1	3	3	2.2	2.04
2.2	1.8	2.8	2	2	2.16
2.8	2.2	2	2	1.2	2.04
2.2	1.8	2.4	1	2.6	2
2.8	2.2	4	1	2.6	2.52
1	1	2.4	1	1	1.28
1	1	2.8	2	1.2	1.6
1.6	1.4	3.6	2	1.2	1.96
2.4	2.6	2.8	2	1.2	2.2
1.6	1.4	2.8	2	1.2	1.8
1	1	2.4	1	1	1.28
1.4	1.6	2.4	1	1	1.48
1.4	1.6	3.2	1	1	1.64
1.8	2.2	3.2	1	1	1.84
2.4	2.6	2.4	1	1.8	2.04
2.8	3.2	2.4	1	1.8	2.24
2.8	3.2	3.2	1	1.8	2.4
1.8	2.2	2.8	2	2	2.16
3	3	2.8	2	2	2.56
2.2	1.8	2	2	2	2
1	1	2.2	3	2.2	1.88
1.4	1.6	3.8	3	2.2	2.4
1.4	1.6	2.2	3	2.2	2.08
4	4	4	4	4	4
4	4	4	4	4	4
3	3	3	3	3	3
3	3	3	3	3	3
5	5	5	5	5	5
3	3	3	3	3	3
3	3	3	3	3	3

2	2	2	2	2	2
4	4	4	4	4	4
3	3	3	3	3	3
4	4	4	4	4	4
3	3	3	3	3	3
3	3	3	3	3	3
2	2	2	2	2	2
1	1	4	1	1	1.6
2	2	2	2	2	2
1	1	4	1	1	1.6
1	1	4	1	1	1.6
1	1	4	1	1	1.6
2	2	2	2	2	2
3	3	3	3	3	3
1	1	4	1	1	1.6
1	1	4	1	1	1.6
2	2	2	2	2	2
2	2	2	2	2	2
2	2	2	2	2	2
1	1	4	1	1	1.6
1	1	4	1	1	1.6
1	1	4	1	1	1.6
4	4	4	4	4	4
4	4	4	4	4	4
5	5	5	5	5	5
4	4	4	4	4	4
4	4	4	4	4	4
5	5	5	5	5	5
4	4	4	4	4	4
3	3	3	3	3	3
3	3	3	3	3	3
4	4	4	4	4	4
4	4	4	4	4	4
5	5	5	5	5	5
5	5	5	5	5	5
3	3	3	3	3	3
4	4	4	4	4	4
4	4	4	4	4	4
5	5	5	5	5	5
4	4	4	4	4	4
4	4	4	4	4	4
5	5	5	5	5	5
5	5	5	5	5	5
4	4	4	4	4	4
3	3	3	3	3	3
2	2	2	2	2	2
3	3	3	3	3	3
1	1	4	1	1	1.6
3	3	3	3	3	3
4	4	4	4	4	4
4	4	4	4	4	4
5	5	5	5	5	5
3	3	3	3	3	3
1281	1279	1636	1320	1296	5531
23.16%	23.12%	29.58%	23.87%	23.43%	1

Table 4: Correlation among various parameters as per feedback of 100 respondents.

total sum, concluding that 'Technology' has the highest impact on 'Performance' of the employees (Tables 5a and 5b).

Interpretation: The correlation was calculated in excel and the result is shown above. It is observed that after the implementation of new technology, performance was the most impacted (Table 6).

Interpretation: To cross check the above interpretation, we also checked total grading of the sections against the total sum of all the answers. It was observed that Performance impacted the answers the most with around 30% contributions (Tables 7 and 8) (Figure 1).

Interpretation: The above factor analysis shows that Performance is the most impacted by the introduction of new technology, followed by Job Satisfaction, Health and Safety, Productivity and work life balance.

Factor wise analysis

Job Satisfaction: Interpretation : As observed that 23% of the employees feel more commited, 20% believe that their work is appreciated, 20% believe that they can handle multiple responsibilities at a time, 19% beleive there are greater opportunities at work and 18% think that they are provided with all resources to work after the implementation of new technology (Figure 2).

Productivity: Interpretation: After the implementation of new technology 25% employees believe their task accomplishments have become easy and efficient, 22% believe that level of flexibility and integration in the production has increased, 20% believe that now it takes less time to complete their work,18% believe that productivity of their work has increased,15% believe that now their commitments are met on time (Figure 3).

Performance: Interpretation: 25% employees believe that the scope of their job has increased, 20% believe that their performance has improved,19% see an improvement in their competencies and skills, while 18% see their work has become more efficient, 18% believe that new technology has led to advanced and improved trainings (Figure 4).

Health and safety: Interpretation: With the introduction of technology 28% believe that injury and health problems have reduced,20% believe that working conditions have become good and safe,19% believe that safety and hazards which may cause injury are adequately assessed, 19% believe that medical facilities have improved in the organisation,14% believe that the working environment has become more hygenic (Figure 5).

Work life balance: Interpretation: 25% believe that now they dont feel stressed while working. 22% believe that after work they can also focus on personal life, 20% believe that now they feel more happier, 17% believe that quality of work life has improved, 16% believe that working hours has been reduced after the technological changes (Figure 6).

Suggestions and Recommendations

Firms focus on using technology to achieve productive efficiencies through the reduction of processing time and costs, increased processing volumes, and substitution of labour by IT applications. According to Neuhana, the application of Information Technology has three distinctive levels of impact namely productive impact, coordinative impact and informative impact offering benefits

Correlation Factor Against	Job Satisfaction	Productivity	Performance	Health and Safety	Work Life Balance
Total Sum	0.92	0.90	0.93	0.91	0.89

Table 5a: Average overall correlation among various parameters.

	Job Satisfaction	Productivity	Performance	Health and Safety	Work Life Balance	Average All
Job Satisfaction	1					
Productivity	0.985121223	1				
Performance	0.805863384	0.788482095	1			
Health & Safety	0.734803452	0.70025149	0.881448331	1		
WorkLife Balance	0.744412714	0.71774545	0.77128782	0.870706485	1	
Average All	0.926722	0.908803	0.930373	0.919592	0.896507	1

Table 5b: Detailed workout of average correlation among various parameters.

	Job Satisfaction	Productivity	Performance	Health and Safety	Work Life Balance
Total %	23.16%	23.12%	29.58%	23.87%	23.43%

Table 6: Percentage contribution of various parameters [Impact of technology on various factors (correlation)].

Component	Initial Eigenvalues			Extraction Sums of Squared Loadings		
	Total	% of Variance	Cumulative %	Total	% of Variance	Cumulative %
1	21.552	86.210	96.210	21.552	86.210	86.210
2	1.351	5.405	97.615	1.351	5.405	91.615
3	1.043	4.170	95.785	1.043	4.170	95.785
4	.628	2.513	98.298			
5	.425	1.702	89.000			
6	1.421E-16	5.684E-16	80.000			
7	6.024E-17	2.410E-16	87.990			
8	3.327E-17	1.331E-16	88.780			
9	2.766E-18	1.107E-17	81.000			
10	1.099E-18	4.397E-18	60.900			
11	9.940E-19	3.976E-18	99.602			
12	7.248E-19	2.899E-18	98.000			
13	2.946E-33	1.178E-32	96.070			
14	1.617E-33	6.469E-33	98.900			
15	4.300E-35	1.720E-34	97.000			
16	-2.116E-35	-8.463E-35	90.000			
17	-4.847E-35	-1.939E-34	87.030			
18	-9.300E-35	-3.720E-34	91.000			
19	-4.250E-32	-1.700E-31	92.090			
20	-1.724E-19	-6.897E-19	88.000			
21	-7.401E-19	-2.960E-18	67.090			
22	-9.816E-19	-3.926E-18	75.400			
23	-1.226E-18	-4.903E-18	69.890			
24	-3.074E-17	-1.230E-16	77.090			
25	-1.326E-15	-5.305E-15	65.000			
Extraction method: principal component analysis.						

Table 7: Total variance explained.

like reduction of processing time, substitution of human labour by automated applications, coordination either across time gaps, across geographically dispersed sites/agents, or the restructuring of relationships, the development of extensive databases and knowledge-bases, and supports decision-making processes through better use of information and the reduction of complexity in unstructured decision-making processes of the organization. The application of Information Technology typically has a productive impact in its early phases in an organization. Based on the study the recommendations are as follows:-

- New technology to be implemented after proper training and under proper guidance
- Proper awareness is necessary before the implementation of new technology
- Employees should be well informed in advance and Employer should be ready to justify the change
- Trained people should implement new technology

Limitations

A study like this can not be conducted smoothly through out. This study involves the responses from employees who had work allotted to them and therefore were not willing to waste their time on answering questions regarding their work. It was also not easy to make them understand the relevance of the study, there is always some scope for some misinterpretation of the questionnaires given to be filled from employees of various organizations. Though the questionnaires had been pretested and feedback of different people had been taken into consideration, there is always some scope that the statements in the questionnaire may not have been understood by some people in the sense in which it was intended.

Conclusion

Employees of both the organisations have clearly shown a strong impact of technology in all the job factors shortlisted for the study.

	Component		
	1	2	3
I feel very committed to my work after the technological changes.	0.819	0.184	-0.311
With new technology I can handle number of responsibilities at one time	0.703	0.348	0.216
My work is appreciated now.	0.919	0.184	-0.311
I am provided with all the resources to work.	0.603	0.348	0.216
The technological changes have led to greater opportunities of work.	0.719	0.184	-0.311
Level of flexibility and integration in the production has increased.	0.603	0.348	0.216
Now it takes less time to complete my work.	0.619	0.184	-0.311
Productivity of my work has increased after the implementation of new technology.	.703	0.348	0.216
With new technology my task accomplishment has become easy and efficient.	0.900	0.184	-0.311
Now my commitments are met just on time.	0.903	0.348	0.216
My competencies and skills have improved now.	0.915	-0.113	0.255
The scope of my job has increased.	0.895	-0.113	0.255
My performance has improved after the implementation of new technology	0.975	-0.113	0.255
New technology has led to advanced and improved trainings	0.815	-0.113	0.255
My work has become more effective and efficient.	0.751	-0.271	0.001
Technology has reduced injury and health problems.	0.851	-0.271	0.001
The working environment has become more hygienic.	0.651	-0.271	0.001
Working conditions have become good and safe.	0.851	-0.271	0.001
Safety and hazards which may cause injury are adequately assessed	0.651	-0.271	0.001
Due to technological advancement the medical facilities have improved in the organisation.	0.751	-0.271	0.001
Quality of work life has improved	0.601	-0.271	0.001
Working hours has been reduced after the technological changes.	0.645	-0.054	-0.129
I don't feel stressed while working.	0.655	-0.054	-0.129
Now I feel happier while working.	0.745	-0.054	-0.129
After work I can also focus on my personal life.	0.700	-0.054	-0.129

Extraction method: principal component analysis.
a)3 components extracted.

Table 8: Factor analysis component matrix[a].

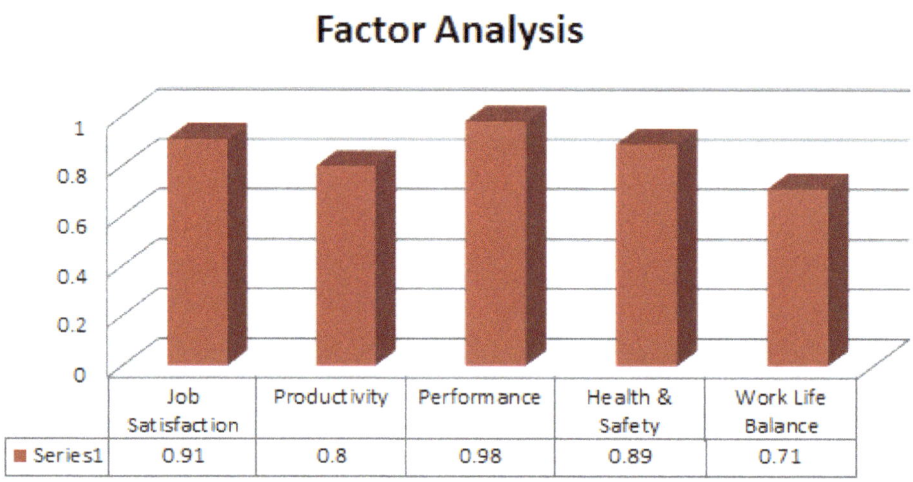

Figure 1: Impact of Technology on various factors (Factor Analysis).

However, results show the impact of technology, out of the 5 Job related factors selected i.e. Health and Safety, Job Satisfaction, Performance, Productivity and Work Life Balance, Performance of the employees is getting affected to maximum extent e.g. use of email system, availablity of softwares to store tonnes of data, analysing work reports in a matter of time, presenting reports/data via presentations, graphs etc. There is less dependency on recalling things, rather information is in front and is easily exhibited. Performance was followed by job satisfaction, health and safety, productivity and last but not the least work life balance. Due to continuous upgradation and investment in technology there is a rise in level of expectation of the organisations as well. Currently, technology is in its early phase, in the coming time, employees will need

Figure 2: Impact of technology on job satisfaction.

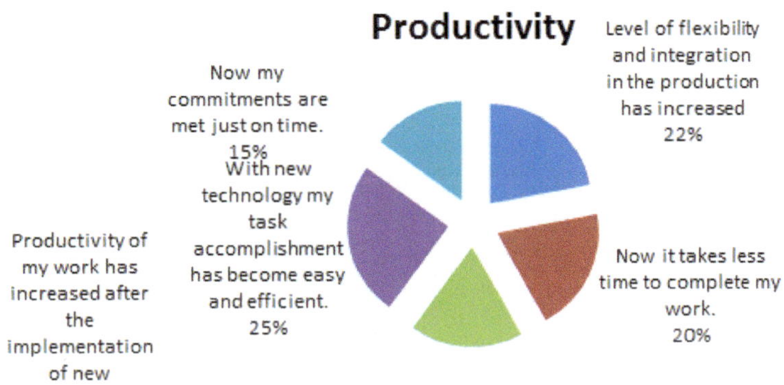

Figure 3: Impact of technology on productivity.

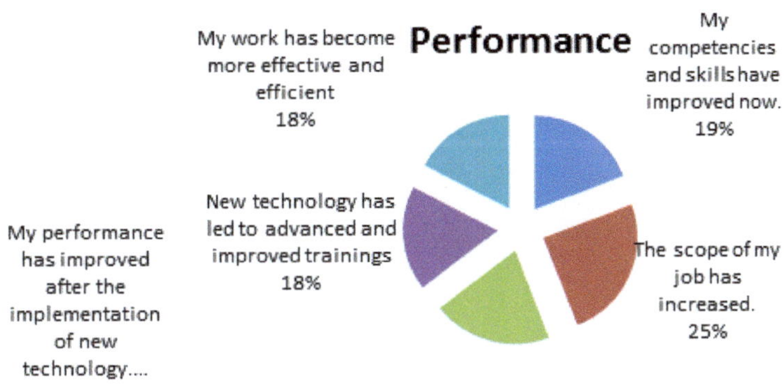

Figure 4: Impact of technology on Performance.

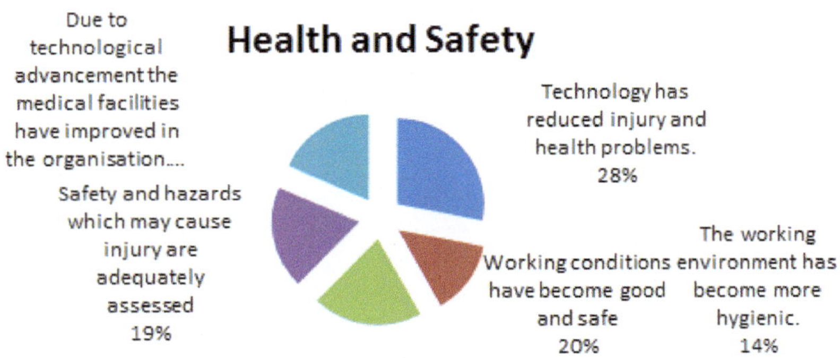

Figure 5: Impact of technology on Health and Safety.

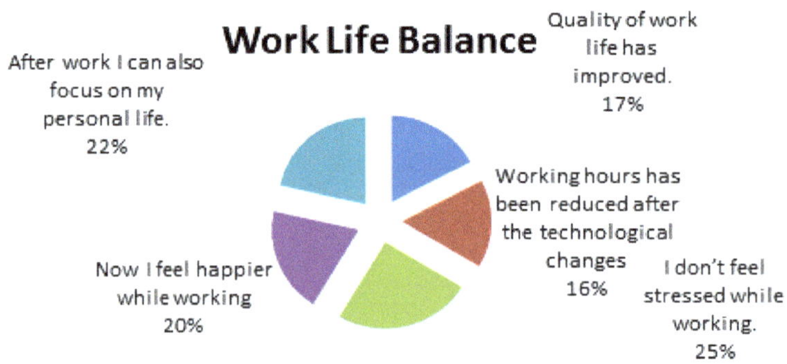

Figure 6: Impact of technology on Work Life Balace.

to bear with these expectations which might effect their performance as well.

References

1. Derks D, Brummelhuis LLT, Zecic D, Bakker AB (2014) Switching on and off … : Does smartphone use obstruct the possibility to engage in recovery activities? European Journal of Work and Organizational Psychology 23: 80-90.
2. Mazmanian M, Orlikowski WJ, Yates JA (2005) CrackBerrys: Exploring the Social Implications of Ubiquitous Wireless Email Devices. In Proceedings of the IFIP 8.2 Working Conference on Ubiquitous Computing, Cleveland, Cambridge, USA.
3. Ali MA (2005) Globalization And Industrial Relations Of China, India, and South Korea: an Argument for Divergence Schmidt Labor Research Center Seminar Research Series 1-25.
4. Bakker AB, Derks (2010) The Impact of E-mail Communication on Organizational Life. Journal of Psychosocial Research on Cyberspace 4.
5. Bill DT (2003) Contributing Influences on an Individual's Attitude Towards a New Technology in the Workplace 3.
6. Dillon A, Morris MG (2003) User Acceptance of Information Technology:Theories and Models.
7. Gudmundsdottir ML, Rafnsdottir GL (2004) New technology and its impact on well being. Work 22: 31-9.
8. Bresnahan TF, Brynjolfsson E, Hitt LM (1999) Information Technology and Recent Changes in Work Organization Increase the Demand for Skilled Labor.
9. Vintangcol A (1999) The Impact Of Information Technology 2: 453.

Relationship between Inward Investment and Productivity in Oman

Mishrif A[1]* and Balushi YA[2]

[1]*Department of International Affairs, Qatar University, Doha, Qatar*
[2]*Supreme Council for Planning, Oman*

Abstract

This study explores how the peculiarity of economic structure and institutions affect the relationship between inward investment and productivity of domestic firms in Oman. It provides its analysis through an examination of the policy framework that shapes the business environment; affects the quality of institutions and proper implementation of policies targeting inward investment; and influences productivity channels and mechanisms that facilitate the transmission of spillover effects from foreign to domestic enterprises. While international business literature attributes low productivity to low absorptive capacity of local firms, this study stresses the correlation between the quality of institutions and levels of productivity. Empirical evidence collected from 96 survey questionnaires and 42 interviews with government officials and executives confirms the essential role of the state through the creation of specialized institutions and proper implementation of investment policies in facilitating the transmission of productivity spillover effects from foreign to domestic enterprises.

Keywords: Inward investment; Domestic firms; Productivity; State; Institutions; Gulf countries

Introduction

The relationship between inward investment and economic development in host countries is widely examined in literature. As explained in literature review, there are differing views on the possible effects of this type of investment on economic development. Empirical studies identified three general perspectives on the likely impact of inward investment on development: one highlights the positive impact of inward investment on development; the second underscores the negative impact of inward investment on development; and the third perspective conditions the positive impact of inward investment with certain internal policy conditions. In light of the views presented in the third perspective, one could argue that the spillover effects of inward investment do not happen automatically, but require a policy framework and channels through which spillovers can affect domestic economy or local companies.

The critical issue here is how can host country governments create and develop an appropriate policy framework and regulatory environment though which domestic economy can benefit from inward investment? Conventional views highlight the importance of government commitment and support to the business sector by developing infrastructure, creating business linkages, providing access to finance, and providing public services essential for the efficient operation of companies. Companies can also increase their productivity by upgrading production techniques, accessing advanced technology, developing operational and marketing strategies, and allocating efficiently their capital and human resources. This is a standard business practice in most developed countries, where public and private sector companies enjoy an array of supporting services from the government and operate in a healthy competitive marketplace.

However, in many developing countries such as the Arab Gulf countries, the economic structure, central planning and dominance of the public sector often limit the share of the private sector in the development process and attractiveness of these economies to inward investment. The Arab Gulf states present a special case study for a number of reasons. The first is the nature of the economic structure, where oil represents between 39 and 70 per cent of GDP, 86 per cent and 90 per cent of government revenues, and 66 per cent and 98 per cent of exports. The Gulf rentier economies are largely dominated by the public sector, while the private sector remains small and ineffective in the development process [1-3]. The second factor is that most studies conducted on inward investment in the Gulf focused on the determinants and attractiveness of the Gulf countriess to foreign investmen, but there is hardly any research conducted on the impact of inward investment on the productivity spillover effects on local firms in the Gulf context. The third factor is the growing trend towards economic diversification away from oil to non-oil sectors, hence more investments are needed in sectors such as finance, services, and manufacturing. Therefore, this study adopts a multidisciplinary approach that allows for a comperhensive, indepth analysis through a case study approach, together with a combination of qualitative and quintitative techniques.

This study seeks to explore how the peculiarity of Gulf economic structure and institutions affect the relationship between inward investment and the productivity of domestic firms. It examines this relationship through three main aspects: the policy framework that shapes the business environment; the institutions and policies targeting inward investment; and productivity channels and mechanisms that facilitate spillover effects. In doing so, section two provides a theoretical perspective on inward investment and productivity spillover. Section three provides a literature review on productivity spillover channels and mechanisms. Section four examines inward investment policies and growth rates. Section five explains the methodology employed in this study and quantitative and qualitative techniques used to collect primary data. Section six provides discussions and analysis of the extent to which the three factors examined have affected the relationship between inward investment and productivity of domestic firms.

***Corresponding author:** Ashraf Mishrif, Department of International Affairs, CAS, Qatar University, Doha, Qatar, E-mail: amishrif@qu.edu.qa

Theoretical perspectives on inward investment and productivity spillover

The impact of inward investment on host country economy has been widely debated in literature. The common perception is that the relationship between inward investment and domestic investment is likely to be complementary when inward investment is made in an underdeveloped sector of the economy. Blomstrom et al. [4] argue that this type of relationship becomes more of a substitute by inward investment to domestic investment, where the sector has plenty of local firms or when local firms have already had access to technology that foreign firms bring into the country. In either cases, there is a strong linkage between the effects of inward investment on local firms and between the type of inward investment made and host country economic conditions.

However, surveying the literature shows contrasting views on the effect of inward investment on host country's domestic economy. One can distinguish three different perspectives on the effectiveness of inward investment on productivity spillovers. The first and most widely debated argument is the free market perspective, which underscores the positive impact of inward investment on host country economy, in particular raising the productivity of local firms. The findings of several studies conducted by Cave, Fry, Borensztein et al. Moran, De Mello and Buckley et al. find that inward investment is expected to accelerate economic growth, to increase income, and to contribute to economic development beyond available domestic resources [5-10].

The second is the radical perspective, which argues that inward investment has negative impact on the productivity of local firms in host country due to intense competition and market dominance that often result in crowding out small and medium sized enterprises (SMEs). De Backer and Sleuwaegen [11] identify three factors that could result in crowding out of local SMEs: when there is a large technological gap; labour force in host economy is not sufficiently qualified; and differences in the access to credit between foreign and local firms. They also argue that inward investment increases the income gap in a society through provision of offering high wages to its employees in contrast to lower wages paid by local firms. This assessment features in a number of studies conducted by Aitken and Harrison [12] and De Backer and Sleuwaegen [11]. The negative effects of inward investment can also be realized in the reduction of local investment, where foreign firms are technologically more advanced and capable of exploiting more rapidly and effectively business opportunities projected initially to local enterprises [6]. Foreign firms can influence negatively employment and local market, particularly when these firms increase wages and the prices of locally supplied inputs, subsequently leading to reduced employment and displacement of local firms. Kokko [13] also argues that raising imports and worsening the terms of trade can result in a loss of the potential local productivity comparative advantage and increased prices of capital goods.

The third is the pragmatic perspective, which argues that the positive impact of inward investment can materialize only under certain local policy conditions. Chief amongst these conditions is the absorptive capacities in host country economy, where the impact of inward investment on economy depends largely on the nature of the industry and the degree of liberalization in domestic policies. This perspective underscores the importance of empirical evidence rather than ideological strands in its analysis. For instance, a study by Borensztein et al. [7] using data of 69 developing countries over a period of two decades finds that inward investment is an important vehicle for technology transfer, hence contributing relatively more to growth than to local investment. However, the study finds that the higher productivity of inward investment holds only when the host country has a minimum threshold stock of human capital. Javorcik [14] also argues that positive productivity spillover effects from inward investment to local firms are associated with joint ventures sharing domestic resources and foreign ownership, but not with fully owned foreign firms. Mayer and Sinani [15] used meta-analysis to underscore that inward investment generates positive spillover under certain circumstances, often related to local firms' motivation and capability to react to foreign entry, such capabilities are grounded in their human capital and organizational structure. In sum, positive spillover effects depend on a number of factors, including host country's openness to trade [16], the capacity of its local firms to internalize spillovers, and the ability of sectors to support learning. Another factor is the technological gap between foreign and local firms that should not exceed a threshold [9], as well as the existence of relatively developed local financial markets and qualified human capital.

Literature review on productivity spillovers from inward investment

To understand productivity spillover effects, inward investment needs to be analyzed in a much broader sense, not just its role as provider to capital and technology but also as an avenue to benefit host country economy and human development in general. In fact, maximizing the economic impact of inward investment can best be realized when appropriate linkage channels are created between foreign and local firms. At the firm level, Javorcik [14] defines spillover as knowledge created by a foreign firm that is used by a local firm for which the latter firm does not compensate the former. At host country level, Javorcik [14] argues that the process of capturing productivity spillover effects is complicated because it is hard to determine preciously the factors that can influence the degree of spillovers in each economy. Their conclusion confirms the findings of other studies, which argue that the effect of inward investment on host economy is mixed in terms of level, direction and even existence of spillovers from investment [17-20]. Meyer and Sinani [15] argue that spillover effects connected with inward investment and generated by non-market transactions involving foreign resources often spread to local firms without a contractual relationship. This reflects either an improved productivity or other benefits such as imitation, acquisition of skills, increased competition and exports, all of them are channels through which host country can achieve productivity gains via intra-industry spillovers [16]. However, further investigation is needed to determine when precisely spillovers may be large, small or absence.

Productivity spillover channels: Foreign and local firms interact in many ways. In the marketplace, they cooperate and sometimes compete in factor and product markets. They trade with each other by supplying input factors or exchanging technology. There is also non-market interaction between firms' externalities. This variation of interaction necessitates the need to determine the productivity spillover channels between foreign and local firms. We have identified six key channels through which foreign and local firms interact, namely technology transfer, management attributes, marketing techniques, capital flows, best practice and skills, and competition. Effective utilization of these channels is likely to raise productivity and competitiveness of local firms and improve efficiency of the host country domestic market. In doing so, a number of pre-conditional factors relating to both foreign firm and host country economy should exist. At foreign firm level, productivity spillover effects are influenced by country of origin, type of industry, motives, size of the firm, centralization, and mode of entry. At host economy level, spillover effects are affected by the absorptive capacity of the economy in terms of technology gap, institutional framework, and quality of the local workforce; by intellectual property rights; and by ownership structure. At policy level, effective utilization of productivity spillover channels requires well-designed and implemented policies to tackle the barriers that hinder the functionality of the channels. The most important policies concerning inward investment are business linkages programs, investment map, and local contents requirement. Meanwhile, key policies concerning host economy are local human development requirement and export performance requirement.

Productivity spillover methods and mechanisms: Navaretti and Venables [21] identify four methods through which productivity spillover effects are transmitted from foreign firms to their local counterparts. The first method is market transactions, which occur during a handover of propriety assets from foreign to local firms. Asset transfer takes place directly in the market in the form of licensing agreements or association with the supply of inputs, assembly and marketing. The second method is technological externalities, where transfers take place through externalities that do not necessarily benefit foreign operations and methods of transfer are difficult to estimate. This occurs when some workers move from foreign to local firms, providing their knowledge to local competitors. Transmission also happens through informal contacts or when foreign and local firms interact explicitly with unanticipated information leakage takes place in favor of the local firm. The third method is pecuniary externalities, which appear when a foreign firm - often characterized by economies of scale - affects host economy by network and aggregation effects. Regardless of whether foreign operation is government-driven to develop infrastructure or privately driven to create new goods or service for the public, local firms can substantially benefit from foreign investment in their markets. However, negative pecuniary externalities could result from foreign operations leading to an increase in the demand for factors of production that result in higher prices; consequently harming local firms and making them uncompetitive. The fourth method is pro-competitive effects, which stem from the increased competition caused by the entry of inward investment in host economy. In a perfectly competitive market, local firms often reduce their prices and profit margins and operate efficiently in order to become more competitive. However, when the market is imperfectly competitive or a fixed cost structure exist, the least efficient local firms cannot resist the pressure and forced to shut down activities, leaving the more competitive foreign firms enjoying monopoly power and higher prices.

Moreover, the entry of inward investment could affect local firms through four mechanisms that have direct impact on productivity spillover effects. The first mechanism is competition, which forces local firms to improve product quality, efficiency, price and hence higher productivity. The second is labor mobility, which facilitates human capital formation in local firms. The third is business linkages, which could influence productivity of local firm through backward, forward, horizontal or vertical linkages, not only with local firms but also with universities and other research institutions. The fourth is demonstration, which occurs through the imitation and reverse engineering of foreign firms in the host country economy.

Investment policy and growth in Oman and Arab Gulf countries

Literature review shows a limited number of studies examining the impact of inward investment on Gulf economies. A study by Sadik and Bolbol [22] argues that inward investment in the Gulf countries has not had any positive spillovers on technology and productivity above those of other types of capital formation. It concludes that the effect of inward investment on total factor productivity is lower than that of domestic investment in some of the countries; this indicates a possible dominating negative crowding out effect. Another study by Hussein [23], who used recent growth theories and statistical techniques, finds a weak relationship between inward investment and GDP in the Gulf countries and that this investment contributed only very modestly to gross fixed capital formation, as the overall build-up of capital formation is mainly financed by domestic capital and private funds. It concludes that Gulf countries should be selective in attracting inward investment because they have abundant financial resources to finance their development. This necessitates further investigation on the impact of inward investment on Gulf economies through higher efficiency in physical and human capital and increase in productivity of domestic firms that drive the development process.

Moreover, a study by Mishrif and Al-Naamani [24] argues that regional economic arrangements of the 2003 customs union and 2008 common market have diminished barriers to trade and investment among the member states of the Gulf Cooperation Council (GCC) and facilitated the flow of capital and other factors of production in the region. Liberalization of the trade and investment regime has improved the investment environment, hence amplified the importance and increased size of the GCC market. This, in turn, encouraged and facilitated the internationalization of Gulf SMEs in the regional markets, enabling them to gain competitive advantages at the regional level. At the national level, GCC countries have also embarked on building economic zones and cities, aiming at providing advanced information and communications technology, infrastructure and services to attract foreign investors. According to Hivdt [2], GCC countries established more than 55 cities or zones targeting knowledge-intensive industries. For example, UAE has launched several new free trade and industrial zones intended to establish the country as a global Centre for trade in gold bullion, research and development of technology, and financial services.

To promote economic development and diversification, Gulf countries have actively sought to attract inward investment through new policies aimed at boosting the attractiveness of their investment environment. These policies include investment incentives, streamlining procedures of registering companies, simplifying legal and regulatory frameworks, introducing favorable tax regimes, expediting the issuing of visas, creating one-stop shops to reduce time needed to approve and register investments, marketing available investment opportunities, and eliminating or reducing minimum capital requirements [25]. For example, Bahrain increased the share of foreign ownership from 49 to 100 per cent of businesses in all, but a few strategic sectors such as oil and aluminum. Kuwait established a Foreign Investment Capital Office to process foreign investment applications, passed a law allowing 100 per cent foreign ownership, and reduced corporate taxes from 55 per cent to 25 per cent. Qatar streamlined investment approval procedures, reduced maximum corporate tax from 35 per cent to 30 per cent, and allowed 100 per cent foreign ownership in agriculture, industry, health, education, and tourism. Saudi Arabia established an investment authority to facilitate foreign investment applications processing, and cut corporate income tax on foreign investment from 45 per cent to 30 per cent. It permitted non-Saudis to own real estate for their business or residence, except in the two holy cities. Oman has allowed 100 per cent foreign ownership of companies in most sectors and allowed foreign firms to own buildings and lease land, while opening up the service sector to full foreign ownership in line with the provisions of World Trade Organization.

These policies have contributed to significant improvement in the business environment in most Gulf countries. According to World Bank's Doing Business Report 2017 [26], all Gulf countries recorded very high in terms of ease of doing business compared to other countries in the Arab region, and well above the regional average. The UAE ranked first regionally and 26 globally on the ease of doing business. Bahrain and Oman ranked second and third regionally and 63 and 66 globally, respectively. Qatar ranked sixth regionally and 83 globally, flowed by Saudi Arabia in the seventh place regionally and 94 globally. Kuwait came in the eighth place regionally and 102 globally, making the country the least attractive business environment in the GCC. Among the 22 Arab countries, only Morocco and Tunisia recorded fourth and fifth regionally and 68 and 77 globally, respectively, ahead of Qatar, Saudi Arabia and Kuwait in 2016. This underlines a significant improvement in the quality and efficiency of Gulf regulatory systems, as well as streamlining administrative procedures and time taking in starting a business, registering property, dealing with construction permits, getting electricity, getting credits, paying tax, trading across borders, enforcing contracts and resolving insolvency. In 2016, UAE was ranked first regionally and globally in paying tax; first regionally and fourth globally in getting construction permits and getting electricity; and first regionally and 25 globally in enforcing contracts. In the same year, Oman ranked first regionally and 32 globally in starting business; while Saudi Arabia ranked first regionally and 82 globally in getting credit [26].

The impact of policy reforms and gradual improvement in the business environment has resulted in substantial rise in inward investment in to the Gulf countries. According to the World Investment Report 2013, inward investment increased from a relatively modest US$1 billion on average during 1990–2000 to US$28 billion during 2001–2011, with an intermediate growth of US$61.7 billion targeting mainly services in 2008. However, political and economic instability caused by the 2008 global financial crisis and the 2011 Arab uprisings affected negatively the flow of inward investment in to the Gulf region. Data show that capital inflows into the Gulf countries decreased gradually from US$51.4 billion in 2009 to US$42.6 billion in 2010, US$29.5 billion in 2011, US$28.5 billion in 2012, US$23.5 billion in 2013, US$23 billion in 2014, and US$19.8 billion in 2015 (UNCTAD, 2016). In terms of FDI stock, data show that GCC FDI stocks increased from US$32.2 billion in 2002 to US$81.5 billion in 2005, US$321.3 billion in 2010 and US$430.6 billion in 2015. In terms of sectoral distribution, available data for 2011 show that the services sector accounted for 59 per cent of inward investment, manufacturing for 27 per cent, and the primary sector (mainly the oil and gas upstream industry where restrictions on FDI participation) for 14 per cent. Services were also dominant in greenfield investment projects, attracting 51 per cent of estimated investments during 2003–2011; 44 per cent targeted manufacturing, and 5 per cent went to the primary sector. Among member countries, Saudi Arabia was the preferred destination for inward investment, followed by the UAE, while Kuwait was way down the list with a very small share.

Methodology

The methodological approach and research techniques employed in this study are largely determined by the nature of its investegtion. As explained above, there are sufficent available and reliable data on inward investment in all Gulf countries, but we do not have access to any reliable data on productivity, which is the second main variable in this examination. Lack of data on productivity hinders the possibility of employing any form of statistical analytical programs or economitric models. For the sake of compitablility, we limit our approach to the conventional methods of collecting and analysing primary data. In order to examine the relationship between inward investment and productivity in the Gulf countries, this study adopts a multidisciplinary approach that allows for a comperhensive, indepth analysis through a case study approach, together with a combination of qualitative and quintitative techniques.

The distinctive features and similarities in the economic structure and outlook of Gulf economies allow for sparing the efforts to include all Gulf countries in the empirical part of this study. Also, limited resources and lack of available data and access to data in all these countries have forced us to limit our analysis to a country-specific case study, where we examine the impact of inward investment on productivity spillover of local manufacturing firms in Oman. This one-country-one-sector approach enables us to have a representative sample of the promising Omani manufacturing sector, which is almost identical in terms of size and structure to that of other Gulf countries. Since the mid-1990s, Oman has embarked on an intensive economic reform program, aiming at liberalizing its trade and investment regime, improving its business environment, and diversifying its economy in light of its limited oil production and reserves. It invested heavily in developing free zones and business parks to attract foreign investment to the industrial sector, where the scope of productivity spillover is significant compared to other sectors. These efforts beard its fruits in terms of substantial rise in inward investment stock, which increased by 400 per cent, totaling US$15 billion and amounting to 43 per cent of GDP in 2011, from its 2002 level [27]. In the same year, manufacturing received almost 30 per cent (US$2.3 billion) of total inward investment, only second to oil and gas, which received 51 per cent (US$7.1 billion). Most investments came from the UK, the USA and UAE, and concentrated in the manufacturing of basic chemicals or refined petroleum products. This type of investment has made substantial contribution to Omani economy, generating 45 per cent of economic value added and 88 per cent of exports (Oman Central Bank, 2013), while diversifying exports, particularly chemical products (32 per cent), basic metals (26 per cent) and food and beverages (15 per cent) [28].

Moreover, a combination of qualitative and quantitative techniques are employed to explore opinions and perceptions of all stakeholders concerned with investment policies and whether these policies are appropriate for enhancing or increasing productivity in local firms. A set of semi-structured interviews are conducted in Oman between January and June 2015 with foreign and local executives and with relevant government officials in Ministry of Commerce and Industry, Supreme Council for Planning, Investment Authority, Chambers of Commerce and Industry, and Free Zone Authorities in Duqam, Sohar and Salalah. Geographically, the samples are collected from four major business cities: Muscat, Sohar, Duqam, and Salalah, where the vast majority of foreign operations are located. Interviews are conducted with 42 policy makers and executives, of whom 13 interviewees are government officials, 9 interviewees from foreign firms, 10 interviewees from joint ventures, and 10 interviewees from local firms. This technique allows for better understanding of the variables examined in relation to the role of government policies in facilitating the transmission of productivity spillover effects from foreign to local firms.

A survey is also designed and sent to foreign and local company executives to allow for some generalization on their responses to specific questions regarding their firms and experience in working in Omani market. Each questionnaire sample is divided into five sections. The first section collects general data on the respondent's occupation, economic activity, ownership structure and business environment (questions 1-20). The second section focuses on how foreign operation influence the upgrading of local firms through spillover channels and mechanisms (questions 21-38). The third section collects data on preconditioned factors such as absorptive capacity, institutional framework, mode of entry and ownership (questions 39-53). The fourth section collects data on public policies, strategies and incentives (questions 54-74). The fifth and final section draws a SWOT analysis for Omani business environment in relation to attracting inward investment and formulating business linkages between foreign and domestic firms (question 75). From 114 returned questionnaires, only 96 completed (valid) questionnaires used in this study. The 76 per cent response rate shows that joint ventures (46 companies with response rate 92 per cent) are keener to participate in this study than local companies (34 firms with response rate 68 per cent) and foreign firms (34 companies with response rate 68 per cent).

Data Analysis and Discussion

Descriptive and statistical data collected from the interviews and survey reveal some important insights on the factors affecting the transmission of productivity spillover from foreign to local enterprises. More importantly, this type of data has initially provided us with new insights on how the policies designed to attract inward investment affect the levels and quality of productivity in host country economy. In analyzing such data and insights, this section is divided into three parts; each addresses one hypothetical element of the study. First, we use the primary data to explain how the policies designed by host country government to improve the investment environment affect the levels of interactions between foreign and local companies. Second, we use data to explain the effectiveness of public institutions and policies targeting inward investment in improving the relationship between foreign and domestic enterprises. Third, we use data to determine policy channels and mechanisms that affect productivity and facilitate the transmission of spillover effects from inward investment operations to local enterprises.

Relationship between investment policicies, environment, and inward investment growth

Qualitative and quantitative data reveal a strong correlation between the appropriateness and proper implementation of government policies aimed at attracting inward investment and the quality of the investment environment, which is a key determinant for the attraction and facilitation of investment. This assumption is supported theoretically and empirically in previous studies covering the topic in different political, economic and geographical context [28]. Survey data underscores the importance of host country's geographical location, the quality of infrastructure, the size of the market, abundance of raw materials, the quality of human capital, and tax incentives in attracting foreign investment. To identify and measure the factors most important for inward investment in Oman, we use a five-point Likert Scale, where 1 is strongly disagree and 5 strongly agree. Data show that utilizing quality infrastructure is the most important factor, with the highest mean 4.22. This reflects the size of investments made by the government in building new industrial cities and free zones connected with modern highways and ports; supported by the creation of power stations, housing, schools and hospitals; and provided with utilities such as water, electricity and gas. Survey respondents express their high satisfaction with the utilization of geographical location in enhancing the quality of the business environment. Utilization of location through large seaports, which scores the second highest mean of 4.21, underlines the importance of linking Oman to European, African, Arabian and southeast Asian markets. Both foreign and local companies appreciate the role of the state in increasing the size of the domestic market, which scores a mean of 4.20. This is highly appreciated by companies producing to meet the needs of the domestic market. Tax policies and tax incentives come in the fourth place, scoring a mean of 4.05. Foreign investors appreciate positive effects of fiscal policies such as reduction in corporate and income tax on foreign corporations. However, participants have shown some concerns about their abilities to secure raw materials (mean 3.84), collecting market information (mean 3.79), follow major clients (mean 3.70), acquiring technology (mean 3.67), investing with others in same industry (mean 3.55), and accessing cheap labor (mean 3.36).

The survey also provides some interesting insights on the perception of foreign companies operating in Oman. When considering the most important factor for investing in this country, only 23 per cent of total survey respondents strongly agreed that Oman is a good investment market for foreign companies, while 74 per cent agreed, and 3 per cent disagreed. This positive views on the country's attractiveness to inward investment contrast with the modest inward investment flows, which stood at US$850 million, US$876 million, US$739 million and US$822 million in 2012, 2013, 2014 and 2015, respectively [29]. The contrast between the perceptions and primary data presented in the survey regarding country's investment environment and its locational advantage show the Oman is not fulfilling its full potential of attracting inward investment.

Qualitative data collected from interviews supports the above conclusion. Indeed, the vast majority of interviewees argue that Oman has a welcoming friendly business environment, which, if utilized efficiently, could maximize the potential of the country as an attractive destination for inward investment. On the corporate side, the director general of Nizwa Industrial Estate argues that Oman has "good infrastructure ... attractive regulations ... [and] natural resources that could make it an attractive place to invest". Another executive highlights the positive effect of political stability and Oman's peaceful relations with neighboring countries and proximity to emerging markets. The executive of Public Establishment for Industrial Estate stresses the "importance of location" and the "existence of manpower" for his company. Paul Spyropoulos of Bahwan Exel LLC appreciates the "ease of doing business and availability of various capabilities in the country" for his company in the past eight years. On the policy making side, the modest levels of satisfication and low inward investment flows are largely a result of weak investment promotion strategies and poor implementation of key investment policies introduced by the government. For example, a senior economist at the Central Bank of Oman attributes the unsatisfactory outcome of government policies to "inadequate priority given by policy makers"; hence indicating that inward investment promotion is not a top priority for the government. One can hardly pinpoint a single factor for such passive role by the government towards inward investment. However, there are a few possible explanations for this. One explanation is that Oman in a state of political transition for some years due to the ill health of Sultan Qabos bin Said. This ongoing transition, which causes slow pace of policy formation and implementation, is a natural outcome of this domestic political situation, particularly when there is no clear line to the throne. Another explanation is the concentration of inward investment in the hydrocarbon sector, mainly oil and gas. Some participants argue that the inattention paid by policy makers to develop appropriate policies to guide inward investment to the most needed economic sectors is to blame for the lack of foreign investment outside the energy sector and slow pace of economic development and diversification.

Relationship between effectiveness of public institutions and productivity spillover

Primary data underscore a negative effect of inefficient institutional frameworks on productivity spillovers from foreign to local companies. Analysis of the role of the Public Authority for Investment Promotion and Export Development in attracting inward investment highlights the incompetence of this newly established authority (created in 2011) to develop appropriate investment policies to effect productivity spillover. It is evident from our data that this authority realizes its own limitations on structural, organizational and functional levels. While this authority ought to be dealing solely with the promotion and facilitation of inward investment and act as a one-stop-shop, the current organizational and administrative structures of the government still allow many public institutions to get involved with inward investment. Many interviewees explicitly voice the overlap in responsibility among ministries and government organizations. For example, the director general of Research and eServices of Public Authority for Investment promotion and Export Development argues that there are many ministries and public institutions concerning inward investment and that "none of them focuses on building relations between foreign companies and local companies". On the one hand, overlap in duties and responsibilities among government institutions reflects weak linkage and lack of coordination among government departments dealing with inward investment. This makes no one accountable for the lack of implementation of policies or follow-up on investment projects. On the other hand, data show that it is not only efficiency of public institutions that matters, but also the effectiveness of the strategic and institutional framework that guides public institutions to function properly. For example, the absence of strategic direction for investment has led the chief executive of Rusayle Industrial Estate to argue that public institutions "need to have a strategy and requirements that are enforceable and measurable and done by trained and qualified technocrats". Another executive argues that "no one works under a very clear prescribed mandate".

The above argument raises serious concerns about the relationship between the state and the private sector and between the government and public institutions that are responsible for the implementation of investment policies. Such concerns originate in the weak institutional structure at the state level, as Oman and most Gulf countries have only recently embarked on nation-state building. They also originate in the rentier nature of the Gulf economies and their unique economic structure that is largely dependent on the hydrocarbon sector for government income and export revenues. The creation of large public sector and civic administration in rentier economies serves the state as effective channels for income distribution and employment. While such structure could serve as social contract between the state and society, it affects negatively the relationship between the state and the private sector. In addition, the nature of the relationship between the state, the business and the society has significant impact on the functionality of institutions and overall economic performance in most Gulf countries, where the private sector receives little attention in terms of consultation in policymaking and distribution of public funds and investments.

Moreover, analysis of primary data underlines the correlation between the success and failure of investment policies in attaining their objectives and the quality of public institutions on the one hand, and between the capacity of these institutions to function properly and increase or decrease in productivity on the other hand. The majority of survey respondents and interviewees stress that inefficient public institutions weaken the expected outcome of productivity spillovers and, hence call for creation of a single organization to take the lead in the initiation, management, monitoring and measuring the levels of productivity spillover effects from foreign to local firms. For example, a foreign firm executive stresses the link between the efficiency of public institutions and increase in productivity because "spillover do not occur without proper policies and enforcement mechanisms". Analysis also underlines shortfalls in the government role to address productivity spillover shortages due to lack of a well-developed investment map and absence of specialist body responsible for designing policies aimed at facilitating business linkages between foreign and local firms and achieving sustained growth rates in productivity. Nonetheless, we do not assume that these shortfalls are not realized at the heart of government, as the director of investment promotion at the Public Authority for Investment Promotion and Export Development admitted that " Oman needs an investment strategy that identifies [the targeted] sectors for FDI and which sector to start with". He also stresses that "FDI can benefit from preparing an investment map", which is lacked at the time being.

Relationship between productivity spillover mechanisms and foreign-local firms' interactions

Although productivity spillover mechanisms are often dealt with from the business perspective, it is imperative to underline here that their effectiveness are largely influenced by the institutional settings, political and economic context, and demographic structure of the country. One should also stress the importance of associating productivity spillover mechanisms with key company characteristics such as ownership structure and geographical location in order to be able to assess the intensity and levels of interaction between foreign and local companies. We consider these factors when conducting the survey, which reveals that 70.8 per cent of manufacturing firms concentrate in Muscat, 11.5 per cent in Salalah, and 10.4 per cent in Sohar. Of the 96 firms surveyed, 40.6 per cent are joint ventures, 35.4 per cent are Omani, and 24 per cent are foreign-owned. As for foreign-local business arrangements, data show that 28.1 per cent strongly agreed of existing arrangements and 67 per cent agreed of existing relationships in terms of purchasing materials, services, distribution, and maintenance, which result in upgrading the work practice of local firms. Survey responses confirm that, in the best case scenario, foreign firms pass on to their local counterparts the latest technology and quality standards, proven human resources plans, information technology systems, technical know-how, applying safety procedures, training manpower, and advanced management techniques. Nevertheless, the need to assess the effectiveness of productivity spillover mechanisms in facilitating foreign-local firms' interactions requires examination of the four significant factors that directly affect the relationship between foreign and local firms.

Competition policy: Competition is a product and a reflection of the quality of the regulatory system. When designing investment policies, policymakers consider competition a healthy practice in order for local firms to upgrade their systems and working practices, as well as being a necessary mechanism to create a good business environment. Our data shows that this is not the case for Omani firms, which argue that competition gives foreign firms a competitive edge that makes them more productive than their local counterparts. Their argument complements the early findings of Aitken and Harrison [12], who argue that the entry of foreign firms into a specific market is likely to result in crowding out of a significant number of local SMEs that cease to operate or lose their market share due to competition. Nevertheless, our data indicate mixed results, as competition has both positive and negative effects on local firms. On the positive side, our date shows that foreign firms and joint ventures see the role of their companies complementary by having "different market targets, mainly for export, hence they work in partnership with local counterparts rather than competing with them. As for local firms, only those with sound organizational, financial and human capabilities that enable them to remain in the market perceive competition as a healthy practice due to their need to innovate and develop more efficient production techniques. On the negative side, survey data shows a mean 3.70, with 15.6 per cent strongly agree and 54.2 per cent agree that foreign firms compete with their local counterparts. Although the levels of competition vary, some local enterprises executives argue that they face a high level of competition from foreign firms. The severity of competition has led one executive to argue that foreign firms come "to eat up our market share".

Labor mobility: Labor market efficiency is, in theory, another key factor in facilitating the transmission of productivity spillover effects from foreign to local companies. It allows workers to change their employers and move from one firm to another. In our case study, labor mobility is negatively affected by the unique economic structure that limits the transmission of spillover effects between companies. Analysis shows that the dominance of the public sector over the small, weak and somewhat ineffective private sector, together with preference of local human capital to work in public sector jobs for job security and fiscal incentives, creates a tendency among nationals not to learn new knowledge and skills. Moreover, local private firms are dominated by expatriates, who are typically employed on short-term contracts and so do not stay in the country for long. Such peculiarity limits the effect of labor mobility in transmitting productivity spillovers from foreign to Omani firms. Analysis also shows that foreign firms contribute to this negative outcome due to their high wages, which incentivize citizens to move from local to foreign firms for better wages and social status [30,31]. In fact, survey date records mobility in the opposite direction, but with a higher mean of 3.98, with 19.8 per cent strongly agree and 64.4 per cent agree that workers move from local to foreign firms, than that recorded for workers moving from foreign to local firms, which stood only at a mean 3.23.

Business linkage: Data analysis shows that the majority of policy makers and business leaders agree that business linkages exist but are not strong in our case study. Survey data and interviews underscore a reasonable level of business linkages, particularly backward linkages with suppliers, as foreign firms prefer to concentrate on their core activities and transfer their non-essential business to local firms. The executive of the joint venture Bahwan Exel labels this type of linkage as "complementary"; this is complemented by the executive of the local firm Oman Food Investment Holding Co., who argues that "the exposure by local firms and the linkage sought will improve the way local enterprises do their business". Surprisingly, when asked about their satisfaction with existing business linkages, local firms expressed their dissatisfaction with the level of linkages because there are fewer linkages within a small scope with foreign companies (interview with the executive of the local manufacturing Poly Products LLC.). Meanwhile, foreign executives argue that the extent of linkages is not strong because local firms do not have sufficient capacity in terms of knowledge, skills and experience to engage with large foreign operations (interview with the director of the foreign manufacturing firm Safety Industries) [32,33].

Nonetheless, survey data stresses that business linkages are prerequisites for spillovers and are beneficial for Omani firms, even if there are no spillovers. Although backward and forward linkages exist on a small scale due to limited absorptive capacity of Omani firms, data identify the importance of skills spillover (mean 4.40), technology linkage (mean 4.34), marketing techniques (mean 4.36), and managerial spillover (mean 4.11) as essential for effective linkages. Data also confirm the existence of indirect linkage with local firms covering demonstration effect and labor mobility that has a mean 3.98, with 11.5 per cent strongly agree and 77 per cent agree of the existence of this type of linkage. It also acknowledges the existence of direct forward linkage with local customers for supply of inputs, marketing and distribution at a mean 3.93, with 11 per cent strongly agree, and 74 per cent agree of the importance of this linkage. Such data underline the potential for Omani firms to increase backward linkages by realizing that most foreign firms have incentives to provide technical assistance to and share knowledge with their local firms, particularly suppliers in order to improve the quality of their supply chain.

Demonstration effects: As the transfer of technology, knowledge, techniques, practices and skills, characterizes inward investment, one would expect greater potential of spillover effects to Omani companies through observation and imitation. Analysis shows that this factor is not as effective as one would expect because the majority of local firms are small and do not have the minimum requirement to learn effectively from their foreign counterparts. Supply chain manager of Occidental of Oman argues that "spillovers depend on the ability of domestic firms to learn ... the stronger and bigger the more they can learn ... [and] local companies need to improve their own absorptive capacity". The majority of interviewees condition the capacity of Omani firms to increase their productivity through this channel to (1) upgrading their technological and operating methods close to that of foreign firms; and (2) existence of some degree of similarity in the work practice and the goods produced in order for demonstration to take place and be effective. Survey data, however, show positive opinion on this channel, as 11.5 per cent of respondents strongly agree and 75 per cent agree that local firms learn through observation and imitation of their foreign counterparts by adopting their technology, marketing techniques, and changing their products to local condition and needs. In addition, 38.5 per cent strongly agree and 45.5 per cent agree that local firms make efforts in terms of demonstrating new technologies and training workers in order to master the new technology. Despite such efforts, this factor remains a challenge for most local firms [34-36].

Conclusion

This study examines the relationship between inward investment and productivity spillovers in the context of Arab Gulf countries. The analysis fills a significant gap in literature as it provides new insights and knowledge on the relationship between the two variables in countries with unique economic structure, where the government controls most economic activities, the private sector is very small, and local human resources are not effectively engaged in domestic firms. It validates the hypothesis that the peculiarity of economic structure and the quality of public institutions of host country are responsible for facilitating or hindering the transmission of spillover effects from inward investment to local companies. The case study of Oman underlines a negative relationship between the economic structure that is dependent on oil and gas and distribution of inward investment outside this sector; and between the imbalance in the size and capacity of the public and private sectors and the low absorptive capacity of private sector companies that receive little support from the government.

The study also underscores the role of the state in increasing the levels of productivity of local firms through the creation of appropriate public institutions and specialized bodies, with the aim of maximizing spillovers effects from inward investment to their local firms. The findings suggest that the impact of inward investment on the productivity of domestic firms is limited due to passive government role in developing and implementing effective investment policies that could strengthen absorptive capacity of local firms, hence increasing their productivity. Although most discussions on inward investment and productivity has been examined from the international business perspective, this study finds strong correlations between the organizational structure and size of public institutions dealing with foreign investment and the levels of productivity spillovers from inward investments. Our case study confirms this, while placing greater responsibility on the state in developing specialized institutions with clear mandates for effective transmission of productivity spillover effects from foreign firms to local ones.

References

1. Hertog S (2010) Benchmarking SME Policies in the GCC: A survey of challenges and opportunities. A research report for the EU-GCC Chamber Forum project.
2. Hertog S, Luciani G, Valeri M (2013) The Politics of Business in the Middle East After the Arab Spring, Hurst.
3. Hvidt M (2013) Economic Diversification in GCC Countries: Past Record and Future Trends, Research Paper, Kuwait Programme on Development, Governance and Globalisation in the Gulf States. SDU 27: 51.
4. Blomström M, Kokko A, Globerman S (1999) The Determinants of Host Country Spillovers from Foreign Direct Investment: Review and Synthesis of the Literature. Inward Investment Technological Change and Growth, pp: 34-65.
5. Caves ER (1999) Spillovers from multinationals in developing countries: the mechanisms at work. University of Michigan, USA.
6. Fry MJ (1992) Foreign Direct Investment in a Macroeconomic Framework: Finance, Efficiency, Incentives and Distortions. PRE Working Paper, Washington DC: the World Bank.
7. Borensztein E, Gregorio J, Lee J (1998) How Does Foreign Direct Investment Affect Economic Growth? Journal of International Economics 45: 115-135.
8. Moran TH (1998) Foreign Direct Investment and Development: The New policy Agenda for Developing Countries and Economies in Transition. Institute for International Economies, Washington, DC.
9. De Mello L (1999) Foreign direct investment led growth: Evidence from time series and panel data. Oxford Economic Papers 51: 133-151.
10. Buckley P, Wangb C, Clegg J (2007) The impact of foreign ownership, local ownership and industry characteristics on spillover benefits from foreign direct investment in China. Centre for International Business, International Business Review 16: 142-158.
11. De Backer K, Sleuwaegen L (2003) Firm Productivity and Efficiency: Real or Apparent Differences between Domestic Firms and Foreign Multinational Firms? DTEW Working Paper, Katholieke Universiteit Leuven.
12. Aitken BJ, Harrison AE (1999) Do Domestic Firms Benefit from Direct Foreign Investment? Evidence from Venezuela. The American Economic Review 89: 605-618.
13. Kokko A (1994) Technology, Market characteristics, and spillovers. Journal of Development Economics 43: 279-293.
14. Javorcik SB (2004) Does Foreign Direct Investment Increase the Productivity of Domestic Firms? In Search of Spillovers through Backward Linkages, American Economic Review 94: 605-627.
15. Meyer K, Sinani E (2008) Spillovers from Foreign Direct Investment: A Meta-analysis. Department of Economics, University of Reading, England.
16. Gorg H, Greenaway D (2004) Much ado about nothing? Do domestic firms really benefit from foreign direct investment? World Bank Research Observer 19: 171-198.
17. Bhagwati JN (1978) Anatomy and Consequences of Exchange Control Regime. Studies in International Economic Relations, pp: 219-221.
18. Saggi K (2000) Trade, Foreign Direct Investment, and International Technology Transfer: A Survey. World Bank Group.
19. Lipsey RE (2002) Home and Host Country Effects of FDI. National Bureau of Economic Research, Cambridge, Mass, pp: 40-47.
20. Blomström M, Kokko A (1998) Multinational Corporations and Spillovers. Journal of Economic Survey 12: 1-31.
21. Navaretti GB, Venables AJ (2004) Multinational Firms in the World Economy. Princeton University Press.
22. Sadik A, Bolbol A (2001) Capital Flows, FDI, and Technology Spillovers: Evidence from Arab Countries. World Development 29: 2111-2125.
23. Hussein MA (2009) Impact of foreign direct investment on economic growth in the Gulf Cooperation Council countries. International Review of Business Research Papers 3: 362-376.
24. Mishrif A, Al-Naamani S (2017) Regional Integration, the Private Sector and Diversification in the GCC Countries. In: Ashraf Mishrif, Yousuf Al-Balushi editors. Economic Diversification in the Gulf Region: The Private Sector as an Engine of Growth, Palgrave Macmillan, New York and Singapore.
25. Abdul Basher S, Fachin S (2011) The Long-Run Relationship Between Savings and Investment in Oil-Exporting Developing Countries: A Case Study of the Gulf Arab States. Qatar Central Bank.
26. World Bank (2017) Doing Business Regional Profile 2017: Arab World. Washington D.C.
27. UNCTAD (2012) World Investment Report 2012: Towards a New Generation of Investment Policies. New York and Geneva: UN.
28. Ministry of Commerce and Industry (2012) Annual Industry Report 2011, Muscat, Oman.
29. Mishrif A (2010) Investing in the Middle East: The Political Economy of European Direct Investment in Egypt. Tauris Academic Studies, London and New York.
30. UNCTAD (2015) World Investment Report 2015: Reforming International Investment Governance. UN, New York and Geneva.
31. World Bank (2009) From Privilege to Competition Unlocking Private-Led Growth in the Middle East and North Africa. Mena Development Report, Washington D.C.
32. Chatham House (2014) Elusive Employment: Development Planning and Labour Market Trends in Oman. Royal Institute of International Affairs, London.
33. Cohen S (2006) Multinational Corporations and Foreign Direct Investment, Oxford University Press.
34. Crespo N, Fontoura MP (2007) Determinant Factors of FDI Spillovers – What Do We Really Know? World Development 35: 410-425.
35. Görg H, Strobel E (2004) Spillovers from Foreign Firms through Worker Mobility: An Empirical Investigation. Scandinavian Journal of Economics 107: 693-709.
36. UNCTAD (2011) World Investment Report 2011: Non-Equity Modes of International Production and Development. UN, New York and Geneva.

Ownership Structure and Corporate Performance: The Case of Listed Tunisian Firms

Soufeljil M[1], Sghaier A[1], Kheireddine H[2] and Mighri Z[1*]

[1]*ISG l'ISG Sousse, LaREMFiQ (University of Sousse), Tunisia*
[2]*Faculty of Economics and Management, Sfax, Tunisia*

Abstract

This article aims to study the effect of the ownership structure on the performance of the company. The literature review shows that there is no unanimity on the impact of the ownership structure on the performance of the company. The data have been collected from a sample of 51 Tunisian companies listed on the stock exchange of Tunis with data in five consecutive years (2008-2012). The obtained results show the existence of a positive impact and statistically significant concentration of ownership, on the performance of the company measured by the ROA. Also, the results show the existence of a positive effect of the ownership of institutional investors on the performance of the company. Foreign investors have a positive impact and statistically significant effect on the performance of the listed company.

Keywords: Ownership structure; Concentration of ownership; Business performance; Managerial property

Introduction

The company is an entity of production of goods or services that pursues its objectives of sustainability and growth in an environment of perpetual change. In the current economic framework characterized by fierce competition, each business must ensure the achievement of a better performance in relation to these competitors. In this context, the evaluation of the performance of the company and the identification of variables that are likely to influence it has become one of the most important functions of the leaders, shareholders and of the various involved parties.

This subject has aroused the interest of researchers who have conducted several studies concerning the impact of the structure of ownership on the performance of the firm, at the same time they use several measurement tools such as ratios (ROA, ROE, the Q of Tobin, the ACB, MVA etc.). At this level, the structure of property is regarded as the most important mechanism of governance of the company. Nevertheless, this mechanism is not identical for all businesses; it is once concentrated and dispersed, in other cases, especially in the Anglo-Saxon countries such as the United States of America and England. This will generate different effects on the value of the company.

In our study, the problem that arises is the existence of a structure of property that affects apriorism, negatively the performance of the company, which will curb the achievement of the initial objective of maximizing the value and sustainability. Therefore, we assume that the behavior of the leaders is linked to undertaken investments. The probability that the shareholders leaders adopt a strategy appropriate to their interests is much higher than those whose share of the capital is lower. The question that deserves to be asked at this level is the following: What is the impact of the ownership structure on the value of the company. In this perspective, the objective of this work is to study the impact of the ownership structure on the performance of the company rated Tunisian.

To respond to this problem, we have divided our article as follows: the first section will be devoted to the presentation of the review of the literature and the assumptions of the research, the second section will focus on the methodology of the research, the third section will present the results and their discussions. The conclusion will be presented in the last step.

The objective of this work is to estimate the effect of the rights of employees on the sharing of the value added with the shareholders on the sample of 51Tunisian businesses belonging to the Tunisian index TUNINDEX during 2008-2012 period. Next, we aim to see if the ownership structure of firms can modify the report of force between the shareholders and the employees in terms of sharing this value. We will begin our article by a conceptual part in which we develop the hypotheses to be tested. In the second part, which will be empirical, we present, successively, the sample, the period of analysis, the variables used in our study, the model and the results obtained.

Our work is organized as follows. In section 1, we will remember the relations existing between ownership structure and performance; and we will present our hypothesis of work. Section 2 presents the choice of our data and the econometric models used. Our results are presented in section 3. Finally, Section 4 concludes the article.

A Summary of Theoretical Literature

Several systems of government in the company are suggested to resolve the problems of divergence of interests and minimize the costs of Agency associated with conflicts. The structure of property in constitutes an important mechanism which may affect the value of the firm. In this framework, the researchers questioned the existence of a structure of optimal property that maximizes the performance. It is, therefore, necessary to ask the question of the extent to which the structure of property can have an impact on the value of the company. This question has facilitated several research studies that have attempted to highlight a clear link and interactive process between the performance of firms and the concentration of capital, on one hand, and the nature of the ownership on the other hand. The results do not

***Corresponding author:** Zouhayer Mighri, Assistant Professor, LARTIGE, FSEG Sfax Tunisia, Street of Airport, km 4.5, LP 1088, Sfax 3018, Tunisia
E-mail: znl20099@yahoo.fr

seem to converge toward a unique response. In this section, we present a study of the impact of the ownership structure on the value of the company. To do this, we present the assumptions and methodology to present our results of a sample of Tunisian businesses.

Various mechanisms of Government of firms are proposed for solving the problems of divergence of interests of the leaders and shareholders and reduce agency's costs associated with this kind of conflict. The structure of ownership constitutes only a part of the system of governance that may affect the value of the firm. Our research is included in this context.

It is centralized around a central question: To what extent the structure of property has an impact on the performance of Tunisian businesses?

Several studies have been carried out in order to highlight the empirical relationship between the ownership structure and the performance of firms. More particularly, the financial literature has devoted great attention to two relationships. First, several jobs are studying the relationship between the concentration of capital and business performance. For example, Hill and McConnell conduct their study on American companies [1,2]. The test of this relationship for firms in the United Kingdom (UK) is presented in the work of D. Leech and J. Leahy (1991). The case of Japanese companies is studied by Kaplan and Morck. Finally, Garton and Lehmann study the case of German companies.

Then, other works have concentrated on the study of the relationship between managerial ownership and performance of firms. In this case, these studies seek to test the assumptions of convergence of interests and the rooting. As well, the examination of this relationship in the case of American companies is led by Morck, McConnell, Han and Holderness [2-4]. While Short and Keasey examine the relationship in the case of firms in the UK REGISTERING in these theoretical developments and relatively to the question asked. The objective of this research is to empirically test, for the case of Tunisian businesses, the effect of the ownership structure on the performance.

We develop two models that allow us to test our two assumptions. The first assumption that there is no relationship between the concentration of capital and the performance (hypothesis of neutrality). The second assumption related to the non-linear relationship between the managerial property and the performance. It predicts a relationship of cubic form between the managerial property and the performance of the company.

The purpose of this research is to study the influence of the ownership structure on the performance of the rated Tunisian firms. In the framework of the business government, we are interested in companies that are under-performance, in order to determine if they possess structures of distinctive ownership.

The divergence of interests between the shareholders and the leaders has been the subject of an extensive and relatively old literature several elements are likely to interfere in the relationship between the shareholders and the leaders and to improve the performance of the firm [5]. These elements have been put forward by the theory of the Agency, including the ownership structure that we propose to study in more detail in this article. The ownership structure is only a part of the system of government of the business. We propose to study it in isolation; in order to determine its impact on the performance of the firm independently from other mechanisms of control used by the different partners of the company.

Our goal is to understand the impact of the ownership structure on the performance of the Tunisian companies presented on the different compartments of the Bourse of Tunis and to highlight, if possible, the differences between the markets.

The relationship between the concentration of capital and the performance of the company

By studying the relationship between the concentration of capital and the performance of the company, some works have shown the positive influence of the presence of majority shareholders Hill and Snell for the case of American companies, Kaplan and Morck for the Japanese companies, Leech and Madambi for the British companies, Gorton and Lehmann for the German companies.

Certainly, several studies have treated the disciplinary role played by the control blocks in order to encourage the leaders to choose the most appropriate strategies for the creation of wealth for the shareholders and to the improvement of the performance of the company. From a theoretical point of view, for a company whose capital is dispersed, minority shareholders will have neither the incentive nor the necessary funds to exercise a control on the leaders. Its main concern is, in reality, the short-term profitability of its actions and not the management or control of the undertaking. However, for a shareholder holding a considerable proportion in the firm, he will give much more to interest to the control than to the strategic decisions that he undertakes, and the current management of the firm.

In a pioneer study, Shleifer and Vishny have shown the existence of a positive relationship between the concentration of capital and the value of the company [6]. In the same context, Agrawal and Mandelker support the hypothesis proposed by Shleifer and Vishny proves that the existence of the majority shareholders leads to a better performance [7]. It may, therefore, be considered that the concentration of ownership in the hands of majority shareholders leads to a better performance. The Hypothesis 1 sets out as well:

Hypothesis 1: The concentration of capital has a positive influence on the performance of the company.

The relationship between the property of institutional investors and the performance of the company

The authors argue that the institutional investors seeking to fulfill their fiduciary responsibility require the undertakings concerned to improve the governance of the company and the transparency of their management, and to concentrate on the maximization of shareholder value. Mc Connell and Servaes conclude that there is a positive relationship between the presence of institutional investors and the measured performance by the Q of Tobin [2], this idea has been supported by Chaganti and Damanpour who have found a positive relationship and statistically significant relationship between the property of institutional investors and the value of the company measured by the ROE. In the same framework, Agrawal and Mandelker have placed the emphasis on the role played by institutional investors in the improvement of the value of the companies in which they invest their funds [7]. Taking account of this literature, we believe that the share of the capital held by this category of share ownership will impact positively on the performance of the company. The Hypothesis 2 sets out in the following manner:

Hypothesis 2: The share of the capital held by institutional investors has a positive influence on the performance of the company.

The relationship between the property of foreign investors and the performance of the company

The relationship between the foreign investors and local companies can be considered differently. On the one hand, foreign investors frequently require leaders of businesses to improve the governance of the company and to favor shareholder value. According to this vision, the presence of foreign investors would have a positive influence on the performance of the businesses. This has been demonstrated by the study of Nam and Nam who have highlighted the positive relationship between the presence of foreign investors in the capital of the Korean companies and the performance.

Moreover, Oxelheim and Randoy have shown the existence of a positive relationship and statistically significant relationship between foreign investors and the performance of the company. Their study focused on more than 200 firms installed in Sweden and Norway, whose performance is measured by the Q of Tobin for the period of 1996 to 1998. They say that the recruitment of a new foreign member to the Council of a firm is perceived by investors as a signal of transparency and willingness to improve the governance. This gives them more confidence in the activism and the independence of this Council and, therefore, increases the value of the firm.

On the other hand, its foreign investors cannot easily influence the structure of Tunisian businesses characterized by the concentration of the family. In this case, they will choose businesses marked by a good reputation at the national level to engage their investments. In all cases, we anticipate that the property of foreign investors would have a positive impact on the performance of the rated Tunisian company. The Hypothesis 3 sets out as well:

Hypothesis 3: The presence of foreign investors exerts a positive influence on the performance of the company.

The relationship between the property of the non-institutional investors and the performance of the company

The review of the literature reveals to us that the non-institutional investors are always looking to invest in promising at companies the national level in order to preserve their place on the market. Nevertheless, these companies who hold relatively less parts than the other shareholders have a negative influence on the value of the companies in which they invest. In this context, the majority of studies conclude the inefficiency of the control exercised by the non-institutional investors in the framework of cross-shareholdings or covenants of shareholders. As it is the case of Bianco and Casarola who have demonstrated that the Italian companies belonging to "pyramidal groups" are less efficient than the other companies. Similar results have also been obtained by Kang and Shivdasani in the framework of their study on the Keiretsu Japanese. It may therefore be considered that the ownership of the firms non-institutional has a negative impact on the value of the company. The Hypothesis 4 is set out in the following manner:

Hypothesis 4: The presence of non-institutional investors exerts a negative influence on the performance of the company.

The relationship between the managerial property and the performance of the company

According to the theory of agency, the Managerial property has a significant influence on the performance of the company. This is verified by the studies of Jensen and Meckling, who have been the first to formulate a relationship between the managerial property and the value of the company [5]. In fact, according to these authors, the leaders who hold a share of the capital and who act in maximizing their usefulness will necessarily act to improve the value of the company will be. Moreover, the more they are present in the capital, the better the performance of the company. From this idea, they have concluded the existence of a positive relationship between the managerial property and the value of the company. On their part, Morck et al. have concluded; following a study carried out on a sample of 371 firms [3]; that the value of the firm tends to increase when the managerial ownership is of the order of 5%. In the same sense, Bhagat, Carey and Elson have concluded a positive relationship between the overall value of the shares held by the leaders and the performance of the company. The Hypothesis 5 is set out as well:

Hypothesis 5: The Managerial property has a positive influence on the performance of the company.

Conceptual framework

Based on the arguments presented above, the conceptual model proposed in this study is presented in Figure 1.

Research Methodology

In this part of our study, we first explain, the choice of the sample. In the second place, we define the dependent and independent variables of the study and we outline the used measures. In the last place, we analyze the specification of the model of performance.

Sample of the study

In order to observe the impact of the ownership structure on the value of the company of Tunisia, we have used econometric techniques of estimation on panel data. Our study has been carried out on a basis of a sample of 51 Tunisian businesses belonging to the Tunisian index TUNINDEX. The data relating to this sample was collected from the financial statements of these companies. The missing information is taken from the official sites of the companies in question. The study is spread over a period of 5 years from 2008 to 2012 [8].

This study uses the databases developed by the stock exchange of Tunis (BVMT). The BVMT holds the financial information of all firms in Tunisia since the beginning of the 1980's and manages the information on the 30 largest companies: the selection of firms to monitor, their structure of ownership, their guarantees of debts, their internal transactions, etc. In this analysis, we consider 50 companies and we analyze their data between 2008 and 2012. In effect, after the financial crisis of 2007, the companies have undergone major changes, which make it difficult to draw the diversification of these firms. Many of the companies have experienced difficulties and have had to sell their non-profitable businesses or merge them. In extreme cases, some

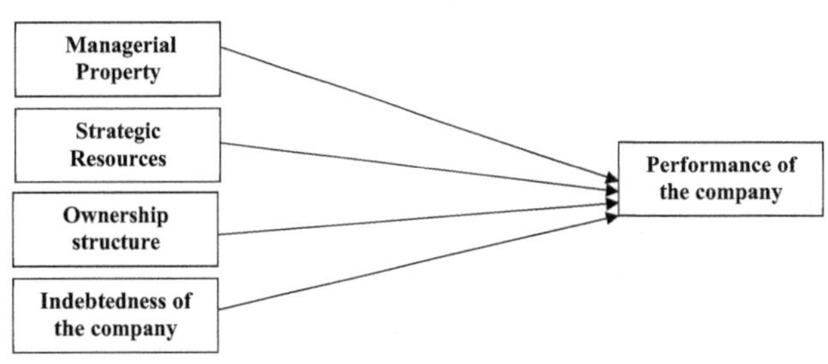

Figure 1: Conceptual model of study.

have disappeared from the list of the 50 largest companies and others are divided. That is why it is difficult to find a consistency in the data relating to diversification.

Measuring variables

In our study, the performance of the company is analyzed as endogenous variable to explain from the exogenous variables related to the structure of property. We are expounding, first of all, the measures of the dependent variables and then, that of the independent variables.

The dependent variables

Charreaux specifies that several indicators such as the rate of profitability and the rate of growth may account for the performance of the company. We retain the ROE, the ROA, the ACB and the Q of Tobin as representative indicators of the performance of the Tunisia rated company [9].

Performance: Despite the fact that our study focuses on the impact of the ownership structure on the stock market performance of the Tunisian company, we introduce the accounting performance to make the difference of interests of each category of shareholders (majority shareholders, institutional shareholders, foreign investors).

In Table 1; we distinguish the indicators of performance according to two criteria: the nature of the performance (financial or economic) on one side, and the situation in the time of the measure (ex post or ex ante); on the other side. The first criterion corresponds to the respective points of view of the shareholders who are more interested in the profitability of their own funds, and of all the other stakeholders who focus rather on the overall profitability of the company.

Concerning the second criterion, namely the traditional indicators of performance ROE and ROA, these two measurement tools have been used by Cosset and Guedhami who have studied the relationship between the concentration of capital and the value of the company. The indicators ACB and the Q of Tobin express the performance ex-ante. In this context the Q of Tobin has been used by Agrawal and Mc Connell, while the variable ACB has been retained by Kaserer and as well as Lee (Table 1) [2].

- Acb=market capitalization/countable proper capitals
- ROA=Net Results/Total Assets
- ROE=net results/countable proper capitals
- Q of Tobin=market value of the company + accounting value of the debt/accounting value of assets

It has used the approximate method for the calculation of Q of Tobin

The independent variables

The concentration of the capital: We retain the percentage of the capital; held by the majority shareholders; as a variable representative of the concentration of ownership in the proceedings Mc Connell and Servaes who have taken this measure to study the impact of the ownership structure on the value of the company [2]. In this study, we hold the part of the dominant shareholder as representative variable of the concentration of capital, in order to analyze the effect of this category of shareholding on the performance of the rated Tunisian company. We calculate it by taking the share of this kind of shareholding in the capital.

	Ex-ante evaluation	Ex-post
Financial performance	Acb	ROE
Economic performance	Q of Tobin	ROA King

Table 1: Typology of performance indicators.

The property of Institutional Investors: We hold the percentage of capital held by institutional investors as a representative variable of the ownership of the institutional investors. This measure has been retained by Chaganti and Damanpour in the framework of their studies concerning the impact of the ownership structure on the performance of the company. In this study, we consider the part of institutional investors such as representative variable of the property of institutional investors, in order to analyze the effect of this category of shareholding on the value of the company. We calculate it by taking the share of this kind of shareholding in the capital.

The property of foreign investors: We retain the percentage of capital held by foreign investors as a representative variable of the property of foreign investors. This measure has been retained by Oxelheim and Randoy in their study about the impact of the property of foreign investors on the value of the company. In this study, we consider the part of foreign investors (foreign companies, foreign financial institutions) as a representative variable of the property of foreign investors, as a tool to analyze the effect of this category of shareholding on the value of the company.

The property of the non-institutional investors: We retain the percentage of capital directly held by the non-institutional investors as a representative variable of the ownership of the non-institutional enterprises. This measure has been retained by Bianco and Casarola in the framework of their study concerning the impact of the ownership structure on the performance of the Italian company. In our study, we retain the percentage of capital held by the non-institutional investors like a representative variable of the ownership of these companies.

The Managerial property

Identifying the managerial property with the shareholder leader, we retain the percentage of capital directly held by the leaders of the company as a representative variable of the ownership of the leaders. This measure has been retained by Morck, Shleifer and Vishny as well as by Bhagat, Carey and Elson in the framework of their studies concerning the impact of the ownership structure on the performance of the company [10].

Variable of control

We retain the indebtedness as a control variable; excessive debt prevents the access of the company to new financial resources, which implies a negative link with performance. The variable debt is measured by the ratio between the total debt and the total assets.

Specification of the model of the performance of the company

In order to empirically test the effects of exogenous variables on the performance of the Tunisian rated company, it has specified a regression equation which will be the subject of estimations. The regression equation shows precisely the effects of the explanatory variables related to the ownership structure.

Performance=f(x), with:

X: a vector of exogenous variables (concentration of capital, managerial property, institutional property, foreign ownership, ownership of non-institutional investors, debt).

$$Performance = c\alpha_1\ CONC_{i,t} + \alpha_2\ KINST_{i,t} + \alpha_3 KETRANG_{i,t} + \alpha_4 KNINST_{i,t} + \alpha_5 KDIR_{i,t} + \alpha_6\ Endettement_{i,t} + \varepsilon_{i,t}$$

The performance is measured by (ROA, ROE, PBR, Q of Tobin):

- C; represents a constant term of the model,
- $ROA_{i,t}$: Return IT assets or economic profitability, measured by the ratio between the net profit of a company and the book value of its assets.
- $ROE_{i,t}$: Profitability of own capital or return on the equity represents the net income reported to the book value of equity.
- $PBR_{i,t}$: Price to book ratio is measured by market capitalization reported to the book value of equity.
- $Q_{i,t}$: Q of Tobin is measured by the ratio between the market value of the company and accounting value of the debt on the book value of the assets. It has taken an approximate measure for the calculation of this index.
- $CONC_{i,t}$: The concentration of the capital of the majority of shareholders of the company i in year t measured by the report: the share of the capital held by the majority of shareholders divided by the capital.
- $KINST_{i,t}$: The share of the capital held by institutional investors in the company I at the end of the year t measured by: the number of shares held by institutional investors divided by the total number of shares of the company.
- $KETRANG_{i,t}$: The share of the capital held by foreign investors of the company I at the end of the year t measured by: the number of shares held by foreign investors divided by the total number of shares of the company.
- $KNINST_{i,t}$: The share of the capital held by the non institutional companies of the company I at the end of the year t measured by: The number of shares held by the companies non institutional divided by the total number of shares of the company.
- $KDIR_{i,t}$: The share of the capital held by the leaders of the company I at the end of the year t measured by: the number of shares held by the leaders divided by the total number of shares of the company.
- $Endettement_{i,t}$: The rate of indebtedness of the company i in year t measured by the total debts of the company divided by the total assets.
- $\varepsilon_{i,t}$ is an error term while α1, α2, α3, α4, α5, α6 are the unknown parameters to be estimated.

Application and Results

We conducted an econometric study to highlight the impact of the ownership structure on the performance of the Tunisian rated company. For this, we selected seven explanatory variables; but view the inadequacy of data which is related to the share of the capital held by the family and the property of the state which we consider essential for the explanation of our problem; we have limited our study on five representative variables of the shareholding in the Tunisian rated businesses (concentration of capital, managerial property, institutional property, foreign ownership, ownership of the enterprises not institutional). We have used the software e-Views 6 to perform the econometric regression. The review of the presence of the problem of multi-collinearity between the explanatory variables by the matrix of Pearson correlation and between the dependent and independent variables taken two by two, shows that the correlation coefficients between the independent variables taken two by two are not statistically significant with a threshold of 10%. The values taken by these correlation coefficients have not exceeded a maximum of 0.3. This value is less than the threshold fixed by Gujarati (2003) which enhances the presence of a problem of multi-collinearity [11]. As well, we can say that the multi-collinearity between the variables rises no problem in the framework of this study. In what follows, we will study the structure of ownership and its influence on the performance of the company to know the ROA, ROE, the ACB and the Q of Tobin. Econometric estimations show the following results (Table 2):

In what follows, we will discover the results on the basis of the share of the capital held by each explanatory variable, followed by the economic analysis in accordance with the results obtained in previous studies.

Discussion and Conclusions

Impact of the concentration of capital on the performance of the company

The obtained results show that the variable concentration of capital has a positive and statistically significant impact on the performance of the company measured by the ROA at the threshold of 5%. This result is consistent with that of Shleifer and Agrawal who found a positive relationship between the concentration of capital and the value of the company, while highlighting the vital role played by these investors in the management of the company, thanks to their number of votes in the Council of Administration [6,7].

However, this impact has a negative and statistically significant effect on the measured performance by the ROE and the Q of Tobin. This result corroborates with those obtained by Kirchmair and Grant; who have concluded a negative influence between the concentration of capital and the value of the company. This idea was supported by Thomson, Pedersen and Kvist; who have carried out a study for the period (1990-1998) [12,13]. They have found a negative relationship between the concentration of ownership and the measured performance by the ROE and the Q of Tobin. Thus, the higher the share of the shares by the majority of shareholders the, less efficient will be the company.

Dependent variables	Model 1	Model 2	Model 3	Model 4
	ROA	ROE	Acb	Q of Tobin
Independent variables				
C	0.246*** (12.741)	-0.130 (0.642)	5.658*** (4.748)	2.234*** (4.872)
CONC	0.087**	-1.828***	-2.187	-2.741***
	(2.206)	(-9.148)	(-1.238)	(-4.146)
KDIR	-0.438***	-4.058**	-8.111*	-1.769
	(-3.113)	(-2.932)	(-2.034)	(-1.098)
KINST	-0.020	0.866***	1.222	2.279**
	(-0.721)	(4.696)	(0.590)	(2.788)
KNINST	0.084	3.667***	3.442	1,937
	(1,140)	(3.574)	(1.121)	(1.666)
KETRANG	0.010	2.061***	2.886	3.542***
	(0.294)	(6.998)	(1.608)	(4.893)
Indebtedness	-0.275***	-0.468***	-5.178***	-1.868***
	(-29.541)	(-8.375)	(-7.139)	(-5.714)
R^2	0.9926	0.9171	0.8352	0.8325

Note: The T values are between parentheses *, **, *** correspond to the significance of the statistics at the threshold of 10%, 5%, 1% respectively.

Table 2: Results of regressions.

Rejection of the hypothesis H1 according to which the concentration of the capital has a positive influence on the value of the company measured by the ROE and the Q of Tobin at the threshold of 1%, 5% and 10%. And acceptance of the same hypothesis (H1) for the performance measured by the ROA.

Impact of institutional investors on the performance of the company

Concerning the institutional property Kinst; the results of our estimation shows that the share of the capital held by institutional investors exerts a positive influence on the performance ex-post ROE and has no influence on the ROA. However, concerning the performance ex-ante, the share of the capital held by these investors has no influence on the ACB and positively influences the Q of Tobin at the threshold of 5% and 10%. This has been confirmed by the assumption of the efficiency of the Direction Statement by Jensen [8]; who predicted the existence of a positive relationship between institutional ownership and the performance of the company based on the fact that the institutional investors are more effective in the control of leaders than the minority of shareholders. On their side, Chaganti and Damanpour also show the existence of a positive relationship between the presence of institutional investors and the ROE [14,15]. This idea was supported by Thomson, Pedersen and Kvist who found a positive influence between the share held by institutional investors and the value of the company. As well, the higher the share of the shares held by institutional investors is, the more efficient will be the company.

Acceptance of the hypothesis H2 according to which the share of capital held by institutional investors has a positive influence on the value of the company.

Impact of foreign investors on the performance of the company

The share of the capital held by foreign investors exerts a positive influence on the performance ex ante measured by the Q of Tobin (H3) and has no significant effect on the ACB. We know that the performance indicators ex ante reflects the impact of estimated costs of Agency and the organizational structures [9]. However, concerning the performance ex post, the share of the capital held by foreign investors positively influences the ROE to threshold 1%, and has no influence on the ROA.

These results can be interpreted by the fact that foreign investors cannot influence the management of the companies in which they invest thanks to the solid family control which characterizes the Tunisian company. In these conditions, they would invest in companies that have good corporate governance and a higher value of future market. These results corroborate with the study of Nam and Nam who have highlighted the positive relationship between the presence of foreign investors in the capital of the Korean companies and the performance of the company. This idea was supported by the study of Oxelheim and Randoy who found a positive influence between the foreign investors and the value of the company [16-19].

Acceptance of the hypothesis H3 according to which the presence of foreign investors exerts a positive influence on the value of the company.

Impact of non-institutional investors on the performance of the company

Our estimation shows that the property of the non-institutional investors has no influence on the ROA as well as on the performance indicators ex ante the ACB and the Q of Tobin. This result was confirmed by the study of Madani W., who has used a sample of industrial Tunisian enterprises during the period (1999-2002). His study shows that the share of capital held by the non-institutional investors has no impact on the performance measured by the ROA and the ROE. These results can be interpreted as a validation of the thesis of the neutrality proposed by Demstez according to which all the structures of property are equivalent. However, the share of the capital held by these investors exerts a positive influence on the value of the Tunisian rated company measured by the ROE at the threshold of 1%; in contrast to the results obtained by Bianco as well as Kang; who have found a negative relationship between the property of the non-institutional investors and the performance of the firm [20,21].

Rejection of the hypothesis H4 according to which the presence of non-institutional investors exerts a negative influence on the value of the company.

Impact of the Managerial property on the performance of the company

We are studying the effects of the Managerial property on the performance of the company. Our results show that the Managerial property has a negative influence on the value of the company measured by the ROA, ROE and the ACB; whereas, it has no influence on the Q of Tobin. As well, the detention of an important share of the capital by the leaders is inversely related to the performance of the Tunisian rated company. The more this proportion is important, the less efficient will be the company. This result corroborates that of Morck et al. who found that the performance of the company tends to increase when the property of the leaders increases to 5%. But, it declines when the property of the leaders becomes more important and reaches the threshold of 25% of the capital. The same idea was supported by Davies et al. Our result confirms the thesis of the rooting [22].

Rejection of the hypothesis H5 according to which the managerial property has a positive influence on the value of the company.

As expected, the control variable "Debt" is significantly related to the performance of the company. This negative relationship implies that the higher the indebtedness is the less efficient will be the company.

Conclusion

In the framework of this research, we have tried to study the impact of the ownership structure on the performance of Tunisian businesses through the measurement tools: ROA, ROE, PBR, and Q of Tobin. We have based our study on a sample of 51 Tunisian companies listed on the stock exchange of Tunis. The obtained results have verified 3 assumptions: H1 (measured by the ROA), H2, H3 among the five proposals set forth above. In effect, our estimation shows that the share of the capital held by the dominant shareholder Institutional Investors and foreign investors exerts a positive influence on the performance of the company. However, it has proved that the assumptions H1 measured by the ROE and the Q of Tobin, H4 and H5 are not validated. In effect, our regression shows that the concentration of capital has a negative influence on the performance of the company. In addition, the ownership of non-institutional investors has a positive effect on the value of the company. Whereas, the Managerial property has a negative impact on the performance.

The goal of this research is to better understand the relationship between the ownership structure and performance in the context of

Tunisia. More specifically, we examined the effect of the structure of the property (the concentration of capital and managerial property) on accounting performance, measured by performance of own capital/ performance on the active, for a population of 51 Tunisian businesses listed for the period 2008-2012.

Based on the analysis of the regressions developed, the results of the relationship between the structure of ownership and the performance are as follows:

First, there is no relationship between the concentration of capital and the performance, measured by the ROA and the ROE. It follows that we maintain our hypothesis of departure, according to which the concentration of the property has no effect on the performance. This result confirms the thesis of the sustained neutrality by Demsetz. For this author, all structures of ownership are equivalent. The performance of firms is essentially constrained by the environment and the conditions for the operation of the business. Therefore, the detention of the capital by the leaders is a response of the endogenous process of profit maximization.

Secondly, a positive relationship between the family property and accounting performance. These results corroborate those of H. of Angelo and B.F. Smith suggesting that firms controlled by families tend more to maximize the performance because the control in businesses belongs, to their families. Also, the family shareholders have better information on the performance compared to other types of shareholders because of their close relationship with the leaders and administrators.

In contrast, the detention of the capital of other Tunisian businesses, foreign investors has no effect on the performance. Similarly, the percentage of voting shares held by institutional investors has not an impact on the performance measured by the ROA and the ROE, unlike the results found in the study of M.A. Omri on the Tunisian companies listed on the stock exchange. In effect, the institutional investors are involved in the control and management of these companies listed. The mutations affecting mainly the insurance sector and the banking sector affect the degree of interest which puts the institutional in relation with the companies in which they are shareholders. Institutional investors can influence the modes of organization by giving these companies their skills in varied areas. This could improve the performance.

Thirdly, the results show that there is a positive and significant relationship between the managerial property and the performance measured by the ROA, but not significant when the performance is measured by the ROE. This is consistent with Kesner who shows that the proportion of the shares held by the members of the board of directors is positive and significant in the measurement of the performance: the ROA. This result confirms the thesis of the convergence of interests. According to this thesis, the value of the firm increases with the proportion of control held by the managers. As well, the greater the percentage of capital held by managers is the lower the gap compared to the traditional objective of maximization of value. Indeed, leaders identify their interests with those of shareholders and are less likely to use the free flow to the unproductive expenditures.

Finally, the analyzes suggest that the assumed relationship between non-linear managerial property and the performance does not exist for the case of our study. Our result confirms the studies of Chung, Barnhart, Bhagat which have led to a positive linear relationship between the managerial ownership and performance. Then, what is not consistent with Himmelberg that the Managerial property is an endogenous variable. These authors extend the work of Demsetz by adding new variables to explain the variation in the structure of property (such as the size of the firm, spending on research and development, the costs of advertising, the rates of investment and the cash flows) [23]. The results of their regression corroborate the idea of the existence of a non-linear relationship between the managerial property and the performance of the company.

However, these results are tainted with certain limits. As we have adopted the hypothesis of the stability of the structure of property on our period of study, this could have an effect on the results. Although it has not identified significant changes on this period of time, the use of data relating to the ownership structure could give more reliable results.

Furthermore, although the results of this research contribute to explain part of the research's problem; the relationship between governance and business performance in the context of Tunisia; future researches in more depth will be needed in order to better identify the effect of the mechanisms of the governance, and this will be done by an extension applied primarily on:

- A period of study longer than five years;
- Other variables of discipline as the percentage of detention of external directors measuring the intensity of the control of the Board of Directors and the debt.

References

1. Hill CWL, Jones GD (1992) Stakeholder-agency theory. Journal of Management studies 29: 131-154.
2. Mcconnell JJ, Servaes H (1990) Aditional evidence on Equity Ownership and Corporate value. Journal of Financial Economics 27: 595-612.
3. Morck R (1988) Management Ownership and Market valuation. Journal of Financial Economics 20: 293-315.
4. Han KC, Suk DY (1998) The effect of ownership structure on firm performance: Aditional evidence. Review Financial Economics 27: 143-155.
5. Jensen MC, Meckling WH (1976) Theory of the Firm: Managerial Behavior, Agency Costs and Ownership Structure. Journal of Financial Economics 3: 305-360.
6. Shleifer A, Vishny RW (1986) Large shareholders and corporate control. Journal of political Economy 94: 461-488.
7. Agrawal A, Mandelker G (1990) Large shareholders and the Monitoring of Managers: the case of Antitakover charter Amendments. Journal of Financial and Quantitative Analysis 25: 143-161.
8. Jensen M (1993) The Modern Industrial Revolution: exist and the failure of internal control systems. Journal of Finance 48: 831-880.
9. Charreaux G (1997) Le Gouvernement des entreprises corporate governance: Théorie et faits. Economica, collection Recherche en gestion.
10. Morck R, Shleifer A, Vishny W (1988) Management Ownership and Market valuation. Journal of Financial Economics 27: 595-612.
11. Chang SJ, Hong J (2000) Economic performance of group-affiliated companies in Korea: Intragroup Resource sharing and Internal Business Transactions. Academy of Management Journal 43: 429-448.
12. Balsam S, Lipka R (1998) Share Prices and Alternative Measures of Earnings Per Share. Accouting Horizons 12: 234-249.
13. Fama E, Jensen M (1983) Separation of ownership and control. Journal of law and Economics 26: 301-325.
14. Weiss C, Hilger S (2010) Ownership Concentration Beyond Good and Evil: Is There an Effect on Corporate Performance. Working Paper series-SSRN.
15. Mtanios R, Paquerot M (1999) Structure de propriété et sous performance des firmes : une étude empirique sur le marché au comptant, le règlement mensuel et le second marché. Finance contrôle Stratégie 2: 157-179.

16. Pigé B (1998) Enracinement des dirigeants et richesse des actionnaires. Finance, contrôle, stratégie, 131-158.

17. Lapointe P (2000) Structure de propriété, investisseurs institutionnels et performance de l'entreprise: le point de connaissance. Université Laval version 3 juillet 2000.

18. Alexandre H, Paquerot M (2000) Efficacité des structures de contrôle et enracinement des dirigeants. Finance contrôle stratégie 3: 5-29.

19. Ma S (2009) The Impact of Ownership and Ownership Concentration on the Performance of China's Listed Firms. Working Paper series-SSRN.

20. Fama E (1980) Agency problems and the theory of the firm. Journal of Political Economy 88: 288-307.

21. Magni CA (2007) Residual Income and value creation: A Investigation into the Lost-Capital Paradigm. MPRA Paper series, University Library of Munich, Germany.

22. Penrose E (1959) The Theory of the Growth of the Firm. Oxford univ press.

23. Syed HR (2009) Impact of Ownership Structure on Performance of Firms-Evidence from KSE-100 Index Firms. Working Paper series-SSRN.

When the Employer Neglects his Contractual Obligation Push and Pull Factors for Employees to Come to Work Which is not Paid: A Case of Zimbabwean Parastatals

Maunganidze F, Mashavira N and Mapira N*

Department of Human Resource Management, Great Zimbabwe University, Masvingo, Zimbabwe

Abstract

The paper establishes the reasons why employees from selected parastatals continue coming to work even though they have not been paid their salaries for months. A qualitative study was conducted using 2 different interview guides, one for employees and the other one for human resource managers who acted as key informants. Twenty employees, 10 from each pararstatal were interviewed and 4 key informants, 2 from each organization also took part in the study. Participants were selected using purposive sampling. Data were analysed using thematic analysis. It has emerged from the study that employees in parastatals continue reporting for duty for different reasons which included desire for professional growth, hope that the fortunes of their respective organisations may turn for the better, abuse of organisational resources and vending at the workplace. Some participants also highlighted a number of social reasons such as seeking company from fellow workmates, avoiding lengthy periods with spouses who were deemed to be demanding and difficultly to handle. As recommendations, it is argued that organisations value and prioritise the welfare of their employees and engage in sound corporate governance decisions.

Keywords: Parastatal; Motivation; Job dissatisfaction; Corruption; Salary; Wage theft

Introduction and Background

Among other things, employees work in order to earn an income in the form of a wage or salary. Unfortunately, in Zimbabwe, as in many other parts of the world there is no guarantee of regular and adequate wages and salaries even for employed workers [1].

Zimbabwe is currently experiencing economic challenges that have severed the well-functioning of its various production sectors [2]. Zhou [3] has it that the period 2000-2009 experienced some deep seated economic woes from which many companies including state owned enterprises are still struggling to recover. On that note, the government is failing to service its wage bill that is reported to gobble over 80 percent of its national budget, leaving less than 20% for other operations. Employment costs between January and June 2016 consumed 96.8% of the total revenue. The poor economic performance obtaining in Zimbabwe has also had a ripple effect to both public and public sectors. At best, this has seen workers of most companies in Zimbabwe being paid late every month in the past couple of years and at worst, going for months without being remunerated. Most organisations including state owned enterprises are paying their employees as and when money is available without talking about arrears [4]. This is not in line with contracts of employment which stipulates specific time periods when employees should be paid after rendering their service. Some of the companies have gone for months without paying employees. Muchichwa [1] in a study by the Labour and Economic Development Institute of Zimbabwe (LEDRIZ) conducted a research with 442 companies and established that an estimated 80,000 employees have not received their salaries and benefits on time. It is argued that the majority of these employees have gone for more than 12 months without receiving their monthly salaries yet their respective employees still expect them to report for duty without fail. Non-payment of salaries is no longer a characteristic of the private sector, but has extended its wings into the public sector where employees are also not getting their salaries on time. Both the government and state owned enterprises employees have been subjected to untimely payment of their salaries [1]. Muchichwa (opcit) argues that the number of employees going without pay is on the increase contributing to family disintegration, higher poverty rates as well as an increased number of the working poor.

The importance of timeous payment for job done in organisations cannot be ignored for this is instrumental to the well-functioning of the whole system. Without the pay incentive organisations are likely to experience low output, thefts, corruption, absentisms among other related social ills. Best practice and international standards, specifically, the International Lanbour Organisation (ILO) Protection of Wages Convention, 1949, No. 95 clearly stipulates the regular payment of wages to workers and the priority of such payments over other financial obligations of the employer.

State owned enterprises in most African countries are known for deep fiscal problems. These entities are characterised by inefficiencies, losses, budgetary burdens as well as provision of poor products and services [5]. Zimbabwe is not spared from these challenges facing other parastatals on the African continent. In recent years, most state owned enterprises in Zimbabwe were plagued by salary gate. Top executives in these parastatals were known to be paid absurd salaries and allowances. Some would even go home with financial and non-financial rewards amounting to US$500 000 per month [1,2,6,7]. Such poor corporate governance and other ills are the responsible factors that have contributed to management failing to pay employees for months.

***Corresponding author:** Farai Maunganidze, Department of Human Resource Management, Great Zimbabwe University, Masvingo, Zimbabwe
E-mail: fmaunganidze@gzu.ac.zw

ECSAFA (2004) has it that parastatals are bodies set up by specific Acts of Parliament. These bodies are managed by Boards of Directors appointed by the government. Parastatals are established outside the Central Government and engage in commercial economic, service oriented or social activities requiring significant levels of autonomy and freedom from bureaucratic interference. The affairs of state owned enterprises are subject to the scrutiny of Parliament and their respective Ministries, thereby placing their responsibility in the hands of the Minister in charge of that particular ministry.

The Zimbabwean public companies are wholly owned by government. They are not for profit making but serve to provide a service where the private companies cannot. They are just an extension of the government. Zimbabwe has a number of parastatals which include the following; National Railways of Zimbabwe (NRZ), Air Zimbabwe, Zimbabwe Broadcasting Corporation (ZBC), Zimbabwe National Water Authority (ZINWA), Zimbabwe National Family Planning (ZNFP), National Archives (NA), Zimbabwe Institute of Public Administration and Management (ZIPAM), Premier Service Medical Aid Society (PSMAS), National Social Security Authority (NSSA) among others.

According to Nyoni [8] employees of non performing state owned enterprises have resorted to putting up at their companies head offices to push for salary payments after months of reporting for work without getting any payment. The Grain Marketing Board (GMB) employees left their homes and camped at the parastatal's Dura House which is its headquarters demanding their over 10 months' salary which they were owed by the organisation.

In an interview with some of the disgruntled employees by Nyoni, they had to say [8];

I have been coming to work every day for the past 15 months without pay, but I can't continue donating my labour to a company that does not care for its workers and their families. As it stands, I can't even bring food to the table, yet every day my children see me leaving for work.

I am a failed parent because I can't even send my children to school and industry in Bulawayo has collapsed, meaning I am the sole breadwinner with no bread to bring home," Terrence Tshuma, a father of five, said.

It has emerged from Nyoni [8] and Muchichwa [1] that the industrial action is different from other forms as those displayed by some employees of the National Railways of Zimbabwe and Hwange Colliery is incorporating their immediate family members such as spouses and children in order to force management to act on the issue of salaries. It is thus clear that non-payment of employees not only affect the employees, but their immediate family members as well. Muchichwa technically calls the non-payment of salaries by organisations for longer periods "wage theft" [1].

Due to high unemployment rate and limited economic growth, Zimbabwean workers are not able to fight 'economic theft' [1]. They just hope that one day, fortunes will turn for the better and they would be in a position to enjoy the sweat of their labour in the form of descent and timely salaries.

Despite being unpaid for over 10 months, it is interesting to note that some employees of state owned parastatals still hope that one day they would be paid their dues [8]. The Labour Act clearly stipulates that labour rendered should be paid for and this could be the source of these employees hope.

Underlying theoretical framework

This study is informed by three theories of motivation namely Adam's Equity Theory, Vroom's Expectancy Theory and Maslow's Hierarchy of Needs. According to Mullins and Brooks [9,10], Equity Theory stipulates that individual employees are keen to be treated fairly in terms of what they bring into the organisation (inputs) and what they get in return (outputs). Employees compare themselves with significant others in as far as their inputs and outputs are concerned [11]. When employees perceive an imbalance between their inputs and outputs, compared to significant others, they either adjust on their inputs or their outputs. In this case, employees may either adjust their commitment to the organisation (inputs) or they may adjust on their outputs in the form of some unsolicited benefits. The effort is aimed at addressing the perceived imbalance between one's inputs and outputs at the workplace. This theory can be used to explain the likely response of state owned enterprises to the non-payment of their salaries by their respective organisations. They may compare their inputs and outputs with those of their counterparts in some other organisations who are being paid well and on time. In order to address the perceived sense of inequity, state owned enterprise employees may start altering their outputs through such behaviours as theft and abuse of resources. Alternatively, they may alter inputs in the form of commitment.

Expectancy Theory argues that an individual will decide to behave or act in a particular way because they are motivated to select a specific behavior over other behaviours due to what they expect the result of that selected behavior will be. According to Schultz and Schultz and Mullins [9,12], the theory by Vroom emphasises much on the needs of organisations to relate rewards directly to performance and to make sure that the rewards provided are those deserved and wanted by the recipients. In this study, commitment of employees to do their work and to produce is a function of their faith in the organisation to reward them accordingly. State owned enterprises should therefore reward the commitment by its workforce by prioritising them in as far as remuneration and opportunities are concerned. It is, however, important to note that when employees expect no benefits from their effort and behaviours, then, they may not engage in those behaviours that promotes the organisation. Due to non-payment of salaries, employees may see no reason to commit themselves to the goals of the organisation since they expect no reciprocity from the system.

Mullins and Robbins, Judge & Campbell [9,13] note that according to Maslow's hierarchy of needs, money is important for the lower order needs. The lower order needs comprise physiological, security and social needs. The first two are directly related to the aspect of money which one should earn, according to this study, from their employer. Kalchmanov and Kaliannan have it that money is a strong motivator [14]. In line with Maslow's hierarchy of needs, money satisfies lower order needs. In other words, money does not motivate employees to do their best, thus higher order needs. Employees who are not getting satisfying salaries or who are not paid on time are then likely to have reduced motivation to address the higher order needs. Desire for growth and self actualising can only be relevant after one would have addressed the lower order needs according to Maslow. Considering this theory, state owned enterprises employees are struggling to address lower order needs hence commitment to the organisation and the desire to see it grow is compromised.

Early writers such as FW Taylor of the famous scientific management believed in economic needs motivation. He argued that workers would be motivated by obtaining the highest possible wages through working in the most efficient and productive way. Physiological fatigue would limit performance. It was believed that motivation was simple, all what workers would want was more money in the form of high wages. The issue of working and being motivated by money has been called rational-economic concept of motivation. This approach and some subsequent arguments have led to the debate among scholars over the role of financial rewards in the motivation of employees [9]. It has also been established by Mullins [9] that for the majority of people, money is clearly important and a motivator at the workplace. However, the extent of money being a motivator as well as its importance depends upon the employees' personal circumstances and the other satisfaction they derive from work [15].

Findings and Discussion

Reasons for coming to work

'Economic' Reasons for coming to work: The study has revealed that a significant number of participants come to work with an intention to engage on some fraudulent behaviours. Fifteen (75%) of the participants highlighted that one of the main reason why they continued coming to work despite not being paid their dues was engaging in some fraudlent behaviours. It has emerged that the majority of these (80%) had positions which allowed them to deal with some resources, either financial or material. In order to cushion themselves from the continuously declining economy coupled with the organisation's inability to pay on time, employees with access to some resources would engage in fraudlent behaviours. These behaviours included stealing, misapproroiation of funds, possession of parallel receipt books. Participant 16 had to say;

I know we can go for months without being paid but if I do not come to work, I tend to lose more because coming to work will allow me to make use of my office in order to make money. If I don't do that my family will starve to death and I may not be able to send my children to school.

The above remark by one of the participants of not being paid for months concurs with the findings by Muchichwa and Sibanda [1,4] who have it that some of the state owned enterprises can go for months without paying their workforce and only pay them when as and when they get some money. Some of the employees then settle for some unorthodox means of earning a living through fraudulent means. The importance of money is also revealed. As noted by Kalchmanov and Kaliannan highlight that money in the form of a salary is a strong motivator [14]. This is in line with the argument by Maslow who argues that money satisfies lower order needs, those which are important for basic living. By failing to pay their workers, state owned enterprises are going against the best practice as noted by the International Labour Organisation. ILO's Protection of Wages of 1949, number 95 clearly stipulates that wages of employees should be prioritised ahead of other expenses.

Three of the key informants admitted that there has been a steady increase in cases involving fraudulent and corruption related behaviours in their organisations. Fraudulent behaviours may be linked to Equity Theory by Adams which states that when employees perceive that their inputs are exceeding their outputs vis-à-vis the inputs and outputs of significant others, they can alter their outputs. Outputs can be altered through unorthodox means as witnessed in this study. George and Jones, Mullins and Brooks also have it that when employees perceive some form of imbalances between their inputs and outputs, they may alter their outputs and/or inputs. In this case, employees are attending to their outputs [9-11].

It has also been established that 4 (20%) of the participants indicated that one of the reasons why they come to work even when they are not being paid is to sell their wares. It has been argued that the workplace is a conductive environment for one to engage in some personal economic activities such as selling some imported goods from neighbouring countries. These may include clothes, electronic gadgets and jewellery. According to participant 3;

I travel to South Africa or Botswana once every month to buy some wares to resell to my workmates and some surrounding organisations. My employment circle has become a very good market place for many of us here. Our wares are relatively cheap as we do not pay any rentals or bills. We just use these premises to do our business. If I do not come to work, it means I lose out.

Such behaviours automatically mean low levels of commitment to one's job. Focus is on one's personal interests not on the growth of the organisation. This also tallies with the arguments by George and Jones, Mullins and Brooks, in relation to Adams Equity Theory [9-11]. When employees perceive some form of imbalance, they find ways of bringing equity between their inputs and outputs, even though unorthodox means. In this case, employees are channeling their energies to personal economic developments at the expense of organisational development. Commitment to the welfare of the organisation is reduced in order to restore equity. Mullins and Schultz & Schultz also have it that employers [9,12], according to the Expectancy Theory, should reward commitment as employees expect it that way. If this not done, as in the case of the parastatals under study who are failing to pay their salaries, employees will have no reason to engage in positive behaviours or behaviours that reflect high levels of commitment. Among other things, workers trade their effort for money, which in this case, is not being paid.

Abuse of infrastructure such as phones, internet, company vehicles and other resources has been cited as one of the economic reasons why employees in parastatals continue coming to work even though they can go for months without receiving their salaries. Participant 7 had this to say;

When I come to work, I make sure I do all my calls, including international calls. I also print all my assignments since I am a student at one of the tertiary institutions. I am also forced to come to work because that is where I get free internet for my academic work.

Similar sentiments were also echoed by two of the key informants who had it that at times employees come to work to pursue their academic endeavours and to use the organisation's resources. It has emerged from the key informants that management was considering getting stricter with organisational resources. As already mentioned, when employees perceive some imbalances between their inputs and outputs, they make efforts to either alter inputs and outputs. This is in line with the arguments by George and Jones, Mullins and Brooks in relation to the Equity Theory by Adams [9-11]. Employees will generally lose interest in the welfare of an organisation if they feel they are being shortchanged by the same system that should be taking care of them.

Socially related reasons: A number of social reasons have emerged as to why employees continue coming to work. Eighteen (90%) of the shop floor participants highlighted that the reason for them coming to work on a daily basis even though they had gone for months without remuneration was to meet fellow friends whom they had been with for years. In relation to this theme, participant 17 had to say;

If I do not come to work, how will I spend my day? Days at home can be very long and stressful. I am therefore better off at work where I chit chat with my friends and even before you know it, it is already 17:00 h and we are going home.

This trend is in line with Maslow's hierarchy of needs of 1963, particularly the social needs [9,13]. Being an employee at an organisation does not take away the need for one to be social and to belong to a certain grouping. It is also important to note that of these 55.5% of these were males. This could be linked to the African traditional culture in general and Zimbabwean in particular which argues that males are more outgoing and are culturally 'allowed' enjoying outdoor activities more than their female counterparts. Three of the key informants however highlighted that indeed people form social circles but these could not be the reasons why they come to work as they can as well meet outside the work premises. The workplace could however be more strategic than most of the alternative meeting places. The workplace is more central and there is free and conducive space to meet and socialise.

Still under social related reasons for one to come to work, the study has revealed that (6) 30% of the participants alluded to the fact that one of the reasons why they come to work despite being unpaid for several months was to have time with their 'loved' ones who were employed at the same organisation with them. Participant 11 had to say;

My girlfriend and I work here and by not coming to work, it means I won't see her for that day. So coming to work guarantees that we see each other without fear of being seen by my future-in-laws whom I am not yet prepared to see as of now.

Of those participants who had romantic relationships at the workplace, (4) 66.6% of them were not married. Employees on average spend about 40 h at the workplace and in some cases, romantic relationships may develop, especially to those who are not married. It is also now a common trend that people are postponing marriages with a desire to personally develop first; hence, a significant number of employees in organisations are not yet married. One (16.7%) reported to have been a divorcee and was male while the other one (16.7%) was married. This theme was however not mentioned by all the four key informants.

Another important social theme that motivates employees to come to work was that of need to maintain good social contacts so that one has company in times of future positive and negative social gatherings. Nine (45%) of the participants argued that they have sought to invest in social relations at the workplace so that they have a fall back when they need people during their ups and downs in life such as funerals and weddings. According to P8;

I have since incorporated most of my workmates into my inner social circle. They are now as good as my blood relatives and these are the people who would stand by me in times of funerals, parties and weddings. You see we have children and soon they could be engaging in some weddings and these are the people I bank on during such events. I then have to continuously come to work to make sure these relationships are kept intact.

The theme of company on social events such as funerals and weddings tallies highly with the collectivistic nature of Africans in general and Zimbabweans in particular whereby life is lived as a society and one's joys and sorrows are shared by the whole community.

The study has also revealed that 3 (15%) of the participants indicated that one of their reason for coming to work even though it is rarely paid for was running away from 'troublesome' spouses. Participant four had to say;

Spending the day at home would mean spending the day arguing with my wife and I do not want it that way. The best for me is to minimise the time we are together by making sure I spend the whole day at work.

They highlighted that being away from home saved them from unnecessary arguments with their spouses which are inevitable when they spend the day together at home. In relation to marital related arguments, Muchichwa argued that wage theft by state owned enterprises were leading to family disintegration and an increase in the working poor [1]. Table 1 below depicts the social reasons for coming to work although employees are not getting rewarded on time.

Although key informants alluded to the fact that social ties were important within an organisation, they argued that these ties were not the reason why employees would come to work. They argued that employees do come to work to perform specific tasks which are in relation to the organisational growth.

Psychological related reasons: One of the themes that emerged from the study was that of psychological well-being that they derive from being at work. Eight (40%) of the participants highlighted that they come to work mainly to grow in their respective professional fields. This confirms the argument presented by such scholars as Maslow's higher order needs, Herzberg's two factor theory, particularly the motivators as well McGregor's theory X and Y, in this case, focus is more on the latter [9,13].

It is however important to note that these theories do not completely disregard the importance of money. Money still serves an important function to an extent that its absence may cause challenges both to an organisation as well as individual workers. According to Maslow's hierarchy of needs, one has to satisfy basic needs before they move on to higher order needs and money is usually instrumental in the satisfaction of lower order needs [9,13]. Kulchmanov and Kaliannan have it that money remains the strongest and compulsory factor for employees [14], which can satisfy only basic needs. Findings from this study then are in contradiction with the arguments by most theories of motivation which states that growth needs should come after basic needs have been met and in order for these to be met; there is need for remuneration in the form of money. It is however important to note that the majority of these theories were derived from economically stable societies where one's salary is definite and it is in most cases above the poverty datum line.

Another theme which relates to an individual's psychological well-being was the notion of job security. The study has revealed

Social reasons sub-themes	Participants
Sense of belonging and to socialise with fellow workmates	P1, P2, P3, P4, P5, P7, P8, P9, P10, P11, P12, P14, P15, P16, P17, P18, P19, P20
Romantic relationships	P6, P11, P12, P15, P18, P20
Guaranteeing company in future social events	P3, P5, P6, P7, P8, P11, P13, P17, P18
Avoiding marital disputes	P9, P14, P16

Table 1: Social reasons for coming to work.

that 17 (85%) of participants argued that one reason why they keep on presenting themselves to an employer who is failing to honour the contractual obligation of remunerating for work done was the issue of job security or what Pilbeam and Corbridge termed job for life [15]. According to Participant 10;

I have to carefully look after this job till I retire. So far I have been with the employee for 28 years. Where would I go if I leave this place?

It is important to note that the findings of this study differ from the arguments presented by Pilbeam and Corbridge who has it that employees are no longer valuing job security as before [15]. The difference could be emanating from the fact that Pilbeam and Corbridge focused on developed countries where economies are rather stable and employment opportunities are vast [15]. In contrast, in Zimbabwe, the unemployment rate is high and employment is not easy to come across. One will realise it is important to keep the job that they have. Three of the key informants highlighted that the economy is very depressed and employers should bear with their respective employers as the options are limited. These findings concur with the arguments presented by Muchichwa [1] who has it that the prevailing high unemployment rate obtaining in Zimbabwe is one of the major reasons why employees find it difficult to move out of an unrewarding relationship with an employer who is failing to meet their contractual obligation of paying wages and/or salaries.

Participants also highlighted the fact that they are sure that as long as they have worked, it is clear that that they will eventually be paid. This theme was raised by (16) 80% of the participants. These argued that although the salaries were delayed, they will still get their money. Seventy five percent of these argued that they believed they would one day get a lump some of their dues. Participant 11 had to say;

Each and every day I work would one day be paid for, so I feel I am investing and they are keeping my money. When I receive it in bulk, I am able to do something more meaningful than when I receive my salary on a monthly basis.

The Labour Act clearly stipulates that labour rendered should be paid and these employees could be basing their arguments on this. The remaining 25% were of the opinion that although they would eventually be paid, their amounts would come in parts. All the key informants however alluded to the fact that although the salaries are erratic, they will eventually be paid according to the Labour Act.

Conclusion

The study sought to unravel the factors that lead employees of some state owned enterprises to continue reporting for work despite being paid their salaries intermittently or at worst, going for months without receiving their salaries. Such a scenario is not in line with the both the international standards and the local Labour Act. The study was informed by Adams's Equity Theory, Vroom's Expectancy Theory and Maslow's Hierarchy of Needs.

It has emerged from the findings that employees are driven by a number of factors to report for work. The reasons have been categorised as social, psychological and economic. Participants highlighted that they report to their respective work stations in order to grow their professional lives, to seek company at the workplace as well as avoiding potential conflicts with spouses. The study has also revealed that some employees are keen to report to work even though they have not been receiving their dues for months because they tend to abuse some resources such as money, internet and vehicles among other resources. Work premises, it has been established, can also be used by some participants to study. Some participants highlighted that they come to work simple to sell their wares to fellow employees.

In general, employees of the majority of state owned enterprises, although they are reporting to work, they are not coming to work to offer their labour. Most of them are present at the workplace for other reasons, nothing to do with the mission and vision of their respective organisations. Most of the employees are no longer committed to their work. They have lost interest in the welfare of their organisations.

Recommendations

Management of state owned enterprises must review their human resource policies if they wish to take full advantage of their personnel. Motivated employees are more committed and productive than disgruntled workers.

In order to make sure that operations at state owned enterprises are above board and compatible with best practice, the government and Boards must ensure that sound corporate governance decisions are made, especially on executive pay. In most cases, company executives are earning unrealistically high salaries and enjoying huge benefits at the expense of ordinary employees who are going for months without being paid their salaries.

Employees must also be made to realize their own contribution to the deplorable state of their respective organizations. Abuse of resources coupled with limited commitment on the part of workers only help to plunge their organizations deeper. Employees must be made aware of their potential ability to turn the fortunes of their respective organizations for the better.

References

1. Muchichwa N (2016) Working without pay: Wage theft in Zimbabwe. The Labour and Economic Development Research Institute of Zimbabwe, Harare.
2. Ncube F, Maunganidze L (2014) Corporate governance and executive compensation in Zimbabwean state owned enterprises: A Case of institutionalized predation. Management 4: 131-140.
3. Zhou G (2012) Three Decades of Public Enterprise Restructuring in Zimbabwe A Will-Of-The-Wisp Chase? International Journal of Humanities and Social Science 2: 175-184.
4. Sibanda DN (2014) Unpaid wages: The landscape.
5. Mwaura K (2007) The failure of corporate governance in state owned enterprises and the need for restructured governance in fully and partially privatised enterprises: The case of Kenya. Fordham International Law Journal 31: 31-47.
6. Mutanda D (2014) The impact of the Zimbabwean crisis on parastatals. International Journal of Politics and Good Governance 5: 1-14.
7. Mahove C (2014) Obscene salaries: Ministers slept on duty, ignored code. The Worker.
8. Nyoni MM (2016) Sleep-ins over non-payment of salaries new protest form. Newsday.
9. Mullins LJ (2011) Essentials of organisational behaviour. Pearson, London.
10. Brooks I (2009) Organisational behaviour: Individuals, groups and organisations. Pearson Education limited, Essex.
11. George JM, Jones GR (2012) Understanding and managing organisational behaviour. Pearson Education Limited, Essex.
12. Schultz D, Scultz SE (2010) Psychology and work today. Pearson, Boston.
13. Robbins SP, Judge TA, Campbell TT (2010) Organisational behaviour. Pearson, Essex.

Role of a Project Manager in Managing Agile Projects

Soumita Banerjee*

University of Bridgeport, Bridgeport, USA

***Corresponding author:** Soumita Banerjee, University of Bridgeport, Bridgeport, Connecticut-06604, USA, E-mail: sobanerj@my.bridgeport.edu

Abstract

With the advent of the agile project management methods, the role of a project manager has enhanced to satisfy the needs. The traditional project management principles are not enough to manage today's large, complex projects. In this paper, we will review the role of a project manager in managing agile projects and how it is different from traditional project manager's approaches. A comprehensive literature review on the changing roles of a project manager in an agile project is the theoretical foundation of the paper.

Keywords: Agile; Project manager; Waterfall; Sprint; Scrum; Scrum master

Introduction to Agile Project Management

The principle of the project management is to manage a project successfully so that it can produce the desired outcome within the specific budget and time. The role of a project manager is not same in managing different projects. The project management techniques are designed carefully so that the project manager can run the project successfully by minimizing the risks and other negativities. One of the recent project management techniques is the agile project management.

With the initiation of business management practices, today's business environment has become versatile and uncertain. The requirements of clients are changing. Therefore, the business processes accommodate to fulfill client's demands. A project is defined as "a collection of simultaneous and sequential activities which together produce an identifiable outcome of value [1]." A project is a unique set of activities with definite objectives, specific time to complete and identified budget.

The project management team manages the internal and external factors which have an impact on the project. To avoid any risky circumstances, the project management team acts quickly so that project timelines and priorities can be achieved. The quality of taking quick actions to manage the project is known as agility [2]. The contemporary financially unstable and technology driven environments are unreliable for traditional project management methodologies. Changing customer demands, minimizing budget and tightening the delivery deadline are the three key factors of managing a project in agility - "The ability to move quickly and dramatically to get around any and all obstacles [2]." Agile project management process develops a realistic and repeatable methods to increase the flexibility of the project.

According to Chin et al., the reasons to implement agile project management practices in an organization are as follows:

1. Business-centric decision making is quick and easy.
2. The project team is focused on achieving the business goal.
3. The conflict of having multiple goals can be avoided.
4. Managing changes are easy to reach the project goals.
5. Roles and responsibilities can be shared by individuals and the micro management of management can be avoided.

Transforming to agility

According to Chris et al., one of the common project management methods is known as Waterfall project management principle [3]. According to this concept, the project is divided into different phases. One phase needs to be completed before another phase begins. Skilled individuals are associated with the project irrespective of teams and geographic locations. A successful project can bring changes in the organizational operation and it may have a long-term impact on the business (Figure 1).

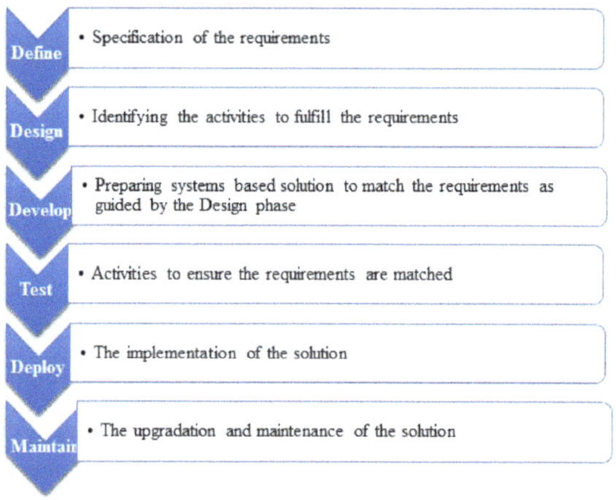

Figure 1: Project implementation phases in waterfall concept.

Limitations of waterfall concept

Waterfall process develops several limitations to achieve the project objectives [3].

- The project plan and activities are planned in the initial phase of the project. All the activities might not require later on.
- A project takes a longer time to complete as one phase needs to be completed before another phase begins.
- The project manager is responsible for prioritization of daily activities.
- Once the project begins, changes in project objectives are difficult to accommodate.
- Documentation is considered to measure the accountability of the team members.

Agile methodology

Agile methodology can be defined as "Iterative and incremental style of development that dynamically adjusts to changing requirements and enables better risk management [4]." The agile projects are customer defined, aligned to client's expectation and measurable activities specific. It focuses on delivering the client's needs at the earliest, forming the project plan as per client's demands and implementing changes to provide the best solution to the client [5]. In agile methods, the interactions of the individuals are valued to develop a software solution for the changing requirements of the client.

Scrum is another agile method, developed by Jeff Sutherland. According to Hoda et al. Scrum refers to short development phases of a large project [4]. The daily short interaction of Product Owner, Scrum Master, and the team is one of the key characteristics of the scrum method. The product owner maintains the accurate business standpoint, the scrum master is a facilitator and the team, consists of 5-7 executives, executes on the project activities. The responsibilities of the team include sprint planning and scrum meeting. A Sprint is a specific timeframe (usually 2-4 weeks) to work on a set of activities. In a sprint review meeting, the set of activities is identified and reviewed. The Scrum master organizes a daily meeting of 15 minutes to discuss any issues or concerns [4]. By using Sprint and Scrum methods, agile project management techniques empower the project managers and the team to successfully manage risks, define scope, maintain budget and follow timelines.

According to Lee et al. agility is defined as "the continuous readiness of an entity to rapidly, inherently proactively or reactively, embrace change, through high-quality, simplistic, economical components and relationships with its environment [6]." Agility is the promptness in accepting a change or action. There are two dimensions. It can be accepting and adapting to changes or ability to re-engineer the existing process. Agile methodology is "a set of flexible techniques [7]." It helps the software development team to sustain in a volatile environment. The teams are responsible for managing the software development process, resolving issues, making decisions and delegating tasks to other teams. The expertise in managing changes by using agile methodologies make it easily acceptable by the software development teams.

Limitation of agile process

Turk et al. mentioned that agile process combines technical and managerial processes to adapt the changes in a software development process during development phase or in the environment of the software development [8]. Following are some limitations of agile process:

- Support is limited to distributed development situations and subcontracting,
- Support is limited while developing reusable objects and involving large teams,
- Unavailability of adequate support while developing critical, large, safety critical and complex software,
- An agile project is unpredictable and difficult to control in development culture.

The agile process focuses on the interaction between people, process, and tools. It also fosters customer's involvement in providing best solution [9].

Project manager in agile project

According to Turbit et al., a project manager is a way to connect to the steering committee [10]. The responsibilities of a project manager include the following:

- Managing people in an unpredictable and stressful environment - In agile projects, project timelines are critical. Project Manager ensures the sprint of the project is completed on time.
- Motivating everyone to remain focused on reaching the goal. In a large agile project, challenges and issues create frustration among team members. Project manager motivates his team members to avoid any issues that degrade employees' performance.
- Modifying work-pressure and timelines to keep the pace - The project is divided among several segments which need to be completed phase wise in a specific timeline. The project manager assigns tasks to individual and balances the workload.
- Managing issues and escalating to the right authorities - Project manager informs the right person at the right time to resolve the issue.
- Communicating changes to the stakeholders – Project manager informs all the stakeholders about the status of the project.
- Fighting for the proper resource – Project manager manages approvals for required resources from the authorized people.
- Preparing project plans and making changes if necessary – Project manager helps to prepare project plans and ensure the project plan is being followed. If any changes required, he ensures changes are updated in the project plan and communicated to all.
- Developing risk management plans – Project manager identifies risks and develops risk management plans.
- Resolving issues to keep the project moving – Project manager ensures any interpersonal conflict, political issues, technical skill scarcity, shortage of the budget should not harm the project. He takes preventive actions to avoid risks.

Project manager as a scrum master

As a scrum master, a successful project manager attains a daily meeting with the team members. This helps the project manager to identify any issues that the team members have faced or shared the update among all the team members [11]. As a scrum master, the project manager is responsible for sharing status reporting, communicating changes, risks, project plans and to identify any missing roles. Contrary to waterfall method, roles are distributed among all the team members. The key people in an agile method are the team members, scrum master, and the client.

According to Eriksson, in an agile method, 'command and control' method is not applicable [11]. The scrum master role is like 'servant leader' who leads his team and perform his part. The scrum master is more flexible and versatile than a project manager.

Project manager roles and responsibilities expand in an agile method. As a project manager of an agile project, he manages project financials, project status report, change management, governance, role identification and business communication to the stakeholders.

As a Scrum Master, a project manager plans a sprint. One of the major responsibilities of the project manager as a scrum master is to divide a large project into different phases, accomplish the sprint objectives and maintain the smooth flow of the project.

Case Study

The case study is about a project where the agile methodology was followed. The objective of the project is the implementation of Mobile Work Management Systems at Denver Water, Colorado by following the agile project management approach. Denver Water field work used to be communicated to its customer service technicians by phone, paper or radio. The scope of the project was to develop the "mPlatform mobile work management application" which makes the work more efficient and easier for the field technicians. The budget of the project was approximately $1 million and the maximum time allocation was 6 months. Mr. Mike Aragon was the "product owner" of this project. He was trained in agile methodologies. He was involved in many other IT projects previously which followed waterfall method. According to him, it was a challenge to follow waterfall method due to lack of daily involvement with customers or users. He followed agile methodologies in the following way:

- At first, a pilot team was formed which consisted of selective field technicians from different fields of operation. The pilot team had 5 field technicians who have rich experience and necessary computer skills.
- The pilot team worked as a sample of the end-users. Their daily feedback and suggestions were carefully considered to modify the product as per their needs.
- Another core team was developed which was formed by the supervisors of different fields of operations. As the product owner, Mr. Aragon was responsible for prioritizing the best suggestions, received from the pilot team and the core team, and implements the same in the project.
- The prioritization was done based on the cost-benefit analysis and the business value analysis. Mostly, the suggestions of the pilot team were implemented as they were the future end-users of the application.
- As the product owner, Mr. Aragon was careful to avoid any insecurity of losing jobs among the field technicians due to not using the application correctly.
- The risk management plan was developed with the help of the pilot team. This pilot team was involved in identifying the potential risks and to generate suggestions to mitigate the risks.
- The agile methodology was also applied in training the field technicians. Instead of week-long classroom training, the pilot team members were being deployed as the on-the-job trainers for the field technicians.
- After seven months of scrum process, the application was "go-live" in 2 days. The volume of the end-user support calls was very minimum as the entire field technicians were carefully trained by the pilot team members. The application was successfully implemented throughout the organization's field technicians and the project was successful by following the agile methods.

The project was beneficial by following the agile methodologies. It was able to meet the objective of the project within time and the budget. The deployment of the project was a huge success. According to Mr. Aragon, producing the same results by following the traditional waterfall approach was difficult. Therefore, the success of this project makes it a benchmark for the following projects in Denver Water organization.

Findings: How role of a scrum master differs from a PM

According to Frederico et al., the role of a project manager and a scrum master differs from each other [12]. In an agile project environment, the roles of a project manager and a scrum master are as follows:

- A project manager manages the project – scope, cost, timeline and the overall quality of the project. A scrum master manages each scrum to reach the project goals.
- A project manager might manage multiple projects at a time. A scrum master usually focused on a specific project team.
- A project manager manages the budget and the risks of the project. A scrum master motivates the team members, facilitates sprint planning and scrum meetings.
- A project manager focuses on processes and allocates tasks to the team members. A scrum master helps to improve team dynamics and acts as a servant leader if required by the project.
- A project manager is a communicator between the management team and the team members. A scrum master is the facilitator and trains the product owner.
- A project manager informs the management about the project progress and coordinates with other teams. A scrum master motivates the team members and increases the team bonding.

Conclusion

The project manager and the scrum master are not two separate entity. The role of a project manager expands as a scrum master. The objective of a project manager is to complete a project successfully within specific budget and timeline. With the advent of the agile method, the involvement of a project manager increases. In agile project management, the distribution of the roles and responsibilities are specific to the individuals. Therefore, the role of a project manager as a scrum master is now more specific, crisp and concise. In an agile method, the focus of a project manager is not limited to the entire project but as a scrum master, it is every scrum that needs to be successful. This new point of view makes it more methodical and quantitative to achieve the success.

Recommendations

In this competitive world, the role of a project manager or a scrum master is critical to the success of a project. Be it a project manager or a scrum master, the objective of successful execution of a project remains same. In order to achieve success, the clarity of roles and responsibilities is necessary. Moreover, a project manager and a scrum master can be same individual or different individuals. Both the roles are important for a successful project in agile methods. Therefore, the skills to become a project manager in managing agile projects need to be learned and applied since the early phase of career development. The skills of segmenting a large project into small parts, involving and contributing with the team as a scrum master, communicating and negotiating with the stakeholders and achieving the success need to be learned over the time. Therefore, be it a scrum master or a project manager, an individual needs to learn the project management techniques continuously to improve themselves and gain more successes.

Lessons Learned

According to Granot et al., the success of a project depends on the careful planning, managing co-related activities and scheduling the tasks [13]. Careful planning includes developing strategies, managing resources and handling risks. In an agile project, the responsibilities of a project manager are not only limited to careful planning and managing activities; but also to involve in segmenting the project and participate with the team to become successful in the phase-wise implementation of the project. The agile project management gives the flexibility to choose where to start from and where to reach at first before moving further. Therefore, it is one of the most popular project management practices now. With the future perspective, the role of a project manager will be enhanced in order to follow the agile project management methodology.

References

1. Pich MT, Loch CH, de Meyer A (2002) On Uncertainty, Ambiguity, and Complexity in Project Management. Manage Sci 48: 1008-1023.
2. Gary C (2004) Agile project management. Amacom, New York.
3. Chris D, Ragsdale P, Mike (2012) Information Technology Projects and Business Engagement: New Strategies. J Am Water Works Ass 104: 44-50.
4. Hoda R, Noble J, Marshall S (2008) Agile project management. Computer Science Research Student Conference, New Zealand.
5. Michael K, Voord VM (2008) Agile project management. Embedded Systems Conference Boston, Boston.
6. Gwanhoo L, Weidong X (2010) Toward Agile: An Integrated Analysis of Quantitative and Qualitative Field Data on Software Development Agility. Mis Quart 34: 87-114.
7. Maruping LM, Venkatesh V, Agarwal Ritu (2009) A Control Theory Perspective on Agile Methodology Use and Changing User Requirements. Inform Syst Res 20: 377-399.
8. Turk D, France R, Rumpe B (2014) Limitations of agile software processes. Third International Conference on Extreme Programming and Flexible Processes in Software Engineering, Italy.
9. Vijayasarathy LEOR, Turk D (2008) Agile Software Development: A survey of early adopters. J Inform Technol Manage 19: 1-8.
10. Turbit N (2005) The Project Perfect White Paper Collection.
11. Eriksson Ulf (2015) The Role of the Project Manager in Agile Development.
12. Frederico A (2015) What's the difference between a project manager and a scrum master?
13. Granot D, Zuckerman D (1991) Optimal Sequencing and Resource Allocation in Research and Development Projects. Manage Sci 37: 140-156.

Who Regulates the Mobile Money Operations by Telco's? The Need for an Effective and Robust Legislative and Regulatory Framework in Ghana

Tagoe NA*

Export Trade, Agricultural & Industrial Development Fund Operations,Accra, Ghana

Abstract

Ghana has evolved with the rest of the world in technological advancement. Mobile phones have so many peripheral merits besides phone calls and text messaging. Mobile Network Operators (MNO) has ventured into rendering financial services other than the usual mandate of providing telecommunication services. Mobile Money Operations (MMO) by the Telco's in Ghana has become a tool to mobilize and encourage savings for the mostly unbanked populace of Ghana, and again as vehicle towards the ultimate aim of moving the economy into a cashless economy. However, there are unseemly implications if these activities of the Telco's are not strongly regulated by the appropriate regulatory bodies. Telecommunication activities in Ghana are normally regulated by the National Communications Authority (NCA), apparently the financial services activities of Telco's are beyond the purview of NCA and naturally falls within the mandate of the Bank of Ghana (BoG). This article seeks to implore the BOG to come out with a much stronger and robust legislative framework than what is currently available. The article compares and analyses some legislative frameworks of countries such as Nigeria, Kenya and Tanzania. Finally, the paper gives recommendations on regulating the MMO of Telco's.

Keywords: Mobile money operations; Mobile network operators; Bank of Ghana; National communications authority; Regulatory and legislative framework

Introduction

There is growing recognition of the importance of mobile phones. The mobile phone revolution and the introduction of mobile money have brought unprecedented benefits: improving clients' lives and livelihood, and enhancing a more stable and secure financial systems particularly across Africa. For instance, In Kenya and Nigeria, mobile phones can be used to verify the authenticity of a drug [1]. Another use of the mobile services by the Telco's is mobile marketing. Mobile marketing offers direct communications with consumers at anytime and anyplace [2].

At the centre of the current revolution of the mobile telecommunication is mobile money. According to Jerkins [3], mobile money could be described as monies assessed and used through the use of mobile phones. Mobile money could be used for transactions such as utility bills payment, remittances to family and friends, purchase of goods and services, payroll payment, airtime top up and micro insurance.

Mobile money has served both as a compliment to traditional banking services and in other cases served as the only form of non-traditional banking services [4]. In Africa, the fastest growing brand of mobile money in one country has been the M-PESA both in Kenya and Tanzania [4,5]. Mobile money does not only enhance people's lives, it serves as an outlet through which a more inclusive financial sector could be built. Furthermore, mobile money serves as an opportunity for the unbanked and new clients who feel the conventional banks are too congested, time consuming, and charge higher fees and commission. Therefore, affordability and convenience of the service become key determinants in negotiating banking choices by rational clients. Some of the reasons for the unbanked population in Ghana include account opening requirements (KYC), cost of financial service and distance to financial service outlets [6].

Indeed, mobile money operation in Ghana is fairly recent. However, the field is fast growing in Ghana. With 2.5 billion people still lacking access to basic financial services globally (GSMA, 2012) [7], much of which comes from the sub-regions in Africa, the essential role of mobile money operation: as an alternative entry point for the unbanked rural areas becomes important. In Africa, the fastest growing brand of mobile money in one country has been the M-PESA both in Kenya and Tanzania [4,5,8].

Despite the beneficial consequences of mobile money operation, it remains a major challenge for mobile network corporations to meet the growing clientele needs. Ofcourse, Mobile Network Operators do not operate in a vacuum. They operate within internal and external circumstances. Thus, depending on the context and specificities of constraints thereof, further deployment can be done. Regulatory issues have been a major determinant in the landscape of operation for most telecom industries. Indeed, a favourable and friendlier regulatory architecture could facilitate further penetration of the telecom market. Paradoxically, this has not been the case and this hugely undermines the operation of telecom operators [9]. Emerging evidence suggests that in contexts where institutionally marked barriers in the form of regulations do not allow mobile money operators to design and set up effective distribution network and/or put in mechanisms that can facilitate easy registration and identification of clients (which has investment wisdom) can hamper free flow of operation [10].

***Corresponding author:** Nii Ardey Tagoe, Msc, Officer, Credit and Projects, Export Trade, Agricultural and Industrial Development Fund Operations, Accra, Ghana, E-mail: nardtag@gmail.com

The questions that remain less discussed are: Who should regulate MNOs? How should MNOs be regulated? And should this regulation be a fair play ground? This paper, therefore, situates its arguments in drawing attention to the need for a strong regulatory framework in the emerging mobile money industry. This article seeks to draw government and other regulatory bodies' attention on the need to ensure safety of clients' monies in order not to disincentives or further distant them from financial system. This article also serves as an entry point for further recommendation in terms of regulatory and legislative framework in the Telco industry in Ghana and beyond.

The next section gives an overview of MMO in Ghana. This is followed by a section that synthesizes and discusses the regulatory and legislative frameworks available in other countries. The last section concludes with some recommendations.

Overview of MMO in Ghana

The role of the Bank of Ghana include other things such as to regulate, supervise and direct the banking and credit system and ensure the smooth operation of the financial sector whereas the role of the NCA includes granting licenses and authorisations for operation of communication systems and services ensure fair competition among licensees, Establish and monitor quality of service indicators for operators and service providers, Consumer Education and Protection, Equipment Standards and Type Approval and International Frequency Coordination [11].

Mobile money started in Ghana in the year 2008. The population of Ghana is over 25 million and over 80% of the population is unbanked whiles mobile phone usage as at 2013 is over 100% (i.e. 27.51 million users) (Appendix A).

Mobile money usage

The illustration above gives the trend of mobile money registered customers and annual usage. The number of registered mobile money customers increased by 64.1% from 2013 to 2014. The total annual value of mobile money transactions increased by 393% from 2013 to 2014. Table 1 gives an increasing trajectory for mobile money operations is Ghana.

In March 2014, The BoG at the Strategic Payments System Roadmap for Ghana deliberated on the way forward of electronic payments systems including mobile money. In Ghana, whiles new mobile money agents are been registered and approved by NCA, the BoG also needs to approve these new agents as part of payment system providers, thus the need for greater collaboration between NCA and BoG [12].

According to the National Communications Authority, the total number of mobile phone subscribers in Ghana as at February 2015 was 31,028,253. Three out of the six mobile network operators in Ghana are involve in mobile money operations. These are Scancom (MTN), Millicom (Tigo) and Airtel. As at 2012, MTN had 3 million mobile money subscribers, Airtel had 900,000 mobile money subscribers and Tigo had 3.75 million mobile money Subscribers [4].

According to the Bank of Ghana (2014), two of the key objectives of the payment system in Ghana are: (a) to discourage the use of cash for transactions whilst encouraging the use of paper-based instruments for payments as part of the short-term development plan; (b) to develop an integrated electronic payment infrastructure that will enhance interoperability of payment and securities infrastructures. Although, there is the Payment System Policy and Oversight division at BoG, which in part oversees the activities of MMO. The BoG recognizes the Telco's as participants in payment system but only in the capacity as providing the telecommunication infrastructural arrangement for the payment system [13]. Thus the central bank and commercial banks plays the active roles because the BoG recognizes them as financial intermediaries while the Telco's play a passive role because they are recognized as MNO. There is no concrete legislative framework for MMO. The BoG sees the MMO as part of other electronic payments such as Ghana Interbank Payment and Settlement Systems Limited (GhIPPS).

The BoG issued Guidelines to Branchless Banking in 2008 which purported to provide the basis of mobile financial services in Ghana. In analyzing these guidelines, one could see that it only provides the basics for branchless banking for the traditional commercial banks and non-bank financial institutions. Further guidelines or legislative framework should address the following: Who will monitor and control the mobile money agents to make sure they compile with Ghana's Anti-Money Laundering Act as well as the Anti-Money Laundering and Financing of Terrorism (AML/CFT) standards as set by the Financial Action Task Force (FATF). Currently, the BoG finds it even difficult to regulate, monitor and control Microfinance, Savings & Loans and other money lending institutions. The Guidelines define the Telco's as agent in the Branchless Banking. Apparently, these Telco's are actively involved in the mobile money operations. They are not mere agents but principals or play a lead role in MMO.

Discussions

The Telco's MMO makes it unclear as to the regulatory distinction between telecommunication and financial services. For instance, in Ghana, at prima facie it's unclear as to whether it falls under the purview of the National Communications Authority (NCA) or BOG. MMO is a simple financial intermediation activity but can also be compared to a complex financial transaction in terms of the operations of the Telco's. Therefore a strong systems needs to be out in place before Ghana is hit by a financial crises caused by MMO. The Central Bank of Nigeria does not allow Telco's to engage in MMO but allow other operators to use the networks of the Telco's.

Indicators	2013	2014
Total number of mobile phone subscribers	20,346,016	21,721,814
Registered mobile money customers (Cumulative)	3,303,837	5,424,650
Active mobile money customers	963,495	2,369,997
Registered Agents (Cumulative)	17,467	26,889
Active Agents	10,404	20,722
Total volume of Mobile Money Transactions (Annual)	36,796,146	106,431,007
Total value of Mobile Money Transactions (Annual, GH¢'Million)	2,351	11,592
Balance on Float (GH¢)	62,809,945	223,325,189
Source: Bank of Ghana (2014) Payment System Statistics.		

Table 1: Mobile money usage.

In future, it could possible to transfer mobile money from MTN to Tigo or Airtel and vice versa. It would even be possible to transfer mobile money from one operator in Ghana to the other in Nigeria. These are major transformations that need strong legislative controls.

There are no limits on these mobile money transactions because no regulatory and supervisory control exists. This could be a great avenue for money launderers to infiltrate and wash clean their dirty monies.

Mobile money helps cultivate the habit of savings both in adults and the youth. The Bank of Ghana's (BOG) know-your-customer (KYC) policy disqualifies a lot of people from opening bank accounts. Not all bankable (everybody above 18 years) Ghanaians can provide a proof of residence, a form of identity (i.e. passport, national voter's ID and national health insurance card) and also a proof of source of income.

The mobile money service is in the emerging/transition stage now. The service will grow and consolidate and might pose serious problems if regulatory actions do not start now. The rapid growth of MMO has initiated the urgency for the need of an effective and robust regulatory and legislative framework [14].

Can the Telco's effectively and efficiently manage the financial services operations?

Capacity - Can the management of Telco's run MMO as financial services effectively and efficiently? No, they need the services of expertise in the banking and finance industry to run it. MMO might look very simple but it's a complex financial transaction. It needs to be managed well otherwise it could lead to a financial crisis.

Infrastructure - MMO does not need any huge investments in physical infrastructure. The Telco's already have the platforms and technological infrastructures in place. A MMO operation runs on a branchless banking operations model.

Customer base of Telco's - According to NCA, the total number of subscribers of MTN, Airtel and Tigo was as 22,186,257 at February 2015. This number is more than the total number of the banked population of Ghana. Assuming, MMO becomes fully developed/ matured and most subscribers are registering for the mobile money service. This will create an oligopoly and Ghana's financial services sector will be controlled by a few Telco's engaged in MMO.

MMO models and some legislations in Nigeria, Kenya and Tanzania

According to Jimoh who happens to be the Head of Payment System Policy and Oversight, Central Bank of Nigeria [6]. The three regulatory frameworks are as follows:

- **Bank-focused model:** This is where a bank delivers banking services to customers using the mobile phone as a mode of delivery. This model can only be deployed by licensed deposit-taking financial institutions including Microfinance Banks and Discount Houses.
- **Bank-led model:** This is where a bank or consortium of banks, partnering with other organizations, jointly seeks to deliver banking services by leveraging on the mobile banking system. The model could only be possible where; there exists collaboration between a licensed bank and an organization duly verified by the partner bank.
- **Non-bank-led model:** The model allows a corporate organization that has been duly approved by the Central Bank to deliver mobile payments services to consumers. The model is applicable to any organization other than a licensed deposit money bank and telecommunication companies.

Ghana could adopt the three regulated frameworks of Nigeria or adopt what the article termed as Telco-Bank led model. This is where Telco's are actually in MMO and partner banks to carry out the activities. Here, the MMO of the Telco's must be ring fenced from the Mobile Network Operations for taxation and clear business operating line purposes.

Nyaga 2014 lists a few legislative frameworks that regulate mobile money in parts of eastern Africa.

In Kenya, these include:

- Central Bank of Kenya Act (enacted 1966, amended through 2009), creating the Central Bank of Kenya and defining its mandate.
- Banking Act (enacted 1991, amended through 2010), regulating the activities of banking institutions within the financial sector in Kenya.
- Guideline on Agent Banking (2010), providing for the appointment of agents to extend banking services within Kenya.
- Draft Electronic Retail Transfers Regulation and Draft E-Money Regulation (stake holder consultations have been organized and comments to the draft are now being integrated), regulating electronic money issuance and exchange, as well as its transfer between different parties within Kenya.
- The Kenya Information and Communications Act (enacted 1998, amended in 2010), providing the mandate of Communications Commission of Kenya (CCK) and a framework to regulate the information, communications, media, and broadcasting subsectors.
- A range of Kenyan information and communications regulations made by the Minister in charge of Information and Communications in tandem with the CCK to regulate various aspects of the communications sector that include consumer protection, competition, tariffs, numbering, inter-connection, quality of service, etc.
- The Kenyan Competition Act (enacted 2009), which includes some elements of consumer protection and provides for the creation of an autonomous Competition Authority to replace the Monopolies and Prices Commission

In Tanzania, these include:

- The Bank of Tanzania Act (enacted 2006), creating the Bank of Tanzania and defining its principal functions.
- The Banking and Financial Institutions Act (enacted 2006), providing the legal framework for undertaking licensed banking operations within the United Republic of Tanzania.
- There are a number of guidelines from the Bank of Tanzania that are relevant to mobile money including the National Payment Systems Guidelines for retail payments, rules and regulations for retail payments, and the guidelines for introducing electronic payments.

- The United Republic of Tanzania Communications Regulatory Authority (TCRA) Act no. 12 (enacted 2003), establishing and providing the mandate for the communications regulator. The Electronic and Postal Communications Act (enacted 2010), principally repealing the Broadcasting Services Act and the Tanzania Communication Act with the aim of putting in place a comprehensive regulatory framework for electronic and postal communication.
- The Fair Competition Act (enacted 2003), fostering competition in different sectors, while at the same time protecting consumers. As part of this Act, the Tanzanian government has set up the Fair Competition Commission (FCC) to administer the law, and the Fair Competition Tribunal (FCT) to provide a judicial forum where appeals of various commission decisions can be made.

Analysis of legislative and regulatory frameworks in Kenya, Tanzania and models in Nigeria

From the above listed regulations in both Kenya and Tanzania, we can see that MMO by the Telco's has made it very difficult to clearly distinguish the financial regulations from telecommunication regulations. Both Central Banks in Kenya and Tanzania has adopted flexible and calm posture waiting how the MMO will eventually span out before they react. Nigeria, on the other hand, has blocked the Telco's from getting involved in MMO because of the complexities and uncertainties.

In Kenya, the Communications Commission of Kenya defers specifics of M-PESA oversight to the Central Bank of Kenya and in Tanzania, there is a MoU between the Bank of Tanzania and the Tanzania Communications Regulatory Authority.

Conclusions/Recommendations

The government and other regulatory bodies should provide an enabling environment for MMO because of the merits. MMO presents a new set of operational challenges for the central bank [14]. The paper would recommend a Telco and Commercial Banks partnership led model which would be easier to regulate.

Telco – Bank led Model – This is where Telco's are actually in MMO and partner banks to carry out the activities. Here, the MMO of the Telco's must be ring fenced from the Mobile Network Operations for taxation and clear business operating line purposes. This model calls for a robust legislative and regulatory framework otherwise the Telco's would form an oligopoly because of their subscriber base and would also take advantage to charge higher fees, engage in activities outside the boundaries of Banking and Non-Banking Financial Institutions as players in the Financial services industry such as insurance and moving funds around. In effect, the MMO business unit of Telco's would be duly decoupled from the MNO and operate as either a Banking Institution or Non-Banking Financial Institution, whichever is appropriate. The National Telecommunication commission should still remain as the regulator of the core operations of the Telco's while the BOG takes up the regulatory role of the mobile money and other financial services provided by the Telco's.

However, decoupling the MMO from MNO's would mean the MMO business unit would fall under financial services industry which is primarily regulated by BoG. This would create accessibility problems because many unbankable persons in Ghana would be prequalified from opening accounts as they would not meet the basic account opening criteria. Subsequently not all MMO users would be required to open accounts, many of them would only be required to register with their phone numbers.

Apparently, this is where the Branchless banking of BOG would work effectively. Here, all the agents would be duly registered by the MMO unit and the Telco shall be held responsible for any lapses caused by the agents. Therefore the Telco's shall strictly monitor and evaluate the MMO agents on a regular basis to ensure proper record keeping and strict adherence to regulations.

Government could get more revenue where financial services of the Telco's are properly supervised so the appropriate taxes could be collected. The government has a major role in developing mobile money ecosystems and regulators are responsible for providing environments that enable ecosystem development to happen [3].

Nobody can predict what would happen in the mobile money industry three to five years from now. The paper admits the need for mobile money services by the telecommunication networks but it needs to be properly regulated before it get out of control or goes bust.

References

1. Qiang CZ, Yamamichi M, Hausman V, Altman D, Unit IS (2011) Mobile applications for the health sector. Washington: World Bank.
2. Scharl A, Dickinger A, Murphy J (2005) Diffusion and success factors of mobile marketing. Electronic Commerce Research and Applications 4: 159-173.
3. Jerkins B (2008) Developing Mobile Money Ecosystems. IFC and the Havard Kennedy School, Washington, DC.
4. William I (2013) Regulatory frameworks and Implementation patterns for Mobile Money in Africa: The case of Kenya, Ghana and Nigeria. Ghana ICT Conference, Accra.
5. Hughes N, Lonie S (2007) M-PESA: Mobile Money for the "Unbanked" Turning Cellphones into 24-Hour Tellers in Kenya. Innovations 2: 63-81.
6. Jimoh MI (2013) International Conference for Payment Systems 2013.
7. GSMA (2012) Mobile Money for the Unbanked (MMU) Deployment Tracker.
8. Mas I, Morawczynski O (2009) Designing Mobile Money Services Lessons from M-PESA. Innovations 4: 77-91.
9. Pénicaud C (2013) State of the Industry: Results from the 2012 Global Mobile Money Adoption Survey. GSMA, London, UK.
10. Leishman P (2011) Is There Really any Money in Mobile Money? GSMA Mobile Money for the Unbanked position paper.
11. NCA (2012) What We Do.
12. Bank of Ghana (2014) Overview of Payment System in Ghana.
13. Bank of Ghana (2011) Participants in Payment System.
14. Nyaga JK (2014) Mobile Banking Services in the East African Community (EAC): Challenges to the Existing Legislative and Regulatory Frameworks. Journal of Information Policy 4: 270-295.

Working Capital Management and Profitability: Evidence from Manufacturing Sector in Malaysia

Jakpar S[1]*, Tinggi M[1], Siang TK[1], Johari A[2], Myint KT[2] and Sadique MS[2]

[1]*Faculty of Economics and Business, University Malaysia Sarawak (UNIMAS), Malaysia*
[2]*School of Business, Curtin University Sarawak Campus, Malaysia*

Abstract

The purpose of this study is to examine the effect of working capital management on firm's profitability. The study is based on a sample of 164 manufacturing firms listed on the Main Board of Bursa Malaysia, covering a span of five years from 2007 to 2011. A discriminatory panel regression and Pearson correlation are used to test the hypotheses. The empirical evidence found that there is existence of significant positive relationship between exogenous variables, the average collection period, inventory conversion period and firm's size and its endogenous variable, which is firm's profitability. The findings also show a significant inverse relationship between debt ratio (leverage) and firm's profitability, but the firm's capability to translate working capital into cash promptly, as proxy in log cash conversion cycle has no impact on firm's profitability.

Keywords: Working capital management; Manufacturing sector; Profitability

Introduction

This study attempts to examine the relationship between the working capital management and firm's profitability. In this research, a panel data have been used for a sample of 164 manufacturing firms listed on Bursa Malaysia over a period of 5 years from 2007 to 2011.

Many findings of past studies were revisited and analyzed to link working capital management with firm's profitability. However, there is still ambiguity regarding the appropriate variables which might serve as proxies for working capital management that would affect firm's profitability. Thus, this research paper is conducted in order to find the appropriate proxy for exogenous variables that will impact the firm's profitability. Similarly it is also found that few studies have been conducted by researcher in Malaysia to determine the impact of working capital management on profitability, particularly in the manufacturing sector, which serves as the second largest sector contributing to Malaysia economy. To become a major contributor to the economic growth of a country, this sector is certainly expected to be well-managed in order to remain efficient and viable. Therefore, this research paper is carried out to investigate how the working capital in the manufacturing sector in Malaysia is managed towards attaining profitability.

In 2008, the global financial crisis and the collapses of colossal organizations such as General Motors and Lehman Brothers have affected the industries business operation worldwide. In the aftermath, the firm's managers are forced to recognize the importance of managing the firm's resources effectively, particularly in the areas of working capital in order to prevent more losses or bankruptcy. Manufacturing sector is not exempted from the impact of the financial crisis. As found earlier, the manufacture sector is important to Malaysia economic growth, through its high export demand and generating employment opportunities. Thus, without doubt, it is imperative for Malaysian analyst to conduct a further study on working capital management, in the field of manufacturing domain.

Based on the Department of Innovation, Industry, Science & Research (DIISR) data from Australia, about half of its total 294 manufacturing firms reported bankruptcy status after the financial crisis in 2008. Similarly, the impact was also widely felt in Malaysia. According to Bank Negara Malaysia report, the gross domestic product (GDP) contributed from the manufacturing export demand, declined by 8.8% in the fourth quarter of 2008; reported a negative growth of 17.6% in the first quarter of 2009 and, finally, a negative 14.5% in the second quarter of 2009. The recession has left the firms with no choice but to retrench workers and hence increase the unemployment rate. Therefore, it is valuable to know what the Malaysia manufacturing manager would attempt to do, in order to sustain profitability and maintain their working capital to an optimal level, right after the financial crisis in 2007.

Extant research which is conducted in the other part of world, but using different exogenous variables report mixed results in its attempt to determine their impact on organization's profitability. The findings are perplexing managers and major stakeholders during the process of making vital financial decision. Mathuva [1] finds that there is a positive relationship between independent variables, which are measured by average payment period and inventory turnover with firm's profitability. This study runs contrary to findings from Deloof [2], Falope and Ajilore [3], which suggest that there is a significant negative relationship between profitability and the inventory turnover.

This study focuses on evaluating and identifying the significant relationship between the management of working capital and the manufacturing firm's profitability in Malaysia.

Our findings show that there is insignificant negative relationship between the log cash conversion cycle and firm's profitability. However, there is an evidence of positive and significant relationship between the average collection period, inventory conversion period and its profitability. Similarly, this research study also reported that the

***Corresponding author:** Shaharudin Jakpar, Faculty of Economics and Business, University Malaysia Sarawak (UNIMAS), Malaysia
E-mail: jshaharudin@unimas.my

size of firms has a significant positive relationship with profitability of firms. However, other findings show a negative significant relationship between debt ratio (leverage) and firm's profitability.

The results of this study should be great of importance to managers and major stakeholders, such as investors, creditors, and financial analysts especially after the recent global financial crisis which can help them to establish a proper tradeoff policy between firm's liquidity and its performance. The empirical result of this study will benefit the owner and management of the manufacturing firms, to understand the liquidity-performance relationship much better, in order for the management to maintain an appropriate level between liquidity and profitability so as to ensure that the business will function more effectively. They would be expected to know at what extent they should maintain firm's liquidity in order to achieve a satisfactory level of firm's performance. It will also help them to know the optimal level of receivables and inventory level which will be useful for their receivable and inventory control management. Besides, this study is also useful for selected industries' manager, who are anticipated to understand which working capital and corporate finance theory that should actually be adopted by them. Furthermore, this research aim to be a platform for other researchers to conduct more in-depth studies which will contribute more to the field of corporate finance in Malaysia.

Theoretical framework

In this study, two types of theories have been adopted, which are trade-off theory and pecking order theory. The trade-off theory implies that firms with high level of liquidity may potentially encounter low profitability problem. In other word, there is a plausibility of negative relationship between liquidity and profitability. A study conducted by Filbeck and Krueger [4] has revealed that there is an existence of significant inverse relationship between profitability and liquidity of companies in United Kingdom. Dittmar et al. [5] indicate that when the firms are liquid, the firms generate huge amount of net working capital, follow by diminishing level of profitability. However, in a situation of over trading, the trade-off theory will highlight the firms will, actually be confronted with the problem of holding too little liquid once the firms generate high level of profitability.

Second, the pecking order theory implies that there is an opposite relationship between the levels of debt and profitability. It means that, if the firms has higher debt ratio, the firms would have low or decreasing profitability and vice versa. Myers and Majluf found an inverse relationship between profitability and debt. Profitable firms with higher level of retained earnings will not be over-dependant on external financing. Thus, a pecking order theory suggests that the firms should rather use the internal fund instead of the required external fund or debt to finance their operation in order to overcome the problem which will potentially affect the firm's value. As reported in a study by Raheman and Nasr, as the firms' leverage increase, it will have a significant and negative impact on its profitability (Figure 1) [6,7].

Research Objectives

General objective

The purpose of this analysis is to examine the relationship between management of working capital and firm's profitability for a sample of 164 manufacturing firms listed on Bursa Malaysia over a period of 5 years from 2007 to 2011.

Specific objective

The specifically objectives of this study are:

i. To empirically examine whether there is a significant relationship between the working capital management and firm's profitability; and,

ii. To determine which theory would best fit in explaining the relationship between the working capital management and firm's profitability.

Literature Review

Cash conversion cycle and firm's profitability

The relationship between working capital management and firm's profitability in Nigeria Stock Exchange (1996 to 2005) and New York Stock Exchange (2005 to 2007), respectively [3,8]. The results of the study show a significant and positive relationship between firm's profitability and cash conversion cycle. They also opine that higher cash conversion cycle will lead to higher profitability of the firms and vice versa.

There is a negative significant relation between return on asset and cash conversion cycle [2,9-14].

Samilogu and Demirgunes also elucidated the linkage between the management of working capital and firm profitability and they found that the cash conversion cycle has no effect on firm's profitability [15].

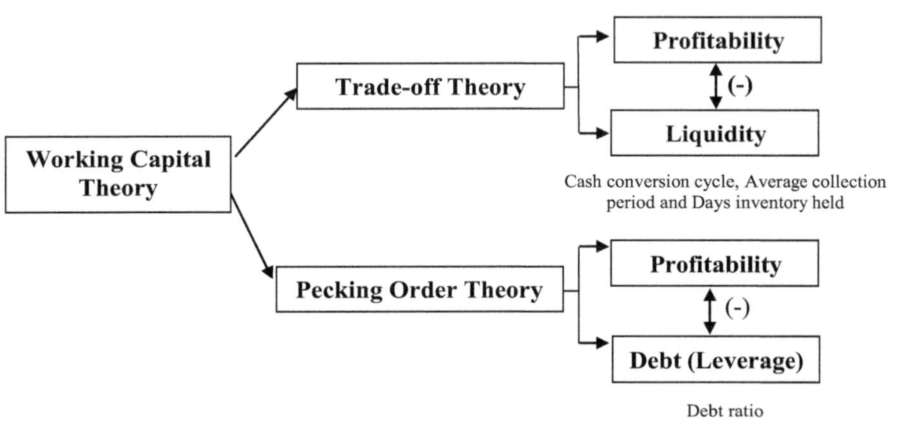

Figure 1: Summaries of theoretical framework.

Average collection period and firm's profitability

There is a significant and negative relationship between net operating profitability and the average collection period. This seems to suggest that the profitability will decrease if the number of days' collection from debtor increases [2,7,8,14,16-19].

Inventory conversion period and firm's profitability

There is a significant and negative relationship between net operating profitability and the inventory conversion period in days. It specifies that shortening the number of days of inventories turnover can maximize the firm profitability and hence create shareholder wealth [1,4,7,12,14,16,17,20,21].

Debt ratio and firm's profitability

The studies done by Dong and Su in Vietnam stock market in 2006 to 2008 show that the debt ratio, as a measure by debt leverage is positively associated with gross operating profit [11]. The result implies that when the debt ratio increases, the firm's profitability will simultaneously rise.

The debt ratio as the proxy for debt leverage is significantly and inversely associated with profitability. In a situation when the firms are less profitable, the firm will be reliant on higher leverage to meet its financial obligation [7,12,16,17,22,23]. They also indicate in this study that when the firms leverage increase, it will have a significant and negative impact on its profitability

Al-Mwalla examined the effect of working capital management policies on the firm's profitability over the period of 2001 to 2009 in Amman Stocks Market [24]. The result, however, shows that the leverage does not have an exact significant impact on firm profitability.

Firm size and firm's profitability

There is a significant and positive relationship between firm's profitability and size of firms which is measured by natural logarithm of sales [3,7,11,17,24,25]. The studies indicate that a larger firm can increase the company value by taking advantage of any favorable investment opportunity.

There is no evidence of a statistically significant relationship between firm size and its gross operating profit [8,26].

Manufacturing sector	Number of firms selected
Consumer products	83
Industry products	81
Total	164

Table 1: Sample Distribution and Descriptions (2007-2011).

Data and Methodology

In this study, the financial data are collected from the DataStream and the annual report of relevant companies listed at the Bursa Malaysia (KLSE) in Malaysia. The sample consists of 164 firms in manufacturing sector over a period of five years spanning from 2007 to 2011. The financial data of those companies include firm's Net Sales, Purchases Inventory, Cost of Goods Sold, Net Income, Total Assets, Total Liabilities and Account Receivable.

The model that is used in this study is Pooled Ordinary Least Squares (OLS), Random and Fixed effect Regression Model.

Research design (sample selection)

The original sample was consisting of about 400 listed companies on the main board of Bursa Malaysia but was finally narrowed down to 164 firms with an available data. The sample data were obtained from DataStream and Bursa Malaysia website (Table 1 and Figure 2).

Description of variables

The endogenous or dependent variable in this study is return on asset, as a measure for firm's profitability. Exogenous or independent variable consists of ash conversion cycle, average collection period, average payment period, inventory turnover period, debt ratio and firm size as a proxy for component of working capital management.

Measurement of variables

The endogenous and exogenous variables stated below are have been used to test the hypotheses in this study (Table 2).

Hypotheses

The hypotheses are derived based on our objectives. The five hypotheses are stipulated to examine the relationship between working capital management and firm's performance in term of profitability (ROA).

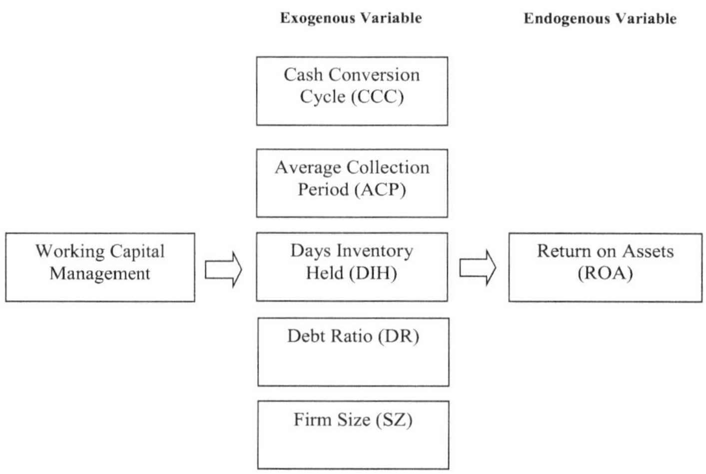

Figure 2: The relationship between working capital management and firm's profitability.

Description	Measurement	Variable
Return on asset (ROA)	(Net income)/(Total assets)	Dependent
Cash Conversion Cycle (CCC)	(Average Collection Period)+(Average Payable Period)+(Inventory Turnover Period)	Independent
Average Collection Period (ACP)	(Account Receivable)/(Net Sales × 365)	Independent
Inventory Conversion Period (ICP)	(Inventory)/(Cost of Goods Sold × 365)	Independent
Debt Ratio (DR)	(Total Liabilities)/(Total Assets)	Independent
Firm Size (SZ)	Natural Logarithm of Sales	Independent

Table 2: Proxy Variables Description with Measurement.

H_1: There is a relationship between log cash conversion cycle and firm's profitability

H_2: There is a relationship between log Average collection period and firm's profitability

H_3: There is a relationship between log Inventory turnover and firm's profitability

H_4: There is a relationship between debt ratio and firm's profitability

H_5: There is a relationship between firm size and firm's profitability.

Data analysis

Correlation coefficient test: Correlation coefficient is used to measure the strength of the relationship between two variables such as dependent variable and independent variable. It is conducted to determine the relationship between the five independent variables namely Average Collection Period, Inventory Conversion Period, Cash Conversion Cycle, Debt Ratio and Firm Size with the dependent variable of return on assets ratio. The values of correlation coefficient are ranged from −1.00 to+1.00. A positive correlation coefficient means that the when the values of one variable increase, the value of the other correlated variable will simultaneously rise whereby a negative correlation coefficient indicates that as one variable increases, the other decreases.

Panel regression analysis: The model of Pooled Ordinary Least Square (OLS), Random Effect and Fixed Effect Model are used in this study in order to estimate the impact of working capital management on profitability. The regression model as follows:

$$ROA_{it=}C_{+}\beta_1(LCCC_{it})+\beta_2(LACP_{it})+\beta_3(LICP_{it})+\beta_4(DR_{it})+\beta_5(SZ_{it})+\varepsilon_{it}$$

Where,

C = Constant term

ROA = Return on Assets

LCCC = Natural logarithm of Cash Conversion Cycle

LACP=Natural logarithm of Account Collection Period

LICP=Natural logarithm of Inventory Conversion Cycle

DR=Debt Ratio

SZ=Firm Size (measured by Log of Sales)

ε=Error Term

Breusch and Pagan Lagrangian multiplier test: The Breusch and Pagan Lagrangian Multiplier Test are applied to test the hypothesis in order to differentiate which model is appropriate for our research study. The null hypothesis stipulates that the variance of the error term is constant, H_0: $\acute{o}^2_\lambda = 0$. If the null hypothesis is rejected, the random effect model is thus more appropriate for the research study and vice versa. The following is the hypothesis of Breusch and Pagan Lagrangian Multiplier Test:

H_0: $\sigma^2_\lambda = 0$

H_A: $\sigma^2_\lambda = 0$

Hausman test: Besides the Breusch and Pagan Lagrangian Multiplier Test, we also use the Hausman Test to test the hypothesis that whether fixed-effect or random-effect regression should be the choice for this research study. The null hypothesis states that there exist no co-variance between the firm specific effect and the regressor, H_0: $Cov(\lambda, x_{it}) = 0$ If the null hypothesis is rejected, the random-effect regression is not appropriate for this study. As a result, we will probably prefer the fixed-effect regression for our study. The following is the hypothesis of Hausman Test:

H_0: $Cov(\lambda, x_{it}) = 0$

H_A: $Cov(\lambda, x_{it}) = 0$

Descriptive statistics result

The following table presents the descriptive statistics for dependent variable: Return on Assets (ROA) and independent variables: Natural Logarithm of Cash Conversion Cycle (LCCC), Natural Logarithm of Average Collection Period (LACP), Natural Logarithm of Inventory Conversion Period (LICP), Debt Ratio (DR) and Firm Size (SZ).

Table 3 reports descriptive statistics of all the data in this study. The return on assets (ROA) has a mean of 4.83 percent of total asset, and standard deviation is 7.2 percent. The maximum value for the ROA is 41.17 percent and the minimum value is -28.35. Correspondingly, the log of cash conversion cycle (LCCC) is used to test the liquidity of the companies which has shown an average of 4.63 with a standard deviation of 0.64. The maximum value is 5.76 which indicate that the firms take 5 years and above to convert its capital into cash. However, the minimum value is 1.39 or more than 1 year for the company to change it working capital into cash.

In addition, the log of average collection period (LACP) is also used as a proxy to verify the liquidity of the companies which is defined as the ability of the firm to covert it receivables into cash. The mean value of LACP is 4.1 years with the standard deviation of 0.58. Maximum time taken by a firm to collect it receivable is 5.75 years while the minimum level is 1.95 years. Correspondingly, the log of inventory conversion period (LICP) also applies in this research study to check for the level the liquidity of the company. The outcome shows that the means of log of inventory conversion period is 4.40, and the standard deviation is 0.64. The maximum value of log of inventory conversion period (LICP) is 5.81 while the minimum level for this purpose is 2.20.

Besides that, the mean value for debt ratio (DR) is 0.39 with standard deviation of 0.18. The maximum level of debt used by a company is 0.84 while the minimum is 0.02. Result from descriptive statistics also shows that the average firm size (SZ) which is measured by terms of log of sales is 19.24 while the standard deviation is 1.31. The maximum value of log of sales is 23.33 and the minimum value for this purpose is 15.40.

Correlation coefficient results

Table 4 above reports the correlation coefficients among the variables considered in the study. The return on assets is negatively correlated with the log of cash conversion cycle, log of average collection period and debt ratio. The negative correlation between return on assets indicates that when those stated proxy variables increase it may have adverse effect on the firm's profitability. Information from correlation coefficients also indicates that the log inventory conversion period and firm size is positive associated with the return on asset.

Panel regression analysis results

The panel model of regression analysis has been used in this research study, in an attempt to further investigate the relationship between the working capital management and firm's profitability. To run the data, the E-Views 7 Software were used to analyze the panel data for the total number of 820 company year observations, which represents the sample size of 164 listed firms from manufacturing sector over a 5 year period from 2007 to 2011. The following is the regression estimation result where profitability of firm which is measured by return on assets is regressed against natural logarithm of cash conversion cycle (LCCC), natural logarithm of average collection period (LACP), natural logarithm of inventory conversion period (LICP), debt ratio (DR) and firm size (SZ).

$$ROA_{it=}C+\beta_1(LCCC_{it})+\beta_2(LACP_{it})+\beta_3(LICP_{it})+\beta_4(DR_{it})+\beta_5(SZ_{it})+\varepsilon_{it}$$

Based on the result presented on Table 5 above, it shows that the coefficient determination, R-square is approximately 0.2804. This indicates that the independent variables explained about 28.04 percent of the variation in return on assets which represent the profitability of the firms. The model also points out that the intercept of the equation is -0.390219 which shows that the ROA is expected to decrease by 0.390219 when the entire variables are remaining constant and unchanged.

From the Table 5 above, the finding shows that there is a negative relationship exists between the log cash conversion cycle (LCCC) and return on assets of the company. It also demonstrates that the log cash conversion cycle is statistically significantly affecting the firm's profitability. The null hypothesis which shows that there is no relationship between the log cash conversion cycle and firm's profitability is therefore rejected at 5 percent significant level, indicating a significant alternative hypothesis of a one percent decrease in log cash conversion cycle would increase profitability by 0.0311 percent.

Furthermore, the result illustrated that there is a positive association

	ROA	LCCC	LACP	LICP	DR	SZ
Mean	0.04839	4.631501	4.097567	4.402449	0.393530	19.23812
Median	0.046650	4.672829	4.189655	4.382027	0.402350	19.11237
Maximum	0.411700	5.961005	5.749393	5.808142	0.840900	23.32860
Minimum	-0.283500	1.386294	1.945910	2.197225	0.023600	15.39961
Std. Dev.	0.071960	0.642805	0.580518	0.635178	0.179166	1.314705
Skewness	0.166850	-0.668896	-0.717392	-0.153358	0.052863	0.308278
Kurtosis	5.473043	4.052917	3.709073	2.628077	2.229377	3.121150
Jarque-Bera	212.7660	99.02606	87.51406	7.940380	20.67213	13.48965
Probability	0.000000	0.000000	0.000000	0.018870	0.000032	0.001177
Sum	39.68610	3797.830	3360.005	3610.008	322.6944	15775.26
Sum Sq. Dev.	4.241028	338.4097	276.0041	330.4260	26.29029	1415.600
Observations	820	820	820	820	820	820

Table 3: Descriptive Statistics.

	ROA	LCCC	LACP	LICP	DR	SZ
ROA	1.000000					
LCCC	-0.064009	1.000000				
LACP	-0.191015	0.483427	1.000000			
LICP	0.040960	0.786376	0.179288	1.000000		
DR	-0.310077	-0.175859	0.060099	-0.140587		
SZ	0.326631	-0.312453	-0.396213	-0.263031	0.193900	1.000000

Table 4: Pearson Correlation Coefficients

Variable	Coefficient	Std. Error	t-Statistic	Prob.
C	-0.390219***	0.006665	-4.672173	0.0000
LCCC	-0.031141**	0.004954	2.117926	0.0345
LACP	0.010492***	0.005977	5.704041	0.0000
LICP	0.034091***	0.012653	-12.86727	0.0000
DR	-0.162805***	0.001862	12.66614	0.0000
SZ	0.023591***	0.006665	-4.672173	0.0000
R-squared	0.280431		**Adjusted R-squared**	0.276011
S.E. of regression	0.061229		**F-Statistic**	63.44642
Prob. (F-Statistic)	0.000000			

***Significant at 1% level; **Significant at 5% level.

Table 5: Model I: The Result of Pooled Ordinary least Square (OLS).

between the firm's profitability and log average collection period (LACP). The finding also stated that the log average collection period has a statistically significant impact on firm's profitability. Therefore, the null hypothesis will be rejected at significant level of 1 percent. This indicates that when the log average collection period increases by one percent, it will lead to an approximately 0.0105 percent growth in profitability.

Additionally, the result above also finds that there is statistically significant and positive relationship between the log inventory conversion period (LICP) and firm's profitability. The null hypothesis is rejected at 1 percent level of significance and highlighting that there is a relationship between the log of inventory conversion period and firms' profitability. It gives an idea that a one percent increase in log inventory conversion period would yield a 0.0341 percent increase in profitability.

The finding also explains that the debt ratio (DR) is significantly affecting the firm's profitability. The result illustrates that there is inverse relationship between the two variables, indicating that for every one percent decreases in debt ratio would result in a 0.1628 percent growth in profitability.

Besides that, the finding also demonstrate evidence of is a positive relationship between firm's profitability and the firm size (SZ) which is calculated by log of sales. The null hypothesis is rejected at 1 percent significant level since the firm size is statistically significant affecting the firm's profitability, suggesting that a one percent increase in firm size increases profitability by 0.0236 percent.

Based on the result using by random effect model in Table 6, it can be observed that the coefficient determination, R-square value is 0.1361. This means that 13.61 percent of the variation in return on assets is explained by the independent variables. Additionally, this model also point out that the intercept of the equation is -0.5174 which shows that the ROA is expected to decrease 0.5174 when the entire variables are remaining constant and unchanged.

The cash conversion cycle was used as the control variable to test the efficiency of working capital. The regression shows that there is a significant and negative relationship between the firm's profitability and log cash conversion cycle (LCCC). Thus, the null hypothesis is rejected at 1 percent significant level suggesting that a one percent decrease in the cash conversion cycle increases firm's profitability by 0.0201 percent.

Additionally, the finding also shows that the log average collection period (LACP) is positively and significantly affecting the firm profitability. Thus, we fail to accept the null hypothesis at 5 percent significant level. This means that a one percent increase in log average collection period increases profitability by approximately 0.0131 percent.

Furthermore, the log inventory conversion period (LICP) is found to be significant and positively associated to firm's profitability. Therefore, this implies that the null hypothesis of no significant relationship between the log inventory conversion period and firm profitability is rejected at 1 percent significant level. It means to suggest that firm profitability will grow by 0.0298 percent for every one percent increase in log inventory conversion period.

Moreover, this finding also illustrates a negative relationship between the debt ratio (DR) and firm's profitability. It shows that the debt ratio is significantly affecting the firm's profitability. Hence, the null hypothesis is rejected at 1 percent significant level highlighting that a 1 percent decrease in the debt ratio would increase firm's profitability by about 0.1413 percent.

This model also explained that there exists a statistically significant and positive relationship between the firm size (SZ) and firm's profitability. Thus, the null hypothesis is rejected, suggesting that a one percent increase in firm size would yield a 0.0275 percent increase in profitability.

Based on the fixed effect model in Table 7, the R-square is approximately 0.7281. This means that the independent variables explain about 72.82 percent of the variation in return on assets. This model also point out that the intercept of the equation is -1.067701

Variable	Coefficient	Std. Error	t-Statistic	Prob.
C	-0.517436***	0.072534	-7.133705	0.0000
LCCC	-0.020112***	0.007455	-2.697622	0.0071
LACP	0.013167**	0.006207	2.121284	0.0342
LICP	0.029791***	0.006937	4.294772	0.0000
DR	-0.141261***	0.017866	-7.906625	0.0000
SZ	0.027522***	0.002996	9.185946	0.0000
R-squared	0.136116		Adjusted R-squared	0.130810
S.E. of regression	0.042491		F-Statistic	25.65125
Prob. (F-Statistic)	0.000000			

***Significant at 1% level; **Significant at 5% level.

Table 6: Model II: The Result of Random-Effect Regression.

Variable	Coefficient	Std. Error	t-Statistic	Prob.
C	-1.067701***	0.167543	-6.372682	0.0000
LCCC	-0.012149	0.008945	-1.358190	0.1749
LACP	0.019530**	0.008204	2.380403	0.0176
LICP	0.032301***	0.008925	3.619087	0.0003
DR	-0.116095***	0.028320	-4.099406	0.0000
SZ	0.051763***	0.007738	6.689734	0.0000
R-squared	0.728172		Adjusted R-squared	0.658023
S.E. of regression	0.042082		F-Statistic	10.38033
Prob. (F-Statistic)	0.000000			

***Significant at 1% level; **Significant at 5% level.

Table 7: Model III: The Result of Fixed-Effect Regression.

which shows that the ROA is expected to decrease 1.067701 when the entire variables are remaining constant and unchanged.

From Table 7, the estimation results from the model show that there is insignificant and negative relationship exists between the log cash conversion cycle (LCCC) and firm's profitability. It simply means that, the log cash conversion cycle is not significantly affecting the firm's profitability suggesting, that for every one percent increase in log cash conversion cycle will not lead to any change in firm's profitability.

Furthermore, this finding also illustrates that there is a positive relationship between the average collection period (LACP) and firm's profitability. The log average collection period is significantly influencing the firm's profitability. Therefore, the null hypothesis is rejected at 1 percent significant level, suggesting evidence a one percent level increase in log average collection period will lead to an approximately 0.0195 percent growth in profitability.

Additionally, the result also explains that there is a positive relationship exists between the log inventory conversion periods (LICP) with the firm's profitability. The finding seems to demonstrate that the log inventory conversion period is significantly affecting the firm's profitability. Thus, the null hypothesis is rejected, suggesting that a one percent increase in log inventory conversion period would increase profitability by 0.0323 percent.

The relationship between debt ratio (DR) and firm's profitability is significantly negative in this regression model. Therefore, the null hypothesis is rejected at 1 percent level, indicating that there is a significant relationship between debt ratio and firm's profitability. It means to highlight that the profitability would grow by an approximately 0.1161 percent, while the debt ratio would decrease by one percent.

As mentioned earlier, the firm size (SZ) is measured by log of sale.

Effects Test	Statistic	d.f.	Prob.
Cross-section F	6.578490	(163,651)	0.0000
Cross-section Chi-square	798.256151	163	0.0000

Table 8: Breusch and Pagan Lagrangian Multiplier Test Results.

Test Summary	Chi-Sq. Statistic	Chi-Sq. d.f.	Prob.
Cross-section random	20.928791	5	0.0008

Table 9: Hausman Test Results.

This finding shows that the log of sales is significant and positively associated with the firm's profitability. Thus, the null hypothesis is rejected at 1 percent level. It would mean that for every one percent increase in firm size would increase firm's profitability by 0.0517 percent.

Breusch and Pagan Lagrangian multiplier test

Based on Table 8, the null hypothesis is rejected at 1 percent significant level. This indicates that the random effect model is more appropriate compared to Pooled ordinary least squares (OLS), because of the presence of error term which is not constant, that will affect the efficiency of the Pooled Model.

Hausman test

From Table 9, the null hypothesis is rejected because the p-value is statistically significant at 1 percent level. It also means that there is a co-variance between the error term and the regressor, making random effect statistically not efficient. Therefore, the fixed effect model is more appropriate for this study compared to random effect model.

Based on the summaries of the results of panel regression analysis in Table 10, we find evidence that the best model to explain the empirical research for this study is the fixed effect (FE) regression model.

Results and Discussion

The main purpose of this research is to investigate the relationship between the management of working capital and profitability of 164 manufacturing firms listed in Malaysia over 5 years period from 2007 to 2011. This study also attempts to analyze evidence regarding which theory would be appropriate to explain the relationship between profitability and the working capital management. The hypotheses are finally formulated to examine the relationship between the working capital management and firm profitability which is measured by return on assets. The following discussion of the result is based on the fixed effect model regression (Model III).

HA_1: There is a relationship between log cash conversion cycle and firm's profitability

The empirical result suggests that the log cash conversion cycle which is used to measure the liquidity of firms is found to have no

ROA	Pooled OLS	Random Effect	Fixed Effect
C	-0.390219 (-8.014764)***	-0.517436 (-7.133705)***	-1.067701 (-6.372682)***
LCCC	-0.031141 (-4.672173)***	-0.020112 (-2.697622)***	-0.012149 (-1.358190)
LACP	0.010492 (2.117926)**	0.013167 (2.121284)**	0.019530 (2.380403)**
LICP	0.034091 (5.704041)***	0.029791 (4.294772)***	0.032301 (3.619087)***
DR	-0.162805 (-12.86727)***	-0.141261 (-7.906625)***	-0.116095 (-4.099406)***
SZ	-0.031141 (12.66614)***	0.027522 (9.185946)***	0.051763 (6.689734)***
Observation	820	820	820
LM Test (Pooled *vs.* RE)	798.256151 (0.0000)*** (random effect is more appropriate)		
Hausman Test (RE *vs.* FE)		20.928791 (0.0008)*** (random effect is not appropriate)	

***Significant at 1% level; **Significant at 5% level.

Table 10: Summaries of the Results of Panel Regression Analysis.

control over the firm's profitability. Thus, this hypothesis is rejected. This finding is different from results found in the previous studies done [2,9-14], which stated that there is indeed an existence of negative relationship between the profitability of the firms and cash conversion cycle. However, this result is still consistent with findings by Samilogu and Demirgunes who indicates that the cash conversion cycle is not significant at all in affecting firms' profitability. Finally it also means that our finding is not consistent with the Trade-off Theory [15].

HA_2: There is a relationship between log average collection period and firm's profitability

The log average collection period is used to measure the firm's liquidity and is found to have a significant and positive relationship with the firm's profitability. Therefore, this hypothesis is not rejected suggesting that longer collection period is creating increased profitability, which may seems to highlight those firms may suffer from over trading. As the statistical result portrays, it is totally the opposite with the prior studies [2,7,8,14,16-19]. They found that average collection period have a significant negative relationship on the firm's profitability. Additionally, this finding also seems to suggest that it is not consistent with the Trade-off theory. If the Trade-off theory holds, the profitability should be negatively correlated with the firm's liquidity which is measured by average collection period.

HA_3: There is a relationship between log inventory conversion period and firm's profitability

This hypothesis is not rejected because the log inventory conversion period which is used to measure the liquidity of firm is positively correlated to firm's profitability in our study. It would be the firms can create the value and increase the performance by increasing the inventory conversion period. This theory nevertheless is consistent with the management accounting philosophy that inventory that is reported using absorption costing will show increased profit, as the costing of closing inventory will be deferred to next accounting period. This result, however, is not supported by the evidence from the prior studies [1,4,7,12,14,16,17,20,21], which stated that inventory turnover period have a negative relationship on the firm's profitability. In summary, this result is not consistent with the Trade-off theory which implies that the liquidity should be negatively correlated to profitability of the firms.

HA_4: There is a relationship between debt ratio period and firm's profitability

This hypothesis is not rejected as the debt ratio is significantly and negatively associated with the profitability. This result is consistent with the Pecking Order Theory which indicates that the debt ratio should be negatively correlated with the profitability. This finding also proving by earlier research study [7,12,16,17,22,23], which finds evidence that there is negative relationship between profitability of a firms and debt ratio.

HA_5: There is a relationship between firm size and firm's profitability

Moreover, the result also explained that there is positive relationship between the size of firms and firm's profitability. Thus, this hypothesis is not rejected, suggesting that firm with has grown big has the potential to control markets and supplier chain for its own benefit and reap competitive edge. Several previous studies have shown to support this result, seems to suggest that there is positive relationship between the firm size and profitability of a firm [3,7,11,17].

Conclusion

This study is aimed at investigating the relationship between the working capital management and firm's profitability. For the purpose of analysis, a sample of 164 manufacturing firms over a 5 years period from 2007 to 2011 was selected. The sample data were obtained from DataStream and Bursa Malaysia website. To run and analyze the data, the descriptive statistic, correlation coefficient analysis, and panel regression analysis were used.

Consequently, the empirical results from Model III suggest that the log cash conversion cycle is insignificantly and negatively correlated to profitability. This implies that the log cash conversion cycle have no control over the firm's profitability. Furthermore, the results from the regression analysis also showed that the log average collection period has a significant positive relationship with the profitability of the firm. This means that the longer the credit period granted by the firms to their customer, the higher the firms gain their profitability. In many cases this form of results highlighted the fact that the company is suffering from over-trading.

In addition, the finding also illustrated that the log inventory conversion period is significantly and positively associated with the profitability of the firms. Thus, when the number of day of inventory turnover period increases, the profitability of a firm increases and vice versa, a proposition of the absorption costing approach. This indicates that the manager will be influenced to report longer period of inventory so as to enhance the firm's profitability.

Furthermore, the results from the regression analysis also indicated that the debt ratio has negative relationship with the profitability of firms. In other words, the firm's profitability decreases when the debt ratio increases. This means that the profitable firm is not depending on debt refinancing to pay off their obligations. Additionally, the firm size showed positive relationship with the firm profitability suggesting when the firm size increases it will lead to more profit. This implies that the larger firms would often have strong earning power compared to smaller firms.

Implications

Several implications can be observed from the findings of this study about the relationship between the working capital management and the firm's profitability. First, the empirical results drawn in this study suggest that the log cash conversion cycle is found to have no control over the profitability. Thus, this shows that even though the firms has improved its cash conversion cycle by improving collection of accounts receivable, moving inventory faster and paying it supplier longer, the profitability of the firms would not be affected.

Secondly, the outcomes also show that there is a positive relationship between the log average collection periods with the firm's profitability. This suggests that, when the log average collection periods increase, it will lead to growth in profitability. Therefore, the manager would be encouraged keep its customers credit period longer in order to increase the firm's profitability. In fact, customers are mostly looking for the company which offer them the longer period of payment.

Third, the finding also shows that there is a positive relationship between the log inventory conversion periods toward the firm's profitability. This implies that if the firms have higher inventory conversion period, the profitability will increase. This is opined by Fraser and Ormiston which indicates that the type of industry is important in assessing inventory turnover period [27], as highlighted on study on jewelry or farm equipment retailed industry which often recorded higher inventory conversion period accompanied by higher profit margin.

Next, the result from the regression analysis also showed that the debt ratio is negatively correlated with the profitability of the firms. This means that when the profitability of a firm increases, the firms are mostly depending less on the debt or leverage. Based on the Pecking Order Theory, it suggests that the firms should use the internal fund rather than external financing to pay off the company debt or obligation. Thus, the profitable firms are often relying on the retained earnings to pay off their obligation.

Lastly, the outcomes also show that there is a positive relationship between the size of firms and the firm's profitability. This implies that, when the firm size is getting bigger, the profitability of a firm will potentially increase. In other words, this means that the firm with bigger size has an effect on enhancing firm profitability compared to smaller firm.

References

1. Mathuva D (2009) The influence of working capital management components on corporate profitability: A survey on Kenyan listed firms. Research Journal of Business Management 3: 1-11.
2. Deloof M (2003) Does working capital management affect profitability of Belgian firms? Journal of Business Finance and Accounting 30: 573-588.
3. Falope OI, Ajilore OT (2009) Working capital management and corporate profitability: Evidence from panel data analysis of selected quoted companies in Nigeria. Research Journal of Business Management 3: 73-84.
4. Filbeck G, Krueger T (2005) Industry related differences in working capital management. Journal of Business 20: 11-18.
5. Dittmar A, Mahrt-Smith J, Servaes H (2002) Corporate Liquidity.
6. Myers S, Majluf N (1984) Corporate Financing and Investment Decision When Firms Have Information That Investors Do Not Have. Journal of Financial Economics 13: 187-221.
7. Raheman A, Nasr M (2007) Working capital management and profitability – case of Pakistani firms. International Review of Business Research Papers 3: 279-300.
8. Gill A, Biger N, Mathur N (2010) The relationship between working capital management and profitability: Evidence from the United States. Business and Economics Journal 10: 1-9.
9. Lazaridis I, Tryfonidis D (2006) Relationship between working capital management and profitability of listed companies in the Athens stock exchange. Journal of Financial Management and Analysis 19: 26-35.
10. Uyar A (2009) The relationship of cash conversion cycle with firm size and profitability: An empirical investigation in Turkey. International Research Journal of Finance and Economics 4: 186-193.
11. Dong HP, Su JT (2010) The relationship between working capital management and profitability: A Vietnam case. International Research Journal of Finance and Economics, pp: 59-67.
12. Raheman A, Afza T, Qayyum A, Bodla MA (2010) Working capital management and corporate performance of manufacturing sector in Pakistan. International Research Journal of Finance and Economics 47: 151-163.
13. Mohamad NEA, Saad N (2010) Working capital management: The effect of market valuation and profitability in Malaysia. International Journal of Business and Management 5: 140-147.
14. Saghir A, Hashmi FM, Hussain MN (2011) Working capital management and profitability:Evidence from pakistan firms. Interdisciplinary Journal of Contemporary Research in Business 3: 1092-1105.
15. Samiloglu F, Demirgunes K (2008) The effect of working capital management on firm profitability: Evidence from Turkey. International Journal of Applied Economics and Finance 2: 44-50.
16. Charitou MS, Elfani M, Lois P (2010) The effect of working capital management on firm's profitability: Empirical evidence from an emerging market. Journal of Business & Economics Research 8: 63-68.
17. Karaduman HA, Akbas HE, Caliskan AO, Durer S (2011) The relationship between working capital management and profitability: Evidence from an emerging market. International Research Journal of Finance and Economics 62: 61-67.
18. Hussain F, Hamid K, Akash R, Khan M (2011) Day of the week effect and stock returns: (Evidence from Karachi stock exchange-Pakistan). Far East Journal of Psychology and Business 3: 25-31.
19. Mojtahedzadeh V, Tabari SHA, Mosayebi R (2011) The relationship between working capital management and profitability of the companies (Case study: listed companies on TSE). International Research Journal of Finance and Economics 76: 158-166.
20. Afeef M (2011) Analyzing the impact of working capital management on the profitability of SME's in Pakistan. International Journal of Business and Social Science 2: 173-183.
21. Azam M, Haider SI (2011) Impact of working capital management on firms' performance: Evidence from non-financial institution of KSE-30 index. Interdisciplinary Journal of Contemporary Research in Business 3: 481-492.
22. Al-Debi'e M (2011) Working capital management and profitability: The case of industrial firms in Jordan. European Journal of Economics, Finance and Administrative Sciences 36: 1450-2275.
23. Ray S (2012) Evaluating the impact of working capital management components on corporate profitability: Evidence from Indian manufacturing firms. International Journal of Economic Practices and Theories 2: 127-136.
24. Al-Mwalla M (2012) The impact of working capital management policies on firm's ability and value: The case of Jordan. International Research Journal of Finance and Economics 85: 147-153.
25. Vural G, Sokmen AG, Cetenak EH (2012) Affects of working capital management on firm's performance: Evidence from Turkey. International Journal of Economics and Financial Issues 2: 488-495.
26. Eljelly A (2004) Liquidity-profitability tradeoff: An empirical investigation in an emerging market. International Journal of Commerce and Management 14: 48-61.
27. Fraser LM, Ormiston A (2013) Understanding Financial Statements. (10th edn.), Pearson Education Limited, United States.

Permissions

All chapters in this book were first published in JBFA, by OMICS International; hereby published with permission under the Creative Commons Attribution License or equivalent. Every chapter published in this book has been scrutinized by our experts. Their significance has been extensively debated. The topics covered herein carry significant findings which will fuel the growth of the discipline. They may even be implemented as practical applications or may be referred to as a beginning point for another development.

The contributors of this book come from diverse backgrounds, making this book a truly international effort. This book will bring forth new frontiers with its revolutionizing research information and detailed analysis of the nascent developments around the world.

We would like to thank all the contributing authors for lending their expertise to make the book truly unique. They have played a crucial role in the development of this book. Without their invaluable contributions this book wouldn't have been possible. They have made vital efforts to compile up to date information on the varied aspects of this subject to make this book a valuable addition to the collection of many professionals and students.

This book was conceptualized with the vision of imparting up-to-date information and advanced data in this field. To ensure the same, a matchless editorial board was set up. Every individual on the board went through rigorous rounds of assessment to prove their worth. After which they invested a large part of their time researching and compiling the most relevant data for our readers.

The editorial board has been involved in producing this book since its inception. They have spent rigorous hours researching and exploring the diverse topics which have resulted in the successful publishing of this book. They have passed on their knowledge of decades through this book. To expedite this challenging task, the publisher supported the team at every step. A small team of assistant editors was also appointed to further simplify the editing procedure and attain best results for the readers.

Apart from the editorial board, the designing team has also invested a significant amount of their time in understanding the subject and creating the most relevant covers. They scrutinized every image to scout for the most suitable representation of the subject and create an appropriate cover for the book.

The publishing team has been an ardent support to the editorial, designing and production team. Their endless efforts to recruit the best for this project, has resulted in the accomplishment of this book. They are a veteran in the field of academics and their pool of knowledge is as vast as their experience in printing. Their expertise and guidance has proved useful at every step. Their uncompromising quality standards have made this book an exceptional effort. Their encouragement from time to time has been an inspiration for everyone.

The publisher and the editorial board hope that this book will prove to be a valuable piece of knowledge for researchers, students, practitioners and scholars across the globe.

List of Contributors

Celikdemir DZ and Paker IT
Department of International Logistics Management, Faculty of Economics and Administrative Sciences, Yasar University, Turkey

Beg K
Department of Commerce, Aligarh Muslim University, Aligarh, India

Selvaraj N and Suganya M
Commerce Department, Saraswathi Narayanan College, Madurai, Tamilnadu, India

Balajikumar P
Management Department, Saraswathi Narayanan College, Madurai, Tamilnadu, India

Sarkodie EE and Addai I
Department of Accounting Studies Education, College of Technology Education, Kumasi, Ghana

Asiedu DK
University of Education, Winneba, College of Technology Education, Kumasi, Ghana

Amala V Venkatasami
GIM, Coimbatore, India

James AP
BSc (Hons) MA (PCET) DBA, 41 Burgess Road, Stratford, London, UK

Machayi J and Ahmed EM
Faculty of Business, Multimedia University, Malaysia

Elsadig Musa Ahmed
Faculty of Business, Multimedia University, Cyberjaya, Malaysia

Anwar Ammar
Faculty of Management, Multimedia University, Cyberjaya, Malaysia

Ambreen Khursheed
FMS Faculty Office, University of Central Punjab, Lahore, Pakistan

Affes H and Sardouk H
Faculty of Economics and Management of Sfax, University of Sfax, Tunisia

Ahmed MH
Risk Management and Insurance, Arab East Colleges, Business Administration Department, KSA, Saudi Arabia

Khan N and Iqbal N
Management Sciences, Indus International Institute DG Khan, Pakistan

Ullah A
Department of Business Administration, Port City International University, Chittagong, Bangladesh

Islam T
Faculty of Business Studies, University of Dhaka, Bangladesh

Rahman M
Department of Business Administration, Northern University, Bangladesh

Rehman OU
Lecturer at CFCBE, CECOS University, Peshawar, Pakistan

Khaliq IH
Warid Telecom Pakistan and Pacific Western University, USA

Naeem B and Abbas Q
Department of Management Sciences, COMSATS Institute of Information Technology, Lahore, Pakisthan

Khalid S
Lecturer, Department of Education, University of Sargodha, Sargodha, Pakistan

Björn Preuß
Department of International Management and Economics, Copenhagen Business School, Denmark Department of Economics, Radboud University Nijmegen, The Netherlands

Nassar S
Marmara University, Institute of social science, Accounting and Finance Department, Istanbul/Turkey

Selvaraj N, Balajikumar P and Alagukanna AS
Saraswathi Narayanan College, Madurai, Tamilnadu, India

Jones LM
Walden University, College of Management and Technology, 100 Washington Avenue South, Suite 900, Minneapolis, Minnesota, USA

Selvaraj N
Saraswathi Narayanan College, Madurai, Tamilnadu, India

Narayana T
School of Commerce, University of South Australia, Australia

Ramiah V
Associate Professor of Applied Finance, UniSA Business School, Australia

Taghi Vahidi
The Branch of Marketing Managemen, Islamic Azad University of Shahrood, Shahrood, Iran

Ratna R
PhD Scholar (IIT Kharagpur) and Assistant Professor (HR and OB), Amity Business School, Amity University, Noida-201301, Uttar Pradesh, India

Kaur T
Academic Co-ordinator, Quality Assurance and Enhancement Cell, Amity University, Amity Lucknow Campus, Uttar Pradesh, India

Mishrif A
Department of International Affairs, Qatar University, Doha, Qatar

Balushi YA
Supreme Council for Planning, Oman

Soufeljil M, Sghaier A and Mighri Z
ISG l'ISG Sousse, LaREMFiQ (University of Sousse), Tunisia

Kheireddine H
Faculty of Economics and Management, Sfax, Tunisia

Maunganidze F, Mashavira N and Mapira N
Department of Human Resource Management, Great Zimbabwe University, Masvingo, Zimbabwe

Soumita Banerjee
University of Bridgeport, Bridgeport, USA

Tagoe NA
Export Trade, Agricultural and Industrial Development Fund Operations, Accra, Ghana

Jakpar S, Tinggi M and Siang TK
Faculty of Economics and Business, University Malaysia Sarawak (UNIMAS), Malaysia

Johari A, Myint KT and Sadique MS
School of Business, Curtin University Sarawak Campus, Malaysia

Index